A New Grammar of
Biblical Hebrew

ALSO BY THE SAME AUTHOR

(with Ted A. Hildebrandt). *The Book of Proverbs: A Classified Bibliography*. Sheffield: Sheffield Phoenix Press, 2010.

Proverbs. The Complete Biblical Library. Old Testament Study Bible. Springfield, MO: World Library Press, 1998.

Card-Guide to Biblical Hebrew. Quakertown, PA: Stylus, 1996; rev. ed., 1997.

Hebrew Bible Insert: A Student's Guide to the Syntax of Biblical Hebrew. Quakertown, PA: Stylus, 1996.

A Cumulative Scripture Index of Hebrew Grammar & Syntax. Winona Lake: Eisenbrauns, 1996.

(with James C. Pakala). *Directory & Profile: Collection Evaluation & Development Section of the American Theological Library Association*. Collection Evaluation and Development Committee of the ATLA, 1986.

A New Grammar of
Biblical Hebrew

Frederic Clarke Putnam

וִיהִי נֹעַם אֲדֹנָי אֱלֹהֵינוּ עָלֵינוּ
וּמַעֲשֵׂה יָדֵינוּ כּוֹנְנָה עָלֵינוּ
וּמַעֲשֵׂה יָדֵינוּ כּוֹנְנֵהוּ׃

And may the favor of the Lord our God be upon us;
And the work of our hands establish for us;
And the work of our hands, establish it.
Psalm 90.17

Sheffield Phoenix Press

2010

Copyright © 2006, 2010 Frederic Clarke Putnam

Published by Sheffield Phoenix Press
Department of Biblical Studies, University of Sheffield
Sheffield S3 7QB England

www.sheffieldphoenix.com

All rights reserved.
No part of this publication may be reproduced or transmitted in any form or by any
means, electronic or mechanical, including photocopying, recording or any information
storage or retrieval system, without the publisher's permission in writing.

A CIP catalogue record for this book
is available from the British Library

Typeset by Vikatan Publishing Solutions (P) Ltd., Chennai, India
Printed by Lightning Source Inc.

ISBN 978-1-907534-03-4 (hardback)
ISBN 978-1-907534-04-1 (paperback)

Notice: BWHEBB [Hebrew] and BWGRKL [Greek] Postscript® Type 1 and TrueTypeT fonts Copyright © 1994-2009 BibleWorks, LLC. All rights reserved. These Biblical Greek and Hebrew fonts are used with permission and are from BibleWorks, software for Biblical exegesis and research. If you use or derive any materials from this work, please respect this copyright by displaying this notice. Thank you.

To Emilie,
with thanks for unfailing
love & support

CONTENTS

List of Enrichment Sections	ix
Preface	xi
Acknowledgements	xiii
Abbreviations	xv
Introduction	xvii

PART I: READING & PRONOUNCING HEBREW — 1

Introduction	3
1. The Hebrew Alphabet	5
2. The Vowels	11
3. Syllables	21

PART II: NOMINAL & VERBAL GRAMMAR (I) — 29

4. The Noun	31
5. The Hebrew Verb	41
6. The Preterite	55
7. Nominal Modification (II): Prepositions	65
8. Commands & Prohibitions	73
9. Nominal Modification (III): The Construct	79
10. The Perfect (*Qatal*, Suffix Conjugation)	87
11. Nominal Modification (IV)	95
12. The Participle	103
13. Pronominals (I)	109
14. Pronominals (II): Suffixes	117
15. Stative Verbs & היה	127
16. The Infinitives & Summary of *Qal*	135
17. Questions, Negatives, Numerals	143

PART III: VERBAL GRAMMAR (II) & READING HEBREW — 151

18. Other Stems	153
19. The D-Stems (*Piel, Pual, Hitpael*)	163
20. The H-Stems (*Hifil, Hofal*)	173
21. The *Qal* Passive/Identifying (Parsing) Verbal Forms	181
22. Guttural Verbs	189
23. Basic Tools	195
24. Other Kinds of Verbal Roots	203
25. "Pre-reading" Biblical Narrative	211
26. I-נ Verbs	221
27. Pre-reading a Biblical Poem	231

28. Hollow (II-ו/י) Verbs	235
29. The *Masora*	243
30. I-י/ו Verbs	249
31. Geminate (ע"ע) Verbs	255

APPENDICES — 263

A.	Supplementary Vocabulary	265
B.	Hebrew – English Glossary	269
	The Most Common "Proper" Nouns	280
C.	Glossary of Morphosyntactical Terms	283
D.	Paradigms	289
E.	Bibliography	301

LIST OF ENRICHMENT SECTIONS
(AT THE END OF EACH LESSON)

Section	Topic
1.4	Acrostic Poetry
2.8	Implicit/Assumed Information
3.8	The Divine Name
4.11	Hendiadys
5.10	Translation & the Exercises
6.11	Narrative Backbone (& Ancillary Information)
7.11	Directions
8.10	Verbal Euphony in Poetry
9.6	Semantic Clusters
10.8	The Perfect as Performative?
11.8	Reading a *Bulla*
12.6	Participles & Poetic Compression
13.8	Disjunctives in Poetry
14.8	Ruth 3.16
15.8	Genesis 13.2
16.7	Gerundive Infinitives Construct
17.7	Irrealis
18.8	*Nifal* vs. *Hitpael*?
19.8	The Nature of D/*Piel*
20.8	Modality
21.5	Nominal Formation
22.11	Vocabulary
23.6	Using the Lexicon
24.8	Narrative Aperture
25.10	Pre-reading Ruth 2.1-7
26.7	Participant Reference
27.7	Reading a Poem
28.8	Dating Haggai
29.6	The *Masora Marginalis* to Genesis 37.18-22
30.6	Pay Attention While Reading

Preface

The flood tide of introductory grammars of Biblical Hebrew since c. 1990 raises the question: "Why another?" This grammar exists, first, because I needed a grammar from which to teach that would reflect a discourse- and genre-based understanding of Biblical Hebrew[1]. When the supplementary handouts overtook the regular textbook that I was using, I realized that it would be simpler just to fill in the gaps; this book is the result.

Secondly, students who pursued postgraduate studies encouraged me to persevere in seeking to have it published by reporting that they were better-prepared in Hebrew than their classmates (and even, in some cases, were as well-prepared as their professors). A number of people downloaded earlier permutations from my website (www.fredputnam.org) and reported using it to learn to read Hebrew. The learning and preparation of all of these students was, of course, their own responsibility; I am honoured to have had some part in it.

The positive response of others whom I respect, including linguists, translators, and professors of Hebrew, likewise encouraged me to bring it to fruition.

---

1. Unless otherwise qualified, the terms "Biblical Hebrew" and "Hebrew" refer interchangeably to the language of the biblical text (MT as represented by *BHS*); "Classical Hebrew" refers to both biblical and epigraphic materials.

Acknowledgements

I am thankful for the suggestions and corrections of many students through the years, especially Linda Dietch (whom I also thank for her marvelous family story in footnote 39), Chris Drager, John Muhlfeld, Abigail Redman, and Robert Van Arsdale; for those offered by Rick Houseknecht of Biblical Seminary and Michael Hildebrand of Toccoa Falls College, both of whom have used this text to teach Biblical Hebrew; and for the extensive editorial help of Julie Devall and Jordan Siverd of Gregorian Publishing (although not even all of these together could catch all of my errors).

Most of all, I thank my wife and our daughters for their patience through the years with "Daddy's writing".

My goal in this, as in all things, is that people of the Book might grow in their ability to read it, and thus to delight in its beauty and truth. *S.D.G.*

Frederic Clarke Putnam
Hatfield, Pennsylvania
Epiphany MMX

Abbreviations

BIBLICAL BOOKS				GRAMMAR		
Canonically[2]		**Alphabetically**		**Verbal Stem**		
Genesis	Gn	Am	Amos	**D**	*piel*	(doubled stem)
Exodus	Ex	Dn	Daniel	**Dp**	*pual*	(passive doubled stem)
Leviticus	Lv	Dt	Deuteronomy	**Dt**	*hitpael*	(t-prefix doubled stem)
Numbers	Nu	Ec	Ecclesiastes	**H**	*hifil*	(h-prefix stem)
Deuteronomy	Dt	Es	Esther	**Hp**	*hofal*	(passive h-prefix stem)
Joshua	Js	Ex	Exodus	**N**	*nifal*	(n-prefix stem)
Judges	Jg	Ezk	Ezekiel	**Q**	*qal*	("simple" stem)
1 Samuel	1 Sam	Ezr	Ezra	**Qp**	*qal passive*	(passive of the "simple" stem)
2 Samuel	2 Sam	Gn	Genesis			
1 Kings	1 Kgs	Hb	Habakkuk	**Verbal Conjugation**		
2 Kings	2 Kgs	Hg	Haggai	**Coh**	**Coh**ortative	
Isaiah	Is	Ho	Hosea	**F**	Imper**f**ect (*yiqtol*, imperfective)	
Jeremiah	Jr	Is	Isaiah	**J**	**J**ussive	
Ezekiel	Ezk	Jb	Job	**NC**	I**n**finitive **C**onstruct	
Hosea	Ho	Jg	Judges	**NA**	I**n**finitive **A**bsolute	
Joel	Jl	Jl	Joel	**P**	**P**erfect (*qatal*, perfective)	
Amos	Am	Jn	Jonah	**Pr**	**Pr**eterite (*wayyiqtol*, imperfect with *waw*-consecutive/conversive)	
Obadiah	Ob	Jr	Jeremiah			
Jonah	Jn	Js	Joshua			
Micah	Mi	La	Lamentations	**Ptc**	**P**ar**t**i**c**iple	
Nahum	Na	Lv	Leviticus	**V**	Imperati**v**e	
Habakkuk	Hb	Ma	Malachi			
Zephaniah	Zp	Mi	Micah	**Person, Gender, Number**		
Haggai	Hg	Na	Nahum	**1**	first person ("I, me, my"; "we, us, our")	
Zechariah	Zc	Ne	Nehemiah	**2**	second person ("you"; "your")	
Malachi	Ma	Nu	Numbers	**3**	third person ("he, she, it, they", "him, her", &c.)	
Psalm	Ps	Ob	Obadiah			
Job	Jb	Pr	Proverbs	**f**	feminine	
Proverbs	Pr	Ps	Psalm	**m**	masculine	
Ruth	Ru	Ru	Ruth	**p**	plural	
Song of Songs	SS	SS	Song of Songs	**s**	singular	
Lamentations	La	Zc	Zechariah			
Ecclesiastes	Ec	Zp	Zephaniah			
Esther	Es	1 Chr	1 Chronicles			
Daniel	Dn	1 Sam	1 Samuel			
Ezra	Ezr	1 Kgs	1 Kings			
Nehemiah	Ne	2 Chr	2 Chronicles			
1 Chronicles	1 Chr	2 Sam	2 Samuel			
2 Chronicles	2 Chr	2 Kgs	2 Kings			

2. As the books are arranged in *Biblia Hebraica Stuttgartensia*.

Introduction

This grammar of Biblical Hebrew, the language of the religious literature of ancient Israel, and the expressive medium of religious texs held dear by those of several of the world's major religions, seeks to inculcate in students the conviction that language makes sense, that the forms of Biblical Hebrew and their functions are not random, but rather motivated by the constraints of their linguistic medium, including both the genre within which they are used and the discourse structures of that genre.

Characteristics

1. *Frequency*. As much as possible, those aspects of the language which are most frequent, common, or "usual" are studied before the less common. The **verb** is presented beginning with the two conjugations (imperfect and preterite) whose parallel morphology (common subject affixes) accounts for more than forty percent of all verbal forms in Biblical Hebrew. **Vocabulary** is introduced in approximate order of frequency, allowing, of course, for the order of topics. The combined "supplementary" vocabulary lists (Appendix A) and those in the chapters introduce all words used fifty times or more in Biblical Hebrew (approximately 650 words in all). The verbal stems are the exception to this pattern of frequency; I find it more helpful pedagogically to link these by form and function rather than frequency. Furthermore, students find it helpful to interrupt the cascade of weak verbal roots with non-morphological topics in order to allow students time to assimilate the characteristics of each type of root.

    There are a number of *statistics* scattered throughout the lessons, such as how often a particular conjugation, stem, or other form occurs. They are not intended to imply or establish a form's relative importance or significance; they are included because students frequently ask how often they can expect to see this or that phenomenon. Most are rounded off to the nearest whole number.

2. *Simplicity*. First-year students need to learn enough grammar and syntax to get them into the text. Beginning to understand a language comes from extensive interaction with the language *as it occurs*, not from memorizing paradigms and vocabulary, necessary as that is. This text presents basic grammar as quickly as has proven practical, with the goal that students begin reading the text fairly early in their first semester of study. Noun formation is described very simply, and primarily in terms of recognition. For example, the guttural verbal roots are presented in one brief lesson, rather than a half-dozen lengthy ones.

    This is also the reason for offering explanations that are "pedagogical" rather than "technical" or "technically accurate" (e.g., footnotes 20, 34, 80). Most students tend to find technically precise explanations or definitions less than helpful; these explanations offer enough information for them to progress in their understanding without bogging them down in technical detail. The teacher or faculty member can always direct interested students to the appropriate discussions for further information.

3. *Continuity with previous language study*. Semiticists traditionally arrange verbal charts (paradigms) from the third to the first persons (3rd-2nd-1st [e.g., she/he-you-I]), and pronominal paradigms in the opposite order (1st-2nd-3rd). This is both contrary to the experience of students who have studied other languages in high school or college (where all paradigms are arranged 1st-2nd-3rd person), and confusing to beginning students (who need to remember that the order varies according to the type of paradigm). This text uses the order

1st-2nd-3rd for all paradigms. Students who pursue advanced studies in Hebrew or Semitics will need to orient themselves to the academic paradigms.

4. *A linguistic orientation.* Explanations in this grammar assume that language in general is an aspect of human behavior. Hebrew was a human language, a form of behavior that—like every other language—can be more or less (and more rather than less) understood by other human beings. This reflects the further conviction that languages—and the utterances in which they are incarnate—thus exist and function within larger societal patterns and systems; each part of any such system must, as much as possible, be understood in relation to the system of which it is a part, upon which it depends, and to which it contributes.

    This text therefore aims at inculcating this understanding of language in general, and of Biblical Hebrew as an example of a particular stage of a specific language. Furthermore, since language is an aspect of *human* behavior, Biblical Hebrew is an example of the linguistic behavior of human beings—authors and speakers—in a particular time and place, and therefore must be read as an example of normal human communication, regardless of the speaker's [author's] understanding of his or her mission or purpose in writing, and equally, without regard for the reader's view of the Bible as human or divine (or human and divine) in origin. Biblical Hebrew is not some extraordinary language, chosen for its ability to communicate at or beyond certain levels of human understanding. It was merely one aspect of an everyday human language, and should be read as such.

    A specific application of this idea is that verbal conjugations are explained in terms of their function in biblical genres. The string of preterites (*wayyiqtol*, "waw-conversive/consecutive plus imperfect") in a biblical story outlines the backbone of the narrative, or the narrative chain; it is a form with a discourse-level function that is related to the discourse-level functions of verbal conjugations, types of clause, etc.

    At the same time, however, I have tried to avoid linguistic jargon and trivia, or at least to explain them when they are introduced. The term "function" tends to replace the word "meaning," and verbal conjugations are explained in terms of their contextual function (rather than "defined" by a list of possible translation values). There is a glossary of terms in Appendix C.

5. *Exercises.* Most of the exercises are biblical texts taken from *Biblia Hebraica Stuttgartensia* (BHS). In order to allow teachers to assign texts that best suit the purposes and goals of their particular course and program, there are often more exercises than can be completed. [n5.10 explains the purpose and function of the exercises.]

6. *Appendices.* Appendices include supplementary vocabulary lists (above); an alphabetical list of proper nouns (persons and places) that occur fifty times or more in the Hebrew Bible; pronominal and verbal paradigms, including a table of some easily confused verbal forms; a glossary of morphosyntactic terms; and an annotated bibliography.

7. *Schedule & Workload.* This grammar was designed for two semesters (twenty-six weeks). The lessons assume that an average student who follows a normal schedule of eight to twelve hours of study per week in addition to time in class will achieve an average grade in the course.

    The lessons introducing the "weak" verbal roots begin in Lesson 24. They are interspersed with lessons on reading biblical genres (25, 27) and the *Masora* (29), because students found it helpful to have "buffers"—time in which to absorb one set of forms before encountering the next.

    Students and I have found it practical to work through Lessons 1-22 in one semester, meeting twice per week; in the second semester we alternate studying a lesson with working through an extended biblical text, for example, the story of Abraham ("Additional Resources Online", below). This makes them encounter verbal forms and vocabulary in the text before meeting them "formally" in the grammar, which in turn lets them connect the more abstract presentation with a biblical passage. We also begin reading at sight from the biblical text about one-third of the way through the first semester, usually in an extra "reading session" of 30-45 minutes before or after the official class.

    After completing this study, students should be able to develop their understanding of Hebrew grammar and syntax by reading the biblical text with the aid of standard reference works. By the end of their second semester/term of Hebrew, students should have read at least ten chapters directly from the Hebrew Bible, in addition to many partial and whole verses in the exercises.

8. *References*. References to HBI are to the *Hebrew Bible Insert: A Student's Guide to the Syntax of Biblical Hebrew* (Putnam 1996), a booklet covering nominal, adjectival, pronominal, verbal, and clausal syntax, the "major" masoretic accents, and verbal paradigms.
9. *Additional Resources Online*. Reading notes on Abraham (Gn 12-25), Ruth (1-4), Jonah (1-4), and other materials may be downloaded without charge from www.fredputnam.org

Notes for Teachers

1. My courses entail many "discussions" or "conversations"—which appear *ad hoc* and *ad lib* to students, but are in fact carefully planned—that would make this work too long, tedious, and "chatty". An example of this is the all-too-brief discussion of vocabulary (Lesson 2), which merely hints at a discussion of lexical and theoretical semantics and translation that resurfaces throughout their first year of study. In order to avoid this tediousness, and to protect other teachers from the need to disavow (at least some of) my idiosyncracies, I leave to you the task of filling in the gaps that are thereby necessarily created. In other words, because schools, teachers, and students are individual, what is effective in the context of a particular course, its teacher, and the curriculum of which they are part may not be in another, as all good teachers know.
2. Students and I have occasionally found it helpful to combine the lessons on resources (#23), reading (#25, 27), and the *masora* (#29) in order to fit a changed schedule.

Part I

Introduction & Lessons 1-3
Reading & Pronouncing Hebrew

This section introduces the writing system of Biblical Hebrew (alphabet, vowels), and how to pronounce words (accent, syllables). It also addresses the nature of vocabulary (gloss and meaning). By the end of these three chapters, you should be able to look at a Hebrew word, spell and pronounce it, analyze its parts (syllables, *dageš*, *šewa*), and recognize more than thirty of the most common words in Biblical Hebrew.

One of the biggest barriers to learning to read Hebrew is moving our eyes from right to left. Indo-European culture assumes a left-to-right orientation that affects our perception and experience of just about everything.

If you are asked to write a comic strip for Hebrew- or Arabic-speaking readers, be sure to put the punch line in the left-most (first, to us) panel!

In the USA, highway signs list the town to the left of the distance, again based on the assumption that people read left to right, and that "where" you are going is more important than "how far"—we don't usually ask "What is forty-three miles from here?" but "How far is it to …?"

This cultural pattern means that reading right-to-left is a major hurdle for most students—a hurdle that is not merely physical, but mental and emotional—because reading right-to-left *feels* wrong (especially for those who have learned reading techniques such as quickly returning the eyes to the beginning of the next line … at the *left* margin).

When we add to this the non-alphabetic nature of the vowel symbols, and sounds that are not part of the vocal system of most English speakers, the task becomes daunting. The importance of the material in these opening chapters, and the value of pronouncing Hebrew aloud as much as possible, therefore, can hardly be overstated. Accordingly, you should read the examples in the chapters aloud, and read the exercises aloud, in order to attune both eye and ear to the patterns of Hebrew.

INTRODUCTION

These reformatted biblical quotations[3] illustrate some of the similarities and differences between Hebrew and English, which you will notice as soon as you try to read them.

.1   .dg m dg ry dnא lpp m b llš lpp ry
         o y   o ou   :a e eo   y e   :a e eo ou

.2   .slא knrd slmc ry vg llw א dnא knrd
         O :a   :i :   : e a ou :i   :i i   a   :i :

.3   .uoy ssruc tht h sא dsruc dnא ouy ssslb tht h sא dsslb
         e: a e   i e: a   e :e: a e i e:e:

.4   .lluf tn sא s ht ty s ht tnא nur srvr ht llא
         :   o iea e   e ea e   o :i   :ei e   a

.5   .rp ht srdsnc tht h sא dsslb
         oo e   :e i:o a: e   i e:e:
         wo

.6   .tpw dnא nd ts w nlbb fא srvr ht b
         :e   a   a e   oya o   :ei e   y

Although they are certainly not written in Hebrew, these sentences exemplify some of the main *differences between Hebrew and English orthography* [writing].

1. Hebrew is read from right to left.
2. Hebrew vowels are written around (mainly below, but also above and beside) the consonants; they are mainly dots (called "points") and dashes that are much smaller than the consonants.
3. Words cannot begin with a vowel—there must be a consonant, even if it is silent to our ears (e.g., the א (*alef*) in these sentences).
4. Hebrew has a sign (׃) that shows that there is no vowel between two consonants (e.g., the last vowel point in #4 and #6).

At the same time, however, there are significant *differences between this example and Biblical Hebrew* (apart from the obvious difference of using English [Latin] symbols):

1. The vowels are [much] smaller signs, not part of the Hebrew alphabet (i.e., they are not "letters").
2. Biblical Hebrew has no capital letters.
3. Biblical Hebrew is punctuated by accent marks that correspond more or less indirectly to English [European] punctuation (see Lesson 25.3).

---

3. P.H. Mason & Hermann Hedwig Bernard, *Gently Flowing Waters: An easy, practical Hebrew grammar: with exercises for translation...arranged in a series of letters from a teacher of languages to an English duchess in two volumes: To which is attached* Ma'eyney ha-Yeshū'ah: The fountains of salvation, *being a translation, with notes critical and explanatory of Isaiah LIII. Also: Ha-Mafteaḥ, key to the exercises.* Vol. 1, Letters I-XV (Cambridge: J. Hall & Son, 1853).

Lesson 1

The Hebrew Alphabet

The Hebrew alphabet has twenty-two letters, some of which have more than one form. Two letters distinguished only by the position of a dot (שׂ, שׁ) were a single sign until the Masoretes added the points (lines in Ps 119.161-68, the "ש" section, begin with both).

Follow your teacher's example	Pronunciation	Trans-literation[4]	Final Form	Form	Name (accent is bolded)
	silent	ʾ		א	**a**lef
	boat	b		בּ	**b**et
	vent	v	b/v	ב	("bait")
	goat	g	g		גּ	**gi**mel
			g/g		ג	
	door	d	d		דּ	**da**let
			d/d		ד	
	hope	h	h		ה	he ("hay")
	vent	v	v or w		ו	vav/waw
	zoo	z	z		ז	**za**yin
	Hugh	ch (loch)	ḥ		ח	het
	title	t	ṭ		ט	tet
	yet	y	j or y		י	yod
	keel	k	k		כּ	kaf
	hew	ch (loch)	k	ך	כ	
	liquid	l	l		ל	**la**med
	moon	m	m	ם	מ	mem
	night	n	n	ן	נ	nun
	sigh	s	s		ס	**sa**mek
	silent	ʿ		ע	**a**yin
	paper	p	p		פּ	pe
	ford	f	p	ף	פ	("pay")
	eats	ts	ṣ	ץ	צ	**sa**de
	keel	k	q		ק	qof
	r-right	r (flapped)	r		ר	reš ("raysh")
	sigh	s	ś		שׂ	sin ("seen")
	shall	sh	š		שׁ	šin ("sheen")
	tonight	t	t		תּ	tof
			t		ת	

4. Transliterating represents the sounds of one language with the letters of another. There is no universal transliteration scheme for Hebrew (see Jg 21.25). Once you can read and pronounce Hebrew, you should be able to "read" any transliteration scheme.

This "square script"—in contrast to the cursive found in manuscripts and the "archaic" forms used in inscriptions—was standardized after the invention of the printing press. Adapted from the Aramaic alphabet, this alphabet is found in published Hebrew Bibles and prayerbooks, as well as in academic books and journals. Most of these comments (below) on the shapes of the letters do not apply to extra-biblical inscriptions or original biblical manuscripts (no biblical author would easily recognize these letters!). These comments, some of which overlap, are intended as guidelines, not as rules for memorization.

1. Hebrew is written and read from *right to left*. Practice writing and reading the alphabet *in that order*.
2. There is only *one* alphabet; i.e., there are no "capital" or "small" letters.
3. Like some other Semitic scripts, this alphabet is "consonantal"—i.e., none of the letters of the alphabet directly represent vowels (cf. "a", "e", "i", "o", "u"), although a few consonants could be used to indicate the presence of long vowels.
4. The letters listed with and without a dot (ב/ב, ג/ג, ד/ד, כ/כ, פ/פ, ת/ת) are called the *bᵉgad-kᵉfat* letters (בגד־כפת), a nonsense phrase made up of the letters themselves (the rabbis were fond of such mnemonic devices). At one time these letters had two pronunciations, distinguished by the presence or absence of the *dageš lene*, but only ב/ב, כ/כ, and פ/פ are distinguished in modern Hebrew. When spelling a Hebrew word with English letters (transliterating), the letter without *dageš* is either underlined or followed by "h" to show that it is "soft" (e.g,. "b̲/bh", "k̲/kh", "p̲/ph").

    This difference is sub-phonemic, i.e., it does not distinguish one word from another in Biblical Hebrew. In English, on the other hand, this same difference would be quite meaningful (phonemic): one's response to "Come to su__ __er!" would probably be affected by whether the middle consonant was *f* or *p*!
5. Four letters are called "gutturals" (א, ה, ח, ע), so-called because they represent sounds made in the throat (Latin *guttur*).
6. Since some pairs of letters *sound alike*, you will need to learn to recognize Hebrew words by both sight and sound, and to distinguish them by sight.

א	ע		silent
ס	שׂ	s	as in *s*igh
ח	כ ךְ	ch or *ḥ*	as in lo*ch*, Ba*ch* or *h*ew, *H*ugh
ב	ו	v	as in *v*ent
כּ	ק	k	as in *k*eel
ט	ת תּ	t	as in *t*ough

7. Five letters have a special form used only at the end of a word. Four of these *final forms* have "descenders"; note their length relative to other letters.

Initial/Medial Form		Final Form	
כבד	כ	ךְ	ארךְ
מלךְ	מ	ם	אדם
נביא	נ	ן	אבן
פלא	פ	ף	אלף
צדה	צ	ץ	ארץ

8. Some pairs of letters are *similar* in *appearance*:

		To distinguish them, note the ...
ד	ר	*tittle*—the small extension of the horizontal stroke—on *dalet* and *bet*
ב	כ	
ה	ח	left side—open or closed
ם	ס	lower corners—square or round
ט	מ	open at top or bottom
ג	נ	shape of bottom—"arched" or flat
ה	ת	shape of left leg—straight or bent; *tittle* on right side of *ḥet*
ו	ז	shape of top
צ	ע	
שׂ	שׁ	dot on left or right; this is a later (medieval/Masoretic) distinction
ך	ן	*šewa* + *tittle* in final *kaf* (which also has a longer [wider] top stroke)

9. The Dead Sea (Qumran) Scrolls also reveal that Hebrew scribes often inscribed a line onto the parchment, and then suspended the text from the line (rather than resting the letters on the line, as in English). This is why so many letters have a horizontal stroke near the top of the letter, and why Hebrew tends to use descenders rather than ascenders.

Sixteen letters fit within a "square" and several of these are roughly square in appearance, i.e., roughly the same height and width. Listed alphabetically (from right to left), they are:

א ב ד ה ה ח ט כ מ מ ס ע פ צ ר ש ש ת

Three non-final forms (י, ל, ק) and the four final forms with descenders (#9, above) differ from the standard in *height*. The non-final forms are:

- *yod* is only half of the height and width of the other letters (its top is even with the others)   ויהי
- *lamed* extends above the other letters[5]   לילה
- *qof* [and four final forms (#9, above)] extend below the others   מקרא

Five letters are also narrower than the standard *width* (ג ו ז י נ). Each is roughly one-half as wide as the square. *Yod* (the "jot" of Mt 5.18), at roughly one-fourth of the square, is the smallest letter in the Hebrew alphabet.

10. The names of the letters are transliterated into English. Disyllabic names are accented on the first syllable (e.g., ***a'** lef*, ***gi'** mel*). [Transliteration is usually italicized.]

1.2 Concepts

| acrostic | ascender | descender | medial form | tittle |
| alphabet | consonant | final form | square script | transliteration |

---

5. In the Dead Sea (Qumran) Scrolls, the height of the ascender on the *lamed* is often greatly exaggerated, so that their location is obvious (also obvious at a glance is whether or not a photograph in a book or article is correctly oriented).

1.3 Exercises

1. Practice *reciting* the Hebrew alphabet, and *writing* it from right to left, with the final forms following their medial forms.
2. Esther 3.13 is one of twenty-six verses that contain every letter in the alphabet.[6] *Copy* it in Hebrew; practice *spelling* the words by naming the Hebrew letters from right to left (words linked by a horizontal line, called *maqqef*, are considered separate words); and *find* all ten final forms. Which final form does not occur in this verse?

ונשלוח ספרים ביד הרצים אל־כל־מדינות המלך
להשמיד להרג ולאבד את־כל־היהודים מנער ועד־זקן טף ונשים ביום אחד
בשלושה עשר לחדש שנים־עשר הוא־חדש אדר ושללם לבוז׃

3. Discuss the significance of Jesus' statement in Matthew 5.18.
4. This is an alphabetical list of most of the proper names that occur more than 175 times in Biblical Hebrew ("c", "d", "h" are titles and generic nouns). Write their *English form*, and practice spelling them aloud in Hebrew. Use the references—the first time that name occurs—to check your work.

	Example:	גד	"gimel-dalet"	"Gad"		
	Gn 25.26	יעקב	m.	Gn 17.5	אברהם	a.
	Gn 13.10	ירדן	n.	Ex 4.14	אהרן	b.
	Josh 10.1	ירושלם	o.	Gn 14.20	אל	c.
	Gn 32.28	ישראל	p.	Gn 1.1	אלהים	d.
	Gn 9.18	כנען	q.	Gn 41.52	אפרים	e.
	Gn 29.34	לוי	r.	Gn 10.10	בבל	f.
	Gn 19.37	מואב	s.	Gn 35.18	בנימן	g.
	Ex 2.10	משה	t.	Jg 2.13	בעל	h.
	Gn 10.14	פלשתי	u.	1 Sam 16.13	דוד	i.
	Gn 12.15	פרעה	v.	Gn 29.35	יהודה	j.
	Gn 36.37	שאול	w.	Ex 14.13	יהושע	k.
	2 Sam 5.14	שלמה	x.	Gn 30.24	יוסף	l.

N.B.: When transliterated, some of these will not resemble their English counterparts, for one or more of these reasons. [This grammar uses the "received" transliteration.]

  a. The "J" that begins many names in English Bibles represents initial י; within names י often appears as "i" or merely indicates the presence of a vowel (see, e.g., exercises d, r, u [above]), but there are exceptions (below). This is because Latin used the letter "i" to transliterate י (as the corresponding Greek letter *iota* had been used centuries earlier in the Septuagint), and also because the letter "j" was not distinguished orthographically from "i" until the 17th century. The English Bible has inherited the transliteration of biblical names from these two sources. (In some ecclesiastical traditions, for example, "Jesu", representing an older "Iesu" is pronounced "Yesu" or "Yezu".)

---

[6] The complete list: Ex 16:16; Dt 4:34; Js 23:13; 2 Kgs 4:39; 6:32; 7:8; Is 5:25; 66:17; Jr 22:3; 32:29; Ezk 17:9; 38:12; Ho 10:8; 13:2; Am 9:13; Zp 3:8; Zc 6:11; Ecc 4:8; Est 3:13; Ezr 7:28; Ne 3:7; 2 Chr 26:11; Dn 2:45; 3:22; 4:20; 7:19 (all Daniel references are in Aramaic). If, however, *sin* and *šin* are counted separately there are only fourteen vv. (Dt 4:34; 2 Kgs 7:8; Is 66:17; Jr 22:3; 32:29; Ezk 17:9; 38:12; Ho 10:8; 13:2; Zc 6:11; Est 3:13; Ecc 4:8; Ezr 7:28; 2 Chr 26:11). Two vv. include all five final forms (Ezk 38:12; Zp 3:8).

	י > "j"			י > "i"	
יוֹסֵף	jôsēf	**J**oseph	יִרְמְיָהוּ	yirmᵉyāhû	Jerem**i**ah
יְהוּדָה	yᵉhûdā	**J**udah	אֱלֹהִים	ᵉlōhîm	Eloh**i**m
אֲחִיָּהוּ	ᵃhayyāhû	**J**... Ahi**j**ah	הַלְלוּ־יָהּ	halᵉlû-yāh	Hallelu**i**ah

b. The gutturals (א, ה, ח, ע) are either ignored when names are transliterated (יחזקאל > Ezekiel) or represented by a second vowel (אהרון > A**a**ron), reflecting the transliterations of the Septuagint and Vulgate.

c. Two forms of *waw* represent long vowels (note the dots):

	וּ > "û"			וֹ > "ô"	
שָׁאוּל	šā'ûl	Sa**u**l	יוֹסֵף	jôsēf	J**o**seph

d. The letter צ is often represented by "z" in traditional biblical transliteration, by either either *ts* or *ṣ* in academic transliteration.

	צ > "z"	
צִיּוֹן	ṣiyyôn	**Z**ion
צִדְקִיָּהוּ	ṣidqyhû	**Z**edekiah
מַלְכִּי־צֶדֶק	malkî-ṣedeq	Melchi**z**edek

e. The letter שׁ is often represented by "s" in traditional biblical transliteration, but by *š* in academic transliteration.

	שׁ > "s"	
שְׁלֹמֹה	šᵉlomo	**S**olomon
יְרוּשָׁלַםִ	jerûšālaim	Jeru**s**alem

1.4 *Enrichment: Acrostic Poetry*

No one knows why the biblical poets wrote acrostic [alphabetically organized] poems (the most famous is Ps 119); perhaps they were a type or style of poem, like sonnets in English. Other acrostics are, e.g., Lam 1-4 (each chapter), Pr 30.10-31, Ps 9-10 and Ps 37. Psalms 111 and 112 are also acrostics. After the opening "Halleluiah" (1a), each line (not each verse) begins with the next letter of the alphabet:

	Psalm 112			Psalm 111	
1a	הַלְלוּ יָהּ		1a	הַלְלוּ יָהּ	
b	אַשְׁרֵי־אִישׁ יָרֵא אֶת־יְהוָה		b	אוֹדֶה יְהוָה בְּכָל־לֵבָב	
c	בְּמִצְוֺתָיו חָפֵץ מְאֹד:		c	בְּסוֹד יְשָׁרִים וְעֵדָה:	
2a	גִּבּוֹר בָּאָרֶץ יִהְיֶה זַרְעוֹ		2a	גְּדֹלִים מַעֲשֵׂי יְהוָה	
b	דּוֹר יְשָׁרִים יְבֹרָךְ:		b	דְּרוּשִׁים לְכָל־חֶפְצֵיהֶם:	
3a	הוֹן־וָעֹשֶׁר בְּבֵיתוֹ		3a	הוֹד־וְהָדָר פָּעֳלוֹ	
b	וְצִדְקָתוֹ עֹמֶדֶת לָעַד:		b	וְצִדְקָתוֹ עֹמֶדֶת לָעַד:	
4a	זָרַח בַּחֹשֶׁךְ אוֹר לַיְשָׁרִים		4a	זֵכֶר עָשָׂה לְנִפְלְאֹתָיו	
b	חַנּוּן וְרַחוּם וְצַדִּיק:		b	חַנּוּן וְרַחוּם יְהוָה:	
5a	טוֹב־אִישׁ חוֹנֵן וּמַלְוֶה		5a	טֶרֶף נָתַן לִירֵאָיו	
b	יְכַלְכֵּל דְּבָרָיו בְּמִשְׁפָּט:		b	יִזְכֹּר לְעוֹלָם בְּרִיתוֹ:	
6a	כִּי־לְעוֹלָם לֹא־יִמּוֹט		6a	כֹּחַ מַעֲשָׂיו הִגִּיד לְעַמּוֹ	
b	לְזֵכֶר עוֹלָם יִהְיֶה צַדִּיק:		b	לָתֵת לָהֶם נַחֲלַת גּוֹיִם:	
7a	מִשְּׁמוּעָה רָעָה לֹא יִירָא		7a	מַעֲשֵׂי יָדָיו אֱמֶת וּמִשְׁפָּט	
b	נָכוֹן לִבּוֹ בָּטֻחַ בַּיהוָה:		b	נֶאֱמָנִים כָּל־פִּקּוּדָיו:	
8a	סָמוּךְ לִבּוֹ לֹא יִירָא		8a	סְמוּכִים לָעַד לְעוֹלָם	
b	עַד אֲשֶׁר־יִרְאֶה בְצָרָיו:		b	עֲשׂוּיִם בֶּאֱמֶת וְיָשָׁר:	
9a	פִּזַּר נָתַן לָאֶבְיוֹנִים		9a	פְּדוּת שָׁלַח לְעַמּוֹ	
b	צִדְקָתוֹ עֹמֶדֶת לָעַד		b	צִוָּה־לְעוֹלָם בְּרִיתוֹ	
c	קַרְנוֹ תָּרוּם בְּכָבוֹד:		c	קָדוֹשׁ וְנוֹרָא שְׁמוֹ:	
10a	רָשָׁע יִרְאֶה וְכָעָס		10a	רֵאשִׁית חָכְמָה יִרְאַת יְהוָה	
b	שִׁנָּיו יַחֲרֹק וְנָמָס		b	שֵׂכֶל טוֹב לְכָל־עֹשֵׂיהֶם	
c	תַּאֲוַת רְשָׁעִים תֹּאבֵד:		c	תְּהִלָּתוֹ עֹמֶדֶת לָעַד:	

1. Lines in biblical poetry are conventionally referred to by verse number and a letter, so that, e.g., the three lines of v. 10 are referred to as Ps 111.10a, 10b, 10c.
   a. Which line recurs three times in these two psalms with only the difference of one letter?
   b. Which lines begin with letters distinguished by only the position of a dot?
2. If you have a Hebrew Bible, look at Ps 119.161-168. These eight lines are grouped together under one letter, even though some begin with *sin* and some with *šin*. Which verses begin with which letter? [This incidentally demonstrates that these were originally one letter; the distinguishing dots were added by the Masoretes in the medieval period.]
3. The "colon" at the end of each verse (which is actually two "diamonds"—look closely!) is called *sof pasuq*, which means "end of *pasuq*"; *pasuqîm* (plural of *pasuq*) correspond to verses in English.

Lesson 2

The Vowels

Like English, Hebrew has a full range of vowel symbols. Unlike English, Hebrew vowels are not "letters" (i.e., they are not part of the alphabet) but are small signs placed under, between, or above consonants. The Masoretes—scribes who added the vowel markings—were unwilling to change the consonantal text, and so, apparently following the example of other Semitic languages, devised a system of "dots" and "dashes" to represent the various vowel sounds, which were added to the consonantal text. The vowel points were intended to eliminate ambiguity in pronunciation—all but three points represent only one sound each. [Contrast the variety of sounds represented by "ou" in English: c*ou*gh, th*ou*gh, r*ou*gh, thr*ou*gh, g*ou*ge, etc.] The Masoretes used another set of signs (§2.2) to represent half-vowels (e.g., beaut*i*ful), whereas English uses the regular vowel signs (a, e, i, o, u) to represent both full- and half-vowel sounds.[7]

2.1 *Full Vowels*

The Full Vowels

Vowel Class	Name of Vowel	Vowel Point	מ + Vowel Point	Transliteration & Pronunciation		Length: L(ong) or S(hort)
A	qameṣ	ָ	מָ	mā	father	L
	pataḥ	ַ	מַ	ma	rot	S
E	ṣere-yod	ֵי	מֵי	mê	they	L
	ṣere	ֵ	מֵ	mē		L
&	segol	ֶ	מֶ	me	bet	S
I	ḥireq-yod	ִי	מִי	mî	mean	L
	ḥireq	ִ	מִ	mī	mean	L or
				mi	bit	S
O	ḥolem-waw	וֹ	מוֹ	mô		L
	ḥolem	ֹ	מֹ	mō	moan	
&	qameṣ-ḥatuf	ָ	מָ	mō		S
U	šureq	וּ	מוּ	mû	moon	L
	qibbuṣ	ֻ	מֻ	mū	moon	L or
				mu	moot; book	S

---

7. Pronounciation of vowels, full and half, varies from one teacher to the next according to, for example, which variety of modern Hebrew one prefers. You will need to listen closely to your teacher's example, which may not be quite the same as those listed here.

1. The vowel is read *after* the consonant that it is *under* (i.e., that it follows). In other words, the vowel is either below or to the left of its consonant (cf. the first column under "pronunciation").
2. A vowel that includes a letter of the alphabet—called a "vowel letter"—(יִ , יֵ , וֹ, וּ) is always long.
3. Apart from the qualitative distinction between long and short *ḥireq* (/ee/ v. /i/), "length" refers primarily to duration (how long the sound of the vowel is maintained) rather than to vowel quality. For example, the difference between *šureq* and *qibbuṣ* is more like the difference between "b**oo**n" and "b**oo**t" than between "b**oo**n" and "b**u**n" (English long and short /u/). Their tonal quality is the same, but their duration differs (in the English words this is due to the nature of the following consonants).
4. Although there are five "classes" of vowels (a, e, i, o, u), the "o/u", and "i/e" vowels are so closely related that they often interchange, leaving three functional classes (a, i, u).
5. Some long vowels do not sound like their English counterparts, for example, "long e" sounds like English *a* as in "w*ay*", so check the "pronunciation" column carefully. You must learn their Hebrew sounds and names.
6. *Qameṣ* and *qameṣ-ḥatuf* look alike. *Qameṣ-ḥatuf* is quite rare, and occurs only in unaccented, closed syllables (Lesson 3, below).
7. *Pataḥ-yod* and *qameṣ-yod* at the end of a word are both pronounced as the diphthong *ai*, as in *ai*sle.
8. When ה, ו, and י follow a vowel, but are not themselves followed by another vowel, they are called "vowel letters" or *matres lectionis* ("mothers [i.e., helpers] of reading"). This practice started many centuries before the vowel points were used (c, below). When used as a vowel letter, the ה, ו, and י are considered vowels, not consonants (e.g., יֵ is referred to as a single unit of spelling: *ṣere-yod*).

	Vowel Letter or Consonant?	Explanation	Transliteration	Pronunciation
אִישׁ	*yod* = vowel letter (*mater*)	*yod* is not followed by a vowel	ʾîš	eesh
אִשָּׁה	*he* = vowel letter (*mater*)	*he* ends the word (is not followed by a vowel)	ʾiššā	ish**a**
בַּיִת	*yod* = consonant	*yod* followed by a vowel	ba**y**it̠	**ba**yit
עַיִן			ʿa**y**in	**a**yin
יוֹם	*yod* = consonant	*yod* is the first letter of the word (& followed by a vowel)	**y**ôm	**y**ōm
	waw = vowel letter (*mater*)	*waw* is not followed by a vowel		

a. When they begin a word, or are followed by a vowel point, they are consonants (not *matres*).
b. When they are written with the vowel letter (*mater*), they are called "full" (Hebrew *malēʾ*, Latin *plene*, "full").
c. When *ḥolem* lacks *waw*, and *ṣere* and long *ḥireq* lacks *yod*, they are called "defective" (Hebrew *ḥaser*, "lacking").
d. Forms with and without *matres* are pronounced alike. This discussion may sound excessively technical, but all of these terms are routinely used in commentaries and reference works dealing with the Hebrew text.
e. Inscriptions show that *matres* were in use by the 10th century BCE, but they were not used consistently. When the Masoretes began to add the vowel points (c. CE 800), they incorporated the vowel letters that were already present in the text into their system, but did not add more vowel letters to the consonantal text, since that would have entailed changing the biblical text. Many words thus occur both with and without a vowel letter.

I.2. The Vowels

f. This lack of standardization also explains why *ḥireq* and *qibbuṣ* have more than one value. If there was no vowel letter in the text, the Masoretes simply used the "defective" form of the vowel, which is why *ḥireq* and *qibbuṣ* can be either long or short.

2.2 Half-Vowels

Both Hebrew and English have half-vowels, e.g., "i" in "beaut*i*ful" and "a" in sof*a* (in regular conversation, not exaggeratedly, as "bee-yoo-**tee**-ful"). English orthography does not distinguish full and half vowels; the Masoretes distinguished them by using different signs.

The Half-Vowels

Type	Name	Sign	Consonant + Sign		Length	Sound
šewa	*šewa*	ְ	מְ	mᵉ		
a	*ḥatef-pataḥ*	ֲ	הֲ	hᵃ	Half	*uh*
e	*ḥatef-segol*	ֱ	הֱ	hᵉ		
o	*ḥatef-qameṣ*	ֳ	הֳ	hᵒ		

1. The *ḥatef*-vowels combine one of the full vowel signs with vocal *šewa* (ְ).
2. *Ḥatef*-vowels mainly occur after the gutturals (below) instead of vocal *šewa*. The *ḥatef*-vowels are most important when discussing guttural verbs (below).
3. The half-vowels all sound alike ("uh", as in "Uh-huh").
4. Vocal *šewa*, which is also a half-vowel, is the first vowel point in the Bible: בְּרֵאשִׁית, "in the beginning" (Gn 1.1). It is also the sound in the first syllable of its own name: *shᵉva*. It is thus the almost necessary sound between some combinations of consonants—a sound that is usually ignored in English orthography (cf. the slight separation between, e.g., the first two letters of "break" or "pray").

2.3 A Brief History of Hebrew Orthography

Hebrew was first written with consonants and perhaps an occasional vowel letter. This meant that a cluster of consonants was potentially ambiguous. [These examples exaggerate the difficulties, since a word's function is largely determined by the context.]

מלכ[8] *king, he reigned/was/became king, she reigned, they reigned, queen, one who rules* [male or female], "*her/his* [act of] *ruling, Be king!,* or *to be/come king*

As inscriptions show, by the 10th century BCE, *matres lectionis* were being used to indicate the presence of long vowels. This first took place at the end of words, and simplified reading by reducing a word's potential function:

מלכו *his king, the one ruling him, they reigned, his* [act of] *ruling,* or *Reign!* (masc. pl.)
מלכה *her king, queen, she reigned, her* [act of] *ruling,* or *Reign!* (masc. sg.)

Although many biblical books were written after the *matres lectionis* had begun to be used, spelling was never standardized, and so the *matres* were inserted haphazardly. In the 7th–9th centuries CE, the Masoretes began adding "points" to the consonantal text in order to preserve traditional

---

8. The archaic ("paleo-Hebrew") alphabet did not use final forms; they were, however, in use by the time of the Dead Sea Scrolls.

pronunciation,[9] but they did not attempt to standardize the use of *matres* before adding the vowel points, even though this meant inconsistencies in spelling (they considered the *matres* part of the "consonantal" text). The vowel points eliminated most of the ambiguity:

מַלְכָּה ≈ queen מְלָכָה ≈ Be king! (masc. sg.) or She reigned [was queen]
מַלְכָּהּ ≈ her king מֹלְכָה ≈ she [the one] who reigns or the reigning one [female]

This overview helps explain the general scholarly freedom to suggest different pointings—repointing a word is not considered to be "changing the text", since the vowel points were not original. It also explains why the same word can be spelled with and without a vowel letter, since the Masoretes were unwilling to add *matres* to the consonantal text.

Biblical texts may be "unpointed", "consonantal" (both without vowel points), or "pointed" (often called "Masoretic"). Pointing is largely restricted to printed (typeset) Bibles and Hebrew prayerbooks; Modern Hebrew is largely unpointed.

2.4 Regarding Vocabulary

The vocabulary lists include all the words that occur more than fifty times in the Hebrew Bible, except proper names of persons and places (which are listed in Appendix B). Words are introduced *very generally* in order of descending frequency, so that words that occur more frequently in the biblical text are learned first. A complete Hebrew–English glossary for this grammar appears in Appendix B. Learning vocabulary is a process of familiarization through repetition—some students learn best by repeatedly writing the list until the glosses are learned, others by reviewing them orally or by means of cards (Hebrew on one side, English on the other). It also helps to learn word by a biblical context in which it occurs.

Each list consists of Hebrew words alongside one or more suggested English *glosses* for that word. A gloss is merely a word used to translate a word—it is *not* a definition or meaning. The gloss(es) listed with each word are English words that frequently represent that Hebrew word in translations—they are *not* the word's "basic" or "central" or "real" meaning. Words represent referential ranges, so that many glosses may be appropriate for a given word (although not every gloss will fit every context in which that word occurs).

In general, words have ranges of reference (also called their "semantic range"). The only apparent exceptions are highly technical terms, whether medical (*pneumococcys*), mathematical (*cosine*), theological (*hypostatic union*), etc.[10] The more limited a word's area of reference, the more "technical" or specialized it is, and *the more its content is determined by what it refers to*. The less specific a term is—the broader its range of reference—*the more its content is determined by its context* (linguistic, cultural, etc.). "Dog", for example, conveys less information than [is less specific than] "Labrador", and so can fit a larger variety of contexts. The latter expression is limited to contexts that refer to a Labrador (again, unless it is being used metaphorically).

In addition to semantic range, words also have what might be called a "load", as in the expression "a loaded word". "Semantic load" refers to the combination of their denotation ("dictionary meaning") and connotation (associated emotive function). In English, for example, "beefy", "chunky", "heavy", "solid", "big-boned", and "fat" could all be used to refer to a person's build, but many people would consider "solid" a compliment (or at least a polite euphemism) and "fat" a deliberate insult, even though "insulting" is not part of the dictionary's definition. This point probably refers more to issues of translation than to the Hebrew lexicon, since we know the semantic load of words that we use in our own languages far more instinctively than we can know those in another language no longer spoken.

Furthermore, when comparing the vocabularies (lexicons) of different languages, the greater the extent to which words' ranges overlap, the more they appear to "mean the same thing". Since Biblical

---

9. There were several centers of scribal activity, where competing systems of pointing (and thus of pronunciations) developed; this one is called the "Tiberian". Each group of Masoretes was therefore attempting to preserve the pronunciation that it had "received". Nor did the Masoretes consider points to "add to" the biblical text, perhaps because the points do not affect its consonantal shape.

10. Many of these, however, can also be used metaphorically.

Hebrew is a textual language—i.e., there are no longer any native speakers of Biblical Hebrew—we are left to make educated guesses about the semantic range of some words, and the corresponding semantic range in English. These are "educated" guesses, however, based on its biblical use and the evidence from cognate Semitic languages, such as Akkadian, Ugaritic, and Aramaic, from its use in rabbinic (Mishnaic) Hebrew, and from medieval rabbinic commentators and grammarians.

1. *Terms of relationship.* The following Hebrew terms are usually glossed by the first English term, although their range of application is often much broader, as the second gloss suggests:

אָב	father, male ancestor	אֹהֶל	tent, home
אָח	brother, male relative	בַּיִת	house, household
אָחוֹת	sister, female relative	שֵׁבֶט	tribe
אֵם	mother, ancestress	מִשְׁפָּחָה	clan, [extended] family
בֵּן	son, descendant; used to address a younger [unrelated] male (e.g., 1 Sam 3.16)	בֶּן אָח	son of a brother (nephew)
בַּת	daughter, female descendant; used to address a younger [unrelated] female (e.g., Ruth 2.8)	בֶּן בֵּן	son of a son (grandson)

These are the usual glosses because these Hebrew and English words usually refer to the same aspect of reality. In each case, however, the Hebrew terms may also refer to relationships outside the nuclear family. Because parents and their children (the nuclear family) are the usual referents of the English terms, it is tempting to think of the first gloss listed for each term as its "real meaning" and the other gloss as an "extended" or "metaphorical" meaning, perhaps even concluding that every related male, for example, was considered a "brother". We do not know whether or not this was how they thought about these words, since we cannot ask them, and they left no dictionaries. The brief genealogical table of Gn 46.8–27, which describes Jacob's family at their journey to Egypt, illustrates this point. Note the use of the words "son" and "bore" in these verses:

²³ Now the *sons* of Dan were Hushim, ²⁴and the *sons* of Naphtali were Jazeel, Guni, Jezer, and Shillem. ²⁵These are the *sons* of Bilhah, whom Laban gave to Rachel his daughter; and she *bore* these to Jacob, all seven lives (Gn 46.23–25).

This diagram shows the generational spread described by "son" in these verses (those called "sons" are in *italics*):

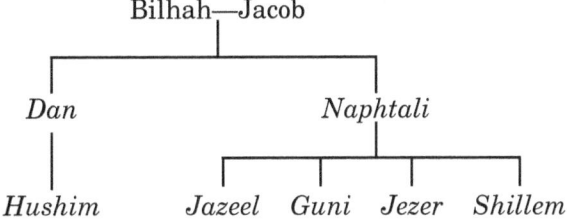

Since Hushim, Jazeel, Guni, Jezer, and Shillem were Bilhah's [and Jacob's] grandsons, *not* her sons, the word בֵּן cannot have the same reference as "son" in everyday English. Furthermore, the verb glossed "bear/give birth to" ("and she *bore* these to Jacob") cannot have the usual English function of "give birth", but has an "extended" function that is revealed only by the context. Note that the same pattern describes the descendants of Jacob's other three wives (Gn 46.8–27).

Since the range of reference of the usual English glosses is much more restricted than that of the Hebrew terms, the word "son" may be misleading if it suggests a closer genealogical or chronological relationship than the context allows. [On the other hand, English also uses some of these terms generically—"son" and "daughter" can refer to a younger unrelated male or female.]

The tiny lexical base (vocabulary) of Biblical Hebrew (c. 8400 words) means that we have only a very incomplete record of the Israelite lexicon, so that it is difficult to see how Abraham could have used the vocabulary of the OT to ask Sarah, "I'd prefer my steak less well done than last night, but the cakes could be a little softer than yesterday; maybe an oak fire would be better than sycamore. Oh, and could you also mend my favorite robe; that same seam is unraveling. Don't forget to use the green thread—the blue showed up too much last time. And we need to remind the servant girls that they can only wash their hair every new moon due to the drought." Of course he must have been able to say this (or something very much like it), but it is not entirely clear how he would have done so using the resources of Biblical Hebrew.

2. Many common glosses suggested by Hebrew-English reference tools may be traditional, but changes in either our understanding of Hebrew or English usage may mean that that gloss no longer functions accurately. It may even misrepresent the Hebrew. These glosses are sometimes included in the vocabulary lists with "trad." ("traditionally"). For example:

	Traditional Gloss	**Potential Gloss(es)**	**Discussion**
פֶּן	lest	so that ... not	*Lest* is a perfectly good, if uncommon, English word that indicates negative purpose.
כבס	full (wash by treading)	wash	The archaic verb *to full* (from Latin, *via* Old French) means to "wash", and is the origin of expression like "whiter than fuller's cloth" (i.e., recently washed).
עַיִן	eye, fountain	eye fount	*Fountain* normally refers to a stream of water that is mechanically shot into the air or poured out, whereas עַיִן refers to a natural source of water (as opposed to a well or cistern).
סֵפֶר	book	text scroll document record	Codices ("proto-books") were not in use until the third century CE, so that the rendering "book" for סֵפֶר is culturally misleading. We know that many Iron Age documents, apparently including even legal texts, were written on pieces of broken pottery (*shards*; called *ostraca* when written on). [There is a specific term for *scroll* (מְגִלָּה; from the verb גלל, *to roll*).]
ילד	bear, give birth	the same	This refers to both immediate birth and to physical *ancestry*, or "eventual" birth (cf. on Gn 36, above).
צְדָקָה	righteousness	innocence rightness justness righteousness triumph	Terms built on the root צדק are traditionally glossed with "righteous", "righteousness", etc., but in many places the thrust of the term is forensic *innocence* relative to a particular situation or accusation, not to an absolute or universal moral state. It is even possible that "innocence" is the primary reference and that the idea of "righteousness" is the global extension of particular innocence. Each passage needs to be studied in order to see which gloss is most appropriate, but not even careful study will guarantee certainty or consensus in every case.

3. It is often easier to explain what a word signifies than it is to give an appropriate gloss in another language, as the discussion of "give birth" shows. If you have studied another language, you may have thought, "There's no way to say that in English", which is, of course, not true. So far as is known, whatever one language can express others can express as well. The difference may be that what one language says in a single word, another can say only with a phrase, a sentence, or even a paragraph.

For example, Lot is called "[Abraham's] brother's son" and David referred to his nephews as "sons of [his sister] Zeruiah", which suggests that Biblical Hebrew lacked a simple lexeme that meant what English means by "nephew". Both Biblical Hebrew and English can refer unambiguously to a sibling's immediate offspring, but Biblical Hebrew lacks a single word that has this function (much as modern English lacks a specific term for the parents of one's son- or daughter-in-law, although there are terms for this relationship in some languages).

This discussion suggests that the referents of words are not to be confused with the words that we use to express them. English "son" is usually the most contextually appropriate gloss for Hebrew בֵּן, but this does *not* imply, and *must not* be misunderstood to imply, that בֵּן somehow "literally" or "basically" or "fundamentally" *means* "son", or even that it means "the same thing as is meant by the English noun 'son'", but rather that two language groups have chosen these particular words to refer [usually] to what turns out to be the same entity.

2.5 Concepts

full vowel	lexeme	meaning	semantic range
function	lexicon	*penult*	*šewa*
gloss	*malē'* (*plene*) spelling	range [of reference]	*ultima*
half (*hiatef*) vowel	*matres lectionis* (sg., *mater*)	reference	vowel letter
hiaser spelling			

2.6 Vocabulary

.1	אָב	*father; male ancestor*	.9	יָד	*hand (power, authority)*
	אָבוֹת	*fathers*[11]			
.2	אִישׁ	*man (not Mankind/humanity), husband; each (as subject of a plural verb)*	.10	יוֹם	*day; when* (preceding the infinitive construct [§16.2])
	אֲנָשִׁים	*men, husbands*			
	אַנְשֵׁי	*men of, husbands of*	.11	כֹּהֵן	*priest*
.3	אֵל	*god, God* (used of Israel's God and other gods)	.12	כָּל־ כֹּל	*all, whole; each, every* [NB: This is a noun, *not* an adjective; "all" is an adjective in English.]
	אֱלֹהִים	*gods, God* (used of Israel's God and other gods)			
.4	אִשָּׁה	*woman, wife*	.13	לֵבָב לֵב	*heart* (a person's moral center; often used where English uses "mind")
	אֵשֶׁת	*wife of*			
	נָשִׁים	*women, wives*	.14	מֶלֶךְ	*king; monarch*
	נְשֵׁי	*women/wives of*			
.5	אֶרֶץ	(f.) *land, country* [of a geo-political region], *earth* (as in "heaven and earth")	.15	נֶפֶשׁ	(f.) *life, self*; trad., *soul*
.6	בַּיִת	*house, home, household*	.16	עֶבֶד	*servant, slave*; someone bound in some way to another person, for whom he or she works
	בָּתִּים	*houses, etc.*			
.7	בֵּן	*son, male descendant* (cf. בִּנְיָמִין, Benjamin, "son of [my] right hand")	.17	עִיר	(f.) *city*
.8	דָּבָר	*word, thing; event, affair, matter*		עָרִים	*cities*

1. Most words in Biblical Hebrew are accented on the last syllable (עָרִים → a · **rîm**), called the *ultima*.
2. Some are accented on the next-to-last syllable (דֶּרֶךְ → **de** · rek), the *penult*.[12]

---

11. Some *plurals* with unexpected or unpredictable forms (e.g., אָבוֹת, *fathers*) are listed.
12. Di-syllabic (two-syllable) nouns with two *seghols* (דֶּרֶךְ), *sere-seghol* (סֵפֶר, "document"), *seghol-patah* (זֶרַע, "seed"), two *patahs* (דַּעַת, "knowledge") are called "segholates", and are accented on the first syllable.

3. The terms "ultima", "penult", and "antepenult" (the syllable before the penult) are commonly used in scholarly literature—including some commentaries—that discusses the spelling (pointing) or pronunciation of words; you need to know what they refer to.
4. When the penult is accented, you will see a Masoretic accent over the consonant that begins that syllable, either *rebia'* (for full-width letters: e.g., דֶּ֫רֶךְ; note that it is larger than *ḥolem*, and centered over the consonant), or *zaqef* (for narrow letters; e.g., נֶ֫פֶשׁ). Words without these marks are usually accented on the ultima.

2.7 Exercises

1. Learn the names and sounds of the full- and half-vowels. Practice writing them with different consonants.
2. This list includes all but one of the proper names of people and places that occur between 174 and 77 times in Biblical Hebrew. *Pronounce* and *spell* each name aloud, and *write* them in their English forms, and *identify* each *waw* or *yod* as a consonant or vowel letter (and be able to explain your identification). Use the references (the name's first canonical occurrence) to check your work. Unlike the [alphabetical] list in Lesson I, these are listed in descending order of frequency. For more practice with the alphabet, rearrange the list so that it is in alphabetical order (vowel letters count!).

Example: יְבוּסִי Jebusite   *yod, šewa, bet, šureq, samek, ḥireq-yod*
1st *yod* = consonant (followed by vowel)
waw = vowel letter (not preceded or followed by vowel)
2nd *yod* = vowel letter (not followed by vowel)

Gn 17.19	יִצְחָק	.m		Gn 9.18	כְּנַעַן	.a
1 Kgs 13.32	שֹׁמְרוֹן	.n		Gn 10.22	אֲרָם	.b
Nu 26.29	גִּלְעָד	.o		2 Sam 5.7	צִיּוֹן	.c
2 Sam 3.3	אַבְשָׁלוֹם	.p		Gn 2.14	אַשּׁוּר	.d
1 Kgs 11.26	יָרָבְעָם	.q		Gn 41.51	מְנַשֶּׁה	.e
2 Kgs 24.11	נְבוּכַדְנֶאצַּר	.r		2 Kgs 23.31	יִרְמְיָה	.f
Gn 29.32	רְאוּבֵן	.s		1 Sam 26.6	יוֹאָב	.g
Gn 10.16	אֱמֹרִי	.t		Nu 34.20	שְׁמוּאֵל	.h
2 Sam 8.16	יְהוֹשָׁפָט	.u		2 Kgs 16.20	חִזְקִיָּה	.i
Gn 30.11	גָּד	.v		Jg 18.30	יְהוֹנָתָן	.j
Gn 14.14	דָּן	.w		Gn 19.38	עַמּוֹן	.k
Gn 13.18	חֶבְרוֹן	.x		Gn 25.30	אֱדוֹם	.l

a. *Ḥatef*-vowels are usually transliterated in English Bibles as the corresponding full vowel (e.g., אֱדוֹם → "Edom"), but not in academic transliteration (e.g., ["ᵉdôm"]).
b. *Šewa* usually appears in English names as *e*, although it can also be transliterated as *i*.
c. As with the first list of names (§1.3), the transliterated form may not resemble their form in English. This is because their form in English is based on their transliteration in Greek (in the Septuagint), Latin (in the Vulgate), or both.
3. Transliterate the first four verses of 1 Chronicles into their English equivalents, and practice reading them aloud. You will need to know two more things: (1) the sign ׃ (*sof pasuq*, "end of *pasuq*") marks the end of the verse; and (2) the ו prefixed to the last word in this verse is a conjunction that can be glossed as "and".

1.1 אָדָם שֵׁת אֱנוֹשׁ׃

1.2 קֵינָן מַהֲלַלְאֵל יָרֶד׃

1.3 חֲנוֹךְ מְתוּשֶׁלַח לָמֶךְ׃

1.4 נֹחַ שֵׁם חָם וָיָפֶת׃

Congratulations! You have now read four verses of the Bible in Hebrew! (Only 22,199 to go!)

2.8 Enrichment: Implicit/Assumed Information

Notice that the author of Chronicles does not tell us that these are personal names, how they are related (or even *that* they are related), and that he also expects his readers to know that the first nine words outline a single line of descent, but that v. 4 branches from a father to his three sons. In fact, to a reader who knows nothing of Genesis 5 and 6, these verses are gibberish. They demonstrate the principle of *assumed information*—information that a speaker or author does not mention, because he or she assumes that the readers or hearers already know it (both speaker and audience thus "share" the information). Assumed information typifies all communication, but is especially noticeable when the author lived (or lives) in another culture or time.

In much of Western culture, for example, if someone arrived at an early-afternoon meeting and said "Sorry I'm late—the service was slow", most hearers would probably assume a scenario of lunch at a restaurant, including being seated, waiting to order, ordering, eating, paying, etc., none of which need be expressed, since we assume this as part of our own cultural setting. In the same way, the biblical authors never tell us why men tended to meet women at wells (e.g., Gn 24; Ex 2), but assume that their readers know that women drew and hauled water, and—in a culture without plumbing or public water—that an efficient way for a traveler to meet someone from the area was merely to wait at a well, since sooner or later someone would show up. In the same way, many middle- and upper-class North Americans would probably assume that a husband and wife of about the same age met in college, since, in fact, many do meet in college.

Reading 1 Chronicles 1.1–4 shows us that the "Chronicler" (as the author of Chronicles is often called) expected his readers to be familiar with the genealogies of Genesis. He did not expect his work to be read as an independent account of God's dealings with Israel, but as a supplement or parallel to Genesis—Kings. This also explains that when he "ignored" the sins of David and Solomon, or the history of the Northern Kingdom—he was not trying to mislead his readers, but assuming that they knew the rest of the story.

Lesson 3

SYLLABLES

The final aspect of pronouncing Biblical Hebrew is to recognize combinations of consonants and vowels as syllables. This primarily entails distinguishing silent from vocal *šewa*, and *dageš lene* from *dageš forte*, which will enable you in turn to recognize a syllable as either open or closed. Although the ability to recognize syllables and identify their type will help you recognize some verbal forms, its main value is enabling you to pronounce Hebrew.

3.1 *Šewa*[13]

The sign for *šewa* (ָ) has at least two functions. It can represent a *half-vowel* (above) or mark the *absence* of a vowel. This section describes how to distinguish these functions.

a. Vocal *šewa* (ָ) is a half-vowel (above), like the "i" in *beautiful*, or the "a" in *sofa*.
b. Silent *šewa*. When two consonants occur with no vowel between them, the Masoretes inserted *šewa* as a "place-holder". In English, consonants can be placed side by side, as in *pl*aced, but in Hebrew, every consonant—except the last letter of the word—must be followed by a vowel point. This *šewa* is also called *šewa quiescens*.

N.B.: The three *hatef*-vowels (מֲ / מֱ / מֳ) are always vocal.

There are **three basic rules** for distinguishing vocal and silent *šewa*.

1. If the preceding vowel is short, the *šewa* is silent; if the preceding vowel is long, *šewa* is vocal; *qameṣ* /*qameṣ ḥatuf* and *ḥireq* are ambiguous.

after a short vowel	יַמְלִיכוּ	*yamlîkû*
after a long vowel	יֵשְׁבוּ	*yēšᵉbû*

2. *Šewa* after (under) a letter written with *dageš* ("dot") is always vocal; *šewa* before a letter with *dageš* is always silent.

after *dageš*	יִפְּלוּ	*yippᵉlû*
before *dageš*	יִכְתֹּב	*yiktōb*

3. When there are two *šewa*s in a row, the first is always silent and the second always vocal (unless they are under the last two letters of a word, where they are both silent).

1st silent, 2nd vocal	יִשְׁמְרוּ	*yišmᵉrû*
both silent (end of word)	וַיֵּבְךְ	*wayyēbk*

These three basic rules will allow you to distinguish most *šewa*s; the following guidelines[14] merely amplify them (despite all the rules, there are exceptions and ambiguities).[15]

---

13. This discussion refers only to šewa itself; ḥatef-vowels are always pronounced.
14. Most of these rules were developed by Rabbi Elias Levitas (d. 1549 CE).
15. For more information, see Joüon & Muraoka (1991, §§5o, 8, 10, 18, 19).

Šewa is vocal when it ...			
a. follows the first letter in a word		בְּרֵאשִׁית	bᵉrēšît
b. follows another šewa (except at the end of the word)		יִשְׁמְרוּ	yišmᵉrû
c. follows any consonant with dageš (cf. "j")		יְכַפְּרוּ	yᵉkappᵉrû
d. follows the first of two identical consonants		רוֹמְמוּ	rômᵉmû
e. follows any syllable with a long vowel		יֵשְׁבוּ	yēšᵉbû
f. precedes a bᵉgad-kᵉfat letter **without** dageš (a tendency, not a rule)		יֵשְׁבוּ	yēšᵉbû
Šewa is silent when it ...			
g. precedes another šewa (cf. "b", "k")		יִשְׁמְרוּ	yišmᵉrû
h. follows a guttural consonant		יִהְיֶה	yihye
i. follows the last letter of a word (cf. "k")		הָלַךְ	hālak
j. precedes dageš (cf. "c")		יִכְתֹּב	yiktōb
k. follows *both* of the *last two* letters in a word (both šewas are silent, and the consonants are pronounced as a cluster; cf. "b", "g")		כָּתַבְתְּ וַיֵּבְךְּ	kātabt wayyēbk

Most of these "rules" merely invert another rule (cf., e.g., "b", "g", "k"), but allow you to examine a given šewa from more than one vantage point, as this table demonstrates:

בְּרֵאשִׁית	vocal	under first letter of word (a) [and thus does not follow a short vowel (#1)]; follows dageš (c)
יִשְׁמְרוּ	1st: silent	follows short vowel (#1); precedes another šewa (g)
	2nd: vocal	follows another šewa (b)
תִּכְתֹּב	silent	follows short vowel (#1); precedes dageš (j)
רוֹמְמוּ	vocal	between two identical consonants (d); follows long vowel (e)
יֵשְׁבוּ	vocal	follows long vowel (e); precedes bᵉgad-kᵉfat letter without a dageš (f)

3.2 Dageš

1. *Dageš lene*. When the Masoretes pointed the text, they distinguished the pronunciation of six letters (ב ג ד כ פ ת) as either "hard" or "soft". Although we explain this as the difference between "b" (בּ) and "v" (ב), or "p" (פּ) and "f" (פ), it may have been more like the difference between, e.g., the "p" in "pit" and "tip" (hold your hand in front of your mouth). This is a difference in sound (pʰ/p), but not in function (i.e., if you say "pit" with a big puff of air it still refers to a hole in the ground, a seed, etc.). The same is true of *dageš lene*—whether a consonant is hard or soft, the word is the same.

2. *Dageš forte*. Instead of writing a doubled letter twice (e.g., su**pp**er), Biblical Hebrew writes it once, with *dageš forte* ("strong *dageš*") to show that it is doubled.[16] A letter with *dageš forte* is therefore a doubled letter (although this rarely affects our pronunciation apart from the bᵉgad-kᵉfat letters).[17] In transliteration, letters with *dageš forte* are written twice:

אִשָּׁה	'iššā	"woman, wife"
יִפֹּל	yippōl	"he will fall" ("... falls")
אִמִּי	'immî	"my mother"

---

16. *Dageš forte* both doubles and "hardens" the beged-kefet letters.
17. Five letters do not double: א, ה, ח, ע, ר.

a. Like a doubled consonant in English, the first of the doubled consonants indicated by *dageš forte* closes one syllable and the second opens the next syllable:

supper	***sup*** · *per*	(contrast "*su* · *per*")
אִשָּׁה	*'iš* · ***šā***	"woman, wife"
יִפֹּל	*yip* · ***pōl***	"he will fall"

b. Also like a doubled consonant in English (and unlike *dageš lene*), *dageš forte* affects the word's function:[18]

su*pp*er	su*p*er
di*nn*er	di*n*er
גָּדַלְתִּי	I am great
גִּדַּלְתִּי	I made [someone or something] great

c. *Dageš* in a non- *bᵉgad-kᵉfat* letter can be only *forte*. In a *bᵉgad-kᵉfat* letter, however, *dageš* can be either *forte*, showing that the letter is doubled, or *dageš lene* ("weak dot"), which means that the letter is merely "hard" (but not doubled). [Since they cannot double, the gutturals and ר rarely occur with *dageš*.]

3. There are four basic rules for distinguishing *dageš forte*:

***Dageš* is always *forte* when it ...**			
1. is in a non- *bᵉgad-kᵉfat* letter	חִצִּים	*ḥiṣ* · ***ṣîm***	arrows
2. follows a full vowel (long or short)	עַתָּה	*'at* · ***tā***	now
***Dageš* is always *lene* when it ...**			
3. follows *šewa*	מִשְׁתֶּה	*miš* · ***te***	feast
4. begins a word[19]	דָּבָר	*da* · ***var***	word, thing

N.B.: Identifying the type of *dageš* is challenging only when *dageš* occurs in a *bᵉgad-kᵉfat* letter. *Dageš* in a letter following *šewa* is always *lene* (the *šewa* is always silent); *dageš* after any full vowel is always *forte*. Neither *dageš* follows a *ḥatef*-vowel.

3.3 *Identifying Syllable Boundaries*

1. Every syllable in Biblical Hebrew begins with a consonant, except the conjunction when it has the form - וּ (below).
2. Every syllable in Biblical Hebrew contains one—and only one—vowel, which may be either a full or a half vowel;[20] the number of vowels in a word determines the number of syllables.

מַיִם	***ma*** · *yim*	water
בְּרִית	*bᵉ* · ***rît***	covenant, treaty, agreement
יִשְׁתַּחֲוֶה	*yiš* · *ta* · *ḥᵃ* · ***ve***	he bows down

---

18. The Hebrew examples are part of the verbal system (below).
19. There is one exception to this that we need not worry about.
20. Grammarians disagree on the nature of *šewa*. Some (e.g., Blau, Lambdin, Seow) agree with this statement. Others (e.g., Kelley, GKC [§26m]) explain the consonant with a half-vowel as the first part of the syllable of the following full vowel, since, in this theory, every syllable must have a full vowel. On the other hand, Joüon-Muraoka (§27c, da) finds a single *šewa* with three functions. No explanation yet accounts for every *šewa* (nor did the Masoretes explain their use of *šewa*).

3. There are two types of syllables in Biblical Hebrew. *Open* syllables consist of a consonant + vowel (CV); *closed* syllables consist of consonant + vowel + consonant (CVC).[21] The nature of the syllable, and whether or not it is accented, then determine the length of its vowel.

When a syllable ends in ...	it is:	and its vowel is:
a vowel, vowel letter, א	open	long (rarely short)
a consonant (including ה)	closed	short (if the syllable is unaccented) *or* long (if the syllable is accented)

4. Therefore ...
   a. any consonant except א (and ה without *mappiq*) may close a syllable
   b. in the middle of a word a consonant must be either doubled by a *dageš forte*, or followed by silent *šewa* in order to close a syllable
   c. ה can close a syllable only when written with *mappiq* (הּ-), which occurs only at the end of a word

5. As in English, a double letter (with *dageš forte*) closes one syllable and opens the next (above).

supper	sup · per				
אִשָּׁה	'iš · **šā**	woman, wife	בִּתִּי	bit · **tî**	my daughter
יִפֹּל	yip · **pōl**	he will fall	יִפָּלֵא	yip · pā · **lē'**	it is marvelous
כִּפֶּר	kip · **pēr**	he atoned	וַיֹּאמֶר	vay · **yō'** · mer	[and] he said

6. Some syllables seem to be both open and closed. A short vowel precedes *šewa* (like a closed syllable), but is followed by a *bᵉgad-kᵉfat* letter without *dageš lene* (as though the *šewa* were vocal). Some grammarians call this *šewa media* (i.e., "middle"), others say that this apparent anomaly reflects the history of the language, rather than a particular pronunciation. See footnote 15 (above). For example:

	Suggests *dageš forte*:	Suggests *dageš lene*:
מַלְכֵי	*pataḥ* is short	but כ lacks *dageš lene*
אֶתְכֶם	*segol* is short	

3.4 Furtive Pataḥ

When a word ends in a strong guttural (ה, ח, ע) that is *not* preceded by an *a*-class vowel (*pataḥ* or *qameṣ*), the Masoretes wrote *pataḥ* between the final vowel and the final guttural. This *pataḥ furtivum* ("furtive") was written slightly to the right to show that it is pronounced after the non-*a*-vowel and before the guttural. [This is all much easier to illustrate than explain!] These words thus appear to have two consecutive vowels, but the furtive vowel was used only as a signal to listeners that the word ended in a guttural, not with the long vowel.

רוּחַ	*rûᵃḥ*	wind, breath; spirit
רֵעַ	*rēᵃ'*	friend, neighbour, companion

3.5 Concepts

Adonai (§3.8)	generic noun	long vowel	short vowel	vocal *šewa*
closed syllable	*dageš lene*	*mappiq*	silent *šewa*	Yhwh (§3.8)
dageš forte	furtive *pataḥ*	open syllable	Tetragrammaton (§3.8)	

---

21. Each has various sub-types, which we leave to the reference grammars (see Bibliography).

3.6 Vocabulary

18.	אָדָם	humanity, humankind, man; Adam (cf. אִישׁ)	26.	הַר	mountain; mountain range, hill country, high country (especially in contrast to valleys; cf. Jg 1.19)
19.	אָח	brother, male relative	27.	ישׁב	dwell, live, settle; sit; stay, remain
20.	אכל	eat, devour, consume	28.	עַיִן	eye; well, water-source (cf. En-gedi [עֵין־גְּדִי] "the well of the kid")
21.	אמר	say, speak; think	29.	פָּנִים	face, presence (always plural)
22.	בַּת	daughter, female descendant (cf. Bathsheba [בַּת־שֶׁבַע] "daughter of an oath", or "seventh daughter")	30.	שׁלח	stretch out, reach; let go, send [away]
	בָּנוֹת	daughters	31.	שֵׁם	name, fame, reputation
23.	גּוֹי	people [group], nation, folk	32.	שׁמע	hear, listen (שׁמע + בְּקוֹל, hear the voice of ≈ obey)
24.	דֶּרֶךְ	(f.) road, way, path, journey; custom	33.	שָׁנָה	year (cf. רֹאשׁ הַשָּׁנָה, Rosh hashanah, "the head of the year" [New Year])
25.	הלךְ	come, go, walk, travel; a general term for travel/motion			

3.7 Exercises

1. Identify each *dageš* as either *forte* or *lene*, and each *šewa* as silent or vocal. Be prepared to explain how you determined your answer.

   a. אֲנָשִׁים   k. כָּבֵד
   b. אִשָּׁה   l. כֹּהֵן
   c. בְּטֶרֶם   m. כְּלִי
   d. בַּיִת   n. כֹּפֶר
   e. בֵּן   o. מִזְבֵּחַ
   f. דְּבַר   p. מִלְחָמָה
   g. דָּבָר   q. מֶלֶךְ
   h. דָּם   r. מִשְׁפָּט
   i. דֶּרֶךְ   s. נְאֻם
   j. וַיֹּאמֶר   t. עֲלֵיהֶם

2. Divide each word into syllables, and identify (the chart format is optional)
   a. each **syllable** as open or closed
   b. each **vowel** as long, short, or half
   c. each ***dageš*** as *forte* or *lene*
   d. each ***šewa*** as silent or vocal

Example:		יְכַפְּרוּ			תִּכְתְּבוּ		
Syllables	רוּ	פְּ	כַפ	יְ	בוּ	תְּ	תִּכ
Open/Closed	O	O	C	O	O	O	C
Vowel length	L	H	S	H	L	H	S
Dagešōt		forte				lene	lene
Šewas		vocal[22]	vocal			vocal	silent

---

22. *Dageš forte* technically represents two of the same letter, separated by [an invisible] silent *šewa*. This method of analyzing *dageš forte* is extremely artificial, and for pedagogical purposes only. The first of the doubled letter closes a syllable, and second opens the next syllable. Do not supply the "invisible" silent *šewa* that is "between" the doubled letters.

a.	בְּטֶרֶם	f.	מִלְחָמָה
b.	דָּבָר	g.	מִשְׁמֶרֶת
c.	דֶּרֶךְ	h.	מִשְׁפָּט
d.	כָּבֵד	i.	נְאֻם
e.	לַיְלָה	j.	תִּשְׁעִים

After you have done this, practice pronouncing these and the rest of your vocabulary.

3.8 Enrichment: The Divine Name

Most English Bibles distinguish "the LORD" (small capital letters) from "the Lord" (capitalized first letter). This distinguishes the personal *name* of God ("the LORD") from the generic noun or *title* that means "lord" or "master", referring to both humans ("my master") and God ("the/my Lord").

	Hebrew	Pronunciation	Interpretation
The Tetragrammaton (*tetra* "four" + *gramma* "letter") is the personal name of God.	יהוה		
For unknown reasons (although we might speculate that it was in order to avoid breaking the commandment of Ex 20.7), the divine name (יהוה) was read as though it were pointed with the vowels of אֲדֹנָי.	יהוה + vowels of אֲדֹנָי	*Adonai* (usually)	"Lord"
This yielded a form (יְהֹוָה) that came to be misread as "Jehovah" (which is not a biblical word or name). [The initial *ḥatef-pataḥ* was written as *šewa* under the -יְ.]	יְהֹוָה		"the Lord" "my Lord" "my Master"
Some read the form as שְׁמָא (i.e., "the Name" in Aramaic), although many read the Tetragrammaton as though it were הַשֵּׁם, "the Name" in Hebrew.	———	*Adonai*	
The original pronunciation of the divine name was thus lost.	יְהוָה		
Some clues to its pronunciation			
• In the Psalter, Exodus (twice) and Isaiah (three times), the first syllable of the divine name is used as a shortened form of the whole: הַלְלוּ־יָהּ (e.g., Ps 150.1, 6), which suggests the pronunciation of the first syllable.	יָהּ	*Yah*	
• Greek texts occasionally transliterate [and abbreviate] the divine name as Ιαω, which suggests a pronunciation like *Yahweh* (-ω- to approximate the sound of ו).	Ιαω		
The orthography is thus often restored as (using Masoretic pointing).	יְהוֶה *or* יַהְוֶה	*Yah · veh*	3 ms *hifil* imperfect of היה: "he causes to become/happen"

Regardless of the exact history of its pronunciation (which is largely conjectural), the main point is that the Tetragrammaton, YHWH, is a *personal* or *proper name* (not a title), whereas אֲדֹנָי (Lord, Master) and אֱלֹהִים (God) are common nouns that were used as titles for the true God. When we realize that the term glossed as "the LORD" is a proper name we can better understand the constant reference to "the LORD your God" (which often seems tautologous—who else would be God?), which would have reminded Israel that Y<small>HWH</small> was the God to whom Israel owed covenantal fealty, not Molech, Dagon, Baal, or any other pagan deity (all of whom could be called אֵל or אֱלֹהִים, "God", or אֱלֹהֵינוּ, "our God" by their worshippers).

יהוה אֱלֹהֶיךָ	Y<small>HWH</small> your God (Dt 6.1)
יהוה הוּא הָאֱלֹהִים	Y<small>HWH</small> is God [i.e., not Baal] (1 Kgs 18.39); probably in the sense: Y<small>HWH</small> is the [true] God!
וִידַעְתֶּם כִּי־אֲנִי יהוה׃	"... and that you may know that I am Y<small>HWH</small>."
וַיָּבֹא מֹשֶׁה וְאַהֲרֹן אֶל־פַּרְעֹה וַיֹּאמְרוּ אֵלָיו	So Moses and Aaron went to Pharaoh and said to him,
כֹּה־אָמַר יהוה אֱלֹהֵי הָעִבְרִים	"Thus says Y<small>HWH</small>, the god of the Hebrews: ..." (Ex 10.2b-3a).[23]
נְאֻם יהוה לַאדֹנִי	Y<small>HWH</small>'s declaration to my master/lord: ... (Ps 110.1)
כֹּה אָמַר אֲדֹנַיִךְ יהוה וֵאלֹהַיִךְ	Thus says your master, Y<small>HWH</small>, even your god: "... (Is 51.22)

1. When it immediately follows or precedes the term אֲדֹנָי (Lord, Master), יהוה is pointed with the vowels that correspond to אֱלֹהִים (אֲדֹנָי יְהוִה) so that it would be read as *'Elohim* rather than *'Adonai* (thus avoiding the reading *'Adonai 'Adonai*). This occurs about three hundred times in Biblical Hebrew.
2. Since the potential abuse of the name of God is a grave concern to many, some journals and books do not spell it out (e.g., as "Yahweh"), even when citing a biblical text in which it occurs (the journal or book might be thrown in the trash or otherwise treated callously, thus dishonoring "the Name"). Instead, they may follow the scribal practice of abbreviating it as "י, or transliterate it without vowels ("Yhwh" or "Y<small>HWH</small>"), or both.
3. Although the reasoning that led Israel to avoid or stop pronouncing the divine Name may have been (or at least sound) superstitious, its origin was positive—the desire to obey the commandment and avoid the curse. This was a "hedge" about the law: something that is never pronounced cannot be abused or misused. Some scholars suggest that the pronunciation of the Name was never known to any but the priests, and perhaps even passed from one high priest to the next, but there is no biblical evidence to support this theory.
4. The frequent use of these two terms to refer to the same God occasioned a great deal of discussion through the ages. Some rabbis suggested that יהוה refers to God in his covenantal, relational rôle, whereas אֱלֹהִים points to his godhood and power, and that the compound form יהוה אלהים (one half of its occurrences are in Gn 2–3) deliberately identified the creator God of Genesis 1 (only אלהים) as the covenantal and relational God (יהוה) of the rest of the book of Genesis.
5. These are not, of course, the only divine names or titles in Scripture, but they are by far the most common.

---

23. The point of Ex 10.2b-31 is that both Israelites and Egyptians [Pharaoh] will realize that the plagues that are afflicting Egypt are the work of the God of the Hebrews (i.e., Y<small>HWH</small>), not of some other god (cf. Ex 20.2).

Part II

Lessons 4–17
Nominal Grammar
Verbal Grammar (I)

This section introduces the forms of the noun and basic [strong] verb, and how they function in phrases, clauses, and sentences (morphosyntax), so that when you finish of these lessons, you should be able to read nominal phrases and verbal and non-verbal clauses.

You should be able to recognize and interpret the forms of the noun, adjective, pronouns (independent and suffixed), and basic verb, and in the exercises you will have read a number of clauses and phrases of Biblical Hebrew, so that the basic aspects of phrasal and clausal syntax should have become relatively familiar.

More specifically, you should be able to identify nouns as definite or indefinite; to identify which noun an adjective is modifying, whether or not that adjective is attributive, predicate (or substantive, if no noun is present); to recognize and identify construct chains as primarily subjective, objective, or adjectival; to identify (parse) verbal forms of the *qal* stem of the basic verb; and to identify the constituent elements of compound forms (e.g., a "word" made up of conjunction + preposition + article + noun).

Some of these concepts—e.g., nouns and verbs themselves, singular, plural, conjunctions, the imperative—will be familiar from English and other languages, even though their forms are quite different in Hebrew. Other aspects of these chapters—e.g., person, gender, number of verbal forms—will be familiar to students of languages which mark verbal forms to show agreement with their subjects. The construct—Hebrew's way of showing the "of" relationship between substantives—will be largely unknown to most students, although its function is the same as "of" in English (along with some other common English syntagms).

These lessons also introduce the concept of "discourse"—that words function (have "meaning") primarily in context, and that their context is not primarily the individual clause or sentence, but the entire story, sermon, poem, etc. in which they occur.[24] In fact, we will see that grammar (the combination of words and their forms to create meaningful texts) normally functions at the level of the paragraph (story, etc.) as well as within clauses and sentences.

Finally, because all languages are individual, some aspects of Hebrew, such as word order, as well as the non-semantic signals of clausal function (i.e., the distinction between conjunctive and disjunctive clauses, and the significance of that difference) will be entirely new ground for nearly all students.

The "enrichment" paragraphs in these lessons are extremely important, as they illustrate and apply the exegetical significance of the lessons. They are integral to the grammar, not merely "extras".

---

24. The term "discourse" refers to the entire episode, whether that is a story (narrative), a set of instructions, a declaration about future events (prophecy), poem, conversation, &c. "Discourse" can also refer to the entire world within which the episode occurs or is described (the "universe of discourse").

Lesson 4

The Noun

Many languages, like English, depend on endings, word order, or both to show a word's function in a sentence or clause, and to show the functional relationships between words. English adjectives, for example, usually come between the article and the noun that they modify (e.g., "the *red* book", "a *wise old* prophet"). A word's function or role in English is normally indicated by its position in the sentence:

a. The hungry man ate an apple.
b. A hungry apple ate the man.

Since word order in English is usually subject-verb-object (SVO), these sentences differ in function, even though all six words are identical (counting "a/an" as two forms of one lexical item).

Another way to show both function and association is to put an ending on a word—called an *inflection*[25]—different endings indicate the word's rôle in the sentence and the functional relationships between words in a clause. In the previous sentences, for example, we know that "hungry" describes "man" in a, but that it describes "apple" in b, since adjectives in English precede the word that they modify. Many languages, however, use fairly sophisticated inflectional systems to show agreement, or *concord* between words. Greek, Latin, and German, for example, use sets of endings called "cases" to indicate the rôle that different words play in the sentence (e.g., the nominative and accusative indicate the subject and object, respectively).

Endings may also indicate "gender" to show which words modify (or are modified by) other words. In French, for example, many adjectives add the letter "e" to the end of the lexical form when they modify feminine nouns. "Inflected" languages—in which endings show the function of and relationship between words (the case and gender + number, respectively)—often do not depend on word order to show syntax as heavily as does English. English, for example, uses gender only with third person pronouns ("his", "she", "its"), and only nouns are inflected for number (by the addition of the suffix "-s"), which means that word order is crucial to function in English (as the above sentence illustrates).

Although Hebrew nouns, adjectives, and verbs are inflected, sentences in Hebrew prose have a fairly restricted word order (although not nearly as rigid as word order in English). Inflection in Hebrew shows how words are related, but not syntactical function (as, e.g., subject or object). Nominal endings indicate *gender* (masculine, feminine) and *number* (singular, plural) in order to show *concord* between words, revealing which words "belong together".

4.1 *Gender*

Every content word (noun, finite verb, pronoun, adjective, participle)[26] in Biblical Hebrew belongs to one of two classes, called "masculine" and "feminine". Grammarians assign gender based on the gender of any verbs and adjectives that modify the word, and of pronouns that refer to it; i.e., feminine nouns are only modified by feminine adjectives and referred to by feminine pronouns,

---

25. To "inflect" is to "bend", the term reflects the view that the endings are "bent" forms of the lexical, or "regular/straight" form.
26. A language's lexicon (the list of all the words in that language) can be crudely divided between *content words* (verbs, nouns, adjectives, adverbs) and *function words* (everything else).

and *vice versa* for masculine nouns. Pairs of words that refer to *animate* objects reflect so-called *natural* gender:

Masculine Nouns			Feminine Nouns
man, husband	אִישׁ	אִשָּׁה	woman, wife
bull, ox	פַּר	פָּרָה	cow
(male) lamb	כֶּבֶשׂ	כִּבְשָׂה	ewe (female) lamb
king	מֶלֶךְ	מַלְכָּה	queen
son	בֵּן	בַּת	daughter
brother, [male] relative	אָח	אָחוֹת	sister, [female] relative
father, ancestor	אָב	אֵם	mother, ancestress

Nouns that are feminine tend to end in either ה- or ת-. Masculine nouns can end in any letter of the alphabet, but tend *not* to end in ה- or ת-. Although endings are clues to a noun's gender, they are only secondary clues, since we can be confident of a noun's gender only if it occurs as the subject of a verb, if it is modified by an adjective, or if it is referred to by a pronoun. The gender of words that are never modified in these ways cannot be identified with certainty; their apparent gender is assigned based on their endings. Adjectives and participles, on the other hand, always have the ending that matches the gender [and number, below] of the word that they refer to or modify.

4.2 Number

Number is the other part of the concord system of Biblical Hebrew. In addition to suggesting gender, every noun's ending indicates whether the noun refers to one or more than one, and, together with its gender, shows which words modify it. Again, as with gender (above), the number of an adjective or participle is determined by the word that it modifies or refers to, so that the reader or hearer can track how words in the clause or phrase relate to each other.

4.3 *The Forms of the Noun*

	Singular		Plural	
Masculine	סוּס[27]	horse or horse of	סוּסִים	horses
			סוּסֵי	horses of [28]
Feminine	סוּסָה	mare	סוּסוֹת	mares or mares of
	סוּסַת	mare of		
	מַלְכוּת	kingdom or kingdom of		

1. Masculine singular nouns are considered *unmarked*—i.e., they normally have no special ending.
2. Feminine singular nouns are considered *marked*, since they usually end in either ה-, or ת-, although some are unmarked (e.g., עִיר, city; אֶרֶץ, land).
   a. The construct singular ending (ת-) and the plural ending (וֹת-) *replace* the final ה-.
   b. If the lexical form ends in ת-, the singular has only one form (e.g., מַלְכוּת); the plural ending (וֹת-) follows the ת-.
3. Masculine plural nouns usually end in either יִם- or יֵ-. These endings are added directly to the end of the singular form. The *only* function of the ending יֵ- is to signal that a noun is both *plural* and *construct* (the "of" function; see Lesson 9).
4. Feminine plural nouns usually end in וֹת- (occasionally in יִם- or יֵ-).

27. Although סוּס and סוּסָה are related, they are considered separate nouns.
28. Hebrew uses a form called the "construct" to indicate the "of" relationship (Lesson 9).

5. Although most nouns follow the paradigm above, the plural of some cannot be predicted from their singular. ["Irregular" plurals are listed with their singulars in the vocabulary lists.]

father (m.)	אָב	אָבוֹת	fathers
man (m.)	אִישׁ	אֲנָשִׁים	men
woman (f.)	אִשָּׁה	נָשִׁים	women
house (m.)	בַּיִת	בָּתִּים	houses
daughter (f.)	בַּת	בָּנוֹת	daughters
city (f.)	עִיר	עָרִים	cities

Endings therefore merely *suggest* a noun's gender—they do not determine it. Nouns in the vocabulary lists that end in ה- or ת- are feminine, and other nouns are masculine, unless marked with "f." or "m."[29]

masc. sg. noun with "fem." plural	אָב	father	אָבוֹת	fathers
fem. sg. noun not in ה- or ת- with masc. plural	יָד	hand	יָדַיִם	hands [dual]
fem. sg. noun with "masc." plural	אִשָּׁה	woman	נָשִׁים	women
fem. sg. noun not in ה- or ת- with fem. plural	אֶרֶץ	land	אֲרָצוֹת	lands

There are, however, tendencies in the gender of nouns. For example, parts of the body (e.g., יָד, *hand*; רֶגֶל, *foot/leg*; זְרוֹעַ, *arm/shoulder*) are feminine (although שַׁד, *breast* is masculine!). Tools or objects that people use (e.g., חֶרֶב, *sword*) also tend to be feminine.

4.4 Dual

Biblical Hebrew also uses a *dual* ending (ַיִם-; accented on the penult) to refer to things that occur in pairs (e.g., parts of the body), or with units of measure to indicate two of that unit (e.g., "two hundred", "two thousand"). It shows that such things were thought of primarily in pairs, even though they are usually glossed as simple plurals ("feet", "wings", not "two feet", "two wings").

	Singular		Dual		
ear	אֹזֶן		אָזְנַיִם	ears	אָזְנֵי	ears of
hand	יָד		יָדַיִם	hands	יְדֵי	hands of
nose	אַף		אַפַּיִם	nostrils		
foot	רֶגֶל		רַגְלַיִם	feet	רַגְלֵי	feet of
palm	כַּף		כַּפַּיִם	palms	כַּפֵּי	palms of
sandal	נַעַל		נַעֲלַיִם	sandals	נַעֲלֵי	sandals of
wing	כָּנָף		כְּנָפַיִם	wings	כַּנְפֵי	wings of
year	שָׁנָה		שְׁנַיִם	two years		
hundred	מֵאָה		מָאתַיִם	two hundred		
thousand	אֶלֶף		אַלְפַּיִם	two thousand		

A few other words have dual form, but lack any obviously dual quality or function:

יְרוּשָׁלַ͏ִם	Jerusalem	מַיִם	water
מִצְרַיִם	Egypt[30]	שָׁמַיִם	sky, heaven

---

29. If a noun never occurs as the subject of a verb, *and* is never modified by an adjective or participle, lexicographers assign its gender based on its endings.

30. Egypt was divided into "Upper" and "Lower" Egypt, but this does not seem to be the reason for the form of its name.

4.5 Nominal Modification (I): The Article

To specify or *modify* something is to identify it more closely in order to narrow the field of possible referents. For instance, the main difference between "Please get a book" and "Please get the big tan book that is on the table" is that the second is more specific—the [a particular book, not just any book] big [not small or medium] tan [not red, yellow, blue, etc.] book that is on the table [not on the shelf, floor, etc.]. The adjectives "big" and "tan", and the relative clause "that is on the the table" all modify the word "book".

(1) Please get a book.
(2) ... *the* book
(3) ... *my* book
(4) ... *my tan* book
(5) ... *my small tan* book
(6) ... *my small tan* book *that is on the table*
(7) ... *my small tan* book—*my copy of The Princess and Curdie*—*that is on the table*

Thus, to modify nouns and other substantives, English uses the definite article (2), possession (3; either pronominal ["my", "her"] or nominal ["Susan's", "the prophet's"]), adjectives (4–5), relative clauses (6), apposition (7), and other means. In this example the phrases grow increasingly specific, so that (7) virtually assures us of getting the right book.

Like many languages, English uses these means of modification in virtually any combination, e.g., "a book that is on the table" (relative clause), or "my copy of *The Princess and Curdie*" (possession and identification). The complexity or fulness of a description is determined by the redundancy factor of language. That is, speakers and authors tend to include as much information as necessary for effective communication.[31] This is not an absolute value, and may apply more to casual conversation than to formal communication. On the other hand, authors who overestimate readers' knowledge may write what they think is clear, but their readers may not understand (or may misinterpret) what they are trying to say.

Hebrew can also modify nouns by attaching, for example, the article, some prepositions, and possessive pronominal forms directly to the noun (rather like the -*s* plural in English).[32] This first section describes the article, followed by a description of the most common conjunction.[33]

4.5.1 The Article: Function

The article in Biblical Hebrew corresponds roughly to English "the"; Biblical Hebrew has no indefinite article.[34] Words with the article are *articular*; words lacking the article are *anarthrous*. Articular nouns are grammatically "definite" and anarthrous nouns are often "indefinite", but Biblical Hebrew also has several other common ways to show a word's definiteness or indefiniteness (e.g., the "construct", below). Since English and Biblical Hebrew use their articles differently, articular words in the biblical text are not necessarily glossed using an English definite article.

---

31. The linguistic tendency toward efficiency explains why we rarely speak like sentence (7). If there were no other book nearby, we might say only, "Please get my [or even "the"] book", since that would communicate enough information.
32. Biblical Hebrew also modifies nominal function by means of separate words, such as prepositions, adjectives, relative clauses, the construct chain (the "of" relationship), nominal apposition, and hendiadys.
33. A conjunction links lexemes, phrases, or clauses; it does not "modify" a noun. It is included here for pedagogic reasons.
34. The actual situation is slightly more complicated. Generic English nouns (e.g., "cow", "house", "son"— i.e., not proper names) must be modified by either an article ("the", "a/an") or a possessive (e.g., "her", "our", "their"); since they are not used "absolutely", the sentence *Shepherd saw dog is "ill-formed" (both nouns require an article). Biblical Hebrew, however, has no word(s) whose function is limited to that of "a/an", although the word "one" (אֶחָד) occasionally fills that rôle.

That a word is indefinite does *not* mean that it is non-specific. For example, the phrase "a dog" in the sentence "She saw a dog" refers to a *specific* dog (the dog that she saw), even though the word "dog" is grammatically *indefinite*. Because Biblical Hebrew and English differ in their use of the article, words that are anarthrous in Hebrew often end up being definite in English. This is especially common in biblical poetry, where the article is relatively infrequent, but also occurs in prose.[35]

4.5.2 *The Article: Form*

The article consists of a syllable prefixed to a word: • הַ (*he-patah* plus *dageš forte* in the first letter of the word; the size of the *dageš forte* is deliberately exaggerated). This combination of *patah* + *dageš forte* is sometimes called the "pointing of the article" when it occurs at the beginning of a word. The article in Hebrew has only one form (i.e., it is not inflected for gender or number); apart from doubling the first consonant, it rarely affects the form of its word (#3, below).

1. This chart lists words with and without the article (the transliteration shows the doubling).[36]

[a] king	*melek*	מֶלֶךְ	הַמֶּלֶךְ	*hammelek*	the king
years	*šānîm*	שָׁנִים	הַשָּׁנִים	*haššānîm*	the years
[a] name	*šēm*	שֵׁם	הַשֵּׁם	*haššēm*	the name

2. When a word begins with a *bᵉgad-kᵉfat* letter, *dageš lene* "becomes" the *dageš forte* of the article:

[a] house	*bayit*	בַּיִת	הַבַּיִת	*habbayit*	the house
words	*dᵉbārîm*	דְּבָרִים	הַדְּבָרִים	*haddᵉbārîm*	the words

3. The article affects the form of a few words (in addition to doubling the first letter) in which a short vowel in the lexical form "lengthens" to *qames* when the article is added:

box (ark)	אֲרוֹן	הָאֲרוֹן	the box (ark)
land, earth	אֶרֶץ	הָאָרֶץ	the land, earth
garden	גַּן	הַגַּן	the garden
mountain, hill country	הַר	הָהָר	the mountain, hill country
festival	חַג	הֶחָג	the festival
people, nation	עַם	הָעָם	the people, nation
bull	פַּר	הַפָּר	the bull

4. In two situations the first letter of the word does not double, so that the pointing of the article is *not* • הַ (*he-patah* followed by *dageš forte*):
   a. Words that begin with *yod* or *mem* followed by vocal *šewa*.

Judahites	*yᵉhûdîm*	יְהוּדִים	הַיְהוּדִים	*hayhûdîm*	the Judahites
kings	*mᵉlākîm*	מְלָכִים	הַמְלָכִים	*hamᵉlākîm*	the kings

---

35. The opposite is also true. For example, the subject of Genesis 14.13a is an otherwise unknown fugitive, who is identified with the article: וַיָּבֹא הַפָּלִיט וַיַּגֵּד לְאַבְרָם *The fugitive* came and reported to Abram ... (Gn 14.13). To identify him in English, however, as "*the* fugitive" could mislead casual readers or hearers, who would conclude—based on their experience of English—that the article means that he was mentioned before this point in the story.
36. Transliterations are illustrative (pedagogical) rather than technically precise.

b. Words that begin with a guttural (ע ח ה א) or *reš* (ר).[37]

hill country	*har*	הַר	הָהָר	*hāhār*	*the hill country*
cities	*'ārîm*	עָרִים	הֶעָרִים	*he'ārîm*	*the cities*

5. These are all of the possible forms [pointings] of the article:

הַ	before words beginning with all letters except א, ה, ח, ע, ר	הַבַּיִת הַמֶּלֶךְ	*the house* *the king*
הַ	before ה, ח before -מְ (sometimes) and -יְ before -נְ (vocal *šewa*)	הַחֶרֶב הַמְרַגְּלִים הַיְהוּדִים הַנְּעָרִים	*the sword* *the spies* *the Jews* *the youths*
הָ	before -א, -ר, and (usually) -ע	הָאִישׁ הָעִיר הָרֹאשׁ	*the man* *the city* *the head*
הֶ	before -הָ before unaccented -הָ before unaccented -עָ	הֶחָכָם הֶהָרִים הֶעָרִים	*the wise man* *the mountains* *the cities*

N.B.: You do not need to memorize this list, or the table in #5; the main point is to recognize a word as *anarthrous* or *articular*.

4.6 The Conjunction waw (-וְ)

Conjunctions are particles or function words that *join* words, phrases, or clauses (cf. "junc*ture*", "junc*tion*"). English has a multitude of conjunctions, many of which also specify the relationship between the clauses or phrases as contrast ("but"), alternatives ("or"), concession ("although"), etc. Hebrew has a number of conjunctions, but the most common by far is the letter ו, which is prefixed to the first word in the clause or phrase.

4.6.1 Function

The conjunction *waw* (also pronounced *vuv*) shows, for example, *that* clauses are related, but it does not imply anything about *how* they are related. The *function* of the *waw* depends entirely on the relationship between the two clauses which it joins. It therefore can represent the function of nearly any English conjunction, such as "and", "but", "or", "because", "so that", "although". None of these represent its "real" or "literal" function. On the other hand, these glosses are not equally permissible—or even possible—in a given context. *The first step* in interpreting any *waw* is to understand the content of the clauses that it joins so that we can determine their relationship.

1. Vocal *šewa* usually links the conjunction to its word; adding the *waw* to a word does not affect the word itself (apart from the usual loss of initial *dageš lene* due to the vocal *šewa* under the conjunction):

---

37. On gutturals see §22.1; their lack of doubling is their only characteristic that affects the article (for doubling, see §3.2b).

a man	אִישׁ	וְאִישׁ	and a man
a day	יוֹם	וְיוֹם	but a day
a camel	גָּמָל	וְגָמָל	and a camel

2. The vowel under the conjunction may be affected by the first letter of the word. When prefixed to a word beginning with a *bilabial* ("two lips") consonant (ב מ פ), or to a word that has *šewa* as the first vowel, the conjunction becomes *šureq* (וּ). This is the only time that a Hebrew syllable begins with a vowel.

a house	בַּיִת	וּבַיִת	and a house
transgression	פֶּשַׁע	וּפֶשַׁע	or a transgression
a proverb	מָשָׁל	וּמָשָׁל	even a proverb
from the king	מֵהַמֶּלֶךְ	וּמֵהַמֶּלֶךְ	and from the king
their names	שְׁמוֹתֵיהֶם	וּשְׁמוֹתֵיהֶם	but their names

4.6.2 Form

These are all of the possible forms (pointings) of the conjunction *waw*:

Conjunction	Prefixed to …		Examples	
-וְ	all words except the following		וְיִשְׂרָאֵל	and Israel
-וּ	words beginning with *šewa*		וּנְעָרוֹת	or maidens
			וּבֶגֶד	and a garment
	words beginning with ב מ פ		וּמַלְכָּה	or a queen
-וַ	words beginning with *ḥatef-pataḥ*		וַחֲלוֹם	but a dream
	certain verbal forms		וַיִּכְתֹּב	[and] he wrote
	יהוה		וַיהוה	and Y<small>HWH</small>
-וֶ	words beginning with ḥatef-segol		וֶאֱמֶת	and truth
-וֵ	אֱלֹהִים		וֵאלֹהִים	and God
-וִ	words beginning with יְ		וִיהוּדָה	and Judah
-וָ	words beginning with *ḥatef-qameṣ*		וָעֳנִי	and affliction
	words beginning with an accented syllable		וָאָרֶץ	and earth
			וָלַיְלָה	and night
	a verbal form (all 1cs preterites)		וָאֶכְתֹּב	[and] I wrote

N.B.: You need not memorize this chart. The point is that any form beginning with a *waw* begins with the conjunction, *no matter how the* waw *is pointed.*[38]

---

38. About ten nouns in Biblical Hebrew begin with *waw*; none occurs more than 9 times; most occur once. No lexical item begins with -וּ.

4.7 Compound Forms ("Words")

A single form (word) can thus be comprised of several elements, such as the conjunction, article, and noun (always in that order). The goal is to be able to identify the components of the compound form on the right:

noun	article + noun	conjunction + article + noun
בַּיִת *a house*	הַבַּיִת *the house*	וְהַבַּיִת *and the house*
מֶלֶךְ *a king*	הַמֶּלֶךְ *the king*	וְהַמֶּלֶךְ *or the king*
נָשִׁים *women*	הַנָּשִׁים *the women*	וְהַנָּשִׁים *or the women*

4.8 Concepts

affix	bilabial	form	modification/modify	preposition
anarthrous	conjunction	function	noun	*qal*
article	context	gender	number	separable
articular	dual	inseparable	plural	singular
aspect	feminine	masculine	[nominal] prefix	

4.9 Vocabulary

.34	אָדוֹן	lord, master			
	אֲדֹנָי	(*my*) [*divine*] *Lord, Master* (note the ending)	.43	מִזְבֵּחַ	*altar; place of sacrifice*
.35	אֹהֶל	*tent; dwelling/home*	.44	מַיִם	*water;* מֵי *waters of*
.36	אֵשׁ	*fire*	.45	מִשְׁפָּט	*judgment, justice; justly; custom*
.37	הַ	*the* (for other forms, see §4.5.2(5))	.46	עבר	*cross over, pass through/by; trespass*
.38	וְ	*and, but, or, even, …*	.47	עוֹלָם	*long/remote time* (i.e., time without visible or imaginable end); *age*[*s*] (trad. "forever")
	וּ	וְ - before words that begin with ב, מ, פ or have initial vocal *šewa*			
.39	חֶרֶב	*sword, dagger, knife*	.48	עמד	*stand* (*stop; stay* (*in place*))
.40	יהוה	Y*hwh* (proper name)	.49	צָבָא	*army, host; military duty;* cf. the phrase יהוה צְבָאוֹת Y*hwh* [*of*] *hosts*
	יָהּ יָהּ	Y*h* (proper name; shortened form)			
.41	יָם	*sea;* יַמִּים *seas;* הַיָּם *the sea; west*	.50	רֹאשׁ	*head, top, peak* (of mountain); *beginning* (cf. #16)
.42	לקח	*take, get, acquire; buy; marry* (a wife)			

4.10 Exercises

Grammatical exercises are generally designed to help you to learn to see contextual examples of patterns so that you can begin to recognize them as they occur in the biblical text, not with the goal of assigning precise or exact functions to words, phrases, etc. The point of these particular exercises is that you learn to recognize some nominal affixes—the plural nominal endings, article,

II.4. *The Noun*

and conjunction *waw*—and to identify the vocabulary form of nouns when combined with these affixes.

1. Provide a gloss for each noun, identify its gender and number, and write out its lexical [vocabulary list] form.

   a. אָבוֹת (Ex 34.7)   h. מִזְבְּחוֹת (2 Kgs 21.3)
   b. אִישׁ (Nu 31.53)   i. נְבִיאַי נָבִיא *prophet* (1 Kgs 18.4)
   c. אֲנָשִׁים (2 Sa 7.14)   j. נְפָשׁוֹת (Lv 27.2)
   d. בָּנוֹת (Ezk 14.16)   k. נָשִׁים (1 Kgs 11.1)
   e. בָּנִים (Hos 11.10)   l. עָרַי (Ps 69.36)
   f. בָּתִּים (Ex 1.21)   m. רוּחוֹת (Ps 104.4)
   g. הָרִים (2 Kgs 19.23)   n. שָׁמַי (Ps 148.4)

2. Provide English glosses for these phrases. Be prepared to analyze and explain their elements (e.g., the spelling of the article or conjunction). If a word has more than one gloss translate it both ways (e.g., אִישׁ as both "husband" and "man"); Give the lexical form of words that do not have their lexical form. Note the hints on the left.

   a. אָדָם וֵאלֹהִים   i. יוֹם וְלַיְלָה   לַיְלָה *night*
   b. אִישׁ וְאִשָּׁה   j. הַמֶּלֶךְ וְהַשָּׂרִים   שַׂר *noble*
   c. וּבַיִת   k. הַנְּבִיאִים וְהַמֶּלֶךְ   נָבִיא *prophet*
   d. וְהַבַּיִת   l. עָרִים וְאֲרָצוֹת
   e. בָּנִים וּבָנוֹת   m. הֶעָרִים וְהֶהָרִים
   f. הָהָר וְהֶהָרִים   n. הֶעָרִים וְהַבָּתִּים
   g. כֹּהֲנִים וּמְלָכִים   o. שָׁלוֹם וּמִלְחָמָה   מִלְחָמָה *war*
   h. כֶּסֶף וְזָהָב   p. הַשָּׁמַיִם וְהָאָרֶץ   שָׁמַיִם *heaven(s), sky*

4.11 *Enrichment: Hendiadys*

Hendiadys (Greek for "one through two") is the name given to two words that can be linked to refer to a single entity. A common hendiadys, שָׁמַיִם וָאָרֶץ—*heaven and earth*, refers to the entire created order (perhaps what we call the "universe"), for which there is no specific lexeme in Biblical Hebrew.

Jonah used a unique hendiadys to tell the sailors that he feared [served] "Y<small>HWH</small>, the god of heaven, who made *the sea and the dry land*" (אֶת־הַיָּם וְאֶת־הַיַּבָּשָׁה (Jon 1.9)). Since the sailors wanted to get *from* the sea *onto* dry land (1.13), Jonah's way of identifying the creator was crafted to catch their attention! And it worked, as their response shows: a great fear (1.10), duplicated after they throw Jonah into the sea (1.16).

The satan [accuser] tells Y<small>HWH</small> to afflict Job himself (rather than merely destroy his property and family), by saying "Only put forth your hand and strike *his bone and his flesh* [אֶל־עַצְמוֹ וְאֶל־בְּשָׂרוֹ] ..." (Jb 2.5), not a reference to internal and external physical affliction, but to Job's entire body.

Hendiadys is also a *verbal* function, when two verbs describing the same event or when one verb modifies the following verb. In 1 Kgs 17.20, the two verbs (וַיִּקְרָא ... וַיֹּאמַר ...) must refer to the same event since calling and speaking are not discrete acts (i.e, to call is to speak).

וַיִּקְרָא אֶל־יְהוָה וַיֹּאמַר יְהוָה אֱלֹהָי   And *he called* to Y<small>HWH</small>, and *said* "Y<small>HWH</small> my God, ..."
(1 Kgs 17.20)

Occasionally as many as three verbs describe one event; the combination in Jg 9.7 suggests that Jotham was probably shouting so that the rulers of Shechem could hear him from atop Mount Gerizim:

וַיִּשָּׂא קוֹלוֹ וַיִּקְרָא וַיֹּאמֶר לָהֶם שִׁמְעוּ אֵלַי   And *he lifted* his voice and *called* and *said* to them "Listen to me, ..." (Jg 9.7)

Lesson 5

The Hebrew Verb[39]

The verb may be thought of as the "motor" of the sentence: it makes the sentence "run" or "go". It does this by identifying what the subject of the sentence did, or by describing the subject itself.[40]

a. Moses wrote Psalm 90.
b. Moses was humble.

Sentence (a) tells us what Moses did (it identifies a deed that he performed), but does not describe him; sentence (b) describes Moses himself, without telling us anything about what he has done. Both functions can be combined in a single sentence, which can be either *compound* (c) (i.e., two or more *parallel* clauses) or *complex* (d) (i.e., at least one clause is *subordinate* to another):

c. Moses was a humble man, and he wrote Psalm 90.
d. Moses, who was a humble man, wrote Psalm 90.

Since English is a "slot" language in which a word's function is determined by its position, we normally recognize the verb in an English clause or sentence by its *position*—the verb is the word following the subject (which is the first word or group of words in the sentence).

e. The *bears* killed forty-two men.
f. The Levite *bears* the ark.

In (e) the word "bears" is the subject (since it begins the sentence and is preceded by the article "the"), and "killed" is the verb. In (f), however, "bears" is a verb, identifying or naming what the Levites (the subject) did to the ark. In either case, we know that "killed" and "bears" are the predicates of their respective sentences because they follow their subjects.[41]

In (a) through (f), as in languages in general, the verbs define or describe the subject or its action(s). Verbs are therefore part of the *comment* of their clause.

A clause consists of a *topic* (or "subject") and a *comment* (or "predicate"). In sentence (a), "God" is the topic and "created heaven and earth" is the comment (it describes an action of the subject). A sentence always consists of at least one clause, although a clause may not be a complete sentence. All three of the following sentences represent "complete" thoughts, but the thought represented by (h) is "more complete" than that in (g), and (i) is the most complete of the three. Only (g) consists of a single clause.

---

39. Much of the rest of this book addresses the functions and forms of the verb in Biblical Hebrew, not because verbs are somehow more fundamental or basic or "important" than nouns, but because the verbal system is the most complex aspect of Hebrew grammar.

40. This distinction between action and state is discussed further below (§15.1).

41. We sometimes recognize that a word is the verb because of its context, not because of its form or syntax:
    a. "Bank!" the flight instructor screamed.
    b. "Bank" was his laconic reply to "Where are you going?"
    c. "Bank ahead" called the lookout on the riverboat.

Linda Dietch, a former student, told me that this example reminded her "… of my dad's answer when I asked why he wasn't around when my mom went into labor with my older brother: 'I fell at the bank.' He fractured a vertebrae in his back and so he and my mom were hospitalized at the same time. My sympathy turned to irritation when I learned that he had fallen out of a tree stand at a river bank. He went on a hunting trip, leaving my mom alone when she was 8.5 months pregnant with their first child!".

g. Job was patient.
h. Job was patient, even when he was tested.
i. Job was patient, even when his flocks and herds were stolen, his servants and children killed, and he himself afflicted with boils.

Like nouns, verbs in Biblical Hebrew are inflected for several reasons: (1) to indicate that the form is a verb; and (2) to show the person, gender, and number (§5.1.3) of the noun(s) that it modifies (its "subject"). Their inflection also indicates (3) the general function or nature of the clause (especially in narrative); and (4) the general time frame of the event or state that they describe. Verbal affixes (the "bits and pieces" that inflect the form) can be prefixed or suffixed to the verbal root (§5.1.1).

Verbal inflection is therefore part of the concord system (§4.1–2), since its affixes indicate its subject (the word that it modifies or comments on), and the relationship between the event or state that it describes and those described by verbs in other clauses. English has lost most of its inflectional system; only third person singular forms are inflected by adding "s" ("I/you/we/they sing" *vs.* "he/she sings").

5.1 *Form*

In discussing the verbal conjugations (Lessons 5, 6, 8, 10, 12, 13), "stems" (Lessons 18–21), and weak verbal roots (Lessons 24, 27, 28, 30, 31) the term "diagnostic" refers to those few vowel points (including *dageš*) that enable us to distinguish one form from another, or to determine the stem and root of a particular form. This is one aspect of a verb's *morphology*, or "shape", which is created by its subject affixes (§5.1.1) and by the vowel points that the Masoretes added to the consonantal text to tell readers how to read a particular form. We have already looked at the basic morphology of the noun (e.g., endings for gender and number); now we turn to the morphology of the verb in Biblical Hebrew.

5.1.1 *Subject (PGN) Affixes*

Verbs modify their subjects by identifying what the subject is or does. In English the verb follows the subject (word order again), but Hebrew verbs have affixes (prefixes and suffixes) that agree with the person, number, and gender of the subject.

1. The *person* [**P**] of the verb (first, second, third) shows the relationship of the speaker or narrator to the action or state described by the verb:

Person	The speaker/narrator ...		
1st	... describes himself as doing the action, or as existing in the state described by the verb	"I know" "I thought"	"We see" "We went"
2nd	... directly *addresses* (speaks to) the subject of the verb	"You know" "You thought"	"You see" "You went"
3rd	... talks or writes *about* the subject of the verb	"He knows" "They thought"	"She sees" "He went"

2. The verb's *gender* [**G**] (masculine, feminine) and *number* [**N**] (singular, plural) agree with the number and gender of its subject, so that the form of the Hebrew verb is sufficient to identify its subject (unlike the verb in English, which requires an explicit subject).

The three features of person-gender-number [**PGN**] are indicated by the form of the verb itself, whereas the subject of an English sentence is always a separate word, either a noun ("Moses", "a servant") or pronoun ("he", "they"). The subject in Hebrew *may* be expressed by a noun or pronoun, but the narrator's decision to identify the subject by using a separate word (whether it is a proper name or a common noun), phrase, or clause is one of the ways that he shapes the story.

Furthermore, although "he went" in English describes the action of one male ("he"), the form of the English verb ("went") tells us nothing about its subject. The verb in Hebrew, however, identifies its subject as singular or plural, masculine or feminine, and first, second, or third person. Although "you" is completely ambiguous in English (singular? plural? male? female?), there is a specific

Hebrew verbal form for each 2nd person number-gender combination (2ms, 2fs, 2mp, 2fp), all of which are represented by "you" in contemporary English.

The range of subjects to which a given verbal form may refer is thus modified by verbal suffixes and prefixes—affixes attached to the end and beginning of the verbal root (below)—so that the verb agrees with the person, gender, and number [**PGN**] of its subject. There are two main sets of verbal PGN affixes, one for each of the two main sets of conjugations.

5.1.2 *Verbal Root*

Every verbal form consists of a set of consonants called the "verbal root". The root usually has three, but sometimes two (rarely four) of these consonants, which we will call "radicals".[42] Verbal roots have been abstracted by grammarians from the forms of the verb.[43]

מָשַׁלְתִּי	*I ruled/reigned*	מְשֹׁל	*Rule! (masc. sg.)*
יִמְשֹׁל	*He shall rule/reign*	הַמֹּשְׁלִים	*Those (masc. pl.) who rule ...*
מָשַׁל	*He ruled/etc.*	הִמְשִׁילוּהוּ	*They caused him to rule*

When early grammarians recognized that these and other forms share the consonants מ-שׁ-ל, and that they all refer in some way to "rule", "govern[ment]", "dominion", etc., they concluded that these three consonants—in this order—were the "root" of a verb מָשַׁל, "rule/govern", as well as the root (or source) of nouns referring to rule or government. Since many roots in the Semitic languages—including Biblical Hebrew—have three radicals, the Semitic languages are said to be "triradical".

Many lexical tools (lexicons, theological wordbooks and dictionaries, concordances, etc.) list both verbal forms and nouns under the verbal root that they are either "derived from" or "related to" (e.g., these nouns that contain משל and refer to governance are listed after the verbal root מָשַׁל).

מֶמְשָׁלָה	*rule, dominion, realm, kingdom*
מֹשֶׁל	*rule, dominion; authority* (2x)
מִשְׁלָה	*rule, dominion; ruler*

In order to use any of these tools you must know whether it lists words alphabetically or by root, and be able to identify the putative "roots" of nouns, since the nouns will be listed under [after] the verbal forms.

5.1.3 *Conjugation*

Hebrew verbs have two main sets of forms—the *perfect* (which has a more or less unique set of PGN affixes) and the *imperfect* (which "shares" PGN affixes and other characteristics with other conjugations). The main difference between these two main sets of conjugations[44] is that the perfect uses PGN *endings* to agree with the subject, whereas the imperfect uses PGN *prefixes and endings* to agree with the subject. The perfect is thus also called the "suffix conjugation" and the imperfect is called the "prefix conjugation". Their functions also differ (below). Although it is tempting to describe or think of these as tenses, they are not as fundamentally time-oriented as Indo-European tenses; any connotation of "tense" in Biblical Hebrew depends more heavily on the surrounding context and syntax than in, for example, English.

Some conjugations in Biblical Hebrew, such as the preterite and imperative, have a single or primary function—to narrate a series of past events and to give commands, respectively. The perfect and imperfect, on the other hand, have various functions, depending on, for example, whether or not they have a prefixed conjunction (-וְ). And some—more specifically, the imperfect—also has other functions that are discerned largely from their context, such as when the imperfect functions as a third-person "imperative", as in "He should/must/ought to ..."

---

42. The term "radical" refers to the consonants of the verbal root (Latin *radix*, "root").
43. Some grammars and most lexicons use the "root" sign (√) when they discuss verbal roots.
44. The term "conjugation" is more neutral than either "tense" or "aspect", both of which are potentially misleading with regard to Biblical Hebrew.

Finally, the descriptions of the functions of the various conjugations in this book refer primarily to their function in biblical *narrative* or *instructional* discourse.[45]

5.1.4 *Stem (binyan)*

There are eight main ways of constructing verbal forms in Biblical Hebrew in order to show the type of action being described by the verb. The medieval grammarians referred to these combinations of vowels and affixes as *binyanîm* ("buildings"), since they were "built" on or from the root; today called "stems". [see §18.1][46]

In *form*, some stems have a doubled middle radical (*piel, pual*), some have stem prefixes (*hifil, hofal, nifal*), one has both (*hitpael*), and one has neither (*qal*). Note that all of these names, except for "qal" have the letters "p" or "f" and "l". This is because the early rabbinic grammarians used the verbal root פעל *p'l* ("do, make") as their paradigm verb, following the example of the Arabic gramarians.

Where English uses pronouns, helping verbs, and prepositions to show the type of action described by a verb ("David *hid* the sword", "David *hid* [*himself*]", "David *was hidden*", "The sword *was hidden by David*"), Hebrew shows the *function* of the verbal form by, e.g., doubling the middle letter of the verbal root, and varying the forms and vowels of the prefixes.

Doubled II-radical		**Prefix**		**Both**		**Neither**	
Piel	משל	Hifil	המשיל				
Pual	משל	Hofal	המשל	Hitpael	התמשל	Qal	משל
		Nifal	נמשל				

We begin with the *qal* (Q)[47] stem, since more than two-thirds of all verbal forms in the Bible are in the *qal*. The word "*qal*" means "light"; *qal* is the only stem that has no stem prefix (its only prefix is the subject [PGN] prefix in imperfect and preterite), and no doubled letters (in the strong verb).[48]

5.2 *The Imperfect*

The prefix conjugation—the "imperfect"—primarily describes events or states that are either present or future to the time of the speaker. It therefore tends to be more frequent in direct quotations and poetry than in narrative. (Biblical Hebrew rarely anticipates events, whereas anticipation is not infrequent in English, as in "He would soon discover …".) It is therefore unlike the English imperfect (or the French *imparfait*), which refers to a continuous action in the past (e.g., "He was walking")—the Hebrew imperfect does not refer to the past.[49]

5.2.1 *Form*

The imperfect[50] uses *prefixes* and some *suffixes* to show the person, gender, and number of its subject. Every form of every imperfect has a PGN prefix; half of the forms also have endings. The affixes of the imperfect are:

---

45. In biblical poetry, conjugations seem to be used more for poetic reasons than for any temporal reference.
46. They can also be called "constructions" or "patterns". In some languages the term "stem" refers to the "unchangeable" part of a verbal or nominal form. In Semitic studies the three radicals are called the "root"; the verbal stems (combinations of vowels, prefixes, and doubling) are built "on" or "from" those roots.
47. The name of the stem sounds like "Cal" (a nickname for "Calvin"), not *kwal* (unlike English "q", Hebrew ק does not require a following "u").
48. This means that doubling is not a sign of the *qal*, as it is of some other stems (below).
49. This statement refers primarily to biblical narrative, not to poetry.
50. The imperfect is also called "*yiqtol*" (the 3ms form of the *qal* imperfect of the verb קטל *qtl*, "kill"), or the "prefix conjugation" (since every form has a prefix). The name "imperfect" reflects the view that it describes action that was yet-to-be-complete.

Person	Gender	Singular		Plural	
1st	Common	אֶ -	I	נְ -	We
2nd	Masc.	תָּ -	You	תְּ - וּ	You
	Fem.	תְּ - י		תְּ - נָה	
3rd	Masc.	יִ -	He/It	יִ - וּ	They
	Fem.	תְּ -	She/It	תְּ - נָה	

1. Two sets of forms (2ms/3fs, 2fp/3fp) are identical, and can be distinguished only by context.
2. The dash (-) represents the consonants of the verbal root, which either follows, or is "surrounded by" the PGN affix.
3. A form with a *yod* prefix is always *masculine*.
4. The six forms with a - תּ prefix all require endings, context, or both to distinguish their PGN.
5. These affixes *must be memorized*, since they are used in the imperfect and preterite[51] of all verbs, and the second-person endings are used in the imperative of all verbs.
6. Although the subject prefix is always followed by a vowel, none is listed here because the prefix vowel varies from stem to stem.

5.2.2 *Qal Imperfect*

The term *qal* (related to the verb קלל *qll*, "be light, slight, trifling") means "light", and was used because the *qal* lacks the doubling and prefixes (or both) that occur in the other stems (Lessons 18–21). The term "*qal*[52] imperfect" refers to a particular combination of three elements: the radicals of the verbal root, the PGN affixes of the imperfect, and the vowels that characterize the *qal* imperfect, a combination that yields the following paradigm:

Person	Gender	Singular		Plural	
1st	Common	אֶמְשֹׁל	I rule	נִמְשֹׁל	We rule
2nd	Masc.	תִּמְשֹׁל	You rule	תִּמְשְׁלוּ	You rule
	Fem.	תִּמְשְׁלִי		תִּמְשֹׁלְנָה	
3rd	Masc.	יִמְשֹׁל	He rules	יִמְשְׁלוּ	They rule
	Fem.	תִּמְשֹׁל	She rules	תִּמְשֹׁלְנָה	

1. The vowel for the *qal* PGN prefixes is *ḥireq* (except 1cs—remember the close relationship between the *i/e* vowels). Two other stems also have *ḥireq* as their prefix vowel (*nifal*, *hitpael*,[53] Lessons 18, 19).
2. The first radical (*not* the PGN prefix) is followed by silent *šewa*.
3. The vowel after the second radical in the *qal* imperfect is often *ḥolem* (all forms except those with a vocalic ending). Because this vowel helps distinguish one stem from another, it is often called the "stem" or "theme" vowel.
4. Verbs that have a guttural (ה, ח, ע) as their second or third radical (e.g., שמע, שלח) usually have *pataḥ* as their theme vowel. This *pataḥ* is the only difference between these verbs and מְשֹׁל.

51. The *preterite* is the conjugation that identifies the "main storyline" of biblical narratives (Lesson 6).
52. It is also called "G" for *Grundstamm* (German: "basic stem").
53. The names of the stems reflect the verbal root פעל ("do, make"), which was used as the paradigm verb by the early Jewish grammarians. The names (which are the 3ms perfect of פעל for each stem) are often written with a sign for ʿayin: *nifʿal, hitpaʿel* to show the presence of the middle radical. This is left out for the sake of simplicity.

Person	Gender	Singular		Plural	
1st	Common	אֶשְׁמַע	I hear	נִשְׁמַע	We hear
2nd	Masc.	תִּשְׁמַע	You hear	תִּשְׁמְעוּ	You hear
	Fem.	תִּשְׁמְעִי		תִּשְׁמַעְנָה	
3rd	Masc.	יִשְׁמַע	He hears	יִשְׁמְעוּ	They hear
	Fem.	תִּשְׁמַע	She hears	תִּשְׁמַעְנָה	

5. Verbs with א as their third radical (III-א verbs) have *qameṣ* where שמע has *pataḥ*, because the א cannot close the syllable (e.g., מצא: אֶמְצָא, תִּמְצָא, etc.). Since the א is silent, it is not followed by silent *šewa*, the second syllable is open, and the vowel is long.

Person	Gender	Singular		Plural	
1st	Common	אֶמְצָא	I find	נִמְצָא	We find
2nd	Masc.	תִּמְצָא	You find	תִּמְצְאוּ	You find
	Fem.	תִּמְצְאִי		תִּמְצֶאנָה	
3rdğ	Masc.	יִמְצָא	He finds	יִמְצְאוּ	They find
	Fem.	תִּמְצָא	She finds	תִּמְצֶאנָה	

5.2.3 *Function (HBI §2.2.2)*

The function of the imperfect depends on its context, especially on the genre (literary type) of material, and sometimes on whether or not the conjunction (-וְ) is prefixed to the form. In the lengthy narratives of Genesis, for example, the imperfect is relatively infrequent, whereas it is by far the most frequent verb form in Leviticus (most of which is instruction, commandment, and prohibition, with little narration).

1. The imperfect usually occurs in direct or indirect quotations,[54] and generally refers to *future* or *present* events.[55]

כָּל־הַשֹּׁמֵעַ יִצְחַק־לִי:	Everyone who hears *will laugh* for me (Gn 21.6).
וְרַב יַעֲבֹד צָעִיר:	"... and the older *shall serve* the younger" (Gn 25.23).
וַיֹּאמֶר אָנֹכִי אֶגְאָל:	He said, "*I will redeem*" (Ru 4.4).
זֹאת בְּרִיתִי אֲשֶׁר תִּשְׁמְרוּ	This is my covenant which *you shall keep* (Gn 17.10).

It occurs in both main and secondary clauses, as in Gn 17.10. "This is my covenant" is the *main* clause—it is the primary part of the sentence—and the relative clause (introduced by the relative אֲשֶׁר) is *secondary* or supplemental to it.

2. The following list of functions of the imperfect is not meant to intimidate beginning students, but rather to arm you against simply equating the imperfect with the [English] future by demonstrating some of the variety of expression possible within a single conjugation. When beginning your study of Hebrew, assume that an imperfect verb refers to the present or future, unless a modifying particle occurs, or there is enough context to show that it has

---

54. An indirect quotation reports what someone said, thought, or felt, and is usually introduced by "that": "He said *that* she had finished". A direct quotation would be: "He said, 'She finished'." Indirect quotations also occur with verbs of perception (e.g., "see", "hear"), and emotion (e.g., "fear", "rejoice").

55. Since those have not yet occurred, they may be called *irrealis* ("not real"). This does not mean that the events will not happen, merely that they had not happened as of the time of the quotation.

some other use (or your teacher directs you otherwise). You will find this list more helpful when you begin reading the biblical text.

a. The imperfect occurs in conditional sentences, generally preceded by אִם (*if*) or אִם לֹא (*if not*; also with אוּלַי, *perhaps*):

אִם־יִגְאָלֵךְ טוֹב יִגְאָל   "If *he will redeem* you—good, *let him redeem*.
וְאִם־לֹא יַחְפֹּץ לְגָאֳלֵךְ   But if *he is* not *pleased* [*willing*] to redeem you …" (Ru 3.13).
אִם־תִּגְאַל גְּאָל וְאִם־לֹא יִגְאַל   "If *you will redeem*, redeem! But if *he will not redeem*" (Ru 4.4)

b. The imperfect can be negated by לֹא or אַל (both ≈ *not*). Depending on the context, a negated second person imperfect may express a *prohibition*:[56]

לֹא נֵרֵד כִּי־הָאִישׁ אָמַר אֵלֵינוּ   "… we *will not go down*, for the man said to us,
לֹא־תִרְאוּ פָנָי   'You *shall not see* my face …" (Gn 43.5).
וַיֹּאמֶר לֹא תִשְׁלָחֻהוּ:   He said, "*Do not send*" (2 Kgs 2.16).
לֹא תִּרְצָח   "You *shall not murder*" (Ex 20.13).
לֹא תִּגְנֹב   "You *shall not steal*" (Ex 20.15).

c. When it is not first in its clause, the imperfect may be modified by a particle:

וְכָל־עֵשֶׂב הַשָּׂדֶה טֶרֶם יִצְמָח   and *every* wild herb *had not yet sprouted*, …
(Gn 2.5; טֶרֶם ≈ *not yet*); = "no herb had *yet* sprouted"
עַד אֲשֶׁר־תָּשׁוּב חֲמַת אָחִיךָ:   "… until your brother's anger *turns away*"
(Gn 27.44; עַד אֲשֶׁר ≈ *until*)
אוּלַי יִישַׁר בְּעֵינֵי הָאֱלֹהִים   "Perhaps it will be good in God's eyes …"
(Nu 23.27; אוּלַי ≈ *perhaps*)

d. When the imperfect occurs with the conjunction (וְ) it *always begins* its clause, is usually followed by its subject, and generally refers to the future. It seems to imply that the imperfect is closely linked to the preceding verb (which is often an imperative or another imperfect). Many times the verb merely describes the next in a logical or chronological sequence of events, but, depending on the *context* and on the *relationship* between the function ("meaning") of the verbal roots, this syntagm may also imply purpose or result.

נַעֲשֶׂה אָדָם … וְיִרְדּוּ בִדְגַת הַיָּם   "Let us make mankind … *so that they may rule* …"
(Gn 1.26).
אוּלַי יִתְעַשֵּׁת הָאֱלֹהִים לָנוּ וְלֹא נֹאבֵד: "Perhaps God will save us, *so that we do not perish*" (Jon 1.6).
וְנִחְיֶה וְלֹא נָמוּת   "… that we *may live* and *not die*" (Gn 43.8).

3. Hebrew lacks forms that correspond to what are called "helping", "auxiliary", or "modal" verbs (e.g., "may, might, will/would, shall/should, ought").[57] Imperfect forms can apparently serve any of these functions, but the nuance of any given imperfect form is open to debate (see the examples above). This is especially clear in biblical poetry, where a single form might be rendered as either "*May* Yhwh *bless* you" (precative—a prayer), "Yhwh *blesses* [*is blessing*] you" (present indicative), or "Yhwh *will/shall*[58] *bless* you" (future). Even published translations differ, and their renderings tend merely to follow tradition. For now, unless the context demands a modal interpretation, we will use the simple present or future to represent the imperfect (unless the context, especially a particle, indicates that the verb is functioning modally, as in Gn 17.18).

---

56. The imperative (Lesson 8) in Biblical Hebrew is used only for positive commands, not for prohibitions.
57. The verbal root יכל, glossed as "[be] able", "can", or "could", is introduced with the infinitives (below).
58. The distinction between "will" and "shall" is complex, but this grammar uses "will" in the first person for simple futurity, and "shall" for intent, determination, or choice. In the second and third persons, "shall" is much stronger than "will" (e.g., "You shall not steal"). In American English, at least, this distinction is largely lost. "Shall" is viewed as more "correct" or "formal"; emphasis tends to be by means of vocal stress ("You *will* not get any dessert!").

וַתֹּאמֶר הָאִשָּׁה ...	The woman said ... "From the fruit of the trees of the
מִפְּרִי עֵץ־הַגָּן נֹאכֵל:	garden we *may eat*" (Gn 3.2)
אֶת־שְׁנֵי בָנַי תָּמִית	"My two sons *you may put to death* ..." (Gn 42.37)
לוּ יִשְׁמָעֵאל יִחְיֶה לְפָנֶיךָ:	"If only Ishmael *might live* before you!" (Gn 17.18; לוּ, *if only*)

4. This brief discussion of conjugational function shows that, as in vocabulary (Lesson 2), so in grammar, there is no direct or one-to-one correspondence between Biblical Hebrew and English (i.e., they are non-isomorphic). The function of a given form depends on a complex interplay of its lexical function, the genre in which it occurs, and the content of its immediate and larger contexts (perhaps especially, its relationship to the preceding clause). The verbal conjugation therefore has no "basic", "fundamental", or "central" function *in the other language*. This in turn implies that no word or form has a "literal" function in another language (again, especially when the languages are as varied in form and function as Biblical Hebrew and English).

5.3 The "Sign of the Object"

Hebrew uses a particle to point out the *definite direct object* of the verb. The particle אֵת (or אֶת־) occurs only before definite direct objects (in Ex 34.13, the object precedes the verb).

... אֶשְׁלַח אֶת־עֲבָדַי אֵלֶיךָ	... I will send *my servants* to you ... (1 Kgs 20.6)
... וְאֶת־אֲשֵׁרָיו תִּכְרֹתוּן	..., and *their Asherahs* you shall cut down (Ex 34.13)

5.4 *Maqqef*

A horizontal line (־), written evenly with the top horizontal stroke of, e.g., ד (ד־) can link two or more words into a single accentual unit, so that they are pronounced as though they were one form (although they are still separate "words"). This is especially common when the first consists of a single syllable, such as the sign of the object (Ex 34.13, above).

כָּל־אֵלֶה	all these
בֶּן־אֲחִינֹעַם	son of Ahinoam
עַל־הָעִיר	against the city

5.5 Parsing Verbs

To parse is to identify the "parts" (Latin: *pars*) of a thing. Parsing verbal forms allows us to check our understanding of a form, since our ability to understand it depends on identifying or recognizing it accurately. Parsing a Hebrew verb entails identifying the following elements or "parts" (some do not yet apply):

Lexical form	The radicals of the verbal root
Gloss(es)	One or more of the glosses linked to its *lexical form*
PGN	The person, gender, and number of the subject form (e.g., 3fp)
Stem	For now, we are studying the *qal*
Conjugation	E.g., imperfect, preterite, imperative, perfect
Prefixes	There are only four possibilities for this column: the conjunction *waw*, the interrogative הֲ– (§18.1.2), inseparable prepositions (Lesson 7), the article (only on participles [Lesson 12])
Suffixes	This refers *only* to the PGN of pronominal suffixes (Lesson 14; *not* the PGN of the subject)

The "parsing form" at the end of this lesson may be reproduced and used throughout your studies.

5.6 Frequency

The occurrence and distribution of the conjugations vary widely, the perfect and infinitive absolute being the most (29%) and least frequent (less than 1%), respectively. The conjugations are not distributed evenly through the Bible; e.g., imperatives (positive commands) are more frequent in the poetic books (Pss) than in, for example, the specifically "covenantal" books (Ex, Lv, Dt).

More than one-fifth (22%) of all verbs in Biblical Hebrew are imperfect. Together with the preterite (Lesson 6), *two-fifths of all verbal forms (42%)* use the same set of subject [PGN] affixes.

Conjugation	Occurrences	% of Total
Perfect	21032	28.4%
Imperfect	16110	21.8%
Preterite	14977	20.3%
Imperative	4270	5.8%
Infinitive Absolute	796	1.1%
Infinitive Construct	6985	9.4%
Participle	9787	13.2%
Total	**73957**	

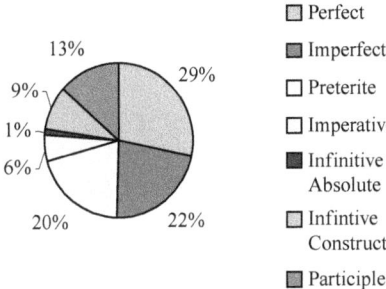

5.7 Concepts

affix	dynamic equivalence	interlinear	parse	radical
aspect	function	*maqqef*	person	root
comment	functional equivalence	modification	PGN	stem
conjugation	gender	morphology	predicate	subject
context	imperfect	number	prefix	topic
diagnostic			*qal*	translate/translation

5.8 Vocabulary

rule, reign	מָשַׁל	.59	no, not	אַל	.51
tree (sg. & coll.), wood	עֵץ	.60	One form with two functions: the preposition *with*; direct object marker (not translated)	אֵת ‎/ אֶת־	.52
voice, sound	קוֹל	.61	go down, descend	ירד	.53
(f.) breath, wind, spirit	רוּחַ	.62	utensil, tool;[59] container, pot	כְּלִי	.54
cultivated ground (trad. "field"); contrast מִדְבָּר	שָׂדֶה	.63	no, not	לֹא	.55
official; leader, ruler	שַׂר	.64	war, battle	מִלְחָמָה	.56
heaven(s), sky	שָׁמַיִם	.65	be[come] king; reign, rule (as monarch, king)	מלך	.57
watch, guard, keep, protect	שמר	.66	place	מָקוֹם	.58

---

59. The function of the "utensil" or "tool" may be specified: כְּלֵי מִלְחָמָה utensils of war ≈ weapons.

5.9 Exercises

1. After learning the PGN affixes of the imperfect and the 3ms *qal* imperfect of מָשַׁל, gloss these clauses in English, using the simple future, and parse the verbs.

   a. יִמְשְׁלוּ הַכֹּהֲנִים   c. תִּשְׁמַעְנָה הַבָּנוֹת   e. יִמְלֹךְ דָּוִד
   b. תִּשְׁמְעִי   d. תִּשְׁלָחוּ   f. יִמְשֹׁל שְׁלֹמֹה

2. After reading the "enrichment" section (below), prepare an interlinear version of these clauses and sentences, and be ready to discuss the task of representing one language by another.

   a. יִשְׁמַע הַמֶּלֶךְ — 2 Sam 14.16
   b. יִשְׁמֹר אֶת־נַפְשֶׁךָ — Ps 121.7; ךָ- *your* (m.s.)
   c. תִּמְשְׁלִי עַל־הָעִיר — עַל *upon, over*
   d. יִמְשְׁלוּ הָאֲנָשִׁים עַל־הָאָרֶץ — עַל *upon, over*
   e. יִמְלֹךְ דָּוִד עַל־כָּל־הָאָרֶץ — David; עַל *over, upon* (prep.); כָּל *all of*
   f. אֶכְרֹת בְּרִית אִתְּכֶם — בְּרִית, *covenant*; אִתְּכֶם *with you* (m. pl.)
   g. לֹא תִּרְצָח — Ex 20.13; רצח *murder*
   h. לֹא תִּגְנֹב — Ex 20.15; גנב *steal*
   i. יִשְׁמְעוּ הַבָּנִים וְהַבַּת אֶת־קֹל־הָאֱלֹהִים — קֹל [*the*] *voice of*
   j. תִּזְכְּרִי אֶת־הַבְּרִית — בְּרִית (see "f", above)
   k. וְאָזְנֶיךָ תִּשְׁמַעְנָה דָּבָר מֵאַחֲרֶיךָ — Is 30.21; וְאָזְנֶיךָ *and your ears*; מֵאַחֲרֶיךָ *from behind you*
   l. יִקְרְבוּ אֶל־הַמִּזְבֵּחַ — קרב *approach, come near* [*be*] *near*; אֶל *to* (prep.)
   m. תִּכְתֹּב אֶת־כָּל־הַדְּבָרִים אֶל־הָעֶבֶד — כתב *write*; כָּל *all of*; אֶל *to, unto* (prep.)

5.10 Enrichment: Translation & the Exercises

Translation from one language [and therefore one culture] into another raises a host of questions which we will not attempt to answer. One of the foremost questions is whether the translator is primarily responsible to the original text or to the audience for which the translation is intended. Does the translation primarily face the original or the reader(s)? The answer to this question determines many of the differences between the so-called "dynamic" or "functional equivalence" versions and the more-or-less "literal" versions.

The exercises in an introductory grammar afford us an opportunity to practice recognizing grammatical forms and their function, and to check our identification and understanding by representing them in English. In other words, the goal is *not* "translation" as we often think of it—rendering or representing a passage written in one language (in this case, Biblical Hebrew) by means of a fluid passage in another language (e.g., English). Especially in later lessons, where the exercises consist of biblical passages, such "fluent" translations often merely show that we are familiar with one of the standard English versions (or that we checked our work against theirs!). In fact, without first-hand speakers to interview, no one knows Biblical Hebrew well enough to produce a "polished" or "smooth" translation without a great deal of guesswork, much of which merely reflects the "received" or traditional translation or interpretation.

Furthermore, the goal of exercises should reflect our overall reasons for studying Biblical Hebrew—that we learn to read the biblical text as carefully as possible, that we be able to understand and evaluate translational choices made by the various versions in English (and, possibly, other languages), and that we be able to evaluate the comments in published tools (commentaries, lexical aids, etc.). We are not trying to see "more deeply" into the text, but to make sure that we are actually reading the text, rather than skimming across its surface, basing our "understanding" on what it says (and does not say), rather than on what we have heard said about it.[60]

Therefore, your primary goal in rendering the clauses, phrases, sentences, and verses into English should be to represent what is in the Hebrew text—to prepare an "interlinear"—that will provide a basis for studying the Hebrew text and looking at other versions. Your "translation" of the exercises should, therefore, be fairly "literal", even "wooden"—it is actually a *gloss*, not a translation—rather than free and impressionistic (see the discussion of "gloss" in terms of vocabulary in Lesson 2). This does not not mean that it should be unintelligible (e.g., following Hebrew word order rather than English); your work should be well-formed English. Free and impressionistic versions are the appropriate fruit of much study and interpretation, *not* for this point in your Hebrew career.

This list of "rules" for glossing Biblical Hebrew into English are merely suggestions—feel free to use or modify them in ways that are most fruitful for the specific goals of your own studies.

1. Every element is verbally represented in English; every English element represents an element in the Hebrew text.
2. Words in English that correspond to elements of compound forms in Hebrew are linked by dashes (e.g., וַיֹּאמֶר, *and-he-says*).
3. Each Hebrew lexeme is rendered by the same English lexeme (e.g., אֶרֶץ is rendered by *land*; אֲשֶׁר by *who/that*, הִנֵּה by *behold*, and וְ by *and*).[61]
4. Synonyms are distinguished (e.g., -לְ *to*, אֶל *unto*).
5. The object marker אֵת is indicated by "[o]" or the like.
6. Linking words that are necessary for sensible English (e.g., relative pronoun, article, copula) are added in brackets [*is*], *italics*, or underlined.
7. Only proper names (persons, places) are capitalized.
8. Only two punctuation marks are used:
   a. "!" indicates that the verb that it follows is an imperative (#16b).
   b. "?" indicates the presence of the interrogative prefix (-הֲ).
9. In longer passages, verse numbers are minimized (verse divisions and numbers were not original).
10. Rules for the construct (Lesson 9):
    a. Words in construct are indicated by "-of" as the last element in their English word-group.
    b. All elements of a construct are visually linked by en-dashes (i.e., *the-house-of–the-king*).
    c. Words that are construct to a definite form are represented with the definite article "the".
11. Verbs are rendered as "he" and "she" for 3ms and 3fs, respectively, regardless of the "gender" of their subject in English, e.g., *and-[o] the-city she-was-captured*.
12. The translation of *hifil* verb forms (Lesson 20) includes the word "cause" if the form is causative.
13. Verbal forms are rendered as consistently as possible:
    a. imperfects as future: *I-will-[future]*
    b. preterites as past: *and-she-[past]*;
    c. imperatives are immediately followed by an exclamation point (e.g., *Go! to the land …*).

---

60. This is not meant to denigrate the use of commentaries and other exegetical tools, but merely to suggest that if our primary obligation is to the text, we ought to be sure that our primary interaction is *with the text*.

61. The latter is not "who" or "that", but the combined form "who/that".

These rules probably sound great—after all, don't we want to get as "close" to the original as possible? Here's the result for Jonah 1.1–3:

1 וַיְהִי דְבַר־יהוה אֶל־יוֹנָה בֶן־אֲמִתַּי לֵאמֹר:
And-he-was the-word-of Y<small>HWH</small> unto Jonah the-son-of Amittai to-say

2 קוּם לֵךְ אֶל־נִינְוֵה הָעִיר הַגְּדוֹלָה וּקְרָא עָלֶיהָ כִּי־עָלְתָה רָעָתָם לְפָנָי:
Rise! Go! unto Nineveh the-city the-great and-call against-her for she-has-gone-up their-evil before-me

3 וַיָּקָם יוֹנָה לִבְרֹחַ תַּרְשִׁישָׁה מִלִּפְנֵי יהוה וַיֵּרֶד יָפוֹ וַיִּמְצָא אֳנִיָּה בָּאָה תַרְשִׁישׁ
And-he-rose Jonah to-flee Tarshish-ward from-before Y<small>HWH</small> and-he-went-down Joppa and-he-found ship going Tarshish

וַיִּתֵּן שְׂכָרָהּ וַיֵּרֶד בָּהּ לָבוֹא עִמָּהֶם תַּרְשִׁישָׁה מִלִּפְנֵי יהוה:
And-he-gave her-fare and-he-went-down in-her to-go with-them Tarshish-ward from-before Y<small>HWH</small>

Carefully following the rules yields a text that is neither Hebrew nor English ("Heblish"?); if it communicates meaning to anyone, he or she will *already know Hebrew* and so can reconstruct the Hebrew text behind our "translation".

Although we might think that such a version demonstrates our knowledge of Hebrew and our faithfulness to the Hebrew text, it actually shows that we don't understand how language works. The first priority of any attempt to communicate is *to communicate*, and this rendering of Jonah communicates little. Since most users of this grammar know the story of Jonah, as well as English, we can figure out what is going on in the "Heblish Version", even though it is not normal English. In order to test our understanding of Hebrew, therefore, we need to render the Hebrew text into "good"—or at least "normal"—English (since it was written, as far as we know, in "good" ["normal"] Hebrew). For example:

> Y<small>HWH</small>'s word came to Jonah son of Amittai, saying, "Get up and go to the great city of Nineveh, and call out against her that[62] their wickedness has come up into my presence."
>
> But Jonah rose to flee to Tarshish away from Y<small>HWH</small>'s presence. He went down to Joppa, found a ship going to Tarshish, paid its fare, and went down into it to go with them to Tarshish away from Y<small>HWH</small>'s presence. (Jonah 1.1–4)

Whether or not this is the best possible translation of these verses into English is beside the point at the moment. It certainly *communicates* more to the reader than the "inter-linear" version, and so—from that point alone—is more "successful".

---

62. Ambiguities are one of the delights of translation. In this case, the word כִּי can introduce either the reason for Jonah's mission ("since", "because", "for"), or the content of his message ("that").

Parsing Form

Lexical Form	Gloss	P/G/N	Stem	Conjugation	Prefix	Pronominal Suffix	Key
							Lexical Form: the vocabulary form of the word
							Gloss: of the lexical form
							P/G/N: person (1,2,3), gender (m, f), & number (s, p)
							Stem: *qal* (Q), *qal* passive (Qp), *nifal* (N), *piel* (D), *pual* (Dp), *hitpael* (Dt), *hifil* (H), *hofal* (Hp)
							Conjugation: perfect (P), imperfect (F), preterite (Pr), imperative (V), cohortative (C), jussive (J), participle (Ptc), infinitive construct (NC), or infinitive absolute (NA)
							Prefix: The conjunction, article, [prefixed] preposition, & interrogative –h are the only possibilities for this column)
							Pronominal suffix: P/G/N of pronominal suffix
							N.B.: The last two columns (prefixes, pronominal suffixes) are only used if these elements are present. Lexical form, gloss, stem, & conjugation are *required* for all verbal forms. Infinitives have no P/G/N.

Lesson 6

The Preterite

Languages tend to use one particular verbal conjugation for the "main sequence" of events in a story ("narrative"). In Biblical Hebrew that form is the *preterite* (which means "past"), the conjugation that identifies the main sequence of events in a biblical narrative.[63] In telling a story, English uses the simple past for the sequence of events, as in this example (the preterites are in *italics*).

> George *walked* toward the cliff, wondering what had happened to his friends. Standing on the edge, he *gazed* down its face, looking for some sign of them, but no one was there. He *sighed*, *put* his hands to his mouth, and *shouted* yet again. There was still no answer, but then something far below him *moved* on the face of the cliff.

The main storyline consists of five events: George walked, gazed, sighed, put, and shouted, and something moved. The other verbal forms ("wondering", "had happened", "standing", "looking", and "was"), also identify events (or non-events), but do not describe the *next event* on the storyline. Both "wondering" and "standing" tell us that George was doing two things at the same time (wondering as he walked; standing as he gazed). "Looking for" modifies "gazed", narrowing its focus (no pun intended) to tell us that George was not merely admiring the scenery. The three verbs "sighed", "put", and "shouted" identify a sequence of actions (and perhaps, by their close proximity, suggest that they were executed rapidly and without interruption). The form "had happened"—an example of the English "past perfect"—refers to something that occurred before George walked toward the cliff.[64] Both occurrences of "was" are negated ("no one", "no answer")—they are examples of *irrealis*, giving the reader information about something that did not occur.

It may be helpful to think of a story as made up of a number of *threads*,[65] each of which keeps track of a certain type of information. The thread provided by pronouns is obvious in the sentences above: "his", "he", and "him" enable the narrator to refer to George without repeating his name (just as "them" refers back to "his friends").[66] Another thread is the simple past tense that outlines the story (George walked, gazed, sighed, put, and shouted, and [then] something moved).

וַיָּרָץ הָעֶבֶד ... And the servant *ran* ... (Gn 24.17a)
וַיֹּאמֶר הַגְמִיאִינִי ... And *he said*, "Let me swallow ..." (Gn 24.17b)
וַתֹּאמֶר שְׁתֵה ... And *she said*, "Drink ..." (Gn 24.18a)

---

63. Although the existence of a preterite "conjugation" in Biblical Hebrew is debated, this grammar uses the term to refer to the past narrative *function* of these verbs, rather than to their form, since this form and function are so closely related in Biblical Hebrew (avoiding the debate about the existence of the preterite as a morphological class).

64. Of course, the narrator decides how to express this simultaneous action. How would the story change if it read "Walking toward the cliff, George wondered ..." In this case, "wondered" is the main narrative verb (preterite), modified by "walking". The biblical narrators made the same choices, as we shall see.

65. This is not the same as the literary term "narrative thread", which refers to a story's basic plot.

66. Pronouns have a similar function in Biblical Hebrew (see §13.1.2).

The preterite (= "past") in Biblical Hebrew (also called "*wayyiqtol*"[67]) is also a thread—a cohesive device that links an event to the preceding event. The preterite in Biblical Hebrew thus has the same function as the italicized verbs in the "story" (above)—it tells the reader that the event that it describes was the next event in the story (see §6.10).

Verbal PGN is a cohesive device in Biblical Hebrew that enables us to track verbal subjects. In Gn 24.17, for example, the second verb וַיֹּאמֶר, *and he said*, is 3ms. Since it has no expressed subject, and has the same PGN as the preceding verb, they have the same subject, but וַתֹּאמֶר, *and she said*, is 3fs, which tells us that Rebecca (already introduced in the story) answered the servant's request. Furthermore, since they are described by three consecutive preterites, readers will assume that these events are consecutive and consequentially related.[68]

6.1 *Form*

The PGN afffixes of the preterite are the same as those of the imperfect. The only difference between their forms is that the preterite is always preceded by *waw* followed by *pataḥ* with a *dageš forte* in the PGN prefix (this is sometimes called the "pointing of the article" (וַ), since it has the same vowel and doubling), so that the PGN prefix is doubled by the *dageš forte* (except the guttural -א [1cs: "I"]). The result of this combination of the conjunction, pointing, and prefix is the following set of subject affixes, which is unique to the preterite (cf. the PGN prefixes of the imperfect, §5.2.1).

Person	Gender	Singular		Plural	
1st	Common	וָא -	I ...	וַנ -	We ...
2nd	Masc.	וַתּ -	You ...	וַתּ - וּ	You ...
	Fem.	וַתּ - ִי		וַתּ - נָה	
3rd	Masc.	וַיּ -	He/It ...	וַיּ - וּ	They ...
	Fem.	וַתּ -	She/It ...	וַתּ - נָה	

1. Apart from the prefixed *waw* and *dageš forte* the forms of the preterite are identical to those of the imperfect.
2. *Every form* that begins with *waw* followed by a letter with *dageš* (or *waw + qameṣ* followed by *'alef*) is *preterite*.

6.1.1 *The qal preterite of* מׁשל

Person	Gender	Singular		Plural	
1st	Common	וָאֶמְשֹׁל	I ruled/reigned	וַנִּמְשֹׁל	We ruled/reigned
2nd	Masc.	וַתִּמְשֹׁל	You ruled/etc.	וַתִּמְשְׁלוּ	You ruled/etc.
	Fem.	וַתִּמְשְׁלִי		וַתִּמְשֹׁלְנָה	
3rd	Masc.	וַיִּמְשֹׁל	He ruled	וַיִּמְשְׁלוּ	They ruled
	Fem.	וַתִּמְשֹׁל	She ruled	וַתִּמְשֹׁלְנָה	

---

67. The term "*wayyiqtol*" transliterates the 3ms form of the *qal* preterite of the verb קטל (וַיִּקְטֹל). This conjugation is also called "imperfect plus *waw*-consecutive" and "imperfect plus waw-conversive", which reflect views that the *waw* either "converted" the function of the imperfect from present-future to narrative, or showed that its event was "consecutive to" or "consequent upon" the preceding event. All of these terms are used by various authors and resources.

68. Other cohesive devices are temporal and locative expressions (e.g., אָז, "then", הַיּוֹם, "today"; שָׁם, "there, in that place").

1. Note the difference in form (the vowel under the conjunction) and function between the imperfect (Dt 10.2) and preterite (Jr 32.10) of the same verb:

וְאֶכְתֹּב עַל־הַלֻּחֹת אֶת־הַדְּבָרִים   and *I will write* on the tablets the words (Dt 10.2); 1cs Q F +*w*

וָאֶכְתֹּב בַּסֵּפֶר   and *I wrote* in the document (Jr 32.10); 1cs Q Pr

2. When the verbal PGN is 1cs ("I"), with the guttural prefix א, the *waw* is followed by *qameṣ*, and there is no *dageš forte* in the א, since it is a guttural, and so does not double (cf. Jr 32.10, above):

וָאֶשְׁלַח אֶת־מֹשֶׁה וְאֶת־אַהֲרֹן   and *I sent* Moses and Aaron … (Jos 24.5); 1cs Q Pr

3. As with the imperfect, preterites of II- and III-guttural and III-א verbal roots[69] have an *a*-vowel after the second radical instead of *ḥolem*.

    וָאֶקְרָא לְךָ בִּשְׁמֶךָ   and *I called* you by your name (Is 44.4).   1cs Q Pr

    וַיִּשְׁמַע דָּוִד וַיִּשְׁלַח אֶת־יוֹאָב   And David *heard* and *sent* Joab (2 Sam 10.7)   3ms Q Pr (both)

4. Because only four consonants function as prefixes in the preterite, all preterites begin in one of six ways—there are no exceptions—regardless of the vowel following the prefix.

וָא - וָאֶ -	1cs preterite: *I*	וַנ -	1cp preterite: *we*
וַתּ -	2ms/2fs/3fs preterite: *you, she* 2/3fp preterite: *they*	וִי - וַיּ -	3ms/p preterite: *he, they*

N.B.: In parsing the preterite, there is no need to specify the conjunction in the "prefix" column, since the term "preterite" assumes the prefixed *waw*.[70] Your teacher may want you to spell this out.

Lemma	Lexical Form	Gloss	P/G/N	Stem	Conjugation	Prefix
וַיִּמְשֹׁל	מָשַׁל	*rule, reign*	3ms	Q	Pr	

6.2 I-א *Verbal Roots*

The *qal* preterite (and imperfect) of most strong verbs looks like מָשַׁל (above), but five verbs look quite different. These five verbs begin with the letter א (they are therefore called I-א[71] or "initial א" verbal roots). Because א is silent when followed by silent *šewa*, the prefix vowel of the *qal* imperfect and preterite is *ḥolem*, not *ḥireq*, and there is no *šewa* under the א (i.e., the *šewa* was left out and the א functions as a "place marker", a little like "silent *e*" in English). The five I-א verbs[72] are:

---

69. On this terminology, see §6.2 (below).
70. There are a few examples of preterites without prefixed *waw*.
71. The Roman numeral "I" refers to the position of the *'alef* as the *first* radical of the verbal root. The same pattern can also refer to the second (II) and third (III) letters in the verbal root. These terms (I-, II-, III-) will be used without further comment.
72. Other verbal roots begin with א, but their forms follow the pattern of the "guttural" verbal roots (Lesson 22).

Verbal Root	Gloss	Occurrences
אמר	*say, speak*	5000+
אכל	*eat, consume, devour*	827x
אבד	*perish; stray*	191x
אפה	*bake, cook*	54x
אבה	*desire, be willing, agree*	25x

1. Their prefix vowel in Q F and Pr is *ḥolem*; there is no *šewa* under the א, which is silent.

נֹאכַל	We [shall] eat	1cp Q F
וַתֹּאמֶר	You/She said	2ms/3fs Q Pr
וַיֹּאמְרוּ	They said	3mp Q Pr
נֹאבַד	We [shall] perish	1cp Q F

2. In 1cs *qal* imperfect and preterite the 1cs prefix (א) assimilates with the first radical, so that only one א is written:

אֹמַר	I shall say	1cs Q F
וָאֹכַל	I ate	1cs Q Pr

3. The main reason for introducing this set of verbal roots at this point is so that we can use אמר in the exercises. Here is its paradigm for the *qal* preterite:[73]

Person	Gender	Singular		Plural	
1	Common	וָאֹמַר	*I said*	וַנֹּאמֶר	*We said*
2	Masc.	וַתֹּאמֶר	*You said*	וַתֹּאמְרוּ	*You said*
	Fem.	וַתֹּאמְרִי		וַתֹּאמַרְנָה	
3	Masc.	וַיֹּאמֶר	*He said*	וַיֹּאמְרוּ	*They said*
	Fem.	וַתֹּאמֶר	*She said*	וַתֹּאמַרְנָה	

N.B.: אמר is so frequent that the clause וַיֹּאמֶר יהוה *Y*HWH *said* represents one-half of one percent of all the words in Biblical Hebrew (וַיֹּאמֶר alone occurs nearly 2000 times).

6.3 Functions (HBI §2.2.3)

The introduction to this chapter said that the preterite identifies the main storyline of the narrative; this is its main function, but it also has other—much less frequent—functions.

6.3.1 Narrative "backbone"

The preterite describes a series of events in the main flow of a narrative (also called the "main sequence" or "backbone" of the narrative). Preterites are usually translated with the simple past. Each preterite always begins its clause, so that the string of preterites describes the string of past events (see also the examples above) [all of the verbs in these examples are Q Pr]:

---

73. The paradigm for the *qal* imperfect of אמר is nearly identical to this paradigm of its preterite.

וַיִּקְרְאוּ־צוֹם וַיִּלְבְּשׁוּ שַׂקִּים	and *they proclaimed* a fast and *put on* sackcloth (Jonah 3.5)
וַיִּשָּׁבַע הַמֶּלֶךְ וַיֹּאמַר	and the king *swore* [an oath] and *said* … (1 Kg 1.29)
וָאֶכְתֹּב בַּסֵּפֶר וָאֶחְתֹּם … וָאֶשְׁקֹל הַכֶּסֶף בְּמֹאזְנָיִם:	and *I wrote* in the document, and *I sealed* [it], … and *I weighed* the silver with scales (Jr 32.10).

Tracing the string of preterites in Gn 1 reveals the prominence of divine speech in creation (these are only the last few verses of the creation story):

וַיֹּאמֶר אֱלֹהִים …	and God *said* … (Gn 1.26)
וַיִּבְרָא אֱלֹהִים אֶת־הָאָדָם …	and God *created* human beings, … (Gn 1.27)
וַיְבָרֶךְ אֹתָם אֱלֹהִים	and God *blessed* them
וַיֹּאמֶר לָהֶם אֱלֹהִים …	and God *said* to them (Gn 1.28b)
וַיֹּאמֶר אֱלֹהִים …	and God *said* … (Gn 1.29)
וַיַּרְא אֱלֹהִים אֶת־כָּל־ …	and God *saw* everything … (Gn 1.30)

Calling the "preterite chain" the narrative "backbone" does not mean that events described by preterites are the only events—or even "essential" or most important events—of the story.[74] It *does* mean that in the narrator's mind, the events described by these verbs comprise the main sequence, or flow, of the narrative. As you might expect from its function, the preterite is far more common in books that are largely narrative (e.g., Gn, 1–2 Sam, Est) than in books that are mainly covenantal (e.g., Lv, Dt) or poetic (e.g., Jb, Pss, Pr, SS). In 1 Sam 3.4–5, the string of preterites outlines a series of events (the speeches introduced by "[and] he said" are brief):[75]

וַיִּקְרָא יְהוָה אֶל־שְׁמוּאֵל	Y<small>HWH</small> *called* Samuel
וַיֹּאמֶר הִנֵּנִי:	and he *said*, "Here I am!" (1 Sam 3.4)
וַיָּרָץ אֶל־עֵלִי	He *ran* to Eli
וַיֹּאמֶר הִנְנִי כִּי …	and he *said*, "Here I am, because …"
וַיֹּאמֶר לֹא־קָרָאתִי …	But he *said*, "I did not call …"
וַיֵּלֶךְ	So he *went*
וַיִּשְׁכָּב:	and he *lay down* (1 Sam 3.5).

This string of preterites extends (with interruptions, see §6.6, §6.10) through the rest of the chapter (and the rest of Samuel[76]). When first reading a biblical narrative, a helpful first step is to identify the preterites, since they normally yield the [bare] outline of the story (see Lesson 25).

6.3.2 *Narrative Summary*

Although each preterite in a string usually describes the next event in a series, a preterite may also summarize an entire sequence of events, usually at the end of a larger discourse. This function can be recognized by *content* of the preterite clauses, and the relationship between the events that they describe. "God humbled" (Jg 4.23) summarizes the events of Jg 4.13–22, whereas the next preterite (4.24) describes a further event that had begun on the same day.

---

74. For example, in any story, *what* is said is as important as *that* something was said (e.g., the content of the initial divine speech (Gn 1.26) is crucial, although its content is not "on" the storyline).

75. Note the context-dependent renderings (or non-rendering) of the initial *waw*.

76. The books of 1-2 Samuel, 1-2 Kings, 1-2 Chronicles, and Ezra-Nehemiah each form a single book in the Hebrew Bible.

וַיַּכְנַע אֱלֹהִים בַּיּוֹם הַהוּא אֵת יָבִין מֶלֶךְ־כְּנַעַן לִפְנֵי בְּנֵי יִשְׂרָאֵל׃ — So on that day, God *humbled* Jabin king of Canaan before the sons of Israel (Jg 4.23),

וַתֵּלֶךְ יַד בְּנֵי־יִשְׂרָאֵל הָלוֹךְ וְקָשָׁה — and the hand of the sons of Israel *grew* continually harsher

עַל יָבִין מֶלֶךְ־כְּנָעַן — against Jabin king of Canaan

עַד אֲשֶׁר הִכְרִיתוּ אֵת יָבִין מֶלֶךְ־כְּנָעַן׃ — until they [had] destroyed Jabin king of Canaan (Jg 4.24).

6.3.3 *Past Perfect*

A preterite can apparently refer to an event that took place before the previous event. This function is discernable only from context. Although Yʜᴡʜ might be repeating himself, in the context, Ex 4.19 seems to refer back to 4.11–12; it seems unlikely that Laban interrupted Jacob and Leah's wedding night (Gn 29.24).

וַיֹּאמֶר יהוה אֶל־מֹשֶׁה — Now Yʜᴡʜ *had said* to Moses … (Ex 4.19)

וַיִּתֵּן לָבָן לָהּ אֶת־זִלְפָּה שִׁפְחָתוֹ לְלֵאָה בִתּוֹ שִׁפְחָה — Now Laban *had given* her Zilpah his maid—[to be] his daughter Leah's maid (Gn 29.24)

6.3.4 *Compound Reference*

Consecutive preterites can describe a single event. In Ru 1.9 and 14, the three women wept aloud ("lifted their voices and wept"), which we might call "compound" or "multiple" reference:

וַתִּשֶּׂאנָה קוֹלָן וַתִּבְכֶּינָה — And they *lifted* their voices and *wept* (Ru 1.9)

וַיִּקְרְאוּ אֶל־לוֹט וַיֹּאמְרוּ — And they *called* to Lot and *said* … (Gn 19.5)

6.4 *Word Order*

Although there is some variety in the order of elements in preterite clauses, *every preterite begins a new clause* (as the above examples illustrate), which can be called a "preterite clause". *Nothing*—adverb, subject, object, negative, prepositional phrase—precedes the preterite. After the preterite the order is generally **subject—object**(s) (direct or indirect); **adverbial** expressions are usually clause- or sentence-final. This structure of main narrative clauses is the main reason that Hebrew is often referred to as a **V-S-O** (verb-subject-object) language.

6.5 *The Imperfect & Preterite*

The imperfect and preterite together "cover" all of the verbal "tenses" and many of the verbal "moods" used in English:

Imperfect (contextual)	Present
	Future
	Modal (*may/might, should, ought*, etc.)
Preterite	Past Narrative (the main line of events)

1. They do not directly correspond to what we think of as "tenses", "moods", or "aspects", since their function depends on the type of material—the *genre*—within which they occur, so that this chart applies primarily to their function in *narrative*, not to their use in poetry, legal or instructional materials, or other genres.
2. The imperfect can also be preceded by the conjunction *waw*, which means that you will need to distinguish these forms from the preterite; the clue is the pointing under the *waw*:

וְיִמְשֹׁל	conjunction + 3ms Q imperfect (present/future)	*and he shall rule*
וַיִּמְשֹׁל	conjunction + 3ms Q preterite (narrative past)	*and he ruled*
וְאֶמְשֹׁל	conjunction + 1cs Q imperfect (present/future)	*and I shall rule*
וָאֶמְשֹׁל	conjunction + 1ms Q preterite (narrative past)	*and I ruled*

6.6 *Disjunctive Clauses (HBI §3.2.2)*

Since the preterite names consecutive narrative events, other information (e.g., flashbacks, contemporaneous action) is contained in clauses that begin with *waw* followed by "something-other-than-a-verb". This information is often *parenthetic*, adding information to the narrative about a character or circumstance that the reader needs to understand the story. It may also *contrast* two characters or their circumstances, or *introduce* a new character to the story, or describe something that did not happen (a negative clause).

Disjunctive clauses in narrative may be non-verbal, have a perfect or a participle as predicate, or an imperfect with a modifying adverb. Genesis 12.6b, for example, heightens God's promise in the next clause (12.7) by telling the reader that the promised land was not uninhabited:

וְהַכְּנַעֲנִי אָז בָּאָרֶץ׃	(now the Canaanites were then in the land) (Gn 12.6b)
לְזַרְעֲךָ אֶתֵּן אֶת־הָאָרֶץ הַזֹּאת	"... to your seed I shall give this land." (Gn 12.7)

The syntax of the disjunctive clause (*w* + subject ["the Canaanites"]) means that this is not the next event in the story (the Canaanites were [already] in the land), but it contains information crucial to the story.

Furthermore, the disjunctive syntax of this clause derives from—and is determined by—its function in the story; the word order is not merely another way of saying "the same thing". In other words, a disjunctive clause is a signal that its contents do *not* describe the next event in the story (whether it is a positive or negative statement). Furthermore their syntax does not *of itself* indicate the function of a disjunctive clause; it merely indicates its non-sequentiality. [See §6.11.]

6.7 *Frequency*

About one-fifth (20%) of all verbal forms in the Bible are preterites, but this frequency is much higher in narrative than in poetry. In Genesis (for example) more than two-fifths of all verbs are preterite, but in the Song of Songs less than one percent are preterite.

6.8 *Concepts*

clause	disjunctive [clause]	narrative	perfect	VSO
waw-consecutive	flashback	narrative backbone	pluperfect	*wayyiqtol*
waw-conversive	genre	parenthetic information	preterite	word order
diagnostic(s)				

6.9 Vocabulary

67.	אוֹיֵב	enemy	75.	לֶחֶם	bread, food
68.	אַף	(I) also, even, all the more (cj.) (II) nose, nostril; anger (n.)	76.	מִדְבָּר	wilderness (uncultivated or "unclaimed" land)
69.	בְּרִית	covenant, treaty, agreement	77.	מִשְׁפָּחָה	clan, extended family (smaller than a tribe)
70.	בָּשָׂר	flesh, meat; humanity (as "flesh")	78.	עָבַד	serve (cf. עֶבֶד)
71.	חֹדֶשׁ	month, new moon	79.	עֵת	time (i.e., a particular moment)
72.	חָזַק	be[come] strong; sieze, grasp, hold onto	80.	פָּקַד	do something [good or bad] for/to [someone] (trad. "visit")
73.	עֶרֶב	evening	81.	צֹאן	flock (sheep, goats)
74.	כָּרַת	cut [off]; with בְּרִית as object, make a treaty	82.	קָרַב	approach, come/draw near

6.10 Exercises

1. After studying the PGN affixes of the preterite and the 3ms *qal* preterite of מֹשַׁל, represent these clauses in English using the simple past ("He said") for the preterite and simple future ("He will say") for the imperfect. Parse the verbs.

   a. וַתִּמְשְׁלוּ d. וְתִכְרְתִי g. וַיִּמְלֹךְ שָׁאוּל
   b. וָאֶשְׁמַע e. וַתִּכְרְתִי h. וְיִמְלְכוּ
   c. וַיִּשְׁלָחוּ f. וַתִּשְׁמֹרְנָה i. וַתִּקְרְבִי

2. Gloss these clauses and sentences in English, parsing the verbal forms. Remember that the purpose of the exercises is primarily to understand why the text means what it does.

   a. וַיֹּאמֶר חִזְקִיָּהוּ אֶל־יְשַׁעְיָהוּ ...
   2 Kgs 20.8; אֶל *to*; Hezekiah; Isaiah

   b. וַיִּכְרְתוּ שְׁנֵיהֶם בְּרִית:
   Gn 21.27; שְׁנֵיהֶם *they both* [*the two of them*]

   c. וַיִּשְׁפֹּט יִפְתָּח אֶת־יִשְׂרָאֵל שֵׁשׁ שָׁנִים
   Jg 12.7; שֵׁשׁ *six*; Jephthah; Israel

   d. וַיִּכְרְתוּ אֶת־רֹאשׁ שֶׁבַע בֶּן־בִּכְרִי
   2 Sam 20.22; רֹאשׁ *head of*; בֶּן *son of*; Sheba, Bichri

   e. וְאָזְכֹּר אֶת־בְּרִיתִי:[77]
   Ex 6.5; זכר *remember*; בְּרִיתִי *my* [final יִ-] *covenant*

   f. וַיִּשְׁלַח דָּוִד וַיִּדְרֹשׁ לָאִשָּׁה וַיֹּאמֶר ...
   2 Sam 11.3; לְ- *for the*; דרשׁ *seek*; David

   g. וַיִּזְבְּחוּ־שָׁם לַיהוָה:
   Jg 2.5; שָׁם *there, in that place*

   h. וְאַתֶּם לֹא־תִכְרְתוּ בְרִית לְיוֹשְׁבֵי הָאָרֶץ הַזֹּאת
   Jg 2.2; אַתֶּם *you* (mp); יוֹשֵׁב *inhabitant* (ms Q Ptc); הַזֹּאת *this* (modifies אֶרֶץ)

   i. וַיִּשְׁכַּב יְהוֹיָקִים עִם־אֲבֹתָיו וַיִּמְלֹךְ יְהוֹיָכִין בְּנוֹ
   2 Kgs 24.6; שׁכב *lie down, sleep*; עִם *with*; אֲבֹתָיו *his fathers*; בְּנוֹ *his son*; Jehoiakim, Jehoiachin

---

77. The two "diamonds" mark the end of a biblical verse (*sof pasuq*, "end of *pasuq*").

j. וַיִּשְׁמְרוּ אֶת־הַבַּיִת לַהֲמִיתוֹ	Ps 59.1; לַהֲמִיתוֹ, *to kill him (put him to death)*
k. וַיִּשְׁאֲלוּ בְנֵי־יִשְׂרָאֵל בַּיהוָה	Jg 20.27; שאל *ask;* -בְּ often introduces the object of שאל; בְּנֵי *sons of*
l. וַתַּהַרְגוּ אֶת־בָּנָיו	Jg 9.18; הרג *kill* (Q Pr; the guttural (ה) affects the prefix syllable); בָּנָיו *his sons*

6.11 *Enrichment: Narrative Backbone (& Ancillary Information)*

Tracing preterite and disjunctive clauses in a narrative reveals its skeleton (the preterites) and information that the author considered "ancillary" to the storyline (disjunctive clauses). In 1 Samuel 3, for example (next page), the first three verses contain seven disjunctive clauses and two secondary (parallel) clauses, which together set the stage (or background) for the rest of the story (disjunctive clauses are in *italics*):

Now the young man Samuel was serving Yhwh *in Eli's presence,*	1a וְהַנַּעַר שְׁמוּאֵל מְשָׁרֵת אֶת־יהוה לִפְנֵי עֵלִי
but Yhwh's *word was rare in those days*—	b וּדְבַר־יהוה הָיָה יָקָר בַּיָּמִים הָהֵם
no vision was breaking through. [parallel clause]	c אֵין חָזוֹן נִפְרָץ׃
Then one day	2a וַיְהִי בַּיּוֹם הַהוּא
when Eli was sleeping in his place	b וְעֵלִי שֹׁכֵב בִּמְקֹמוֹ
(now his eyes had begun to be dim—	c וְעֵינוֹ הֵחֵלּוּ כֵהוֹת
he could not see), [parallel clause]	d לֹא יוּכַל לִרְאוֹת׃
and the lamp of God had not yet gone out,	3a וְנֵר אֱלֹהִים טֶרֶם יִכְבֶּה
and Samuel was sleeping in Yhwh's *temple, where the ark of God was,*	b וּשְׁמוּאֵל שֹׁכֵב בְּהֵיכַל יהוה אֲשֶׁר־שָׁם אֲרוֹן אֱלֹהִים׃

Following these introductory—scene-setting—disjunctive clauses, the *events* of the specific story begin with the preterites in verse 4 (preterites are in **bold**):

Yhwh **summoned** Samuel	4a וַיִּקְרָא יהוה אֶל־שְׁמוּאֵל
and he **said**, "Here I am".	b וַיֹּאמֶר הִנֵּנִי׃
And he **ran** to Eli	5a וַיָּרָץ אֶל־עֵלִי
and he **said**, "Here I am, for you called me."	b וַיֹּאמֶר הִנְנִי כִּי־קָרָאתָ לִּי
But he **said**, "I did not call. Go back to sleep."	c וַיֹּאמֶר לֹא־קָרָאתִי שׁוּב שְׁכָב
So **he went** and **he lay down**.	d וַיֵּלֶךְ וַיִּשְׁכָּב׃
And Yhwh **called** Samuel again,	6a וַיֹּסֶף יהוה קְרֹא עוֹד שְׁמוּאֵל
And [so] Samuel **got up**,	b וַיָּקָם שְׁמוּאֵל
[**and** he] **went** to Eli,	c וַיֵּלֶךְ אֶל־עֵלִי
and he **said**, "Here I am, for you called me."	d וַיֹּאמֶר הִנְנִי כִּי קָרָאתָ לִי
But he **said**, "I didn't call, my son. Go back to sleep."	e וַיֹּאמֶר לֹא־קָרָאתִי בְנִי שׁוּב שְׁכָב

Calling the information in verses 1–3 "background" does not mean that this is unimportant or non-essential to the story. It does mean, on the other hand, that these clauses "set the stage" for the sequential events, which begin in verse 4.

After Samuel goes twice to Eli the author finally explains why Samuel did not recognize Yhwh's voice, setting off his explanation syntactically in a disjunctive clause (*waw* + noun):

(*Now Samuel did not yet know* Yhwh,	7a וּשְׁמוּאֵל טֶרֶם יָדַע אֶת־יהוה
nor had Yhwh's *word yet been revealed to him*)	7b וְטֶרֶם יִגָּלֶה אֵלָיו דְּבַר־יהוה׃

The author used disjunctive clauses (*w* + a noun ["Samuel"] (7a) and *w* + adverb ["not yet"] (7b)), to tell readers that these clauses will describe events or situations that do **not** follow **sequentially** the events just described (see §6.6 (above)). Furthermore, because these statements are negative, they "describe" *non-events* (*irrealis*), or things that did not happen and which therefore are not (and cannot be) part of the storyline (since they hadn't yet occurred), but their information is crucial to the reader's understanding of the sequence of events in the story. They answer a question that would probably occur to most readers, namely, how Samuel could be serving Y<small>HWH</small> (3.1) and not recognize his voice. Having given the reader this needed information, the preterite chain then resumes the narration of the sequence of events:

And Y<small>HWH</small> **again** called Samuel a third time	וַיֹּסֶף יהוה קְרֹא־שְׁמוּאֵל בַּשְּׁלִשִׁית	**8a**
and he **got up and he went** to Eli	וַיָּקָם וַיֵּלֶךְ אֶל־עֵלִי	**8b**
and he **said**, "Here I am, because you called me"	וַיֹּאמֶר הִנְנִי כִּי קָרָאתָ לִי	**8c**
and Eli **discerned** that Y<small>HWH</small> was calling the young man.	וַיָּבֶן עֵלִי כִּי יהוה קֹרֵא לַנָּעַר׃	**8d**
And Eli **said** to Samuel ...	וַיֹּאמֶר עֵלִי לִשְׁמוּאֵל	**9a**

Lesson 7

Nominal Modification (II): Prepositions

Prepositions precede (are *pre-position*ed to) other words in order to show their *function* or *rôle* in the clause or phrase. In English, for example, the difference in function between "George went *to* the store" and "George went *from* the store" is determined by the prepositions "to" and "from", which indicate which way George went relative to the store. Prepositions thus modify a noun's *syntagmatic function*, rather than its reference (which is modified by the article (§4.3), construct (Lesson 8), adjectives and the relative particle (Lesson 11). Prepositions in Biblical Hebrew do not affect the form of the word that they modify (remember, there are no "case endings" in Hebrew). There are three types of prepositions in Biblical Hebrew:

1. *inseparable*—the prepositions -בְּ, -כְּ, and -לְ are always prefixed to the word that they modify (like the conjunction -וְ)
2. *separable*—the preposition מִן may be either separate from or prefixed to the word that it modifies
3. *separate*—most prepositions in Biblical Hebrew are separate words (as are prepositions in English)

7.1 *The Inseparable Prepositions*

The prepositions -בְּ (*in, with, against*), -כְּ (*like, as, according to, about* [*approximately*]), and -לְ (*to, for, at, belonging to*), are always prefixed to the word that they govern, becoming the first syllable in the word (cf. the conjunction -וְ).

1. If the word is anarthrous, the preposition is prefixed using vocal *šewa* (but if the first vowel in the word is *šewa*, they use *ḥireq*).

a house	בַּיִת	בְּבַיִת	in a house
a king	מֶלֶךְ	כְּמֶלֶךְ	like a king
a woman	אִשָּׁה	לְאִשָּׁה	to/for a woman
garments	בְּגָדִים	בִּבְגָדִים	in/with garments
young men	נְעָרִים	כִּנְעָרִים	like young men

2. The first letter of a word that begins with a *bᵉgad-kᵉfat* letter loses *dageš lene*, since the preposition is followed by a [half-] vowel:

a house	בַּיִת	לְבַיִת	to a house
a son	בֵּן	כְּבֵן	like a son
tool	כְּלִי	בִּכְלִי	with a tool

3. If the first letter of the word has a *ḥatef*-vowel, the preposition uses the full vowel that matches the half-vowel:

an ark/box	אֲרוֹן	בַּאֲרוֹן	in a box ("in *the* box" = בָּאֲרוֹן)
a fool	אֱוִיל	לֶאֱוִיל	to a fool

4. When they are added to an *articular* word, these three prepositions *replace* the -הַ of the article, but *not* its pointing (hence the importance of being able to recognize the article's pointing). These three are the *only* prefixes that replace the -הַ of the article:

	Articular				Anarthrous	
the house	הַבַּיִת	בַּבַּיִת	in the house		בְּבַיִת	in a house
the son	הַבֵּן	כַּבֵּן	like the son		כְּבֵן	like a son
the woman	הָאִשָּׁה	לָאִשָּׁה	to/for the woman		לְאִשָּׁה	to/for a woman

5. When they are added to the name and titles of God (below), their vowel is *sere* (with אלהים) or *pataḥ* (with יהוה and אדני):

God	אֱלֹהִים	לֵאלֹהִים	for God
Yhwh	יהוה	בַּיהוה	in Yhwh
the Lord	אֲדֹנָי	לַאדֹנָי	for/to the Lord

6. When the *conjunction* is prefixed to a word with an inseparable preposition (-לְ -כְּ -בְּ), it is simply added in front of the preposition (-בְּ and -כְּ will lack *dageš lene*):

like the house	כַּבַּיִת	וְכַבַּיִת	and like the house
for the king	לַמֶּלֶךְ	וְלַמֶּלֶךְ	even for the king

7. The prepositions -לְ (c. 20,000x) and -בְּ (c. 15,700x) account for well more than half of all prepositions in Biblical Hebrew. There are several reasons for their frequency:

   a. -לְ often indicates an [*indirect*] *object*, much like English "to" or "for":

וַיִּזְבְּחוּ־שָׁם לַיהוָה׃	They sacrificed there *to* Yhwh (Jg 2.5)
לֹא־תִקַּח אִשָּׁה לִבְנִי	"Do not take a wife *for my son* …" (Gn 24.6)
וְלֹא דָרַשׁ לַבְּעָלִים׃	And he did not seek [*for*] the Baals (2 Chr 17.3)

   b. The preposition -לְ is also one of several ways in which Biblical Hebrew indicates *possession*; the -לְ is prefixed to the "owner". The context determines whether the syntagm corresponds to a phrase "an X of Y" ("Y's X") or clause ("Y has/had an X"). This is how Hebrew shows that the owner is a particular person, and implies that he or she has more than one:

נָבִיא לַיהוה	a prophet *of* Yhwh (1 Kgs 18.22); (implication: Yhwh has more than one prophet)
מִזְמוֹר לְדָוִד	a psalm *of David* (Ps 3.1); (implication: David wrote more than one psalm)
וּלְרִבְקָה אָח	Now Rebekkah *had* a brother (Gn 24.29); (implication: Rebekkah had more than one brother)

   c. The preposition -לְ frequently shows purpose or result, much like English "to", in the sense of "in order to" or "so that" (Lesson 16).
   d. The preposition -בְּ has a wide range of functions, as its glosses suggest (e.g., *in, with, by, on, against*), and is also used to form temporal clauses (as is the preposition -כְּ; Lesson 16).

7.2 The Separable Preposition (מִן)

1. The preposition מִן, "from", can be prefixed to its noun, or written as a separate word. When separate, it is usually linked to the word that it governs with *maqqef*:

a house	בַּיִת	מִן־בַּיִת	*from a house*
the son	הַבֵּן	מִן־הַבֵּן	*from the son*
the woman	הָאִשָּׁה	מִן־הָאִשָּׁה	*from the woman*

2. Like the inseparable prepositions (-בְּ, -כְּ, -לְ), מִן is often joined to the word that it governs, becoming its first syllable. When this happens, the *nun* of מִן assimilates[78] completely to the first letter, which therefore doubles, so that the *nun* shows up only as a *dageš forte* in the first letter. This assimilation is called *nunnation*. In the first example, **minbáyit > mibbáyit* (* means that the form is hypothetical; > means "developed into").

a house	בַּיִת	מִבַּיִת	*from a house*
a son	בֵּן	מִבֵּן	*from a son*
a king	מֶלֶךְ	מִמֶּלֶךְ	*from a king*

3. This means that we now know three causes of doubled letters:

The word's spelling:	אִשָּׁה	*a woman/wife*
The article:	הַבֵּן	*the son*
Nunnation:	מִמֶּלֶךְ	*from a king*

N.B.: You should **always ask why a letter is doubled**, since this often helps identify the word's lexical form, or distinguish the elements of a "compound word" (below).

4. Since *reš* and the gutturals (א, ה, ח, ע) do not double, מִן appears as -מֵ (remember that the *i/e* vowels are closely related) when it is joined to a word beginning with one of these letters:

a woman	אִשָּׁה	מֵאִשָּׁה	*from a woman*
a city	עִיר	מֵעִיר	*from a city*
a land	אֶרֶץ	מֵאֶרֶץ	*from a land*

5. Since מִן does not replace the -ה of the article, but is prefixed to it, *siere* also joins מִן to articular words:

the house	הַבַּיִת	מֵהַבַּיִת	*from the house*
the woman	הָאִשָּׁה	מֵהָאִשָּׁה	*from the woman*
the king	הַמֶּלֶךְ	מֵהַמֶּלֶךְ	*from the king*

7.3 Summary: Compound Forms

A substantival form (one "word") can thus consist of as many as four elements: a noun plus up to three prefixes (conjunction, preposition, article [and always in that order]).[79] This chart shows how

---

78. In *assimilation* one consonant becomes exactly like another—usually the one after it. In English the prefix *in-* ("not") assimilates to the first letter of words beginning with *m, r, l* (e.g., *im*mobile, *ir*replaceable, *il*legal), but not to the first letter of every word (cf., e.g., *in*violate). Note that assimilation produces a doubled letter in English as well as in Biblical Hebrew.

they are combined; you should learn to "take apart" the forms listed on the right by identifying their elements:

Noun	+	Article	+	Preposition	+	Conjunction
בַּיִת		הַבַּיִת		לַבַּיִת		וְלַבַּיִת
a house		the house		to the house		and to the house
מֶלֶךְ		הַמֶּלֶךְ		מֵהַמֶּלֶךְ		וּמֵהַמֶּלֶךְ
a king		the king		from the king		even from the king
אִישׁ		הָאִישׁ		כָּאִישׁ		וְכָאִישׁ
a man		the man		like the man		or like the man

7.4 Independent ("Separate") Prepositions

All other Hebrew prepositions are separate words, although they are often connected to their noun by *maqqef*. Those that end in a long vowel (e.g., לִפְנֵי) often cause an initial *bᵉgad-kᵉfat* letter in the following word to lose *dageš lene*.

a house	בַּיִת	תַּחַת־הַבַּיִת	under the house
his father	אָבִיו	תַּחַת־אָבִיו	in his father's place
a house	בַּיִת	לִפְנֵי־בַיִת	before/in front of a house
the king	הַמֶּלֶךְ	לִפְנֵי־הַמֶּלֶךְ	before/in the presence of the king
Dan	דָּן	עַד־דָּן	as far as Dan
the Jordan	הַיַּרְדֵּן	עֵבֶר־הַיַּרְדֵּן	beyond the Jordan
Moses	מֹשֶׁה	אֶל־מֹשֶׁה	to[ward] Moses

7.5 Syntax

Hebrew prose often repeats the preposition before each element of a multiple object, and uses the conjunction between prepositional phrases. Since this repetition is normal, it is most likely non-emphatic.

| בֵּין בֵּית־אֵל וּבֵין הָעָי | *between Bethel and Ai* (Gn 13.3); not "[right smack dab] between both Bethel and Ai" |
| מִדָּן וְעַד־בְּאֵר שֶׁבַע | *from Dan to [as far as] Beersheba* (1 Sam 3.20) |

7.6 Direction/Goal

Hebrew indicates that an action or event is directed to or toward a person, thing, or location in three different ways: (1) lexically, by prefixing a *preposition* (e.g., אֶל) to the object (§7.4); (2) morphologically, by suffixing the letter ה- to the object (§7.6.1); and (3) contextually (§7.6.2).

7.6.1 The Accusative/Directional Ending (ה ָ-)

A suffixed ה ָ - on some words indicates the direction or goal of verbs of motion—where the subject of the verb is going:

וַיָּקָם וַיָּבֹא הַבַּיְתָה	and he got up and went *to the house* (2 Kg 9.6)
וַיָּשָׁב יוֹסֵף מִצְרַיְמָה	and Joseph returned *to Egypt* (Gn 50.14)
וַיִּפְרֹשׂ כַּפָּיו הַשָּׁמַיְמָה	and he spread his hands *toward the sky* (2 Ch 6.13)
וַיָּסוּרוּ שָׁמָּה	and they turned aside *to that place* (Jg 18.15)

---

79. We will see another combination—but still a maximum of four elements—when we discuss pronominal suffixes.

Since Ugaritic[80] suggests that this is a remnant of an accusative case ending,[81] it has come to be called "accusative ה-". Unlike prepositions, the accusative ה- occurs on only a few words, the most frequent of which are listed here.[82]

1. *Nouns* (common and proper)

Lexical Form		With Accusative/Directional ה-	Frequency[83]	
			Locative	Total (c.)
אֶרֶץ	אַרְצָה	to[ward] the ground	87x	2500x
מִצְרַיִם	מִצְרַיְמָה	to[ward] Egypt	29x	680x
בַּיִת	הַבַּיְתָה	to[ward] the house	20x	2000x
מִדְבָּר	הַמִּדְבָּרָה	to[ward] the wilderness	18x	270x
הַר	הָהָרָה	to[ward] the mountain / hill country	14x	550x
שָׁמַיִם	הַשָּׁמַיְמָה	to[ward] heaven/the sky	12x	420x
שְׁאוֹל	שְׁאוֹלָה	to Sheol	10x	65x
עִיר	הָעִירָה	to[ward] the city	9x	1090x
בַּיִת	בַּיְתָה	to[ward] the house, inward	8x	2040x
יְרוּשָׁלַיִם	יְרוּשָׁלַיְמָה	to[ward] Jerusalem	5x	640x
שַׁעַר	שַׁעְרָה	to[ward] the gate	4x	360x

2. *Locatives*

	Lexical Form	With Accusative/Directional ה-	Frequency	
			Locative	Total
there	שָׁם	שָׁמָּה	to[ward] there/that place	142x	831x
where?	אָן	אָנָה	to where?	39x	42x

3. *Direction* (see §7.11)

	Lexical Form	With Accusative/Directional ה-	Frequency	
			Locative	Total
sea; west	יָם	יָמָּה	to[ward] the west (sea); westward	64x	392x
north	צָפוֹן	צָפֹנָה	to[ward] the north; northward	53x	153x
east	קֶדֶם	קֵדְמָה	to[ward] the east; eastward	26x	86x
south; Negev	נֶגֶב	נֶגְבָּה	to[ward] the south (Negev); southward	29x	110x
south	תֵּימָן	תֵּימָנָה	southward	13x	24x

7.6.2 Directional Objects

In addition to prepositions and the directional ה-, the place toward which someone is moving may simply be named, and the "movement to[ward]" understood from the combination of a verb

---

80. The "Semitic" languages are spoken by the people groups traditionally identified with the "sons of Shem" listed in Gn 10. They are commonly divided between Eastern (Akkadian, which includes the dialects of Assyria and Babylonia) and Western (Ugaritic; Aramaic, Canaanite [of which Hebrew, Moabite, Edomite, &c. are dialects]; Arabic, and Ge'ez [Ethiopic]). Comparative linguistics is the study of the links between related languages, and uses one language to explain features of another.
81. Like the rest of the Semitic family, Hebrew certainly had case endings early in its history.
82. Although the statistics show that the directional ה- is relatively infrequent (e.g., "to[ward] the house" is expressed some 130 times with the preposition אֶל-, but only twenty-eight times with the directional ה-), there are many forms with directional ה- in Biblical Hebrew, which means that you will need to recognize them.
83. Occurrences of the directional form and total occurrences of the word are listed on the right.

of motion and the name of the place. Objects may also indicate a location rather than a direction (2 Sam 11.9).

...וַיִּקְרָא לְרָחֵל וּלְלֵאָה הַשָּׂדֶה אֶל־צֹאנוֹ׃	... and he summoned Rachel and Leah *to the field*, to his flock (Gn 31.4)
מִן־הָאָרֶץ הַהִוא יָצָא אַשּׁוּר	From that land he went out *to Ashur* (Gn 10.11)
וַיִּשְׁכַּב אוּרִיָּה פֶּתַח בֵּית הַמֶּלֶךְ	Uriah slept *at the door* of the king's house (2 Sam 11.9)
וְיָרַדְתְּ הַגֹּרֶן	... and go down *to the threshing floor* (Ru 3.2)

N.B.: These are *not* three different functions, merely different ways of realizing the same function.

7.7 Prepositional Clauses

Hebrew rarely uses the verb "to be" for clauses that describe the location of a person or thing. Instead, Biblical Hebrew simply juxtaposes the noun and prepositional phrase, leaving the time frame ("tense") to be inferred from the context:

וְדָוִד בְּמִדְבַּר־זִיף	David [*was*] *in* the wilderness of Ziph (1 Sa 23.15)
וְיוֹתָם בֶּן־הַמֶּלֶךְ עַל־הַבָּיִת	and Jotham, the king's son, [*was*] *over* the palace (2 Kg 15.5)
וּכְבוֹד־יהוה עַל־הַבָּיִת	and Yhwh's glory [*was*] *over* the temple (2 Ch 7.3)
וְהַכְּנַעֲנִי אָז בָּאָרֶץ	now the Canaanites [*were*] then *in* the land (Gn 12.6)

7.8 Concepts

accusative	directional	preposition
assimilation	inseparable preposition	prepositional phrase
comparative linguistics	locative	Semitic
compound form(s)	nunnation	separable preposition

7.9 Vocabulary

gift, offering, tribute	מִנְחָה	.92	*behind, after* (locative & temporal)	אַחַר אַחֲרֵי	.83
to, as far as; until, while	עַד	.93	*to, toward*	אֶל־ אֵל	.84
leave, forsake, abandon	עָזַב	.94	*cubit; forearm*	אַמָּה	.85
on, upon, over; against; concerning	עַל	.95	*in, with, by, on, against, ...; when, while* (with inf. const.)	בְּ-	.86
with	עִם	.96	*between*	בֵּין	.87
innocent, just; righteous (adj.)	צַדִּיק	.97	*on behalf of, about; away from; behind*	בְּעַד	.88
innocence; righteousness (n.)	צֶדֶק		*like, as, according to; about, approximately* (with numbers); *when, while* (with inf. const.)	כְּ-	.89
lie down, sleep; have sexual relations with	שָׁכַב	.98			
under, beneath; instead of, in place of[84]	תַּחַת	.99	*to, for* (indicates indirect object); *have* (showing possession)	לְ-	.90
			from, out of; some of; than (in comparisons)	מִן	.91

---

84. For example, Josh 6.20 says that Jericho's wall fell down תַּחְתֶּיהָ, "under itself" ("in its own place"), straight down on its foundation.

7.10 Exercises

1. When you have studied the inseparable prepositions and מִן, and can recognize the presence of the article, identify the elements of these forms and provide English glosses for them.

   a. וּלְבֵן   c. וְעַל־הַמִּזְבֵּחַ   e. וּמֵהַבַּיִת
   b. וּמֵהֶהָרִים   d. מִכֹּהֵן   f. וְלָאֲנָשִׁים

2. Represent these *phrases* and *clauses* in English, parsing the verbal forms.

   a. וַיִּשְׁכַּב שְׁמוּאֵל עַד־הַבֹּקֶר — 1 Sam 3.15; בֹּקֶר *morning*; Samuel

   b. לֹא־תִכְרֹת לָהֶם בְּרִית — Dt 7.2; לָהֶם *for/with them*

   c. וַיִּקְרָא שָׁם אַבְרָם בְּשֵׁם יהוה: — Gn 13.4; קרא *call*; שֵׁם *the name of*; שָׁם *there*; Abram

   d. וְאֶכְתֹּב עַל־הַלֻּחֹת אֶת־הַדְּבָרִים — Dt 10.2; כתב *write*; לוּחַ *tablet*

   e. וַאֲנִי וְכָל־הָעָם אֲשֶׁר אִתִּי נִקְרַב אֶל־הָעִיר — Josh 8.5; אֲנִי *I*; עַם *nation, people*; אֲשֶׁר *who* (relative particle); אִתִּי *with me*

   f. וַיִּקְרַב אַהֲרֹן אֶל־הַמִּזְבֵּחַ וַיִּשְׁחַט אֶת־עֵגֶל הַחַטָּאת — Lv 9.8; שחט *slaughter*; עֵגֶל *calf of*; חַטָּאת *sin-offering*; Aaron

   g. וַיִּשְׁאֲלוּ בְנֵי־יִשְׂרָאֵל בַּיהוָה — Jg 20.27; שאל *ask* (middle-guttural verbs have a *ḥiatef-*vowel rather than *šewa*; an initial *begad-kefat* letter following a word ending in וּ-, ִי -, or ֵי - often lacks *dageš lene*)

   h. וַיִּסְפֹּר שְׁלֹמֹה כָּל־הָאֲנָשִׁים — 2 Chr 2.16; ספר *count*; Solomon

   i. וַיִּקְרָא אֱלֹהִים לָאוֹר יוֹם — Gn 1.5; קרא *call, name*; אוֹר *light*

   j. וַיִּשְׁמַע מֹשֶׁה לְקוֹל חֹתְנוֹ — Ex 18.24; קוֹל *voice of*; חֹתְנוֹ *his father-in-law*; Moses

   k. וַיִּכְרֹת יְהוֹשֻׁעַ בְּרִית לָעָם בַּיּוֹם הַהוּא — Josh 24.25; עַם *nation, people*; הַהוּא *that*; Joshua

   l. וַיִּשְׁכַּב דָּוִד עִם־אֲבֹתָיו — 1 Kgs 2.10; יו ָ - *his* (the י- shows that the noun is plural); David

   m. וַיִּשְׁמַע אֱלֹהִים אֶת־נַאֲקָתָם וַיִּזְכֹּר אֱלֹהִים אֶת־בְּרִיתוֹ אֶת־אַבְרָהָם אֶת־יִצְחָק וְאֶת־יַעֲקֹב: — Ex 2.24; נַאֲקָתָם *their* [ם ָ - 3 mp] *groaning, complaint, lament*; בְּרִיתוֹ *his covenant*; זכר *remember*; אֶת has both functions in this verse

7.11 Enrichment: Directions

As the Abram/Abraham stories progess, the divine promises become increasingly specific. YHWH first promised to *show* Abram a "land" (Gn 12.1), then that he would *give* "this land" to his descendants (Gn 12.7). In Gn 13.14–15, he tells Abram that what he can see "from the place where [he was] standing", using the cardinal directions with the accusative ה- to identify the general extent of the now-promised land, which he declares that he will give to *both* Abram and his descendants.

צָפֹנָה וָנֶגְבָּה וָקֵדְמָה וָיָמָּה: *... to the north, and to the Negev* [south], *and to the east, and to the sea* [west] (Gn 13.14–15)

What we cannot tell from the story is the extent of the land that Abram could see, since we do not know (1) where he was standing; or (2) the precise topography of his day.

In the ancient Near East [ANE], orientation was toward the east (cf. Lat. *orient*); *yāmîn* could mean either "right side", "right hand", or "south". In the northern hemisphere today we "orient" ourselves and our maps to the north, which reflects magnetic means of direction-finding (e.g., lodestones, compass). Without such tools, sunrise functioned as the primary directional indicator.

South	North	West	East	
יָמִין	שְׂמֹאול	אָחוֹר	קֶדֶם	Jb 23.8–9
			עַל־פְּנֵי יְרוּשָׁלַם מִקֶּדֶם	
		וְיָמָּה	מִזְרָחָה	Zc 14.4
נֶגְבָּה	צָפוֹנָה			

Job says that God and his work cannot be found in any direction (Jb 23.8–9), but whether he refers to the cardinal directions (east, west, north, south) or his own point of view ("in front", "behind", "on [my] left", "on [my] right") is unclear, since all four words can have both frames of reference.

In Zc 14.4, the Mount of Olives is said to be "facing" Jerusalem "on the east"; when it splits "from sunrise [east] to the sea [west]", its two halves will move "northward" and "toward the Negev [south]" (all four forms have "directional" ה-).

Lesson 8

COMMANDS & PROHIBITIONS

The imperfect conjugation can function modally with the sense of "should" or "must" (Lesson 5); the *imperative* conjugation is used for positive commands.[85] Like the imperative in English, which has only an implicit subject ("Go to bed!"), commands in Biblical Hebrew rarely name the subject. Like the imperfect and preterite, however, the imperative in Biblical Hebrew identifies the gender and number of its subject, using the PGN *endings* (only) of the second person imperfect.

8.1 *Form*

The imperative occurs only in the second person, and uses the subject [PGN] endings of the imperfect *without* the subject prefixes.

Person	Gender	Singular	Plural
2nd	Masc.	no ending or ־ָה	־וּ
	Fem.	־ִי	־ְנָה

8.2 *The Qal Imperative*

When the affixes of the imperative and the vowels of the *qal* imperative are added to the verbal root, the paradigm of the *qal* imperative is:

Person	Gender	Singular		Plural	
2nd	Masc.	מְשֹׁל מָשְׁלָה	*Rule!*	מִשְׁלוּ	*Rule!*
	Fem.	מִשְׁלִי		מְשֹׁלְנָה	

1. The *ḥireq* under the first radical with vocalic endings avoids consecutive vocal *šewa*s (when the prefix is removed from the imperfect, the *šewa* under the first radical becomes vocal).[86]
2. It is not uncommon for the 2ms imperative to have the ending ־ָה, which, in the *qal*, yields a form that looks just like 3fs *qal* perfect (מָשְׁלָה), and can be distinguished from it only by the context.
3. As in the imperfect and preterite, II- and III-guttural verbal roots form their imperative with *pataḥ* rather than *ḥolem*; III-א roots have *qameṣ*.

---

85. Imperatives are relatively infrequent, accounting for only about one in twenty of all verbs in Biblical Hebrew. Although we might expect to see them in the covenantal "legal" books, they are proportionately most frequent in Psalms (12% of all verbs), Song (11%), Jeremiah (7%), and Isaiah (7%); cf. Leviticus (2%) and Deuteronomy (4%).

86. This explanation is pedagogical, not technical.

Person	Gender	Singular		Plural	
2nd	Masc.	שְׁמַע / שִׁמְעָה	מְצָא / מְצָאָה	שִׁמְעוּ	מִצְאוּ
	Fem.	שִׁמְעִי	מִצְאִי	שְׁמַ֫עְנָה	מְצֶ֫אנָה

8.3 Function (HBI §2.2.4c)

1. Positive *commands* use the imperative.

קְרָא נָא גַּם לְחוּשַׁי הָאַרְכִּי	*Summon* Hushai the Archite ... (2 Sa 17.5).
אֶ֫רֶץ אֶ֫רֶץ אֶ֫רֶץ שִׁמְעִי דְּבַר־יְהוָה:	Land, land, land, *hear* Yhwh's word (Jr 22.29).
בֶּן־אָדָם עֲמֹד עַל־רַגְלֶ֫יךָ	Son of man, *stand* on your feet! (Ezk 2.1)
שִׁמְעוּ אֶת־הַדָּבָר הַזֶּה	*Hear* this word! (Am 3.1)

2. *Prohibitions* (negative commands) are formed with the *imperfect* (*not* imperative) negated by לֹא or אַל. There may be a slight tendency for prohibitions with לֹא to be more universal or permanent than those with אַל (which would then refer to an immediate or specific situation), but this must be determined for each case; it is not a general rule.

לֹא תִּגְנֹב:	*Do not steal* (Ex 20.15).
לֹא תַעֲבֹר בִּי	*Do not cross over* against me (Nu 20.18).
לֹא־תִקְרָא אֶת־שְׁמָהּ שָׂרָי	*Do not call* her name Sarai (Gn 17.15).
אַל־נָא תִקְבְּרֵ֫נִי בְּמִצְרָ֫יִם	*Do not bury me* in Egypt (Gn 47.29).
רַק אֶת־בְּנִי לֹא תָשֵׁב שָׁ֫מָּה:	But my son *do not take back* there (Gn 24.9).

8.4 Other Volitional Verbs

The term "volitional" refers to speech in which the speaker asserts his or her will (volition) toward another person. The imperative (above) is the most obvious form of volitional speech, but not all declarations of a speaker's will are directed to the hearer. Some may indirectly command another person ("He should ...", "Rebecca ought to ...", "Let Ezra do it" [*not* in the sense of "allow" or "permit"]), or summon a group (of which the speaker is part) to do something ("Let's ...", "We should ...").

8.4.1 Cohortative (HBI §2.2.4a)

The first person forms of the imperfect can show *volition*—the subject's determination to do something. This is technically another modal use of the prefix conjugation, although this form can occur with an added ־ָה. It is parsed in the conjugation column as "c" (for "cohortative").

נִכְרְתָה בְרִית אֲנִי וָאָ֫תָּה	You and I *will make* a covenant (Gn 31.44) or "We—you and I—will make a covenant"
וְאֶשְׁלְחָה סֵ֫פֶר	I *will send* a letter ... (2 Kgs 5.5)
נִשְׁלְחָה אֲנָשִׁים לְפָנֵ֫ינוּ	We *will send* men before us ... (Dt 1.22)
נִזְבְּחָה לַיהוָה:	We *will sacrifice* to Yhwh (Ex 5.17)

When it occurs with the conjunction after another cohortative, imperfect, or imperative, the cohortative may be *telic*, showing purpose or result; this is determined by the context and the relationship between the functions of the two verbs:

תְּהִי אָלָה ... וְנִכְרְתָה בְרִית עִמָּךְ׃	Let there be an oath ... that we *may make* a covenant with you (Gn 26.28)
קְרָא נָא גַּם לְחוּשַׁי ... וְנִשְׁמְעָה מַה־בְּפִיו	Call Hushai ..., *that we may hear* (2 Sam 17.5)
... וְנַפִּילָה גוֹרָלוֹת וְנֵדְעָה ...	... we'll cast lots *so that we may know* ... (Jn 1.7)

8.4.2 *Jussive (HBI §2.2.4b)*

In the third person the prefix conjugation can also have volitional force, which is called *jussive* (Latin *jussus*, a command). This functions rather like a third person imperative, that is, "Let him ..." in the sense of "He should/must/ought ...",[87] but probably *not* with the sense "Allow him to ...". Because there is no special form[88] for this function, grammarians differ on which verbs are jussive and which are not, especially in biblical poetry; in Gn 41.35, for example, Joseph is offering Pharaoh advice, so the verbs are probably jussive:

וְיִקְבְּצוּ אֶת־כָּל־אֹכֶל ... וְיִצְבְּרוּ־בָר	"*Let them gather* all the food ... and *let them store* grain ..." (Gn 41.35); i.e., "They should ..."
יִשְׁמְעוּ הָעִבְרִים׃	"*Let* the Hebrew *hear*!" (1 Sam 13.3); i.e., not permission, but exhortation.
יִשְׁמֹר אֶת־נַפְשֶׁךָ׃	*May* he *guard* your life *or* He shall guard your life (Ps 121.7)

8.5 *The Volitional Particle* (נָא)

The imperative, cohortative, and jussive may be followed by the particle נָא (with or without *maqqef*). Although נָא is often translated "please", or "I pray" (in the archaic sense of "ask"), its function seems to be inconsistent, which means that its function is not clear. A verb followed by נָא, however, is *always* volitional. When a volitional verb is negated, it may be preceded by אַל־נָא or לֹא־נָא:

שִׁמְעוּ־נָא הַחֲלוֹם הַזֶּה אֲשֶׁר חָלָמְתִּי׃	"*Hear* this dream which I dreamed (Gn 37.6).
וַיֹּאמְרוּ לוֹ אֱמָר־נָא שִׁבֹּלֶת	They said to him, "*Say* 'Shibbolet' " (Jg 12.6).
וַיֹּאמֶר אַל־נָא תַעֲזֹב אֹתָנוּ	He said, "*Do not abandon* us,[89] ..." (Nu 10.31).

8.6 *The Volitional Summary Particle* (וְעַתָּה) *(HBI §3.3.8)*

The particle וְעַתָּה (וְ + עַתָּה; traditionally, "And now") usually introduces an imperative, cohortative, or jussive, which directs the hearer to pursue a course of action based on the preceding discourse. Volitional forms occur frequently without וְעַתָּה, but you should expect to find a volitional verb (negative or positive) after וְעַתָּה whenever you come across it. When it occurs without a volitional form, it functions as a temporal particle, "now". Note that the volitional form is often *not* the following word; additional information or reasons can precede the command or declaration of intent.

וְעַתָּה בְנִי שְׁמַע בְּקֹלִי	*Now therefore*, my son, *listen* to my voice (Gn 27.8)
וְעַתָּה יִגְדַּל־נָא כֹּחַ אֲדֹנָי	*Now therefore, let* the power of my Lord *be great* (Nu 14.17)
וְעַתָּה כִּתְבוּ לָכֶם אֶת־הַשִּׁירָה הַזֹּאת	*Now therefore, write* this song (Dt 31.19)
וְעַתָּה יִשְׁמַע־נָא אֲדֹנִי הַמֶּלֶךְ	*Now therefore, let* my lord the king *hear* (1 Sam 26.19)

---

87. Since Biblical Hebrew does not use helping verbs to show what is called "mood", the choice of which helping verb to use in English reflects the translator's interpretation.

88. The imperfect and jussive can be distinguished in a *few* types of verbal roots because their vowels differ (below).

89. Pronominal objects are always attached to either the verb itself or, as here, the direct object marker itself (אֹתָנוּ > אֵת+־נוּ).

8.7 Concepts

cohortative	imperative	prohibition
command	jussive	volitional

8.8 Vocabulary

love, loyalty, kindness (trad. "lovingkindness")	חֶסֶד	.108	stone (cf. אֶבֶן הָעֵזֶר, Ebenezer, "the stone of help"; 1 Sam 7.12)	אֶבֶן	.100
possess, subdue; dispossess [someone] (hifil)	ירשׁ	.109	ground (cf. Gn 2.7)	אֲדָמָה	.101
silver	כֶּסֶף	.110	boundary; territory (i.e., land inside a boundary)	גְּבוּל	.102
write	כתב	.111	blood	דָּם	.103
night (m.)	לַיִל לַיְלָה	.112	gold	זָהָב	.104
something appointed (place, time); season	מוֹעֵד	.113	remember	זכר	.105
work, deed, thing done (m.)	מַעֲשֶׂה	.114	seed (sg. & coll.)	זֶרַע	.106
untranslatable particle indicating volition (trad. "please"); follows imv., coh., juss.	נָא-	.115	strength; army; wealth	חַיִל	.107

8.9 Exercises

After learning the forms of the *qal* imperative, gloss the clauses, parsing the verbs. Since the imperative is always second person, you can simply label the PGN by gender and number (e.g., "ms" or "fp"). N.B.: Not all verbal forms in these biblical quotations are imperative.

a. וַיֹּאמֶר שְׁמֹר אֶת־הָאִישׁ　　1 Kg 20.39

b. שִׁכְבִי עַד־הַבֹּקֶר:　　Ru 3.13; עַד until; בֹּקֶר morning

c. וַיֹּאמֶר פַּרְעֹה אֶל־יוֹסֵף אֱמֹר אֶל־אַחֶיךָ　　Gn 45.17; אָחִיךָ your [ךָ- 2ms] brothers; Pharaoh, Joseph

d. לֹא תִּגְנֹב:　　Ex 20.15; גנב steal

e. וְעַתָּה בָנִים שִׁמְעוּ־לִי　　Pr 5.7; וְעַתָּה (see §8.6); לִי to me; Jehoshaphat

f. וַיֹּאמֶר יְהוֹשָׁפָט אֶל־מֶלֶךְ יִשְׂרָאֵל דְּרָשׁ־נָא כַיּוֹם אֶת־דְּבַר יְהוָה:　　1 Kgs 22.5; דרשׁ seek, search; מֶלֶךְ king of; כַיּוֹם today; דְּבַר word of

g. בְּנִי תּוֹרָתִי אַל־תִּשְׁכָּח　　Pr 3.1; בְּנִי my son (vocative); תּוֹרָתִי my teaching; שׁכח forget

h. וַיֹּאמֶר מֹשֶׁה אֶל־אַהֲרֹן אֱמֹר אֶל־כָּל־עֲדַת בְּנֵי יִשְׂרָאֵל קִרְבוּ לִפְנֵי יְהוָה　　Ex 16.9; עֲדַת assembly of; לִפְנֵי before, in the presence of

i. וַיִּשְׁמַע יהוה אֶת־קוֹל דִּבְרֵיכֶם　　Dt 5.28; קוֹל the sound of; דִּבְרֵיכֶם your words

j. וַיִּקְרָא פַרְעֹה אֶל־מֹשֶׁה וּלְאַהֲרֹן וַיֹּאמֶר לְכוּ זִבְחוּ לֵאלֹהֵיכֶם בָּאָרֶץ:　　Ex 8.21; קרא אֶל call to, summon; לְכוּ go (2mp Q V of הלך); זבח sacrifice; כֶם- your (2mp); Pharoah, Moses, Aaron

k.	זְכֹר אַל־תִּשְׁכַּח	Dt 9.7; שׁכח *forget*
l.	וְעַתָּה כִּרְתוּ־לָנוּ בְרִית:	Josh 9.6; לָנוּ *for [with] us*
m.	וַיִּקְרָא אֶל־גֵּיחֲזִי וַיֹּאמֶר קְרָא אֶל־הַשֻּׁנַמִּית	2 Kgs 4.36; קרא אֶל *call to, summon*; Gehazi, Shunamite
n.	שְׁאַל־נָא אֶת־הַכֹּהֲנִים	Hg 2.11; שׁאל *ask*
o.	וְעַתָּה בְנִי שְׁמַע בְּקֹלִי	Gn 27.43; יִ - *my* (1cs)
p.	שְׁמַע יִשְׂרָאֵל יְהוָה אֱלֹהֵינוּ יְהוָה אֶחָד:	Dt 6.4; אֱלֹהֵינוּ *our* [-נוּ 1cp] *god*; אֶחָד *one*

8.10 *Enrichment: Verbal Euphony in Poetry*

The first eight lines of Psalm 100 contain seven commands: "Shout …! Serve ..! Enter …! Know …! Enter …! Thank …! Bless …!" Even though Hebrew poetry does not use rhyme, the repeated PGN affix וּ- on the string of 2mp imperatives links this series of commands by both form and sound (imperatives are *italicized*). Nearly every line in the psalm (after the title [1a]) begins with a word ending in –*u*, and several (2a-b, 4a-b) end with a word that begins with the preposition בְּ- (*with*). Read these lines aloud until you can begin to hear their repeated sounds.

Shout to Yhwh, all the earth;	הָרִיעוּ לַיהוָה כָּל־הָאָרֶץ: **1b**
Serve Yhwh **with** joy;	עִבְדוּ אֶת־יְהוָה בְּשִׂמְחָה **2a**
Come before him **with** a glad shout;	בֹּאוּ לְפָנָיו בִּרְנָנָה: **2b**
Know that Yhwh is God.	דְּעוּ כִּי־יְהוָה הוּא אֱלֹהִים … **3a**
Enter his gates **with** thanks,	בֹּאוּ שְׁעָרָיו בְּתוֹדָה **4a**
His courts **with** praise,	חֲצֵרֹתָיו בִּתְהִלָּה **4b**
Thank him,	הוֹדוּ־לוֹ **4c**
Bless his name;	בָּרֲכוּ שְׁמוֹ: **4d**

Reading the Hebrew text reveals effects such as this aural repetition (which is invisible in English), so that we can enjoy both *what* they said and *how* they said it.

Lesson 9

Nominal Modification (III): The Construct

The English word "of" signals many relationships, including possession ("the sword of Goliath"), relationship ("son of David"), and modification ("an altar of gold"). These can also be signalled by the "possessive 's'" ("God's kingdom", "the scribe's son") or an adjective ("a golden altar"), or even by juxtaposing two nouns ("a stone wall").

Hebrew expresses these relationships with the construct chain, in which each word is "linked to" the following word. Words are said to be in either the "construct" or "absolute" state. Nouns thus have one of two states:[90] they are either "absolute" (from Latin, meaning "unconnected" or "independent") or "construct". About **one-third** of all nouns in Biblical Hebrew occur in the construct state.

9.1 The construct Chain

To modify (in language) is to restrict. A major way to modify a word's referent in English and Hebrew is by means of the "of" relationship. Consider, for example, "the girl's book", "the author's book", and "his book". In each case the words before "book" restrict what "book" can refer to. In order to show this relationship, Biblical Hebrew places two or more substantives side-by-side in a sequence of words called a *construct chain*, in which each word is linked to the following word by the "of" relationship:

1. אֲבִי מֶלֶךְ — *a father of a king* or *a king's father*
2. אֲבִי הַמֶּלֶךְ — *the father of the king* or *the king's father*
3. בַּת הַמֶּלֶךְ — *the daughter of the king* or *the king's daughter*
4. סֵפֶר הַתּוֹרָה — *the document of the teaching/law*
5. בֵּית מֶלֶךְ הָאָרֶץ — *the house of the king of the land*
6. בֵּית מֶלֶךְ יִשְׂרָאֵל — *the house of the king of Israel*

1. Each noun is *in construct* to the *following* word.
2. The order is not arbitrary, and may not be changed (e.g., #1 cannot mean "a father's king").
3. The last word in a construct chain is in the absolute state.[91] The vocabulary form of a noun is also its form in the *absolute*.
4. A construct chain therefore consists of a series of words, each of which (except the last) is modified by the rest of the series.

9.1.1 Forms

1. Masculine singular and feminine plural nouns have the same endings in both states. Feminine singular and masculine plural nouns, however, have separate endings for absolute and construct. The ת- of the fem. construct singular and the וֹת- of the plural replaces the ה- of the singular; if the absolute ends in ת-, the absolute and construct singular endings are the

---

90. Unfortunately, the words "construct" and "absolute" can refer to a word's *function* (i.e., "linked" or "independent") or its *form* (since the construct spelling of many words differs slightly from their absolute [lexical] form). You will need to note which sense applies.
91. We shall note the single exception to this when we discuss pronominal suffixes (Lesson 14, below).

same. The ם- of the masculine plural absolute drops off, and the form has *ṣere* instead of *ḥireq*, as in the following table.[92]

	Singular		Plural	
	Absolute	Construct	Absolute	Construct
Masc.	סוּס *horse*	סוּס *horse of*	סוּסִים *horses*	סוּסֵי *horses of*
Fem.	סוּסָה *mare*	סוּסַת *mare of*	סוּסוֹת *mares*	סוּסוֹת *mares of*

2. Even if the ending is the same (as in ms and fp), the vowels of words in construct often differ from their lexical form, since the accent changes [lessens] slightly when a word is in construct.

	Singular		Plural	
	Absolute	Construct	Absolute	Construct
Masc.	בַּיִת *house*	בֵּית *house of*	בָּתִּים *houses*	בָּתֵּי *houses of*
	בֵּן *son*	בֶּן *son of*	בָּנִים *sons*	בְּנֵי *sons of*
Fem.	אִשָּׁה *wife*	אֵשֶׁת *wife of*	נָשִׁים *wives*	נְשֵׁי *wives of*
	בַּת *daughter*	בַּת *daughter of*	בָּנוֹת *daughters*	בְּנוֹת *daughters of*

3. This does not apply to long internal vowels (cf. סוּס, above), i.e., those written with a *mater* (which are thus called "unchangeably long"):

	Singular		Plural	
	Absolute	Construct	Absolute	Construct
Masc.	אִישׁ *man*	אִישׁ *man of*	אֲנָשִׁים *men*	אַנְשֵׁי *men of*
Fem.	עִיר *city*	עִיר *city of*	עָרִים *cities*	עָרֵי *cities of*

4. Three fairly common nouns form their construct singular by adding ־ִי (פְּרִי has the same form in both states):

	Singular		Plural	
	Absolute	Construct	Absolute	Construct
	אָב *father*	אֲבִי *father of*	אָבוֹת *fathers*	אֲבוֹת *fathers of*
	אָח *brother*	אֲחִי *brother of*	אַחִים *brothers*	אֲחֵי *brothers of*
	פֶּה *mouth*	פִּי *mouth of*		
	פְּרִי *fruit*	פְּרִי *fruit of*		

5. The construct singular of nouns with two vowels with either *waw* or *yod* between them "collapses" or "simplifies" into a single long vowel (*-awe-* > *-ô-*; and *-ayi-* > *-ê-*):

	Singular		Plural	
	Absolute	Construct	Absolute	Construct
	מָוֶת *death*	מוֹת *death of*		
	בַּיִת *house*	בֵּית *house of*	בָּתִּים *houses*	בָּתֵּי *houses of*
	עַיִן *eye; spring*	עֵין *eye/spring of* [93]	עֵינַיִם *eyes*	עֵינֵי *eyes of*

---

92. The following paradigms list the singular and plural forms for each word—regardless of the point being illustrated—as they occur in Biblical Hebrew. If a form is not listed, it does not occur.

93. עֵין is the first part of the names of many water sources, e.g., עֵין־גְּדִי (*En-gedi*) "Well of [the] Kid".

9.1.2 Syntax

1. Although the form of a word often signals that it is in the construct, the primary signal of a construct chain is an *uninterrupted series of two or more substantives*, the last of which is often definite, being either an articular noun or proper name.[94]

כּוֹכְבֵי הַשָּׁמַיִם	the stars of the sky
בֶּן דָּוִד	the son of David, David's son
עָרֵי יְהוּדָה	the cities of Judah, Judah's cities
בְּנוֹת צְלָפְחָד	the daughters of Zelophehad, Zelophehad's daughters
מִזְבַּח הַזָּהָב	the altar of gold, the golden altar

2. The definiteness of the *last* element in a construct chain determines the definiteness or indefiniteness of *every* element in that chain. If the last element is definite, the entire chain is definite; if it is indefinite, then the entire chain is indefinite. A substantive can be definite because it is articular, or because it is a proper name, or because it is construct to another word that is definite.

a man's son	בֶּן אִישׁ	בֶּן הָאִישׁ	the son of the man, the man's son
houses of a city	בָּתֵּי עִיר	בָּתֵּי הָעִיר	the houses of the city, the city's houses
a king's song	שִׁיר מֶלֶךְ	שִׁיר דָּוִד	the song of David, David's song

3. On the other hand, some words in construct with a definite noun may be definite, but are not exclusive. The phrase תּוֹעֲבַת יהוה, *an abomination of* Yhwh, for example, describes many things in Scripture, none of which is "*the* [implicitly: only] abomination of Yhwh".

4. Nothing can come between words in a construct chain except the locative ה- without breaking the chain. This includes prepositions and the conjunction וְ, which can only be prefixed to the first word in the chain.

5. Articular words, proper names (and substantives with a pronominal suffix, below) cannot occur within a chain. When they occur, the construct chain ends. Since they are all definite, they make the entire chain definite. This means that the first noun in a construct chain cannot have the article or be a proper name.[95]

6. Each word in a construct "belongs to" the next word. This is never reversed. כּוֹכְבֵי הַשָּׁמַיִם (the first example above) cannot mean "the sky of the stars".

7. Most construct chains have either two or three parts (as above), but construct chains can [rarely] have as many as six elements (six-element chains are extremely rare[96]). In these examples, English words linked by dashes represent a single Hebrew form:

לִפְנֵי כָּל־קְהַל עֲדַת בְּנֵי יִשְׂרָאֵל	in-the-presence-of all-[of] the-assembly-of the-congregation-of the-sons-of Israel (Nu 14.5) [six elements]
וְאֶל־כָּל־מִשְׁפַּחַת בֵּית־אֲבִי אִמּוֹ	and-to all-[of] the-clan-of the-household-of the-father-of his-mother (Jg 9.1) [six elements]
לְכָל־עֲבוֹדַת מִשְׁכַּן בֵּית אֱלֹהִים	for-all-[of] the-labour-of the-tabernacle-of the-house-of God (1 Ch 6.33; cf. 1 Ch 28.13, 20) [five elements]
מִסְפַּר יְמֵי־חַיֵּי הֶבְלוֹ	the-number-of the-days-of the-life-of his-vanity [his vain life] (Qo 6.12) [five elements]

---

94. Or a noun with a pronominal suffix (Lesson 14).
95. The apparent exception to this, the phrase יהוה צְבָאוֹת (traditionally rendered "Lord of hosts" but now "Sovereign Lord" [NIV] or the like), may be probably more apparent than real. It occurs fifteen times in the form יהוה אֱלֹהֵי צְבָאוֹת, "Yahweh, God of hosts" (e.g., 2 Sam 5.10; 1 Kgs 19.10, 14; Ps 89.9), which may suggest that יהוה צְבָאוֹת is a shortened form of the same phrase. It also occurs six times as יהוה אֱלֹהִים צְבָאוֹת (Ps 59.6; 80.5, 20; 84.9; אֱלֹהִים צְבָאוֹת occurs twice [Ps 80.8, 15]). יהוה may not, therefore, be in construct to צְבָאוֹת, but rather in apposition to an implicit [culturally understood] אֱלֹהֵי צְבָאוֹת. On the other hand, however, יהוה צְבָאוֹת may be a true exception.
96. In Nu 14.5, the form לִפְנֵי is a compound preposition the second element of which is פָּנִים, *face, presence*; in Jg 9.1, the last form is compounded from אֵם, *mother*, and ־וֹ, *his*.

9.1.3 Function

Construct chains are functionally *attributive*—they modify a word by limiting its range to the "of" term. "Brother", for example, could refer to many males; "brother *of David*" limits the potential referents to seven. This modification often shows possession, but it can also carry any of several nuances, such as those identified for "of" in English, or the genitive in Greek or German.

Construct chains have three primary functions: objective, subjective, or adjectival. For example, "the love of God" can refer to one's love *for God* ("God" is the object of the love) or God's love *for someone/thing* ("God is the subject of the love); "the word of Y<small>HWH</small>", on the other hand, refers consistently to a message from Y<small>HWH</small> (Yhwh is the source of the message).

Possession—a common function of the construct—is an example of the subjective function, so that "Goliath's sword" refers to "the sword that Goliath has (had/owns/uses/etc.)". The following list of functions of the construct is not meant to suggest that the biblical authors chose to use a particular "type" of construct (any more than we think about "which" function of "of" we are using). It merely illustrates the types of relationships that the construct can indicate.

Since the entire chain cumulatively modifies the first word, *only the first word* in a construct chain can be the subject, object, or indirect object of a clause, or the object of a preposition. This will become increasingly clear as you read more Hebrew.

1. *Possession*. The item named by the first word belongs to the second.

    חֶרֶב גָּלְיָת   Goliath's sword or the sword of Goliath (1 Sa 21.10)

    כִּסֵּא שְׁלֹמֹה   Solomon's throne or the throne of Solomon

2. *Attribution*. The second word modifies the first, and is often glossed like an adjective. This type of construct chain often has a pronominal suffix (Lesson 14) on the final word (the ִי in Ps 2.6).

    מִזְבַּח הַזָּהָב   the gold altar or the altar of gold (Nu 4.11)

    הַר קָדְשִׁי   my holy mountain or the mountain of my holiness (Ps 2.6)

3. *Relationship*. The construct chain describes people who are related to one another.

    בַּת־מֶלֶךְ   a king's daughter; a daughter of a king (2 Kg 9.34)

    אֲבִי כְנַעַן   Canaan's father; the father of Canaan (Gn 9.18)

4. *Definition*. Generic terms are often defined more closely by a proper name:

    נְהַר־פְּרָת   the river Euphrates (Gn 15.18)

    אֶרֶץ כְּנַעַן   the land of Canaan (Gn 17.8)

5. The noun כֹּל—"all, every, each" is in construct to the noun that it modifies. Its construct form is כָּל (with or without *maqqef*):

    כָּל־עַם הָאָרֶץ   *all* the people of the land (2 Kgs 11.20)

    לְכָל־בְּנֵי הַמֶּלֶךְ וּלְשָׂרֵי הַצָּבָא   to *all* the king's sons and to the leaders of the army (1 Kg 1.25)

9.2 The "Possessive" lamed

A construct chain is either entirely definite ("*the* servant of *the* king", "*the* city of *David*") or entirely indefinite ("*a* servant of *a* king"). To show possession when the owner is specific but the thing possessed is not ("*a* servant of *the* king", "*a* prophet of Y<small>HWH</small>"), Hebrew prefixes the preposition לְ (cf. §7.1) to the "owner". The context determines whether the construction is a phrase "a X of Y" ("Y's X") or clause ("Y has/had an X"). This often implies that a person had more than one prophet, psalm, &c.

II.9. Nominal Modification (III): The Construct

נְבִיא לַיהוה	*a* prophet *of* Y<small>HWH</small> (1 Kgs 18.22)
מִזְמוֹר לְדָוִד	*a* psalm *of David* (e.g., Ps 3.1)
וּלְרִבְקָה אָח	Now *Rebeccah* had *a* brother (Gn 24.29)
וּלְנָעֳמִי מֹידָע לְאִישָׁהּ	Now *Naomi* had *a* relative by [*or* of] her husband (Ru 2.1)

9.3 Concepts

absolute	attributive; attribution	modification; to modify	possessive	state
adjectival	construct (chain)	objective	relationship	subjective

9.4 Vocabulary

prophet	נָבִיא	.125	love, like; desire (cf. Amnon, 2 Sam 13)	אָהַב	.116
inheritance, property	נַחֲלָה	.126	(f.) mother; ancestress	אֵם	.117
young man[97]	נַעַר	.127	gather, take in	אָסַף	.118
guilt, trespass, sin	עָוֹן[98]	.128	chest, box; ark (of the covenant)	אָרוֹן	.119
inward part	קֶרֶב	.129	garment, clothing	בֶּגֶד	.120
inside, within	בְּקֶרֶב		morning	בֹּקֶר	.121
foot, leg	רֶגֶל	.130	glory, honor, wealth	כָּבוֹד	.122
peace, health, welfare	שָׁלוֹם	.131	camp, army	מַחֲנֶה	.123
teaching, instruction (trad., "law")	תּוֹרָה	.132	messenger (מַלְאָכִי, Malachi, "my messenger"); angel	מַלְאָךְ	.124

9.5 Exercises

Gloss these phrases and clauses, parsing the verbal forms, and identifying any construct chains. Use the "rules" for glossing the construct (Lesson 5):

1. Words in construct are indicated by '-of' as the last element in their English word-group.
2. All elements of a construct are visually linked by em-dashes (i.e., *the-house-of the-king*).
3. Words that are construct to a definite form are represented with the definite article "the".

---

97. This word can focus on *age* ("youth", "young man"), especially when opposed to "elder" or "aged" (e.g., Ex 10.9; Dt 28.50; Josh 6.21; 1 Sam 17.33,42; 2 Kgs 4.29 ... 35; Is 3.5; Est 3.13), but can also reflect social standing; for example, it identifies an especially trusted or personal *servant*, such as one who accompanies his master on an errand or journey (e.g., Gn 22.3,5,12,19; Ex 33.11; Jg 7.10; 9.54; 19.3,9 ..., 19 [N.B.: distinguished from other (previously unmentioned) servants!]; 1 Sam 14.1,6; 16.18; 20.21,35 ...; 25.5,8 ...; 2 Kgs 4.19,22,24,25; 5.20; 6.15,17; Ru 2.5,6; Est 2.2; 6.3,5), to an *heir* (e.g., Gn 25.27; 34.19; 37.2; 41.12; 2 Sam 18.5,12 ...), or a young man who is in some way "*special*" (e.g., Jg 13.5,7,8 ...; 17.7,11 ...; 1 Sam 1.22,24 ...;2.11,13 ...; 3.1,8; 4.21; 9.3,5 ...; 16.11; 1 Kgs 11.28; 1 Chr 12.28). Some occurrences, by modifying it with "small" or "little" seem to encompass *both* (e.g., Jg 8.20; 1 Sam 20.35; 1 Kgs 3.7 (cf. 1 Ch 22.5; 29.1); 2 Kgs 5.14). The narrative sometimes includes the age of the נַעַר (e.g., Gn 37.2 (17 years) ; 2 Chr 34.3 (16 years; cf. 34.1)). Calling someone a נַעַר thus often implies that he is a person of *rank* or *relative importance*.

98. The Masoretes pointed this word with what looks like two consecutive vowels. It is pronounced, however, as though a *waw* preceded the *ḥolem*: `a · **wôn** (i.e., according to its theoretical spelling: עָווֹן).

a. בַּת מֶלֶךְ	e. בֵּית בְּנֵי אֵשֶׁת הַכֹּהֵן	i. לְכָל־אַנְשֵׁי־יְהוּדָה
b. בֵּית בֶּן הַמֶּלֶךְ	f. רוּחַ אֱלֹהִים	j. בֶּן לְדָוִד
c. נְבִיאֵי יהוה	g. שְׁמוֹת בְּנֵי־דָוִד	k. עָרֵי יִשְׂרָאֵל
d. מַלְכֵי יִשְׂרָאֵל	h. מִבְּנוֹת הַמֶּלֶךְ	l. בֶּן־אִשָּׁה מִן־בְּנוֹת דָּן

---

a. וַיִּשְׁלְחוּ אַנְשֵׁי גִבְעוֹן אֶל־יְהוֹשֻׁעַ אֶל־הַמַּחֲנֶה   Josh 10.6; Gibeon, Joshua

b. וַיֹּאמְרוּ עַבְדֵי פַרְעֹה אֵלָיו ...   Ex 10.7; אֵלָיו *to him*

c. בְּנֵי רָחֵל אֵשֶׁת יַעֲקֹב יוֹסֵף וּבִנְיָמִן: Gn 46.19; Rachel, Jacob, Joseph, Benjamin

d. וַיֹּאמֶר מֹשֶׁה הִנֵּה דַם־הַבְּרִית   Ex 24.8; הִנֵּה *here is*; Moses

e. וְיֶתֶר דִּבְרֵי יָרָבְעָם כְּתוּבִים עַל־סֵפֶר דִּבְרֵי הַיָּמִים לְמַלְכֵי יִשְׂרָאֵל: 1 Kgs 14.19; יֶתֶר *rest of*; כְּתוּבִים *are written*; note the possessive לְ near the end; Jeroboam, Israel

f. אֵלֶּה רָאשֵׁי אֲבוֹת הַלְוִיִּם לְמִשְׁפְּחֹתָם: Ex 6.25; אֵלֶּה *these [are]*; לְ *according to*; (name); ם ָ - *their* (3 mp); Levites

g. וַיִּשְׁכַּב יְהוֹאָשׁ עִם־אֲבֹתָיו וַיִּקָּבֵר בְּשֹׁמְרוֹן עִם מַלְכֵי יִשְׂרָאֵל וַיִּמְלֹךְ יָרָבְעָם בְּנוֹ תַּחְתָּיו: 2 Kgs 14.16; אֲבֹתָיו *his fathers*; וַיִּקָּבֵר *and he was buried*; בְּנוֹ *his son*; תַּחְתָּיו *in his place*; Jehoash, Samaria, Jeroboam

h. וַיְהִי גְּבוּל בְּנֵי רְאוּבֵן הַיַּרְדֵּן   Josh 13:23; וַיְהִי *and it was* (3 ms Q Pr , היה); Reuben, Jordan

i. וַיִּמְצָא מַלְאַךְ יהוה אֶת־הָגָר   Gn 16.7; מצא *find*; Hagar

j. וַיִּשְׁלַח הָעָם שִׁלֹה   1 Sam 4.4; עָם *people*; שִׁלֹה *to Shiloh*;

    וַיִּשְׂאוּ מִשָּׁם אֵת אֲרוֹן בְּרִית־יהוה צְבָאוֹת   וַיִּשְׂאוּ *and they took*; שָׁם *there* (+ מִן)

k. אֵלֶּה הֵם מִשְׁפְּחֹת הַגֵּרְשֻׁנִּי: Nu 3.21; אֵלֶּה הֵם *these [are]*; Gershonites

9.6 Enrichment: Semantic Clusters

You now have a large enough Hebrew vocabulary that you will begin to find it helpful to group and learn words by their *semantic domain*—their shared "area of reference". Here are few examples, taken from the vocabulary in Lessons 2–9 (numbers are the number of the lesson):

II.9. Nominal Modification (III): The Construct

Human relationships (family)		
father; male ancestor	אָב	2
brother, male relative	אָח	3
man, husband; each	אִישׁ	2
(f.) mother; ancestress	אֵם	9
woman, wife	אִשָּׁה	2
women, wives	נָשִׁים	2
son, male descendant	בֵּן	2
daughter, female descendant	בַּת	6
daughters	בָּנוֹת	2
clan, extended family	מִשְׁפָּחָה	3

Human relationships/rôles (society)		
lord, master	אָדוֹן	4
humanity, humankind, man; Adam	אָדָם	3
enemy	אוֹיֵב	6
people [group], nation, folk	גּוֹי	3
priest	כֹּהֵן	2
king, monarch	מֶלֶךְ	2
messenger; angel	מַלְאָךְ	9
rule, reign	מָשַׁל	5
servant, slave	עֶבֶד	2
official, leader, ruler	שַׂר	5

Parts/Aspects of the Body/Person			
heart	לֵבָב	לֵב	2
(f.) life, self		נֶפֶשׁ	2
eye [water-source, well]		עַיִן	3
face, presence		פָּנִים	3
head, top, peak		רֹאשׁ	4
voice, sound		קוֹל	5
(f.) breath, wind, spirit		רוּחַ	5
(II) nose, nostril; anger (n.)		אַף	6
foot, leg		רֶגֶל	9

Terms that Refer to Deity		
(my) [divine] Lord, Master	אֲדֹנָי	4
god, God	אֵל	2
gods, God	אֱלֹהִים	
Yhwh (proper name)	יהוה	4
Yah (proper name)	יָהּ יָה	

Seeing how terms are related to each other will help you remember their gloss(es), since you will learn them according to their semantic function, rather than merely in isolation. As you learn more words, a semantic "map"—cross-referenced lists or diagrams that link words by function or reference—will also help you realize the [sometimes slight] differences between apparent synonyms, although this often comes only by studying the occurrences of a pair (or set) of closely related words to see how each one is used.

Lesson 10

The Perfect (*Qatal*, Suffix Conjugation)

The imperfect primarily refers to the present or future, and the preterite explicitly narrates series of events. Both are "prefix" conjugations. The other main verbal paradigm of Biblical Hebrew, the "perfect", has an extremely broad set of functions that are both *temporal*—ranging from pluperfect (in, e.g., narrative flashbacks) to simple past, present, and even future—and *volitional* (especially as imperative). The main distinction in form between the imperfect and preterite, on the one hand, and the perfect, on the other, is that the perfect uses a unique set of PGN affixes—all of which are suffixes (hence "suffix conjugation")—to refer to the person, gender, and number of its subject. Its other name, *qatal*, reflects the 3ms *qal* perfect of קטל, "kill", a common paradigm verb.

The perfect is the most frequent conjugation in Biblical Hebrew. More than one-quarter (28%) of all biblical verbs are perfects.

10.1 *Form*

The perfect[99] uses *suffixes* to agree with the person, gender, and number [PGN] of its subject.

Person	Gender	Singular	Plural
1st	Common	תִי - *I*	נוּ - *we*
2nd	Masc.	תָ - *you*	תֶם - *you*
	Fem.	תְ -	תֶן -
3rd	Masc.	--- *he/it*	וּ - *they*
	Fem.	ה - *she/it*	

1. The 3ms perfect has no ending; it is the lexical (or "vocabulary") form of the verb.
2. Second person endings all consist of ת + vowel point, as does 1cs.
3. The *šewa* of the 2fs perfect ending is silent; this is the only time that a Hebrew word ends with two consonants (see "*Dageš, šewa,* & Syllables", Lesson 3): מָשַׁלְתְּ ≈ *mašalt*.
4. The 3fs (ה -) and 3cp (וּ -) endings consist of a vowel.
5. The 2mp (תֶם-) and 2fp (תֶן-) endings consist of a closed syllable.
6. The third person plural ("they") is called "common" (as are both first person forms) because the same suffix (וּ-) is used for subjects of either gender.
7. These endings are used throughout the perfect of all verbs (the only difference is the loss of *dageš lene* in the ת-endings of some forms of the verb), and so *must be memorized*.

---

99. The perfect is also called "*qatal*" (= 3ms *qal* perfect of the traditional paradigm verb) or "suffix conjugation".

10.2 The Qal Perfect

Person	Gender	Singular		Plural	
1st	Common	מָשַׁלְתִּי	I ruled	מָשַׁלְנוּ	We ruled
2nd	Masc.	מָשַׁלְתָּ	You ruled	מְשַׁלְתֶּם	You ruled
	Fem.	מָשַׁלְתְּ		מְשַׁלְתֶּן	
3rd	Masc.	מָשַׁל	He ruled	מָשְׁלוּ	They ruled
	Fem.	מָשְׁלָה	She ruled		

The slight vocalic differences under the *radicals* of the verbal root reflect the nature of the ending (whether an open or closed syllable or a vowel) and are fairly consistent throughout the entire verbal system, not just the *qal* perfect. You do not need to memorize these guidelines, but they may help you find your way around the verbal paradigms.

1. If the PGN ending *begins with a consonant* (all except the third person forms), there is silent *šewa* after the third radical (i.e., before the ending), and the second radical's vowel is *pataḥ* (-שַׁ-).
2. If the ending is a *closed syllable* (2mp, 2fp), the second radical has *pataḥ*, and the vowel after the first radical is a half-vowel (*šewa* [-מְ]).
3. If the ending is a *vowel* (3fs, 3cp), the second radical has vocal *šewa* (-שְׁ-).
4. If the ending is a closed syllable (2mp, 2fp) or vowel (3fs, 3cp), it is accented; otherwise, the accent falls on the antepenultimate [next-to-last] syllable. This is part of the reason for the variations in the vowels within the verbal root.
5. The perfect may describe a simple past event ("I ruled"), ingression ("He began/came to rule"), or ongoing action ("She was ruling").

מָשַׁלְתִּי	mā·**šal**·tî	מָשַׁלְנוּ	mā·**šal**·nû
מָשַׁלְתָּ	mā·**šal**·tā	מְשַׁלְתֶּם	mᵉ·šal·**tem**
מָשַׁלְתְּ	mā·**šalt**	מְשַׁלְתֶּן	mᵉ·šal·**ten**
מָשַׁל	mā·**šal**	מָשְׁלוּ	mā·šᵉ·**lû**
מָשְׁלָה	mā·šᵉ·**lā**		

10.2.1 Stative Verbs

Some verbs have either *ṣere* or *ḥolem* after the second radical in the 3ms *qal* perfect (the lexical form). The rest of their forms are like משׁל. These verbs describe a state or condition, and are called "stative" verbs (Lesson 15). The most common stative verbs in Biblical Hebrew are:

גָּדַל	be[come] large, great		מָלֵא	be[come] full
זָקֵן	be[come] old		קָדֹשׁ	be[come] holy, set apart, reserved
טָהֵר	be[come] ceremonially clean, pure, acceptable		קָרֵב	be[come] near, close
טָמֵא	be[come] ceremonially unclean, impure		רָחֹק	be[come] distant, far
כָּבֵד	be[come] heavy, important; wealthy		שָׁלֵם	be[come] whole, complete, healthy, at peace

10.2.2 III-א Verbs

Verbs that end in א (III-א verbs) look slightly different because "syllable-final" א becomes silent and cannot close the syllable (§6.2). Their forms differ from those of משׁל (above) and other strong verbs in three ways.

1. They lack silent *šewa* after the א, which functions as a reminder of historical spelling (cf. the now-silent *e* in English, which was pronounced in Chaucer's day).
2. Since the second syllable is thus open, they have *qameṣ* after the second radical rather than *pataḥ* (§22).
3. Since the *qameṣ* after the second radical therefore precedes the ending, the ת of the second person endings lacks *dageš lene* (and 2fs lacks the final silent *šewa*).

Person	Gender	Singular		Plural	
1st	Common	מָצָ֫אתִי	I found	מָצָ֫אנוּ	We found
2nd	Masc.	מָצָ֫אתָ	You found	מְצָאתֶם	You found
	Fem.	מָצָ֫את		מְצָאתֶן	
3rd	Masc.	מָצָא	He/It found	מָצְאוּ	They found
	Fem.	מָצְאָה	She/It found		

4. In most other III-guttural verbal roots, 2fs *qal* perfect has two *pataḥ*s (note the accent).

שָׁלַ֫חַתְּ *šā·la·ḥat* you sent   שָׁמַ֫עַתְּ *šā·ma·'at* you heard

10.3 Function (HBI §2.2.1)

The function of the perfect is heavily contextual. It depends primarily on the *genre* or literary type of the discourse within which it occurs. Its function also reflects the content of its clause and its relationship to the surrounding context, as well as the action or state described by the verbal root itself. A primary factor in its temporal and modal function is syntactical—whether or not it occurs with the prefixed *waw* (-וְ).[100]

1. *Without the conjunction*, the perfect nearly always refers to the *past* in narrative—either the simple past ("he saw"), continual past ("he was seeing"), perfect ("he has seen") or pluperfect ("he had seen"). The function is controlled by the context. In narrative, the perfect tends to be preceded by another word, either a subordinating conjunction such as כִּי, the relative (אֲשֶׁר), or, in a disjunctive clause (§6.6, and below), by its subject, object (Gn 42.4), prepositional phrase (2 Sam 5.5), or a negative (לֹא).

בְּחֶבְרוֹן מָלַךְ עַל־יְהוּדָה ... וּבִירוּשָׁלַ֫ם מָלַךְ ... עַל כָּל־יִשְׂרָאֵל וִיהוּדָה:	In Hebron *he reigned* over Judah ..., and in Jerusalem *he reigned* over all Israel and Judah (2 Sam 5.5).
וְאֶת־בִּנְיָמִין אֲחִי יוֹסֵף לֹא־שָׁלַח יַעֲקֹב	(Joseph's brothers went down [preterite] ...), but Benjamin, Joseph's brother, Jacob *did not send* ... (Gn 42.4)
וַהֲדַד שָׁמַע בְּמִצְרַ֫יִם כִּי־שָׁכַב דָּוִד עִם־אֲבֹתָיו	Now Hadad *heard* in Egypt that David *slept* with his fathers ... (1 Kgs 11.21)

This function of the perfect is especially common in *disjunctive clauses* (§6.6, §6.10), which describe events that happened alongside or before the preceding preterite (a flashback), contrast or compare two events (Gn 1.5), or inject a non-event (i.e., with a negative) into a string of preterites (Jg 11.17).

וַיִּקְרָא אֱלֹהִים לָאוֹר יוֹם וְלַחֹ֫שֶׁךְ קָרָא לָ֫יְלָה	God called [preterite] the light "Day", and the darkness *he called* [perfect] "Night" (Gn 1.5).
וְלֹא זָכְרוּ בְּנֵי יִשְׂרָאֵל אֶת־יְהוָה	but the sons of Israel *did not remember* Yhwh ... (Jg 8.34)
וַיִּשְׁלַח יִשְׂרָאֵל מַלְאָכִים אֶל־מֶ֫לֶךְ אֱדוֹם ... וְלֹא שָׁמַע מֶ֫לֶךְ אֱדוֹם וְגַם אֶל־מֶ֫לֶךְ מוֹאָב שָׁלַח וְלֹא אָבָה	Israel sent [preterite] messengers to the king of Edom, ... but the king of Edom *did not listen*, and also to the king of Moab [they] *sent*, but he *did not agree* (Jg 11.17).

---

100. This discussion refers primarily to narrative and instructional biblical prose.

The disjunctive clause shows that the event that it describes is *not necessarily* the next event in the story. Its relationship to the storyline (simultaneous, overlapping, antecedent [flashback], proleptic, etc.) must be determined by the relationship of its *content* to its *cotext*.[101] This is an especially common function of the perfect in biblical narrative.

This does *not* mean that events described in disjunctive clauses are insignificant or less important, but rather that they stand outside the main sequence (often like a "by the way" comment in English), telling the reader something that he or she either will need to know in order to fully understand something that is going to be described in the narrative.

From another perspective, non-events (*irrealis*) are often just as important as events, so that we should always ask why the narrator is telling us that this or that *didn't* happen.

2. *Stative* verbs (§15.1) may describe either a *past* or *present* state, condition, or situation in the perfect, including verbs that describe an emotion, thought, perception, or condition. Their function is determined by the syntax and context; 2 Sam 7.22 is a direct quotation; Dt 34.9 is a disjunctive clause.

גָּדַלְתָּ אֲדֹנָי יְהוִה   *You are great*, Lord Y<small>HWH</small> (2 Sam 7.22)
וִיהוֹשֻׁעַ בִּן־נוּן מָלֵא רוּחַ חָכְמָה   Now Joshua ben Nun *was full* of a spirit of wisdom (Dt 34.9)

3. Any *perfect with a prefixed* ו- begins a clause, and is often followed by its subject or object. This tends to occur in direct quotations (within either narrative or prophecy), where the perfect tends to refer to the present or future, and may function as a series of instructions (Lv 3.8), predictions, or commands (Ru 3.2). Again, the nuance depends heavily upon the literary genre and immediate context.

... וְסָמַךְ אֶת־יָדוֹ עַל־רֹאשׁ   He *shall lean* his hand on [its] head, ...
... וְשָׁחַט אֹתוֹ   and *slaughter* it ..., and the sons of Aaron
וְזָרְקוּ בְּנֵי אַהֲרֹן אֶת־דָּמוֹ   *shall sprinkle* its blood (Lv 3.8).
וְרָחַצְתְּ וָסַכְתְּ וְשַׂמְתְּ שִׂמְלֹתַיִךְ עָלַיִךְ   *Wash, perfume yourself, put on* your robe,
וְיָרַדְתְּ הַגֹּרֶן   and *go down* to the threshing floor (Ru 3.2)
כִּי יִמְלְאוּ יָמֶיךָ וְשָׁכַבְתָּ אֶת־אֲבֹתֶיךָ   When your days are full [complete], and you *lie down* with your fathers, ... (2 Sam 7.12).

The predicate of a disjunctive clause that interrupts a sequence of *waw* + perfect clauses may be *imperfect* or *imperative*. This often happens within a series of instructional or imperatival *w*+perfects, and reflects the non-instructional line of the disjunctive clause.

וְקִרְבּוֹ וּכְרָעָיו יִרְחַץ בַּמָּיִם   And its inner part and legs *he shall* [*must*] *wash* with water (Lv 1.9)
וְאֵשׁ הַמִּזְבֵּחַ תּוּקַד בּוֹ   And the fire of the altar *shall* [*must*] *be kept burning* on it (Lv 6.2 [ET 6.9])[102]

10.4 *The Imperfect, Preterite, & Perfect*

As this chart suggests, a verb's conjugation in Biblical Hebrew narrative is primarily related to the function of its clause within a particular genre, and the relationship of the contents of the clause to the main line of that genre. These are not absolute rules: for example, an imperfect may begin a prophetic discourse, as may a participle (not listed), a perfect may introduce a series of preterites, &c. Within direct quotations, any verbal conjugation may be used.

---

101. The terms "context" and "cotext" are often distinguished. "Cotext" refers to the surrounding *words*, and "context" to the entire sociological and conceptual "world" within which the discourse occurs ("context" in this sense can also be called the "universe of discourse").

102. This nomenclature is the normal way of indicating different verse numberings between the Hebrew and English text (ET); it means that Leviticus 6.2 in the Hebrew text is 6.9 in the English Bible (Leviticus 6.1 in Hebrew is 6.8 in the English text).

II.10. *The Perfect (Qatal, Suffix Conjugation)*

Conjugational Functions	Primary Temporal Reference	Primary **Function**		Subject person gender number
		Main "storyline"	"Added" information (disjunctive clauses)	
preterite	past	narrative		
***waw* + perfect**	present-future-modal	instruction prophecy		any
perfect	past		narrative	
imperfect	present-future-modal		instruction prophecy	
cohortative imperative jussive	future	commands (used in direct quotations)		1st only 2nd only 3rd only

10.5 *Concepts*

antecedent	cotext	genre	perfect	*qatal*
content	disjunctive clause	instructional material	performative	stative verb
context	flashback	narrative	proleptic	suffix conjugation

10.6 *Vocabulary*

.133	אָבַד	*perish*	.141	מַטֶּה	*tribe; rod, staff* (m.)[103]
.134	אֹזֶן	*ear*	.142	עַם	*people* [group], *nation*
.135	בְּהֵמָה	*cattle; animals*	.143	סֵפֶר	*text, document;*[104] *writing*(s)
.136	בַּעַל	*master, owner, husband, Baal*	.144	רֵעַ	*friend, companion*
.137	בָּקָר	*herd* (large cattle, such as donkeys, camels, cows, horses)	.145	שָׂפָה	*lip, language; edge, shore*
.138	הָיָה	*be, become* (often ל introduces the result), *happen, occur*	.146	שֵׁבֶט	*tribe; rod, staff*
.139	כַּף	*palm of hand, sole of foot*	.147	שָׁבַע	*swear* [an oath] (N only)
.140	מִצְוָה	*command*[ment], *order*	.148	שָׁפַט	*judge* (vb.)

103. The noun מַטֶּה refers to a tribe slightly more frequently (196/248 = 79%) than שֵׁבֶט (143/193 = 74%). מַטֶּה is more common in Ex & Nu, whereas שֵׁבֶט is distributed more widely and evenly, as this table shows (statistics are for these books, not total occurrences):

	מַטֶּה				שֵׁבֶט	
	staff	*tribe*	*other*		*staff*	*tribe*
Ex	20	6		**26**	4	1	3
Nu	5	103		**108**	8	1	7
Dt					19		19
Jg					16	1	15
Sam	2			**2**	18	3	15
Kgs		2		**2**	13		13
Pss	1		1	**2**	11	9	2
Pr					**8**	8	

104. "Book"—the traditional gloss for סֵפֶר—is misleading; codices, the forerunners of bound volumes—"books" as we think of them—were not used until the second century CE. A סֵפֶר could be written on nearly any material (e.g., a broken piece (sherd) of pottery (writing makes it an *ostracon*), a piece of papyrus or parchment, a clay tablet). The noun מְגִלָּה (related to the verb גלל, "to roll") refers explicitly to a "scroll", although it is relatively infrequent in Biblical Hebrew (21x) compared to סֵפֶר (185x).

10.7 Exercises

After learning the PGN subject endings of the perfect, parse and gloss (using the simple past) these forms.

a.	אָבַדְתִּי	e.	מָצָאת	i.	וַנִּקְרַב
b.	וַתִּמְצָא	f.	יָשְׁפְטוּ	j.	קָרַבְנוּ
c.	קָרָאתָ	g.	קָרַבְנוּ	k.	וּשְׁמַרְתֶּן
d.	וַתִּקְרָא	h.	וַיִּזְכֹּר	l.	שָׁפְטוּ

a. וּשְׁלֹמֹה יָשַׁב עַל־כִּסֵּא דָוִד אָבִיו — 1 Kgs 2.12; כִּסֵּא *seat, throne*; אָבִיו *his father*; Solomon, David

b. לֹא־עָבַדְתָּ אֶת־יהוה אֱלֹהֶיךָ בְּשִׂמְחָה — Dt 28.47; ךָ- *your (2 ms)*; שִׂמְחָה *joy, rejoicing, happiness*

c. וְהַמֶּלֶךְ דָּוִד שָׁלַח אֶל־צָדוֹק וְאֶל־אֶבְיָתָר — 2 Sam 19.12; David, Zadok, Abiathar

d. וְלֹא שְׁמַעְתֶּם בְּקוֹלִי: — Jg 6.10; יִ- *my (1cs)*; שמע בְּקוֹל *listen to the voice of (obey)* ...

e. מָלַךְ אֱלֹהִים עַל־גּוֹיִם
אֱלֹהִים יָשַׁב עַל־כִּסֵּא קָדְשׁוֹ: — Ps 47.9 (each line is a clause); קָדְשׁוֹ *his* [וֹ- 3ms] *holiness*

f. לֹא־הָלַכְתָּ בְּדַרְכֵי יְהוֹשָׁפָט אָבִיךָ
וּבְדַרְכֵי אָסָא מֶלֶךְ־יְהוּדָה: — 2 Chr 21.12; ךָ- *your (2ms)*; Jehoshaphat; Asa

g. כִּי שָׁמַרְתִּי דַּרְכֵי יהוה
וְלֹא רָשַׁעְתִּי מֵאֱלֹהָי: — 2 Sam 22.22; כִּי *for, that, because*; רשׁע *be wicked; act wickedly*; here מִן *against*; יִ- *my*

h. וְלֹא שָׁמַרְנוּ אֶת־הַמִּצְוֹת וְאֶת־הַחֻקִּים — Ne 1.7; חֹק *statute, rule, regulation*

i. וַיֹּאמֶר אֶל־בְּנֹתָיו לָמָּה זֶּה עֲזַבְתֶּן אֶת־הָאִישׁ — Ex 2.20; בְּנֹתָיו *his* [וֹ- 3ms] *daughters*; לָמָּה זֶּה *Why?*

j. זָכַרְתִּי בַלַּיְלָה שִׁמְךָ יהוה
וָאֶשְׁמְרָה תּוֹרָתֶךָ: — Ps 119.55; ךָ- *your (2ms)*; יהוה (vocative); ignore the final ה- on וָאֶשְׁמְרָה

k. וְאָהַבְתָּ אֵת יהוה אֱלֹהֶיךָ בְּכָל־לְבָבְךָ
וּבְכָל־נַפְשְׁךָ וּבְכָל־מְאֹדֶךָ: — Dt 6.5; ךָ- *your (2ms)*; מְאֹד *strength, might, power*

l. לְמַעַן יִשְׁמְעוּ וּלְמַעַן יִלְמְדוּ
וְיָרְאוּ אֶת־יהוה אֱלֹהֵיכֶם
וְשָׁמְרוּ לַעֲשׂוֹת אֶת־כָּל־דִּבְרֵי הַתּוֹרָה הַזֹּאת: — Dt 31.12; לְמַעַן *so that, in order that*; למד *learn*; ירא *fear*; כֶם- *your (2mp)*; שׁמר here *be careful*; לַעֲשׂוֹת *to do; by doing*

10.8 Enrichment: The Perfect as Performative?

A possible function of the perfect not mentioned in the lesson, is the perfect as *performative*. A performative is a verb that accomplishes or realizes the act that it describes, so that to say, e.g., "I *promise* that …" is to make the promise—no further action is required (cf., e.g., "I *declare* …", "I *announce* …", "I *claim* …"). A crude test of a performative is whether or not the word "hereby" can be inserted into the statement, as well as such functional tests as whether or not the speaker has the authority to accomplish the act that he or she is naming.

II.10. *The Perfect (Qatal, Suffix Conjugation)*

A common example of a performative in the prophetic literature is the formula "Thus says Yhwh" (כֹּה אָמַר יהוה), so that although אָמַר is 3ms *qal* perfect, it refers to the following quotation, rather than to a past speech.

The performative function may also explain statements with a perfect as predicate, especially divine pronouncements, such as the promise of the land to Abram [sic]:

לְזַרְעֲךָ נָתַתִּי אֶת־הָאָרֶץ הַזֹּאת   To your seed I [hereby] *give* this land (Gn 15.18)

Why does this statement use the perfect, since the former promises (Gn 12.7; 13.15, 17), use the imperfect to refer to a clearly future event (Abram does not yet have any heirs to whom the land might be given)? One explanation is that the performative function is better suited to the divine self-malediction in the covenantal ratification ceremony (Gn 15.17).

In Gn 17.5, two verbal clauses—with a imperfect (יִקָּרֵא) and *waw* + perfect (וְהָיָה)—referring to the future, precede a perfect (נְתַתִּיךָ). The content and context of the divine promise suggest that this is a performative, especially since Abram [now Abraham] was not yet a "multitude of nations", and would not even be a father for some time (the verse is divided into clauses).

וְלֹא־יִקָּרֵא עוֹד אֶת־שִׁמְךָ אַבְרָם   "And your name shall no longer be called 'Abram',
וְהָיָה שִׁמְךָ אַבְרָהָם   but your name shall be 'Abraham',
כִּי אַב־הֲמוֹן גּוֹיִם נְתַתִּיךָ:   because I [hereby] *make* you a father of a multitude of nations" (Gn 17.5).

The possibility of performative functions here and in other places again cautions us against assuming a simple relationship or equation between verbal conjugations—or verbal function—in Biblical Hebrew and other languages.

Lesson 11

Nominal Modification (IV)

Biblical Hebrew uses prepositions to show a noun's syntagmatic function (Lesson 7). It limits or modifies the range of a noun's reference by means of the article (§4.3), construct chain (Lesson 9), relative particle אֲשֶׁר (§11.2), or adjectives (cf. the examples in §4.3).

11.1 *Adjectives*

11.1.1 *Form*

Adjectives in Hebrew use the same endings as the noun. The lexical form of the adjective is masculine singular. The endings are added to the lexical form, unless it ends in ה -, in which case the gender-number endings replace ה - (e.g., יָפֶה). Endings often affect the word's vocalization.

Gender	Singular	Plural	
Masc.	טוֹב	טוֹבִים	*good*
Fem.	טוֹבָה	טוֹבוֹת	
Masc.	גָּדוֹל	גְּדֹלִים	*large, great*
Fem.	גְּדֹלָה	גְּדֹלוֹת	
Masc.	יָפֶה	יָפִים	*handsome, attractive; beautiful*
Fem.	יָפָה	יָפוֹת	

Adjectives use the endings that agree with the *grammatical gender* of the word that they modify, so that their endings do *not* always match the ending of the noun that they modify. This is especially true for feminine nouns that do not end in ה-, ת-, or וֹת- (plural). When an adjective modifies a collective noun (e.g., צֹאן), it may agree with its grammatical number (and be singular), or with the noun's collective sense (and be plural).

אִשָּׁה יָפָה	*a beautiful woman*	Both nouns have the form (ending) associated with their genders, so the adjectives and nouns have the same endings.
סוּסִים טוֹבִים	*good horses*	
עָרִים גְּדֹלוֹת	*great cities*	All three nouns are feminine (despite their form); so the adjectives have the feminine ending.
יָד חֲזָקָה	*a strong hand*	
נָשִׁים יָפוֹת	*beautiful women*	
עַם גָּדוֹל	*a great people* [*nation*]	Both adjectives agree with the noun, one with its grammatical number, the second with its collective sense.
הָעָם הַהֹלְכִים	*the people who walk* (Is 9.1)	

11.1.2 *Function*

Adjectives in Biblical Hebrew have three functions, which are indicated by 1) whether or not the adjective and its substantive agree in *definiteness*; 2) the *word order* of the adjective and substantive; and 3) the immediate *syntax*. The three functions may be called *attributive*, *predicate*, and *substantive*.

1. An *attributive* adjective and its noun agree in definiteness—both are either definite or indefinite—and form a noun phrase, like an adjective in English:

הַמֶּלֶךְ הַגָּדֹל	the *great* king
בְּחַיִל כָּבֵד מְאֹד	… with a very *heavy* [i.e., lavish] retinue (1 Kg 10.2)

2. A *predicate* (or "verbal") adjective and its noun form a non-verbal clause, glossed using a form of "to be".[105] The adjective is usually indefinite, the noun definite, but both may be indefinite, especially in poetry. The adjective, which *predicates* something about the noun, may precede or follow it.

הַמֶּלֶךְ גָּדֹל	The king *is* [*was*] great.
גָּדֹל הַמֶּלֶךְ	
טוֹב הַדָּבָר	The word *is good* (1 Kgs 2.38).
כִּי־כָבֵד הָרָעָב בָּאָרֶץ	for the famine *was heavy* [i.e., harsh, severe] in the land (Gn 12.10).
כָּל־דַּרְכֵי־אִישׁ זַךְ בְּעֵינָיו	All a man's ways *are clean* in his eyes (Pr 16.2).

3. When there is an adjective but no noun, the adjective "becomes" a noun—it is *substantive* (or "nominal"), and may function as a noun or as a relative clause. Indefinite substantive adjectives occur much more frequently in poetry than prose. Some adjectives occur so frequently as substantives that they can be considered nouns (e.g., more than 90% of the occurrences of זָקֵן, "old", are substantive, hence the gloss "elder"). An adjective in a construct chain is always substantive (Pr 15.28; Ex 12.21).

הַגָּדֹל	the great one/man; he [one] who is great
לֵב צַדִּיק יֶהְגֶּה לַעֲנוֹת	The heart of *the righteous* ponders in order to answer (Pr 15.28); this could also be attributive: "A righteous heart …"
וַיִּקְרָא מֹשֶׁה לְכָל־זִקְנֵי יִשְׂרָאֵל	Moses summoned all of *the elders of* Israel … (Ex 12.21)

4. When both noun and adjective are indefinite (as is fairly common in poetry), the adjective's function must be determined from its context. For example, when the modified noun is the subject or object of a clause or sentence ("*The great king* went to war"), or object of a preposition ("for *the great king*"), then the adjective is *attributive*. When the noun and adjective form their own clause ("The king *is great*"), the adjective is *predicate*.

	Adjective with Noun	
	Indefinite Noun	**Definite Noun**
Predicate	טוֹב מֶלֶךְ מֶלֶךְ טוֹב A king is good.[106]	טוֹב הַמֶּלֶךְ The king is good.
Attributive	מַלְכָּה טוֹבָה a good queen[107]	הַמַּלְכָּה הַטּוֹבָה the good queen

---

105. It may seem that we are *adding* "is", "was", &c. to the text. Not so. The predicate translation renders the Hebrew text according to the requirements of English syntax and grammar. Some translations (e.g., KJV, NKJV, NAS) italicize words to show that there is no form in the Hebrew text that directly corresponds to that English term. It is unfortunate that this practice gives the appearance of "adding to" to the text.

106. When an anarthrous adjective follows an indefinite noun, the context—the clausal syntax—determines whether the adjective is predicate or attributive. Hence מֶלֶךְ טוֹב could be either *a good king* or *a king is good*.

107. See the preceding note.

II.11. *Nominal Modification (IV)*

	Adjective without Noun	
	Indefinite Noun	**Definite Noun**
Substantive	טוֹב	הַטּוֹב
	a good one/person/man	*the good* one/person/man
	he who is good / whoever is good / [the / any] one who is good	
	טוֹבָה	הַטּוֹבוֹת
	a good woman	*the good* women
	she who is good	the women who are good

5. English adds "-er" to an adjective to show comparison ("taller", "holier") or uses the adverb "more" ("more wise", "more sure"). There is *no comparative* form in Biblical Hebrew, which compares two things by using the preposition מִן to introduce the thing *to which* something is being compared (the word introduced by "than" in English comparison). Comparative adjectives are always predicate.

וְכַעַס אֱוִיל כָּבֵד מִשְּׁנֵיהֶם — ... but a fool's wrath *is heavier than* both (Pr 27.3)

וְטוֹב־רָשׁ מֵאִישׁ כָּזָב׃ — ... and a poor [man] *is better than* a man of a lie [liar] (Pr 19.22)

גָּדוֹל יְהוָה מִכָּל־הָאֱלֹהִים — Yhwh is *greater than* all gods. (Ex 18.11)

כִּי חָזָק הוּא מִמֶּנּוּ — ... for [they—i.e., the people] are *stronger than* we (Nu 13.31)

6. The "comparative *min*" also occurs with stative verbs, where the subject of the verb is compared to someone/thing else (1 Kgs 10.23).

וַיִּגְדַּל הַמֶּלֶךְ שְׁלֹמֹה מִכֹּל מַלְכֵי הָאָרֶץ — And King Solomon *became greater than* all the kings of the land ... (1 Kgs 10.23)

7. The word כֹּל, *all*, is a *noun* in Hebrew; it therefore does *not* agree with the noun that it modifies, but usually occurs in construct with it as כָּל־, *all of, each of, every* ... (more than 4000x). With pronominal suffixes (Lesson 14) it is written כֻּל־ (c. 200x).[108] When it [occasionally] occurs with the article, it refers to "everything" (i.e., "the whole [thing]"; 2 Sa 19.31; cf. Lv 1.9, 13; more than one-quarter of the occurrences of הַכֹּל are in Ec).

כְּכֹל הַתּוֹרָה הַזֹּאת — according to *all* [*of*] this teaching/instruction (Dt 4.8)

וְיֶתֶר כָּל דִּבְרֵי אָסָא — Now the rest of *all* [*of*] the words of Asa (1 Kgs 15.23)

מְנוֹרַת זָהָב כֻּלָּהּ — a lampstand *entirely* [all of it] of gold (Zc 4.2)

וַיֹּאמֶר מְפִיבֹשֶׁת אֶל־הַמֶּלֶךְ — And Mephiboshet said to the king,

גַּם אֶת־הַכֹּל יִקָּח — "Let him just take *everything* ..." (2 Sa 19.31).

8. The word מְאֹד, *very, much*, can strengthen adjectives and verbs, and so is often called an "adverb". מְאֹד is not inflected for gender or number. It comes at the end of the phrase or clause, following the word that it modifies. [N.B.: מְאֹד is strengthened by repetition (Nu 14.7).]

קָרוֹב אֵלֶיךָ הַדָּבָר מְאֹד — ... the word is *very near* to you (Dt 30.14)

טוֹבָה הָאָרֶץ מְאֹד מְאֹד׃ — The land is *very, very* good (Nu 14.7)

יָפָה הִיא מְאֹד — ... she was *very* beautiful (Gn 12.14).

אִישׁ בָּרִיא מְאֹד — ... a *very* fat man (Jg 3.17).

9. Adjectives follow construct chains; they do not interrupt them.

כָּל־מַעֲשֵׂה יְהוָה הַגָּדֹל — all of the *great* work of Yhwh (Dt 11.7 ∥ Jg 2.7)

וְאֵלֶּה דִּבְרֵי דָוִד הָאַחֲרֹנִים — These are the *last* words of David (2 Sam 23.1)

---

108. The "x" is shorthand for "times" or "occurrences" [in Biblical Hebrew]. This means "two hundred times".

11.1.3 The Most Common Adjectives

This lists by frequency all adjectives used 50 times or more in Biblical Hebrew (* indicates those which occur often or primarily as substantives).

רַע	bad, evil, disastrous (661x);	רָחוֹק	far, distant (85x)
רָעָה	fem. as subst.: disaster, tragedy, evil, wickedness		
טוֹב	good, pleasant; happy [of the heart] (612x)	קָרוֹב	near (78x)
רַב	much, many (475x)	עָנִי	*afflicted, distressed, poor (76x)
צַדִּיק	just, innocent, righteous (206x)	מֵת	dead (72x)
זָקֵן	*old (187x); elder	זָר	strange, different, illicit (71x)
אַחֵר	another, other (166x)	כְּסִיל	*stupid, dull, insolent (70x); fool
חָכָם	wise, skilled (138x)	מָלֵא	full (67x)
קָדוֹשׁ	holy, set apart (115x)	אֶבְיוֹן	*poor (61x)
מְעַט	few; subst.: a little (96x)	חָזָק	hard, strong (56x)
חָלָל	dead, killed (94x); subst.: the dead	קָטֹן	small, little, insignificant (54x)
טָהוֹר	clean, pure (94x)	חָדָשׁ	new (53x)
תָּמִים	whole, complete, entire, blameless (91x)	שָׁוְא	worthless (52x); in vain (adverb); subst.: worthlessness
טָמֵא	[ceremonially] unclean, impure (88x)	אַחֲרוֹן	behind, last (50x)

11.2 The Relative Particle

A relative clause modifies a noun or substantive by *relating* something about it. English relative clauses are introduced by a relative pronoun ("who", "which") and follow the word that they modify—"the prophet *who said*". Hebrew relative clauses are introduced by the relative אֲשֶׁר (more than 5500 times in Biblical Hebrew).

1. Like the relative pronoun in English, אֲשֶׁר normally follows the word that it modifies:

    עֳנִי עַמִּי אֲשֶׁר בְּמִצְרָיִם ... the affliction of my people *who are in Egypt* (Ex 3.7)
    הַמְּלָכִים אֲשֶׁר מִצְּפוֹן בָּהָר ... the kings *who were on the north in the hill country* (Jos 11.2)
    בֹּעַז אֲשֶׁר מִמִּשְׁפַּחַת אֱלִימֶלֶךְ: ... Boaz, *who was from Elimelek's clan* (Ru 2.3)
    עִם־יִשְׂרָאֵל אֲשֶׁר עִם־שָׁאוּל וְיוֹנָתָן: ... with [the] Israel[ites] *who were with Saul and Jonathan* (1 Sam 14.21)

    N.B.: English allows "implicit" relative clauses—i.e., those that do not begin with a relative pronoun, such as "the kings from the north" instead of "the kings *who were* from the north". In biblical narrative, however, relative clauses are nearly always explicit (written with אֲשֶׁר).

2. When a relative clause modifying a "locative noun" ends with שָׁם, "there", the combination אֲשֶׁר ... שָׁם often functions as a relative locative adverb (אֲשֶׁר ... שָׁם, "where"):

    בְּאֶרֶץ גֹּשֶׁן אֲשֶׁר־שָׁם בְּנֵי יִשְׂרָאֵל ... in the land of Goshen, *where the sons of Israel* [were], ... (Ex 9.26)
    מִן־הַמָּקוֹם אֲשֶׁר־אַתָּה שָׁם "... from the place *where you are* ..." (Gn 13.14)
    בְּהֵיכַל יהוה אֲשֶׁר שָׁם אֲרוֹן ... in Yhwh's temple, *where the ark ... was* (1 Sa 3.3)

3. When this type of relative clause describes a person, group, or thing, it is usually predicate ("who/which was/were/is/etc. there"):

    אֶת־הָאֱמֹרִי אֲשֶׁר־שָׁם: ... the Amorites *who were there* (Nu 21.32)

4. The compound form כַּאֲשֶׁר (כְּ + אֲשֶׁר) is a comparative particle, "as, just as," that often precedes a verb (especially verbs of command, instruction, etc.); following the introductory particle וַיְהִי it is often temporal in the sense of "when":

וְעָשָׂה יְהוָה לָהֶם כַּאֲשֶׁר עָשָׂה	Yhwh shall do to them *just as* he did ... (Dt 31.4)
כַּאֲשֶׁר יֹאמַר מְשַׁל הַקַּדְמֹנִי	*As* the proverb of the ancients says, (1 Sam 24.14)
וַיְהִי כַּאֲשֶׁר זָקֵן שְׁמוּאֵל	Now *when* Samuel was old, ... (1 Sam 8.1)

N.B.: Biblical Hebrew has three syntagms that correspond roughly to the relative clause in English: (1) clauses introduced by the particle אֲשֶׁר; (2) clauses formed by a substantive adjective (§11.1.2); and (3) clauses formed by a substantive participle (§12.2). Although these sound the same when rendered into English, the אֲשֶׁר clause modifies a noun; the substantival adjective and participle have no noun to modify.

11.3 Non-verbal Clauses

A clause is a group of words that makes a *comment* (the predicate) about a *topic* (the subject). Although the word "predicate" is often used casually to refer to verbs, a predicate can be nearly any part of speech or connected group of words (syntagm). A clause can be a sentence, or merely part of a sentence (e.g., relative clauses, above). In these two examples, David is the subject; the rest of the clause tells us something about David:

a. David *wrote many songs.*   ascribes an action to David (something that he did)
b. David *was a mighty warrior.*   explains who/what David was (what kind of warrior he was)

Hebrew clauses that sound like (a) are *verbal* clauses (a verb is the main part of the predicate), but clauses like (b) tend to be *non-verbal*, with either a predicate adjective (Ex 9.27), noun, prepositional phrase, or adverb as the predicate. We will consider a clause non-verbal when it lacks an imperfect, preterite, perfect, imperative, predicate participle (Lesson 12), or infinitive (Lesson 16). We will also consider the more specific word in a non-verbal clause to be the subject, with (1) proper names and definite nouns more specific than generic nouns; (2) personal pronouns more specific than proper names and definite nouns; and (3) demonstratives more definite than personal pronouns.

יְהוָה הַצַּדִּיק	Yhwh is the righteous one (Ex 9.27)
אֲנִי יְהוָה	I am Yhwh (Ex 6.2); pronoun as subject
אָחִי הוּא	he is my brother (Gn 20.5); pronoun as subject
וַיֹּאמֶר אֲלֵהֶם אֱלִישָׁע	Elisha said to them, "*This* is not the way,
וְלֹא זֶה הַדֶּרֶךְ וְלֹא זֶה הָעִיר	nor [וְלֹא *and not*] is *this* the city. ..." (2 Kgs 6.19)

A clause is either *syndetic* (linked to its preceding cotext by a conjunction) or *asyndetic* (lacking a conjunction; these are relatively infrequent in biblical narrative). Disjunctive and preterite clauses are by definition syndetic, as is any other clause beginning with *waw*. Other types of clauses are also syndetic, such as those that begin with subordinating particles, such as כִּי, אֲשֶׁר, לְמַעַן, etc. It is not the first word or form that determines that a concatenation of words is a clause, however, but the presence of a topic and a comment.

11.4 Nominal Apposition

Nouns can also be modified by other nouns. In *apposition* one noun follows another, but they do not form a construct chain (since the first noun is usually definite, it cannot be in construct). If the first noun is a generic term (e.g., "the king"), the apposed noun is usually a personal name. If the first noun is a personal name, the second usually identifies him or her by office, position, or relationship (i.e., the aspect of that person that is contextually appropriate). A major clue to the presence of apposition is that proper names and definite nouns do not occur in construct:

(a)	הַמֶּלֶךְ דָּוִד	*King* David (2 Sa 3.31; Samuel-Kings uses this syntagm)
(b)	דָּוִיד הַמֶּלֶךְ	*King* David (1 Ch 26.26; Chronicles uses this syntagm)
(c)	יְהוֹשֻׁעַ בִּן־נוּן	Joshua *son of Nun* (Ex 33.11)
(d)	שָׂרַי אֵשֶׁת אַבְרָהָם	Sarai, *Abram's wife* (Gn 16.1)
(e)	דָּוִד עֶבֶד יהוה	David, *the servant of* YHWH (Ps 36.1)
(g)	רוּת הַמּוֹאֲבִיָּה אֵשֶׁת מַחְלוֹן	Ruth, *the Moabitess, Mahlon's wife* (Ru 4.10)
(f)	בָּרוּךְ בֶּן־נֵרִיָּהוּ הַסֹּפֵר	Baruch, *son of Neriah, the scribe* (Jr 36.32)

In (c) – (e), a construct chain is apposed to the proper name; in (f), a second apposition ("the scribe") further describes Baruch; in (g), a second apposition, which is also a construct chain describes Ruth as "Mahlon's wife". Understanding this requires reading the string of words to see how they are related to each other, as well as general knowledge of biblical context. These examples also illustrate the frequent interdependence of construct chains and apposition.

11.5 Concepts

adjective	attributive	comment	relative	substantive
apposition/apposed	clause	predicate	subject	topic

11.6 Vocabulary

copper, bronze	נְחֹשֶׁת	.158	other, another (adj.)	אַחֵר	.149
service, servitude, labour, work	עֲבוֹדָה	.159	who, which, what, that; when	אֲשֶׁר	.150
mouth	פֶּה	.160	[just] like, as; when	כַּאֲשֶׁר	
mouth of (construct)	פִּי		large, big, great (adj.); be/become large, great (st. vb.)	גָּדוֹל	.151
holiness, "apartness"	קֹדֶשׁ	.161	old; elder (adj.); be/become old (st. vb.)	זָקֵן	.152
holy, sacred (adj.)[109]	קָדוֹשׁ		good (adj.); be/become good (st. vb.)	טוֹב	.153
much, many (adj.)	רַב	.162	honest, upright, right (adj.); thus, so (adv.)	כֵּן	.154
bad, disastrous; evil, wicked (adj.)	רַע	.163	before (temporal & locative), *in the presence of, in front of*	לִפְנֵי	.155
bad, disastrous, evil, wicked (adj.)	רָשָׁע	.164	wadi (temporary stream *or its valley*; rarely perennial stream, e.g., Jabbok)	נַחַל	.156
gate (of a city)	שַׁעַר	.165	horse, stallion (m.)	סוּס	.157
			mare	סוּסָה	

11.7 Exercises

1. After studying the forms of טוֹב, גָּדוֹל, יָפֶה (§11.1.1), gloss these phrases and clauses, parsing any verbal forms. Be prepared to explain their structure and the function of the adjectives.

g. הָאִישׁ הַגָּדוֹל אֲשֶׁר בַּשָּׂדֶה	d. גָּדוֹל הָאֱלֹהִים	a. הָאִישׁ הַטּוֹב
h. הָעִיר בַּמִּדְבָּר קְטַנָּה	e. הֶעָרִים עַל־הֶהָרִים	b. הָאִשָּׁה יָפָה מְאֹד
i. זָקֵן אֲבִי הַכֹּהֵן	f. הַבָּקָר אֲשֶׁר עַל־הֶהָרִים	c. הָאִישׁ אֲשֶׁר בַּבַּיִת

---

109. "Holy" and "sacred" are synonyms with different histories: "holy" comes from Old English *hālig*, "sacred" from Latin *sacrare*.

2. Gloss these phrases and clauses, parsing the verbs and identifying the function of any adjectives.

a.	טוֹב יהוה לַכֹּל	Ps 145.9; remember that כֹּל is a *noun*
b.	וַיִּירְאוּ הָאֲנָשִׁים יִרְאָה גְדֹלָה	Jon 1.10; ירא *fear, be afraid*; יִרְאָה *fear* (noun); an object from the same root as its verb is called a "cognate accusative", which is a common syntagm in Biblical Hebrew
c.	וְקָרָא זֶה אֶל־זֶה וְאָמַר קָדוֹשׁ קָדוֹשׁ קָדוֹשׁ יהוה צְבָאוֹת מְלֹא כָל־הָאָרֶץ כְּבוֹדוֹ׃	Is 6.3; זֶה *this* [one]; צָבָא *host, army*; מְלֹא *fulness, that which fills* (n.m.); כְּבוֹד+וֹ, *glory+his* [Your gloss should differ from most English versions.]
d.	וַיֹּאמֶר הָאִישׁ הַזָּקֵן שָׁלוֹם	Jg 19.20; the last word is a quotation
e.	וַיֹּאמֶר שִׁמְעוּ דְּבַר־הַמֶּלֶךְ הַגָּדוֹל מֶלֶךְ אַשּׁוּר	2 Kg 18.28; Assyria
f.	אֲנָשִׁים רְשָׁעִים הָרְגוּ אֶת־אִישׁ־צַדִּיק בְּבֵיתוֹ עַל־מִשְׁכָּבוֹ	2 Sam 4.11; הרג *kill*; צַדִּיק *innocent*; מִשְׁכָּב+וֹ *bed+his*; בֵּית+וֹ *house+his*
g.	וַיָּבֹאוּ כֹּל זִקְנֵי יִשְׂרָאֵל וַיִּשְׂאוּ הַכֹּהֲנִים אֶת־הָאָרוֹן׃	1 Kgs 8.3; וַיָּבֹאוּ *they* [m.p.] *went*; וַיִּשְׂאוּ *they carried*
h.	שַׁחוּ רָעִים לִפְנֵי טוֹבִים וּרְשָׁעִים עַל־שַׁעֲרֵי צַדִּיק׃	Pr 14.19; שַׁחוּ *they bow* (down); לִפְנֵי *in the presence of*; רָע / רֶשַׁע *bad, evil, wicked*; the verb is elided from the second line
i.	וִהְיִיתֶם קְדֹשִׁים כִּי קָדוֹשׁ אָנִי׃	Lv 11.45; וִהְיִיתֶם *and you* [m.p.] *shall be*; אֲנִי *I*; כִּי *because, for* (*that*)
j.	וַהֲלַכְתֶּם אַחֲרֵי אֱלֹהִים אֲחֵרִים אֲשֶׁר לֹא־יְדַעְתֶּם׃	Jr 7.9; אַחֲרֵי *after*
k.	וְהַבַּיִת אֲשֶׁר־אֲנִי בוֹנֶה גָּדוֹל כִּי־גָדוֹל אֱלֹהֵינוּ מִכָּל־הָאֱלֹהִים׃	2 Chr 2.4; אֲנִי *I*; בּוֹנֶה *building* (a participle functioning as a predicate adjective); נוּ- *our*
l.	וּמֶלֶךְ אֲרָם צִוָּה אֶת־שָׂרֵי הָרֶכֶב לֵאמֹר לֹא תִּלָּחֲמוּ אֶת־הַקָּטֹן אֶת־הַגָּדוֹל כִּי אִם־אֶת־מֶלֶךְ יִשְׂרָאֵל לְבַדּוֹ׃	2 Chr 18.30; Aram; צִוָּה [he] *commanded*; לֹא תִּלָּחֲמוּ *Do not fight*; רֶכֶב *chariot*; לֵאמֹר *saying*; כִּי אִם *but*; לְבַדּוֹ *only* (him alone)
m.	עִיר גְּדוֹלָה גִּבְעוֹן כְּאַחַת עָרֵי הַמַּמְלָכָה וְהִיא גְדוֹלָה מִן־הָעַי וְכָל־אֲנָשֶׁיהָ גִּבֹּרִים׃	Josh 10.2; אַחַת *one of*; מַמְלָכָה *kingdom*; הִיא *she, it*; הָ- *her, its*; גִּבּוֹר *warrior*; Gibeon, Ai

11.8 Enrichment: Reading a Bulla

This is a greatly enlarged drawing of a *bulla*, the clay impression of a seal; the original is thumbnail-sized.

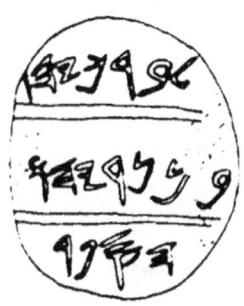

לברכיהו
בן נריהו
הספר

of Berechyahu
ben Neryahu
the scribe

or (using more familiar forms of the names):
Belonging to Baruch
son of Neriah
the scribe
(cf. Jr 36.32)

This is a greatly enlarged copy of a typical *bulla*, with an inscription consisting of the owner's name (with *lamed* of possession), followed by "son of", his father's name, and his occupation. The appositions between "Baruch" and "son of Neraiah" on the one hand and "the scribe" on the other, identify both men by their fathers' names and their occupation or position in society. The *bulla* is thus the owner's "signature".

1. Both names end in *-yahu*, a variant of *-yah* that occurs in Biblical Hebrew. [Jeremiah's name occurs with both endings: יִרְמְיָה (8x; only in Jr 27.1–29.1) and יִרְמְיָהוּ (>110x; in the rest of the book; never in 27.1–29.1).]
2. Since the names of the father and son, as well as the occupation, match the biblical references, this particular bulla most probably records the personal seal of the scribe named Baruch ben Neraiah who worked for Jeremiah, and would have been affixed to documents (long since deteriorated) that he wrote, transcribed, or witnessed.
3. The same form of personal identification was in use long before the Israelite monarchy and the period of the canonical prophets. In Josh 1.1, Joshua is identified as יְהוֹשֻׁעַ בִּן־נוּן מְשָׁרֵת מֹשֶׁה, *Joshua son of Nun, servant of Moses*; Joshua—not his father—was Moses' assistant; Baruch was a scribe, according to the information on this bulla.
4. This bulla appeared on the antiquities market without any reference to its provenance. This means that its interpretation lacks the controls that its discovery *in situ* (in place) would have provided, such as depth, occupational or destruction layer, etc.
5. You can find more information on the paleo- or archaic Hebrew (Canaanite) alphabet at many sites on-line.

Lesson 12

THE PARTICIPLE

The verbal system of Biblical Hebrew includes forms that are called both "participles" and "verbal adjectives", since they are based on verbal roots and are functionally adjectives. Unlike English participles (forms that end in "-ing"), Hebrew participles can be identified by their vowels, a prefixed -מ (in most verbal stems),[110] and syntax. More than one-tenth (about 13%) of all verbal forms in Biblical Hebrew are participles. They are especially common in biblical poetry.

12.1 *Form*

All participles are inflected for gender and number in order to agree with the word that they modify. They use the same endings as adjectives and nouns. Like adjectives, participles agree with the *grammatical* gender of the word that they modify. The *qal* has two participles—active and passive.

		Qal Active Participle		Qal Passive Participle	
		Singular	Plural	Singular	Plural
Masc.	abs.	מֹשֵׁל	מֹשְׁלִים	מָשׁוּל	מְשׁוּלִים
	const.		מֹשְׁלֵי	מְשׁוּל	מְשׁוּלֵי
Fem.	abs.	מֹשֶׁלֶת	מֹשְׁלוֹת	מְשׁוּלָה	מְשׁוּלוֹת
		מֹשְׁלָה			
	const.[111]			מְשׁוּלַת	

1. The *qal active* participle always has an *o*-vowel (*ḥolem* or *ḥolem-waw*) after the *first* radical.
2. The *qal passive* participle always has a *u*-vowel (*šureq*, rarely *qibbuṣ*) after the *second* radical.
3. Unlike the other verbal conjugations, participles can be articular. Like the infinitive construct, they can occur with prepositions and pronominal suffixes (Lesson 14).

12.2 *Function (HBI n2.2.5)*

The participle in Biblical Hebrew is an adjective, with the same functions as the adjective—attributive, predicate, and substantive. The rules for identifying participial function are the same as for the adjective (§11.1.2).

1. *Attributive*, or *adjectival* participles usually follow, and agree in definiteness with the word that they modify. Although they are attributive, their verbal nature means that they can be glossed in several ways, often as relative clauses (cf. Pr 8.34; Dt 1.38); for example, Is

---

110. The term "stems" refers to various patterns of vowels and prefixes used to modify the function of the verbal root (Lesson 18).
111. There are about thirty-five feminine construct *qal* participles in Biblical Hebrew; few of these are strong verbal roots. The most frequent occurs in the phrase זָבַת חָלָב וּדְבַשׁ, "*flowing* with milk and honey" (20x; always fsc Q Ptc from the root זוב, "flow").

40.3 could also be rendered "a voice which was calling, ..." Their temporal reference (past, present, future) is entirely contextual:

אַשְׁרֵי אָדָם שֹׁמֵעַ לִי	How happy is the man *who listens* to me, ... (Pr 8.34)
קוֹל קוֹרֵא בַּמִּדְבָּר	A voice *calling*, "In the wilderness ..." (Is 40.3)
יְהוֹשֻׁעַ בִּן־נוּן הָעֹמֵד לְפָנֶיךָ	Joshua son of Nun, *who stands* before you (Dt 1.38)
מִשְׁפָּט כָּתוּב	judgment *that is written* (Ps 149.9)
שַׁלֻּם ... שֹׁמֵר הַבְּגָדִים	Shallum ..., *the keeper of* [*who keeps* or *the one who keeps*] the garments (2 Kgs 22.14)
וַיְשַׁלַּח אֶת־הָעָם נֹשְׂאֵי הַמִּנְחָה׃	He sent away the people *who had carried* the tribute (Jg 3.18)

2. *Predicate*, or *verbal* participles may precede or follow the word that they modify; the words *dis*agree in definiteness. In narrative, predicate participles tend to occur in disjunctive clauses, where they function much like finite verbs. A predicate participle is technically "tenseless"—its temporal reference depends on the context, as does its nature as simple or continuous action. Note that the last five examples in this list occur in disjunctive clauses (§6.6):

אֱלֹהִים מֹשֵׁל בְּיַעֲקֹב	God *rules* in Jacob (Ps 59.14)
צִדְקָתוֹ עֹמֶדֶת לָעַד	His righteousness *stands* for ever (Ps 112.9)
וְהֵם לֹא יָדְעוּ כִּי שֹׁמֵעַ יוֹסֵף	But they did not know that Joseph *was listening* (Gn 42.23)
וַעֲתַלְיָה מֹלֶכֶת עַל־הָאָרֶץ׃	Now Athaliah *was ruling* over the land (2 Kg 11.3)
וּפְלִשְׁתִּים עֹמְדִים אֶל־הָהָר מִזֶּה	Now the Philistines *were standing* on the hill on this side (1 Sam 17.3)
וּמַלְכַּת־שְׁבָא שֹׁמַעַת אֶת־שֵׁמַע שְׁלֹמֹה	Now the queen of Sheba *heard* the report of Solomon ... (1 Kgs 10.1)
וְהִיא יֹשֶׁבֶת בִּירוּשָׁלָ͏ִם	Now she *lived* in Jerusalem (2 Kgs 22.14)

Depending on the context, and the semantic *load* of the verbal root, a predicate participle following הִנֵּה or וְהִנֵּה may suggest the speaker's sense of immediacy:

כִּי־הִנְנִי בוֹרֵא שָׁמַיִם חֲדָשִׁים וָאָרֶץ חֲדָשָׁה	For I am *about to create* [*creating*] a new heaven and a new earth (Is 65.17)
הִנֵּה אָנֹכִי עֹשֶׂה דָבָר בְּיִשְׂרָאֵל	I am *doing* [*about to do*] a thing in Israel (1 Sa 3.11)
וְהִנֵּה אָנֹכִי יֹרֵד אֵלֶיךָ	I am *going to come down* [*coming*] to you (1 Sa 10.8)

3. When there is no substantive for the participle to modify, it is "its own noun", and thus *substantival* (nominal), glossed by a pronominal relative clause ("he who ...", "the one who ...", "whoever ... ", etc.). As Jos 2.24 suggests, all participles in construct chains are substantive.

הוֹלֵךְ בְּיָשְׁרוֹ יְרֵא יְהוָה	*Whoever walks* in his honesty fears Yhwh (Pr 14.2)
יְהוָה שֹׁמְרֶךָ	Yhwh is *the one who watches* you [= "your watcher"] (Ps 121.5)
כָּל־יֹשְׁבֵי הָאָרֶץ	All the *inhabitants* of the land (Jos 2.24)

4. Some verbs occur primarily as substantive participles (e.g., the verbal root איב occurs 281 times; all but two are substantive participles). Words listed as nouns that have the vowel pattern *o-e* (i.e., *ḥolem - ṣere*) are *qal* participles that were used primarily as substantives (e.g., שֹׁפֵט, *judge*; סֹפֵר, *scribe*).

הִנֵּה אָנֹכִי נֹתֵן אֶת־אֹיִבְךָ בְּיָדֶךָ	I am about to give [predicate ptc.] *your enemy* into your hand (1 Sam 24.4)

5. Since they are *verbal* adjectives, participles can govern direct and indirect objects. They also occur with pronominal suffixes (Lesson 14); the suffix may indicate pronominal possession or it may identify the [pronominal] direct object of the action described by the participle:

שֹׁמְרֶךָ ... שׁוֹמֵר יִשְׂרָאֵל׃ *He who watches* you ... *he who watches* Israel (Ps 121.3b, 4b)

אֲנִי יהוה רֹפְאֶךָ I am Yhwh, [*he*] *who heals* you (Ex 15.26); or *your healer*

12.3 Concepts

active	nominal	participle	predicate	verbal
adjectival	attributive	passive	substantive	

12.4 Vocabulary

166.	אַיִל	*ram*	175.	יֵשׁ	*there is/are* (opposite of אֵין/אַיִן)
167.	בָּחַר	*choose* (the preposition בְּ- often introduces its object)	176.	מָוֶת	*death*; מוֹת, *death of*
168.	גִּבּוֹר	*mighty man, warrior*	177.	נֶגֶד	*in front of, before, opposite*
169.	דּוֹר	*generation, life-span*	178.	מְלָאכָה	*work, occupation*
170.	דָּרַשׁ	*seek, inquire* (cf. מִדְרָשׁ)	179.	סָפַר / סֹפֵר	*count; write, record* / *scribe, secretary, recorder* (ms Q Ptc)
171.	הָרַג	*kill*	180.	פֶּתַח	*opening, entrance*
172.	זֶבַח	*sacrifice* (n.)	181.	שָׁאַל	*ask* [*for*], *request*
173.	חוּץ	*outside* (noun and prep.); *street*	182.	שֶׁמֶן	*oil* (usually olive oil)
174.	חָכְמָה	*wisdom, skill*			

12.5 Exercises

After learning the forms of the *qal* participle, *gloss* these phrases and clauses, *parsing* the verbs, and *identifying* each participle's function as either attributive, predicate, or substantive (adjectival, verbal, nominal).

1. וַעֲתַלְיָה מֹלֶכֶת עַל־הָאָרֶץ׃ — 2 Chr 22.12; Athaliah

2. הָעָם הַהֹלְכִים בַּחֹשֶׁךְ רָאוּ אוֹר גָּדוֹל יֹשְׁבֵי בְּאֶרֶץ צַלְמָוֶת אוֹר נָגַהּ עֲלֵיהֶם׃ — Is 9.1; רָאוּ *they saw* (3cp Q P); צַלְמָוֶת *death-shadow*; נגה *it shined*; עַל + הֶם- (*their/them*) > עֲלֵיהֶם

3. וְיֵדְעוּ כִּי־אֱלֹהִים מֹשֵׁל בְּיַעֲקֹב לְאַפְסֵי הָאָרֶץ — Ps 59.14b; וְיֵדְעוּ *and they will know* (3 mp QF); אֶפֶס *end*; Jacob

4. וּשְׁמוּאֵל שֹׁכֵב בְּהֵיכַל יְהוָה אֲשֶׁר־שָׁם אֲרוֹן אֱלֹהִים׃ — 1 Sam 3.3; הֵיכָל *temple*; שָׁן *there, in that place*; Samuel

5. הָרֹפֵא לִשְׁבוּרֵי לֵב — Ps 147.3; רפא *heal*; שׁבר *break*

6. יֵשׁ צַדִּיק אֹבֵד בְּצִדְקוֹ — Ec 7.15; וֹ + בְּ- + צֶדֶק, *in* + *righteousness* + *his*

7. יֵשׁ־אֱלֹהִים שֹׁפְטִים בָּאָרֶץ׃ — Ps 58.12

8.	וַיֶּאֱהַב יִצְחָק אֶת־עֵשָׂו ... וְרִבְקָה אֹהֶבֶת אֶת־יַעֲקֹב:	Gn 25.28; four names!
9.	כִּי־אֱלֹהִים שֹׁפֵט	Ps 75.8
10.	אַשְׁרֵי שֹׁמְרֵי מִשְׁפָּט עֹשֵׂה צְדָקָה בְכָל־עֵת:	Ps 106.3; אַשְׁרֵי *happy* (trad., *blessed*); עשׂה *do*; צְדָקָה *righteousness, innocence*; עֵת *time*
11.	וְכָל־יִשְׂרָאֵל וִיהוּדָה אֹהֵב אֶת־דָּוִד כִּי־הוּא יוֹצֵא וָבָא לִפְנֵיהֶם:	1 Sam 18.16; הוּא *he*; יֹצֵא ms Q Ptc < יצא *go out, leave*; בָּא ms Q Ptc < בוֹא *come/go in*; הֶם + לִפְנֵי *before* + *them*; David
12.	וּדְבוֹרָה אִשָּׁה נְבִיאָה אֵשֶׁת לַפִּידוֹת הִיא שֹׁפְטָה אֶת־יִשְׂרָאֵל בָּעֵת הַהִיא:	Jg 4.4; הִיא *she*; הַהִיא *that*; עֵת *time*; Deborah, Lapidot
13.	כֹּה אָמַר־יְהוָה אֶל־שַׁלֻּם בֶּן־יֹאשִׁיָּהוּ מֶלֶךְ יְהוּדָה הַמֹּלֵךְ תַּחַת יֹאשִׁיָּהוּ אָבִיו	Jr 22.11; ו + אָבִי *father* + *his*; Shallum; Josiah; Judah
14.	וְהַשֹּׁכֵב בַּבַּיִת יְכַבֵּס אֶת־בְּגָדָיו וְהָאֹכֵל בַּבַּיִת יְכַבֵּס אֶת־בְּגָדָיו:	Lv 14.47; יְכַבֵּס *he will wash*; יו + בגד *garments* + *his* (suffixed to a plural noun; cf. #6)
15.	וּפְלִשְׁתִּים עֹמְדִים אֶל־הָהָר מִזֶּה וְיִשְׂרָאֵל עֹמְדִים אֶל־הָהָר מִזֶּה	1 Sam 17.3; מִזֶּה *on one [this] side* (מִן + זֶה) Philistines
16.	לָכֵן כֹּה־אָמַר יְהוָה אֱלֹהֵי יִשְׂרָאֵל עַל־הָרֹעִים הָרֹעִים אֶת־עַמִּי	Jr 23.2; לָכֵן *therefore* (לְ + כֵּן); עַל *concerning*; both participles are from the root רעה *shepherd, tend* (the mp ending "replaces" the final ה- of the root)
17.	יֹאמְרוּ גְּאוּלֵי יְהוָה	Ps 107.2a; גאל *redeem*

12.6 Enrichment: Participles & Poetic Compression

Participles are especially common in the book of Proverbs, probably because they allow highly compressed syntax, perhaps also to impart a "timeless" and "universal" air to the sayings. In Pr 17.9, for example, the use of four participles allows the proverb to be compressed into only eight words:

מְכַסֶּה־פֶּשַׁע מְבַקֵּשׁ אַהֲבָה	*Whoever* conceals a transgression *seeks* love;
וְשֹׁנֶה בְדָבָר מַפְרִיד אַלּוּף:	And *whoever* repeats a matter *separates* a friend [friends] (Pr 17.9)

At times, however, compression can be confusing. How should we read these lines? Which is primary—seeking or concealing, repeating or separating? Since our experience suggests that talking about offenses can destroy relationships, but that this is not the only reason for relationships to fail, we would probably read Pr 17.9b as suggested above (rather than "Whoever separates friends repeats a matter").

In 17.9a, however, either participle could be read as the subject, so that an alternative interpretation (and translation) would be "Whoever seeks love conceals a transgression". This line may even be deliberately ambiguous, written in order to allow or even encourage both understandings. The decision to *gloss* it in one way or the other, however, is essentially arbitrary, since either participle can be predicate or substantive.

Word order is not always a reliable guide to syntax or function, especially in biblical poetry, so that we must reflect on the content of the proverb in order to translate it appropriately.

In Pr 12.1a, however, the parallelism helps us determine that the first participle is the subject (substantive) and the second the predicate, since the predicate is elided from the second line, and since "loves discipline" parallels "hates correction", we follow the first reading:

אֹהֵב מוּסָר אֹהֵב דָּעַת	*Whoever loves* discipline *loves* knowledge;
וְשֹׂנֵא תוֹכַחַת בָּעַר׃	And *whoever hates* correction [loves] stupidity (Pr 12.1)

It may seem that we have merely read the Hebrew as though it followed English word-order, but our interpretation (and therefore translation) is actually based on the parallels between the two lines. The general principle here is the frequent omission [elision] of the predicate from the second of two parallel lines of biblical poetry.

Two passive participles (Lesson 19) allow even greater compression in Pr 27.5—only five words:

טוֹבָה תּוֹכַחַת מְגֻלָּה מֵאַהֲבָה מְסֻתָּרֶת׃   *A revealed* rebuke is better than *concealed* love (Pr 27.5)

This could also be rendered so that the English syntax corresponds to the Hebrew:

Better a rebuke revealed than love concealed.

Nothing is gained beyond (perhaps) a certain "poetic" feel due to the rhyme of "revealed" and "concealed"; both renderings are as compressed as English allows. Or, if we wanted to add a poetic structure that is not present in the Hebrew sentence, we could invert the order of the last two words so that we read **noun** – *adjective* … *adjective* – **noun**, creating a grammatical chiasm, but this may be overly clever.

Better a **rebuke** *revealed* than *concealed* **love**.

Lesson 13

PRONOMINALS (I)

One challenge in writing or speaking is keeping track of who is acting or speaking, and whether or not this is a new person or someone already mentioned in the discourse. Another challenge is to write so that the result "holds together", or is "cohesive". Pronouns are a *cohesive* device (§6), a linguistic "glue" that binds together a discourse. English tracks clausal subjects pronominally (e.g., "Then *he* went ..." or "After *she* had taken ..."), rather than by repeating the subject's name. Pronouns are thus called "anaphoric" (Greek *ana*, "above"), since they usually refer *back* to someone or something previously mentioned (traditionally called the "antecedent").[112]

Biblical Hebrew has two sets of pronouns—individual words, called "independent pronouns", and suffixes, called "pronominal suffixes" (Lesson 14). Both sets are inflected for person, gender, and number to link them to their "antecedent".

Independent personal pronouns identify the subject of the clause; these "subject" pronouns, however, are not merely cohesive—they also function on the level of discourse, a "higher-level" function that explains why Biblical Hebrew has independent subject pronouns alongside the PGN of the finite verb.[113] (§13.1.2). The third person independent pronouns (along with a few other forms) also function as *demonstrative adjectives* ("this", "these", "that", "those").

Pronominal suffixes show pronominal possession ("my", "her", "their"), indicate the pronominal objects of verbs and prepositions, and the pronominal subjects of the infinitive construct (§16.1.1).

13.1 *Independent Pronouns*

Pronominal forms in Biblical Hebrew have person, gender, and number. Independent pronouns usually identify the subject of their clause; about 20% of all independent personal pronouns occur with the conjunction *waw* as part of the first form in disjunctive clauses (*w* + pronoun).

13.1.1 *Form*

Person	Gender	Singular			Plural		
1st	common	אָנֹכִי	אֲנִי	*I*	נַחְנוּ	אֲנַחְנוּ	*we*
2nd	masc.		אַתָּה	*you*		אַתֶּם	*you*
	fem.		אַתְּ			אַתֶּן	
3rd	masc.		הוּא	*he, it*		הֵמָּה הֵם	*they*
	fem.	הוּא	הִיא	*she, it*		הֵנָּה	

---

112. Pronouns can be *cataphoric*, referring to something that follows ("Although *he* awoke early, John ...")"; this function is rare in Biblical Hebrew.

113. Apart from commands, English sentences have explicit subjects, either nominal or pronominal (English also uses a "dummy" subject, as in "*It*'s raining" and "*There*'s one in here"). Independent subject pronouns in Biblical Hebrew often "sound" redundant (or "emphatic") to English readers when they occur alongside a verbal form that indicates the PGN of its subject. They are not actually redundant, because: (1) all communication is as efficient as possible (superfluity is only apparent, never real); and (2) their function is related to the larger context in which they occur, including the genre and the relationship of their clause to the preceding clause. This will become more clear as you begin to read the biblical text.

1. The basic form is distinct for each person; gender and number is distinguished by the end of the form:

Person	Form	
1st	אֲ-	I, we
2nd	-אַתְּ	you
3rd	ה-	he, she, it, they

2. The "double forms" differ primarily in frequency and distribution:
   a. אֲנִי (1cs) is more than twice as frequent (803x) as אָנֹכִי (c. 350x), but in some biblical books one form dominates, for example

	אֲנִי	אָנֹכִי
Dt	55x	6x
Ezk	1x	155x

   b. The longer 1cp form (אֲנַחְנוּ, "we") occurs about 115 times in Biblical Hebrew, the shorter form (נַחְנוּ) only six times.
   c. The longer 3mp form (הֵמָּה, "they") is slightly more frequent (c. 55%) than הֵם; as with 1cs (אֲנִי/אָנֹכִי), they are not distributed evenly:[114]

	הֵמָּה	הֵם
Gn	4x	17x
Ex	5x	17x
Lv	1x	18x
Ps	25x	3x
Ezk	57x	8x[115]

   d. "She/It"—הוּא (3fs written with -*w*-)—is "normal" in the Torah, but is written הִיא in the rest of the Bible.[116]

13.1.2 *Function (HBI §1.5.1)*

1. An independent pronoun *always* means that you are looking at a *clause*, whether or not the pronoun comes first in the clause.
2. Independent personal pronouns usually identify the *subject* of a verbal or non-verbal clause ("I", "she", "we"). They do *not* show pronominal possession (e.g., "my", "your") or the pronominal objects of verbs or prepositions (e.g., "him", "for them"). The examples illustrate its use with various types of predicates—a noun (Gn 3.19; Ex 6.2), adjective (Ezk 42.14), finite verb (Gn 41.15), and participle (Nu 33.51):

כִּי־עָפָר אַתָּה	For *you* are *dust*, ... (Gn 3.19)
אֲנִי יהוה	*I* am Y<small>HWH</small> (Ex 6.2).
כִּי־קֹדֶשׁ הֵנָּה	For *they* [fp] are *holy* (Ezk 42.14).
וַאֲנִי שָׁמַעְתִּי עָלֶיךָ	And *I heard* about you ... (Gn 41.15)
כִּי אַתֶּם עֹבְרִים אֶת־הַיַּרְדֵּן	When *you cross* the Jordan ... (Nu 33.51)

114. When two 3mp pronouns occur in the same v., both forms may be used (7x), although both are repeated in some vv. (הֵמָּה (17x) or הֵם (7x)).

115. In Ezekiel, the clause כִּי בֵּית מְרִי הֵמָּה/הֵם, *for they are a rebellious household*, occurs seven times, six times with הֵמָּה as the subject, once with הֵם.

116. The 3fs form הִיא—with *yod*—occurs ten times in the Torah out of more than 150 occurrences in those books.

3. Independent pronouns also occur in non-verbal clauses, apparently signaling the non-verbal predication:

יהוה הוא הָאֱלֹהִים	Yhwh [—*he*] is [the] God! (1 Kg 18.39).
כִּי־טוּב כָּל־אֶרֶץ מִצְרַיִם לָכֶם הוּא:	For the goodness of all of the land of Egypt [*it*] is yours (Gn 45.20).

4. Independent pronouns often occur with the conjunction -וְ, creating a disjunctive clause (§6.6). After a conversation between Joseph and his brothers, the narrator finally explains why Joseph's brothers thought that they were secure in talking in front of him (Gn 42.23). The added information of Jg 11.39 makes the virginity of Jephthah's daughter explicit.

וְהֵם לֹא יָדְעוּ כִּי שֹׁמֵעַ יוֹסֵף כִּי הַמֵּלִיץ בֵּינֹתָם:	Now they did not know that Joseph could understand [participle] them, because the interpreter was between them (Gn 42.23).
וְהִיא לֹא־יָדְעָה אִישׁ	… (now she had not known a man) … (Jg 11.39)

The change of subject that is often signalled by an independent pronoun may also imply a contrast between the events or actions described by two clauses, especially when a disjunctive clause begins with *w* + pronoun (cf. 2 Chr 13.11 (Exercise #16)). The contrast is thus appropriately signalled in English by rendering the conjunction as, for example, "but", "now", "but as for her".

Although the contrasting clause—"every great matter they shall bring to you"—is left out of Exercise #6 (Ex 18.22), the disjunctive clause that ends the sentence again signals a contrast, here by beginning the clause with the object (*waw* + non-verb) rather than the subject.

5. The only affix that can be attached to the independent personal pronouns is the conjunction -וְ.

13.2 *Demonstratives*

Demonstratives *point out* or *point to* a person or object ("this", "that", "these", "those"), and can be thought of as making an articular word even more definite or specific (contrast "this scroll" with "the scroll").

13.2.1 *Form*

	Gender	Singular		Plural	
"Near"	masc.	זֶה	*this*	אֵלֶּה	*these*
	fem.	זֹאת			
"Far"	masc.	הוּא	*that*	הֵמָּה	*those*
	fem.	הִיא		הֵנָּה	

The paradigm of the demonstratives overlaps the paradigm of the personal pronouns (above). The "far" demonstratives are the same as the third person personal pronouns. They are demonstrative primarily when they are attributive (§13.2.2(5), below).[117]

13.2.2 *Function (HBI §1.5.2)*

1. Since demonstratives are essentially adjectives, they can be either predicate or attributive. Unlike adjectives, they are not substantive.
2. Like adjectives, demonstratives agree with the grammatical gender and number of the word that they modify.

---

117. Their discourse functions may differ, but there is little functional difference between "*That* is the king" and "*He* is the king".

3. When they are *predicate*, (1) demonstratives are *anarthrous*; (2) they tend to *precede* the word that they modify; and (3) they are usually the *subject* of the clause (זֹה, the second demonstrative in 2 Kgs 6.19, occurs eleven times in Biblical Hebrew):

זֹאת הָאָרֶץ	*This* is the land (Nu 34.2)
הִיא הָעִיר הַגְּדֹלָה	*That* [it] is the great city (Gn 10.12)
אֵלֶּה שְׁמוֹת	*These* are the names (Ex 1.1)
וַיֹּאמֶר אֲלֵהֶם אֱלִישָׁע לֹא זֶה הַדֶּרֶךְ	Elisha said to them, "*This* is not the way,
וְלֹא זֹה הָעִיר	nor is *this* the city. ..." (2 Kgs 6.19)

4. *Attributive* demonstratives *follow* the word that they modify, and are *articular*:

הַמָּקוֹם הַזֶּה	*this* place (Gn 28.17)
בָּעִיר הַהִיא	in *that* city (Js 20.6)
כָּל־הַיּוֹם הַהוּא	all *that* day (Nu 11.32)

5. An articular "third person pronoun" is therefore actually an attributive demonstrative:

בַּיָּמִים הָהֵמָּה	in *those* days (Jr 3.16)[118]
בָּעֵת הַהוּא	at *that* time (Nu 22.4)
הָעִיר הַזֹּאת	*this* city (Gn 19.20)

6. Usually the demonstrative immediately follows the noun that it modifies. If the noun is modified by an adjective (or is in construct), the attributive demonstrative follows the entire phrase, after any adjectives, or after the final word of the construct chain, or both. In Gn 2.12, the adjective after the attributive demonstrative is predicate:

הַדָּבָר הַגָּדוֹל הַזֶּה	*this* great thing (1 Sa 12.16)
הָרָעָה הַגְּדֹלָה הַזֹּאת	*this* great evil (Gn 39.9)
כַּאֲשֶׁר הֵבֵאתִי אֶל־הָעָם הַזֶּה	Just as I brought upon *this* people
אֵת כָּל־הָרָעָה הַגְּדוֹלָה הַזֹּאת	all *this* great disaster (Jr 32.42)
וּזְהַב הָאָרֶץ הַהִוא טוֹב	and the gold of *that* land is good (Gn 2.12)

13.3 *Interrogative Pronouns*

Biblical Hebrew uses two *uninflected* interrogative pronouns to ask questions about persons ("who?", "whom?") and things ("what?" "how?"). Both are normally "fronted"—they begin their clause.

13.3.1 *The Interrogative* מִי

The uninflected interrogative מִי, "who", is always *definite*, and always asks about a *person*.

1. If there is no verb, מִי is usually the subject of a non-verbal clause (but cf. Ru 2.5, #3, below):

וַיֹּאמֶר פַּרְעֹה מִי יְהוָה	Pharaoh said, "*Who* is YHWH, ...?" (Ex 5.2)
מִי אַתֶּם	"*Who* are you (m.p.)?" (Jos 9.8)
מִי הָאֲנָשִׁים הָאֵלֶּה	*Who* are these men ...?" (Nu 22.9)
בַּת־מִי אַתְּ	"*Whose* daughter are you?" (Gn 24.23)
מִי עָשָׂה הַדָּבָר הַזֶּה	"*Who* did this thing?" (Jg 6.29; cf. Jg 15.6)
מִי־שָׁמַע כָּזֹאת	*Who* has heard [such a thing] as this?
מִי רָאָה כָּאֵלֶּה	*Who* has seen [such things] as these? (Is 66.8)

---

118. The phrase "[in] those days" accounts for nearly three-quarters of all occurrences of the 3mp demonstrative.

2. When מִי is the object of the verb, it has the sign of the object, but still begins the question (and is rendered "whom"):

אֶת־מִי תַעֲבֹדוּן "*Whom* will you serve?" (Jos 24.15)

אֶת־מִי אֶשְׁלַח וּמִי יֵלֶךְ־לָנוּ "*Whom* shall I send, and who shall go for us?" (Is 6.8)

3. מִי also functions as the object of prepositions (in Ru 2.5, the ל shows possession):

אַחֲרֵי מִי יָצָא מֶלֶךְ יִשְׂרָאֵל After *whom* has the king of Israel gone out? (1 Sam 24.15)

לְמִי הַנַּעֲרָה הַזֹּאת: *To whom* does this young woman *belong*?" (Ru 2.5)

13.3.2 *The Interrogative* מָה

The uninflected interrogative מָה, "what", is always *indefinite*, and does *not* refer to persons. If there is no verb, מָה is the subject of a non-verbal clause.

וְאָמְרוּ־לִי מַה־שְּׁמוֹ "... and they say to me, '*What is* his name?'

מָה אֹמַר אֲלֵהֶם *What* shall I say to them?" (Ex 3.13)

מֶה־עָשָׂה לְךָ הָעָם הַזֶּה "*What* did this people do to you?" (Ex 32.21)

וּמִי־יֹאמַר־אֵלָיו מַה־תַּעֲשֶׂה: And who says to him, '*What* are you doing?'" (Qo 8.4)

מָה הַחֲלוֹם הַזֶּה אֲשֶׁר חָלָמְתָּ "*What is* this dream which you dreamed?" (Gn 37.10)

1. מָה also occurs in indirect questions:

לֹא יָדְעוּ מַה־הוּא They did not know *what* it [was] (Ex 16.15)

2. מָה may also ask "why", often in combination with ל (לָמָה or לָמָּה, "for what?"):

מָה אֲנַחְנוּ יֹשְׁבִים פֹּה "*Why* are we sitting here ...?" (2 Kgs 17.3)

לָמָה לֹא־הָלַכְתְּ אֵלָי "*Why* didn't you come to me?" (Nu 22.37)

וַיֹּאמֶר דָּוִד לְשָׁאוּל And David said to Saul,

לָמָּה תִשְׁמַע אֶת־דִּבְרֵי אָדָם "*Why* do you listen to men's words, ...?" (1 Sam 24.10)

3. מָה is spelled with three different vowels, depending on the first letter of the following word; there is no difference in function:

מָה *What?*

מַה־ *What?*

מֶה *What?*

13.4 *Frequency*

There are 8,629 independent pronominal forms in Biblical Hebrew:

Personal (subject)	5,001
Demonstratives	2,651
Interrogative	977 (מָה (554x), מִי (423x))

13.5 *Concepts*

antecedent	demonstrative	interrogative	pronoun
cohesion	independent pronoun	pronominal subject	

13.6 Vocabulary[119]

Person	Gender	Singular				Plural			
1st	common	*I*	אָנֹכִי	אֲנִי	.191	*we*	אֲנַחְנוּ	נַחְנוּ	.183
2nd	masc.	*you*		אַתָּה	.192	*you*		אַתֶּם	.184
	fem.	*you*		אַתְּ	.193	*you*		אַתֵּן	.185
3rd	masc.	*he, it*		הוּא	.194	*they* (3 mp pers. pron.); *those* (mp dem.)	הֵם	הֵמָּה	.186
	fem.	*she, it*	הוּא	הִיא	.195	*they* (3fp pers. pron.); *those* (fp dem.)		הֵנָּה	.187
		Who?		מִי	.196	*this* (ms dem. pron.)		זֶה	.188
		What?	מַה־	מָה	.197	*this* (fs dem. pron.)		זֹאת	.189
				מֶה		*these* (cp dem. pron.)		אֵלֶּה	.190

13.7 Exercises

After learning the personal and interrogative pronouns, and the demonstratives, *gloss* these clauses, *parsing* any verbal forms.

1. אֲנִי יהוה — Ex 6.8

2. וַיֹּאמְרוּ מֵחָרָן אֲנָחְנוּ: — Gn 29.4; Haran; the last two words are a quotation

3. וְהוּא שָׁפַט אֶת־יִשְׂרָאֵל אַרְבָּעִים שָׁנָה: — 1 Sam 4.18; אַרְבָּעִים *40*

4. אַתָּה־כֹהֵן לְעוֹלָם עַל־דִּבְרָתִי מַלְכִּי־צֶדֶק: — Ps 110.4; דִּבְרָתִי *order of*; Melchizedek

5. וְאַתֶּם שִׁמְעוּ דְבַר־יהוה — Jr 29.20

6. וְהֵם לֹא יָדְעוּ כִּי שֹׁמֵעַ יוֹסֵף — Gn 42.23; Joseph

7. וְשָׁפְטוּ אֶת־הָעָם בְּכָל־עֵת ... וְכָל־הַדָּבָר הַקָּטֹן יִשְׁפְּטוּ־הֵם — Ex 18.22; עֵת *time* (in the sense of measured, or passing time); קטן *small*; on the second clause, cf. §13.1.2(4)

8. וַיֹּאמֶר מִי־אָתְּ וַתֹּאמֶר רוּת ... כִּי גֹאֵל אָתָּה: — Ru 3.9; Ruth; גֹאֵל *redeemer* (ms Q Ptc < גאל, *redeem*)

9. וַאֲנַחְנוּ נְבָרֵךְ יָהּ מֵעַתָּה וְעַד־עוֹלָם הַלְלוּ־יָהּ: — Ps 115.18; ברך *bless*; עַתָּה *now*; הלל *praise* (D); Yah

10. וְאַתָּה אָמַרְתָּ בִלְבָבְךָ הַשָּׁמַיִם אֶעֱלֶה מִמַּעַל — Is 14.13; ךָ- *your* (m.s.); הַשָּׁמַיִם assumes "to"; עלה *go up, ascend*; מִמַּעַל *above*

11. וַיֹּאמֶר מִי־אֲנִי יהוה אֱלֹהִים וּמִי בֵיתִי — 1 Chr 17.16; יהוה אֱלֹהִים is vocative; בֵיתִי *my house*

12. וְאָנֹכִי עָמַדְתִּי בָהָר — Dt 10.10

---

119. The personal pronouns are listed paradigmatically.

13. שֹׁמְרִים אֲנַחְנוּ אֶת־מִשְׁמֶרֶת יהוה אֱלֹהֵינוּ וְאַתֶּם עֲזַבְתֶּם אֹתוֹ:	2 Chr 13.11; מִשְׁמֶרֶת *observance* (cognate accusative); נוּ- *our*; אֹתוֹ *him* (direct object) [cf. §13.1.2(4)][120]
14. וַיֹּאמֶר אֲלֵהֶם גִּדְעוֹן לֹא־אֶמְשֹׁל בָּכֶם וְלֹא־יִמְשֹׁל בְּנִי בָּכֶם יהוה יִמְשֹׁל בָּכֶם:	Jg 8.23; אֲלֵהֶם *to them* (m.p.); Gideon; בָּכֶם *over you*; בְּנִי *my son*
15. וְהִיא לֹא יָדְעָה כִּי אָנֹכִי נָתַתִּי לָהּ הַדָּגָן וְהַתִּירוֹשׁ	Ho 2.10; נָתַתִּי *I gave*; לָהּ *to her*; דָּגָן *grain*; תִּירוֹשׁ *new wine*
16. וַיַּעַן הַמֶּלֶךְ שְׁלֹמֹה וַיֹּאמֶר לְאִמּוֹ וְלָמָה אַתְּ שֹׁאֶלֶת אֶת־אֲבִישַׁג הַשֻּׁנַמִּית לַאֲדֹנִיָּהוּ וְשַׁאֲלִי־לוֹ אֶת־הַמְּלוּכָה כִּי הוּא אָחִי הַגָּדוֹל מִמֶּנִּי	1 Kgs 2.22; וַיַּעַן *and he answered* (3ms Q Pr < ענה *answer*); Solomon; Abishag; Shunamite; Adonijah; מְלוּכָה *kingship, kingdom*; מִמֶּנִּי *than I* (comparative use of מִן)

13.8 Enrichment: Disjunctives in Poetry

The discussion of disjunctive clauses (§6.6) is usually limited to biblical prose, but it also applies to biblical poetry. A common poetic signal of a shift in perspective is a line beginning with *waw* + an independent pronoun (or a substantive), especially 1cs (referring to the poet) and 2ms (referring to Yhwh). Note the contrasts in the following verses (participants are in bold; *w* + pronoun is in *italics*):

יהוה מָה־רַבּוּ צָרָי	Yhwh, how **my enemies** have increased;
רַבִּים קָמִים עָלָי:	**Many** rise against me;
רַבִּים אֹמְרִים לְנַפְשִׁי	**Many** say about me,
אֵין יְשׁוּעָתָה לּוֹ בֵאלֹהִים	'He has no salvation in God'.
וְאַתָּה יהוה מָגֵן בַּעֲדִי	*But you*, **Yhwh**, are a **shield** on my behalf—
כְּבוֹדִי וּמֵרִים רֹאשִׁי:	**My glory**, and **the one who raises my head** (Ps 3.2–4).
פֶּן־יֹאמַר אֹיְבִי יְכָלְתִּיו	Lest **my enemy** say, 'I have overcome him!'
צָרַי יָגִילוּ כִּי אֶמּוֹט:	**My foes** exult when I fall.
וַאֲנִי בְּחַסְדְּךָ בָטַחְתִּי	*But I* trust in your love;
יָגֵל לִבִּי בִּישׁוּעָתֶךָ	**My heart** exults in your salvation;
אָשִׁירָה לַיהוה כִּי גָמַל עָלָי:	I will sing to Yhwh, for he has done good for **me** (Ps 13.5–6).
נַפְשֵׁנוּ כְּצִפּוֹר נִמְלְטָה מִפַּח יוֹקְשִׁים	Our soul like a bird has been delivered from **the birders' snare**;
הַפַּח נִשְׁבָּר וַאֲנַחְנוּ נִמְלָטְנוּ:	**The snare** is broken, *but we* are delivered (Ps 124.7).

---

120. The contrast in this v. is *not* signaled by the use of different conjugations. Instead, the *waw* + non-verb (in this case, the independent pronoun) makes this a disjunctive clause, to which the choice of conjugation is subordinate. Contrast is a function of the difference in *content* between the clauses.

Lesson 14

Pronominals (II): Suffixes

Independent "subject" pronouns indicate the subject of their clause. In order to show pronominal *possession*, and verbal and prepositional pronominal *objects*, Biblical Hebrew attaches "pieces" of the independent pronouns to substantive and verbal forms. Like the independent pronouns, these suffixes are inflected to agree with the person, gender, and number of their antecedent. There are 45,590 pronominal suffixes in Biblical Hebrew (*versus* about 8,629 independent pronominal forms).

14.1 Form

Person	Gender	Singular	Plural
1st	com.	ִי- *my, me*	נוּ- *our, us*
2nd	masc.	ךָ-	כֶם -
	fem.	ךְ -	כֶן - *your, you*
3rd	masc.	־ה ־ו ־וֹ	הֶם -
		־ֻנּוּ ־הוּ *his, him, its*	־ָם
		[מוֹ- poetic]	*their, them*
	fem.	־ָהּ *her, its*	הֶן -
		־ָה	־ָן

1. There are no *cases* in Biblical Hebrew (unlike, e.g., Greek, Latin, German), so that the form of the suffix is the same regardless of its function, which is determined entirely from its context.
2. There is no difference in function between different forms (i.e., all forms listed under 3ms refer to "he", "him", or "his").
3. מוֹ- (3ms) occurs only in poetry; ־ֻנּוּ - (3ms) occurs on verbs.
4. Pronominal suffixes are added to nouns as follows:
   a. Suffixes are added directly to *masculine* and *feminine singular* nouns, sometimes with a helping vowel. When a feminine noun ends in ה-, the ה- is replaced by ת- (the feminine singular construct ending), and the suffixes are added to the form with ת - (תּוֹרָה > תּוֹרָתִי, *my teaching*).

	Absolute	Construct	Construct + suffix	
son	בֵּן	בֶּן	בְּנִי	*my* son (2 Sam 19.1)
			בְּנֵךְ	*your* (fs) son (2 Kgs 6.28)
			בְּנָהּ	*her* son (2 Kgs 4.6)
city	עִיר	עִיר	עִירוֹ	*his* city (2 Sam 17.23)
land	אֶרֶץ	אֶרֶץ	אַרְצֵנוּ	*our* land (Jos 9.11)
maid/servant	שִׁפְחָה	שִׁפְחַת	שִׁפְחָתְךָ	*your* maid/servant (1 Sam 1.18)
teaching	תּוֹרָה	תּוֹרַת	תּוֹרָתִי	*my* teaching (Is 51.7)
mistress/lady	גְּבִירָה	גְּבֶרֶת	גְּבִרְתָּהּ	*her* mistress (Ps 123.2)

b. When suffixes are added to *plural* nouns, there is a ִי- between the noun and the suffix; some forms are found only on plural nouns:

Person	Gender	Singular		Plural	
1st	com.	ַי-	*my, me*	ֵינוּ-	*our, us*
2nd	masc.	ֶיךָ-	*your, you*	ֵיכֶם-	*your, you*
	fem.	ַיִךְ-		ֵיכֶן-	
3rd	masc.	ָיו-	*his, him, its*	ֵיהֶם-	*their, them*
	fem.	ֶיהָ-	*her, its*	ֵיהֶן-	

1) *Masculine plural* nouns drop the final ם- of their ending and add the suffixes after the ִי- of the plural.
2) *Feminine plural* nouns add -ֵי- after their plural (וֹת-) ending, and before the suffix (בְּנוֹת > בְּנוֹתֵיכֶם, *your* [masc pl] *daughters*). The third plural suffixes ָם- and ָן-, however, can are added directly to the plural ending (בְּנוֹתָם).

words	דְּבָרִים	דִּבְרֵי	דְּבָרֶיךָ	*your* (ms) words (Josh 1.8)
sons	בָּנִים	בְּנֵי	בָּנֶיהָ	*her* sons (Is 66.8)
days	יָמִים	יְמֵי	יָמָיו	*his* days (Jb 14.5)
garments	בְּגָדִים	בִּגְדֵי	בְּגָדֶיךָ	*your* garments (1 Kg 22.30)
lands	אֲרָצוֹת	אַרְצוֹת	בְּאַרְצוֹתָם	*in their* (mp) lands (Gn 10.5)
daughters	בָּנוֹת	בְּנוֹת	בְּנוֹתֵיכֶם	*your* (mp) daughters (Ezr 9.12)

c. The 1cs suffix (ַי-) is added to plural nouns with the vowel *pataḥ*, which is the only difference between "my" used with singular and plural nouns.

	Absolute		Construct + Suffix	
horse	סוּס		סוּסִי	*my* horse
horses	סוּסִים		סוּסַי	*my* horses
son	בֵּן		בְּנִי	*my* son (Pr 3.1)
sons	בָּנִים		בָּנַי	*my* sons (1 Sam 12.2)
daughter	בַּת		בִּתִּי	*my* daughter (Ru 3.16)
daughters	בָּנוֹת		בְּנוֹתַי	*my* daughters (Ru 1.11)

d. Suffixes are added to the *construct* form of the noun. We may therefore say that a noun with a pronominal suffix is in construct *to the suffix*, and that the pronominal suffix is the last "element" or "member" of the construct chain (even if it is a chain of only one "form", composed of two elements).

5. Pronominal suffixes are also used to show the pronominal object of a *preposition*. They are combined with prepositions in one of three ways:
a. Suffixes are added *directly* to בְּ and לְ (their paradigms are identical, apart from the preposition; different glosses illustrate the variety of the prepositions' function):

1st		בִּי	*by me*	לָנוּ	*to us*
2nd	m.	לְךָ	*to you* (ms)	בָּכֶם	*with you* (mp)
	f.	בָּךְ	*against you* (fs)	לָכֶן	*for you* (fp)
3rd	m.	לוֹ	*for him*	בָּהֶם	*in them* (mp)
	f.	בָּהּ	*with her*	לָהֶן	*to them* (fp)

b. Singular suffixes and 1cp are added to -כְּ[121] and to some forms of מִן and עִם with a "helping" syllable:

1st	כָּמוֹנִי	like me	כָּמוֹנוּ	like us
2nd	כָּמוֹךָ	like you (ms)	כָּכֶם	like you (mp)[122]
3rd	כָּמוֹהוּ	like him	כָּהֶם	like them (mp)
	כָּמוֹהָ	like her	כָּהֵן	like them (fp)
1st	מִמֶּנִּי	from me	מִמֶּנּוּ	from us[124]
2nd	מִמְּךָ	from you (ms)	מִכֶּם	from you (mp)
	מִמֵּךְ	from you (fs)	מִכֶּן	from you (fp)
3rd	מִמֶּנּוּ	from him[123]	מֵהֶם	from them (mp)
	מִמֶּנָּה	from her	מֵהֶן	from them (fp)
1st	עִמִּי עִמָּדִי[124]	with me	עִמָּנוּ[125]	with us
2nd	עִמְּךָ	with you (ms)	עִמָּכֶם	with you (mp)
	עִמָּךְ	with you (fs)	---[126]	
3rd	עִמּוֹ	with him	עִמָּם עִמָּהֶם	with them (mp)
	עִמָּהּ	with her	---[127]	

6. Most prepositions add suffixes by means of a *yod* between the preposition and suffix, so that the suffixes look like those added to plural nouns (each line in this example uses a different preposition, and glosses of the prepositions are varied to show use):

1st	לְפָנַי	in my presence	לְפָנֵינוּ	before us
2nd	אֵלֶיךָ	to you (ms)	אֲלֵיכֶם	to you (mp)
	עָלַיִךְ	against you (fs)	עֲלֵיכֶן	concerning you (fp)
3rd	אַחֲרָיו	after him	אַחֲרֵיהֶם	after them (mp)
	תַּחְתֶּיהָ	under her / it	תַּחְתֵּיהֶן	under them (fp)

N.B.: The noun אֵל, *god/God* occurs only with the 1cs suffix (אֵלִי, *my God*); all other suffixes are added to the construct of אֱלֹהִים (e.g., אֱלֹהֶיךָ, *your God*). The preposition אֶל/אֵל uses *pataḥ* to link the 1cs suffix (אֵלַי, *to me*); all other forms have *yod*, as in the paradigm.

---

121. The preposition -כְּ does not occur with 2nd person feminine suffixes.
122. כְּמוֹכֶם occurs once (Jb 12.3).
123. The 3ms and 1cp suffixes with מִן (both are מִמֶּנּוּ) can be distinguished only by context.
124. Be careful not to confuse this with forms of the verbal root עמד *stand*.
125. Cf. עִמָּנוּ־אֵל *God [is] with us* ("Immannuel" (with and without *maqqef*; e.g., Is 7.14; 8.8, 10).
126. The preposition עִם does not occur with 2nd person feminine plural suffixes.
127. The preposition עִם does not occur with 3rd person feminine plural suffixes.

The key to analyzing a compound form is to know the pronominal suffixes and the vocabulary (which will let you identify the central lexeme (content word)).

		וּבְבֵיתִי	*and in my house* (Is 3.7)	
-ִי		-בֵּית	-בְּ-	-וּ
1cs suffix		noun	prep.	cj.
		כִּדְבָרֶיךָ	*according to your words* (1 Kg 3.12)	
-ךָ	-ֶי-	-דְּבָר	-כְּ	
2ms suffix	plural	noun	prep.	
		בְּבָנֵינוּ	*with our sons* (Ex 10.9)	
-נוּ	-ֵי- (supply the final nun)	-בָּנ	-בְּ	
1cp suffix	plural	noun	prep.	
		וּבִבְנוֹתֵינוּ	*and with our daughters* (Ex 10.9)	
-נוּ	-ֵי-	-בְּנוֹת	-בְּ-	-וּ
1cp suffix	plural	noun	prep.	cj.
		מִמְּצוּקוֹתֵיהֶם	*from their troubles* (Ps 107.6, 13, 19, 28)	
-הֶם	-ֵי-	-מְצוּקוֹת	-[מִן]-	
3mp suffix	plural	noun	prep.	

14.2 Function (HBI §1.5.1b)

1. Pronominal suffixes are added to nouns with all of the nuances of the construct chain (possession, relationship, etc.):

דְּבָרֶיךָ	*your* (ms) words (Josh 1.8)	source: words spoken by "you"
בָּנֶיהָ	*her* sons (Is 66.8)	relationship: sons born to her
יָמָיו	*his* days (Jb 14.5)	days during which he lived
בְּגָדֶיךָ	*your* (ms) garments (1 Kg 22.30)	ownership: garments owned by "you"
בְּאַרְצוֹתָם	*in their* lands (Gn 10.5)	ownership: lands lived in by "them"

2. Because pronouns are definite, pronominal suffixes make the word to which they are suffixed definite as well, and end the construct chain. Every word with a pronominal suffix is therefore both *construct* and *definite*. In 1 Sam 26.19, דִּבְרֵי is construct to עֶבֶד, which is construct to the 3ms suffix:

יִשְׁמַע־נָא אֲדֹנִי הַמֶּלֶךְ אֵת דִּבְרֵי עַבְדּוֹ	"…, may my master the king hear *the* words of *his* servant (1 Sam 26.19)
יָדָיו וְרַגְלָיו	*his* hands and *his* feet (Jg 1.6); two construct chains
בִּימֵיכֶם	*in your* days (Jl 1.2)

3. Pronominal suffixes indicate the *objects* of prepositions:

וַיֹּאמֶר לָהֶם	He said *to them*, … (Gn 9.1)
וְאָמַרְתָּ אֵלָיו	And you shall say *to him* … (Ex 9.13)
שָׁלַח אֵלַי לְנָשַׁי וּלְבָנַי וּלְכַסְפִּי וְלִזְהָבִי וְלֹא מָנַעְתִּי מִמֶּנּוּ׃	He sent *to me for my wives and for my sons and for my silver and for my gold*; and I have not withheld [anything] *from him* (1 Kgs 20.7).
אֲשֶׁר נוֹתְרוּ אַחֲרֵיהֶם בָּאָרֶץ	who were left *behind them* in the land … (2 Ch 8.8)
וַעֲמָשָׂא בָּא לִפְנֵיהֶם	And Amasa went in *before them* (2 Sa 20.8)

4. Pronominal suffixes indicate the *object of a verb*, either by being suffixed directly to the verbal form, or by being suffixed to the sign of the object. The form of the sign of the object often changes to אֹת– when a pronominal suffix is added (§14.4).

וַעֲבַדְתֶּם אֹתָנוּ׃	... then you shall serve *us* (1 Sam 17.9).
וְאַתֶּם עֲזַבְתֶּם אוֹתִי	..., but you have deserted *me*, ... (Jg 10.13)
אֶל־הַמֶּלֶךְ אֲשֶׁר־שָׁלַח אֶתְכֶם	... to the king who sent *you* (2 Kgs 1.6)

5. As with nouns (§7.1), the preposition לְ can show pronominal *possession* and *indirect objects* (verbs of speaking occur with both לְ and אֶל).

כִּי־לִי כָּל־הָאָרֶץ׃	"... for all the earth is *mine*" (Ex 19.5).
וַתֹּאמֶר אֵלָיו אָבִי	She said *to him* "Father, ..." (Jg 11.36)
וַיֹּאמֶר לָהֶם שִׁמְשׁוֹן	Samson said *to them* ... (Jg 14.12)

6. Prepositions rarely occur with the relative (אֲשֶׁר).[128] Instead, the preposition that functions with אֲשֶׁר falls at or toward the end of the relative clause, with a pronominal suffix that agrees in person, gender, and number with the word being modified by the אֲשֶׁר-clause. [The suffix will be, e.g., fp when the referent is *cities* (Gn 19.29), ms when it is *man* (Gn 41.38; Jos 8.24).] In a similar way, when אֲשֶׁר refers to a place, שָׁם, *there*, comes at the end of the clause (Jg 19.26).

אֶת־הֶעָרִים אֲשֶׁר־יָשַׁב בָּהֵן לוֹט׃	... the cities *in which* Lot lived (Gn 19.29)
אִישׁ אֲשֶׁר רוּחַ אֱלֹהִים בּוֹ׃	... a man *in whom* is a divine spirit" (Gn 41.38)
בַּמִּדְבָּר אֲשֶׁר רְדָפוּם בּוֹ	... in the wilderness *into which* they had pursued them (Jos 8.24)
וַתִּפֹּל פֶּתַח בֵּית־הָאִישׁ אֲשֶׁר־אֲדוֹנֶיהָ שָּׁם	She fell at the door of the man's house *where* her master was (Jg 19.26)
וְעָמַדְתִּי לְיַד־אָבִי בַּשָּׂדֶה אֲשֶׁר אַתָּה שָׁם	And I will stand beside my father in the field *where* you are (1 Sam 19.3)

14.3 *Definiteness*

Comparing the article, construct, and pronominal suffixes reveals that Biblical Hebrew has three ways to indicate that a substantive is definite:

1. *Proper* nouns [names] and *pronominals* are definite, since they refer to a specific person or place:

דָּוִד	David	הוּא	he, it, that (when articular)
אַבְרָהָם	Abraham	חֶבְרוֹן	Hebron
מִי	Who?	הֵם	they, those (when articular)

2. *Articular* common substantives are definite:

הַבַּיִת	the house	לַכֹּהֵן	to/for the priest
הֶחָג	the feast	אַחֲרֵי־הַמִּלְחָמָה	after the battle

3. Words in *construct* to something that is *definite*, that is when the construct chain ends in:
   a) a proper noun:

בֵּית אַבְרָהָם	Abraham's household (Gn 17.23)
בֶּן־דָּוִד	David's son (2 Sam 13.1)
אַנְשֵׁי יְהוּדָה	the men of Judah (2 Sam 2.4)

---

128. Contrast the routine and common use of relative pronouns as the objects of prepositions in English.

b) an articular substantive:

כָּל־כְּלֵי הַמִּשְׁכָּן	all the utensils of the Tabernacle (Ex 27.19)
מֵעֵינֵי הַקָּהָל	from the eyes of the assembly (Lv 4.13)
דְּבַר אִישׁ־הָאֱלֹהִים	the word of the man of God (1 Kg 13.4)

c) a pronominal suffix or מִי:

שֹׁמְרֶךָ	he who watches over you (Ps 121.5) [your watcher]
בֵּיתִי וַחֲצֵרוֹתָי	my house and my courts (1 Chr 28.6)
הַר קָדְשִׁי	my holy mountain (the mountain of my holiness; Ps 2.6)
דִּבְרֵי פִיךָ	the words of your mouth (Ps 138.4)
וּמִיַּד־מִי לָקַחְתִּי כֹפֶר	... and from whose hand have I taken a ransom (1 Sa 12.3)

N.B.: A word with a pronominal suffix is both *construct* and *definite*, and the suffix ends a construct chain and makes the entire chain definite. A substantive plus pronominal suffix is thus a miniature construct chain of two elements contained in one form.

14.4 *Verbs with Pronominal Objects*

Biblical Hebrew indicates pronominal objects either by suffixing the pronominal to the object marker (§14.2.4), or by attaching the suffix directly to the verbal form itself.

14.4.1 *Form*

1. The pronominal suffixes that are attached to verbs are much like those used on prepositions, nouns, infinitives construct, participles, and the sign of the object (above), and can be suffixed to any conjugation except the infinitive absolute (Lesson 16). Like most Hebrew pronouns, they are inflected for person, gender, and number. The variation in some forms depends on whether the verb ends in a consonant or vowel (e.g., 3fs).

Person	Gender	Singular		Plural	
1st	common	נִי - ִי -	me, to me	נוּ -	us, to us
2nd	masc.	ךָ -	you, to you	כֶם -	you, to you [129]
	fem.	ךְ -		כֶן -	
3rd	masc.	הוּ - וֹ -	him, to him	ם - ָם -	them, to them
	fem.	הָ - ָה -	her, to her	ן -	

2. A few pronominal suffixes have an alternate form, with *nun*—which is often assimilated—between the suffix and the verbal form. This paradigm lists all the forms of this type of suffix that occur in Biblical Hebrew. In this form, the 3ms and 1cp suffixes are identical, and can be distinguished only by the context.

Person	Gender	Singular	Plural
1st	common	נִּי -	נּוּ -
2nd	masc.	ךָּ -	
3rd	masc.	נּוּ -	
	fem.	נָּה -	

129. This form (2fp) occurs only on participles.

3. The combination of a pronominal suffix and verbal form means that any form that ends with –*uhû* (either וּהוּ- or הוּ ֫-) is a masculine plural verbal form (the first -*u*-) with a 3ms suffix (-*hû*):

וְאִם־תִּדְרְשֻׁהוּ יִמָּצֵא לָכֶם וְאִם־תַּעַזְבֻהוּ יַעֲזֹב אֶתְכֶם:	If you seek *him*, he will be found by you, but if you abandon *him*, he will abandon you (2 Ch 15.2).
יִבְלָעֵהוּ	They will swallow *him* (Ho 8.7)

14.4.2 *Function*

1. Pronominal suffixes identify the *pronominal object* of the verb:

וַיִּשְׁלָחֵהוּ מֵעֵמֶק חֶבְרוֹן	... and he sent *him* from the valley of Hebron (Gn 37.14)
וּמָשַׁחְתָּ אֹתוֹ:	"... and you shall anoint *him*" (Ex 29.7)
וְלֹא הֲרָגוּם:	and they did not kill *them* (Josh 9.26)
פֶּן־נִשְׂרֹף אוֹתָךְ	"... lest we burn *you* ..." (Jg 14.15)
שָׁפְטֵנִי יְהוָה כְּצִדְקִי	Judge *me*, YHWH, according to my innocence (Ps 7.9b)
כִּי שְׁכֵחֻנִי עַמִּי	"... for my people have forgotten *me* ..." (Jr 18.15a)

2. When *parsing* a verb with a pronominal suffix, use the "suffix" column to identify the person, gender, and number of the suffix (e.g., 3fp):

Lemma	Lexical Form	Gloss	PGN	Stem	Conj.	Suffix
שָׁפְטֵנִי	שׁפט	*judge*	2ms	Q	V	1cs
הֲרָגוּםא	הרג	*kill*	3cp	Q	P	3mp

14.5 *Concepts*

definiteness   pronominal possession
pronominal object   pronominal suffix

14.6 *Vocabulary*

cherub (perhaps a winged bull with human head)	כְּרוּב	.205	*door* [*way*]	דֶּלֶת	.197
other side; region beyond [sthg.]	עֵבֶר	.206	*knowledge, understanding*	דַּעַת	.198
power, strength	עֹז	.207	*slaughter; sacrifice*	זֶבַח	.199
rebellion, revolt; transgression	פֶּשַׁע	.208	*tumult, uproar; crowd, multitude*	הָמוֹן	.200
be satisfied, satiated	שָׂבַע	.209	*arm, forearm; strength*	זְרוֹעַ	.201
in this way / manner, thus, so	כֹּה	.210	*fat*	חֵלֶב	.202
in front, east; eastward	קֶדֶם קֵדְמָה	.211	*be pleased* [*with*], *delight* [*in*] (st. vb.)	חָפֵץ	.203
bull, young bull; steer	שׁוֹר	.212	*male offspring / child* *female offspring / child*	יֶלֶד יַלְדָּה	.204

14.7 Exercises

1. After learning the pronominal suffixes, gloss these clauses, and be prepared to explain their structure and function. Clauses d-i can be checked against the biblical references.

   a. יהוה מֶלֶךְ עַמּוֹ   d. אַתָּה הָאִישׁ   2 Sam 12.7   g. מִי הָאֲנָשִׁים   Nu 22.9

   b. הוּא אִישָׁהּ   e. מִי הוּא   Est 7.5   h. לְמִי הַנַּעֲרָה הַזֹּאת   Ru 2.5

   c. הִיא אִשְׁתּוֹ   f. מָה זֹאת   Jg 2.2   i. אֲנִי יהוה אֱלֹהֶיךָ   Is 41.13

2. Before glossing these phrases and clauses, circle or mark the pronominal suffixes, and identify their person, gender, and number.

   a. נִכְרְתָה בְרִית אֲנִי וָאָתָּה וְהָיָה לְעֵד בֵּינִי וּבֵינֶךָ׃   Gn 31.44; נִכְרְתָה is cohortative; עֵד testimony, witness

   b. הִיא עִיר דָּוִד׃   2 Sam 5.7; David

   c. בָּעֵת הַהִיא אָמַר יְהוָה אֶל־יְהוֹשֻׁעַ ...   Jos 5.2; עֵת time; Joshua

   d. וַיֹּאמֶר אִישׁ הָאֱלֹהִים הוּא   1 Kgs 13.26; the last three words are a quotation

   e. וַיֹּאמְרוּ מֵחָרָן אֲנָחְנוּ׃   Gn 29.4; Haran (place name); the last two words are a quotation

   f. וְיֵהוּא מָצָא אֶת־אֲחֵי אֲחַזְיָהוּ מֶלֶךְ־יְהוּדָה וַיֹּאמֶר מִי אַתֶּם וַיֹּאמְרוּ אֲחֵי אֲחַזְיָהוּ אֲנָחְנוּ   2 Kgs 10.13; Jehu, Ahaziah; Judah

   g. וַיֹּאמֶר ... [לָהֶם] וְאַתֶּם לֹא־תִכְרְתוּ בְרִית לְיוֹשְׁבֵי הָאָרֶץ הַזֹּאת וְלֹא־שְׁמַעְתֶּם בְּקֹלִי   Jg 2.2; יֹשֵׁב inhabitant

   h. וַיֹּאמֶר לוֹ יִצְחָק אָבִיו מִי־אָתָּה וַיֹּאמֶר אֲנִי בִּנְךָ בְכֹרְךָ עֵשָׂו   Gn 27.32; בְּכֹר first-born; Isaac, Esau

   i. וְאָנֹכִי תוֹלַעַת וְלֹא־אִישׁ   Ps 22.7; תּוֹלַעַת worm

   j. וְיָשַׁב בָּעִיר הַהִיא   Jos 20.6

   k. ... אֶת־אַבְרָם בְּנוֹ וְאֶת־לוֹט בֶּן־הָרָן בֶּן־בְּנוֹ וְאֵת שָׂרַי כַּלָּתוֹ אֵשֶׁת אַבְרָם בְּנוֹ   Gn 11.31; כַּלָּה daughter-in-law (the people identified by the three proper names] are direct objects of "Terah took ..."); Abram, Lot, Haran

   l. אָנֹכִי עֹמֵד בֵּין־יְהוָה וּבֵינֵיכֶם בָּעֵת הַהִוא   Dt 5.5

14.8 Enrichment: Ruth 3.16

In Ruth 3.7, Ruth, in obedience to Naomi, went to the threshing floor, and, after he fell asleep, lay down at Boaz's feet. When he awoke in the middle of the night,

וַיֹּאמֶר מִי אָתּ   He said, "Who are you?" (Ru 3.9)

Boaz knew that the person lying beside him was female (and therefore used the fs pronoun), but could not identify her.

After Ruth made her request known to Boaz, she slept, but he awakened her early in the morning so that she could get back to the privacy of Naomi's home without anyone knowing that a woman had been at the threshing floor (3.14). Ruth left the threshing floor while it was still dark enough that the two of them could not recognize each other (3.14).

When she arrived at Naomi's house in Bethlehem, Naomi asked:

מִי־אַתְּ בִּתִּי   *"Who are you, my daughter?"* (Ru 3.16)

This is often glossed with a question that asks about the plan's success, for example, "How did it go, my daughter" (NAS, NIV; cf. ESV). The question, however, shows that even Naomi—who was certainly expecting Ruth, and who would have recognized her better than anyone else in Bethlehem—could only tell that it was a younger female (hence "my daughter"), not that she was Ruth.

The parallel between Naomi's question and Boaz's (3.9) implies that when Ruth arrived home it was still [nearly] as dark as midnight. The author recorded this question in order to assure readers that Boaz's plan had succeeded—that Ruth's visit to the threshing floor remained secret, since she arrived at Naomi's house while it was still too dark for anyone to identify her (cf. 3.14), even if they had recognized that she was a woman.

Lesson 15

Stative Verbs & היה

Languages in general have two major types of verb: stative (or static) and dynamic (sometimes called "fientive"). *Stative* verbs describe their subject's state or condition, rather than an action, and are therefore intransitive (do not govern direct objects); the closest parallels to stative verbs in English are the verb "to be" with a predicate adjective (*He was old*) and the verb "become" (*He had become unclean*).

Dynamic verbs—which we have been studying since Lesson 4—describe events or actions, including any type of movement. Dynamic verbs are therefore *active*, but not necessarily transitive, since they do not necessarily occur with what we think of as direct objects ("He ran home" means "He ran to his house").

15.1 *Stative Verbs*

Stative verbs in Biblical Hebrew describe their subject's condition or state—the way things are or were—and so are usually glossed with forms of "to be" or "to become". The forms of "be" that are used to render stative verbs do not have the same function as the forms of "be" found in passive clauses in English.[130]

1. The ball *was thrown*.   passive
2. The ball *was* red.   stative
3. The ball *was polished*.   passive (if "polished" is a participle) or stative (if "polished" is an adjective, as in "It was a polished ball.").
4. וְעֶגְלוֹן אִישׁ בָּרִיא מְאֹד   Now Eglon *was* a very fat man (stative; "fat" is an adjective)
5. יְהִי שֵׁם יהוה מְבֹרָךְ   May Yhwh's name *be blessed* ... (Ps 113.2; passive)

These are the most common stative verbs in Biblical Hebrew.

כָּבֵד	be heavy, wealthy	גָּבַהּ	be high, exalted
מָלֵא	be full	גָּדַל	be large, great
קָדֵשׁ	be holy	זָקֵן	be old
קָרֵב	be near	טָהֵר	be clean, pure
רָחֹק	be far, distant	טָמֵא	be unclean, impure

15.1.1 *Form*

1. The lexical form of most stative verbs (3ms *qal* perfect) has a vowel other than *pataḥ* after the second radical: either *ḥolem* (גָּדַל, be[come] large/great) or *ṣere* (טָמֵא, be[come] unclean).
2. Apart from this difference, the paradigm of the stative verbs is the same as that of משל in the perfect; strong stative verbs tend to have *pataḥ* after the second radical in the imperfect and preterite. [N.B.: Many of these forms do not occur in Biblical Hebrew.]

---

130. For the various passive and reflexive functions, Biblical Hebrew uses different forms of the verb, called "stems" or *binyanîm* (Lessons 18-21).

Qal Perfect (גדל *be large, great*)

Person	Gender	Singular		Plural	
1st	Common	גָּדַלְתִּי	I was/became great	גָּדַלְנוּ	We were/became great
2nd	Masc.	גָּדַלְתָּ	You were/became great	גְּדַלְתֶּם	You were/became great
	Fem.	גָּדַלְתְּ		גְּדַלְתֶּן	
3rd	Masc.	גָּדַל	He was/became great	גָּדְלוּ	They were/became great
	Fem.	גָּדְלָה	She was/became great		

Qal Imperfect/Preterite (כבד *be heavy, wealthy, important*)

Person	Gender	Singular		Plural	
1st	Common	אֶכְבַּד	I was/became wealthy	נִכְבַּד	We were/became important
2nd	Masc.	תִּכְבַּד	You were/became heavy	תִּכְבְּדוּ	You were/became wealthy
	Fem.	תִּכְבְּדִי		תִּכְבַּדְנָה	
3rd	Masc.	יִכְבַּד	He was/became heavy	יִכְבְּדוּ	They were/became heavy
	Fem.	תִּכְבַּד	She was/became important	תִּכְבַּדְנָה	

Qal Imperative (קדשׁ *be holy*)

Person	Gender	Singular		Plural	
2nd	Masc.	קְדֹשׁ	Be holy!	קִדְשׁוּ	Be holy!
	Fem.	קִדְשִׁי		קְדֹשְׁנָה	

3. The 3ms *qal* perfect (lexical form) of many stative verbs is identical or nearly identical to the ms form of the adjective of the same root, e.g.:

large, great	גָּדֹל	גָּדַל	be large, great	
old	זָקֵן	זָקֵן	be old	
strong	חָזָק	חָזַק	be strong (also fientive: *hold, seize, grasp*)	
[ceremonially] clean	טָהֹר	טָהֵר	be [ceremonially] clean	
unclean	טָמֵא	טָמֵא	be [ceremonially] unclean, impure	
heavy, wealthy	כָּבֵד	כָּבֵד	be heavy, wealthy	
full	מָלֵא	מָלֵא	be full	

4. On the other hand, only one form of a stative verb looks like the adjective: **3ms *qal* perfect** is exactly like the **ms** form of the adjective. In all other forms, the stem (or "theme") vowel—the vowel after the second radical—varies according to the type of PGN ending, just as in the fientive [action/dynamic] verbs (as the above paradigms show). In the adjectives, however, the vowel does *not* change:

Adjectival Forms

	Singular	Plural		Singular	Plural	
Masc.	קָרֹב	קְרֹבִים	near,	כָּבֵד	כְּבֵדִים	heavy,
Fem.	קְרֹבָה	קְרֹבוֹת	close	כְּבֵדָה	כְּבֵדוֹת	honored

15.1.2 *Stative Verbs & Time*

Stative verbs can refer to the *present* even when their form is the perfect conjugation, in the sense that they describe a condition that characterizes the subject. This same "presentness" is part of the function of the perfect of a number of verbs of thought, emotion, and perception (e.g., אהב, ידע), especially when they occur within quotations. In Ezk 22.4, they might be rendered as "you are ..." or "you have become ..."

בְּדָמֵךְ אֲשֶׁר־שָׁפַכְתְּ אָשַׁמְתְּ וּבְגִלּוּלַיִךְ אֲשֶׁר־עָשִׂית טָמֵאת	because of your blood which you shed, *you are guilty*, and because of your deeds which you have done, *you are unclean* (Ezk 22.4)
יֹאמַר הָעֶבֶד אָהַבְתִּי אֶת־אֲדֹנִי אֶת־אִשְׁתִּי וְאֶת־בָּנָי	... the servant shall say, '*I love* my master, my wife, and my children' (Ex 21.5)
אֲדֹנִי הַמֶּלֶךְ לֹא יָדָעְתָּ׃	... my master, O king, *you do* not *know* (1 Kgs 1.18)
וַיֹּאמֶר הַמֶּלֶךְ אֶל־שִׁמְעִי אַתָּה יָדַעְתָּ אֵת כָּל־הָרָעָה אֲשֶׁר יָדַע לְבָבְךָ	The king said to Shimei, "*You know* all the evil which your heart *knows*, ..." (1 Kgs 2.44)

15.2 *Fientive [Dynamic/Action] Verbs*

Dynamic Verbs (transitive)		**Dynamic Verbs (intransitive)**	
אָהֵב	*love*	עָבַר	*cross over, pass by/through*
אָכַל	*eat, devour, consume*	הָלַךְ	*go, walk*
אָמַר	*say, speak*	יָרַד	*go down, descend*
יָרַשׁ	*possess, dispossess*	יָשַׁב	*remain, sit, settle, stay*
כָּתַב	*write, inscribe*		
מָלַךְ	*reign [as king]* (also stative: *be king*)	חָזַק	Some verbs can be either *dynamic or stative* in qal: *be strong* (also dynamic: *hold, seize, grasp*)
עָזַב	*forsake, abandon, leave*		
עָמַד	*stand, stop, stay*		
שָׁכַב	*lie down, sleep*		
שָׁמַע	*listen, hear; obey*		
שָׁמַר	*guard, watch, keep*		

15.3 *The Verb* היה

Although the function of "being" is often implicit (cf. predicate adjectives, participles, and adverbial functions), the verb הָיָה is usually glossed as "be" or "become" (the latter especially when followed by לְ).

15.3.1 *Forms of* היה

Because היה ends in a vowel letter rather than a consonant, its forms are not like those of the verbs that we have studied to this point. The primary difference is that the final ה- disappears whenever there is an ending (and in the preterite when there is no ending). [III-ה verbs (היה and other verbs like it) are discussed in Lesson 25.][131] היה is so important to the structure and message of Hebrew narrative that we introduce it here. The chief characteristic of III-ה verbs is that the final ה- (which

---

131. This nomenclature for types of verbal roots was explained in §6.2.

is a vowel letter, not a radical) disappears before PGN endings in all forms. It is replaced by a *yod*, which is a vowel letter for either *ḥireq* or *ṣere*:

Qal Perfect of היה

Person	Gender	Singular		Plural	
1st	Common	הָיִיתִי	I was	הָיִינוּ	We were
2nd	Masc.	הָיִיתָ	You were	הֱיִיתֶם	You were
	Fem.	הָיִית		---	
3rd	Masc.	הָיָה	He was	הָיוּ	They were
	Fem.	הָיְתָה	She was		

1. The vowel letter *yod* (as part of *ḥireq-yod*) "replaces" the final vowel letter ה- before consonantal endings (endings that begin with a consonant).
2. The 3fs ending תָה- "replaces" the final vowel letter ה-.
3. The 3cp vocalic ending וּ- "replaces" the final vowel letter ה-.
4. Because they are preceded by a vowel, the ת- of the PGN endings does not have *dageš lene*.
5. The sign—means that this form does occur in the Bible.

Qal Imperfect of היה

Person	Gender	Singular		Plural	
1st	Common	אֶהְיֶה	I am/shall be	נִהְיֶה	We are/shall be
2nd	Masc.	תִּהְיֶה	You are/shall be	תִּהְיוּ	You are/shall be
	Fem.	תִּהְיִי		תִּהְיֶינָה	
3rd	Masc.	יִהְיֶה	He is/shall be	יִהְיוּ	They are/shall be
	Fem.	תִּהְיֶה	She is/shall be	תִּהְיֶינָה	

1. The vowel letter *yod* replaces the final vowel letter ה- before consonantal endings (2/3fp).
2. The vowel before the final ה- is *segol* (this is only for forms without PGN endings).
3. The vocalic endings ִי - (2fs) and וּ- (2/3mp) "replace" the final vowel letter ה-.

Qal Imperative of היה

Person	Gender	Singular		Plural	
2nd	Masc.	הֱיֵה	Be!	הֱיוּ	Be!
	Fem.	הֲיִי		---	

Qal Preterite of היה

Person	Gender	Singular		Plural	
1st	Common	וָאֱהִי	[And] I was	וַנְּהִי	... we were/became
2nd	Masc.	וַתְּהִי	... you were/became	וַתִּהְיוּ	... you were/became
	Fem.	---		וַתִּהְיֶינָה	
3rd	Masc.	וַיְהִי	... he was/became	וַיִּהְיוּ	... they were/became
	Fem.	וַתְּהִי	... she was/became	וַתִּהְיֶינָה	

Final ה- drops off in the preterite, so that forms without PGN endings end in *ḥireq-yod*.

Do not confuse forms of the *Tetragrammaton* (on left) with היה (on right).

	Forms of היה		
יהוה יְהֹוָה (Yhwh)	הָיָה	*He was [became]*	3ms Q P
	יִהְיֶה	*He will be[come]*	3ms Q F
	יְהִי	*Let him [it] be[come]!*	3ms Q J
	יִהְיוּ	*They will be[come]*	3mp Q F
וַיהוָה (*and* Yhwh)	וְהָיָה	*And he will be[come]*	3ms Q P + *waw*
	וַיְהִי	*And he was [became]*	3ms Q Pr

1. In the *imperfect*, the vowel after the second radical of היה is *segol*.
2. In the *preterite*, the final ה- (a vowel letter) drops off; the -י prefix is not doubled due to the following *šewa*.

N.B.: You do not need to memorize these paradigms, but you will need to be able to recognize and identify the forms of היה.

15.3.2 *Functions*

The verb היה is usually glossed as "be", "become", "happen", or "come to pass". Its function is larger than the English verb "to be", which primarily links a topic with its [adjectival, nominal, or adverbial] comment (e.g., "Goliath was *large*", "Goliath was *a giant*", "Goliath was *in front of the Philistine army*").

The primary distinction in the function of היה is between the 3ms forms and the other forms of היה. Since the non-3ms forms are more easily explained, we discuss them first.

1. All forms of היה can link the subject and predicate; the conjugation of היה indicates the general temporal frame of the clause.

טְמֵאִים הֵם וּטְמֵאִים יִהְיוּ לָכֶם:	They are unclean, and they *are/shall be* unclean for you (Lv 11.35) [both clauses have predicate adjectives]
יַד־יְהוָה הָיְתָה־בָּם	Yhwh's hand *was* against them (Jg 2.15)
כַּאֲשֶׁר הָיִיתִי עִם־מֹשֶׁה אֶהְיֶה עִמָּךְ	As I *was* with Moses, I *shall be* with you (Jos 1.5)
לִי הָיְתָה הַמְּלוּכָה	The kingdom *was* mine (1 Kgs 2.15)

2. Furthermore, with an expressed (nominal, substantive) subject, היה is the predicate of a stative clause to which it adds explicit temporal information (past for the preterite and perfect, and present or future for the imperfect and *w*+perfect). This is not primarily a static description, but often signals some sort of change in the subject's condition or state, and therefore a turn in a story. It thus often marks the beginning of a narrative segment, as these examples illustrate:

וַיְהִי אוֹר	and *there was* light (Gn 1.3)
וַיְהִי עֶרֶב וַיְהִי בֹקֶר	*There was* a morning and *there was* an evening, ... (Gn 1.5); or "A morning *was* and ..."
וַיְהִי רָעָב בָּאָרֶץ	*There was* a famine in the land (Gn 12.10; Ru 1.1); or "A famine *came upon* the land"
וַיְהִי יְהוָה אֶת־יְהוֹשֻׁעַ וַיְהִי שָׁמְעוֹ בְּכָל־הָאָרֶץ:	Yhwh *was* with Joshua, and his fame *was* in all [i.e., throughout] the land (Jos 6.27)

3. When a 3ms form of היה without an expressed (nominal, substantive) subject opens a narrative, the 3ms preterite and *w* + perfect tend to signal a temporal or locational shift in the flow of events which is identified in the next two or three words. Either an *infinitive*

construct (below) with a preposition will follow the form of היה, or a temporal phrase, with a preposition and one or more nouns.

    a. If the form is וַיְהִי (3ms *qal* preterite of היה), it opens a section of a past narrative built on a series of preterites (*italicized* in both passages):

וַיְהִי בָּעֵת הַהִוא וַיֹּאמֶר אֲבִימֶלֶךְ	So at that time, Abimelech *said* (Gn 21.22)
וַיְהִי בַּיָּמִים הָהֵם וַיִּגְדַּל מֹשֶׁה וַיֵּצֵא אֶל־אֶחָיו וַיַּרְא בְּסִבְלֹתָם וַיַּרְא אִישׁ ...	Now in those days, Moses *grew up*, and *he went out* to his relatives, and *he saw* their burdens, and *he saw* a man ... (Ex 2.11)

    b. The form וְהָיָה (*waw* + 3ms *qal* perfect of היה) is either the predicate of a simple clause, or it introduces a series of instruction or prophecy outlined by a series of *waw* + perfects. This form therefore occurs primarily within direct quotations, rather than on the main storyline of the narrative.

וְהָיָה שִׁמְךָ אַבְרָהָם	Your name *shall be* Abraham (Gn 17.5)
וְהָיָה כִּי־יֹאמְרוּ אֲלֵיכֶם בְּנֵיכֶם ... וַאֲמַרְתֶּם	*When* your sons say to you ..., you shall say (Ex 12.26–27)

    c. וְהָיָה may be followed by a temporal particle, such as כִּי ("when" in this context), which in turn is then followed by one or more verb(s) in the imperfect, preterite, or *waw* + perfect conjugations; וַיְהִי is rarely followed by these particles.

וְהָיָה כִּי־יִקְרָא לָכֶם פַּרְעֹה וְאָמַר	*When* Pharaoh summons you and says ... (Gn 46.33)
וְהָיָה כִּי־יֶחֱטָא וְאָשֵׁם וְהֵשִׁיב	*When* he sins and is guilty and returns ... (Lv 5.23)

4. The combination of a form of היה followed by the preposition ל has two predominant functions: possession and change in status.

    a. The combination can indicate *possession* (the "possessive" use of ל), with a temporal nuance added by the conjugation of היה.

וַיְהִי־לוֹ צֹאן־וּבָקָר	... and *he had* flocks and herds (Gn 12.16)

    b. It can also indicate a *change* in its subject's *status* or *condition*. The -ל indicates what the subject has "become" (or, in the future, "will become").

וַיְהִי הָאָדָם לְנֶפֶשׁ חַיָּה:	The man *became* a living being (Gn 2.7)
וְהָיָה לְאוֹת בְּרִית	It shall *be* a sign of a covenant (Gn 17.11)

    c. These functions can be combined when two words are introduced by ל—one indicates the new "owner", and the other the subject's new status.

וַתְּהִי־לוֹ לְאִשָּׁה	... and she became *his wife* (Ru 4.13); "a wife of his"
וַיְהִי־לָהּ לְבֵן	... and he became *her son* (Ex 2.10)
וְהֵמָּה יִהְיוּ־לִי לְעָם:	... and they shall be[come] *my people* (Jr 31.33)
הָיְתָה־חֶבְרוֹן לְכָלֵב בֶּן־יְפֻנֶּה הַקְּנִזִּי לְנַחֲלָה	Hebron became *the inheritance of* Caleb son of Jephuneh the Kenizzite (Jos 14.14)
אֲנַחְנוּ נִהְיֶה לַאדֹנִי לַעֲבָדִים:	We shall be[come] *my lord's slaves* (Gn 44.9)

15.4 Frequency

Some forms of היה—by far the most common verb in Biblical Hebrew (c. 3500x), are extremely frequent in the Bible:

הָיָה	*He was [became]*	3ms Q P	1022x
וְהָיָה	*He will be[come]*	3ms Q P + *waw*	776x
וַיְהִי	*He was*	3ms Q Pr	396x
יִהְיֶה	*He will be[come]*	3ms Q F	334x
יִהְיוּ	*They will be[come]*	3mp Q F	130x
יְהִי	*Let him [it] be[come]!*	3ms Q J	75x

15.5 Concepts

dynamic	intransitive	status, change of
fientive	static	transitive
	stative	

15.6 Vocabulary[132]

.213	אִם	*if, then;* אִם ... אִם ≈ *either ... or*	.221	מָלֵא	*be/become full* (st. vb.); *full* (adj.)
.214	גָּבַהּ	*be/become high, exalted* (st. vb.)	.222	מְעַט	*[a] few, little* (adj.)
.215	טָהֹר	*[ceremonially] clean, pure* (adj.)	.223	קָדֵשׁ	*be/become holy; restricted in use* (st. vb.)
	טָהֵר	*be/become [ceremonially] clean, pure* (st. vb.)[133]	.224	רָחַק	*be/become far, remote, distant* (st. vb.)
.216	טָמֵא	*be/become [ceremonially] unclean, impure* (st. vb.); *unclean, impure* (adj.)		רָחֹק	*far, remote, distant* (adj.)
.217	יָכֹל	*be able [to]* (st. vb., often with infinitive construct, §16.2.6c); *overcome, prevail (over)*	.225	קָרָא	*call, invite, summon; name; read; proclaim* [This overlaps with קרה (Lesson 21).]
.218	יָרֵא	*fear, be afraid of* (thing or person introduced by אֵת, מִפְּנֵי, מִן) (st. vb.)	.226	קָרוֹב / קָרֵב	*near, close* (adj.); *be/become near, close, approach* (st. vb.)
.219	כָּבֵד	*be/become heavy, severe; honored, wealthy* (st. vb.); *heavy, severe; etc.* (adj.)	.227	שָׁלֵם	*be/become whole, complete* (st. vb.)
.220	כִּי	*for, because; that; but; since, while; when, if* [N.B.: These glosses do not exhaust its function, but will suffice for the purposes of this grammar.]			

15.7 Exercises

When you have reviewed the forms and function of היה, gloss these clauses, parsing all verbal forms.

1. יהוה אֱלֹהַי גָּדַלְתָּ מְּאֹד   Ps 104.1b; מְאֹד *very, much*

2. וַיֹּאמֶר אַל־תִּקְרַב הֲלֹם   Ex 3.5; הֲלֹם *[to] here*

---

132. This list includes all stative verbs with strong verbal roots that occur fifty times or more in Biblical Hebrew. Stative verbs from other root types will be introduced later.

133. About one-half of the occurrences of both טהר and טמא are in Lv.

3. וְעֵלִי זָקֵן מְאֹד	1 Sam 2.22; Eli
4. וַיֹּאמֶר הִנֵּה־נָא זָקַנְתִּי לֹא יָדַעְתִּי יוֹם מוֹתִי׃	Gn 27.2; מוֹת is construct singular of מָוֶת
5. וַתִּטְמָא הָאָרֶץ וָאֶפְקֹד עֲוֹנָהּ עָלֶיהָ וַתָּקִא הָאָרֶץ אֶת־יֹשְׁבֶיהָ׃	Lv 18.25; וַתָּקִא *and it vomited* (3fs Pr); יֹשֵׁב *inhabitant* (ms Q Ptc)
6. וַיְהִי בַּיָּמִים הָהֵם וַיִּגְדַּל מֹשֶׁה	Ex 2.11; Moses
7. וְאַבְרָם כָּבֵד מְאֹד בַּמִּקְנֶה בַּכֶּסֶף וּבַזָּהָב׃	Gn 13.2; מִקְנֶה *property*; Abram
8. וַתִּקְרָא אִשָּׁה חֲכָמָה מִן־הָעִיר שִׁמְעוּ שִׁמְעוּ אִמְרוּ־נָא אֶל־יוֹאָב קְרַב עַד־הֵנָּה וַאֲדַבְּרָה אֵלֶיךָ׃ וַיִּקְרַב אֵלֶיהָ וַתֹּאמֶר הָאִשָּׁה הַאַתָּה יוֹאָב וַיֹּאמֶר אָנִי וַתֹּאמֶר לוֹ שְׁמַע דִּבְרֵי אֲמָתֶךָ וַיֹּאמֶר שֹׁמֵעַ אָנֹכִי׃	2 Sa 20.17; הַאַתָּה (2ms pronoun with interrogative -הֲ) *Is it you?*; אָמָה [female] servant; Joab [each line is a separate clause]
9. וַיֹּאמֶר לָהֶם פְּרוּ וּרְבוּ וּמִלְאוּ אֶת־הָאָרֶץ׃	Gn 9.1 (‖[134] Gn 1.28); פרה *be fruitful*; רבה *multiply* (both are 2mp Q imperative)

Locate all of the occurrences of וַיְהִי and וְהָיָה in Genesis 11.27–13.18, as well as any stative verbs, and identify their function.

15.8 Enrichment: Genesis 13.2

Since the 3ms *qal* perfect of stative verbs are identical in form to the masc. sing. adjective, the interpretation of some clauses is open to debate, with potentially significantly different interpretations. In Gn 13.2, for example, does כָּבֵד describe a state or condition, or is it a flashback to Gn 12.16? The three interpretations are all grammatically permissible:

	Now Abram *was* very wealthy (כבד as either 3ms *qal* perfect or ms adj.)
וְאַבְרָם כָּבֵד מְאֹד	Now Abram *became* very wealthy (כבד as 3ms *qal* perfect)
	Now Abram *had become* very wealthy (כבד as 3ms *qal* perfect)

There is probably not a great deal of difference in the long run—however we translate it, Abram was veru wealthy. The larger question is how this wealth affected his relationship with Lot, and thus we might want to get some idea of when the troubles between Lot's and Abram's shepherds may have begun.

Our interpretation of the events of Gn 12, and of the relationship between Gn 12 and 13, will affect how we read this clause. The verb can *only* be interpreted in reference to its clause and the larger context. Gn 12.16 says that however well-to-do Abram had been, his wealth greatly increased after Pharaoh took Sarai, which in turn suggests that Gn 13.2 is meant to remind the reader of what had happened in Egypt (Gn 12.16). This in turn suggests that the third option listed above—the past perfect—is the best in this context. We are here searching in the shadows between philology and interpretation, but its occurrence in a disjunctive clause also suggests a flashback to events before the immediately preceding preterite ("Abram went up from Egypt, …"; Gn 13.1).

---

134. A double vertical line (‖) means that two texts are identical (or nearly so), or else that they are parallel poetic lines.

Lesson 16

The Infinitives & Summary of Qal

Hebrew has two forms that are called "infinitives"—the *infinitive construct* (NC) and the *infinitive absolute* (NA). The names refer to whether or not the particular infinitive can occur with affixes; NC routinely occurs with prepositions and pronominal suffixes, whereas NA does not. The term is traditional but unfortunate, for two reasons: (1) their identity as infinitives does not depend on the presence of a preposition as does the infinitive in English ("to ..."); (2) their function overlaps with that of the English infinitive only occasionally. On the other hand, because they seem merely to name an action or event without further specification, they are genuinely "non-finite" in function.

16.1 *Form*

In nearly all verbs, NC (infinitive construct) is essentially identical to the 2ms imperative. The *qal* infinitive absolute (Q NA) has *qames* after the first radical and *holem* after the second radical. This chart lists 2ms *qal* imperfect and imperative for comparison.

	imperfect (2ms)	imperative (2ms)	infinitive construct	infinitive absolute
משׁל	תִּמְשֹׁל	מְשֹׁל	מְשֹׁל	מָשֹׁל
כתב	תִּכְתֹּב	כְּתֹב	כְּתֹב	כָּתֹב
שׁכב	תִּשְׁכַּב	שְׁכַב	שְׁכַב	שָׁכֹב
שׁמע	תִּשְׁמַע	שְׁמַע	שְׁמַע	שָׁמוֹעַ

16.1.1 *Infinitive Construct (NC): Function (HBI §2.2.6)*

1. Infinitives (NC & NA) are inflected for *stem*, but *not* for person, gender, or number. Instead, they use pronominal suffixes to indicate pronominal subjects ("he", "they"), or nouns to indicate nominal subjects; in some uses the subject is implied from the context.
2. If the subject is a *noun*, it follows the infinitive construct; if the subject is *pronominal* ("he", "they"), it is suffixed (almost every time a pronoun follows an infinitive construct, the infinitive is לֵאמֹר and the pronoun begins the direct quotation).
3. If NC has an *object*, the object may be suffixed (in which case the subject will be a noun), or it may follow the infinitive (in which case the subject may be either a suffix or noun). These clauses illustrate the possibilities:

בְּשָׁמְרוֹ	when *he* guards *or* that *he* may guard
בְּשָׁמְרוֹ אֶת־יַעֲקֹב	when *he* guards Jacob
וַיְהִי אַחֲרֵי קָבְרוֹ אֹתוֹ	After *he* buried *him* (1 Kgs 13.31)
לְלַמְּדָם מִלְחָמָה	to teach *them* war (Jg 3.2) [the pronominal object may be considered "indirect" in English]
וּכְשָׁמְעוֹ אֶת־דִּבְרֵי רִבְקָה אֲחֹתוֹ	and when *he* heard the words of Rebecca his sister (Gn 24.30)

4. NC often occurs with prepositions (as the above examples show); the preposition indicates the function of the subordinate clause. When NC occurs with a preposition *other than* לְ, it tends to be the predicate of a temporal [circumstantial] clause. In these cases its temporal reference—or "tense"—is relative to that of the main clause. Both prepositions -בְּ and -כְּ convey contemporaneous action (*when, while, as*); the temporal aspect depends on the preposition and the cotext.[135]

וְהָיָה כִּשְׁכַב אֲדֹנִי־הַמֶּלֶךְ עִם־אֲבֹתָיו	*When* my lord the king *sleeps* with his fathers, ... (1 Kg 1.21). [The future is indicated by introductory וְהָיָה.]
אַחֲרֵי קָבְרוֹ אֶת־אָבִיו:	... *after he buried* his father (Gn 50.14).
וַיְהִי כִּרְאֹת אֶת־הַנֶּזֶם	*When he saw* the gold ring ... and *when he heard* the words of Rebecca his sister (Gn 24.30).
וּכְשָׁמְעוֹ אֶת־דִּבְרֵי רִבְקָה אֲחֹתוֹ	[The past is indicated by introductory וַיְהִי.]

5. The prepositions that occur most frequently with infinitives are:

-בְּ	when, while	בְּדַבֵּר יִצְחָק אֶל־עֵשָׂו בְּנוֹ	*when* Isaac *spoke* to Esau his son (Gn 27.5)
-כְּ		כִּשְׁמֹעַ עֵשָׂו אֶת־דִּבְרֵי אָבִיו	*when* Esau *heard* his father's words (Gn 27.34)
-לְ	to	... לִשְׁמֹעַ אֵת חָכְמַת שְׁלֹמֹה	*to hear* Solomon's wisdom (1 Kgs 5.14)
	by [X]-ing	וְאִם תֵּלֵךְ בִּדְרָכַי לִשְׁמֹר חֻקַּי	And if you walk in my ways *by keeping* my statutes (1 Kgs 3.14)
אַחֲרֵי	after	אַחֲרֵי שְׁכַב־הַמֶּלֶךְ עִם־אֲבֹתָיו	*after* the king *slept* with his fathers (2 Kgs 14.22)
לִפְנֵי	before	לִפְנֵי בוֹא הַפָּלִיט	*before* the fugitives *came* (Ek 33.22)[136]

6. When the phrase בְּיוֹם (*in the day* [*that*]) precedes NC, it usually has the same contemporaneous function as the prepositions -בְּ and -כְּ (i.e., *when, while, as*), although it can also refer to a specific period of time (daylight, twenty-four hours, etc.). This sometimes affects our reading of the text—does Nu 30.9 mean that the husband must restrain his wife immediately ("*when* he hears"), or either before sundown or within the next twenty-four hours ("*on the day* that he hears")?

כַּאֲשֶׁר בְּיוֹם שָׁלַח אוֹתִי מֹשֶׁה	just as *when* Moses sent me (Jos 14.11)
בְּיוֹם בְּרֹא אֱלֹהִים אָדָם	... *when* God created them (Gn 5.1)
וְאִם בְּיוֹם שְׁמֹעַ אִישָׁהּ יָנִיא אוֹתָהּ	and if, *when* her husband hears, he restrains her, ... (Nu 30.9)

7. With a prefixed לְ, NC (infinitive construct) has four main functions (not all of these are *qal* NC):
   a. *telic* (purpose, result); this is always the case when it occurs with לְמַעַן, and often when it occurs with prefixed לְ:

וַיָּבֹאוּ מִכָּל־הָעַמִּים לִשְׁמֹעַ אֵת חָכְמַת שְׁלֹמֹה	They came from all the peoples *to hear* Solomon's wisdom (1 Kgs 5.14).
וַיִּשְׁלַח תֹּעִי אֶת־יוֹרָם־בְּנוֹ אֶל־הַמֶּלֶךְ דָּוִד לִשְׁאָל־לוֹ לְשָׁלוֹם וּלְבָרֲכוֹ עַל אֲשֶׁר נִלְחַם בַּהֲדַדְעֶזֶר	Toi sent Joram his son to King David *to ask* him for peace and *to bless him* because he had fought against Hadad-ezer (2 Sa 8.10).
... בְּגַן־עֵדֶן לְעָבְדָהּ וּלְשָׁמְרָהּ:	... in the garden of Eden *to serve* [*till*] it and *to guard* it (Gn 2.15)

---

135. This function is precisely analogous to the infinitive with prepositions in Greek.
136. The form לִפְנֵי is not common before infinitives construct.

b. *gerundive* (glossed as "by _____ ing"; the blank is filled by the infinitival verb)

שָׁמוֹר אֶת־יוֹם הַשַּׁבָּת לְקַדְּשׁוֹ   Keep the Sabbath day *by sanctifying* it (Dt 5.12); (the main verb is an imperatival infinitive absolute (16.1.2.1))

כִּי תִשְׁמַע בְּקוֹל יְהוָה אֱלֹהֶיךָ לִשְׁמֹר אֶת־כָּל־מִצְוֺתָיו   When you obey Yhwh your God *by keeping* all his commands (Dt 13.18)

c. *complementary*, completing or explaining a "vague verb" (יכל "be able", כלה "finish", חדל "cease", the *hifil* of יסף "do again, repeat". NC can have this function with or without -לְ. [In Jg 3.18 and Ru 1.18, English style suggests their gerundive gloss.]

... אִם־תּוּכַל לִסְפֹּר אֹתָם   ... if you are able *to count* them (Gn 15.5)

וַתֶּחְדַּל לְדַבֵּר אֵלֶיהָ:   She stopped *talking* to her (Ru 1.18); She ceased *to talk* ...

... כִּלָּה לְהַקְרִיב אֶת־הַמִּנְחָה   ... he finished *offering* the tribute (Jg 3.18)

d. *quotative frame*. The form לֵאמֹר (Q NC [*qal* infinitive construct] of אמר; trad., *saying*) is the most common infinitive construct in Biblical Hebrew, usually following verbs of speech *other than* אמר (although it does occur with אמר):

וַיַּעֲנוּ אֶת־יְהוֹשֻׁעַ לֵאמֹר   They answered Joshua, *saying*, "... (Jos 1.16)

וָאֶשְׁלְחָה עֲלֵיהֶם מַלְאָכִים לֵאמֹר   I *sent* messengers to them, *saying*, "... (Ne 6.3)

וַיְצַו בֹּעַז אֶת־נְעָרָיו לֵאמֹר   Boaz *commanded* his servants, *saying*, "... (Ru 2.15)

N.B.: Although -לְ occurs far more frequently with NC than any other preposition, and even though the -לְ is often glossed as "to", it is *not* the "sign of the infinitive" as the word "to" is in English. [In other words, "go" is not an English infinitive, but "to go" is.] In contrast, מְשֹׁל—*with or without* the prefixed -לְ is an infinitive construct.

8. NC is negated by either בִּלְתִּי or לְבִלְתִּי, expressing negative purpose or result, or a negated gerundive.

צִוִּיתִיךָ לְבִלְתִּי אֲכָל־מִמֶּנּוּ   ... I commanded you *not to eat* from it ... (Gn 3.11)

הִפְגִּעוּ בַמֶּלֶךְ לְבִלְתִּי שְׂרֹף אֶת־הַמְּגִלָּה   They pressed the king *not to burn* the scroll (Jr 36.25)

פֶּן־תִּשְׁכַּח אֶת־יהוה אֱלֹהֶיךָ לְבִלְתִּי שְׁמֹר מִצְוֺתָיו   ... lest you forget Yhwh your God *by not keeping* his commandments ... (Dt 8.11)

16.1.2 *Infinitive Absolute (NA): Function (HBI §2.2.7)*

"Absolute" means that no prefixes (e.g., prepositions) or suffixes are affixed to it except the conjunction *waw* (147x) and interrogative –הֲ (23x).

	infinitive construct	infinitive absolute
משל	מְשֹׁל	מָשׁוֹל
כתב	כְּתֹב	כָּתוֹב
שכב	שְׁכַב	שָׁכוֹב
שמע	שְׁמֹעַ	שָׁמוֹעַ

1. NA usually occurs in a clause with a finite form of the same verb. This makes it fairly easy to recognize, because there are *two forms of the same verbal root* in one clause. It apparently

focuses or strengthens the function of the main verb.[137] Its gloss depends on the function of the main verb (stem and conjugation) and the context.

מִכֹּל עֵץ־הַגָּן אָכֹל תֹּאכֵל׃ וּמֵעֵץ הַדַּעַת טוֹב וָרָע ... מוֹת תָּמוּת׃ — "From [any] tree of the garden you may *freely* eat, but from the tree of the knowledge of good and evil …, you shall *surely* die" (Gn 2.16–17)

אָמוֹר אָמַרְתִּי — "I *most certainly* said …" (1 Sam 2.30)

קָרֹעַ אֶקְרַע אֶת־הַמַּמְלָכָה מֵעָלֶיךָ — I will *certainly* tear the kingdom from you (1 Kgs 11.11)

2. When NA occurs alone, it serves as the main verb in its clause. When it does this, its function is equivalent to that of any conjugation, but is most often imperatival.

וַיֹּאמֶר מֹשֶׁה אֶל־הָעָם זָכוֹר אֶת־הַיּוֹם הַזֶּה — Moses said to the people, "*Remember* this day!" (Ex 13.3)

הָלֹךְ וְקָרָאתָ בְאָזְנֵי יְרוּשָׁלַ͏ִם — *Go* call in the ears of Jerusalem (Jr 2.2)

הָלוֹךְ וְרָחַצְתָּ ... וּטְהָר׃ — *Go* and wash … and *you will be clean* (2 Kgs 5.10)

3. Infinitive absolutes (NA) of two different verbal roots can occur side-by-side, especially NA of הלך, in the sense of continually or constantly.

וַיֵּלֶךְ דָּוִד הָלוֹךְ וְגָדוֹל — David *continued to grow strong* (2 Sam 5.10 [= 2 Ch 11.9]); grew stronger and stronger

... הָלוֹךְ וְתָקוֹעַ בַּשּׁוֹפָרוֹת׃ — … *continually blowing* the horns (Jos 6.9)

... וְעָלוּ עָלֹה וּבָכֹה׃ — … and they were *weeping as they went up* (2 Sam 15.30)

4. NA cannot be directly negated, although the main verb of its clause may be negated with לֹא or אַל.

16.2 *Summary of the Qal Stem*

It is helpful to think of verbal forms in Hebrew as containing certain "diagnostics" that help us identify the stem and form of the verb. The most basic of these are the PGN prefixes and endings for the perfect, imperfect (cohortative, jussive), preterite, and imperative. You must be able to identify these at sight.

Person	Gender	Perfect Sg.	Perfect Pl.	Imperfect Sg.	Imperfect Pl.	Imperative Sg.	Imperative Pl.
1st	common	תִּי -	נוּ -	א -	נ -		
2nd	masc.	תָּ -	תֶּם -	ת -	תּ - וּ -	---	וּ -
2nd	fem.	תְּ -	תֶּן -	תּ - י	תּ - נָה -	ִי -	נָה -
3rd	masc.	---	וּ -	י -	י - וּ -		
3rd	fem.	ָה -		תּ -	תּ - נָה -		

Since the PGN affixes are common to all stems and types of verbal root, they do not enable us to distinguish a verb's stem (which often affects or determines the verb's function). It is instead the vowels that "attach" the subject [PGN] prefixes to the verbal root and the vowel after the second radical that are the primary diagnostic of the verb's stem. We will address this as we encounter each stem (Lessons 18–21).

---

137. The vagueness of this statement reflects the generally vague understanding that biblical scholars have of the significance and function of NA in such cases.

16.2.1 *The Qal Stem*

The sign of the *qal* are the *a*-vowels of the perfect, the (occasional) *holem* of the imperfect, imperative, and infinitive construct, and the *holem* and *šureq* of the *qal* active and passive participles. In imperfect and preterite, the primary signal that a verb is *qal* is the **ḥireq under the prefix**.

The **primary diagnostic for the *qal*** is therefore **negative**: **no prefix or doubling** in the **perfect, imperative, participle**, and **infinitives**, and **ḥireq** as the prefix vowel in the **imperfect (cohortative, jussive)**, and **preterite**. This paradigm summarizes the *qal*. [See also the full paradigm in Appendix D.]

Conjugation	PGN	Fientive Verbs	Stative Verbs
Perfect	3ms	מָשַׁל	כָּבֵד
Imperfect	3ms	יִמְשֹׁל	יִכְבַּד
Preterite	3ms	וַיִּמְשֹׁל	וַיִּכְבַּד
Imperative	[2]ms	מְשֹׁל	כְּבַד
Inf. Const.		מְשֹׁל	כְּבֹד
Inf. Abs.		מָשׁוֹל	כָּבֹד
Ptc. (active)	ms	מֹשֵׁל	
Ptc. (passive)	ms	מָשׁוּל	

1. *Qal* perfects tend to have *a*-vowels; *qal* imperfects and preterites tend to have *o*- or *a*-vowels.
2. The prefix vowel in *qal* imperfect and preterite is *ḥireq*.
3. The "stem" or "theme" vowel (*qal* imperfect, preterite, imperative, infinitives) is either *holem* (fientive roots) or *pataḥ* (stative roots); this only appears when there is no ending or a consonantal ending.
4. *Qal* active participle is nearly the only verbal form with *holem* after the first radical.
5. *Qal* passive participle is the only verbal form with a *u*-vowel between the second and third radicals.
6. *Qal* is the only stem that lacks both a stem prefix (perfect, imperative, infinitives, & participle), and a doubled middle radical. [The significance of this will become clear as we study the other stems.]

16.2.2 *The Conjugations*

We have now reviewed all of the conjugations of the Hebrew verb, as they appear in the *qal* stem of the strong verb. How are the functions of these conjugations related?

1. The *perfect* (P) and *preterite* (Pr) are *complementary*. The predicate of an "interruptive" disjunctive clause may be in the perfect. The predicate of the disjunctive clause may also be either participial or non-verbal, in which case the clause contains background information about the setting. This is one way in which Biblical Hebrew shows a "flashback"—an event that happened before the story—or compares the actions or situations of two characters.
2. The *imperfect* (F) and *w + perfect* (w + P) are *complementary*. If a disjunctive clause "interrupts" the w + perfect chain of instructions, commands, or predictions, the predicate of the disjunctive clause will usually be in the imperfect, signaling that the event is secondary to the main line of the instructions, etc.
3. *Infinitives* construct (NC) are either *circumstantial* (often after וַיְהִי) or *complementary*, filling out "vague verbs", *telic* (showing purpose or result), or else they function as *gerunds*. They may do this after any finite conjugation (imperfect, preterite, perfect, imperative). Infinitives absolute appear to modify the function of the main verb; if the clause lacks a main verb, their function must be determined by context.
4. Participles (Ptc) are functionally *adjectives*, modifying or functioning as nouns, although they occasionally occur with a form of היה, apparently as a way of saying that someone "was doing" something.

5. The conjugations can occur with various affixes [in addition to the subject (PGN)]:

This conjugation ...	can be combined with ...			
	conjunction w-	article	prepositions	pronominal suffixes
imper**F**ect	yes	no	no	yes
Preterite	always	no	no	yes
imperati**V**e	yes	no	no	yes
Perfect	yes	no	no	yes
Participle	yes	yes	yes	yes
i**N**finitive **C**onstruct	yes	no	yes	yes
i**N**finitive **A**bsolute	yes	no	no	no

a. Thus any verbal form with an article, for example, is a participle; a conjunction-less verb cannot be preterite, etc.
b. "Yes" does *not* mean "always".
c. "Always" means "always".
d. "No" means "never".

16.3 *Frequency*

More than one-tenth (11%) of all verbs in Biblical Hebrew are infinitives (6985 occurrences in Biblical Hebrew), but infinitives construct (9%) are far more common than infinitives absolute (1%).

16.4 *Concepts*

circumstantial clause   infinitive absolute   temporal clause
gerundive   infinitive construct   vague verb

16.5 *Vocabulary*

open (vb.)	פָּתַח	.236	there is/are not (opp. 317); no; וְאֵין often ≈ without	אֵין אַיִן	.228
innocence (§2.4/3); righteousness	צְדָקָה	.237	not (adv.); except, unless (cj.) us. מִבְּלְתִּי or לְבִלְתִּי	בַּל בִּלְתִּי	.229
north	צָפוֹן	.238	wine	יַיִן	.230
abundance, multitude, great quantity	רֹב	.239	right (hand, side); cf. Ben*jamin* ("son of my right hand"); south	יָמִין	.231
chase, persecute, pursue	רָדַף	.240	seat, throne	כִּסֵּא	.232
rejoice, be glad	שָׂמַח	.241	number, total	מִסְפָּר	.233
hate	שָׂנֵא	.242	dwelling; Tabernacle	מִשְׁכָּן	.234
break, smash, shatter	שָׁבַר	.243	assembly (trad. "congregation")	עֵדָה	.235

16.6 Exercises

After learning the forms of the *qal* infinitives construct and absolute, and reviewing the *qal* system, *gloss* these clauses, *parsing* the verbs. Remember that infinitives have no PGN; if they have a pronominal suffix, it is identified by PGN in the "suffix" column.

1. 2 Sam 15.10; מְרַגֵּל *spy* (here *secret messengers*); שֹׁפָר *ram's horn*; Absalom; Hebron

    וַיִּשְׁלַח אַבְשָׁלוֹם מְרַגְּלִים בְּכָל־שִׁבְטֵי יִשְׂרָאֵל לֵאמֹר
    כְּשָׁמְעֲכֶם אֶת־קוֹל הַשֹּׁפָר
    וַאֲמַרְתֶּם מָלַךְ אַבְשָׁלוֹם בְּחֶבְרוֹן׃

2. Gn 37.8; interrogative –הֲ; when followed by אִם, the two clauses express alternatives (real or hypothetical)

    וַיֹּאמְרוּ לוֹ אֶחָיו הֲמָלֹךְ תִּמְלֹךְ עָלֵינוּ
    אִם־מָשׁוֹל תִּמְשֹׁל בָּנוּ

3. Gn 3.24; וַיַּשְׁכֵּן *he caused to dwell*; מִקֶּדֶם *[to the] east of*; גַּן *garden*; Eden; חַיִּים *life*

    וַיַּשְׁכֵּן מִקֶּדֶם לְגַן־עֵדֶן אֶת־הַכְּרֻבִים
    ... לִשְׁמֹר אֶת־דֶּרֶךְ עֵץ הַחַיִּים׃

4. Qo 3.6, 8; הַשְׁלִיךְ *throw away* (*hifil* of שׁלך)

    עֵת לִשְׁמוֹר וְעֵת לְהַשְׁלִיךְ׃
    עֵת לֶאֱהֹב וְעֵת לִשְׂנֹא
    עֵת מִלְחָמָה וְעֵת שָׁלוֹם׃

5. Jr 45.1; דִּבֶּר *he said*; Jeremiah, Baruch, Neraiah

    הַדָּבָר אֲשֶׁר דִּבֶּר יִרְמְיָהוּ הַנָּבִיא אֶל־בָּרוּךְ
    בֶּן־נֵרִיָּה בְּכָתְבוֹ אֶת־הַדְּבָרִים הָאֵלֶּה
    עַל־סֵפֶר מִפִּי יִרְמְיָהוּ

6. Ex 15.26; this is not a complete sentence

    וַיֹּאמֶר אִם־שָׁמוֹעַ תִּשְׁמַע לְקוֹל יְהוָה אֱלֹהֶיךָ ...

7. Pr 6.22; שׁכב *lie down*; [the subject of תִּשְׁמֹר (3fs) is "Wisdom"]

    בְּשָׁכְבְּךָ תִּשְׁמֹר עָלֶיךָ

8. 1 Sam 24.21

    יָדַעְתִּי כִּי מָלֹךְ תִּמְלוֹךְ

9. Jos 14.7; בֶּן־אַרְבָּעִים שָׁנָה *40 years old*; רגל *to spy* (D); Moses, Kadeš Barnea

    בֶּן־אַרְבָּעִים שָׁנָה אָנֹכִי בִּשְׁלֹחַ מֹשֶׁה עֶבֶד־יְהוָה אֹתִי
    מִקָּדֵשׁ בַּרְנֵעַ לְרַגֵּל אֶת־הָאָרֶץ

10. 2 Ch 24.1; בֶּן־שֶׁבַע שָׁנָה *7 years old*; Joash

    בֶּן־שֶׁבַע שָׁנִים יֹאָשׁ בְּמָלְכוֹ

11. Dt 6.17 [the *nun* on תִּשְׁמְרוּן does not affect its function]

    שָׁמוֹר תִּשְׁמְרוּן אֶת־מִצְוֹת יְהוָה

12. 1 Sa 8.7; מאס *reject, spurn; refuse*; the second כִּי *but*

    כִּי לֹא אֹתְךָ מָאָסוּ
    כִּי־אֹתִי מָאֲסוּ מִמְּלֹךְ עֲלֵיהֶם׃

13. 1 Sam 23.15; וַיַּרְא *and he saw* (3ms Q Pr < ראה); יצא *go out*; בקשׁ *seek*; David, Saul

    וַיַּרְא דָוִד כִּי־יָצָא שָׁאוּל לְבַקֵּשׁ אֶת־נַפְשׁוֹ

14. Gn 41.49; עַד + כִּי *until*; חדל *stop, cease*

    עַד כִּי־חָדַל לִסְפֹּר כִּי־אֵין מִסְפָּר׃

15. רַק חֲזַק לְבִלְתִּי אֲכֹל הַדָּם כִּי הַדָּם הוּא הַנָּפֶשׁ   תֹּאכַל (2ms Q F); רַק only; Dt 12.23
     וְלֹא־תֹאכַל הַנֶּפֶשׁ עִם־הַבָּשָׂר׃

16. וּמָכֹר לֹא־תִמְכְּרֶנָּה בַּכָּסֶף   מָכַר -רֶנָּה 3fs suffix); רָנָה sell; Dt 21.14

17. וַיֹּאמֶר יוֹאָב אֶל־הַמֶּלֶךְ הֹבַשְׁתָּ הַיּוֹם   2 Sam 19.6–7; הֹבַשְׁתָּ you have shamed;
     אֶת־פְּנֵי כָל־עֲבָדֶיךָ לְאַהֲבָה אֶת־שֹׂנְאֶיךָ   both NCs are gerundive ("by ___ing")
     וְלִשְׂנֹא אֶת־אֹהֲבֶיךָ

16.7 Enrichment: Gerundive Infinitives Construct

As the functions outlined above suggest, not all infinitives construct are created equal. In Deuteronomy 10.12, for example, the first infinitive construct, *to fear*, presents the basic response of the Israelites, whereas the next three—*by walking ... loving ... serving*—expound what "fear" means in this covenantal context:

וְעַתָּה יִשְׂרָאֵל	Therefore, Israel,
מָה יהוה אֱלֹהֶיךָ שֹׁאֵל מֵעִמָּךְ	what does Yhwh your God ask from you
כִּי אִם־לְיִרְאָה אֶת־יהוה אֱלֹהֶיךָ	but *to fear* Yhwh your God
לָלֶכֶת בְּכָל־דְּרָכָיו	*by walking* in all his ways
וּלְאַהֲבָה אֹתוֹ	and *by loving* him,
וְלַעֲבֹד אֶת־יהוה אֱלֹהֶיךָ	and *by serving* Yhwh your God
בְּכָל־לְבָבְךָ וּבְכָל־נַפְשֶׁךָ׃	with all of your heart and all of your being (Dt 10.12).

Lesson 17

Questions, Negatives, Numerals

This lesson addresses three syntactical and functional topics: (1) explicit and implicit questions; (2) negated clauses (at which we have already glanced under the topic of "irrealis" (§6, §6.11, §10.3); and (3) numerals. Combining these in one lesson does not mean that they are unimportant. Numerals occur in nearly 3000 verses (and not just in genealogies and the book of Numbers!), and there are more than 6000 negated statements and nearly 900 explicit questions.

17.1 Asking Questions

Biblical Hebrew asks questions in two basic ways. *Explicit* questions begin with an interrogative form, such as an interrogative pronoun or adverb, or the interrogative particle -הֲ. *Implicit* questions—which are much less common—are required or suggested by the context. Unlike English, Biblical Hebrew has no question mark.

17.1.1 Interrogative Adverbs

1. Biblical Hebrew has a number of interrogative adverbs, which can ask about location, direction ("where"), reason ("why"), or manner ("how"). Since a good many questions in Biblical Hebrew are rhetorical—asked not to gain information, but to make a point (e.g., Gn 4.9; Ps 42.4, 10)—the line between questions and exclamations is often blurred (e.g., אֵיךְ in Is 14.11 and 2 Sam 1.5).

לָמָה לָמָּה	Why?	178x	לָמָה שְׁכַחְתָּנִי	*Why* have you forgotten me?
			לָמָּה־קֹדֵר אֵלֵךְ	*Why* do I go about mourning? (Ps 42.10)
מַדּוּעַ	Why?	72x	מַדּוּעַ אֲדֹנִי בֹכֶה	*Why* is my master weeping? (2 Kgs 8.12)
אֵיךְ אֵיכָה	How? Why? How!	61x	אֵיךְ נָפַלְתָּ מִשָּׁמַיִם	*How* you have fallen from heaven! (Is 14.11)
			אֵיךְ יָדַעְתָּ כִּי־מֵת שָׁאוּל	*How* do you know that Saul is dead? (2 Sam 1.5)
			אֵיכָה יָשְׁבָה בָדָד הָעִיר	*How* the city sits solitary, …! (La 1.1)
אַיֵּה	Where [is]?	56x	אַיֵּה אֱלֹהֶיךָ׃	*Where* is your God (Ps 42.4)
אָן אָנָה	[To] where?	42x	אָנָה אַתָּה הֹלֵךְ	"*Where* are you going?" (Zc 2.6)
אֵי	Where?	31x	אֵי הֶבֶל אָחִיךָ	*Where* is Abel, your brother? (Gn 4.9)
עַד אָנָה	How long?	11x	עַד־אָנָה תְּמַלֶּל־אֵלֶּה	*How long* will you say these things (Jb 8.2)
אֵי־מִזֶּה	From where?	9x	לֹא יָדַעְתִּי אֵי מִזֶּה הֵמָּה׃	I did not know *where* they were *from* (1 Sam 25.11)

17.1.2 Interrogative -הֲ

The interrogative particle -הֲ introduces "yes-no" questions by being *prefixed* to the *first* word of a direct or indirect question.[138]

הֲכֶלֶב אָנֹכִי	Am I a dog? (1 Sam 17.43)
הַעֶבֶד יִשְׂרָאֵל	Is Israel a slave/servant? (Jr 2.14)
הֲשֹׁמֵר אָחִי אָנֹכִי:	Am I my brother's keeper? (Gn 4.9)
וַהֲלוֹא עִמְּךָ שָׁם צָדוֹק וְאֶבְיָתָר	And are not Zadok and Abiathar there with you? (2 Sam 15.35)

2. The vowel under the interrogative -ה varies according to the first letter of the word to which it is attached:

Interrogative	If the word begins with ...	Example	
-הֲ	any non-guttural followed by a full vowel	הֲשָׁמְרָה	Did she keep watch?
-הַ	any guttural followed by a vowel other than *qameṣ* or *qameṣ ḥatuf*,	הַעֶבֶד	Is a servant ...?
	or any non-guttural followed by a half-vowel	הָאֱלֹהִים	Did God ...?
-הֶ	any guttural followed by *qameṣ* or *qameṣ ḥatuf*	הֶאָנֹכִי	Am I ...?

3. The compound form הֲלוֹא (-הֲ + לֹא) introduces a *negative rhetorical* question—that is, a question that assumes a positive answer. These might be represented with or without a "tag question" in English (e.g., "Am I not Yʜᴡʜ?" versus "I'm Yʜᴡʜ, aren't I?"), or even "indeed". The question's cotext (literary context) and content determine which might be more appropriate).

הֲלֹא אָנֹכִי יְהוָה:	Am I not Yʜᴡʜ? (Ex 4.11)
הֲלוֹא אָנֹכִי אֲתֹנְךָ	"Am I not your she-donkey, ...?" (Nu 22.30)
הֲלֹא יְהוָה אֱלֹהֵיכֶם עִמָּכֶם	Is not Yʜᴡʜ your God with you? (2 Chr 22.18)

4. *Polar questions*—"yes/no" questions that pose a choice between opposites—end with אִם לֹא ("... or not" questions; e.g., Jg 2.22), introduce each choice with interrogative –הֲ (Nu 13.18b), or end with אִם followed by an adjective (Nu 13.18c).

לְמַעַן נַסּוֹת בָּם אֶת־יִשְׂרָאֵל	... in order to test Israel by them—
הֲשֹׁמְרִים הֵם אֶת־דֶּרֶךְ יְהוָה	*whether* they will observe the way of Yʜᴡʜ
... אִם־לֹא:	... or not (Jg 2.22).
וּרְאִיתֶם אֶת־הָאָרֶץ מַה־הִוא	and see the land, what it is,
וְאֶת־הָעָם הַיֹּשֵׁב עָלֶיהָ	and the people who live in it
הֶחָזָק הוּא הֲרָפֶה	—*whether* they are strong *or* weak,
הַמְעַט הוּא אִם־רָב:	[whether they are] few or many (Nu 13.18).

5. *Implicit questions* are not marked (interrogative –הֲ occurs only 746x). Some questions are semi-explicit, introduced by a verb such as שָׁאַל, "he asked", but most must be recognized from the context, which means that there is often disagreement about whether or not a

---

138. It is preceded twice by the conjunction -וְ (2 Sa 15.35; Zc 3.1).

particular clause is a question or a statement. In 1 Ch 22.18, David exhorts the leaders of
Israel by asking a rhetorical question (introduced by הֲלֹא). Does the force of the interrogative carry over to the next clause or not? It can be read either way:

הֲלֹא יהוה אֱלֹהֵיכֶם עִמָּכֶם	*Is not* YHWH your god with you?
וְהֵנִיחַ לָכֶם מִסָּבִיב	*And has he not given* you rest all around? *or*
	And he has given you rest all around (1 Ch 22.18).

Nor does the rest of the sentence ("for he has given into my hand the inhabitants of the land, and the land has been subjugated before YHWH and his people.") answer the question, since it fits both readings.

17.2 *Negatives*

Biblical Hebrew has three main negative clause-level adverbs—לֹא, אַל, אֵין/אַיִן—as well as a number of relatively infrequent negatives (e.g., בִּלְתִּי, Lesson 16). These largely and usually negate the clause in which they occur.

1. The adverbs לֹא and אַל negate clauses.

וְלֹא שָׁמְעוּ אֶל־מֹשֶׁה	... but they *did not listen* to Moses (Ex 6.9)
וְיִרְאַת יהוה לֹא בָחָרוּ	... but the fear of YHWH they *did not choose* (Pr 1.29)
לֹא־קָרָאתִי בְנִי	I *did not call*, my son ... (1 Sam 3.6)
וַיֹּאמֶר יְהוֹשָׁפָט אַל־יֹאמַר כֵּן:	Jehoshaphat said, "The king *should not say* so" (1 Kgs 22.8)

2. לֹא and אַיִן can also occur in single-element statements as "No", when the rest of the sentence is understood from the context:

וְאָמַר הֲיֵשׁ־פֹּה אִישׁ וְאָמַרְתְּ אָיִן:	"... and he says, 'Is there a man here?', you shall say, '*No*'." (Jg 4.20)
וַיֹּאמְרוּ לֹא כִּי בָרְחוֹב נָלִין	They said, "*No*. Instead/But, we will spend the night in the square" (Gn 19.2).

3. אֵין negates non-verbal clauses as "There is/was not/no". When it negates a participle, its subject is often a pronominal suffix. When the participle itself is the subject, וְאֵין can function like "without ..." (Lv 26.36).

אֵין כָּמֹנִי בְּכָל־הָאָרֶץ	*There is none* like me in all the earth (Ex 9.14)
כַּאֲשֶׁר אֵינְךָ יוֹדֵעַ מַה־דֶּרֶךְ הָרוּחַ	Just as you *do not* know what the way of the spirit is (Qo 11.5)
וְנָפְלוּ וְאֵין רֹדֵף:	... and they will fall *without* a pursuer (Lv 26.36)

4. וְאֵין also occurs with nouns and participles in the sense of "there is no one who" or "without":

וְאֵין־פּוֹתֵר אוֹתָם לְפַרְעֹה:	... but *there was no* interpreter of them for Pharaoh (Gn 41.8);
	... *no one* to interpret them ...
וְאֵין מוֹשִׁיעַ:	... but *there will be no* [*without a*] deliverer (Dt 28.29)
אֵין יוֹצֵא וְאֵין בָּא:	*No one* went out *and no one* went in (Josh 6.1)

5. אֵין occurs with the possessive preposition לְ to indicate that someone "does not have" something. The לְ is prefixed to the person who "does not have":

וּבֵן אֵין־לוֹ	... and *he had no* son (Dt 25.5)
וְאִם־אֵין לָאִישׁ גֹּאֵל	but if the man *has no* "redeemer, ..." (Nu 5.8)

17.3 Numerals

Like English, Hebrew has two sets of numerals, *cardinal* (e.g., "one", "two", "three") and *ordinal*, which identify *order* (e.g., "first", "second", "third").

17.3.1 Cardinal Numerals

Cardinal numerals are words that refer to the amount or quantity of something ("*ten* years", "*thirty* shekels").

"One" – "Ten"			"Tens"	
"Masculine"	"Feminine"			
אֶחָד	אַחַת	one		
שְׁנַיִם	שְׁתַּיִם	two (the initial *šewa* is silent in the feminine)		
שָׁלֹשׁ	שְׁלֹשָׁה	three	שְׁלֹשִׁים	thirty
אַרְבַּע	אַרְבָּעָה	four	אַרְבָּעִים	forty
חָמֵשׁ	חֲמִשָּׁה	five	חֲמִשִּׁים	fifty
שֵׁשׁ	שִׁשָּׁה	six	שִׁשִּׁים	sixty
שֶׁבַע	שִׁבְעָה	seven	שִׁבְעִים	seventy
שְׁמֹנֶה	שְׁמֹנָה	eight	שְׁמֹנִים	eighty
תֵּשַׁע	תִּשְׁעָה	nine	תִּשְׁעִים	ninety
עֶשֶׂר	עֲשָׂרָה	ten	עֶשְׂרִים	twenty (plural of "ten")

1. Apart from "one" and "two", the main difference between the masculine and feminine forms is the "feminine ending" (ה-).
2. When the feminine forms occur in the construct, the final ה- is replaced by ת- (as in nouns); e.g., עֲשֶׂרֶת / עֲשָׂרָה.
3. The numeral "one" usually follows the noun that it modifies and agrees with it in gender and definiteness. If there is no noun, it functions like an indefinite "one" in English, often with the article.

בְּנֵי אִישׁ־אֶחָד נָחְנוּ	We are the sons of *one* man [*a* man] (Gn 42.11)
תּוֹרָה אַחַת לָהֶם	They [shall] have *one* law (Lv 7.7)
הַכֹּל הוֹלֵךְ אֶל־מָקוֹם אֶחָד	Everything goes to *one* place (Qo 3.20)
שֵׁם הָאֶחָד פִּישׁוֹן	The name of [the] *one* was Pishon (Gn 2.11)

4. The numeral that signals "two" can either precede or follow its noun, which is in the plural. If it precedes, it is in construct, but does not mean "two of ...". "Two" also occurs with pronominal suffixes:

עַמּוּדִים שְׁנַיִם	*two* pillars (2 Chr 3.15)
וְאֵת שְׁנֵי בָנֶיהָ	... and her *two* sons (Ex 18.3)
וַיֹּאמֶר יְהוָה לָהּ שְׁנֵי גוֹיִם בְּבִטְנֵךְ	YHWH said to her, "*Two* nations are in your womb" (Gn 25.23)
וַיֹּאכְלוּ שְׁנֵיהֶם יַחְדָּו	The *two of them* ate together (Jg 19.6)

5. The numerals that represent "three" through "ten" *disagree* in *gender* with the noun that they modify.

שְׁלֹשָׁה אֵלֶּה בְּנֵי־נֹחַ	These *three* were Noah's sons (Gn 9.19)
חֲמִשָּׁה שְׁקָלִים כָּסֶף	*five* shekels of silver (Lv 27.6)

6. Hundreds & thousands:

מֵאָה	100
מָאתַיִם	200 (dual ending)
שְׁלֹשׁ מֵאוֹת	300
...	etc.
אֶלֶף	1,000
אַלְפַּיִם	2,000 (dual ending)
שְׁלֹשֶׁת אֲלָפִים	3,000
...	etc.
רִבּוֹת / רְבָבָה	10,000
רִבּוֹתַיִם	20,000 (dual ending)
שְׁלֹשׁ רִבּוֹת	30,000
...	etc.

7. #6 (above) illustrates how Hebrew forms compound numerals (e.g., "thirteen", "ninety-nine", "one hundred forty-two"): numerals are either juxtaposed or linked with the conjunction וְ. Determining whether to multiply or add large numerals is contextual.

כָּל־נֶפֶשׁ אַרְבָּעָה עָשָׂר	*fourteen* people in all (Gn 46.22)
שֵׁשׁ מֵאוֹת עֶשְׂרִים וְאֶחָד	621 (Ez 2.26)
שִׁשָּׁה וְאַרְבָּעִים אֶלֶף וַחֲמֵשׁ מֵאוֹת	46,500 (Nu 1.21)

8. The preposition -כְּ occurs with numerals in the sense of "approximately" or "about":

כְּאַרְבַּע מֵאוֹת אִישׁ:	*about* four hundred men (1 Sam 22.2)
כְּעֶשֶׂר שָׁנִים	*about* ten years (Ru 1.4)

9. *Age* is usually indicated by the phrase "the *son of X years*":

וְאַבְרָם בֶּן־חָמֵשׁ שָׁנִים וְשִׁבְעִים שָׁנָה	Now Abram was *seventy-five years old* ... (Gn 12.4)
בֶּן־שְׁמֹנֶה שָׁנָה יֹאשִׁיָּהוּ בְמָלְכוֹ	Josiah was *eight years old* when he became king (2 Kgs 22.1)

17.3.2 Ordinal Numerals

Ordinal numberals are adjects that tell the *order* in which something occurred. Apart from the words for "first", they are generally formed by adding ִי - to the cardinal forms. Ordinal numerals are not inflected for gender:

רִאשׁוֹן	*first* (cf. רֵאשִׁית, *beginning*; רֹאשׁ, *head*)
אֶחָד	*first* (occasionally)
שֵׁנִי	*second*
שְׁלִישִׁי	*third*
רְבִיעִי	*fourth* (cf. אַרְבַּע)
חֲמִישִׁי	*fifth*
שִׁשִּׁי	*sixth*
שְׁבִיעִי	*seventh*
שְׁמִינִי	*eighth*
תְּשִׁיעִי	*ninth*
עֲשִׂירִי	*tenth*

1. The ordinals function as attributive adjectives, following their noun and agreeing with it in gender, number, and (usually) definiteness:

   וַיְהִי בַּיּוֹם הַשְּׁבִיעִי   On the *seventh* day ... (Josh 6.15)
   וּבַיּוֹם הָרְבִיעִי פָּרִים עֲשָׂרָה   On the *fourth* day, ten bulls, ... (Nu 29.23)
   אֲנִי רִאשׁוֹן וַאֲנִי אַחֲרוֹן   I am *the first* and I am *the last* (Is 44.6)

2. Ordinals only function from "first" to "tenth"; beyond "tenth", Biblical Hebrew uses cardinal numerals:

   וַיַּעֲשׂוּ אֶת־הַפֶּסַח   They made [celebrated] the Passover in the
   בָּרִאשׁוֹן בְּאַרְבָּעָה עָשָׂר יוֹם לַחֹדֶשׁ   *first* [month] on the *fourteenth* day of the month (Nu 9.5).
   בִּשְׁנַת שְׁתֵּים עֶשְׂרֵה לְאָחָז   In the *twelfth* year of Ahaz ... (2 Kgs 17.1)

17.4 Concepts

cardinal numeral	non-verbal clause	polar question
interrogative	negation	rhetorical question
	ordinal numeral	

17.5 Vocabulary

nine	תֵּשַׁע	.252	one (m., f.)	אֶחָד אַחַת	.244
ten	עֶשֶׂר עֶשֶׂר	.253	two (m., f.)	שְׁנַיִם שְׁתַּיִם	.245
twenty	עֶשְׂרִים		second (ord.; m., f.)	שֵׁנִי שֵׁנִית	
hundred	מֵאָה	.254	three	שָׁלֹשׁ	.246
two hundred	מָאתַיִם				
thousand	אֶלֶף	.255	four	אַרְבַּע	.247
two thousand	אַלְפַּיִם				
first (ord.)	רִאשׁוֹן	.256	five	חָמֵשׁ	.248
first; beginning (n.)	רֵאשִׁית	.257	six	שֵׁשׁ	.249
half	חֲצִי	.258	seven	שֶׁבַע	.250
shekel (approx. 11.4 g, 0.5 oz.)	שֶׁקֶל	.259	eight	שְׁמֹנָה	.251

17.6 Exercises

You will find numerals for the populations of the tribes of Israel in the following verses. Fill in the name of each tribe and its population at the beginning and end of the wandering in the wilderness.

N.B.: The order of two tribes is reversed in Nu 26.

Num 1	Tribe	Population	Num 26	Population
1.21	ראובן		26.7	43,730
1.23			26.14	
1.25			26.18	
1.27			26.22	
1.29		54,400	26.25	
1.31	זבולן		26.27	
1.33			26.37	
1.35			26.34	
1.37			26.41	
1.39			26.43	64,400
1.41	אשר	41,500	26.47	
1.43			26.50	
1.46			26.51	601,730

These verses contain numerals for ages, numbers of people (census lists), etc. Gloss the clauses, transmogrifying the numerals.

a. Gn 5.27; Methusaleh

וַיִּהְיוּ כָּל־יְמֵי מְתוּשֶׁלַח תֵּשַׁע וְשִׁשִּׁים שָׁנָה וּתְשַׁע מֵאוֹת שָׁנָה

b. Gn 7.24; גבר *prevail;* the sign *sof pasuq* [׃] marks the "end of the verse"

וַיִּגְבְּרוּ הַמַּיִם עַל־הָאָרֶץ חֲמִשִּׁים וּמְאַת יוֹם׃

c. Ex 23.12; תַּעֲשֶׂה *you shall do* (2ms Q F < עשה); מַעֲשֶׂה *work, deed;* שׁבת *rest*

שֵׁשֶׁת יָמִים תַּעֲשֶׂה מַעֲשֶׂיךָ וּבַיּוֹם הַשְּׁבִיעִי תִּשְׁבֹּת

d. Ex 24.18b; Moses

וַיְהִי מֹשֶׁה בָּהָר אַרְבָּעִים יוֹם וְאַרְבָּעִים לָיְלָה׃

e. 2 Sam 5.4–5; חֹדֶשׁ *month, new moon;* David, Hebron, Jerusalem, Israel, Judah; each line is a clause

בֶּן־שְׁלֹשִׁים שָׁנָה דָּוִד בְּמָלְכוֹ
אַרְבָּעִים שָׁנָה מָלָךְ׃
בְּחֶבְרוֹן מָלַךְ עַל־יְהוּדָה שֶׁבַע שָׁנִים וְשִׁשָּׁה חֳדָשִׁים
וּבִירוּשָׁלַ͏ִם מָלַךְ שְׁלֹשִׁים וְשָׁלֹשׁ שָׁנָה עַל כָּל־יִשְׂרָאֵל וִיהוּדָה׃

f. Nu 11.19; the second form of יוֹם is dual (i.e., *two days*); the final *nun* on "you shall eat" is not (yet) explained

לֹא יוֹם אֶחָד תֹּאכְלוּן וְלֹא יוֹמָיִם וְלֹא חֲמִשָּׁה יָמִים
וְלֹא עֲשָׂרָה יָמִים וְלֹא עֶשְׂרִים יוֹם׃

Gloss these clauses and sentences, *parsing* the verbal forms.

a. Nu 14.41; לָמָה זֶה *why?;* Moses

וַיֹּאמֶר מֹשֶׁה לָמָּה זֶּה אַתֶּם עֹבְרִים אֶת־פִּי יְהוָה

b. Jr 3.14

וְלָקַחְתִּי אֶתְכֶם אֶחָד מֵעִיר וּשְׁנַיִם מִמִּשְׁפָּחָה

c. Is 44.6; כֹּה *thus;* גֹּאֵל *redeemer* (Q Ptc); מִבַּלְעֲדֵי *apart from, except for, without* (+ 1cs suffix); אַחֲרוֹן *last;* Israel; the second line is a quotation

כֹּה־אָמַר יְהוָה מֶלֶךְ־יִשְׂרָאֵל וְגֹאֲלוֹ יְהוָה צְבָאוֹת
אֲנִי רִאשׁוֹן וַאֲנִי אַחֲרוֹן וּמִבַּלְעָדַי אֵין אֱלֹהִים׃

d. 2 Kgs 10.34; יֶתֶר *[the] rest, remainder;* עשה *do;* גְּבוּרָה *strength, power;* Jehu

וְיֶתֶר דִּבְרֵי יֵהוּא וְכָל־אֲשֶׁר עָשָׂה וְכָל־גְּבוּרָתוֹ
הֲלוֹא־הֵם כְּתוּבִים עַל־סֵפֶר דִּבְרֵי הַיָּמִים
לְמַלְכֵי יִשְׂרָאֵל׃

17.7 Enrichment: Irrealis

If a story is a record of events—a record of "what happened"—why do authors tell their readers that some events did *not* occur? What does negative information (*irrealis*) add to a story?

> As Lydia walked down the street, she saw a dog tied in front of a house. The dog barked and lunged at her, breaking its rope. Suddenly realizing that it was free, it ran after her, but *did not bite her*.

In this admittedly simple illustration, the negative clause (in *italics*) tells the reader something that is *contrary to expectation*. We probably expect that a barking dog that breaks loose and chases someone intends to attack that person, but this dog did not, contrary to our expectation (and, perhaps, to our experience). In fact, in this example, the last (negative) statement also leads us to conclude that the dog caught her, since if it did not, the *irrealis* would not make sense (if the dog didn't catch her, it couldn't have bitten her).

But what if the story read:

> As Lydia walked down the street, she saw a dog tied in front of a house. The dog barked and lunged at her, breaking its rope. Suddenly realizing that it was free, it chased her, but Lydia ran inside *before the dog could catch her*.

In this case the negative information is that the dog did not catch her (most readers would probably infer that if the dog had caught her, it would have attacked her). The *irrealis* is given obliquely and implicitly, in a "privative" clause (related to the root of the word "de*prive*"), rather than in a negative statement. Furthermore, if we rewrite the last clause so that it reads merely "... but Lydia ran safely inside", we would not need the clause in italics, since the word "safely" implies that the dog did not catch her.[139]

In the beginning of the story of Abram, we find a number of *irrealis* clauses:

וַתְּהִי שָׂרַי עֲקָרָה אֵין לָהּ וָלָד׃   And Sarai was barren—she had *no child* (Gn 11.30)

This is one of the precipitating crises of the Abram story—his lack of an heir—set over against the divine promise of descendants (e.g., Gn 12.2; 13.16). Since we are told this at the very beginning of the stories about Abram, we might suspect that this will become an important theme in what follows.

In 1 Sa 3.1b, the author uses a form of *irrealis* to warn readers against mis-reading the preceding incident (the prophetic announcement of Yʜᴡʜ's judgment upon Eli's house). This prophecy follows Eli's word to Hannah (1.17), which might encourage us to think that prophetic revelation was relatively commonplace in Israel at that time. As the opening of 1 Sa 3 shows, however, that was not true:

וּדְבַר־יהוה יָקָר בַּיָּמִים הָהֵם   Now Yʜᴡʜ's word was rare in those days;
אֵין חָזוֹן נִפְרָץ׃   there was *no vision* breaking through (1 Sa 3.1b).

This double statement not only warns against misinterpreting the prophetic activity of the preceding chapter as a normal occurrence, but also helps to set the stage for the restoration of prophetic revelation through Samuel (which is the story of 1 Sa 3).

---

139. There is another type of irrealis, which we might call "semantic", or "positive", irrealis in which a non-negated verb describes a non-event. In Lv 10.3, Aaron's response to Moses' speech was silence: וַיִּדֹּם אַהֲרֹן, *and Aaron was silent*, i.e., Aaron did not speak. This raises a host of complex questions about the relationship between positive and negative statements that are better left for another course of study. Note that in this case, the author does not tell us what Aaron actually did.

Part III

Lessons 18–31
Verbal Grammar (II)
Reading Hebrew

This section introduces the forms and functions of the other stems of the verb, the other ["weak"] forms of the verbal root, as well as the basic tools of Biblical Hebrew (the Hebrew Bible and lexica), and the basic steps of beginning to read biblical narrative and poetry.

By the end of these lessons (the end of the book), you should be able to recognize and read nominal phrases with some fluency, as well as recognize a number of fairly standard forms and formulae at sight. You should also be able to identify all of the forms of the verbal stems and roots.

Depending on your teacher and the goals of your course of study, you will have begun to read from the biblical text, and to discuss how to use your knowledge of Hebrew to study the biblical text.

Lesson 18

OTHER STEMS

Verbal function is primarily modified in English by syntax, using various types of pronouns (e.g., reflexive), "helping verbs", prepositions, etc., as illustrated by the differences between the following sentences:

(1) John *hid*.
(2) John *hid* himself.
(3) John *hid* the ball.
(4) The ball *was hidden* by John.
(5) John *made* Jim *hide* the ball.
(6) John *caused* Jim *to hide* the ball.

Since most readers or speakers of English assume that "hide" without an expressed object is reflexive (the subject hides himself or herself), they will read or hear sentences (1) and (2) as essentially identical—the "reflexive" pronoun (2) merely clarifies the meaning of (1). Sentence (3)—which also uses "hid", the same form of the verb as in (1) and (2)—shows an entirely different relationship between the subject ("John") and the object ("the ball"). Sentences (4), (5), and (6) are morphologically and syntactically different from the others; (5) and (6), like (1) and (2), are functionally identical.

18.1 *The Concept of "Stem"*

Where English uses helping verbs, prepositions, and syntax to indicate verbal nuances, ("David hid the sword", "David hid [himself]", "David was hidden [by Samuel]"), Hebrew modifies the shape of the verb itself, using prefixes,[140] different sets of vowels, and a doubled middle radical in patterns which are called "stems" or *binyanim* ("buildings"). These combinations are traditionally called the "derived" stems because the early grammarians viewed *qal* as the basic ("simple") stem, from which these stems were "derived". Although the vowel patterns and forms of the stems differ, the PGN affixes and the functions of the conjugations are the same in all stems. In these examples, the verbs have different stems:

וַיִּמְלְכוּ בְדַמֶּשֶׂק	they *reigned* in Damascus (1 Kgs 11.24)	3mp *qal* preterite
וַיַּמְלִיכוּ אֶת־אֲבִימֶלֶךְ לְמֶלֶךְ	they *made* Abimelek *king* (Jg 9.6) ["caused" Abimelek to be king]	3mp *hifil* preterite
הֲלֹא מִסְתַּתֵּר עִמָּנוּ	Is not David *hiding* with us? (1 Sam 23.19)	ms *hitpael* ptc[141]
וְלֹא נִסְתְּרוּ מִלְּפָנָי	They *are not hidden* from me (Jr 16.17)	3cp *nifal* perfect
כְּבֹד אֱלֹהִים הַסְתֵּר דָּבָר	The glory of God is *to hide* a matter (Pr 25.2)	*hifil* inf. const.

There are eight basic verbal patterns in Biblical Hebrew,[142] but more than two-thirds of all verbal forms in the Bible are *qal*, and three of the main stems (*hitpael*, *pual*, *hofal*) occur fairly infrequently (less than 3% of all verbal forms). Furthermore, only two verbs occur in all eight stems (ten occur in the seven stems not including *qal* passive),[143] and most occur in various combinations of two to four stems.

140. These are combined with the PGN prefixes of the imperfect (below).
141. This example demonstrates "metathesis", in which two letters change places (a normal occurrence in the *hitpael* when the verbal root begins with a *sibilant* ("s-sound"). The root is סתר, one of a relatively few verbal roots that occur in these three stems.
142. The existence of the eighth stem—the *qal* passive—has been suspected for several centuries, but not confirmed until relatively recently.
143. Not including *qal* passive (Lesson 21).

18.1.1 The Names of the Stems

The stems have been given various names through the centuries, following changes in academic fashion, or the individual grammarian's convictions. The traditional names, except for the *qal*, are the 3ms perfect form of the verb פָּעַל, "do, make", which was the original verb for Hebrew paradigms. The early Hebrew grammarians used פעל because the Arabic grammarians used *fa'ala* as their paradigm verb, and the early Jewish grammarians based their study of Hebrew grammar upon that of the Arabs. It is no longer used as the paradigm verb for Biblical Hebrew because ע does not double in Hebrew (as it does in Arabic).

Since the mid-18th century, the study of the Semitic languages has shown that Hebrew is only one of a family of related languages, including Akkadian, Ugaritic, and Coptic, as well as various Aramaic dialects and Arabic. In order to use terminology that reflects the relationship of Hebrew to, for example, Akkadian, scholars have developed what might be called "pan-Semitic" names for the stems. These names reflect the distinguishing aspect of that stem that is shared by some or all of the Semitic tongues. This grammar will use the "Semitic" designations for the stems as a sort of shorthand, but will always refer initially to both sets of terms.

N.B.: The standard Hebrew-English lexica use the traditional names of the stems, so you will want to know both sets of terms.

3ms Perfect	Traditional Name	"Pan-Semitic" Name	Stem Prefix Vowels		Doubled II-radical?
פָּעַל	Qal	G (the *Grund-*, or "basic", stem)			---
נִפְעַל	Nifal	N (*n*-prefix)	-נִ	-הִ	---
פִּעֵל	Piel	D ("doubled")			yes
פֻּעַל	Pual	Dp (passive of D)			yes
הִתְפַּעֵל	Hitpael	Dt (D with t-infix)	-הִת	-יִת	yes
הִפְעִיל	Hiphil	H (*h*-prefix)	-הִ	-יַ	---
הָפְעַל	Hophal	Hp (passive of H)	-הָ	-יָ	---

The name of the stem which we have studied thus far—the *qal* (from the verb קלל)—means "light", because it lacks a stem prefix (unlike N, Dt, H, Hp) and does not have a doubled radical (unlike D, Dp, Dt).

18.1.2 The Paradigm Verb

Hebrew grammarians turned from פעל to קטל, "kill", as a paradigm verb, since it has no *bᵉgad-kᵉfat* letters (and thus no appearing and vanishing *dageš lene*s), and no gutturals (thus no *ḥatef*-vowels). קטל, however, occurs only three times in Biblical Hebrew (Ps 139.19; Jb 13.15; 24.14), which is rather rare for a "model" verb.[144]

Today, different grammars use different verbal roots as their "model" verb. Since the root משל meets the requirements of a paradigm verb (three "strong" radicals, no gutturals or *reš*, and the first radical is a non-sibilant), we will continue to use it as our paradigm verb. It occurs in only a few stems (which means that most of the listed forms do not exist in Biblical Hebrew), but is fairly frequent in Biblical Hebrew (99x).

18.1.3 The Functions of the Stems

The nuances [the plural is deliberate] of a verb's function in different stems must be determined for each verbal root, but there are some overall tendencies. For example, if a verb is fientive (active) in

---

144. Transliterated as *qtl*, however, it appears in one of the sets of names for the verbal conjugations: *qatal* (perfect), *yiqtol* (imperfect, jussive), *wayyiqtol* (preterite), &c.

the *qal*, it will probably be passive in *nifal*. On the other hand, a verb that occurs in *nifal* but not in *qal* usually "sounds" active when glossed in English.

Qal	tends to be either fientive or stative
Nifal	tends to be the passive of *qal* (or *piel*); if there is no *qal* or *piel*, it tends to be reflexive or reciprocal
Piel	fientive, and nearly always transitive; if *qal* is stative, *piel* is often causative
Pual	passive of *piel*
Hitpael	its nuances are difficult to classify, but are usually passive or double-status (reflexive, reciprocal, etc.)
Hifil	causative of *qal* and *nifal*
Hofal	passive of *hifil*

The stems thus correspond in a *very rough* and *approximate* way to the concept of voice (active, middle, reflexive, passive, etc.) in English.

N.B.: Although the vowel patterns and forms of the stems differ, the PGN affixes of each conjugation (perfect, imperfect, etc.) are the same in all stems as those learned for the *qal*, as are also the functions of the various conjugations.

18.2 *The N-Stem (Nifal)*

The name *nifal* comes from the 3ms perfect in the traditional paradigm verb (נִפְעַל). The primary difference between *nifal* and *qal* is a **prefixed** נ (hence its "Semitic" name, "N"). This נ is visible (orthographic) in the perfect and participle, but assimilates ("nunnates", see §7.2) to the first radical whenever it is followed by silent *šewa*. This means that in every conjugation except the perfect and participle a diagnostic for the *nifal* is a **doubled first radical** preceded by a ***ḥireq*** (under the prefix) and followed by ***qameṣ***. These examples illustrate this process (∗ = hypothetical form):

∗*yinmāšel*	∗*yimmāšel*	יִמָּשֵׁל	3ms N F
∗*hinmāšᵉlû*	∗*himmāšᵉlû*	הִמָּשְׁלוּ	2mp N V

18.2.1 *Form*

***Conjugations with orthographic* [written] -נ**
In the *nifal* perfect and participle, the prefixed *nun* is visible at the beginning of the verbal form.

***Nifal* Perfect**

Person	Gender	Singular	Plural
1st	Common	נִמְשַׁלְתִּי	נִמְשַׁלְנוּ
2nd	Masc.	נִמְשַׁלְתָּ	נִמְשַׁלְתֶּם
	Fem.	נִמְשַׁלְתְּ	נִמְשַׁלְתֶּן
3rd	Masc.	נִמְשַׁל	נִמְשְׁלוּ
	Fem.	נִמְשְׁלָה	

1. Every form of the *nifal* perfect begins with -נִ, followed by a silent *šewa* after the first radical.
2. Every form with no ending or a consonantal ending has *pataḥ* after the second radical.
3. 3ms N P looks just like the 1cp Q F of some verbs, especially statives (e.g., dB;k.nI, "we shall be wealthy"); they can be distinguished by their context.
4. All PGN affixes are the same in all stems.

Nifal Participle

Gender	Singular	Plural
Masc.	נִמְשָׁל	נִמְשָׁלִים נִמְשָׁלֵי
Fem.	נִמְשָׁלָה	נִמְשָׁלוֹת

1. Every form begins with נִ- (nun+ḥireq), and has silent šewa after the first radical and qameṣ after the second radical.
2. The qameṣ after the second radical distinguishes the ms and fs participle from 3ms and 3fs perfect.

Conjugations without orthographic נִ-

The prefixed נִ- appears only in the *nifal* perfect and participle. The other conjugations of the *nifal* have three characteristics in common:

1. The **prefix vowel** is *ḥireq* in all forms.
2. The first radical is **doubled** in all forms, since the *nun* assimilates to the first radical of the verbal root.
3. The doubled **first radical** is followed by *qameṣ*.

If there is no PGN ending, the vowel after the second radical is often *ṣere*, which is thus a secondary diagnostic. *Nifal* preterite is identical to the imperfect (with the prefixed -וַ and *dageš forte* in the PGN prefix).

Nifal Prefix Conjugations

		Imperfect (= Preterite)	
Person	**Gender**	**Singular**	**Plural**
1st	Common	אֶמָּשֵׁל	נִמָּשֵׁל
2nd	Masc.	תִּמָּשֵׁל	תִּמָּשְׁלוּ
	Fem.	תִּמָּשְׁלִי	תִּמָּשַׁלְנָה
3rd	Masc.	יִמָּשֵׁל	יִמָּשְׁלוּ
	Fem.	תִּמָּשֵׁל	תִּמָּשַׁלְנָה

Like *hifil, hofal,* and *hitpael* (H, Hp, Dt, below), but unlike *qal, nifal* imperative and infinitives have a prefix. They thus resemble the imperfect, with ה- instead of the PGN prefix.

Nifal Imperative

Person	Gender	Singular	Plural
2nd	Masc.	הִמָּשֵׁל	הִמָּשְׁלוּ
	Fem.	הִמָּשְׁלִי	הִמָּשַׁלְנָה

The infinitive absolute occurs in two forms; most verbal roots tend to use one form or the other. As in all stems, the infinitive construct is the same as 2ms imperative.

Nifal Infinitives

NC הִמָּשֵׁל
NA הִמָּשֹׁל
    נִמְשֹׁל

18.2.2 Summary of Nifal Diagnostics

This chart summarizes the main clues for identifying a *nifal* form.

Conjugation	Diagnostic	Example	Parsing
Perfect	נִ -	נִכְבַּד	3ms N P
Participle	נִ -	נִכְבָּדִים	mp N Ptc
Imperfect	יִ - ָ	יִכָּרֵת	3ms N F
	תִּ - ָ	תִּמָּשַׁלְנָה	2fp N F
Preterite	וַיִּ - ָ	וַיִּכָּתֵב	3ms N Pr
Imperative & Infinitives	הִ - ָ	הִבָּרֵא	N NC
		הִבָּרְאוּ	mp N V

1. All forms of the *nifal* have a prefix, and most have *hireq* as a prefix vowel (like *qal* imperfect and preterite, *hifil* perfect, and all forms of the *hitpael*). The exception to this is I-guttural roots, which have *ṣere* (below). *Nifal* and *qal* are the only stems that use *hireq* as their prefix vowel (except for *hifil* perfect, which has other distinguishing features).
2. All forms of the *nifal* except perfect and participle begin with the same pattern: prefix+*hireq*-*dageš forte* in first radical+*qameṣ*. This pattern occurs only in *nifal*.
3. Compare *nifal* and *qal* in this skeleton paradigm:

Conjugation	PGN	Qal		Nifal	
Perfect	3ms	מָשַׁל	he ruled	נִמְשַׁל	he was ruled
Imperfect	3ms	יִמְשֹׁל	he shall rule	יִמָּשֵׁל	he shall be ruled
Preterite	3ms	וַיִּמְשֹׁל	he ruled	וַיִּמָּשֵׁל	he was ruled
Imperative	2ms	מְשֹׁל	Rule!	הִמָּשֵׁל	Be ruled!
Inf. Const.		מְשֹׁל	to rule	הִמָּשֵׁל	to be ruled
Inf. Abs.		מָשׁוֹל		הִמָּשֵׁל	
				נִמְשֹׁל	
Participle	ms	מֹשֵׁל	one who rules	נִמְשָׁל	one who is ruled

18.2.3 Function of the Nifal (HBI §2.1.3)

1. The *nifal* is primarily the **passive** and **reflexive** of the active stems (*qal*, *piel*, *hifil*). Note the difference between the active (2 Kgs 21.26; *qal*) and passive (2 Kgs 21.18; *nifal*) of קבר, "bury":

וַיִּקְבֹּר אֹתוֹ בִּקְבֻרָתוֹ בְּגַן־עֻזָּא	He *buried* him [Manasseh] in his tomb in Uzzah's garden,
וַיִּמְלֹךְ יֹאשִׁיָּהוּ בְנוֹ תַּחְתָּיו׃	and Josiah his son reigned in his place (2 Kgs 21.26).
וַיִּשְׁכַּב מְנַשֶּׁה עִם־אֲבֹתָיו	And Manasseh slept with his fathers,
וַיִּקָּבֵר בְּגַן־בֵּיתוֹ בְּגַן־עֻזָּא	and he *was buried* in the garden of his palace, in Uzzah's garden.
וַיִּמְלֹךְ אָמוֹן בְּנוֹ תַּחְתָּיו׃	And Amon his son ruled in his place (2 Kgs 21.18).

2. The sign of the object may precede the *subject* of a passive *nifal*, apparently since the subject is affected by the action of the verb:

וַיִּוָּלֵד לַחֲנוֹךְ אֶת־עִירָד   Irad *was born* to Enoch (Gn 4.18).

N.B.: Unlike English (or NT Greek), passive clauses in Hebrew rarely identify or mention who or what did the action described by the verb (the agent or the means). We do not know if the passive was used *in order to* avoid naming the doer of the deed or if, having decided to use a passive, the author was constrained by the rules of Hebrew syntax so that he could not name the actor. This is true of all passives in Biblical Hebrew, not merely of the *nifal*.

3. When the *nifal* is **adjectival**, it can be glossed by words ending in "-ible", "-able", "-ful", "-some". This function, sometimes called "potential" is common with stative verbs.

| מִכָּל־הָאֹכֶל אֲשֶׁר יֵאָכֵל | Any of the food which *may be eaten* [is ceremonially *edible*] ... (Lv 11.34) [3 ms N F] |
| שָׂרִים רַבִּים וְנִכְבָּדִים מֵאֵלֶּה | leaders more numerous and *honorable* than these (Nu 22.15) [ms N Ptc] |

4. *Nifal* also has a variety of "**double-status**" nuances, in which the subject both does the action described by the verb and is affected by its own action. These functions are variously called generally "reflexive", "middle", "reciprocal", or "tolerative" (depending on the verbal root), and often sound active when glossed into English (the third verb in Gn 19.17 is a passive *nifal*).

הִמָּלֵט עַל־נַפְשְׁךָ ...	"*Escape* for your life ... to the hill country
הָהָרָה הִמָּלֵט פֶּן־תִּסָּפֶה:	so that you are not [lest you be] *swept away*" (Gn 19.17).
וְנִסְתַּרְתָּ בְּנַחַל כְּרִית	... and *hide* at the Wadi Cherith (1 Kg 17.3)
יהוה יִלָּחֵם לָכֶם	Yhwh *will fight* for you (Ex 14.14).

18.3 Frequency

The *nifal* occurs 4,140 times in the Bible (6% of all verbal forms); it is more frequent in the latter prophets and poetic books than in Genesis – 2 Kings.

18.4 Concepts

| active | middle | reciprocal | tolerative |
| double-status | passive | reflexive | |

18.5 Vocabulary

still, yet, again; לֹא עוֹד, *no longer, not [never] again*	עוֹד	.269	*or* (cj.)	אוֹ	.260
[whole] burnt offering	עֹלָה	.270	*light* (n.)	אוֹר	.261
now [at this time]	עַתָּה	.271	*only, surely* (adv.)	אַךְ	.262
"therefore" (esp. when followed by a volitional form cf. §8.6)	וְעַתָּה		*wise, skilled* (adj.)	חָכָם	.263
shepherd (Q Ptc)	רֹעֶה	.272	*court, enclosure, settlement*	חָצֵר	.264
joy, rejoicing, gladness	שִׂמְחָה	.273	*therefore* (לְ + כֵּן); not usually followed by a volitional form)	לָכֵן	.265
sun	שֶׁמֶשׁ	.274	*for the sake of, on account of* (prp.); *in order that/to* (cj.)	לְמַעַן	.266
judge (Q Ptc)	שֹׁפֵט	.275	*very, exceedingly* (adv.); *power, might* (n.)	מְאֹד	.267
			find; be found (N)	מָצָא	.268

18.6 Distribution of the Stems

The occurrence of the stems varies widely, as this table shows. Slightly more than two-thirds of all verbal forms in Biblical Hebrew are *qal*.[145]

Stems	Occurrences	% of Total
Qal[146]	49847	67.4%
Qal Passive	1277	1.7%
Nifal	4125	5.6%
Piel	6879	9.3%
Pual	450	0.6%
Hitpael	1177	1.6%
Hifil	9671	13.1%
Hofal	531	0.7%
Total	**73957**	

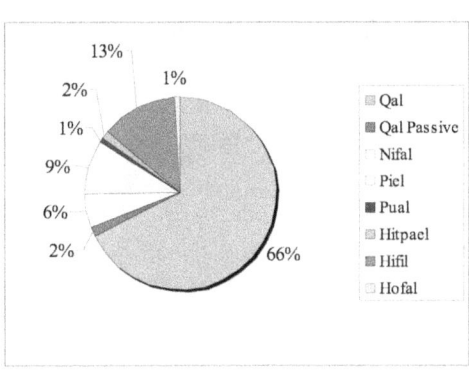

18.7 Exercises

After studying the characteristics of the *nifal*, *gloss* these sentences and clauses, *parsing* the verbs, which contain both *qal* and *nifal* forms.

1. וַיִּקָּבֵר בְּקֶבֶר יוֹאָשׁ אָבִיו — Jg 8.32; קֶבֶר *tomb of*; Joash

2. וְהַחָכְמָה מֵאַיִן תִּמָּצֵא ... וְלֹא תִמָּצֵא בְּאֶרֶץ הַחַיִּים: — Jb 28.12a ... 13b; מֵאַיִן *[from] where?*; חַיִּים *life, living* ("wisdom" is the subject of the clause)

3. אִם־הִמָּצֵא תִמָּצֵא בְיָדוֹ הַגְּנֵבָה ... — Ex 22.3; בְיָדוֹ *in his hand*; גְּנֵבָה *stolen thing*

4. וְאִם־לֹא יִגָּאֵל בְּאֵלֶּה וְיָצָא בִּשְׁנַת הַיֹּבֵל הוּא וּבָנָיו עִמּוֹ: — Lv 25.54; יִגָּאֵל *he/it will be redeemed*; אֵלֶּה *these* [means of redemption]; יצא *go out*; יוֹבֵל *Jubilee*

5. וְלָקַח אֶת־כָּל־הַזָּהָב־וְהַכֶּסֶף וְאֵת כָּל־הַכֵּלִים הַנִּמְצְאִים בֵּית־יְהוָה וּבְאֹצְרוֹת בֵּית הַמֶּלֶךְ — 2 Kg 14.14; וְלָקַח *and he took*; אֹצְרָה *storehouse*

6. נָפְלָה בָבֶל וַתִּשָּׁבֵר — Jr 51.8; Babylon

7. אֵלֶּה תוֹלְדוֹת הַשָּׁמַיִם וְהָאָרֶץ בְּהִבָּרְאָם — Gn 2.4; תּוֹלְדוֹת *generations*; ברא *create*

8. וַאֲרוֹן אֱלֹהִים נִלְקָח — 1 Sa 4.11 [-ֲ is due to *hatef-patah* under -אֲ, not to preterite]

9. כָּל־הַנִּמְצָא כָּתוּב בַּסֵּפֶר — Dn 12.1

10. כִּי יְהוָה אֹהֵב מִשְׁפָּט וְלֹא־יַעֲזֹב אֶת־חֲסִידָיו לְעוֹלָם נִשְׁמָרוּ וְזֶרַע רְשָׁעִים נִכְרָת: — Ps 37.28; חָסִיד *pious, godly, kind* (each line is a clause)

---

145. Statistics vary from source to source. Statistics in this book are based on Dean Forbes & Francis I. Andersen, *Vocabulary of the Old Testament* (Rome: Pontifical Biblical Institute, 1975).

146. Some of *qal*'s relative frequency reflects some common verbs (היה, אמר), but verbs that occur in *qal* and other stems tend to occur most frequently in *qal*.

Zc 9.10b; קֶשֶׁת bow; וְדִבֶּר he will speak (3ms D P+w); אֶפֶס end; מָשָׁל dominion, rule, realm (each line is a clause)	11. וְנִכְרְתָה קֶּשֶׁת מִלְחָמָה וְדִבֶּר שָׁלוֹם לַגּוֹיִם וּמָשְׁלוֹ מִיָּם עַד־יָם וּמִנָּהָר עַד־אַפְסֵי־אָרֶץ:
Ne 13.1; קרא read; יָבוֹא he may enter (3ms Q F); קהל assembly; Moses, Ammonite(s), Moabite(s)	12. בַּיּוֹם הַהוּא נִקְרָא בְּסֵפֶר מֹשֶׁה בְּאָזְנֵי הָעָם וְנִמְצָא כָּתוּב בּוֹ אֲשֶׁר לֹא־יָבוֹא עַמֹּנִי וּמוֹאָבִי בִּקְהַל הָאֱלֹהִים עַד־עוֹלָם:
Ps 139.16; -לָ = כֹּל with suffixes	13. וְעַל־סִפְרְךָ כֻּלָּם יִכָּתֵבוּ
1 Sa 1.13 ("her" refers to Hannah)	14. וְקוֹלָהּ לֹא יִשָּׁמֵעַ
Gn 9.11; מַבּוּל flood (only used of "Noah's flood" and in Ps 29.10); שׁחת destroy (D); the speaker is Yhwh	15. וְלֹא־יִכָּרֵת כָּל־בָּשָׂר עוֹד מִמֵּי הַמַּבּוּל וְלֹא־יִהְיֶה עוֹד מַבּוּל לְשַׁחֵת הָאָרֶץ:
2 Kg 22.13; בְּעַד on behalf of; עַל concerning, about	16. דִּרְשׁוּ אֶת־יְהוָה בַּעֲדִי וּבְעַד־הָעָם וּבְעַד כָּל־יְהוּדָה עַל־דִּבְרֵי הַסֵּפֶר הַנִּמְצָא הַזֶּה ... עַל אֲשֶׁר לֹא־שָׁמְעוּ אֲבֹתֵינוּ עַל־דִּבְרֵי הַסֵּפֶר הַזֶּה
Ps 34.19a	17. קָרוֹב יְהוָה לְנִשְׁבְּרֵי־לֵב
Nu 9.13	18. וְנִכְרְתָה הַנֶּפֶשׁ הַהִוא מֵעַמֶּיהָ
1 Kg 2.10	19. וַיִּשְׁכַּב דָּוִד עִם־אֲבֹתָיו וַיִּקָּבֵר בְּעִיר דָּוִד:
1 Sa 4.22; אִי no; גלה depart	20. וַתִּקְרָא לַנַּעַר אִי־כָבוֹד לֵאמֹר גָּלָה כָבוֹד מִיִּשְׂרָאֵל כִּי נִלְקַח אֲרוֹן הָאֱלֹהִים:
Ps 37.17; זְרוֹעַ arm (fem.); סמך [to] support [Each line is a clause.]	21. כִּי זְרוֹעוֹת רְשָׁעִים תִּשָּׁבַרְנָה וְסוֹמֵךְ צַדִּיקִים יְהוָה:

18.8 Enrichment: Nifal vs. Hitpael?

A much-debated point of interpretation in Genesis pits the *nifal* and *hitpael* (Lesson 19) against each other—the translation of these verses has even been made a test of the orthodoxy of English translations. In Yhwh's covenant with Abraham, Isaac, and Jacob, the divine promise of widespread blessing is repeated five times—three times using the *nifal*, twice with the *hitpael*:

... and in you all the clans of the earth *shall be blessed* (Gn 12.3b) [N]	... וְנִבְרְכוּ בְךָ כֹּל מִשְׁפְּחֹת הָאֲדָמָה:
... and in you all the clans of the earth *shall be blessed* and in your seed (Gn 28.14) [N]	... וְנִבְרְכוּ בְךָ כָּל־מִשְׁפְּחֹת הָאֲדָמָה וּבְזַרְעֶךָ:
... and in him all nations of the earth *shall be blessed* (Gn 18.18) [N]	... וְנִבְרְכוּ בוֹ כֹּל גּוֹיֵי הָאָרֶץ
... and in your seed all nations of the earth *shall bless themselves* (Gn 22.18) [Dt]	... וְהִתְבָּרְכוּ בְזַרְעֲךָ כֹּל גּוֹיֵי הָאָרֶץ
... and in your seed all nations of the earth *shall bless themselves* (Gn 26.4) [Dt]	וְהִתְבָּרְכוּ בְזַרְעֲךָ כֹּל גּוֹיֵי הָאָרֶץ:

The usual approaches to this apparent conundrum assume that all five statements repeat the same promise. They therefore either (1) assign priority to the *hitpael* forms of the promise, claiming that the promise is *middle/reflexive* ("shall bless themselves" i.e., by invoking the name of Abraham—"May you be blessed [*or* May YHWH bless you] as he blessed Abraham!"); (2) claim that all five statements are *passive* ("shall be blessed in/through Abram"), since that is the primary function of the *nifal*; (3) suggest that there is no real difference between the two forms of the promise.

The first interpretation tends to deny that the *hitpael* can be passive; the second seeks to demonstrate that passivity is a normal function of the *hitpael* (as above). The third refuses to assign priority to one or the other.

Perhaps instead of choosing one of these interpretations as *the* "correct" intent of the divine promise, we should conclude that its different forms were intended to be complementary, and they record what are in fact two separate but interlinked promises. The promise(s) could mean that "clans/nations of the earth shall *be blessed* through the divine covenant with Abraham" (Abraham as a channel or means of blessing), and "shall *bless themselves* by or in Abraham" (invoking Abraham's blessings on oneself or someone else). This approach allows the different stems to reflect two different—but related—outcomes of YHWH's prior promise to bless and exalt Abram.

This example illustrates the importance of examining the context(s) within which a verbal root occurs in different stems, and of assuming that morphological differences are intentional and functional, rather than being merely arbitrary, stylistic, or mistaken.

Lesson 19

THE D-STEMS (*PIEL*, *PUAL*, *HITPAEL*)

Piel, *pual*, and *hitpael* are also called "D-stems", since they all have a ***doubled*** (or "geminated") **middle radical**. This *dageš forte* is the primary diagnostic of the D-stems. Like *qal*—but unlike *nifal*—D and Dp have no prefix in the imperative and infinitives; Dt (*hitpael*) always has an orthographic prefix. Further, these stems are relatively stable in form, since the first syllable of the root is closed due to the doubled middle radical.

Many verbs that occur in one or more D-stems also occur in *qal*. The function of the two sets of forms (Q & D) may not be related, just as the functions of *nifal* and *qal* are not necessarily related. Each verbal root-stem combination must be analyzed and evaluated on its own terms, on the basis of its occurrences and use(s) in the biblical text. There is no "pure" or "absolute" one-to-one relationship between them.

The main difference between *piel* and *pual*—in fact, the only difference in many forms—is the vowel under the first radical. If it is a *i*- or *a*-vowel (*hireq* or *patah*) the verb is *piel*; if it is an *o*- or *u*-vowel (*qibbuṣ* or *ḥolem*), it is *pual*. All forms of *hitpael* has a closed prefix syllable (e.g., -מִתְ, -יִתְ, -הִתְ).

19.1 *Form*

Perfect

	Person	Gender	D	Dp	Dt
Singular	1st	Common	מִשַּׁלְתִּי	מֻשַּׁלְתִּי	הִתְמַשַּׁלְתִּי
	2nd	Masc.	מִשַּׁלְתָּ	מֻשַּׁלְתָּ	הִתְמַשַּׁלְתָּ
		Fem.	מִשַּׁלְתְּ	מֻשַּׁלְתְּ	הִתְמַשַּׁלְתְּ
	3rd	Masc.	מִשֵּׁל	מֻשַּׁל	הִתְמַשֵּׁל
		Fem.	מִשְּׁלָה	מֻשְּׁלָה	הִתְמַשְּׁלָה
Plural	1st	Common	מִשַּׁלְנוּ	מֻשַּׁלְנוּ	הִתְמַשַּׁלְנוּ
	2nd	Masc.	מִשַּׁלְתֶּם	מֻשַּׁלְתֶּם	הִתְמַשַּׁלְתֶּם
		Fem.	מִשַּׁלְתֶּן	מֻשַּׁלְתֶּן	הִתְמַשַּׁלְתֶּן
	3rd	Common	מִשְּׁלוּ	מֻשְּׁלוּ	הִתְמַשְּׁלוּ

1. The **middle radical** is **doubled** (has *dageš forte*) in all forms of the D-stems.

N.B.: If the middle radical of a verbal form is a *bᵉgad-kᵉfat* letter, it will have *dageš lene* whenever the first radical is followed by silent *šewa* (e.g., וַיִּשְׁכַּב, *and he lay down*). This means that a *dageš* in the middle radical does not always mean that the verb is a D-form.

2. There is always a full vowel under the first radical in all forms of the D-stems.
3. Like *qal*, *piel* and *pual* have no prefix in the perfect (unlike *nifal*, *hifil*, *hofal*, *hitpael*, which have prefixes in all forms).

4. The PGN indicators are the same in all stems.
5. The closed syllable does not change; the **vowel after the first radical** is **consistent** throughout the perfect of each D stem, as are the prefix and first root syllable of *hitpael*:

D	מִשֵּׁל
Dp	מֻשַּׁל
Dt	הִתְמַשֵּׁל

Prefix Conjugations

			Imperfect (= Preterite)		
	Person	Gender	D	Dp	Dt
Singular	1st	Common	אֲמַשֵּׁל	אֲמֻשַּׁל	אֶתְמַשֵּׁל
	2nd	Masc.	תְּמַשֵּׁל	תְּמֻשַּׁל	תִּתְמַשֵּׁל
		Fem.	תְּמַשְּׁלִי	תְּמֻשְּׁלִי	תִּתְמַשְּׁלִי
	3rd	Masc.	יְמַשֵּׁל	יְמֻשַּׁל	יִתְמַשֵּׁל
		Fem.	תְּמַשֵּׁל	תְּמֻשַּׁל	תִּתְמַשֵּׁל
Plural	1st	Common	נְמַשֵּׁל	נְמֻשַּׁל	נִתְמַשֵּׁל
	2nd	Masc.	תְּמַשְּׁלוּ	תְּמֻשְּׁלוּ	תִּתְמַשְּׁלוּ
		Fem.	תְּמַשֵּׁלְנָה	תְּמֻשַּׁלְנָה	תִּתְמַשֵּׁלְנָה
	3rd	Masc.	יְמַשְּׁלוּ	יְמֻשְּׁלוּ	יִתְמַשְּׁלוּ
		Fem.	תְּמַשֵּׁלְנָה	תְּמֻשַּׁלְנָה	תִּתְמַשֵּׁלְנָה

1. The **middle radical** is **doubled** in all forms of the D-stems (see note above).
2. *Piel* and *pual* have the same prefix vowel (*šewa*) in imperfect, preterite (and participle; below); *hitpael* uses the same prefix vowel (*hireq*) throughout its conjugations:

D, Dp	יְמַשֵּׁל
Dt	יִתְמַשֵּׁל

3. In all forms of *piel* except the perfect, the **first radical** is followed by **pataḥ**.
4. In all forms of *pual*, the **first radical** is followed by **qibbuṣ** (usually) or **ḥolem** (if the middle radical is a guttural or *reš*).
5. The PGN prefixes replace the initial -הִ of *hitpael* (as in the H-stems, below).
6. The preterite of all three stems is identical to the imperfect (with prefixed -וַ plus *dageš forte*). The exception is the -יְ prefix (3ms, 3mp), which lacks the *dageš*:

וַיְדַבֵּר אִתּוֹ אֱלֹהִים	And God *spoke* with him, …(Gn 17.3)
וַיְשַׁלַּח יהוה בָּעָם אֵת הַנְּחָשִׁים הַשְּׂרָפִים וַיְנַשְּׁכוּ אֶת־הָעָם	And Yhwh *sent* among the people fiery serpents, and they *bit* the people (Nu 21.6)

Imperative

	Person	Gender	D	Dt
Sg.	2nd	Masc.	מַשֵּׁל	הִתְמַשֵּׁל
		Fem.	מַשְּׁלִי	הִתְמַשְּׁלִי
Pl.	2nd	Masc.	מַשְּׁלוּ	הִתְמַשְּׁלוּ
		Fem.	מַשֵּׁלְנָה	הִתְמַשֵּׁלְנָה

1. The imperative of *piel* looks exactly like the imperfect without the prefix.
2. The -הִתְ prefix of *hitpael* occurs in all forms except imperfect, preterite, and participle (below).
3. *Pual* does not occur in the imperative.

Infinitives

	D	Dt
Construct	מַשֵּׁל	הִתְמַשֵּׁל
Absolute	מַשֵּׁל	הִתְמַשֵּׁל

1. Both infinitives often look exactly like ms imperative in *piel* and *hitpael*; context will determine which conjugation is being used.
2. *Pual* does not occur as infinitive construct.
3. *Pual* occurs once as infinitive absolute (גֻּנֹּב גֻּנַּבְתִּי, *I was surely stolen*; Gn 40.15).

Participles

	Gender	D	Dp	Dt
Sg.	Masc.	מְמַשֵּׁל	מְמֻשָּׁל	מִתְמַשֵּׁל
	Fem.	מְמַשְּׁלָה	מְמֻשָּׁלָה	מִתְמַשְּׁלָה
Pl.	Masc.	מְמַשְּׁלִים	מְמֻשָּׁלִים	מִתְמַשְּׁלִים
	Fem.	מְמַשְּׁלוֹת	מְמֻשָּׁלוֹת	מִתְמַשְּׁלוֹת

1. Every form begins with -מְ, which is the participial prefix for all stems except *qal* and *nifal*.
2. The prefix vowel is the same as for the imperfect and preterite:

    מְ-   **D, Dp**

    מִתְמַ-   **Dt**

N.B.: When the middle radical is followed by vocal *šewa*, the *dageš forte* is often missing from certain consonants, especially ל, מ, and ק. The middle radical of הלל, *praise*, for example, is never doubled when followed by a half-vowel, although it is written with two *l*s in English: *Halleluiah*.

הַלְלוּ־יָהּ   *Praise* YAH! (Ps 150.1)

וּבִקְשׁוּ אֶת־יהוה   ... and *seek* YHWH! (Ho 3.5)

Summary of the *Hitpael*

1. Due to its prefix (-הִתְ, -יִתְ, etc.), some forms of Dt differ from those given above.
2. If the verbal root begins with a *sibilant* (ז ס צ שׂ שׁ), the ת of the prefix *metathesizes* (switches places with) the first letter of the verbal root (e.g., וָאֶשְׁתַּמֵּר < שמר).[147]
3. If the verbal root begins with צ (e.g., צדק), the ת of the prefix metathesizes with the צ, and partially assimilates to it, becoming ט (e.g., הִצְטַדֵּק).

---

147. In the only I-ז verb in *hitpael*, the ת of the prefix assimilates to, and doubles the ז (הִזַּכּוּ, Is 1.16; this parsing is disputed).

4. If the verbal root begins with a *dental* (ד ט ת), the ת of the prefix assimilates to, and thus doubles, it (e.g., מְדַבֵּר = m.s. *hitpael* Ptc of דבר < *mitdabbēr).[148]
5. The relatively frequent verbal root שחה, "bow, honor, do obeisance; worship"[149] (170x) occurs in forms that begin -הִשְׁתַּ, etc., which have traditionally been parsed as *hitpael* of שחה, with the expected metathesis of the ת and שׁ: הִשְׁתַּחֲוָה, *he bowed*;[150] its participial prefix is -מִ. These are all the forms of this verb in Biblical Hebrew (note the subtle difference between **3ms preterite** and **3mp preterite**, which are the most frequent forms):

PGN	Perfect		Imperfect		Preterite		Imv.
	Singular	Plural	Singular	Plural	Singular	Plural	
1c	הִשְׁתַּחֲוֵיתִי			נִשְׁתַּחֲוֶה	וָאֶשְׁתַּחֲוֶה		
2m		הִשְׁתַּחֲוִיתֶם	תִּשְׁתַּחֲוֶה				הִשְׁתַּחֲווּ
2fs	הִשְׁתַּחֲוִיתָ						הִשְׁתַּחֲוִי
3m	הִשְׁתַּחֲוָה	הִשְׁתַּחֲווּ	יִשְׁתַּחֲוֶה	יִשְׁתַּחֲווּ	וַיִּשְׁתַּחוּ	וַיִּשְׁתַּחֲווּ	
		הִשְׁתַּחֲוּוּ					
3f						וַתִּשְׁתַּחוּ	
						וַתִּשְׁתַּחֲוֶיןָ	
NC	הִשְׁתַּחֲוֹת						
Ptc ms	מִשְׁתַּחֲוֶה						
mp	מִשְׁתַּחֲוִים						

19.2 D-Stem Diagnostics

This chart summarizes the main clues for recognizing a D or Dp form.

Conjugation			Diagnostics	Example	Parsing
Perfect	*dageš forte* in middle radical	no prefix	*i/e*-vowel under I (D)	כִּבֵּד	3ms D P
			u/o-vowel under I (Dp)	כֻּבַּד	3ms Dp P
Imperative & Infinitive			*a*-vowel under I (D, Dt);	כַּבְּדוּ	mp D V
			these forms not in Dp	כַּבֵּד	D NC
Imperfect		*šewa* under prefix	־ְיָ (Dp) ־ְיַ (D)	יְגַדֵּל	3ms Dp F
			־ְתָּ (Dp) ־ְתַּ (D)	תְּכַבֵּדְנָה	2/3fp D F
Preterite			־ְוַיְ (Dp) ־ְוַיַּ (D)	וַיְגַדֵּל	3ms D Pr
Participle			מְ-	מְכַבְּדִים	mp D Ptc

---

148. *in front of a transliterated form means that the form is a hypothetical reconstruction.
149. שחה is often glossed "bow [down]", but this does not fit a number of contexts in which it describes a person who is already bowing (e.g., 2 Sa 14.4, 22; 1 Kg 1.31; 1 Chr 21.21; 29.20; 2 Chr 7.3), or who cannot "bow" because they are, e.g., in bed (1 Kg 1.47).
150. Although this parsing has been challenged (based on Ugaritic), it remains the simplest interpretation of the forms.

1. All D forms have a **doubled middle radical**.
2. The only forms of D & Dp that have a stem prefix are imperfect, preterite and participle; the **prefix** vowel is **always** a **half-vowel**.
3. Dt always has a prefixed stem syllable; the prefix syllable is either –הִתְ (P, V, NC), -יִתְ (F, Pr), or –מִתְ (Ptc).
4. *Comparing the Stems*. This chart reveals the differences and similarities between the various stems. Note the the similarity between the D-stems as a group:

Conjugation	PGN	Q	N	D	Dp	Dt
Perfect	3ms	מָשַׁל	נִמְשַׁל	מִשֵּׁל	מֻשַּׁל	הִתְמַשֵּׁל
Imperfect	3ms	יִמְשֹׁל	יִמָּשֵׁל	יְמַשֵּׁל	יְמֻשַּׁל	יִתְמַשֵּׁל
Preterite	3ms	וַיִּמְשֹׁל	וַיִּמָּשֵׁל	וַיְמַשֵּׁל*	וַיְמֻשַּׁל*	וַיִּתְמַשֵּׁל
Imperative	2ms	מְשֹׁל	הִמָּשֵׁל	מַשֵּׁל		הִתְמַשֵּׁל
Inf. Const.		מְשֹׁל	הִמָּשֵׁל	מַשֵּׁל		הִתְמַשֵּׁל
Inf. Abs.		מָשׁוֹל	הִמָּשֵׁל	מַשֵּׁל	מֻשָּׁל	הִתְמַשֵּׁל
Participle	ms	מֹשֵׁל	נִמְשָׁל	מְמַשֵּׁל	מְמֻשָּׁל	מִתְמַשֵּׁל

*The *yod* prefix is not doubled in *piel* and *pual* preterite—the other PGN prefixes are doubled, just as in *qal*, *nifal*, and *hitpael*.

19.3 *Function of the D-Stems*

19.3.1 *Piel (HBI §2.1.4)*

Piel is an **active** stem. Although the function of verbs in the *piel* is often related to the *qal* of the same stem (if it occurs), the *piel* is not primarily derived from or dependent upon the function of the *qal*, but has its own identify and function, which must be established *for each verb*.

1. If a verbal root occurs in both Q and D, the *piel* often describes the action that **causes** or brings about the state or condition described by the *qal*, especially if the verb is stative in *qal* (1 Ch 29.25; Lam 4.6 is for comparison of both function and form). This use of *piel* is often called "factitive" or "resultative" because it is said to describe the action that results in or brings about the state.

וַיִּגְדַּל עֲוֺן בַּת־עַמִּי מֵחַטַּאת סְדֹם	The guilt of the daughter of my people *is greater* than the sin of Sodom (Lam 4.6; 3ms Q Pr).
וַיְגַדֵּל יהוה אֶת־שְׁלֹמֹה	Yhwh *exalted* Solomon … (1 Ch 29.25; 3ms D Pr).
בָּנִים גִּדַּלְתִּי	I *raised* sons … (Is 1.2; 1cs D P).
טוֹב־לִי כִי־עֻנֵּיתִי לְמַעַן אֶלְמַד חֻקֶּיךָ׃	It is good for me that I have humbled so that *I might learn* your statutes (Ps 119.71; 1cs Q F).
טוֹב־אַתָּה וּמֵטִיב לַמְּדֵנִי חֻקֶּיךָ׃	You are good and [you] do good; *teach* me your statutes (Ps 119.68; ms D V + 1cs).
וַיְקַדֵּשׁ אֶת־הָעָם וַיְכַבְּסוּ שִׂמְלֹתָם	He *sanctified* the people and they *washed* their clothes (Ex 19.14; 3ms D Pr).
וַיֹּאמֶר יְהוֹשֻׁעַ אֶל־הָעָם הִתְקַדָּשׁוּ	Joshua said to the people, "*Sanctify yourselves*" (Jos 3.5).

2. Many verbs, especially those that occur only or primarily in *piel*, sound merely "active" when glossed in English, without any apparent causative function. This is especially true for verbs that occur in *piel* but not in *qal*, and for so-called "denominative" verbs. Denominative verbs are those that supposedly developed from nouns (e.g., דָּבָר > דִּבֶּר), a claim that

generally means that either there is no parallel verb in another Semitic language, or that the noun is more frequent than the verb. We do not yet know how the lexicon of these roots developed (i.e., from verb to noun, or *vice versa*).

וַיְמַן יְהוָה דָּג גָּדוֹל לִבְלֹעַ אֶת־יוֹנָה	Y<small>HWH</small> *appointed* a great fish to swallow Jonah (Jon 2.1; 3ms D Pr).
וַיְדַבֵּר מֹשֶׁה אֶת־הַדְּבָרִים הָאֵלֶּה אֶל־כָּל־בְּנֵי יִשְׂרָאֵל	Moses *spoke* these words to all the sons of Israel (Nu 14.39; 3ms D Pr).
וַיְדַבֵּר שְׁלֹשֶׁת אֲלָפִים מָשָׁל	He *spoke* 3000 proverbs (1 Kgs 5.12).
וַיְקַדֵּשׁ אֶת־הָעָם וַיְכַבְּסוּ שִׂמְלֹתָם	He *sanctified* the people and they *washed* their clothes (Ex 19.14; cf. above).
וְאֶת־הָאֹבֶדֶת לֹא בִקַּשְׁתֶּם	... and the perishing one [female] you *did* not *seek* (Ezk 34.4).
אָזַמֵּר לַיהוה אֱלֹהֵי יִשְׂרָאֵל	I *will sing* to Y<small>HWH</small>, Israel's God (Jg 5.3).
וְלֹא־יָכְלוּ הַכֹּהֲנִים לַעֲמֹד לְשָׁרֵת	The priests could not stand *to serve* (1 Kgs 8.11).
וַיִּגְדַּל עֲוֹן בַּת־עַמִּי מֵחַטַּאת סְדֹם	The guilt of the daughter of my people *has become greater* than the sin of Sodom (Lam 4.6).

19.3.2 *Pual* (HBI §2.1.5)

Pual is the **passive** of *piel*. Many *pual*s are participles (40%), perhaps because passive verbs are basically descriptive. These participles often function as adjectives (e.g., Pr 27.5).

וְשׁוֹמֵר תּוֹכַחַת יְכֻבָּד׃	But whoever regards reproof *shall be honored* (Pr 13.18).
וְאֶפְרַיִם עֶגְלָה מְלֻמָּדָה	And Ephraim is a *trained* [taught] heifer (Ho 10.11)
וַיְבֻקַּשׁ הַדָּבָר וַיִּמָּצֵא	The matter [plot] *was searched out* and found (Est 2.23)
יְהִי שֵׁם יהוה מְבֹרָךְ ...	May Y<small>HWH</small>'s name *be blessed* ...
שֵׁם יהוה מְהֻלָּל׃	... Y<small>HWH</small>'s name is to *be praised* (Ps 113.2a ... 3b)
טוֹבָה תּוֹכַחַת מְגֻלָּה מֵאַהֲבָה מְסֻתָּרֶת׃	Better an *uncovered* rebuke than *hidden* love (Pr 27.5).

19.3.3 *Hitpael* (HBI §2.1.6)

Much like *nifal*, *hitpael* is **passive**, **reflexive**, or **"reciprocal"**. These functions vary from verb to verb, and even from one text to another. Although the *hitpael* occurs more frequently than either *pual* or *hofal* (below), it is relatively uncommon (only twenty-two verbs occur more than ten times in *hitpael*). [In Ps 2.2, the parallel *hitpael* and *nifal* are apparently reflexive and reciprocal, respectively.]

וְהִיא מִתְקַדֶּשֶׁת מִטֻּמְאָתָהּ	She *cleansed herself* from her uncleanness (2 Sam 11.4)
וַיִּתְקַשֵּׁר יֵהוּא ... אֶל־יוֹרָם	Jehu *conspired* ... against Joram (2 Kgs 9.14).
וְאַבְנֵר הָיָה מִתְחַזֵּק בְּבֵית שָׁאוּל	Now Abner *was strengthening* [his position] in the household of Saul (2 Sam 3.6).
יִתְיַצְּבוּ מַלְכֵי־אֶרֶץ וְרוֹזְנִים נוֹסְדוּ־יָחַד	The kings of the earth *take their stand*, and the rulers counsel [*nifal*] together (Ps 2.2).
אִשָּׁה יִרְאַת־יהוה הִיא תִתְהַלָּל	A woman who fears Y<small>HWH</small> —she shall *be praised* (Pr 31.30; final *qames* is due to pausal lengthening).

Compare the *qal*, *piel*, *pual* and *hitpael* of גדל (Ps 144.12 is the only *pual* occurrence of גדל):

רַק הַכִּסֵּא אֶגְדַּל מִמֶּךָּ	Only [with regard to] the throne *am I greater* than you (Gn 41.40); 1cs Q F
בָּנִים גִּדַּלְתִּי	Sons I *have raised* (Is 1.2); 1cs D P
כִּי עַל־כֹּל יִתְגַּדָּל	For he will *exalt himself* over all (Dn 11.37); 3ms Dt F
בָּנֵינוּ כִּנְטִעִים מְגֻדָּלִים בִּנְעוּרֵיהֶם	Let our sons be like *full-grown* plants in their youth (Ps 144.12a); mp Dp Ptc

N.B.: It is not uncommon to read—especially in older works—that the D-stems are emphatic or intensifying. This "intensifying" function has never been demonstrated, and has, in fact, been disproved, so that today we discuss the "functions" (plural) of the *piel*, etc., as illustrated above.

19.4 *Frequency*

There are 8,506 D-forms in the Bible (12% of all verbal forms); *piel* is by far the most common of the three.

D	6,879	9.3%
Dp	450	0.6%
Dt	1,177	1.6%
Total	8,506	11.5%

19.5 *Concepts*

denominative	factitive	passive	pual	reflexive
D-stem	hitpael	piel	reciprocal	resultative

19.6 *Vocabulary*

cover (Q); atone [for] (D)	כָּפַר	.284	kneel (I: Q); bless (II: D)	בָּרַךְ	.276
learn (Q); teach (D)	לָמַד	.285	look for, seek, search (D; not in *qal*)	בָּקַשׁ	.277
hasten, act quickly (D) [often in hendiadys: "do X quickly"]	מָהַר	.286	say, speak (D; in Q only as ptc.)	דָּבַר	.278
capture, seize	לָכַד	.287	living, alive (adj.); life, lifetime (pl. n.)	חַי / חַיִּים	.279
above (prp., also מִמַּעַל); higher (adv., usually מַעְלָה)	מַעַל	.288	wrath, anger; heat	חֵמָה	.280
so that not (i.e., פֶּן is a negative telic particle, trad., "lest")	פֶּן	.289	account, regard, value, reckon	חָשַׁב	.281
remain, be left over (N); spare, leave [behind] (H)	שָׁאַר	.290	young sheep: young ram (m.; rarely written as כֶּשֶׂב); ewe-lamb (f.; also כִּשְׂבָּה)	כֶּבֶשׂ / כִּבְשָׂה	.282
serve, minister to (D)	שָׁרַת	.291	strength, power	כֹּחַ	.283

19.7 Exercises

After studying the characteristics of the D-stems, gloss these sentences and clauses, parsing the verbs.

Ex 22.6; גָּנַב *thief*; שׁלם *[re]pay* (D)	1. אִם־יִמָּצֵא הַגַּנָּב יְשַׁלֵּם שְׁנָיִם:
1 Sam 15.30; חטא *sin*; שׁחה *worship* (Dt); שׁוּב *return* (2ms Q V)	2. וַיֹּאמֶר חָטָאתִי עַתָּה כַּבְּדֵנִי נָא נֶגֶד זִקְנֵי־עַמִּי וְנֶגֶד יִשְׂרָאֵל וְשׁוּב עִמִּי וְהִשְׁתַּחֲוֵיתִי לַיהוָה אֱלֹהֶיךָ:
Mal 2.4; לִהְיוֹת *to be* (Q NC < היה + לְ); אֵת (2nd time) *with*; Levi	3. וִידַעְתֶּם כִּי שִׁלַּחְתִּי אֲלֵיכֶם אֵת הַמִּצְוָה הַזֹּאת לִהְיוֹת בְּרִיתִי אֶת־לֵוִי אָמַר יְהוָה צְבָאוֹת:
Pr 27.1; הלל *boast* (Dt); מָחָר *tomorrow*	4. אַל־תִּתְהַלֵּל בְּיוֹם מָחָר
Ex 12.31 (the speaker is Pharaoh); Moses, Aaron	5. וַיִּקְרָא לְמֹשֶׁה וּלְאַהֲרֹן לַיְלָה וַיֹּאמֶר ... עִבְדוּ אֶת־יְהוָה כְּדַבֶּרְכֶם:
Est 2.23; תלה *impale* (trad., *hang*)	6. וַיְבֻקַּשׁ הַדָּבָר וַיִּמָּצֵא וַיִּתָּלוּ שְׁנֵיהֶם עַל־עֵץ וַיִּכָּתֵב בְּסֵפֶר דִּבְרֵי הַיָּמִים לִפְנֵי הַמֶּלֶךְ:
Ps 148.5; צִוָּה *he commanded* (3ms D P); ברא *create*	7. יְהַלְלוּ אֶת־שֵׁם יְהוָה כִּי הוּא צִוָּה וְנִבְרָאוּ:
Jr 46.26; וּנְתַתִּים *and I will give/put them* (1cs Q P < נתן + וְ); בְּיַד (יָד + בְּ) *in the hand of*; when ק precedes vocal *šewa* it usually lacks *dageš forte*	8. וּנְתַתִּים בְּיַד מְבַקְשֵׁי נַפְשָׁם וּבְיַד נְבוּכַדְרֶאצַּר מֶלֶךְ־בָּבֶל וּבְיַד־עֲבָדָיו
Ex 14.12; Egypt	9. הֲלֹא־זֶה הַדָּבָר אֲשֶׁר דִּבַּרְנוּ אֵלֶיךָ בְמִצְרַיִם ...
Pr 12.8; לְפִי *according to*; שֵׂכֶל *prudence*	10. לְפִי־שִׂכְלוֹ יְהֻלַּל־אִישׁ
Ex 10.11; אֹתָהּ *it/that* (dir. obj. + 3fs) [i.e., the act of serving YHWH]; גרשׁ *drive out/away* [D]; מֵאֵת *from* [מִן + אֵת] (Pharaoh); one clause per line; the first line is a quotation.	11. וְעִבְדוּ אֶת־יְהוָה כִּי אֹתָהּ אַתֶּם מְבַקְשִׁים וַיְגָרֶשׁ אֹתָם מֵאֵת פְּנֵי פַרְעֹה:
1 Sam 23.15; וַיַּרְא *and he saw* (3ms Q Pr < ראה); David, Saul, Ziph, Horshah	12. וַיַּרְא דָוִד כִּי־יָצָא שָׁאוּל לְבַקֵּשׁ אֶת־נַפְשׁוֹ וְדָוִד בְּמִדְבַּר־זִיף בַּחֹרְשָׁה:
Gn 5.24; וְאֵינֶנּוּ *and he was not* (אַיִן + 3ms suffix); Enoch	13. וַיִּתְהַלֵּךְ חֲנוֹךְ אֶת־הָאֱלֹהִים וְאֵינֶנּוּ כִּי־לָקַח אֹתוֹ אֱלֹהִים:
1 Kgs 1.12; מלט *escape* (N), *rescue* (D); Nathan is speaking to Bathsheba; Solomon	14. וּמַלְּטִי אֶת־נַפְשֵׁךְ וְאֶת־נֶפֶשׁ בְּנֵךְ שְׁלֹמֹה:
Ho 3.5	15. וּבִקְשׁוּ אֶת־יְהוָה אֱלֹהֵיהֶם וְאֵת דָּוִד מַלְכָּם
Gn 18.33; וַיֵּלֶךְ *he went* (3ms Q Pr < הלך); כַּאֲשֶׁר *when*; כלה *finish* (D); Abraham	16. וַיֵּלֶךְ יְהוָה כַּאֲשֶׁר כִּלָּה לְדַבֵּר אֶל־אַבְרָהָם
Ho 7.10	17. וְלֹא בִקְשֻׁהוּ בְּכָל־זֹאת:
2 Sam 7.27; פלל *pray* (Dt); תְּפִלָּה *prayer*	18. מָצָא עַבְדְּךָ אֶת־לִבּוֹ לְהִתְפַּלֵּל אֵלֶיךָ אֶת־הַתְּפִלָּה הַזֹּאת:
Josh 22.6; וַיֵּלְכוּ *and they went* (3mp Q Pr < הלך)	19. וַיְבָרְכֵם יְהוֹשֻׁעַ וַיְשַׁלְּחֵם וַיֵּלְכוּ אֶל־אָהֳלֵיהֶם:

20. הַלְלוּ יָהּ   Ps 113.1–3; יְהִי *let/may it be, it should/must be*
     הַלְלוּ עַבְדֵי יְהוָה   (3ms Q J < הָיָה); מִזְרָח *dawn/east;* מָבוֹא *entrance;*
     הַלְלוּ אֶת־שֵׁם יְהוָה: the jussive (יְהִי) is "distributed" to the last line as
     יְהִי שֵׁם יְהוָה מְבֹרָךְ מֵעַתָּה וְעַד־עוֹלָם: well
     מִמִּזְרַח־שֶׁמֶשׁ עַד־מְבוֹאוֹ מְהֻלָּל שֵׁם יְהוָה:

21. לֹא־נָפַל דָּבָר אֶחָד מִכֹּל הַדְּבָרִים הַטּוֹבִים   Josh 23.14
     אֲשֶׁר דִּבֶּר יהוה אֱלֹהֵיכֶם עֲלֵיכֶם

22. וְאָבַד מָנוֹס מִקָּל   Am 2.14–15; מָנוֹס *flight* [i.e., the ability to flee];
     וְחָזָק לֹא־יְאַמֵּץ כֹּחוֹ   קַל *swift;* חָזָק *strong;* מלט *escape* (N)*, deliver,*
     וְגִבּוֹר לֹא־יְמַלֵּט נַפְשׁוֹ:   *rescue* (D)*;* אמץ *strengthen* (D)*;* תפשׂ *use, wield;*
     וְתֹפֵשׂ הַקֶּשֶׁת לֹא יַעֲמֹד   קֶשֶׁת [a] *bow;* רכב *ride;* each line is a clause
     וְקַל בְּרַגְלָיו לֹא יְמַלֵּט
     וְרֹכֵב הַסּוּס לֹא יְמַלֵּט נַפְשׁוֹ:

23. וְעַתָּה הוֹאַלְתָּ לְבָרֵךְ אֶת־בֵּית עַבְדְּךָ   1 Ch 17.27; הוֹאַלְתָּ *you have been pleased* (2ms
     לִהְיוֹת לְעוֹלָם לְפָנֶיךָ   H P < יאל); לִהְיוֹת *to be* (Q NC < היה + ל)
     כִּי־אַתָּה יְהוָה בֵּרַכְתָּ וּמְבֹרָךְ לְעוֹלָם:

19.8 Enrichment: The Nature of D/Piel

There are two D-forms in Ps 29, both occur in the second of two parallel lines, both parallel *qal* verbs. The *qal-piel* parallel of the same verbal root (Ps 29.5) is often cited as proof that the second of two parallel lines is more "intense" (since the *piel* was said to be an intensifying stem), or that it "focuses" or "extends" the content of the first line (see §19.4/N.B.).

קוֹל יהוה שֹׁבֵר אֲרָזִים   Yhwh's voice *breaks* cedars,
וַיְשַׁבֵּר יהוה אֶת־אַרְזֵי הַלְּבָנוֹן: And Yhwh *breaks* Lebanon's cedars (Ps 29.5).

It is true that Ps 29.5b is more specific than 29.5a, but it is more specific (or focused) because the cedars are identified more specifically as "Lebanon's cedars", *not* because of the stem of the predicate. Nor should we necessarily read the act of smashing Lebanon's cedars as somehow more violent, or more destructive, or more *anything*—at least *not on the basis of the verbal stem*. That reading must come from the broader context, possibly even from the use of "cedars of Lebanon" in Biblical Hebrew (the phrase occurs only five times).

At the end of the psalm (29.11), the two stems are again parallel, but this time in different verbal roots. The point, however, is not that the blessing of peace (11b) is somehow greater than the gift of strength (11a); they are coordinate blessings.

עֹז לְעַמּוֹ יִתֵּן יהוה   Yhwh *gives* strength to his people;
יהוה יְבָרֵךְ אֶת־עַמּוֹ בַשָּׁלוֹם: He *blesses* his people with peace (Ps 29.11).

Lesson 20

The H-Stems (*Hifil*, *Hofal*)

The *hifil* (H) and *hofal* (Hp) are also called "H-stems", since they have a **prefixed** -הַ in all conjugations except the imperfect and preterite (where the usual PGN prefixes replace the prefixed -הַ, as they do in the *hitpael*), and participle (where the participial prefix -מַ replaces the -הַ). This -הַ is the primary diagnostic of the H-stems. Like *nifal* and *hitpael* (but unlike *qal*, *piel*, *pual*), the H-stems have a prefix in every form.

The main difference between *hifil* and *hofal* is the **prefix vowel**. If it is *hireq* (perfect only) or *patah* (all other conjugations) the verb is *hifil*; if it is *qames hiatuf* (usually) or *qibbus* (some verbs, e.g., most forms of שׁלךְ), the form is *hofal*. A second difference is the vowel after the **second radical**: in *hofal*, it is always an *a*-vowel (*patah* or *qames*); in *hifil* it is usually an *i/e*-vowel (*hireq*, *sere*, *segol*).

20.1 *Form*

Perfect

	No.	Person	Gender	H	Hp
Singular		1st	Common	הִמְשַׁלְתִּי	הָמְשַׁלְתִּי
		2nd	Masc.	הִמְשַׁלְתָּ	הָמְשַׁלְתָּ
			Fem.	הִמְשַׁלְתְּ	הָמְשַׁלְתְּ
		3rd	Masc.	הִמְשִׁיל	הָמְשַׁל
			Fem.	הִמְשִׁילָה	הָמְשְׁלָה
Plural		1st	Common	הִמְשַׁלְנוּ	הָמְשַׁלְנוּ
		2nd	Masc.	הִמְשַׁלְתֶּם	הָמְשַׁלְתֶּם
			Fem.	הִמְשַׁלְתֶּן	הָמְשַׁלְתֶּן
		3rd	Common	הִמְשִׁילוּ	הָמְשְׁלוּ

1. The **prefixed** -הַ occurs in **all** forms of the perfect.
2. The primary **diagnostic** for *hifil* and *hofal* perfect is the prefixed -הַ and its vowel.
3. The **first radical** is always followed by silent *šewa*, so that the prefixes of the *hifil* and *hofal* form a closed syllable with the first radical (cf. *nifal* perfect & participle, and *qal* imperfect & preterite).
4. Like *nifal* and *hitpael*, the H-stems have a prefix in all forms.
5. The long *hireq* of the *hifil* occurs only in forms that do not have a consonantal ending.
6. The PGN indicators are the same in all stems.

Prefix Conjugations

	Person	Gender	Imperfect H	Imperfect Hp	Preterite H	Preterite Hp
Singular	1st	Common	אַמְשִׁיל	אָמְשַׁל	וָאַמְשֵׁל	וָאָמְשַׁל
Singular	2nd	Masc.	תַּמְשִׁיל	תָּמְשַׁל	וַתַּמְשֵׁל	וַתָּמְשַׁל
Singular	2nd	Fem.	תַּמְשִׁילִי	תָּמְשְׁלִי	וַתַּמְשִׁילִי	וַתָּמְשְׁלִי
Singular	3rd	Masc.	יַמְשִׁיל	יָמְשַׁל	וַיַּמְשֵׁל	וַיָּמְשַׁל
Singular	3rd	Fem.	תַּמְשִׁיל	תָּמְשַׁל	וַתַּמְשֵׁל	וַתָּמְשַׁל
Plural	1st	Common	נַמְשִׁיל	נָמְשַׁל	וַנַּמְשֵׁל	וַנָּמְשַׁל
Plural	2nd	Masc.	תַּמְשִׁילוּ	תָּמְשְׁלוּ	וַתַּמְשִׁילוּ	וַתָּמְשְׁלוּ
Plural	2nd	Fem.	תַּמְשֵׁלְנָה	תָּמְשַׁלְנָה	וַתַּמְשֵׁלְנָה	וַתָּמְשַׁלְנָה
Plural	3rd	Masc.	יַמְשִׁילוּ	יָמְשְׁלוּ	וַיַּמְשִׁילוּ	וַיָּמְשְׁלוּ
Plural	3rd	Fem.	תַּמְשֵׁלְנָה	תָּמְשַׁלְנָה	וַתַּמְשֵׁלְנָה	וַתָּמְשַׁלְנָה

1. The PGN prefixes replace the -הֹ of the perfect.
2. The **prefix vowel** is *pataḥ* in all forms of H except the perfect.
3. The **prefix vowel** is *qameṣ ḥatuf* in all forms of Hp.
4. The **first radical** is followed by *ṣlent šewa* in all forms of H and Hp.
5. The preterite of both stems is like the imperfect, with prefixed -וַ and *dageš forte* in the PGN prefix. *Hifil* preterites without PGN endings have *ṣere* rather than *ḥireq yod* after the second radical (1cs, 2ms, 3ms, 3fs, 1cp):

וַיַּבְדֵּל אֱלֹהִים בֵּין הָאוֹר וּבֵין הַחֹשֶׁךְ:	And God *divided* the light from the dark [… a separation/division between …] (Gn 1.4).
… וַתַּגְדֵּל חַסְדְּךָ	And you *have exalted* your lovingkindness … (Gn 19.19)
יַגְדִּיל תּוֹרָה וְיַאְדִּיר	He *will exalt* and *make glorious* [the] teaching (Is 42.21b).

Imperative & Infinitives

The imperatives and infinitives resemble the imperfect, except that the prefix -הֹ replaces the -תֹּ PGN prefix (cf. *nifal*):

	Gender	H	Hp	N
Sg.	Masc.	הַמְשֵׁל		הִמָּשֵׁל
Sg.	Fem.	הַמְשִׁילִי		הִמָּשְׁלִי
Pl.	Masc.	הַמְשִׁילוּ		הִמָּשְׁלוּ
Pl.	Fem.	הַמְשֵׁלְנָה		הִמָּשַׁלְנָה
NC		הַמְשִׁיל		
NA		הַמְשֵׁל	הָמְשֵׁל	

1. *Hofal* imperative occurs only twice in the Bible: (וְהָשְׁכְּבָה, *Be laid down!* (Ezk 32.19); הָפְנוּ, *Be turned back!* (Jr 49.8)).
2. The **prefix vowel** is *pataḥ* in **hifil** (as in imperfect, preterite, and participle).

3. *Hifil* infinitive absolute and imperative are identical.
4. *Hofal* infinitives construct are extremely rare, and never occur in the strong verb.[151]

Participles

	Gender	H	Hp	Dp
Sg.	Masc.	מַמְשִׁיל	מָמְשָׁל	מְמֻשָּׁל
Sg.	Fem.	מַמְשִׁילָה	מָמְשָׁלָה	מְמֻשָּׁלָה
Pl.	Masc.	מַמְשִׁילִים	מָמְשָׁלִים	מְמֻשָּׁלִים
Pl.	Fem.	מַמְשִׁילוֹת	מָמְשָׁלוֹת	מְמֻשָּׁלוֹת

1. Every form begins with -מ, which is the participial prefix for all stems except *qal* and *nifal* (cf. D, Dp, Dt, above); the first radical is followed by silent *šewa*, so that the prefix syllable is closed.
2. The **prefix vowel** is *pataḥ* in H and *qameṣ ḥatuf* in Hp.
3. The vowel after the second radical is always *qameṣ* in Hp participle (cf. Dp).

20.2 *Summary of H-stem Diagnostics*

This chart summarizes the main clues for identifying a H-stem form.

Conjugation		Diagnostics *Prefix*		Example	Parsing	
Perfect	-ה		*hiireq*[*-yod*] after II	הִכְבִּיד	3ms H P	*he honored*
				הָכְבַּד	3ms Hp P	*he was honored*
Imperative	-ה	-ה	*i/e*-vowel after II	הַכְבֵּד	2ms H V	*Honor [someone]!*
				הַכְבִּידוּ	2mp H V	*Honor [someone]!*
Infinitives				הַכְבִּיד	H NC	*[to] honor*
Imperfect & Preterite	PGN prefix	-יַ		יַכְבִּיד	3ms H F	*he will honor*
				וַיַּכְבֵּד	3ms H Pr	*and he honored*
		-תָ		וַתָּכְבַּד	3fs Hp Pr	*and she honored*
Participle	-מ	-מַ		מַכְבִּיד	ms H Ptc	*one how honors*
				מַכְבִּידוֹת	fp H Ptc	*they who honor*
		-מָ		מָכְבָּדִים	mp Hp Ptc	*they who are honored*

1. All forms have a **prefix**—either -ה (perfect, imperative, infinitives), -מ (participle), or PGN (imperfect, preterite).
2. *Hifil* perfect has **ḥireq** as prefix vowel; all other conjugations of H have **pataḥ**.
3. The "stem vowel" (after the second radical of the root) is either an -*i*- or an -*e*- vowel in all forms of H, and an -*a*- vowel in all forms of Hp.
4. All forms of Hp have *qameṣ ḥatuf* as their **prefix** vowel.
5. *Comparing the Stems.* The following chart reveals differences and similarities between the seven stems. Note the similarity between the H-stems:

151. Hp infinitive construct of ילד (הֻלֶּדֶת) occurs three times (Gn 40.20; Ek 16.4, 5); the other four occurrences of hofal NC are of the root שמם (Lv 26.34, 35, 43; 2 Ch 36.21).

Conjugation	PGN	Q	N	D	Dp	Dt	H	Hp
Perfect	3ms	מָשַׁל	נִמְשַׁל	מִשֵּׁל	מֻשַּׁל	הִתְמַשֵּׁל	הִמְשִׁיל	הָמְשַׁל
Imperfect	3ms	יִמְשֹׁל	יִמָּשֵׁל	יְמַשֵּׁל	יְמֻשַּׁל	יִתְמַשֵּׁל	יַמְשִׁיל	יָמְשַׁל
Preterite	3ms	וַיִּמְשֹׁל	וַיִּמָּשֵׁל	וַיְמַשֵּׁל	וַיְמֻשַּׁל	וַיִּתְמַשֵּׁל	וַיַּמְשֵׁל	וַיָּמְשַׁל
Imperative	2ms	מְשֹׁל	הִמָּשֵׁל	מַשֵּׁל		הִתְמַשֵּׁל	הַמְשֵׁל	
Inf. Const.		מְשֹׁל	הִמָּשֵׁל	מַשֵּׁל		הִתְמַשֵּׁל	הַמְשִׁיל	
Inf. Abs.		מָשׁוֹל	הִמָּשֵׁל	מַשֵּׁל	מֻשֵּׁל	הִתְמַשֵּׁל	הַמְשֵׁל	הָמְשֵׁל
Participle	ms	מֹשֵׁל	נִמְשָׁל	מְמַשֵּׁל	מְמֻשָּׁל	מִתְמַשֵּׁל	מַמְשִׁיל	מָמְשָׁל

N.B.: If the second radical is a *bᵉgad-kᵉfat* letter, it will have *dageš lene* in all forms of *hifil* and *hofal*, *qal* imperfect and preterite, and *nifal* perfect and participle; all forms of the D-stems have *dageš forte*.

20.3 Function of the H-stems

The basic relationship between H and Hp is that *hifil* is always active, and *hofal* is its corresponding passive. Many reference works call *hifil* the "causative" of the *qal*, but many verbal roots occur in *hifil* but not in *qal*, or occur in both stems with little apparent relationship between their functions.

20.3.1 Hifil (HBI §2.1.7)

The *hifil* is an **active** stem. Beyond that it is necessary to determine the nuance of the *hifil* for each verbal root, and, even within each root, for each occurrence of the *hifil*, since its function depends, not only upon the verbal root, but also upon its context, and especially the subjects, objects, and even prepositions with which it occurs.

1. If a verb does not occur in Q, *hifil* is often simply transitive (also "singly" transitive, since it governs *one* object).

וַיהוָה הִשְׁלִיךְ עֲלֵיהֶם אֲבָנִים גְּדֹלוֹת	And Y<small>HWH</small> *threw* great stones at them … (Josh 10.11; 3ms **H** P)
וְאָנֹכִי הַסְתֵּר אַסְתִּיר פָּנַי בַּיּוֹם הַהוּא	I will most surely *hide* my face on that day (Dt 31.19; **H** NA & 1cs **H** F)
וְהִשְׁמַדְתִּי אֶת־בָּמֹתֵיכֶם	… and I will *destroy* your high places (Lv 26.30; 1cs **H** P + *w*)

2. When a verb occurs in Q or N and H, *hifil* is usually **causative** of Q or N. When glossing a *hifil*, it is often helpful to first translate it by saying "A *caused* B *to do* X", and then to look for an appropriate gloss for the entire expression.

   a. The first pair of examples shows עבר in Q and H; the second shows אבד in N and H, and the third illustrates the use of שמע in all three stems (Q, N, H). Note the relationship between the subject, object, and action of the *hifil* verb.

וַיֵּלֶךְ לַעֲבֹר אֶל־בְּנֵי עַמּוֹן	He went *to cross over* to the Ammonites (Jer 41.10; **Q** NC + לְ)
לְהַעֲבִיר אֶת־הַמֶּלֶךְ אֶת־יַרְדֵּן	to *cause* the king *to cross* [≈ to *bring* the king *over*] the Jordan (2 Sa 19.16; **H** NC)

וּפֹשְׁעִים נִשְׁמְדוּ יַחְדָּו	but transgressors will *be destroyed* together (Ps 37.38; 3cp **N** P)
וְאָנֹכִי הִשְׁמַדְתִּי אֶת־הָאֱמֹרִי מִפְּנֵיכֶם	But I *destroyed* the Amorite(s) before you (Am 2.9; 1cp **H** P)

III.20. *The H-Stems (Hifil, Hofal)*

הֲלוֹא שָׁמַעַתְּ כִּי מָלַךְ אֲדֹנִיָּהוּ	Have you not *heard* that Adonijah has become king? (1 Kgs 1.11; 2fs **Q** P)
תִּשָּׁמַע זְעָקָה מִבָּתֵּיהֶם	A cry *shall be heard* from their houses (Jr 18.11; 3fs **N** F)
תַּשְׁמִיעֵנִי שָׂשׂוֹן וְשִׂמְחָה	You *cause* me *to hear* joy and gladness (Ps 51.10a; 2ms **H** F + 1cs)

b. If the verb is transitive in *qal*, H is *doubly* transitive, that is, it takes two objects. The first object is the person (or thing) that the subject causes to perform the action of the verb; the second object is the direct object of that action. In this example the subject is 3ms ("he"), the first object us 1cp ("us"), and the second object is 3fs ("it" [the commandment]):

| וְיַשְׁמִעֵנוּ אֹתָהּ | ... that he may *cause* us *to hear* it (Dt 30.12; 3ms **H** F) |

c. If the verb is stative in *qal*, H is factitive or resultative (see on *piel*, above), a type of causative in which a verb describes or names the process or action that brings the object to the condition or state described by the *qal*:

| כָּל־הַבְּכוֹר ... תַּקְדִּישׁ לַיהוָה אֱלֹהֶיךָ | Every firstborn ... you shall *sanctify* [≈ *set apart*] to Yhwh your God (Dt 15.19; 2ms **H** F). |
| הִגְדַּלְתִּי מַעֲשָׂי | I *increased* my works (Qo 2.4; 1cs **H** P) |

3. In some cases, however, the nature of the object suggests that a *hifil* verb is less than causative. In Is 8.13, the prophet contrasts the Judahites' fear of the northern kings with the fear due Yhwh:

| וְאֶת־יְהוָה צְבָאוֹת אֹתוֹ תַקְדִּישׁוּ | ... but [instead] you shall *sanctify* [≈ *recognize as holy*] Yhwh Sabaoth (Is 8.13; 2mp **H** F) |

4. H can also be called "tolerative" or "permissive", that is, the subject *allows* something [not] to happen:

| וְלֹא־תַשְׁמִיעוּ אֶת־קוֹלְכֶם | Do not *let* your voice *be heard* ≈ *cause* [someone] *to hear* your voice (Jos 6.10; 2mp **H** F) |
| וְלֹא־הִפִּיל מִכָּל־דְּבָרָיו אָרְצָה: | And he [Yhwh] did not *allow* any of his words *to fall* to the ground [i.e., to fail] (1 Sam 3.19; 3ms **H** P [נפל]) |

20.3.2 *Hofal (HBI §2.1.8)*

The *hofal* [Hp] is consistently passive. When it corresponds to *hifil* forms of the same verbal root, it makes the **causative** part of the *hifil* passive. If a verbal root occurs only in Q and Hp, then it will be a simple passive in Hp:

| לַיהוה אָז יָשִׁיר־מֹשֶׁה וּבְנֵי יִשְׂרָאֵל אֶת־הַשִּׁירָה הַזֹּאת | Then Moses and the sons of Israel *sang* this song to Yhwh (Ex 15.1); 3ms **Q** F |
| בַּיּוֹם הַהוּא יוּשַׁר הַשִּׁיר־הַזֶּה | In that day this song *will be sung* (Is 26.1a); 3ms **Hp** F |

The following examples compare Q, H, and Hp (עמד) and Q, H, and Hp (מות). We have not yet studied the hollow verbs, but the point here is the *function* of the various stems, not their form). [Cf. also §20.3.1(2a).]

אַךְ אִם־יוֹם אוֹ יוֹמַיִם יַעֲמֹד	..., but if he *stands* for a day or two days (Ex 21.21; 3ms **Q** F)
מֶלֶךְ בְּמִשְׁפָּט יַעֲמִיד אָרֶץ	A king *causes* a land *to stand* [*preserves*] by justice (Pr 29.4a); 3ms **H** F
יָעֳמַד־חַי לִפְנֵי יהוה	... [the goat] *shall be caused to stand* alive before Y<small>HWH</small> (Lv 16.10); 3ms **Hp** F
וַיָּמָת וַיִּקָּבֵר בְּשָׁמִיר׃	He *died* and was buried in Shamir (Jg 10.2; 3ms **Q** Pr).
... וַיָּמִיתוּ אֶת־הַמֶּלֶךְ בְּבֵיתוֹ׃	... and they *caused the king to die* (*killed*) in his house (2 Kgs 21.23; 3mp **H** Pr).
... וַתּוּמַת שָׁם׃	... and there she *was caused to die* (*was put to death*) (2 Kgs 11.16; 3fs **Hp** Pr)

20.4 Frequency

There are 10,102 H-forms in the Bible (14% of all verbal forms). *Hifil* is the second most frequent stem in Biblical Hebrew; *hofal* is one of the least frequent.

H	9,671	13.1%	
Hp	531	0.7%	
Total	10,102	13.8%	of all verbal forms

20.5 Concepts

causative	permissive	tolerative
doubly transitive	stative	

20.6 Vocabulary

fight (N)	לָחַם	.300	then, at that time	אָז	.292
			formerly, since (מִן + אָז)	מֵאָז	
escape (N); rescue, deliver (D)	מָלַט	.301	be trustworthy, faithful; steady, firm (N); believe, trust (H)	אָמֵן	.293
relent, be sorry, rue (N); comfort, console (D)	נָחַם	.302	truth; trustworthiness	אֱמֶת	.294
hide, conceal [oneself] (N, Dt); be hidden/concealed (N); hide [someone] (H)	סָתַר	.303	[*the*] firstborn	בְּכֹר	.295
cow (female)	פָּרָה	.304	there is/was, here is/was (trad., Behold!)	הִנֵּה	.296
bull (male)	פַּר		[*city*] wall	חוֹמָה	.297
be ruined, spoiled, corrupt (N); ruin, spoil, corrupt (D); destroy (H)	שָׁחַת	.305	ordinance, rule, prescription [something prescribed, required, commanded]	חֹק חֻקָּה	.298
be destroyed, exterminated (N); destroy, exterminate (H)	שָׁמַד	.306	together, simultaneously (adv.); phps. twice as *community* (Dt 33.5; 1 Ch 12.18)	יַחַד יַחְדָּו	.299

20.7 *Exercises*

After learning the characteristics of the H-stems, *gloss* these sentences and clauses, *parsing* the verbs.

1 Kgs 3.7; David	1. וְעַתָּה יְהוָה אֱלֹהָי אַתָּה הִמְלַכְתָּ אֶת־עַבְדְּךָ תַּחַת דָּוִד אָבִי
Ps 8.7	2. תַּמְשִׁילֵהוּ בְּמַעֲשֵׂי יָדֶיךָ
Ps 22.11; בֶּטֶן *belly, womb*; רֶחֶם *womb*	3. עָלֶיךָ הָשְׁלַכְתִּי מֵרָחֶם מִבֶּטֶן אִמִּי אֵלִי אָתָּה:
Dt 32.20	4. וַיֹּאמֶר אַסְתִּירָה פָנַי מֵהֶם
Ps 143.8; בטח *trust*	5. הַשְׁמִיעֵנִי בַבֹּקֶר חַסְדֶּךָ כִּי־בְךָ בָטָחְתִּי
Lv 21.17	6. אִישׁ מִזַּרְעֲךָ ... לֹא יִקְרַב לְהַקְרִיב לֶחֶם אֱלֹהָיו:
Lv 20.24; בדל *separate* (H)	7. אֲנִי יְהוָה אֱלֹהֵיכֶם אֲשֶׁר־הִבְדַּלְתִּי אֶתְכֶם מִן־הָעַמִּים:
Is 8.17; חכה *wait [for]* (D); קוה *wait [for]* (D)	8. וְחִכִּיתִי לַיהוָה הַמַּסְתִּיר פָּנָיו מִבֵּית יַעֲקֹב וְקִוֵּיתִי־לוֹ:
Ex 24.4; שכם *arise/awake/do [X] early*; וַיִּבֶן *and he built* (3ms Q Pr < בנה); מַצֵּבָה *standing stone*; add the numerals for the total	9. וַיִּכְתֹּב מֹשֶׁה אֵת כָּל־דִּבְרֵי יְהוָה וַיַּשְׁכֵּם בַּבֹּקֶר וַיִּבֶן מִזְבֵּחַ תַּחַת הָהָר וּשְׁתֵּים עֶשְׂרֵה מַצֵּבָה לִשְׁנֵים עָשָׂר שִׁבְטֵי יִשְׂרָאֵל:
Gn 1.14; מְאֹרֹת *lights [-givers/bearers]*; רָקִיעַ *vault, firmament*; וְהָיוּ (3cp Q P < היה *be, become*; בדל (see #7); אוֹת *[a] sign*	10. וַיֹּאמֶר אֱלֹהִים יְהִי מְאֹרֹת בִּרְקִיעַ הַשָּׁמַיִם לְהַבְדִּיל בֵּין הַיּוֹם וּבֵין הַלָּיְלָה וְהָיוּ לְאֹתֹת וּלְמוֹעֲדִים וּלְיָמִים וְשָׁנִים:
Zc 13.2; נְאֻם *declaration, utterance*; עָצָב *idol*; טֻמְאָה *uncleanness*; each line is a clause	11. וְהָיָה בַיּוֹם הַהוּא נְאֻם יְהוָה צְבָאוֹת אַכְרִית אֶת־שְׁמוֹת הָעֲצַבִּים מִן־הָאָרֶץ וְלֹא יִזָּכְרוּ עוֹד וְגַם אֶת־הַנְּבִיאִים וְאֶת־רוּחַ הַטֻּמְאָה אַעֲבִיר מִן־הָאָרֶץ:
1 Ch 23.1; שבע *be full, satisfied with; have one's fill of*; David, Solomon	12. וְדָוִיד זָקֵן וְשָׂבַע יָמִים וַיַּמְלֵךְ אֶת־שְׁלֹמֹה בְנוֹ עַל־יִשְׂרָאֵל:
Nu 3.6; Levi, Aaron (in the following verses Yhwh assigns duties to the Levitical clans)	13. וַיֹּאמֶר יהוה אֶל־מֹשֶׁה לֵּאמֹר הַקְרֵב אֶת־מַטֵּה לֵוִי וְהַעֲמַדְתָּ אֹתוֹ לִפְנֵי אַהֲרֹן הַכֹּהֵן וְשֵׁרְתוּ אֹתוֹ:
Ps 17.8; אִישׁוֹן *apple*; צֵל *shadow*; כָּנָף *wing*	14. שָׁמְרֵנִי כְּאִישׁוֹן בַּת־עָיִן בְּצֵל כְּנָפֶיךָ תַּסְתִּירֵנִי:
Dt 31.18; עַל *because of, on account of*; עשׂה *do, make* (3ms Q P); פנה *turn* (3ms Q P)	15. וְאָנֹכִי הַסְתֵּר אַסְתִּיר פָּנַי בַּיּוֹם הַהוּא עַל כָּל־הָרָעָה אֲשֶׁר עָשָׂה כִּי פָנָה אֶל־אֱלֹהִים אֲחֵרִים:
Est 4.4; Esther is the subject of וַתִּשְׁלַח; Mordecai	16. וַתִּשְׁלַח בְּגָדִים לְהַלְבִּישׁ אֶת־מָרְדֳּכַי
1 Sam 25.15; כלם *humiliate, trouble*; מְאוּמָה *anything*; בִּהְיוֹתֵנוּ *while we were* (Q NC < היה + 1cp + בְּ)	17. וְהָאֲנָשִׁים טֹבִים לָנוּ מְאֹד וְלֹא הָכְלַמְנוּ וְלֹא־פָקַדְנוּ מְאוּמָה כָּל־יְמֵי הִתְהַלַּכְנוּ אִתָּם בִּהְיוֹתֵנוּ בַּשָּׂדֶה:

18. גֵּר אָנֹכִי בָאָרֶץ
　　אַל־תַּסְתֵּר מִמֶּנִּי מִצְוֺתֶיךָ׃

Ps 119.19; גֵּר *sojourner; alien* (i.e., non-native)

19. מַשְׁבִּית מִלְחָמוֹת עַד־קְצֵה הָאָרֶץ
　　קֶשֶׁת יְשַׁבֵּר וְקִצֵּץ חֲנִית עֲגָלוֹת יִשְׂרֹף בָּאֵשׁ׃

Ps 46.10; שׁבת *cease, stop;* קצה *end, edge;* קֶשֶׁת *bow;* קצץ *break* (D); חֲנִית *spear;* עגלה *wagon, chariot*

20. וְכָרַתִּי לָהֶם בְּרִית בַּיּוֹם הַהוּא עִם־חַיַּת הַשָּׂדֶה
　　וְעִם־עוֹף הַשָּׁמַיִם וְרֶמֶשׂ הָאֲדָמָה
　　וְקֶשֶׁת וְחֶרֶב וּמִלְחָמָה אֶשְׁבּוֹר מִן־הָאָרֶץ
　　וְהִשְׁכַּבְתִּים לָבֶטַח׃

Ho 2.20 [final ת of כרת doubles the perfect subject ending]; חיה *living thing;* עוֹף *bird;* רמשׂ *creeping thing;* קֶשֶׁת *bow;* בֶּטַח *securely*

20.8 Enrichment: Modality

English uses "helping verbs" to modify the function of the main verb in other ways than causation. Auxiliary verbs modify either the *temporal* reference ("they *have* gone", "they *shall have* gone") or can be *modal* ("you *must/could/should have* gone"). With rare exceptions Biblical Hebrew does not use helping verbs (יכל, *be able*, is the main exception), either modal or temporal. Modality and "tense" are translational (i.e., exegetical) decisions, so that, for example, Ps 5.12 could be rendered in various ways, all of which are grammatically defensible, even though they are not all equally probable. This does not mean that verbal function is somehow inherently ambiguous or indeterminate, but it does underline the importance of lexical value (semantic load) and context, alongside conjugation and stem.

וְיִשְׂמְחוּ כָל־חוֹסֵי בָךְ　　And let all [those] who take refuge in you rejoice

And all [those] who take refuge in you shall rejoice

And all [those] who take refuge in you rejoice

And all [those] who take refuge in you should/must rejoice

And all [those] who take refuge in you may rejoice

And may all [those] who take refuge in you rejoice

יְרַנֵּנוּ לְעוֹלָם　　For ever let them shout

For ever shall they shout (etc.)

וְתָסֵךְ עָלֵימוֹ　　And may you shelter them

And you shall shelter them (etc.)

וְיַעְלְצוּ בְךָ אֹהֲבֵי שְׁמֶךָ׃　　And may those who love your name exult in you

That those who love your name may exult in you (etc.)

Lesson 21

The *Qal* Passive/Identifying (Parsing) Verbal Forms

A number of verbs occur in forms which look like *pual* or *hofal*, but which have come to be recognized as the remnants of a *qal* passive [Qp] stem.[153]

21.1.1 *Form*

The primary criteria for identifying forms as Qp rather than as Dp or Hp is that (1) the verbal root does not occur in *piel* or *hifil*; or (2) these forms function as the passive of the *qal* (i.e., rather than the passive of the *piel* or *hifil*); or both. Note, for example, the function of these verbs in their various stems:

	Q	Qp and N	D	H
אכל	eat; consume, destroy	be eaten, consumed	---	feed
ילד	bear, give birth to	be born	deliver (as a midwife)	beget, become father/ancestor of
לקח	take	be taken	---	---
נתן	give	be given	---	---
שדד	destroy	be destroyed	assault, mistreat	---

This charts some forms of the *qal* passive in these stems (not all are listed, forms not listed do not occur), as well as how relatively infrequent they are.[154]

---

153. The existence of a *qal* passive stem was suggested by Ibn Jikatilla in the 10th century. On the *qal* passive, cf. *Gesenius' Hebrew Grammar* (Oxford: Oxford University), §52e, 53u; Paul Joüon, *A Grammar of Biblical Hebrew*. Trans., Takamitsu Muraoka (Rome: Pontifical Biblical Institute, 1991), §58; Bruce K. Waltke & M. O'Connor, *Introduction to Biblical Hebrew Syntax* (Winona Lake: Eisenbrauns, 1993), §22.6, 23.6.1, 24.6a, 25.1a, 27.1a; Ronald J. Williams, "The Passive *Qal* Theme in Hebrew" *Essays on the Ancient Semitic World*, ed. J.W. Wevers & D.B. Redford (Toronto: University of Toronto, 1970), 43-50.

154. The perfect and participle tend to follow the forms of *pual*, whereas the imperfect and infinitive construct are analogous to *hofal*, as the following distribution for these verbs shows.

Verbal Root	"Stem"	Perfect	Participle	Imperfect	Inf. Const.
אכל	"Pual"	3	1	1	
ילד	"Pual"	26	1		
	"Hofal"				3
לקח	"Pual"	8	1		
	"Hofal"			6	
נתן	"Hofal"			8	
שדד	"Pual"	20			
	"Hofal"			2	
		all ≈ "Dp"	2/3 ≈ "Dp"	16/17 ≈ "Hp"	all ≈ "Hp"

Verbal Root	Perfect	Imperfect/ Preterite	Infinitive Construct	Participle	Gloss	Occurrences (Qp/total)
אכל	אֻכַּל	יֻאְכַל		אֻכָּל	be eaten	5/809
ילד	יֻלַּד		הוּלֶדֶת	יֻלָּד	be born	30/499
לקח	לֻקַּח	יֻקַּח		לֻקָּח	be taken	15/938
נתן		יֻתַּן			be given	8/2007
שדד	שֻׁדַּד	יוּשַּׁד			be destroyed	22/43

21.1.2 *Function (HBI §2.1.2)*

As shown above, the *qal* passive is the passive of the function of the *qal* of the same verbal root.

וְהָאֲשֵׁרָה אֲשֶׁר־עָלָיו כֹּרָתָה ... and the Asherah which was beside it *had been cut down* (Jg 6.28)

וּבָנוֹת יֻלְּדוּ לָהֶם ... and daughters *were born* to them (Gn 6.1)

21.1.3 *Frequency*

It is difficult to garner statistics for the frequency of the *qal* passive. Whether or not to include the "regular" Qp participle, such as בָּרוּךְ, "blessed" (which occurs fairly frequently, and in a number of verbs, but which has a different morphology (i.e., not *pual*- or *hofal*-"like") is problematic. Reference works tend to either (1) identify these forms as *pual* or *hofal* (e.g., DCH); or (2) mention the *qal* passive as a possible identification of *pual* or *hofal* (e.g., BDB, HALOT). The statistics used in this grammar suggest that *qal* passive occurs 1,277 times in Biblical Hebrew (1.7% of all verbal forms).

21.2 *Identifying (Parsing) Verbal Forms*

You may well wonder why we spend so much time identifying [parsing] verbs, especially given the availability of analytical lexicons (which parse every form in Biblical Hebrew), computerized databases, interlinears, and parsing guides. This emphasis does not imply that verbs are somehow more important or "key" to Biblical Hebrew. It merely reflects the nature of the language—Hebrew verbs are more complex than, for example, nouns or numerals, and therefore require more study.

As we begin reading the biblical text, and see verbal forms in their larger linguistic contexts, we will find that they are both more and less complex: more complex because their function is a direct reflection of their literary context (the words, clauses, and sentences around them), and less complex, because they become increasingly easier to recognize as we spend more time in the text itself.

Helpful as they can be, the tools mentioned above form yet another layer between the reader and the Hebrew text, one of the barriers that the study of Hebrew attempts to overcome. Furthermore, the greater our dependence on the "tools", the more tools we need to gather and refer to in order to study the text. If we need to look up the parsing of every other verb form, we spend our study time interacting primarily with the tools, rather than the text. Also, no parsing guide—computerized or not—is infallible, and there are valid differences of opinion between grammarians and commentators regarding the parsing of some forms (most tools identify only one possibility).[154] A major reason for studying Hebrew is to enable the student of Scripture to interact with the text on a more immediate level,[155] as directly as possible with the Hebrew text.

21.2.1 *Verbal Diagnostics (summary)*

This section presents some diagnostics for identifying verbal forms in Hebrew. If one does not seem to work, try another! You will probably recognize something about most verbal forms (an ending,

---

154. These are more common when the verbal form is based on a weak verbal root (Lessons 24-31).
155. "[More] immediate" describes the relationship of the interpreter to the text, not to "layers" of meaning within the text itself (as might be implied by "deeper"). Students of the languages should *apprehend* or *interact with* the text in a different way than those who read it in their native tongue.

the stem, conjugation, lexical form, etc.). Begin from what you recognize, and then develop a routine method that allows you to identify the verb's subject, conjugation, stem, and lexical form.

Stem	Perfect	Imperfect & Preterite	Imperative	Infinitives	Participle
Q	no prefix; *a*-vowels	יִ- ; וַיִּ-	no prefix	no prefix	no prefix; *ḥolem* after first radical
N	נִ-	יִ- ; וַיִּ-	הִ-	הִ- ; נִ-	נִ-
D	no prefix	יְ- ; וַיְ-	no prefix	no prefix	מְ-
Dp	no prefix	יְ- ; וַיְ-	---	no prefix	מְ-
Dt	הִתְ-	יִתְ- ; וַיִּתְ-	הִתְ-	הִתְ-	מִתְ-
H	הִ-	יַ- ; וַיַּ-	הַ-	הַ-	מַ-
Hp	הָ-	יָ- ; וַיָּ-	---	---	מָ-

21.2.2 Diagnostic Questions

1. Is there a *pronominal suffix* or *syntactical prefix* (conjunction, preposition, article, interrogative -ה)?
   a. The conjunction *waw* and interrogative -ה can be prefixed to any verbal form.
   b. A preposition occurs only with infinitives construct and participles.
   c. The article occurs only with participles.
   d. Pronominal suffixes can affect the pointing of, e.g., the prefix vowel; they can also obscure the subject ending of the verb.
2. Is there a *PGN suffix* (i.e., an affix that identifies the person, gender, number of the subject)?
3. Is there a *PGN prefix* (i.e., a prefix that is part of the verbal form, not a syntactical prefix [above], that identifies the person, gender, number of the subject)? Identify the *prefix vowel* (if any).
4. In imperfect and preterite, f the prefix vowel is *ḥireq*, is the *first radical* of the verbal root *doubled*?
   a. Yes → *nifal*
   b. No → *qal* (unless root is I-נ or [certain] geminate verbs)
5. Does the *second radical* of the verbal root have *dageš forte* (i.e., *dageš* preceded by a full vowel)?
   Yes → *piel, pual, hitpael*
6. If you can answer questions 1-5, and know only two forms of each stem (3ms P, 3ms F), you can parse nearly any form.

	Q	N	D	Dp	Dt	H	Hp
3ms perfect	מָשַׁל	נִמְשַׁל	מִשֵּׁל	מֻשַּׁל	הִתְמַשֵּׁל	הִמְשִׁיל	הָמְשַׁל
3ms imperfect	יִמְשֹׁל	יִמָּשֵׁל	יְמַשֵּׁל	יְמֻשַּׁל	יִתְמַשֵּׁל	יַמְשִׁיל	יָמְשַׁל

All stems except *qal* and *nifal* prefix the letter -מ to form the participle; in those stems the prefix vowel for the participle is the same as the prefix vowel of the imperfect and preterite.

21.2.3 Summary

Forms Without a Prefix

1. A verbal form without a prefix must be *qal* (perfect, imperative, participle, infinitive) or *piel* or *pual* (perfect, imperative, infinitive).

Forms with a Prefix

1. A tri-radical form with a prefixed -נ is either *nifal* perfect or participle, *or* 1cp imperfect or preterite (any stem).
2. A tri-radical form with a prefixed -ה is either *hifil*, *hofal*, or *hitpael* perfect, imperative, or infinitive; or *nifal* imperative or infinitive.
3. A tri-radical form with a prefixed -מ is a participle in either *piel*, *pual*, *hitpael*, *hifil*, or *hofal*; or a participle or infinitive construct with prefixed *min* (-מִ).

Prefix Vowel

1. If the prefix is -הִ and there is -ִי- after the second radical, the form is *hifil* perfect.
2. If the prefix is -הִתְ and the second radical is doubled, the form is *hitpael* (perfect, imperative, or infinitive).
3. If the prefix is -הָ the form is *hofal* (perfect or infinitive).
4. *Hifil* is the only stem with a *patah* prefix vowel in imperfect, preterite, imperative, infinitives, and participle (i.e., all conjugations except perfect).
5. If the prefix vowel of an imperfect or preterite form is *hireq*, the form is *qal*, *nifal*, or *hitpael*.

Doubled Radical

1. A tri-tradical form with a doubled second radical must be *piel*, *pual*, or *hitpael* (all conjugations).
2. A tri-radical form with a doubled first radical must be *nifal* imperfect, preterite, imperative, or infinitive.

N.B.: As always, the goal is the ability to "figure out" a verbal form, not to memorize a set of "rules".

21.3 Vocabulary

gather, assemble	קָבַץ	.316	sister, female relative	אָחוֹת	.307
burn incense; cause a sacrifice or incense to smoke (D, H)	קָטַר	.317	trust, be confident in/of	בָּטַח	.308
meet, encounter (only as NC)	קָרָא		burn, consume (Q, D)	בָּעַר	.309
happen, occur	קָרָה	.318	walk, step on, tramp; cause to march, tread down, tread [string] a bow (both Q & H)	דָּרַךְ	.310
toward, against, opposite (Q inf. const. + לְ)	לִקְרַאת		like, just like (variant of -כְּ)	כְּמוֹ	.311
hunger, famine	רָעָב	.319	leader, member of ruling class	נָשִׂיא	.312
burn (oft. specified with בָּאֵשׁ)	שָׂרַף	.320	surrounding, [all] around (adv.)	סָבִיב	
rise early (H; often in hendiadys: "do X early"); often with בַּבֹּקֶר "in the morning"	שָׁכַם	.321	surrounding, [all] around (adv.); מִן + סָבִיב	מִסָּבִיב	.313
throw, cast, hurl (H)	שָׁלַךְ	.322	close, shut (Q); give into someone's power [hand] (H)	סָגַר	.314
			pillar, column	עַמּוּד	.315

21.4 Exercises

After studying the diagnostics of the stems, *gloss* these clauses, *parsing* all verbal forms. If a verb's function is not clear due to its stem, consult a lexicon.

1. וְאֶת־הָעֹלָה הִמְצִיאוּ אֵלָיו לִנְתָחֶיהָ וְאֶת־הָרֹאשׁ וַיַּקְטֵר עַל־הַמִּזְבֵּחַ׃

   Lv 9.13; מצא *present* (H); נֵתַח *piece* [of a cut-up carcass]; -לְ *by*

2. וַיַּעַזְבוּ־שָׁם אֶת־אֱלֹהֵיהֶם וַיֹּאמֶר דָּוִיד וַיִּשָּׂרְפוּ בָּאֵשׁ׃

   1 Ch 14.12; David; אמר probably functions here as "commanded"

3. וַיִּשְׁכַּב אָסָא עִם־אֲבֹתָיו וַיִּקָּבֵר עִם־אֲבֹתָיו בְּעִיר דָּוִד אָבִיו וַיִּמְלֹךְ יְהוֹשָׁפָט בְּנוֹ תַּחְתָּיו׃

   1 Kg 15.24; Asa; Jehoshaphat

4. וְנָתַתִּי מַפְתֵּחַ בֵּית־דָּוִד עַל־שִׁכְמוֹ וּפָתַח וְאֵין סֹגֵר וְסָגַר וְאֵין פֹּתֵחַ׃

   Is 22.22; וְנָתַתִּי *I will put/place/set* (< נתן); מַפְתֵּחַ *key* (something showing that the wearer has authority or ability to open & close?); שֶׁכֶם *shoulder*; David

5. וְהִשְׁלַכְתִּי אֶתְכֶם מֵעַל פָּנָי כַּאֲשֶׁר הִשְׁלַכְתִּי אֶת־כָּל־אֲחֵיכֶם אֵת כָּל־זֶרַע אֶפְרָיִם׃

   Jr 7.15; Ephraim

6. וְאַל־יַבְטַח אֶתְכֶם חִזְקִיָּהוּ אֶל־יהוה לֵאמֹר... לֹא תִנָּתֵן הָעִיר הַזֹּאת בְּיַד מֶלֶךְ אַשּׁוּר׃

   Isai 36:15; נתן *give*; בְּיַד *in[to] the hand of*; Hezekiah; Assyria; the first verb is volitional

7. נִקְבְּצוּ אֵלֵינוּ כָּל־מַלְכֵי הָאֱמֹרִי יֹשְׁבֵי הָהָר׃

   Josh 10.6; אֶל *against* (אֶל and עַל often overlap in function); Amorite(s)

8. וַיִּקָּבְצוּ פְלִשְׁתִּים וַיָּבֹאוּ וַיַּחֲנוּ בְשׁוּנֵם וַיִּקְבֹּץ שָׁאוּל אֶת־כָּל־יִשְׂרָאֵל וַיַּחֲנוּ בַּגִּלְבֹּעַ׃

   1 Sam 28.4; וַיָּבֹאוּ *they came/went*; וַיַּחֲנוּ *they camped*; Philistines, Shunem, Saul, Gilboa; note the difference in function between the N & Q of קבץ

9. כִּי מִמֶּנָּה לֻקָּחְתָּ כִּי־עָפָר אַתָּה וְאֶל־עָפָר תָּשׁוּב׃

   Gn 3.19; the suffix on מִן is 3fs because it refers to אֲדָמָה; עָפָר *dirt, dust*; תָּשׁוּב *you shall return* (2ms Q F < שׁוּב)

10. מַשָּׂא מוֹאָב
    כִּי בְּלֵיל שֻׁדַּד עָר
    מוֹאָב נִדְמָה
    כִּי בְּלֵיל שֻׁדַּד קִיר־מוֹאָב נִדְמָה׃

    Is 15.1; מַשָּׂא *oracle; burden*; לַיִל ‖ לֵיל; שׁדד *destroy, ruin, devastate* (3ms Dp P); Ar (capital(?) city [cf. עִיר] of Moab); נִדְמָה *it is destroyed/undone* (3ms N P); 1a is a "title"; 1b-d are clauses

11. וַתֹּאמֶר יֻתַּן אֶת־אֲבִישַׁג הַשֻּׁנַמִּית לַאֲדֹנִיָּהוּ אָחִיךָ לְאִשָּׁה׃

    1 Kg 2.21; Abishag; Shunamite; Adonijah

12. וַיִּקְבֹּץ מֶלֶךְ־יִשְׂרָאֵל אֶת־הַנְּבִאִים אַרְבַּע מֵאוֹת אִישׁ וַיֹּאמֶר אֲלֵהֶם הֲנֵלֵךְ אֶל־רָמֹת גִּלְעָד לַמִּלְחָמָה׃

    2 Chr 18.5; הֲנֵלֵךְ *shall we go*; Ramoth-gilead

13. הַדְרִיכֵנִי בִּנְתִיב מִצְוֹתֶיךָ כִּי־בוֹ חָפָצְתִּי׃

    Ps 119.35; נָתִיב *path, way*

14. הַבֹּטְחִים בַּיהוה כְּהַר־צִיּוֹן לֹא־יִמּוֹט לְעוֹלָם יֵשֵׁב׃

    Ps 125.1; Zion; יָמוּט *it/he moves/shall be moved*; יָשַׁב *it/he endures/shall endure*; these singular verbs are collectives; their subject is the first word

15. וְלֹא הִסְגַּרְתַּנִי בְּיַד־אוֹיֵב הֶעֱמַדְתָּ בַמֶּרְחָב רַגְלָי׃

    Ps 31.9; מֶרְחָב *wide [i.e., open] place* (cf. רחב, *be wide*)

21.5 Enrichment: Nominal Formation

The lexicon of Biblical Hebrew has many words that are related to each other, so that knowing a verbal root can help you recognize new words, even when they are quite infrequent (e.g., רִפְאוּת, below). These lists also show that noun formation is not arbitrary in Biblical Hebrew. In English, for example, suffixing "r-" to a verb yields the noun that identifies someone characterized by that activity, such as "write+r" (one who writes), but adding "r-" to the beginning of a word does not change its function, since initial "r-" is not a functional prefix in English.

1. Nouns formed by suffixed -וּת are *feminine*, and tend to be abstract:

מלך	reign, rule, be king	מַלְכוּת	royalty, royal authority; kingdom; reign
סכל	be insolent, foolish	סִכְלוּת	folly, insolence (7x; all in Qo)
רפא	heal	רִפְאוּת	healing (only Pr 3.8)
אַלְמָנָה	widow	אַלְמָנוּת	widowhood

2. Nouns can be formed by prefixing -מ to a root:

ירא	fear, be afraid of	מוֹרָא	fear
ישׁב	sit, stay; settle, live, dwell	מוֹשָׁב	dwelling[-place]
ספר	count	מִסְפָּר	number, total
עשׂה	work, do, make, act	מַעֲשֶׂה	deed, act; thing done, work
צוה	command, order, demand	מִצְוָה	command, order, demand
קנה	purchase, buy; acquire	מִקְנֶה	property, acquisition(s); cattle
קרה	happen, befall; meet	מִקְרֶה	happening, occurrence
ראה	see, observe, look [at]	מַרְאֶה	sight, appearance
שׁפט	judge	מִשְׁפָּט	judgment; justice; custom

3. Some of these designate the *place* of the activity described by the corresponding verb:

זבח	sacrifice	מִזְבֵּחַ	altar; place of sacrifice
מלך	reign, rule, be king	מַמְלָכָה	kingdom; sovereignty, rule, reign, dominion
צפה	watch, guard	מִצְפָּה	watchtower (Mizpah)
קדשׁ	be[come] holy	מִקְדָּשׁ	sanctuary; holy place
קום	stand	מָקוֹם	place; standing place
רום	be high, exalted	מָרוֹם	height
רכב	ride	מֶרְכָּבָה	chariot (cf. רֶכֶב, chariot, chariotry)
שׁכב	lie down, sleep	מִשְׁכָּב	bed
שׁכן	live, dwell	מִשְׁכָּן	living/dwelling place; "tabernacle"

4. *Participles* can be substantival so frequently that they essentially function as nouns:

יָשַׁב	live, dwell, settle, remain	יֹשֵׁב	inhabitant; citizen (Q Ptc)
כָּהַן	be/act as priest	כֹּהֵן	priest (Q Ptc)
רָגַל	go about on foot; spy	מְרַגֵּל	spy, scout (D Ptc)
שָׁפַט	judge, administer justice	שֹׁפֵט	[a] judge (Q Ptc)

5. Nouns "from" *geminate* roots can retain the repeated radical of the root (cf. *dageš forte*):

הלל	praise	תְּהִלָּה	praise
פלל	pray	תְּפִלָּה	prayer

6. *False* cognates—words that share the same radicals, but have a different root (i.e., homonyms), as English "Put the money in the *bank*", "a hole in the river *bank*", and "The pilot put the plane into a *bank*"—are usually distinguished by Roman numerals (I, II, etc.) in the lexica; related adjectives, nouns, etc. are identified by the same Roman numeral.

מׁשל I	compare(?); use a proverb	מָשָׁל	proverb, saying; parable
מׁשל II	reign, rule	מֶמְשֶׁלֶת / מֶמְשָׁלָה	rule, dominion, kingdom

Lesson 22

Guttural Verbs

Verbal roots that have א, ה, ח, or ע as one of their root consonants belong to a subset of the basic verb called *guttural* verbs. There are five types, identified according to the position of the guttural consonant. Some verbs with ר also share the characteristics of the guttural verbal roots, since ר does not double.[156]

I-guttural (and I-ר)	פ-guttural	עבר	cross over
I-א	פ״א[157]	אמר	say
II-guttural (and II-ר)	ע-guttural	בער	burn
	ע״ר	ברך	bless
III-guttural	ל-guttural	שלח	send
III-א	ל״א	מצא	find

22.1 The Basic Differences

Four characteristics of the gutturals (one of which they share with ר) cause the vowels of some forms to differ from those of the basic verb.

1. א, ה, ח, ע, ר *do not double* (geminate). In forms of the strong verb that have *dageš forte* in a position occupied by a guttural or ר (e.g., the middle radical in D, Dp, and Dt), the *dageš* is absent; this non-gemination often causes the preceding vowel to lengthen, because a syllable is open rather than being closed by *dageš forte*.
2. א, ה, ח, ע are followed by *ḥatef*-vowels instead of *šewa* (i.e., the half-vowel is *under* the guttural and thus "follows" it in pronunciation).
    a. I-guttural verbs often have a *ḥatef*-vowel after the first radical instead of *šewa*
    b. II-guttural roots have *ḥatef*-vowels instead of vocal *šewa* after the second radical (i.e, before vocalic endings)
3. ה, ח, ע tend to occur with *a*-vowels, either full vowels or *pataḥ furtivum*, so that *pataḥ* may occur where the basic verb (משל) has *ḥolem* or *ṣere*.
4. Since א does not close a syllable, verbs whose roots end in א tend to have long vowels after the second radical. Although ה (i.e., without *mappiq*) does not close a syllable, verbs that end in ה are a type of weak root (below); verbs ending in ה- are strong, and considered III-guttural.

These characteristics cause most of the differences between guttural verbs and the basic verb. In this table, each pair of examples has the same parsing; the second example is the basic verb.

---

156. This lesson presents a great deal of information about guttural verbal roots; the rules merely demonstrate that the patterns are predictable, regular, and reflect the effect of the gutturals on vocalization.

157. The " means that this is to be read as an abbreviation or symbol, not a word. Labels such as פ״א are read from right to left (*pe-'alef*).

Guttural Verb	Basic Verb	Parsing	Nature of the Difference	Reason for the Difference
יַאֲבֵק בָּרֵךְ	יִמְשֹׁל מַשֵּׁל	3ms N F 2ms D V	no *dageš forte*; long vowels instead of short	Since gutturals don't double, the syllable is open; this also affects roots I/II-ר in certain stems (below).
יִשְׁמַע יְשַׁמַּע	יִמְשֹׁל יְמַשֵּׁל	3ms Q F 3ms D F	*a*-vowels (esp. *pataḥ*) after the second radical	Word-final gutturals tend to be preceded by an *a*-vowel.
בָּחֲרוּ עֲמַדְתֶּם	מָשְׁלוּ מְשַׁלְתֶּם	3cp Q P 2mp Q P	*ḥatef*-vowels instead of vocal *šewa*	Gutturals have *ḥatef*-vowels where the basic verb has vocal *šewa*.
יַעֲמֹד יַעֲמִיד	יִמְשֹׁל יַמְשִׁיל	3ms Q F 3ms H P	*ḥatef*-vowels under the first radical instead of silent *šewa* in forms with prefixes (F, Pr)	Initial guttural that closes the prefix syllable (i.e., where the first radical is followed by silent *šewa* in the basic verb) is often followed by the *ḥatef*-vowel that matches the prefix vowel.
יֶחְדַּל	יִמְשֹׁל	3ms Q F	*segol* as prefix vowel instead of *ḥireq*	Initial gutturals, especially ח, may have *segol* as a prefix vowel where the basic verb has *ḥireq*.
מָצָאתִי יִמְצָא	מָשַׁלְתִּי יְמֻשַּׁל	1cs Q P 3ms Dp F	*long* vowel after the second radical, no *šewa* before PGN ending; no *dageš* in ת of PGN ending	III-א forms generally have a *long* vowel after the second radical of the verbal root. The ת of PGN endings lacks *dageš lene* since it is "preceded" by a vowel (final א is not considered consonantal).
צָמִית מָצָתִי וַיִּמְצוּ	מָשַׁלְתְּ מָשַׁלְתִּי וַיִּמְשֹׁל	2fs Q P 1cs Q P 3ms Q Pr	lack final א	[Silent] א drops out of some III-א forms (usually noted in *Mp*; Lesson 29).

22.2 I-Guttural Roots

These verbal roots differ from the basic verb wherever the first radical is followed by *šewa* (*qal* imperfect and preterite; *nifal* perfect and participle; all forms of *hifil* and *hofal*) or doubled (*nifal* imperfect, imperative, infinitive construct). The **D**-stems are **not** affected.

1. 2mp and 2fp *qal* perfect have *ḥatef-pataḥ* under the first radical (משל is for comparison).

   מְשַׁלְתֶּם   2mp Q P   *You served*   עֲבַדְתֶּם

2. Wherever the basic verb has silent *šewa* after the first radical, guttural roots have a *ḥatef*-vowel, with the corresponding full vowel under the prefix (משל is for comparison).

   הִמְשִׁיל   3ms H P   *He enslaved*   הֶעֱבִיד
   אֶמְשֹׁל   1cs Q F   *I [will] seize*   אֶחֱזַק

3. Whenever the initial radical of the basic verb is doubled (*nifal* F, V, NC), the prefix vowel is long (*sere*). Since ר does not geminate, this also applies to verbs that are I-ר.

   תִּמָּשֵׁל   *You/she will be ruled*   3fs N F   יֵעָזֵב   *He/It will be forsaken*
   וַתִּמָּשֵׁל   *and she/it will appear*   3ms N Pr   וְתֵרָאֶה   *and she/it will appear*

22.3 I-א Roots

This sub-set of the I-guttural roots (cf. §6.2), contains only five verbs (אפה, אבה, אבד, אכל, אמר). They differ from other I-guttural verbs (above) only in *qal* imperfect (Q F) and *qal* preterite (Q Pr).

22.4 *II-Guttural Roots*

These verbal roots differ from the basic verb wherever the second radical is doubled (all three D-stems), or followed by vocal *šewa* (all forms with vocal PGN sufformatives, in all stems except *hifil*). The forms of II-guttural verbs are not affected in *hifil*.

1. The D-stems follow one of two patterns:
   a. In some II-guttural roots the vowel after the first radical is *long* (*qames* or *sere* in *piel*, *hitpael*; *holem* in *pual*), since that syllable is open.

בֵּרֵךְ	He blessed	3ms D P	מִשֵּׁל
בֹּרַךְ	He was blessed	3ms Dp P	מֻשַּׁל
מְבֹרָךְ	Blessed	ms Dp Ptc	מְמֻשָּׁל

   b. Other II-guttural roots look just like the basic verb, but without *dageš forte*, so that the vowel after the first radical is *hireq* or *patah* (*piel*, *hitpael*) or *qibbus* (*pual*).[158]

בִּחֵר	He chose	3ms D P	מִשֵּׁל
נִבָּחֵר	We will be chosen	1cp Dp F	נִמָּשֵׁל

2. With vocalic PGN suffixes (וּ-, ָה-, ִי-), these roots have a *hatef*-vowel after the second radical instead of vocal *šewa* (all stems):

גָּאֲלוּ	They redeemed.	3cp Q P	מָשְׁלוּ
בַּחֲרוּ	Choose!	2mp Q V	מִשְׁלוּ
הִגָּאֲלוּ	Redeem yourselves!	2mp N V	הִמָּשְׁלוּ

22.5 *III-Guttural Roots* (III-ח/ע/ה only)

These verbal roots differ from the basic verb mainly by having *patah* after the second radical, or *patah furtivum* after its vowel. *Mappiq* in the final ה of these roots means that the ה is a consonant, not a vowel letter (as it is in roots III-ה; below).

1. If a form has no ending or suffix, the vowel after the second radical is *patah*, except in H (which will, nonetheless, have *patah furtivum*):

יִבְרַח	He flees	3ms Q F	יִמְשֹׁל
יַשְׁמִיעַ	He causes ___ to hear	3ms H F	יַמְשִׁיל
וַיִּשְׁמַע	and he heard	3ms Q Pr	וַיִּמְשֹׁל
וַיַּשְׁמַע	and he caused ___ to hear	3ms H Pr	וַיַּמְשִׁיל

2. If the vowel after the second radical is written with a vowel letter, *patah furtivum* is added (see also the last example in #1, above):

שָׁמוּעַ	Heard	ms Qp Ptc	מָשׁוּל
יַשְׁמִיעַ	He will cause ___ to hear	3ms H F	יַמְשִׁיל

3. 2fs P (all stems) has *patah* after the third radical instead of silent *šewa*:

שָׁמַעַתְּ	You heard	2fs Q P	מָשַׁלְתְּ
הָשְׁמַעַתְּ	You were caused to hear	2fs Hp P	הָמְשַׁלְתְּ

---

158. This is called "virtual doubling" or "gemination", because the Masoretes pointed the word with a short vowel (since the syllable would have been closed if the radical had been doubled)—the term is confusing, since nothing is in fact doubled.

22.6 III-א Roots

These forms differ from the basic verb because א *cannot close* a syllable; at the end of a syllable it becomes silent and the preceding vowel is long, usually *qames* or *sere*. Forms with vocalic endings (וֹ-, ִי-, ָה-), where א begins the final syllable, are like the basic verb.

1. The vowel after the second radical is long, and the PGN ending (ת) does not have *dageš lene*, because the א is silent (and therefore ignored in pronunciation).

מָצָא	He found	3ms Q P	מָשַׁל
מָצָאתָ	You found	2ms Q P	מָשַׁלְתָּ

   Silent א may even be missing (the verbal root is צמא; see table, §22.1):

צָמִת	You are thirsty (Ru 2.9)	2fs Q P	מָשַׁלְתְּ

2. With the ending נָה- (2/3fp F, Pr, V), the vowel after the second radical is *segol* (all stems):

תִּתְמַצֶּאנָה	You/they [will] find your/themselves	2/3pf Dt F	תִּתְמַשֵּׁלְנָה
תִּמְצֶאנָה	You/they [will] find	2/3fp Q F	תִּמְשֹׁלְנָה

22.7 Common Guttural Roots

This table lists all guttural roots with pointing *that is affected* by the presence of a guttural or ר that occur more than two hundred times in Biblical Hebrew, listed by type. Verbs are listed according to the type of weakness that actually occurs (e.g., ירא, "fear", does not occur in the D-stems, and so is listed as III-א, but not as II-ר; ירד, "descend, go down", does not occur in the D-stems, and so is not listed).

I-א		I-guttural (not I-א)	
אמר	say, speak (> 5000x)	עשׂה	do, make; act [perform a deed] (2573x)
אכל	eat, devour, consume (795x)	ראה	see (1294x)
אהב	love (205x)	עלה	go up, ascend (879x)
III-guttural		עבר	cross/pass over/through/by (539x)
שׁמע	hear, listen [to]; obey (1136x)	עמד	stand; stop (519x)
ידע	know, understand; notice, recognize (924x)	ענה	answer; testify (314x)
לקח	take, get, acquire (964x)	עבד	serve, be servant to (289x)
שׁלח	send [away], let go; stretch out, reach, extend (839x)	חזק	be[come] strong (Q); seize, grab; hold (H) (288x)
ישׁע	save, deliver, triumph (205x)	חיה	live, be alive (281x)
III-א		חטא	sin, miss [a target] (237x)
בוא	come, go [in], enter (2530x)	אסף	gather, collect (203x)
יצא	go out, leave, exit (1055x)	עזב	leave, forsake, abandon (212x)
קרא	call; name; invite; read (730x)	**II-guttural (or ר)**	
נשׂא	lift up, carry, bear; forgive (651x)	ברך	bless, worship (D) (328x)
מצא	find, discover (451x)		
ירא	fear, be afraid [of] (377x)		
מלא	be[come] full (250x)		
חטא	sin, miss [a target] (237x)		

22.8 Concepts

doubling	I-guttural	II-guttural	III-guttural	mappiq
gemination	פ-gutteral	ע-guttural	ל-guttural	"virtual doubling"

22.9 Vocabulary

323.	אֹרֶךְ	length	332.	נֶגֶב	south, Negev
324.	הָפַךְ	turn, overturn, destroy	333.	עוֹר	skin, leather
325.	חַיָּה	animal(s) [coll.], living thing	334.	עָנָן	cloud(s)
326.	חָלָל	wounded, slain, dead (adj.)	335.	פַּעַם / פַּעֲמַיִם	footstep; time (i.e., once, thrice) / twice (dual)
327.	חֲמוֹר	male donkey/ass			
328.	יַעַן	on account of, for the sake of (prp.); because [of] (cj.)	336.	שַׁבָּת	rest, sabbath
329.	כֶּרֶם	vineyard	337.	שָׁכַח	forget
330.	מָכַר	sell	338.	תָּמִיד	regularly, continually (adv.)[159]
331.	מַרְאֶה	sight, appearance (cf. ראה)			

22.10 Exercises

After studying the characteristics of the guttural verbs, *gloss* these clauses, *parsing* the verbs.

1. אֵיפֹה הָאֲנָשִׁים אֲשֶׁר הֲרַגְתֶּם — Jg 8.18; אֵיפֹה *Where?*

2. וַיַּחֲלֹם יוֹסֵף חֲלוֹם — Gn 37.5; חלם *dream*; Joseph

3. הַשֶּׁמֶשׁ יֵהָפֵךְ לְחֹשֶׁךְ וְהַיָּרֵחַ לְדָם — Joel 3.4; יָרֵחַ *moon*

4. וַיֶּחֱזַק הָרָעָב בְּאֶרֶץ מִצְרָיִם׃ — Gn 41.56; חזק *sieze, be strong*

5. וַיֹּאמֶר שְׁמָעוּנִי יְהוּדָה וְיֹשְׁבֵי יְרוּשָׁלַםִ הַאֲמִינוּ בַּיהוָה אֱלֹהֵיכֶם וְתֵאָמֵנוּ הַאֲמִינוּ בִנְבִיאָיו וְהַצְלִיחוּ׃ — 2 Ch 20.20; צלח *succeed, prosper*; Judah, Jerusalem

6. וְעַתָּה קוּם עֲבֹר אֶת־הַיַּרְדֵּן הַזֶּה אַתָּה וְכָל־הָעָם הַזֶּה אֶל־הָאָרֶץ אֲשֶׁר אָנֹכִי נֹתֵן לָהֶם לִבְנֵי יִשְׂרָאֵל׃ — Josh 1.2; קוּם *stand, rise* (2ms Q V; this form often introduces another imperative); Jordan

7. אַל־תַּעַזְבֵנִי יְהוָה אֱלֹהַי אַל־תִּרְחַק מִמֶּנִּי׃ — Ps 38.22 (יהוה and אֱלֹהַי are vocative; each line is a clause)

8. הַשְׁמִיעֵנִי בַבֹּקֶר חַסְדֶּךָ כִּי־בְךָ בָטָחְתִּי כִּי־אֵלֶיךָ נָשָׂאתִי נַפְשִׁי׃ ... — Ps 143.8a, bβ (in reading poetry, "bβ" refers to the second half ("β") of the second poetic line ("b"))

9. וַאֲבַדְתֶּם בַּגּוֹיִם וְאָכְלָה אֶתְכֶם אֶרֶץ אֹיְבֵיכֶם׃ — Lv 26.38 (each line is a clause)

10. לָכֵן אֱמֹר לִבְנֵי־יִשְׂרָאֵל אֲנִי יְהוָה — Ex 6.6

---

159. In a construct chain, תָּמִיד refers to something repeated, regular, or perpetual (עֹלָה תָּמִיד, *perpetual offering*).

11. וַתֹּאמֶר הָאִשָּׁה אֶל־הַנָּחָשׁ מִפְּרִי עֵץ־הַגָּן נֹאכֵל:	Gn 3.2; נָחָשׁ snake; גַּן garden
12. וְלֹא אָמְרוּ הָעֹבְרִים בִּרְכַּת־יְהוָה אֲלֵיכֶם בֵּרַכְנוּ אֶתְכֶם בְּשֵׁם יְהוָה:	Ps 129.8; בְּרָכָה blessing
13. וַיֹּאמֶר מֹשֶׁה אֶל־הָעָם אַתֶּם חֲטָאתֶם חֲטָאָה גְדֹלָה	Ex 32.30; חטא sin (v.); חֲטָאָה sin (n.), more commonly חַטָּאת; the second line contains the quotation; Moses
14. תּוֹעֲבַת יְהוָה דֶּרֶךְ רָשָׁע וּמְרַדֵּף צְדָקָה יֶאֱהָב:	Pr 15.9; תּוֹעֵבָה abomination; each line is a clause
15. ... כִּי לֹא־שָׁמַעַתְּ בְּקוֹלִי:	Jr 22.21
16. כִּשְׁמֹעַ עֵשָׂו אֶת־דִּבְרֵי אָבִיו וַיִּצְעַק צְעָקָה גְּדֹלָה וּמָרָה עַד־מְאֹד וַיֹּאמֶר לְאָבִיו בָּרֲכֵנִי גַם־אָנִי אָבִי:	Gn 27.34; צעק cry out [for help]; צְעָקָה cry (n.); מַר bitter (adj.); אָבִי is vocative; Esau
17. וַיֶּאֱהַב שְׁלֹמֹה אֶת־יְהוָה לָלֶכֶת בְּחֻקּוֹת דָּוִד אָבִיו רַק בַּבָּמוֹת הוּא מְזַבֵּחַ וּמַקְטִיר:	1 Kgs 3.3; לָלֶכֶת by walking (Q NC < הלך + ל); רַק only; בָּמָה high place, cultic center; Solomon, David
18. רְפָאֵנִי יְהוָה וְאֵרָפֵא ... כִּי תְהִלָּתִי אָתָּה:	Jr 17.14; תְּהִלָּה praise (n.)
19. בְּבַיִת אֶחָד יֵאָכֵל ... וְעֶצֶם לֹא תִשְׁבְּרוּ־בוֹ:	Ex 12.46; עֶצֶם bone; this is from the instructions about the Passover
20. אָז יִזְעֲקוּ אֶל־יְהוָה וְלֹא יַעֲנֶה אוֹתָם וְיַסְתֵּר פָּנָיו מֵהֶם בָּעֵת הַהִיא	Mi 3.4; זעק cry out [for help]; יַעֲנֶה he will answer (3ms Q F < ענה)
21. וַיְשַׁלַּח יְהוָה בּוֹ אֶת־גְּדוּדֵי כַשְׂדִּים וְאֶת־גְּדוּדֵי אֲרָם וְאֵת גְּדוּדֵי מוֹאָב וְאֵת גְּדוּדֵי בְנֵי־עַמּוֹן וַיְשַׁלְּחֵם בִּיהוּדָה לְהַאֲבִידוֹ כִּדְבַר יְהוָה אֲשֶׁר דִּבֶּר בְּיַד עֲבָדָיו הַנְּבִיאִים:	2 Kg 24.2; גְּדוּד band, troop; multiple national/ethnic names
22. וְנָתַן מַלְכֵיהֶם בְּיָדֶךָ וְהַאֲבַדְתָּ אֶת־שְׁמָם מִתַּחַת הַשָּׁמָיִם	Dt 7.24a

22.11 Enrichment: Vocabulary

A common standard for determining "fluency" in a language is a threshold vocabulary of about 1000 words. This seems to be the point at which most people can begin to communicate with native speakers with some degree of comfort. There are at least two effective ways to approach this goal; many students find that they work well in tandem.

1. Memorize *more vocabulary*, using, for example, Mitchel (see Bibliography), which allows you to learn glosses for words that occur in descending frequency in Biblical Hebrew. If you are learning new words *and* reading the text, you will find that the two often reinforce each other, as when you encounter a newly memorized word (or a closely related form) in the passage that you are reading.
2. Learn words *as they occur* in whatever text you are reading. For example, since fifty of the fifty-two occurrences of קֶרֶשׁ *plank* are in the book of Exodus (describing the Tabernacle), there is not much sense in learning to gloss this word unless you plan to read Exodus. But if you are going to read Exodus, then taking time to learn this word will be worth your while.

Continuing to strengthen your grasp of vocabulary (through memorization), and to see how it functions in a variety of contexts (through reading) will increase your ability to both read and understand the text.

Lesson 23

Basic Tools

In addition to the Hebrew Bible itself, there are many tools designed to help you understand the biblical text. *Lexical aids* suggest glosses (lexicons and word lists), or discuss the use, distribution, and broader function of individual words (theological dictionaries and wordbooks). There are also *grammatical aids* (e.g., reference grammars), and guides to *textual criticism*, the *masora*, and other technical aspects of the biblical text. Most of these are discussed briefly in Appendix F (below). This Lesson focuses on the text of BHS and the major lexical tools.

23.1 *Hebrew Bible*

23.1.1 *Biblia Hebraica Stuttgartensia (BHS)*

Since its completion, BHS has been the basis for nearly every Bible translation, Hebrew-based commentary, and reference work on Biblical Hebrew, whether in print and or electronic. *Biblia Hebraica Stuttgartensia* (BHS), named for its place of publication, is the fourth "scholarly" edition of the Hebrew text. It began to appear in 1967 and was complete ten years later; several corrected versions have appeared since then. A fifth edition, to be known as *Biblia Hebraica Quinta* (5th) is now being released (2010).

Prolegomena III

Foreword (in German, English, French, Spanish, Latin) III
    Part I.   A history of this edition of the Hebrew Bible, explains the differences between it and its predecessor, referred to as either BH³ [3rd ed.] or BHK ["Kittel", its editor].
    Part II.   Explains the basis of the masora in *BHS*, and some of the masoretic notes and readings. The English version of this material is on pp. XI-XVIII.

Sigla et Compendia Apparatum (List of Signs & Abbreviations) XLVII
    I. *Apparatus criticus* (The [Text-] Critical Apparatus) XLVII
        Sources XLVII
            An alphabetical list of abbreviations used in the textual apparatus (at the bottom of each page of the biblical text), with the documents to which they refer.
        Abbreviations LIX
            An alphabetical list of abbreviated Latin expressions used in the textual apparatus, with the full Latin terms.
    II. *Apparatus masorae* (The Masoretic Apparatus) LIII
        Lists alphabetically abbreviations used in the textual apparatus to refer to masoretic materials.

Index Siglorum et Abbreviationum Masorae Parvae (Index of Signs & Abbreviations of the *Masora Parva*) LIII
    Lists the abbreviations in the margins of *BHS* is in alphabetical [Hebrew] order; its Latin translations can be deciphered with the help of Kelley, *et al.* (1998).

Index Librorum Biblicorum (Index of the Biblical Books) .... [no page number]
    Lists the biblical books in the order in which they are printed in *BHS*; titles are in Latin & Hebrew.

The Hebrew Bible 1

The order of the books differs slightly from that found in English Bibles, because they follow the general order of the Septuagint (pre-Christian, Greek translation of the Hebrew text), rather than the Hebrew Bible:

- Ruth, Lamentations, Daniel, Esther, Ezra-Nehemiah, & Chronicles are among the Writings, rather than the historical and prophetic books.
- Samuel, Kings, Ezra-Nehemiah, & Chronicles are each a single book; there is no new title page for the second "book", although the second "half" begins again with chapter 1.
- Because the Latin titles are used, some will not look familiar (e.g., *Regum* = Kings, *Threni* = Lamentations).
- Although BHS claims to reproduce the text of the codex, the book of Chronicles precedes Psalms in the codex, rather than concluding the Bible, as it does in BHS.

Text Pages

The name of the biblical book is listed at the top of each page (Hebrew on the right page, Latin on the left). Page numbers are on the upper inside corners; chapter/verse references on the upper outside corners.

There are four blocks of material on each page. In the center of each page is the biblical text itself. This reproduces the text of Codex Leningrad, which is considered the oldest representative of the best masoretic scribal tradition, manuscripts copied and corrected by the family of Ben Asher. This text therefore represents a single manuscript, and is therefore a single witness to the biblical text (much as Alexandrinus or Vaticanus is to the text of the GNT). The UBS and Nestle-Aland Greek New Testaments contain an *eclectic* text that represents a committee's conclusions about the best reading for each verse, based on a comparison of many manuscripts, so that there is probably no single manuscript of the Greek NT with exactly the same text as the UBS/Nestle-Aland NT. *BHS* presents a single manuscript, and is thus no different in principle from a Greek NT that reproduces the text of only one manuscript, such as B (Codex Vaticanus).

In the outside margin are masoretic notes—*masora parva [mp]* or *masora marginalis*—which contains the Masoretes' comments on anything that they thought worthy of note, often unusual or rare forms. Written in Hebrew and Aramaic, they refer to the words in the text with small circles over them. We will discuss some of these, and how to read them.

At the bottom of each page are two sets of footnotes. The first set, consisting of raised numbers followed by "Mm" and a number, refer you to Weil (1971) for further information about some of the notes in *mp*. The second set of footnotes records whatever variants the editor of that biblical book thought worthy of notice, along with suggested alternate readings that are unsupported by manuscript evidence.

Each verse is preceded by its number. In *prose* passages, the verse number is repeated on the *inner* margin of the line on which the verse begins (but not on the left page if the verse begins at the right margin). In *poetry*, most verses begin at the right margin of the page. There are many differences in verse numbering between the Hebrew and English texts, and quite a few differerences in chapter divisions. You need to know which system a commentary or reference work is using, so that you can be sure that you are looking at the verse that the reference work is discussing.

Some Marks in the Text

:	*sof pasûq*, "end of *pasûq*", marks the end of nearly every "verse", *not* the end of a sentence. The final masora (at the end of each biblical book) lists the number of *pasûqîm* in the book
ס/פ	Solitary unpointed *samek* and *pe* mark textual breaks that were apparently based on content. These "paragraph" endings, called פְּתוּחָה ("open") or סְתוּמָה ("closed") were separated by either *samek* or *pe*, to indicate whether the next section began on the same line (ס) or on the next line (פ, i.e., "Leave the rest of this line open"). Because these have been collated from various reading traditions their occurrences in BHS are no longer consistent with this principle.
	In the inner margin large *samek* headed by a rotated *qameṣ* marks the beginning of a *seder*, a system of indicating the weekly reading in the synagogues. Each is numbered by a small letter with a superscript dot under the *samek*. The final masora for each book also lists the total number of *sᵉdarîm* in that book (except the Minor Prophets, which the rabbis considered one book).

accents	Nearly every biblical word is marked with an accent that shows which syllable is accented, how the word should be sung (cantillated), and how closely it is related to the following word. Your copy of *BHS* should include a card marked *Tabula Accentum* that lists disjunctive and conjunctive accents from strongest to weakest. There are two lists because the accents have different musical value in Psalms, Job, and Proverbs (*Accentus poëtici*). See Lesson 27 and HBI §4.

23.1.1 *Biblia Hebraica Quinta (BHQ)*

This newest edition of *Biblia Hebraica* began to appear in 2004; it will eventually comprise two volumes, the first a biblical text much like BHS, and intended to replace it. The main differences between BHQ and BHS are the inclusion of the text of the *Masorah finalis* at the foot of the biblical text on each page, the *Masorah parva/marginalis* as it stands in Codex Leningradensis (i.e., not as corrected and expanded by Weil for BHS), a much more full textual apparatus that includes abbreviated explanations of the reason for each textual variant. You will also immediately notice the use of English rather than Latin (e.g., titles of books).

The second volume of BHQ will include a text-critical introduction to each biblical book (primarily a descriptive list of the witnesses used in compiling the apparatus), commentaries on textual variants and the *Masorah parva*, and a translation of the *Masorah magna*. These materials will be part of each fascicle as it is published; when the project is complete, the materials will be divided to create the two-volume set.

Since most of the material that describes BHS (above) also applies to BHQ, this section notes only some of the differences.

General Introduction (English, German, Spanish)
The main purpose of this section is to explain the differences between BHQ and BHS (i.e., what justifies the enormous investment of time, effort, and money), and especially to explain the critical apparatus of BHQ. Since the textual apparatus is the reason for this new edition, this is the most extensive section of the Introduction, and describes "The Selection of Cases and Inclusion Witnesses", "The Evaluation of the Evidence", "The Structure and Presentation of Cases", "The Layout of a Page", and so forth.

Following the general introduction are two figures: a "Sample of an Apparatus Entry Illustrating the Presentation of the Text Critical Cases" and a "Sample Page Illustrating the Features of the Layout".

Sigla, Symbols and Abbreviations
Sigla for Textual Witnesses (alphabetical list of abbreviations used in the textual apparatus, with the documents to which they refer).
Symbols Used in the Apparatus.
Abbreviations (alphabetical list of abbreviated English terms used in the textual apparatus).

Definitions and Abbreviations for the Terms Used to Characterize Readings
The Typology Underlying the Characterizations (a "characterization" is the editor's explanation of the reason for a textual variant), followed by an "Index by Type of Characterization" and an "Alphabetical List of the Characterizations and Their Definitions".

Glossary of Common Terms in the Masorah Parva (Index of Signs & Abbreviations of the Masora Parva). An alphabetical list of the abbreviations in the margins of BHQ.

Table of Accents
   Accents for the Twenty-One Prose Books
   Accents for the Three Poetic Books (Psalms, Job, Proverbs)

Text Pages
The pages of the biblical text are similar to those of BHS. There are four blocks of material on each page.

In the center of each page is the *biblical text* itself—the "text block", which reproduces the text of Codex Leningrad, as in BHS.

In the outside margin the *Masora parva* [*mp*] or *Masora marginalis*, is again much as in BHS.

At the bottom of each page are two sets of footnotes. The first set, consisting of unpointed text, is the *Masora magna*, reproduced from Codex L, with the addition of chapter-and-verse numbers.

The second set of footnotes records those textual variants that the editor of that particular portion of the Bible thought worthy of notice, along with a suggested reason for each variant.

The name of the biblical book is listed at the top of each page (Hebrew on the right page, English on the left).

23.2 *Lexica*

As the term is commonly used today, "lexicon" refers to a bi-lingual dictionary that offers a set of glosses to render words from one language into another. As noted above (Lesson 2), however, these are *glosses*, not definitions. For discussions of a word's function within the language as a whole, it is necessary to turn to a theological wordbook or dictionary, which usually discusses each word's frequency, patterns of occurrence, and suggests nuances of function, as well as its relationship to any synonyms and antonyms.

23.2.1 *Lexicons*

BDB	Brown, Francis, S.R. Driver, & Charles A. Briggs. 1907. *A Hebrew and English Lexicon of the Old Testament with an appendix containing the Biblical Aramaic.* Oxford: Clarendon Press.

Words are grouped according to putative root (e.g., nouns, adjectives, and prepositions follow the verbal root from which they supposedly developed; so-called "denominative" verbs follow the noun which was their "source"). The list of abbreviations is helpful; the list of *sigla*—"signs" (p. xix)—is crucial. In addition to its eighteenth-century linguistics, major twentieth-century archaeological and epigraphic finds were not available to the editors. [See the appendix on BDB.]

HALOT	Köhler, L., and W. Baumgartner, eds. 2001. *Hebrew and English Lexicon of the Old Testament.* Study Edition. 2 vols. Leiden: E.J. Brill, 2000.

The most complete modern lexicon of Biblical Hebrew. It generally follows the same classical approach as BDB, except that words are listed alphabetically rather than by root. [Holladay (below) contains the English portion of an earlier German-English edition, without the etymological and cognate information, and fewer references.] The third edition contains a plethora of bibliographic references, supplemented by an extenstive bibliography at the end of the second volume.

DCH	Clines, David J.A., *et al.*, eds. *Dictionary of Classical Hebrew.* Vols. 1 - . Sheffield: University of Sheffield, 1991.

Projected to fill ten volumes, DCH covers all Hebrew (Biblical Hebrew, seals, inscriptions, Ecclesiasticus, DSS) except rabbinic Hebrew. All words, including proper names, are listed alphabetically by actual spelling, which makes nouns and adjectives much easier to find. It includes no etymological or other cognate information, even when the suggested gloss depends on a cognate. It is essentially an analytical concordance, which lists, for example, every subject, object, and preposition with which every verb occurs, as well as synonyms and antonyms. This is unique to DCH; a computerized database should yield similar results.

HOLLADAY	Holladay, W.L. 1971 *A Concise Hebrew and Aramaic Lexicon of the OT.* Grand Rapids: Eerdmans.

An abridgement of an earlier edition of KBL (above), Holladay is more current than BDB (i.e., cognate and extra-biblical evidence), but does not have nearly as much information about usage, occurrences, collocations, etc. as BDB, DCH, or KBL. Words are listed alphabetically, rather than grouped by root, and so are easier to find than in BDB. Popular because it is easy to use, but diligent students will outgrow its resources fairly rapidly.

23.2.2 Theological Dictionaries

TDOT   Botterweck, G.J., and H. Ringgren 1974 - *Theological Dictionary of the OT*. Vols. 1 - . Grand Rapids: Eerdmans.

A translation into English of a massive German work, appearing at the rate of one volume every 2-3 years. Copious information on etymology, usage, context, discussions of function, related terms, etc.

NIDOTTE   van Gemeren, Willem, ed. 1997 *The New International Dictionary of OT Theology & Exegesis*. 5 vols. Grand Rapids: Zondervan.

Detailed studies of nearly every word (even words occurring only one or two times), essays on theological topics (e.g., "Theology of Retribution"), and an essay on the theology of every biblical book (e.g., "Theology of Samuel"). First volume includes essays on exegesis and theology (but not on the language itself).

TWOT   Harris, R.L., G.L. Archer Jr., and B.K. Waltke, eds. 1980 *Theological Wordbook of the OT*. 2 vols. Chicago: Moody.

A basic tool with brief essays. A handy quick reference with more semantic information than a lexicon, but much less than either TDOT or NIDOTTE.

23.3 *The challenges of Lexicons*

If you don't find what you are looking for in a few minutes, then you are looking in the wrong place, or have misidentified the form. Skip it and come back later, or ask your teacher (bring the lexicon for reference). Difficulty often arises from:

1. Confusing letters that look alike (especially ה and ח, שׁ and שׂ);
2. Confusing letters that sound alike (especially א and ע) when you say the word to yourself as you look for it;
3. Looking for a word that is written defectively (i.e., without a vowel letter) in your passage, but is listed in its "full" spelling in the lexicon (i.e., with the vowel letter);
4. Looking in the Aramaic section for a Hebrew word (especially words at the end of the alphabet, since the Aramaic section usually follows the listings for Hebrew);
5. Looking under the wrong "root" (for lexica arranged by "root").
6. Having the wrong parsing.

23.4 *Vocabulary*

bone; essence (i.e., the inmost part)	עֶצֶם	.347	*cult center* (trad., "high place")	בָּמָה	.339
dust, dirt, soil	עָפָר	.348	*redeem, purchase as a kinsman-redeemer; redeemer* (Q Ptc.)	גָּאַל / גֹּאֵל	.340
fruit; descendants, offspring	פְּרִי	.349	*straight, upright; honest* (adj.)	יָשָׁר	.341
chariot(s); chariot force	רֶכֶב	.350	*put on, clothe* (oneself); *wear*	לָבֵשׁ	.342
who, which, what (with dageš forte in the following consonant); = אֲשֶׁר	־שֶׁ	.351	*tongue, language*	לָשׁוֹן	.343
pour [*out*]; *shed* [*blood*]	שָׁפַךְ	.352	*reject, refuse*	מָאַס	.344
lie, falsehood; deception	שֶׁקֶר	.353	*kingdom, realm; kingship, dominion, royal power / authority*	מַמְלָכָה / מַלְכוּת	.345
abomination (something horrific)	תּוֹעֵבָה	.354	[*permanent*] *river*; both הַנָּהָר & הַנָּהָר הַגָּדוֹל refer to Euphrates (rarely as נְהַר פְּרָת)	נָהָר	.346

23.5 Exercises: The Hebrew Bible

1. Fill in the information missing from the following chart (not all biblical books are included):

Hebrew Title	Gloss the Hebrew Title	Latin Title (BHS)	English Title (BHQ)	Page No.
בראשית				1
ויקרא	And he called	Leviticus		
שמואל			Samuel	
		Reges		
ירמיה				
		Micha		
תהלים	Praises			1087
משלי				
שיר השירים		Canticum		
איכה				
דברי הימים				

2. Gloss these clauses, parsing the verbal forms, and using the lexicon where necessary.

a. יִרְאַת יְהוָה טְהוֹרָה עוֹמֶדֶת לָעַד
מִשְׁפְּטֵי־יְהוָה אֱמֶת צָדְקוּ יַחְדָּו׃

Ps 19.10

b. עָבְרוּ בְרִיתִי וְעַל־תּוֹרָתִי פָּשָׁעוּ׃

Ho 8.1; the context suggests that עבר (*cross over/through*) signifies a trespass or transgression; פשע *revolt, rebel, transgress*

c. יְהוָה אַתָּה דִבַּרְתָּ אֶל־הַמָּקוֹם הַזֶּה
לְהַכְרִיתוֹ לְבִלְתִּי הֱיוֹת־בּוֹ יוֹשֵׁב
לְמֵאָדָם וְעַד־בְּהֵמָה כִּי־שִׁמְמוֹת עוֹלָם תִּהְיֶה׃

Jr 51.62; לְבִלְתִּי הֱיוֹת *so that there would not be*; עַל used here as אֶל; שְׁמָמָה *desolation, devastation*

d. וַיָּקָם בָּלָק בֶּן־צִפּוֹר מֶלֶךְ מוֹאָב וַיִּלָּחֶם בְּיִשְׂרָאֵל
וַיִּשְׁלַח וַיִּקְרָא לְבִלְעָם בֶּן־בְּעוֹר לְקַלֵּל אֶתְכֶם׃

Jos 24.9; וַיָּקָם *he rose* (< קום); קלל *curse; belittle;* Balak, Zippor, Moab, Balaam, Beor

e. וַיִּשְׁלַח הַמֶּלֶךְ וַיִּקְרָא לְשִׁמְעִי וַיֹּאמֶר אֵלָיו
הֲלוֹא הִשְׁבַּעְתִּיךָ בַיהוָה

1 Kgs 2.42; Shimei

f. וְאֶת־בִּנְיָמִין אֲחִי יוֹסֵף לֹא־שָׁלַח יַעֲקֹב אֶת־אֶחָיו
כִּי אָמַר פֶּן־יִקְרָאֶנּוּ אָסוֹן׃

Gn 42.4; Benjamin, Joseph, Jacob; אָסוֹן *trouble, disaster*

g. וְשָׁחַט אֶת־בֶּן הַבָּקָר לִפְנֵי יְהוָה
וְהִקְרִיבוּ בְּנֵי אַהֲרֹן הַכֹּהֲנִים אֶת־הַדָּם
וְזָרְקוּ אֶת־הַדָּם עַל־הַמִּזְבֵּחַ
סָבִיב אֲשֶׁר־פֶּתַח אֹהֶל מוֹעֵד׃

Lv 1.5; שחט *slaughter, kill;* זרק *sprinkle;* Aaron; since this is a set of instructions, the main verb form ("backbone") is w*qatal (waw+perfect)

h. וַיִּקְרָא יִרְמְיָהוּ אֶת־בָּרוּךְ בֶּן־נֵרִיָּה
וַיִּכְתֹּב בָּרוּךְ מִפִּי יִרְמְיָהוּ אֵת כָּל־דִּבְרֵי יְהוָה
אֲשֶׁר־דִּבֶּר אֵלָיו עַל־מְגִלַּת־סֵפֶר׃

Jr 36.4; מְגִלָּה *scroll* ("something rolled up" < גלל); Jeremiah, Baruch, Neraiah

i.	וַתִּקְרַבְנָה בְּנוֹת צְלָפְחָד ... וַתַּעֲמֹדְנָה לִפְנֵי מֹשֶׁה	Nu 27.1 ... 2; Zelophehad, Moses
j.	וְיֶתֶר דִּבְרֵי אֲבִיָּם וְכָל־אֲשֶׁר עָשָׂה הֲלוֹא־הֵם כְּתוּבִים עַל־סֵפֶר דִּבְרֵי הַיָּמִים לְמַלְכֵי יְהוּדָה וּמִלְחָמָה הָיְתָה בֵּין אֲבִיָּם וּבֵין יָרָבְעָם:	1 Kgs 15.7; Abijam; Jeroboam; Judah

23.6 *Enrichment: Using the Lexicon*

Lexicons list *glosses*, not definitions, meanings, or descriptions. They therefore rarely give more or less information than a mere word-list *when it comes to exegesis*; their great benefit is the topical or functional arrangement of the occurrences of the word(s), as well as identifying collocations in which they occur, such as a particular combination of a verbal root with certain subjects or prepositions.

The glosses suggested for the various stems often assume that, for example, the *hifil* is the causative of the *qal*, or that the function of *any* stem in which a verb occurs is somehow related to its function in *qal*. This is often (but not always) true, and should *never* be assumed. Since lexica offer glosses instead of definitions, other tools, such as theological dictionaries and wordbooks, are often more helpful than a lexicon when determining the range of a word's function, and where within that range its use in a given passage lies.

The lexica will suggest this if the listing is exhaustive, by assigning each lemma to either a gloss or functional category. You will then need to examine the other passages listed under that gloss or function to be sure that they are related to passage that you are studying.

As an example, consider the verbal root ברך, glossed as *kneel* (Q) or *bless* (D). Many contemporary translations of the Bible render the *piel* as "bless" when its object is human, but "praise" when the object is divine. Ps 103.1, for example, has traditionally been rendered as "*Bless* the Lord, O my soul" (KJV, NAS, ESV), but many contemporary translations read "*Praise* the Lord, O my soul", apparently to avoid implying that anyone can somehow do something that will benefit Yhwh.

HALOT suggests that the function of ברך is either to "endue with special power" (with God as subject), or "declare God to be the source of special power = bless" (with a human subject and a divine object) (HALOT, I:160). Discovering the word's function requires searching the biblical text, looking for patterns of usage, and, perhaps asking whether or not "bless" (in this case) is still the best basic gloss for this verbal root, especially given our cultural understanding of the word "bless".

A question that often concerns students is how to determine the precise "meaning" of a given word—why the author chose this word for this point in the text. This question is not always helpful.

The first danger in asking this question is that it assigns greater precision to the biblical authors than we are willing to accept ourselves. When someone asks us what we meant by a particular word, we are usually quite willling to list two or three synonyms (based on our internal "thesaurus"), rather than replying with the kind of definition found in a dictionary. Only when the word is a so-called technical term, such as might be used within a particular field of study (e.g., "synecdoche" (poetry), "synthetic compound" (organic chemistry)), might we resort to a dictionary-like explanation. Their question might also help us realize that we had chosen the "wrong" word for our hearer(s) (we assumed that they would understand it), or for the occasion (perhaps we used a highly formal word in an informal setting), or for some other reason.

Since they were human beings, using a human language to communicate with other people, we can assume that the biblical authors also used words "as they thought", that is, without necessarily worrying about whether or not it was the "precise" term. Furthermore, there are many constraints upon an author's choice of terms, some of which we can [sometimes] determine, most of which we cannot. In attempting to discern the significance of a particular choice, therefore, we need to be aware of these constraints—or at least to realize *that* the author was constrained—before trying to assess or assign any special meaning or function to a particular word. What are some of those constraints?

1. The immediate *context* is the most obvious constraint. A word must fit its linguistic environment, contribute to the function of the overall text, and generally "make sense" to its hearers or readers. It is in this sense that we may, for example, find ourselves "stuck" for "just the right word" when writing a letter, paper, or sermon.

2. A less obvious constraint is that the author must *know* the word (syntagm, etc.) in order to use it, and would have known its *connotative "load"*—socially emotive associations that are lost to us. This load may privilege or neutralize a particular linguistic expression (lexical choice, morphosyntactic choice, etc.) for the author *and* for that context, in light of his purpose(s) for writing, his own background and his assumptions about his hearers. Further, since connotation is both personal and contextual, as well as societal, we must be extremely cautious about extrapolating the author's motivation by merely studying its occurrences in Biblical Hebrew. This is far more important than the "root" or "basic" meaning of a word, which (cf. Lesson 2) is illusory.

None of this is intended to make us despair, but merely to caution us against over-reading the biblical text, seeking out "hidden treasures" of meaning. The languages in which the Bible was written were ordinary, working languages, spoken, written, and read by ordinary people. They are not secret or hidden "codes" which we need to decipher, but stories, poems, and sermons (and genealogies, and ...) written for us to read and enjoy, and to profit from reading them.

Reading the text in Hebrew (or Greek) forces us to slow down, to give more attention to the text itself, rather than to merely skim over its surface or "reading" it through the lenses of sermons heard or read, lessons learned, or other interpretations. We cannot rid ourselves of every assumption or prejudgement, but we can force ourselves to read more carefully, paying attention to *how* the biblical authors wrote, as well as to *what* (and *why*) they wrote it.

Since reading in Hebrew forces us to slow down, we are prone to pay far more attention to specific linguistic elements of the biblical text than we would ever pay to a book in our own language, such as an author's choice of verbal tense. This is a good thing, but it also encourages us to lose sight of the forest for the trees, which is not helpful.

We need to be sure, therefore, to read the entire story, not merely the individual words that make up that story; the entire poem, not merely the words and lines of that poem; the entire sermon (prophecy), not merely its forms and lexical choices, just as we read any other text in a language that is more familiar to us.

Lesson 24

OTHER KINDS OF VERBAL ROOTS

There are two main types of verbal roots in Biblical Hebrew: those which "have three unchangeable root consonants" (Joüon-Muraoka 1991, §40c), and which are called "strong", and those which lack one or more of their radicals in some forms, and may be called "weak" or "variable".[160] Up to this point we have studied only the forms of verbs with strong roots, but we now turn to the other types.

Although it is tempting to think in terms of "regular" and "irregular" verbs, Hebrew verbs are more or less regular. Even the types of roots to which we now turn are fairly consistent. There are five main types of variable verbs in Biblical Hebrew, named according to the position of the weak letter, using either Roman numerals or the letters of the traditional paradigm verb פעל ("do, make").

24.1 The Types & Effect of Root Weakness

Name		Lexical Form		The Nature of the Variation (effect of the weakness)
Initial Weak	I-נ פ"ן	נפל *fall*		Initial נ assimilates to (and doubles) the second radical of the verbal root whenever the first radical is followed by silent *šewa*.
	I-י/ו פ"י/ו	ישב *sit, settle*		Initial י either disappears or becomes a vowel letter whenever the first radical is followed by silent *šewa* (and in a few other forms).
Middle Weak (Hollow)	II-ו/י ע"ו/י	שׁיר *sing*		Lacking a second radical (thus "hollow"), these roots differ from the basic verb in all forms except the D-stems (where they are rare). Unlike other verbs, their lexical form is Q NC.
Final Weak	ע"ע geminate	סבב *surround*		The second and third radicals are the same ("geminate" means "twinned"); they are weak in most forms except the D-stems.
	III-ה ל"ה	בנה *build*		The final ה of the lexical form is a vowel letter, replacing an original י, which is still present before verbal (PGN) endings; the most consistent weak verbs.

The nature and location of the different weaknesses means that not all forms of a weak verb are, in fact, weak (i.e., some forms look just like the forms of מָשַׁל). This chart shows how each type relates to the strong verb.

Weakness	*Qal*	*Nifal*	D-stems	H-stems
I-נ I-י/ו	Weak in imperfect, preterite imperative, infinitive construct	Weak in perfect & participle	Strong in all forms	Weak in all forms
II-ו/י Geminate	Weak in nearly all forms		Replaced by *polel, polal, hitpolel*	
III-ה	Weak in preterite, jussive, infinitive construct, & all forms with PGN endings			

160. English distinguishes strong from weak verbs by the form of their past tense. Verbs which add "-ed" to form the past are called "strong", since the form of the verbal root does not change ("look", "*look*ed"), whereas verbs that indicate the past by changing a vowel ("run", "ran"), or all or part of their form ("go", "went"; "teach", "taught"; "be", "are") are "weak".

Any verbal form with only two root consonants has a weak root, which you can discover by elimination or by knowing vocabulary. For example, the form וַיֵּבְךְּ must be from one of the following roots: בכך, ביך, בוך, בכה, יבך, נבך. Checking the lexicon shows that only two of these roots occur in Biblical Hebrew: בכה, "weep, cry" (c. 100x) and בוך, "be confused" (3x). Context should let you choose the correct root.

24.1.1 *Consistency among Verbal Forms*

Each verbal stem is fairly consistent, using, for example, the same prefix vowel for each type of weakness. In addition, the III-ה verbs (for example) are weak in many forms, but their weakness is consistent across all stems and conjugations, and—this is especially important—their weakness does not affect any of the diagnostics that we learned for the basic verb, which means that they are fairly easy to recognize.

It is tempting to see the strong and weak forms as vastly different, but they are in fact quite closely tied to the forms of the strong verb (more strongly than, e.g., "be", "was", "are", and "am", or even βλέπω and εἶδον).

1. The subject [PGN] affixes are the same in all verbal forms (e.g., נוּ- is always 1cp perfect, whether the stem is strong or weak).
2. The weaknesses of these verbal roots are only morphological—they only affect the *shape* of the verbal form. They do not affect the function or syntax of the stems or conjugations (i.e., the preterite delineates the narrative backbone, and the *hifil* is generally transitive [occurs with an object]).

24.2 *III-ה Verbs*

The final ה- of the lexical form of these verbal roots is a vowel letter, not a consonant. These verbs originally ended in י, which thus "replaces" the final ה- before consonantal PGN endings and in Q passive participle. This weakness does not affect anything in front of the second radical of the verbal root, which means that their stem diagnostics are identical to those of the basic verb. These roots are also called ל"ה and "final ה".

N.B.: Verbal roots ending in ה- (ה with *mappiq*) are *not weak*, but III-guttural (above); *mappiq* shows that the final ה is a consonant, not a vowel letter (e.g., גבה, "be high"; נגה, "shine/be bright").

24.2.1 *Form*

1. If there is *no PGN ending*
   a) All forms except jussive, preterite, and infinitive construct end in ה. Each *conjugation* has a specific vowel before the final ה, regardless of the stem (on J, Pr, and NC, see below).

Ending	Conjugation	Example	Parsing	Where this Ending Occurs	
ָה -	perfect	בָּנָה	3ms Q P	3ms P only	
ֶה -	imperfect	יִבְנֶה	3ms Q F	1cs F, 2ms F, 3m/fs F, 1cp F only	all stems
	participle	מַבְנֶה	ms H Ptc	ms Ptc only	
ֵה -	imperative	בְּנֵה	ms Q V	2ms V only	
	infinitive absolute	הַבְנֵה	H NA	H & Hp NA	H & Hp only
ֹה -	infinitive absolute	הִתְבַּנֹּה	Dt NA	NA only	all stems except H & Hp
וֹת-	infinitive construct	בְּנוֹת	Q NC	NC f.p. Ptc	all stems

b) In the jussive and preterite of all stems, the final ה drops off forms without a PGN ending, and a "helping" vowel—usually *segol*—is added between the first and second radicals of the root.

	Perfect	Imperfect	Jussive	Preterite	
Q 3ms	בָּנָה	יִבְנֶה	יִבֶן	וַיִּבֶן	*and he built*
1cp	גָּלִינוּ	נִגְלֶה	נִגֶל	וַנִּגֶל	*and we revealed*
N 3ms	נִרְאָה	יֵרָאֶה	[יֵרָא]	וַיֵּרָא	*and he appeared*
D 3ms	צִוָּה	יְצַוֶּה	יְצַו	וַיְצַו	*and he commanded*
Dp 3ms	צֻוָּה	יְצֻוֶּה	יְצֻו	וַיְצֻו	*and he was commanded*
Dt 3ms	[הִתְכַּסָּה]	יִתְכַּסֶּה	[יִתְכַּס]	וַיִּתְכַּס	*and he hid [himself]*
H 3ms	הִשְׁקָה	יַשְׁקֶה	יַשְׁק	וַיַּשְׁק	*and he poured out*
Hp 3ms	הֻשְׁקָה	[יֻשְׁקֶה]	[יֻשְׁק]	[וַיֻּשְׁק]	*and it was poured out*

c) In the *qal* passive (Qp) participle the final radical is י instead of ה:

בָּנוּי	*built*	ms Qp Ptc
גָּלוּי	*revealed*	

2. If there is a *PGN ending*:
   a) *Vocalic* PGN endings are added directly to the second radical of the root. This occurs with וּ- and ִי -, but not with the 3fs perfect ending (ה ָ-; #3 below):

יִבְנוּ	*They will build*	3mp Q F
תִּבְנִי	*You (fs) will build*	2fs Q F
בְּנִי	*Build!*	2fs Q V
צַוּוּ	*Command!*	mp D V

b) With *consonantal* endings י replaces the ה of the lexical form,[161] and comes between the verbal root and the ending. It is preceded by *ḥireq* or *ṣere* (in P), or *segol* (F, V).

בָּנִיתִי	*I built*	1cs Q P
הִשְׁקִיתָ	*You (ms) watered*	2ms H P
תִּבְנֶינָה	*You/they (fp) will build*	2/3fp Q F

3. In 3fs P (all stems), תָה- is added to the second radical of the root:

בָּנְתָה	*She built*	3fs Q P
הָבְנְתָה	*She was caused to build*	3fs Hp P
הִפְנְתָה	*She caused to turn*	3fs H P

4. The infinitive construct in all stems is formed by replacing the final ה with וֹת- :

בְּנוֹת	*to build*	Q NC
הִבָּנוֹת	*to be built*	N NC
הַבְנוֹת	*to cause to build*	H NC

---

161. As mentioned above, י- was the original final letter of the III-ה verbs.

5. The cohortative and imperfect look alike (i.e., cohortative ה is not used), so that it can only be detected from the context.

נִבְנֶה	Let us build!	1cp Q C or
	We shall build	1cp Q F

6. III-ה roots which are also I-ע (עלה, ענה, עשׂה) have *hatef-patah* under the ע and *patah* as prefix vowel in both Q and H. When this is combined with the loss of the final ה in the preterite (#1b, above), some forms of *qal* and *hifil* look exactly alike, and can be distinguished only from the context. Many of these verbs are intransitive in *qal* (e.g., עלה), and so will *not* have a direct object (*He went up*), but will have one in H (*He took* [X] *up*).

עֲשִׂיתֶם	You (mp) made	2mp Q P
תַּעֲלוּ	You (mp) go up/ascend or	2mp Q F or
	You (mp) take [cause to go] up	2mp H F
	[requires an object]	
וַיַּעַל	He went up (Q) or	3ms Q Pr or
	He [caused to go] took up (H)	3ms H Pr
	[requires an object]	
עֲנֵה	Answer [ms]!	2ms Q V

24.3 The Verb היה (Review)

The verb היה (introduced in §15.2) is the most common verb in the Bible (more than 3500x), Its forms are rather unusual due to its final -ה and medial -י-. Since it is a III-ה root, it follows the patterns described above, but whenever the *yod* ends a verbal form (in, e.g., 1cs, 2ms, 3ms, and 3fs preterite), it becomes a vowel letter and the form ends in long *hireq* (ִי).

24.3.1 Common Forms of היה (all qal)[162]

P 1cs	הָיִיתִי	I was		Pr 3ms	וַיְהִי	Now he/it was
						Then there was a/some ...
3cp	הָיוּ	They were		3mp	וַיִּהְיוּ	They were
F 3ms	יִהְיֶה	He shall be		J 3ms	יְהִי	Let/May he/it be/happen
3mp	יִהְיוּ	They shall be		NC	הֱיוֹת הֱיוֹת	to be/[by] being

24.3.2 Function of היה (cf. §15.2.2)

Although היה is often glossed "be" or "become", its most common function in biblical narrative is to introduce a change of setting or circumstance—a shift of scene or focus—in a biblical narrative. The form most commonly used for this function is 3ms *qal* preterite (וַיְהִי), which functions as a discourse-level particle except when followed by a nominal subject.[2] In Ruth 1.1, for example, the first וַיְהִי is *introductory* and thus not represented in the translation, but the second is followed by a subject (רָעָב), and therefore is predicate (and glossed in English). The circumstantial clause is formed with NC, as is frequent in Biblical Hebrew:

וַיְהִי	[signals past reference]
בִּימֵי שְׁפֹט הַשֹּׁפְטִים	In the days when the judges were judging,
וַיְהִי רָעָב בָּאָרֶץ	there was a famine in the land [וַיְהִי has a subject],
וַיֵּלֶךְ אִישׁ	and [so] a man went ... (Ru 1.1)

162. היה also occurs in *nifal*. For a complete paradigm of the III-ה verb, see Appendix D.

The circumstantial element can also be a nominal prepositional phrase, usually with a word of time or place:

וְהָיָה	[signals future reference]
בְּאַחֲרִית הַיָּמִים	at the end of the days
יִהְיֶה הַר בֵּית־יהוה נָכוֹן	the mountain of Yhwh's house [temple] will be established (Mi 4.1)

24.4 Frequency

This lists all III-ה verbal roots that occur *fifty times or more* in Biblical Hebrew, in order of descending frequency.

היה		c. 3500x	חנה	camp, encamp	143x
עשׂה	do, make, act	2573x	פנה	turn (aside)	134x
ראה	see	1294x	בכה	weep	114x
עלה	go up, ascend	879x	ידה	throw (D); thank, praise (H)	115x
נכה	hit, wound, defeat	504x	זנה	fornicate	95x
צוה	command (D)	494x	חרה	be(come) angry, hot	94x
בנה	build	373x	ענה (II)	be humbled, humiliated (Q)	79x
ענה (I)	answer	314x	שׁקה	water, give to drink (H)	79x
חיה	live	281x	חלה	be(come) weak, sick	77x
רבה	increase, multiply	226x	קנה	acquire, get, buy	78x
כלה	cease, finish, end	204x	חזה	see	72x
נטה	stretch out, turn	215x	פדה	buy, ransom	56x
שׁתה	drink	217x	אבה	agree, accept	54x
גלה	reveal, uncover	187x	ירה (III)	teach, instruct (H)	54x
רעה (I)	feed, graze, tend	171x	רצה	be pleased with, like	50x
כסה	cover, conceal (D)	157x	תעה	wander (lost)	50x

24.5 Concepts

circumstantial   strong verb   weak verb

24.6 Vocabulary

answer, reply; respond	עָנָה (I)	.363	build	בָּנָה	.355
be humbled, afflicted; humble, afflict (D)	עָנָה (II)	.364	uncover, reveal	גָּלָה (√I)	.356
			go into captivity/exile	גָּלָה (√II)	
do, make; act	עָשָׂה	.365	live, be/stay alive	חָיָה	.357
command, order (D)	צִוָּה	.366	cease, finish, end, complete (often with inf. const.)	כָּלָה	.358
see	רָאָה	.367	cover, conceal (D)	כִּסָּה	.359
increase, multiply	רָבָה	.368	stretch out; turn	נָטָה	.360
feed, graze, tend; herd	רָעָה	.369	hit, wound, defeat (H)	נָכָה	.361
drink	שָׁתָה	.370	go up, ascend	עָלָה	.362

24.7 Exercises

After you have studied the III-ה verb, *gloss* these sentences, *parsing* all verbal forms.

Is 40.5; יַחַד *together*	1. וְנִגְלָה כְּבוֹד יְהוָה וְרָאוּ כָל־בָּשָׂר יַחְדָּו כִּי פִּי יְהוָה דִּבֵּר׃
Jr 35.17; these are parallel poetic lines, each consisting of two clauses joined by -וְ	2. דִּבַּרְתִּי אֲלֵיהֶם וְלֹא שָׁמֵעוּ וָאֶקְרָא לָהֶם וְלֹא עָנוּ׃
Jonah 1.10; the conjunction כִּי has two different functions	3. וַיֹּאמְרוּ אֵלָיו מַה־זֹּאת עָשִׂיתָ כִּי־יָדְעוּ הָאֲנָשִׁים כִּי־מִלִּפְנֵי יְהוָה הוּא בֹרֵחַ
Ps 30.11 [EV 30.10]; נִי־ = 1cs suffix; חנן *be gracious, show favour*; there are three imperatives in this v.; both occurrences of יהוה are vocative	4. שְׁמַע־יְהוָה וְחָנֵּנִי יְהוָה הֱיֵה־עֹזֵר לִי׃
2 Ch 19.6	5. רְאוּ מָה־אַתֶּם עֹשִׂים
Gn 13.1; Egypt; Abram, Lot; Negev	6. וַיַּעַל אַבְרָם מִמִּצְרַיִם הוּא וְאִשְׁתּוֹ וְכָל־אֲשֶׁר־לוֹ וְלוֹט עִמּוֹ הַנֶּגְבָּה׃
Gn 1.3–4a; the *athnaḥ* (the accent under the first occurrence of אוֹר means "pause here"; see §27.3)	7. וַיֹּאמֶר אֱלֹהִים יְהִי אוֹר וַיְהִי־אוֹר׃ וַיַּרְא אֱלֹהִים אֶת־הָאוֹר כִּי־טוֹב
Gn 1.9; קוה *be gathered* (N)	8. וַיֹּאמֶר אֱלֹהִים יִקָּווּ הַמַּיִם מִתַּחַת הַשָּׁמַיִם אֶל־מָקוֹם אֶחָד וְתֵרָאֶה הַיַּבָּשָׁה וַיְהִי־כֵן׃
Gn 2.18; לְבַד *only, alone*, here with 3ms suffix	9. לֹא־טוֹב הֱיוֹת הָאָדָם לְבַדּוֹ
Gn 2.24	10. וְהָיוּ לְבָשָׂר אֶחָד
Gn 8.20; Noah	11. וַיִּבֶן נֹחַ מִזְבֵּחַ לַיהוָה
Gn 20.12	12. וַתְּהִי־לִי לְאִשָּׁה
Ex 33.18 [נִי־ = 1cs suffix]	13. וַיֹּאמַר הַרְאֵנִי נָא אֶת־כְּבֹדֶךָ׃
Ex 32.4; יִשְׂרָאֵל is vocative; Egypt	14. וַיֹּאמְרוּ אֵלֶּה אֱלֹהֶיךָ יִשְׂרָאֵל אֲשֶׁר הֶעֱלוּךָ מֵאֶרֶץ מִצְרָיִם׃
Dt 9.9	15. לֶחֶם לֹא אָכַלְתִּי וּמַיִם לֹא שָׁתִיתִי׃
1 Sa 4.9; פְּלִשְׁתִּים is vocative; Philistines, Hebrews	16. הִתְחַזְּקוּ וִהְיוּ לַאֲנָשִׁים פְּלִשְׁתִּים פֶּן תַּעַבְדוּ לָעִבְרִים כַּאֲשֶׁר עָבְדוּ לָכֶם וִהְיִיתֶם לַאֲנָשִׁים וְנִלְחַמְתֶּם׃
1 Sa 26.23; אבה *be willing*	17. וְלֹא אָבִיתִי לִשְׁלֹחַ יָדִי בִּמְשִׁיחַ יְהוָה׃
1 Sa 14.35; Saul	18. וַיִּבֶן שָׁאוּל מִזְבֵּחַ לַיהוה
Ne 9.18; נְאָצָה *contempt, blasphemy*; Egypt	19. וַיֹּאמְרוּ זֶה אֱלֹהֶיךָ אֲשֶׁר הֶעֶלְךָ מִמִּצְרָיִם וַיַּעֲשׂוּ נֶאָצוֹת גְּדֹלוֹת׃
Lv 18.8; ערוה *nakedness* [The "nakedness" commandments occur in Lv 18.6-19.]	20. עֶרְוַת אֵשֶׁת־אָבִיךָ לֹא תְגַלֵּה עֶרְוַת אָבִיךָ הִוא׃

24.8 Enrichment: Narrative Aperture

Circumstantial clauses or phrases, as discussed above, often signal narrative onset (or "aperture"), and thus can signal the author's organization of the story (cf. the examples under in §24.3.2). The significance of this is that we need to beware the tendency to rearrange a text in order to suit our own purposes (i.e., the temptation to use the text merely to make our point). To take the first point of a sermon or exposition from the middle of the story (or poem), the second point from the beginning, and our final point from near the end is merely a way of announcing to others that we would have written the passage differently. It is, in other words, to subordinate our own interests to the interests and concerns of its author.

Our message—which purports to re-present the text to our readers or hearers—must serve the text; the text does not exist to serve our sermon.

Noting narrative aperture is one means of being sure that we are paying attention to the authors' arrangement of the material, and that we are attempting to follow their lead rather than to replace it with our own. Since every aperture also means that the previous section has closed, identifying apertures enables us to note the "breaks" in the story that correspond to the paragraphs, etc. of stories in English. Since the chapter breaks in our modern Bibles were not original, we need to be careful not to assume their priority in the organization of the story, even though they may indicate a "shift" of perspective within a larger, more general topic (cf. §26.8).

Semantic markers of aperture are mainly words that signal a change of some type—especially shifts in time (chronology), place (location), and participants (characters). By the same token, continuity of characters across chapter breaks suggests that the break is ill-placed. In Gn 18 (see §26.7) and 44, for example, the main character in the first unit of the chapter is not identified by name, implying in each case that he is the same person identified as the subject of the preceding clause(s). This in turn implies that the stories now separated by the chapter break are a single story that should be read and studied as a whole.

Lesson 25

"Pre-reading" Biblical Narrative

This lesson outlines six steps that will help you find your way through a biblical story by "pre-reading" it in order to prepare to read [translate]. The first four steps—marking preterites, *wayhî*, Masoretic accents, and clause-initial particles—are purely mechanical, and can be done after only a few weeks' study; the last two—quotation formulae and disjunctive clauses (especially)—strengthen our interpretation. This process will prepare you to read, study, and understand biblical stories but without, of course, guaranteeing a valid reading or interpretation. Nor can these the process of itself (i.e., merely by applying it) yield an expository outline. Used carefully, however, it should both help you avoid misinterpreting the story and suggest how the passage might be well interpreted and explained.

25.1 *Preterites*

Preterites (also called "imperfect + *waw*-consecutive" or *wayyiqtol*) form the "backbone" of biblical narratives, and tie them together, much as sticking to the past tense in English tells the reader or hearer "what happened then" or "next". **Locate and mark the preterites** in the narrative by circling, highlighting, underlining, etc. This does at least three things:

1. *Syntax*. Since a preterite always "opens" (comes first in) its clause, marking the preterites indicates where many, or even all, of the main narrative clauses begin. Each preterite clause should be read as a syntactical unit—do not move words "across" a preterite (e.g., we should not read אברם *Abram*, the last word in Gn 12.7a, as part of the following preterite clause).[163]

    Since the subject is often the second word in the preterite clause, marking the preterites also suggests where the subject of each clause can be found (this is far more of a tendency than a "rule").

2. *Flow & Pace*. Preterites outline the story by their spacing and content (lexical function). If the preterites occur in clusters, with relatively larger stretches of material between clusters, there will probably be a great deal of direct quotation, or a large amount of descriptive material (background), introducing or supporting the chain of events (e.g., 1 Sam 3.1-3). They may also be spaced relatively evenly throughout the narrative.

3. *Content*. The content (semantic load) of the preterites also suggests the nature of the story. For example, in Gn 12.1-9, the preterite that opens the discourse (וַיֹּאמֶר) introduces three verses of direct quotation (12.1-3), which is followed by a stretch of six preterites (4-6), five of which are verbs of motion or travel. The next two preterites (7a) introduce another, very brief, divine speech (7b), followed by six more preterites, two of which describe the act of building (7c, 8b), and two of which are again verbs of motion (8a, 9a). Simply noting this suggests that the narrative contained in these verses centers on a person or persons moving from one place to another. Reading the story, therefore, you expect to find information about this type of activity (see Table I, below).

---

163. This does not address whether a particular translation might need or choose to place "Abram" in the following clause.

Preterites in Gn 12.1-9

Gloss	Next Form	Preterite	V.
*and YHWH *said*	יהוה	וַיֹּאמֶר	1
and Abram *went*	אַבְרָם	וַיֵּלֶךְ	4a
and he went with him	אִתּוֹ	וַיֵּלֶךְ	4b
and Abram *took*	אַבְרָם	וַיִּקַּח	5a
and they left to go	לָלֶכֶת	וַיֵּצְאוּ	5b
and they entered the land	אַרְצָה	וַיָּבֹאוּ	5c
and Abram *crossed / passed*	אַבְרָם	וַיַּעֲבֹר	6
and YHWH *appeared*	יהוה	וַיֵּרָא	7a
and he said to your seed	לְזַרְעֲךָ	וַיֹּאמֶר	7b
and he built there	שָׁם	וַיִּבֶן	7c
and he moved on from there	מִשָּׁם	וַיַּעְתֵּק	8a
and he pitched his tent	אָהֳלֹה	וַיֵּט	8b
and he built there	שָׁם	וַיִּבֶן	8c
and he called on the name	בְּשֵׁם	וַיִּקְרָא	8d
and Abram *set out*	אַבְרָם	וַיִּסַּע	9

Words in italics represent the verbal predicate;
regular type glosses the word after the preterite.

If, on the other hand, most or all of the preterites are verbs of speaking (e.g., Gn 17), you know that the "story" largely records a conversation, which in Scripture will tend to be one person telling another what to do (instruction, exhortation) or what he or she [the speaker] will do (prophecy, promise). In fact, in Gn 12.1-3, this is what we find. God tells Abram what to do (1), and then makes certain promises to him (2-3). This leads directly to a second aspect of narrative.

Identifying the preterites in a narrative reveals the beginning of the main narrative clausees, divides the narrative into smaller, more manageable pieces, outlines the flow of the story, suggests its pacing, and reveals some of its content.

25.2 *wayhî-Clauses*

A special preterite is וַיְהִי (3ms Q Pr of היה), which has two primary syntagmatic functions, each of which is related to its function within the larger discourse.

1. *Circumstantial.* When *wayhî* is followed by a **temporal** expression—either a nominal phrase or a verbal clause (e.g., וַיְהִי בַּיּוֹם הַהוּא preposition + infinitive construct)—its clause is *circumstantial.* These usually indicate a change in the temporal or locative setting (cf. Gropp 1995, 202).
2. *Predicate.* When a **subject** follows *wayhî*, the clause introduces a person or object, or describes a change in the larger setting or circumstances of the story.

Taking the next passage in Genesis as an example, the form *wayhî* occurs four times in Gn 12.10-16 (Table II). The first (10) and fourth (16b) have subjects and are therefore predicate, introducing changes in the narrative situation; the second (11) and third (14) are circumstantial, introducing [events at] stages in Abram's journey to Egypt.

WAYHÎ in Gn 12.10-16

Narrative Shift	Gloss	*wayhî* Clause	Gn
A change in situation, implying that the famine began after Abram was is in the land (background information for what follows)	*There was a famine* in the land	וַיְהִי רָעָב בָּאָרֶץ	12.10
The second "stage" of Abram's journey to Egypt (cf. v. 10b)	*When he was about to enter* Egypt, ...	וַיְהִי כַּאֲשֶׁר הִקְרִיב לָבוֹא מִצְרַיְמָה	12.11
The conclusion of Abram's journey to Egypt	*When Abram entered* Egypt, ...	וַיְהִי כְּבוֹא אַבְרָם מִצְרַיְמָה	12.14
A change in Abram's circumstance because of Sarai	*He had* flocks and herds, ...	וַיְהִי־לוֹ צֹאן־וּבָקָר	12.16

The beginning of 12.10 implies that when Abram had arrived and received the promise of God there was no famine; the clause in 12.16 implies that he now had [much?] more than before Pharaoh took Sarai.

When *wayhî* is *predicate* (as defined above), it is *morphologically* bound to (or cohesive with) the main storyline since it is a preterite, which suggests that *wayhî* clauses raise the description of a state or condition to the status of the narrative backbone, even though *they do not narrate a sequential or consequential event* (e.g., Gn 12.10).[164]

This function is analogous to that of a preterite of a non-dynamic stative verb. For example, "Abram *was* very wealthy", describes a general state or condition, while "Abram *became* [or *had become*] very wealthy", describes either the beginning of his wealth ("became") or his prior arrival at a state of wealth ("had become"). There is thus the possibility that predicate *wayhî* clauses may be inceptive, as in the traditional translation of the prophetic formula: וַיְהִי דְבַר־יְהוָה אֶל־יוֹנָה בֶן־אֲמִתַּי, "YHWH's word *came* to Jonah ..." [Jon 1.1]); Gn 12.10 would then signal "A famine *came upon* the land".

In fact, since both types of *wayhî* clauses can signal a change in setting or circumstance (e.g., Gn 12.10), they reveal some of the discontinuities in the story that mark what can be called narrative "seams" or "boundaries", or the onset of the story's narrative "chunks".

Although we need to check our impressions of the function of *wayhî* against the relationship between the content of the *wayhî* clause and the rest of the discourse (especially the preceding clauses), this helps us look beyond the individual form to its literary cotext, and thus to avoid merely "literal" renderings such as "and it happened/came to pass".

25.3 Rabbinic Accents

The Masoretic accents were inserted into the text c. 500-900 CE to help readers pronounce and understand what they read;[165] each is associated with a brief melody that tells the cantor how to chant the text during services. Most of them indicate the accented ("tone") syllable, but they also signal each word's relationship to the following word.[166] There are two types of accents, disjunctive[167] and conjunctive.[168]

---

164. The exception to this "rule of non-narration" is when וַיְהִי (and other forms of *hayah*) are followed by a -לְ in order to show a change in the subject's status; the combination is generally rendered by a form of the verb "become".

165. There are two accentual systems, one used in Psalms, Job, and Proverbs, the other in the rest of the Hebrew Bible.

166. Accents thus testify to a now-codified rabbinic reading of the verse; like the paragraphing and punctuation of a modern English version, they are part of the history of biblical interpretation, not part of the text *per se*.

167. The rabbis called these *melakhîm* ("kings"); Christian grammarians called them *domini* ("lords").

168. The rabbis called these *meshartîm* ("servants"); Christian grammarians called them *servi* ("servants").

A **disjunctive** accent means "*Pause* after this word", that is, *separate* this word from the next one. The pause may be large or small, depending on the relative strength of the accent. The accent's function applies only to the individual word that it marks. These six disjunctive accents are numbered according to the *Tabula Accentum* (included in *BHS*) according to their approximate "weight" or "strength" (there is little difference between #5 and #6).[169]

	Major Disjunctive Accents		
1.	*sillûq*	מֶלֶךְ׃	marks the last word in the verse; it is followed by the two "diamonds" called *sof pasuq* ("end of verse/*pasuq*")
2.	*'aṯnach*	מֶֽלֶךְ	divides the verse into two major sections (often called "halves", but logical halves, not in number of words); there is only one *'aṯnach* per verse[170]
3.	*sᵉgôltā*	מֶ֒לֶךְ֒	the primary divider of the first "half" of the verse (as indicated by *'aṯnach*); written after its word (i.e., "postpositive"), and so does not mark the accented syllable
5.	*zāqēf parva*	מֶ֔לֶךְ	divides either "half" or both "halves" of the verse[171]
6.	*zāqēf magna*	מֶ֕לֶךְ	essentially a variant of #5
7.	*rᵉḇîaʿ*	מֶ֗לֶךְ	resembles holem, but higher, larger, and diamond-shaped
8.	*tifka*	מֶ֖לֶךְ	regularly precedes words with *'aṯnach* (#2) and *silluq* (#1), i.e., before the major divisions of the verse[172]

The Masoretes used these accents to create divisions that were semantic, syntactical, or (often) both, much like English (European) punctuation. Furthermore, these disjunctive accents often precede preterites (and other clauses), reinforcing the first step (above). Just as preterites mark the ebb and flow of the story's events, the major disjunctive accents suggest smaller units of textual organization that also help us "think our way through" the narrative.

We can read "between" the disjunctive accents (much like reading "between" preterites), since the material (words) between disjunctive accents functions as a unit. Although the accents are not original, and occasional accentual interpretations may even be questionable (e.g., 1 Sam 3.3b), they are quite venerable, and often help us read the text; at the very least, they are an important witness to the history of interpretation.

You will soon notice a certain amount of coordination and overlap between these two systems—preterites are normally preceded by disjunctive accents.

When pre-reading, putting a vertical line after words marked with one of these accents visibly divides the text into "meaningful" or "functional" clusters of words. The major disjunctive accents divide 1 Kings 1.1 into five "pieces"; the last word is not separate, but part of the verbal clause, despite *tifka*.

	1 Kings 1.1	
וְהַמֶּ֤לֶךְ דָּוִד֙ זָקֵ֔ן	Now King David was old,	*zaqef*
בָּ֖א בַּיָּמִ֑ים	advanced in days,	*'aṯnach*
וַיְכַסֻּ֖הוּ בַּבְּגָדִ֑ים	and they covered him with garments,	*zaqef*
וְלֹ֥א יִחַ֖ם לֽוֹ׃	but he was not warm.	*tifka – silluq*

169. This table does not include *silluq* (#1), which tends to coincide with *sof pasuq* at the end of (nearly) every verse, or with the relatively rare accent *šalšelet* (#4).

170. It may be missing from short verses (e.g., Gn 18.1; Nu 27.5, 6; 28.1; Jon 1.1), or even longer ones (e.g., Dt 6.22).

171. *Zaqef* can occur more than once in either "half" of the verse.

172, *Tifka* can precede a short word cluster in which the last word has *'aṯnach* or *silluq*, and so can break up a "longer" string of words that might begin with, e.g., a word following *zaqef* and end with *silluq*. In Jon 1.6, *tifka* occurs before the last two words, which are a preterite clause.

The **conjunctive** accents, on the other hand, mean "Don't pause after this word", that is, *link* this word to the next one—they belong together. The strength of the link depends on the relative strength of the accent. The most important conjunctive accent (and the only one that this pre-reading exercise uses) is *munach* (מֶלֶךְ). *Munach* can occur several times in a verse, and even under consecutive words, linking, for example, words in a construct chain. When *munach* occurs under a word that is also marked with a disjunctive accent, the disjunctive accent takes priority (cf. הַשּׁוּנַמִּית in 1 Kgs 1.3). Noticing and marking *munach* keeps together words that belong together.

N.B.: Not every accent occurs in every verse (e.g., Gn 18.1 lacks *'atnach*; many verses lack *zaqef*, *rebîaʻ*); *munach* is often lacking.

25.4 *Clause-Initial Particles*

Another step of this pre-reading process is to mark any "clause-leading" or "clause-initial" particles. These function words usually begin or "introduce" their clause.[173] Having a basic idea of the function of these words, we can strengthen our expectations about the story by noting the relationships that these particles signal between clauses and larger chunks of the narrative.

	Clause-Initial Particles	
אֲשֶׁר	which, who, that	introduces relative clause that usually refers to the preceding word
וְעַתָּה[174]	therefore	introduces volitional conclusions (i.e., calls for action/response: imperative, cohortative, jussive)
כַּאֲשֶׁר	as, just as	introduces comparison
כֹּה	thus, so	introduces clause of manner
	that	introduces content of indirect quotation
כִּי	because, for	introduces reason for, cause of
	when/if	introduces conditions (e.g., laws)
לְמַעַן	in order that, so that	introduces purpose or result (goal)
עַל־כֵּן	therefore	introduces logical conclusion (never calls for action/response)

25.5 *Quotation Formulae*

The narrative burden of many stories is carried by direct quotations, which are often introduced by preterites that someone said, spoke, commanded, etc.

Direct quotations are normally introduced by a verb of speaking (אמר, דבר, שאל, etc.) that is often followed by the subject and addressee (introduced by the preposition לְ-). The syntagm (e.g., "Yhwh said to Abram") helps us locate the beginning (*aperture*) of the quotation; if the form לֵאמֹר occurs, the next word almost always begins the quotation. The end of a speech is not as easily recognized, since other clauses may come between the end of the quotation and the next preterite. For now, merely noting the quotation formulae will alert you to the presence of speeches in the passage.

Many quotation formulae are preterites, but they also occur in other types of clauses (e.g., in Gn 12.12a וְאָמְרוּ, *and they will say*, is a quote within a quote—it falls within Abram's speech), which means that it is not enough merely to check the marked preterites for verbs of speaking; other clauses must also be examined.

---

173. Contrast the conjunction *waw*, which functions at all syntagmatic levels, from phrase to discourse.

174. Without the prefixed *waw-*, עַתָּה; refers to the present: "now". *Weʻattā* clauses are disjunctive (see below) by definition (*w*+non-verb), and mark the transition from argument to conclusion (and action or decision).

When a character instructs or directs another to do something, the narrator often says merely that "and he did so" (וַיַּעַשׂ כֵּן (Jg 6.20; 1 Kg 20.25; Est 2.4; Is 20.2)) or "so they did what Moses [Josuha] had commanded", without describing their actions or repeating the instructions. This means that although the preterites of quotation formulae may carry the narrative *flow* of the story, the content of the quotations often provides much of its *substance*. Key to pre-reading a narrative is therefore **identifying** the **quotations**.

Quotation formulae also serve another purpose: when *repeated* within a unified speech (i.e., a speech made by one person), they do not so much re-introduce the speaker (as though the author expects the reader to have forgotten who was speaking), but signal topical shifts within the speech. Here are three examples from Genesis.

Throughout the creation account (Gn 1.3-26), each occurrence of the quotation formula וַיֹּאמֶר signals the next divine creative activity. There was no one else to speak, so we must ask why the verb and its subject (וַיֹּאמֶר אֱלֹהִים) are repeated. Typically in Biblical Hebrew, the repeated quotation formulae break up and "outline" extended speeches; here, divine speech initiates each creative act.[175] These three examples demonstrate this function of quotation formulae.

1. At the end of that chapter, two quotation formulae divide, or "outline", the divine speech to the newly created man and woman topically (Gn 1.28-30):

Topic	Gloss	Quotation Formula	Gn
The blessing of abundance & dominion	*God blessed them ... and God said to them,"...*	וַיְבָרֶךְ ... וַיֹּאמֶר לָהֶם	3.28
The provision of food	*And God said,"...*	וַיֹּאמֶר אֱלֹהִים	3.29

2. In Gn 9.1-17, the author uses quotation formulae to organize a long divine speech:

Topic	Gloss	Quotation Formula	Gn
	And God blessed Noah and his sons and said to them, "...	וַיְבָרֶךְ אֱלֹהִים אֶת־נֹחַ וְאֶת־בָּנָיו וַיֹּאמֶר לָהֶם	9.1
Divine covenant with all life	*And God said to Noah & his sons with him [saying], "...*	וַיֹּאמֶר אֱלֹהִים אֶל־נֹחַ וְאֶל־בָּנָיו אִתּוֹ לֵאמֹר	9.8
The sign of the covenant	*And God said, "...*	וַיֹּאמֶר אֱלֹהִים	9.12
Reiteration: sign & scope of covt.	*And God said to Noah, "...*	וַיֹּאמֶר אֱלֹהִים אֶל־נֹחַ	9.17

3. Genesis 17 illustrates both points about quotation formulae, including the difference between an extended speech and conversation. The announcement of the covenantal sign of circumcision (Gn 17.3b-17) is divided into three sections by further quotative frames:

New Topic	Gloss	Quotation Formula	Gn
Yhwh's rôle in the covenant	*And God spoke with him [saying], "..."*	וַיְדַבֵּר אִתּוֹ אֱלֹהִים לֵאמֹר	17.3b
Abraham's responsibility under the covenant (circumcision)	*And God said to Abraham, "..."*	וַיֹּאמֶר אֱלֹהִים אֶל־אַבְרָהָם	17.9
Sarah's rôle in the covenantal promise	*And God said to Abraham, "..."*	וַיֹּאמֶר אֱלֹהִים אֶל־אַבְרָהָם	17.15

---

175. More precisely, as is often pointed out, the divine speech *is* the creative act; this theological issue is separate from its function within the *structure* of the narrative.

This is followed by three preterites that describe Abraham's response (*He fell ... he laughed ... he said to himself ...* [17.17]),[176] after which two further quotation formulae introduce the next part the conversation between Abraham and YHWH:

Topic	Gloss	Quotation Formula	Ref.
Abraham asks about Ishmael	*And Abraham said to God, "...*	וַיֹּאמֶר אַבְרָהָם אֶל־הָאֱלֹהִים	17.18
God reassures him about Ishmael	*And God said, "...*	וַיֹּאמֶר אֱלֹהִים	17.19

Noting quotational formulae should fill some of the visual "gaps" in the preterite chain. Just as the preterite chain suggests the pace of the story, quotation plays a rôle in pacing by slowing a narrative.[177] While we read a quotation, no other events are being narrated, which stops the flow of events—the only "event" is the words of the quotation.

If a passage consists largely of quotation (as in, e.g., Gn 1.3-26; 9.1-17; 17.3b-21), not much "happens", even if the passage is fairly lengthy, although, to be fair (and to invoke a false dichotomy), *what* is said (the content of the quotations) often overshadows *that* something is being said (the narrated event).

25.6 *Disjunctive Clauses*

Another key to reading a biblical narrative is the location and content of disjunctive clauses. A *clause* consists of a **topic** (the subject) and a **comment** about that topic (the predicate).[178] A sentence always consists of at least one clause, but a single clause can also be a sentence. In Biblical Hebrew, topics and comments can belong to several "classes" of words, and nearly anything that can be a topic can also be a comment (nearly all of these combinations occur; this chart does not imply that any are more frequent or prominent than others):

"Word-classes" in Clauses

Topic (word-classes)		Comment (word-classes)	
noun (generic)	נָבִיא	noun (generic)	מֶלֶךְ
noun (proper)	אַבְרָם	noun (proper)	דָּוִד
pronoun (independent)	אַתָּה	participle (predicate)	סֹפֵר
pronoun (suffixed to NC)	לְלֶכְתְּךָ	participle (substantive)	הַכֹּתֵב
pronoun (subject PGN affix)	כְּתַבְתֶּן	adjective (predicate)	רַע
participle (substantive)	הַכֹּתֵב	adjective (substantive)	הַגְּדוֹלִים
adjective (substantive)	הַגְּדוֹלִים	infinitive construct	לֶכֶת
infinitive construct	לִהְיוֹת	prepositional phrase (usually locative)	בַּבַּיִת
		finite verb (perfect, imperfect, preterite, imperative)	יֵשֵׁב לֵךְ

Clauses often have other elements that relate primarily to the entire clause—to the relationship between the topic and comment, rather than specifically to one or the other. For example, a prepositional phrase that tells us *where* something occurred may also tell us where the subject/topic was when it happened. Such a phrase relates to the entire predication, not just to one of its elements.

---

176. This rapid succession of preterites—which is quite unlike the surrounding narrative—suggests that the author saw these actions as some sort of narrative "peak" or "climax".

177. In a movie, for example, dialogue often controls pace. Unlike a movie (in which we can both listen to and watch a speaker or listener), text can only mention one thing at a time.

178. The term "comment" seeks to avoid the confusion caused by "predicate", which connotes "verb" to many readers (verbs are only one of a number of potential grammatical forms that can function as a comment in Biblical Hebrew).

Disjunctive clauses begin with the conjunction ***waw* + a non-verb** (i.e., *anything except* a finite verbal form). Backgrounded actions, activities, setting, and *irrealis* (i.e., what *didn't* happen) tend to occur in disjunctive clauses, but it is not primarily the verbal conjugation that determines the relative status or function of a clause. Instead, a disjunctive clause signals the reader that it (the clause) is not on the narrative "backbone", or the preterite "story-line". After noting this, we can address the separate question of what the clause suggests about its status relative to the storyline. Disjunctive clauses have two primary functions:

1. They describe an activity or state that *parallels* that described in the previous clause. The syntax of the disjunctive clause often reverses or inverts the syntax of the clause that it parallels. After Naomi's second statement urging Orpah and Ruth to return to Moab, the contrasting responses of her daughters-in-law are described in a preterite clause ("and Orpah kissed …") and a disjunctive clause ("but Ruth clung …"):

   וַתִּשַּׁק עָרְפָּה לַחֲמוֹתָהּ   and-she-kissed Orpah her-mother-in-law,
   וְרוּת דָּבְקָה בָּהּ   *but*-Ruth she-clung to-her. (Ru 1.14b; cf. 1 Sam 1.2b)

   On the other hand, the wives of Abram and Nahor are introduced in parallel clauses with no implied contrast, the first is asyndetic, and the second disjunctive (Gn 11.29b):

   שֵׁם אֵשֶׁת־אַבְרָם שָׂרָי   The-name-of the-wife-of Abram [was] Sarai,
   וְשֵׁם אֵשֶׁת־נָחוֹר מִלְכָּה   *and*-the-name-of the-wife-of Nahor [was] Milkah.

2. Disjunctive clauses also present *parenthetic* information, which tends to be either flashback (information about earlier events), setting, or other information that the reader will need in order to understand events upcoming in the narrative. For example, the Canaanite presence in the land, noted in a disjunctive clause (Gn 12.6) creates narrative tension with Abram's preceding call (Gn 12.1) and Yнwн's following promise (Gn 12.7):

   וְהַכְּנַעֲנִי אָז בָּאָרֶץ׃   *Now*-the-Canaanite [was] then in-the-land.

   This information is expanded in a later disjunctive clause that helps the reader understand why Abram and Lot could not stay together (Gn 13.7b):

   וְהַכְּנַעֲנִי וְהַפְּרִזִּי אָז יֹשֵׁב בָּאָרֶץ׃   *Now*-the-Canaanite and-the-Perizzite then lived in-the-land.

Genesis 12 contains four disjunctive clauses. They identify Abram's age, which becomes increasingly important in his ongoing search for an heir (Gn 12.4b); the potential tension between Yнwн's promise and the Canaanite presence (Gn 12.6b); Pharaoh's good treatment of Abram for Sarai's sake (Gn 12.16a), as he had predicted (Gn 12.13b); and what Abram was to do after Pharaoh discovered his deception about his relationship to Sarai (Gn 12.19b); it therefore begins with וְעַתָּה, *therefore* (see "clause-initial particles", above).

Marking disjunctive clauses highlights information that is *crucial* to the story; it also reminds us that they probably do *not* describe the next event in the narrative sequence.

25.7 What's Next?

Ater pre-reading, the next step is to *translate* the passage *in writing*; this has at least four purposes: (1) it slows down our reading, compelling us to pay attention to the text itself; (2) it forces us to choose a rendering (rather than merely note all of the possibilities); (3) it quickly reveals that translation entails far more than choosing the "right" gloss or creating a "word-for-word" running gloss; and thus (4) it should protect us against the arrogance that can come from a facility with the biblical languages, as we realize the number and nature of choices and compromises entailed in preparing a written translation.

25.8 Vocabulary

teach, instruct (H)	יָרָה (III)	.379	be willing, agree	אָבָה	.371
ransom, buy (back)	פָּדָה	.380	weep, mourn, wail	בָּכָה	.372
turn (toward)	פָּנָה	.381	fornicate, commit illicit sex	זָנָה	.373
acquire, get, buy	קָנָה	.382	see, observe, gaze [at]	חָזָה	.374
be pleased with, like	רָצָה	.383	be/become weak, sick, ill	חָלָה	.375
pleasure, favor	רָצוֹן	.384	camp, encamp	חָנָה	.376
water, give a drink [to someone or something] (H)	שָׁקָה	.385	be/become angry, hot	חָרָה	.377
wander (lost)	תָּעָה	.386	thank, praise (H)	יָרָה	.378

25.9 Exercise

In the reading passage for the next class, (1) mark (highlight, underline) the preterites; (2) quotation formulae; and (3) any occurrences of *wayhî* (and identify their function as either circumstantial or predicate).

25.10 Enrichment: Pre-reading Ruth 2.1-7

What is the result of pre-reading a passage of biblical narrative? In Ru 2.1-7 the underlining and shading show that the author used two disjunctive clauses flanking two appositional phrases to describe Boaz (1). The next disjunctive clause in these verses also refers to Boaz, this time to his arrival at the field (4). The shading (quotations) shows the increasingly dialogical nature of the story (5-7), as well as the use of preterites within the direct speech of the servant's report on Ruth's actions (v. 7). The sequence of three preterites (3) stands out from the rest of the passage (there are no other consecutive preterites), suggesting that these actions form some sort of anticipatory climax.

Having been pre-read, these verses no longer consist of either a single block of text or 105 individual concatenated words, but are revealed as a series of brief functional units of two to four words that together tell a well-crafted story:

¹וּלְנָעֳמִי מְיֻדָּע לְאִישָׁהּ ‖ אִישׁ גִּבּוֹר חַיִל ‖ מִמִּשְׁפַּחַת אֱלִימֶלֶךְ ‖ וּשְׁמוֹ בֹּעַז: ²וַתֹּאמֶר רוּת הַמּוֹאֲבִיָּה אֶל־נָעֳמִי ‖ אֵלְכָה־נָּא הַשָּׂדֶה וַאֲלַקֳטָה בַשִּׁבֳּלִים ‖ אַחַר ‖ אֲשֶׁר אֶמְצָא־חֵן בְּעֵינָיו ‖ וַתֹּאמֶר לָהּ לְכִי בִתִּי: ³וַתֵּלֶךְ וַתָּבוֹא וַתְּלַקֵּט בַּשָּׂדֶה ‖ אַחֲרֵי הַקֹּצְרִים ‖ וַיִּקֶר מִקְרֶהָ ‖ חֶלְקַת הַשָּׂדֶה לְבֹעַז ‖ אֲשֶׁר מִמִּשְׁפַּחַת אֱלִימֶלֶךְ: ⁴וְהִנֵּה־בֹעַז ‖ בָּא מִבֵּית־לֶחֶם ‖ וַיֹּאמֶר לַקּוֹצְרִים יְהוָה עִמָּכֶם ‖ וַיֹּאמְרוּ לוֹ יְבָרֶכְךָ יְהוָה: ⁵וַיֹּאמֶר בֹּעַז לְנַעֲרוֹ ‖ הַנִּצָּב עַל־הַקּוֹצְרִים ‖ לְמִי הַנַּעֲרָה הַזֹּאת: ⁶וַיַּעַן ‖ הַנַּעַר הַנִּצָּב עַל־הַקּוֹצְרִים וַיֹּאמַר ‖ נַעֲרָה מוֹאֲבִיָּה הִיא ‖ הַשָּׁבָה עִם־נָעֳמִי מִשְּׂדֵה מוֹאָב: ⁷וַתֹּאמֶר ‖ אֲלַקֳטָה־נָּא וְאָסַפְתִּי בָעֳמָרִים ‖ אַחֲרֵי הַקּוֹצְרִים ‖ וַתָּבוֹא וַתַּעֲמוֹד ‖ מֵאָז הַבֹּקֶר וְעַד־עַתָּה ‖ זֶה שִׁבְתָּהּ הַבַּיִת מְעָט:

Key

Double underline	preterite (*wayyiqtol*)
Single underline	disjunctive clause (*waw*+non-finite-verb)
Wavy double underline	clause-initial particle
Shaded	quotation
‖	major disjunctive accent (as described above)

Lesson 26

I-נ Verbs

Verbal roots that begin with נ are weak whenever the first radical of a verbal form is followed by silent *šewa*, since the נ assimilates to the following consonant. Verbs I-נ are therefore weak throughout *hifil* and *hofal*, and in some forms of *nifal* (P, Ptc) and *qal* (F, Pr, V, NC). They are strong throughout all three D-stems, and in some conjugations of *nifal* (F, Pr, V, NC) and *qal* (P, NA, Ptc). This general pattern is the same as the I-י verb (below), so that some forms of these roots are exactly alike, and the lexical form can be determined only by knowing the vocabulary or from context, or both.

Stem	Weak Forms	Strong Forms
Q	F, Pr, V [NC,NA]	P, Ptc [NC, NA]
N	P, Ptc	F, Pr, V [NC,NA]
D, Dp, Dt	None	All forms
H, Hp	All forms	None

When the first radical of a verbal form is followed by silent *šewa* (e.g., יִמְשֹׁל), the initial נ assimilates to the following consonant and doubles it. Each of the following pair of forms has the same parsing; the second verb of each pair is I-נ.

Form	Root	Parsing	Gloss	*Dageš forte*
נִמְשַׁל	משׁל	3ms N P	*He was kept*	In נִגַּשׁ the initial –נ of נגשׁ has assimilated to the ג; the –נ is the prefix of the *nifal* perfect.
נִגַּשׁ	נגשׁ		*He approached*	
יִמְשֹׁל	משׁל	3ms Q F	*He keeps (will keep)*	In יִפֹּל the initial –נ of נפל has assimilated to the פ.
יִפֹּל	נפל		*He falls (will fall)*	
הִמְשִׁיל	משׁל	3ms H P	*He caused to keep*	In הִצִּיל the initial –נ of נצל has assimilated to the צ.
הִצִּיל	נצל		*He rescued*	

1. The primary clue that a verbal form is from a I-נ root is that there are only two radicals, the first of which is doubled (if there is any type of stem or subject prefix).
2. If the second radical of a I-נ root is a guttural or ר, the root is like the basic verb (נ does not assimilate).
3. Roots that are both I-נ and hollow (vowel-medial, e.g., נוּס) follow the rules of the hollow verbs (Lesson 28), not I-נ verbs.
4. Some forms of I-נ roots in Q look exactly like I-י forms (Lesson 30).

26.1 *I-נ Verbal Roots in Qal*

There are three main types of I-נ verb (creatively called Types I, II, and III). Type I occurs in all stems, Type II in Q of some verbal roots; Type III consists of only one verb (נתן). There is no distinction in the other stems (i.e., the differences between Types I, II, & III only appear in *qal*).

26.1.1 Type I (Q F with holem)

This is the most common type of I-נ verb; when the initial נ is followed by silent *šewa* it assimilates to the second radical and doubles it. Type I verbal forms from I-נ roots are therefore weak throughout the H-stems (*hifil, hofal*), in *qal* imperfect (Q F) and preterite (Q Pr), and in *nifal* perfect (N P) and participle (N Ptc). This skeleton paradigm shows the forms of Type I verbs that are affected (*weak*):

	Type I	Q	N	H	Hp
P	3ms	נָפַל	נִפַּל	הִפִּיל	הֻפַּל
F	3ms	יִפֹּל	יִנָּפֵל	יַפִּיל	יֻפַּל
V	ms	נְפֹל	הִנָּפֵל	הַפֵּל	---
	mp	נִפְלוּ	הִנָּפְלוּ	הַפִּילוּ	---
NC		נְפֹל	הִנָּפֵל	הַפִּיל	הֻפַּל
Ptc	ms	נֹפֵל	נִפָּל	מַפִּיל	מֻפָּל

1. Forms in shaded spaces are not weak ("---" means that this form does not occur).
2. The prefix and its vowel are unaffected (except in Hp, where the prefix vowel is always *qibbuṣ*).
3. The endings and vowels after the second radical are the same as those of the basic verb.

26.1.2 Type II (Q F with patah)

These verbs differ from Type I only in *qal* imperfect, preterite, imperative, and infinitive construct; all other forms are the same as Type I (above). The paradigm shows only the *weak* forms of this type of I-נ verb, using נגש and לקח, and lists Q forms only, since the other stems are the same as Type I (above).

Type II (Qal)		√נגש		√לקח	
F	3ms	יִגַּשׁ	he approaches/will approach	יִקַּח	he takes/will take
	3mp	יִגְּשׁוּ	they approach/will approach	יִקְחוּ	they take/will take
Pr	3ms	וַיִּגַּשׁ	and he approached	וַיִּקַּח	and he took
	3mp	וַיִּגְּשׁוּ	and they approached	וַיִּקְחוּ	and they took
V	ms	גַּשׁ	Approach!	קַח	Take!
	mp	גְּשׁוּ	Approach!	קְחוּ	Take!
NC		גֶּשֶׁת	[to] approach	קַחַת	[to] take

1. The root sign (√) is used in studying Hebrew to show that we are discussing or describing forms from a particular verbal root.
2. *Qal* imperfect has *patah* after the second radical.
3. In Q imperative and infinitive construct the initial נ drops off (apocopates).
4. A final ת- is added to Q NC, which has two *seghols* (two *pataḥ*s in II- and III-guttural roots), and looks just like Q NC of some I-י verbs (below).
5. The forms of the verb לקח look just like the forms of a I-נ verb (Type II); any verbal form with קַח- or -קְח is therefore a form of לקח. It is the only I-ל verb that does this. The medial ק loses *dageš forte* before *šewa*; cf. 3 mp Q F (above).

26.1.3 Type III (נתן only)

The most common I-נ verb (nearly 2000x in Biblical Hebrew), נתן, is the only verb of this type. In *nifal* (the only non-*qal* stem in which it occurs), it is like Type II (above). Its main difference from other verbs in *qal* is that the final ן assimilates to consonantal PGN endings:

Q P	1cs	נָתַתִּי	*I gave*
N P	2 mp	נִתַּתֶּם	*You were given (put, set, made)*

The other forms of נתן look like Type II (above), except that its stem vowel is *sere*. In addition, Q NC lacks both נ's.

F	3ms	יִתֵּן	*He gives/will give*
	3mp	יִתְּנוּ	*They [will] give*
Pr	1cs	וָאֶתֵּן	*I gave*
	3ms	וַיִּתֵּן	*He gave*
V	2ms	תֵּן	
		תְּנָה	*Give!*
	2mp	תְּנוּ	
NC		תֵּת	*to give*
	+1cs sfx	תִּתִּי	*my giving*
	+2ms sfx	תִּתְּךָ	*your giving*

A paradigm listing all forms of נתן that occur in Biblical Hebrew follows the I-נ paradigm (Appendix E).

26.2 *Nifal of I-נ Verbal Roots*

Like the strong verb (Lesson 18), I-נ verbal roots appear in two basic forms in *nifal*, with a doubled second radical (P, Ptc) or a doubled first radical (F, Pr, V):

√נפל

P	3ms	נִפַּל
F	3ms	יִנָּפֵל
Pr	3ms	וַיִּנָּפֵל
V	ms	נִפֹּל
NC		נִפֹּל
Ptc	ms	נִפָּל

1. In the perfect and participle, the initial -נ assimilates to the second radical. The -נ is the -נ prefix of the *nifal*.
2. In the other conjugations, the -נ of the *nifal* prefix assimilates to the initial -נ of the verbal root; these forms look just like the strong verb. The visible -נ- is the initial radical of the verbal root.
3. Unlike *qal*, the *nifal* of I-נ verbal roots appears in only one set of forms.

26.3 Hifil & Hofal (H, Hp) of I-נ Verbal Roots

Since the *nun* is assimilated in all forms of the *hifil* and *hofal*,[179] the initial -נ of I-נ verbal roots that occur only in the H-stems (e.g., נגד, נשׂג) never appears:

		√נגד		√נשׂג
		H	Hp	H
P	3ms	הִגִּיד	הֻגַּד	הִשִּׂיג
F	3ms	יַגִּיד	---*	יַשִּׂיג
Pr	3ms	וַיַּגֵּד	וַיֻּגַּד	וַיַּשֵּׂג
V	ms	הַגֵּד	---	---
NC		הַגִּיד	---	---
Ptc	ms	מַגִּיד	---	מַשִּׂיג

*Forms marked with "---" do not occur; Hp of נשׂג does not occur.

26.4 Frequency

This table lists all I-נ verbs that occur fifty times or more in Biblical Hebrew.

נתן	give	1994x	נבא	prophesy (N)	115x
נכה	hit, wound, defeat (H; once each in N, Dp)	504x	נצב	take one's stand/place (N, H)	75x
נשׂא	lift, carry, forgive	651x	נבט	look at, pay attention (once in D; therefore "always" -בט)	70x
נפל	fall	433x	נצח	lead (D)	65x
נגד	tell; declare, report, announce (H; always -גד)	369x	נצר	watch, guard	63x
נטה	stretch out; turn	215x	נטע	plant	57x
נצל	snatch, rescue, deliver (H)	208x	נדח	be scattered (N); scatter (H)	51x
נגע	touch; reach, come to	150x	נכר	recognize (H); a few times in N, D; therefore usually -כר	50x
נסע	depart, break camp	146x	נשׂג	overtake (H; always -שׂג)	50x
נגשׁ	approach, come near	125x			

---

179. This assimilation always takes place because the first radical of every form in H and Hp is followed by silent *šewa*.

26.5 Vocabulary

prophesy (N)	נָבָא	.387	depart, break camp, travel	נָסַע	.395
look at, pay attention to (H)	נָבַט	.388	fall	נָפַל	.396
tell; report, declare, announce (H)	נָגַד	.389	take one's stand/place; be assigned (N)	נָצַב	.397
touch; reach, come to	נָגַע	.390	lead (D)	נָצַח	.398
blow, assault; plague	נֶגַע		rescue, deliver; snatch (all H)	נָצַל	.399
come near, approach	נָגַשׁ	.391	watch, guard, keep, protect	נָצַר	.400
be scattered (st. vb.)	נָדַח	.392	lift, carry; forgive	נָשָׂא	.401
plant	נָטַע	.393	give	נָתַן	.402
pretend (N); recognize (H)	נָכַר	.394			

26.6 Exercises

After you have studied the I-נ verb, *gloss* these texts, *and then* parse all of the I-נ verbs in Genesis 11.27-13.14.

1. וַיִּשְׁאַל יַעֲקֹב וַיֹּאמֶר הַגִּידָה־נָּא שְׁמֶךָ
Gen 32.30; 2ms V with הָ - ending; Jacob

2. וַיָּרֶב הָעָם עִם־מֹשֶׁה וַיֹּאמְרוּ תְּנוּ־לָנוּ מַיִם וְנִשְׁתֶּה
Ex 17.2; ריב *strive* (3ms Q Pr); Moses

3. וַיֵּרַע הַדָּבָר בְּעֵינֵי שְׁמוּאֵל כַּאֲשֶׁר אָמְרוּ תְּנָה־לָּנוּ מֶלֶךְ לְשָׁפְטֵנוּ וַיִּתְפַּלֵּל שְׁמוּאֵל אֶל־יְהוָה׃
1 Sa 8.6; וַיֵּרַע *but it was wrong (evil, wicked)*; 2ms V with הָ - ending; פלל *pray;* Samuel

4. וַיֹּאמֶר שָׁאוּל אֶל־יוֹנָתָן הַגִּידָה לִּי מֶה עָשִׂיתָה וַיַּגֶּד־לוֹ יוֹנָתָן
1 Sa 14.43; Saul, Jonathan

5. הַבֵּט מִשָּׁמַיִם וּרְאֵה מִזְּבֻל קָדְשְׁךָ וְתִפְאַרְתֶּךָ
Is 63.15; זְבֻל *dwelling*

6. אַל־תִּירָא מִפְּנֵיהֶם כִּי־אִתְּךָ אֲנִי לְהַצִּלֶךָ נְאֻם־יְהוָה׃
Jr 1.8; ירא *fear, be afraid*

7. וַיִּקָּחֵנִי יְהוָה מֵאַחֲרֵי הַצֹּאן וַיֹּאמֶר אֵלַי יְהוָה לֵךְ הִנָּבֵא אֶל־עַמִּי יִשְׂרָאֵל׃
Am 7.15 (לֵךְ 2ms QV הלך); the speaker is Amos

8. וַתִּקַּח מִפִּרְיוֹ וַתֹּאכַל וַתִּתֵּן גַּם־לְאִישָׁהּ עִמָּהּ וַיֹּאכַל׃
Gen 3.6

9. כִּי הִצַּלְתָּ נַפְשִׁי מִמָּוֶת
Ps 56.14a [ET 15a]; this nomenclature means that the English and Hebrew texts are divided differently; in English this verse is Ps 56.15

10. יוֹמָם הַשֶּׁמֶשׁ לֹא־יַכֶּכָּה וְיָרֵחַ בַּלָּיְלָה׃
Ps 121.6; כָה - is a 2ms suffix; יָרֵחַ *moon*

11. וְאִישׁ אֶחָד מִבְּנֵי הַנְּבִיאִים אָמַר אֶל־רֵעֵהוּ בִּדְבַר יְהוָה הַכֵּינִי נָא וַיְמָאֵן הָאִישׁ לְהַכֹּתוֹ׃
1Kg 20.35

12. אֶת־קַשְׁתִּי נָתַתִּי בֶּעָנָן וְהָיְתָה לְאוֹת בְּרִית בֵּינִי וּבֵין הָאָרֶץ׃
Gn 9.13; קֶשֶׁת *bow* (n.)

Gn 34.16	וְנָתַנּוּ אֶת־בְּנֹתֵינוּ לָכֶם וְאֶת־בְּנֹתֵיכֶם נִקַּח־לָנוּ וְיָשַׁבְנוּ אִתְּכֶם וְהָיִינוּ לְעַם אֶחָד׃	13.
Ex 20.7; שָׁוְא *vanity, in vain*; נקה *acquit, leave unpunished*	לֹא תִשָּׂא אֶת־שֵׁם־יְהוָה אֱלֹהֶיךָ לַשָּׁוְא כִּי לֹא יְנַקֶּה יְהוָה אֵת אֲשֶׁר־יִשָּׂא אֶת־שְׁמוֹ לַשָּׁוְא׃	14.
Jos 3.6; Joshua	וַיֹּאמֶר יְהוֹשֻׁעַ אֶל־הַכֹּהֲנִים לֵאמֹר שְׂאוּ אֶת־אֲרוֹן הַבְּרִית וְעִבְרוּ לִפְנֵי הָעָם וַיִּשְׂאוּ אֶת־אֲרוֹן הַבְּרִית וַיֵּלְכוּ לִפְנֵי הָעָם׃	15.
Jg 4.7; מָשַׁךְ *draw* [*pull*] [*out*]; הָמוֹן *host, multitude; tumult, confusion*; Kishon, Sisera, Jabin	וּמָשַׁכְתִּי אֵלֶיךָ אֶל־נַחַל קִישׁוֹן אֶת־סִיסְרָא יָבִין וְאֶת־רִכְבּוֹ וְאֶת־הֲמוֹנוֹ וּנְתַתִּיהוּ בְּיָדֶךָ׃ שַׂר־צָבָא	16.
2 Kgs 19.7; שְׁמוּעָה *report, rumour*; וְשָׁב 3ms Q P + *w* < שׁוּב, *return, go back*	הִנְנִי נֹתֵן בּוֹ רוּחַ וְשָׁמַע שְׁמוּעָה וְשָׁב לְאַרְצוֹ וְהִפַּלְתִּיו בַּחֶרֶב בְּאַרְצוֹ׃	17.
Jr 1.9; נָתַתִּי *may be performative* (§10.9)	וַיִּשְׁלַח יְהוָה אֶת־יָדוֹ וַיַּגַּע עַל־פִּי וַיֹּאמֶר יְהוָה אֵלַי הִנֵּה נָתַתִּי דְבָרַי בְּפִיךָ׃	18.

26.7 Enrichment: Participant Reference

Noting the preterites, quotation formulae, and *wayhî*-clauses in a biblical narrative helps us study the text more carefully (Lesson 25), but other types of information in narrative also need to be recognized and accounted for. One that can be especially helpful in understanding the author's intention in a passage is *participant identification*. You have probably noticed that the biblical authors tend to identify the main characters (actors) in the story, either by name, or title, or both.

In Genesis 16, for example, the use of appositional descriptors underlines the dysfunctionality of the triad of Sarai, Hagar, and Abram (to name them in the order in which they appear in the story). The passage begins with three disjunctive clauses (Gn 16.1) that set the stage for the story by identifying the major participants, Sarai and Hagar:

1a	וְשָׂרַי אֵשֶׁת אַבְרָם לֹא יָלְדָה לוֹ	Now Sarai, Abram's wife, had not born [a child] to/for him,
1b	וְלָהּ שִׁפְחָה מִצְרִית	and she had an Egyptian maid,
1c	וּשְׁמָהּ הָגָר׃	and her name was Hagar (Gn 16.1).

Sarai is identified by her relationship to Abram, and Hagar in relationship to her, as well as by her ethnicity. Abram is mentioned only to establish his relationship to Sarai—to "remind" readers that Sarai was his wife.

In Gn 16.2, Sarai is explicitly named as the subject of the leading preterite, but this is a necessary identification. Since two women were named in v. 1, the 3fs preterite וַתֹּאמֶר requires an explicit subject in order for the reader to know—as the quotation begins—which woman spoke to Abram. At the end of the verse, when Abram acquiesced to Sarai, both actors, already named at the beginning of the verse, are again called by name. On the other hand, Sarai does not mention Hagar's name, referring to her merely as "my maid" (שִׁפְחָתִי).

וַתֹּאמֶר שָׂרַי אֶל־אַבְרָם ...	And *Sarai* said to *Abram*, "...
וַיִּשְׁמַע אַבְרָם לְקוֹל שָׂרָי׃	and *Abram* listened to *Sarai's* voice (Gn 16.2).

In Gn 16.3, both Sarai and Hagar are identified as fully as they were in v. 1, and Abram is named "in both directions"—Sarai as his wife, and he as her husband, probably to highlight the tangled relationships that are being created:

וַתִּקַּח שָׂרַי אֵשֶׁת־אַבְרָם	And *Sarai, Abram's wife*, took *Hagar, the Egyptian*, her maid, ...
אֶת־הָגָר הַמִּצְרִית שִׁפְחָתָהּ	
וַתִּתֵּן אֹתָהּ לְאַבְרָם אִישָׁהּ לוֹ לְאִשָּׁה׃	and she gave her to *Abram her husband*, to become his wife (Gn 16.3).

When the relationship between Hagar and Sarai deteriorates (Gn 16.4), the author places Sarai and Abram on the same level by introducing both of their quotations with both names:

| וַתֹּאמֶר שָׂרַי אֶל־אַבְרָם ... | And *Sarai* said to *Abram*, "... (Gn 16.5) |
| וַיֹּאמֶר אַבְרָם אֶל־שָׂרַי ... | and *Abram* said to *Sarai*, "... (Gn 16.6) |

Throughout this brief conversation, Hagar is again demoted implicitly, since she is not called by her name, but merely called "my/your maid". At the end of the story, however, Hagar is named three times—always as the subject of the verb ילד (a preterite [15a], a perfect in a relative clause [15b], and an infinitive construct in a temporal clause within the final disjunctive clause [16]).

וַתֵּלֶד הָגָר לְאַבְרָם בֵּן	And *Hagar* bore Abram a son,
וַיִּקְרָא אַבְרָם שֶׁם־בְּנוֹ	and Abram called the name of his son,
אֲשֶׁר־יָלְדָה הָגָר	whom *Hagar* bore ... (Gn 16.15)
וְאַבְרָם בֶּן־שְׁמֹנִים שָׁנָה וְשֵׁשׁ שָׁנִים	(now Abram was eighty-six years old when
בְּלֶדֶת־הָגָר אֶת־יִשְׁמָעֵאל לְאַבְרָם׃	*Hagar* bore Ishmael to Abram). (Gn 16.16)

Although she is not called Abram's "wife" after v. 3, at the end of the story she is no longer defined in terms of her relationship to Sarai, but in her own right as the mother of Ishmael, which implies some change in her standing within the home.

In Genesis 18.1-5, the author's ways of refering to the participants suggests that Gn 18.1-15 (the story of Abraham's hospitality and the repeated promise of an heir) was meant to be read as the consummation of the story recorded in Gn 17 (the institution of the covenantal sign of circumcision and its attendant promises).

The narrator identifies the subject of the first clause by name (יהוה), but does not name another subject until Gn 18.6a (below); he instead uses pronominal suffixes, an independent pronoun, and PGN affixes. Nor does he identify the pronominal object of the preposition (אֵלָיו). The significance of this lack of identification again comes from the tendency of Hebrew narrative to identify participants (one of the functions of the passive stems is to *avoid* identifying the subject).

In fact, apart from "Yhwh" (18.1a) the participants in these verses are identified only by pronouns and generic nouns (i.e., שְׁלֹשִׁים אֲנָשִׁים; 18.2a):

וַיֵּרָא אֵלָיו יהוה בְּאֵלֹנֵי מַמְרֵא	Yhwh appeared to *him* among the oaks of Mamre	1a
וְהוּא יֹשֵׁב פֶּתַח־הָאֹהֶל ...	(now *he* was sitting at the entrance to the tent ...)	1b
וַיִּשָּׂא עֵינָיו	and *he* lifted *his* eyes	2a
וַיַּרְא ... עָלָיו	and *he* saw ... near *him*	2b
וַיַּרְא	and *he* saw	2c
וַיָּרָץ לִקְרָאתָם ...	and *he* ran to meet *them* ...	2d
וַיִּשְׁתַּחוּ אָרְצָה׃	and *he* bowed to the ground.	2e
וַיֹּאמַר ...	and *he* said, "... (18.3)	3a
וַיֹּאמְרוּ ...	and *they* said, "...	5d

During his speech (3b-5c), he does not identify himself except as "I" (as 1cs verbal PGN affix) and עַבְדְּךָ "your servant". There is no contextual clue to his identity, except that he was a male, who was authorized to offer the hospitality of his home to three strangers, and who was also conscious of the social niceties of abasing himself ("your servant").

Only after the "three men" accept this unnamed person's offer of hospitality (18.4-5) does the author call him "Abraham" (18.6a), and then, as if to confirm or reinforce his identity, names "Abraham" as the subject of two of the next three narrative clauses:

וַיְמַהֵר אַבְרָהָם הָאֹהֱלָה אֶל־שָׂרָה	And *Abraham* hastened to the tent, to Sarah,	**6a**
וַיֹּאמֶר ...	and *he* said, "...	**6b**
וְאֶל־הַבָּקָר רָץ אַבְרָהָם	and [then?] to the herd ran *Abraham*, and ...	**7a**

The point is that this repeated "non-identification" of the subject, followed by his repeated identification *by name* is that these verses—and the story that they open—were written as part of the preceding story: they do not record a meal isolated from the promises and commandments of Gn 17, but rather the meal that ratifies the covenant that had just been sealed by circumcision (17.23-27).[180] This contextual setting also explains the promises about Sarai's rôle in the covenant's fulfillment (18.9-15; cf. 17.15-16), and Yhwh's musings about telling Abraham what he [Yhwh] was about to do (18.17-19).

Because we read the biblical stories having heard them in sermons and Bible lessons, we often find it difficult to read them *as they were written*, so that in this case (for example), we already "know" that Abraham is the main participant in verses 1-5, even though he is never identified (English versions tend to supply "Abraham" in these verses). Paying close attention to the Hebrew text—especially in light of the normally explicit nature of Hebrew narrative—reveals the misleading nature of this chapter break, and encourages us to read the story *in light of* the covenantal statements of Gn 17.

Finally, this table lays out all participant references in Ruth 2.1-7. You can study the manners of reference (proper name, noun, independent pronoun, pronominal suffix, verbal PGN affix), and their relationship to the person(s) mentioned. This sort of exercise will help you focus on *how* the author is telling his story, which is in turn a clue to how he or she intends us to understand it.

Person referred to & Manner of Mention

Others	Boaz	Ruth	Naomi	"Voice"	V.
	לְנָעֳמִי		נָעֳמִי	author	1
	מְיֻדָּע לְאִישָׁהּ				
	אִישׁ גִּבּוֹר חַיִל				
	מִמִּשְׁפַּחַת אֱלִימֶלֶךְ				
	וּשְׁמוֹ בֹּעַז				
		וַתֹּאמֶר רוּת הַמּוֹאֲבִיָּה		author	2
אֲשֶׁר אֶמְצָא־חֵן בְּעֵינָיו				Ruth	
			נָעֳמִי	author	
		וַתֹּאמֶר לָהּ		author	
		לְכִי בִתִּי		Naomi	

---

180. For another account of a covenant ratification followed by a meal between the parties, see Ex 24.4-11.

		וַתֵּלֶךְ	author	3
		וַתָּבוֹא		
הַקֹּצְרִים		וַתְּלַקֵּט	author	
		מִקְרֶהָ	author	
אֲשֶׁר מִמִּשְׁפַּחַת אֱלִימֶלֶךְ		בֹּעַז	author	
		בֹּעַז	author	4
לַקֹּצְרִים		וַיֹּאמֶר	author	
עִמָּכֶם			Boaz	
וַיֹּאמְרוּ		לוֹ	author	
לְנַעֲרוֹ		וַיֹּאמֶר בֹּעַז	author	5
הַנִּצָּב עַל־הַקּוֹצְרִים				
		הַנַּעֲרָה הַזֹּאת	Boaz	
וַיַּעַן הַנַּעַר			author	6
הַנִּצָּב עַל־הַקּוֹצְרִים				
וַיֹּאמַר				
	נָעֳמִי	נַעֲרָה מוֹאֲבִיָּה הִיא הַשָּׁבָה עִם־נָעֳמִי מִשְּׂדֵה מוֹאָב	Boaz's servant	
		וַתֹּאמֶר	Boaz's servant	7
		וַתָּבוֹא		
		וַתַּעֲמוֹד		
		שִׁבְתָּהּ		

Lesson 27

PRE-READING A BIBLICAL POEM

Poetry has been called the "other use [or "kind"] of language"; it does not communicate like "ordinary" speech or thought, but rather functions as language "for its own sake"; this suggests that it needs to be read in a different manner. Nor is this "other kind" of language limited to the "poetic books" (so-called), but also occurs widely throughout the prophetic books, so that nearly one-half of the Hebrew Bible is poetic.

A major challenge in reading a biblical poem in Hebrew is that a careful translation will often not "sound right". There are several reasons for this: (1) poetry's linguistic "compression" often yields ambiguous syntax, especially in non-verbal clauses; (2) poetry often uses unusual or rare vocabulary; (3) verbal conjugations in poetry do not have the same functions as in narrative; (4) scholars disagree about the nature and structure of biblical poetry, so that the results of their studies differ; and (5) the translation tradition in English often controls or determines the English text.

All of these reasons (there are more) mean that it is crucial to translate the Hebrew text *before* studying, or checking, published translations.[181]

This lesson presents some points to consider when trying to understand a biblical poem; it aims to protect us from interpreting the text based only on our impressions by encouraging us to pay close attention to specific aspects of the text itself. These "steps" should prepare you to begin to read a biblical poem as a poetic text.

27.1 *Lineation: One Clause per Line*

Begin by dividing the poetic text into clauses, and then making each clause a separate poetic line. [A clause consists of a subject (topic) and predicate (comment).][182] In doing this, you *must not assume* (1) that a verse contains a certain number of lines; or (2) the validity of the layout in either BHS or the English versions.

27.1.1 *Nominal/Substantive Subjects & Objects*

First, list the nouns in the poem, keeping construct chains together. There are nine in Ps 117, three of which are in construct:

Nouns	Construct	Absolute
1	כָּל־גּוֹיִם	יהוה
	כָּל־הָאֻמִּים:	
2		חַסְדּוֹ
	וֶאֱמֶת־יהוה	
		יָהּ

---

181. You will also find that commentaries and reference grammars often justify traditional renderings. These comments are not meant to disparage the work of Bible translators, in light of the very severe constraints under which translators work—there is simply not time to do detailed research, and so the tendency is to default to the standard. [Other considerations also skew the process, such as the public's desire for what is familiar.]

182. Poetic passages in BHS were arranged typographically by the editor(s); don't assume that the lines, or even the half-lines (separated by an extra space, called a *caesura* [Lat., "cut"]), correspond to poetic lines—they may or may not.

Nouns tell us what a poem is *about*—its topic. Two of these six nominal phrases refer to humanity ("all" people), the other four refer to Yhwh. The repeated divine name (in two forms) suggests an *inclusio* or "envelope" (because the same form "envelops" a section of text).

27.1.2 *Verbal Predicates*

After listing the nominal forms, list the verbs, again in sequence; it can be helpful to divide this list by conjugation (there is no column for conjugations that do not occur), and to parse each verbal form.

Verbs	Imperative	Perfect	Parsing
1	הַלְלוּ		2mp DV
	שַׁבְּחוּהוּ		2mp DV+3ms
2		גָּבַר	3ms QP
	הַלְלוּ		2mp DV

Verbs tell us what the poet says *about* the topic revealed by the list of nouns: three of these forms (all *piel* imperative) describe an act of worship or praise, one (גבר) describes rank or position. The *inclusio* suggested by the list of nouns (above) is even more apparent here where the same form (הַלְלוּ) is repeated. As it does in Ps 117, any aspect of verbal morphology (conjugation, PGN, stem)—or more than one, in combination—can reveal the poem's structure.

27.1.3 *Clausal Lineation*

In order to have some control over our "reconstruction" of the poem, we can make each clause a single poetic line, based on its subject and predicate (no matter how long or short the resultant line).[183] When the two lists are thus combined, they yield very nearly all of Psalm 117, except for one conjunction (2a) and two prepositional phrases (2a, 2b):

	Subject	Object	Imperative	Perfect
1a[184]	כָּל־גּוֹיִם	יהוה	הַלְלוּ	
1b	כָּל־הָאֻמִּים׃		שַׁבְּחוּהוּ	
2a	חַסְדּוֹ			גָּבַר
2b	וֶאֱמֶת־יהוה			
2c		יָהּ	הַלְלוּ	

When we add the conjunction and prepositional phrases to the lines, we realize that the first prepositional phrase is "part of" the predicate of 2a, and that the second *is* the predicate of 2b. The resultant full text is organized by line, so that we can translate the poem and then begin to analyze the particulars of its semantics and syntax.

	Predicate	Subject	Object	Predicate	Conj.
1a		כָּל־גּוֹיִם	יהוה	הַלְלוּ	
1b		כָּל־הָאֻמִּים׃		שַׁבְּחוּהוּ	
2a		חַסְדּוֹ		גָּבַר עָלֵינוּ	כִּי
2b	לְעוֹלָם	וֶאֱמֶת־יהוה			
2c			יָהּ	הַלְלוּ	

183. A quick glance at nearly any translation of a biblical poem will reveal single clauses divided between two lines (or more), largely based on the theory that poetic lines had roughly the same length.

184. Each line is identified by its verse number and a letter; this is conventional in reference works, commentaries, and other sources.

You may wonder what you have learned that makes it worth doing this rather than merely translating the poem. The point is that this is intended to help ensure that you read *this* text in Hebrew, rather than merely repeat what you have heard or read that it says. This is only a beginning—the first few of many things to consider in studying a biblical poem—but it should help give some form to the poetic text before you.

27.5 Vocabulary

sanctuary, holy place	מִקְדָּשׁ	.411	[a] blessing	בְּרָכָה	.403
dead (adj.)	מֵת	.412	breath, idol; vanity; Abel	הֶבֶל	.404
[a] witness	עֵד עֵדָה	.413	cry out [for help], shout (cf. צעק)	זָעַק	.405
reach, overtake (H)	נָשַׂג	.414	strange, foreign; illicit	זָר	.406
only, surely (often begins clause)	רַק	.415	disgrace, reproach	חֶרְפָּה	.407
cry out [for help], shout (cf. זעק)	צָעַק	.416	sin, miss [a mark]	חָטָא	.408
bird, insect [any flying thing]	עוֹף	.417	sin, error, fault; sin-offering	חַטָּאת	
bow, worship, do obeisance; show respect or honor (mainly Dt)	שָׁחָה	.418*	Why?	מַדּוּעַ	.409
			sunrise, east	מִזְרָח	.410

* Because of its initial sibilant, the root שחה never appears as שחה, but only with the initial -שׁ and the -ת- of the prefix inverted: -שְׁתַּ- (metathesized). Forms that end in *šureq* (חוּ-) are singular, those in -חֲווּ or -חֲוּ- (*waw* followed by *šureq*) are plural. Since it is fairly frequent (172x), here is a skeleton paradigm:

		√שחה				**Dt**	
P	3ms	הִשְׁתַּחֲוָה	F	3ms	יִשְׁתַּחֲוֶה	Pr	3ms	וַיִּשְׁתַּחוּ
	3cp	הִשְׁתַּחֲווּ		3mp	יִשְׁתַּחֲווּ		3mp	וַיִּשְׁתַּחֲווּ
V	mp	הִשְׁתַּחֲווּ					3fp	תִּשְׁתַּחֲוֶינָה
Ptc	ms	מִשְׁתַּחֲוֶה					NC	הִשְׁתַּחֲוֹת*[185]

27.6 Exercises

This is the text of **Ps 114**, laid out more or less as in the Hebrew Bible. Divide it into lines (you should end up with sixteen), list the verbal predicates, and identify any repetitions.

1. בְּצֵאת יִשְׂרָאֵל מִמִּצְרָיִם   בֵּית יַעֲקֹב מֵעַם לֹעֵז:
2. הָיְתָה יְהוּדָה לְקָדְשׁוֹ   יִשְׂרָאֵל מַמְשְׁלוֹתָיו:
3. הַיָּם רָאָה וַיָּנֹס   הַיַּרְדֵּן יִסֹּב לְאָחוֹר:
4. הֶהָרִים רָקְדוּ כְאֵילִים   גְּבָעוֹת כִּבְנֵי־צֹאן:
5. מַה־לְּךָ הַיָּם כִּי תָנוּס   הַיַּרְדֵּן תִּסֹּב לְאָחוֹר:
6. הֶהָרִים תִּרְקְדוּ כְאֵילִים   גְּבָעוֹת כִּבְנֵי־צֹאן:
7. מִלִּפְנֵי אָדוֹן חוּלִי אָרֶץ   מִלִּפְנֵי אֱלוֹהַּ יַעֲקֹב:
8. הַהֹפְכִי הַצּוּר אֲגַם־מָיִם   חַלָּמִישׁ לְמַעְיְנוֹ־מָיִם:

In this psalm you should see three sections that are clearly defined by the parallels between lines. The the question is *not* "Does this line parallel the other line of this *verse*?" but rather "How can we describe the relationship between this line and the next line (and the preceding)?"

---

185. The end of this word is pronounced as though there were two *waws*, the first a consonant, the second the *mater lectionis*: -*wôt*.

27.7 Enrichment: Reading a Poem

Analyzing the lineation, semantics, syntax, and morphology of a biblical poem often reveals patterns that are obscured by the differences between languages. This table presents one approach to the preliminary study of a poem—"preliminary", because this analysis is not the poem's meaning, but is instead a way of forcing ourselves to pay attention to every aspect of a poem. We have no way of knowing in advance what will or will not help us establish the meaning of any particular poem; we therefore pay as close attention as possible to everything.

Ps 117

L.	MT/BHS	Semantics	Word Count	Syntax	Predicate
1a	הַלְלוּ אֶת־יהוה כָּל־גּוֹיִם	a . b . c	5: 1.2.2	P/v – O – S/cc	2mp DV
1b	שַׁבְּחוּהוּ כָּל־הָאֻמִּים:	a¹+b¹ . c¹	3: 1.2	P/v+O – S/cc	2mp DV
2a	כִּי גָבַר עָלֵינוּ חַסְדּוֹ	a . b . c	4: 2.1.1	ki – P/v – pp – S/cc	3ms QP
2b	וֶאֱמֶת־יהוה לְעוֹלָם	c¹ . a¹	3: 2.1	w+S – P/pp	
2c	הַלְלוּ־יָהּ:	a . b	2: 1.1	P/v – O	2mp DV

Key

L.	line no.
MT/BHS	The Masoretic text as represented by BHS
Semantics	Each letter represents a functional semantic unit in the line (a construct chain, e.g., is a single functional unit); repeated units in parallel lines have the same letter, with a superscript numeral if they are not exactly identical.
Word Count	The total number of words—groups of letters between spaces or linked by *maqqef*—in the line, followed by the number of forms in each of the semantic units identified in the "semantics" column.
Syntax	The syntax of the clause (these are all that apply to Ps 117):

	P	Predicate
	/	consists of
	v	[finite] verb
	pp	prepositional phrase
	O	object ("direct" or "indirect")
	S	subject
	/	function
	cc	construct chain
Predicate		The parsing of the verbal predicate.

Translation can be done in at least two stages: a very wooden, "interlinear" translation, designed to show the underlying Hebrew text, followed by a rendering into "sensible" and well-formed English:

1a	praise-ye! Yhwh all-of nations
1b	commend-ye-him all-of peoples
2a	for he-is-strong over-us his-lovingkindness
2b	and-the-truth-of Yhwh for-long-time
2c	praise-ye! Yh
1a	Praise Yhwh, all nations!
1b	Commend him, all peoples!
2a	For his lovingkindness is strong over us,
2b	And Yhwh's truth is strong for a long-time.
2c	Praise Yh!

Lesson 28

Hollow (II-ו/י) Verbs

Hollow verbal roots consist of two root consonants with a medial vowel. Their lexical form is *qal* infinitive construct (they are the only verbs not listed by 3ms *qal* perfect). Some verbs, for example, קוּם, *rise, stand*, have medial *šureq* (- וּ -), others have medial *ḥireq* (-ִי-, e.g., שִׁיר, *sing*). The lexica identify their roots in different ways, so if you do not find the root listed with medial -וּ-, try the same root with -ִי- (or *vice versa*). This skeleton paradigm compares the basic forms of the verb:

√קוּם		Q	N	H	Hp
P	3ms	קָם	נָקוֹם	הֵקִים	הוּקַם
F	3ms	יָקוּם	יִקּוֹם	יָקִים	יוּקַם
V	2ms	קוּם	הִקּוֹם	הָקֵם	
NC		קוּם	הִקּוֹם	הָקִים	הוּקַם
Ptc	ms	קָם	נָקוֹם	מֵקִים	מוּקָם

The hollow verbs are weak in all forms (apart from rare occurrences in the D-stems, when they have doubled medial -י-, regardless of the stem vowel of the lexical form.

28.1 *Hollow Verbs in Qal (Q)*

	Qal	√קוּם (II-ו)	√שִׂים (II-י)
	3ms	קָם	שָׂם
P	2mp	קַמְתֶּם	שַׂמְתֶּם
	3cp	קָמוּ	שָׂמוּ
	3ms	יָקוּם	יָשִׂים
F	2fs	תָּקוּמִי	תָּשִׂימִי
	2fp	תְּקֹמְנָה	תְּשֵׂמְנָה
Pr	3ms	וַיָּקָם	וַיָּשֶׂם
	3mp	וַיָּקֻמוּ	וַיָּשִׂימוּ
V	2ms	קוּם	שִׂים
	2mp	קוּמוּ	שִׂימוּ
NC		קוּם	שִׂים
NA		קוֹם	שׂוֹם
Ptc	ms	קָם	שָׂם
	fs	קָמָה	שָׂמָה

1. There is no difference between II-י and II-ו in the *qal* perfect and participle.
2. Since the 3ms Q perfect and ms Q participle are identical, they cannot always be identified with certainty.
3. The original [lexical] vowel appears in the conjugations other than the perfect and participle.
4. In Q jussive and 2/3fp Q F, the stem vowel is often *ḥolem* in verbs II-ו and *segol* in roots II-י:

		Qal	√קוּם	√שִׂים
J	2/3fp		תָּקֹמְנָה	תְּשֵׂמְנָה
	3ms		יָקֹם	יָשֵׂם

28.1a Unique Hollow Verbs

Although most hollow verbs have either medial -ו- (like קוּם) or -ִי - (cf. שִׂים), three are unique in *qal*:

1. בּוֹא, "come, go, enter" (c. 2350x in Biblical Hebrew), is III-א, so its stem syllable is always open, and its stem vowel is always long (*qameṣ* in Q P and Ptc; and -וֹ- elsewhere in Q):

		Qal	√בּוֹא
P	2ms		בָּאתָ
F	3ms		יָבוֹא
Pr	2ms/3fs		וַתָּבוֹא
V	2ms		בּוֹא
	2mp	בּוֹאוּ	בֹּאוּ
NC			בּוֹא

2. בּוֹשׁ, "be ashamed" (126x in Biblical Hebrew), has *ḥolem* (with or without ו) in all forms of Q, and *ṣere* as its prefix vowel in Q F and Pr.

		Qal	√בּוֹשׁ
P	1cp		בּוֹשְׁנוּ
F	2mp		תֵּבוֹשׁוּ
Pr	3mp		וַיֵּבוֹשׁוּ
V	2fp		בּוֹשְׁנָה
NC			בּוֹשׁ
Ptc[186]	mp		בּוֹשִׁים

3. מוּת, "die" (737x in Biblical Hebrew) has *ṣere* in Q P forms without consonantal endings, as well as in Q Ptc. Its other forms look like קוּם (above).

		Qal	√מוּת
P	3ms		מֵת
	3fs		מֵתָה
Ptc	mp		מֵתִים

---

186. There is one *qal* participle of בּוֹשׁ (Ek 32.30).

28.2 Hollow Verbs in Nifal (N)

		Nifal	קוּם√ (II-ו)	שִׁיר√ (II-י)
P	3ms		נָקוֹם	נָשׁוֹר
	2mp		נְקוּמֹתֶם	נְשׁוּרֹתֶם
	3cp		נָקוֹמוּ	נָשׁוֹרוּ
F	3ms		יִקּוֹם	יִשּׁוֹר
	2fs		תִּקּוֹמִי	תִּשּׁוֹרִי
	2mp		תִּקּוֹמוּ	תִּשּׁוֹרוּ
Pr	3ms		וַיִּקּוֹם	וַיִּשּׁוֹר
V	2ms		הִקּוֹם	הִשּׁוֹר
	2mp		הִקּוֹמוּ	הִשּׁוֹרוּ
NC			הִקּוֹם	הִשּׁוֹר
Ptc	ms		נָקוֹם	נָשׁוֹר

1. The stem vowel in N is either *ḥolem* (most forms) or *šureq* (*nifal* perfect with consonantal PGN endings).
2. The prefix vowel in N is either *qameṣ* (P, Ptc) or *ḥireq* (F, V, NC, NA).
3. As in H (below), there is a helping vowel before consonantal PGN endings.
4. As in the basic verb, the prefixed -נ is orthographically present in N P and Ptc, and assimilates to the first radical in the other conjugations in *nifal*.
5. Unlike the basic verb, the prefix vowel in the perfect and participle is long, since the syllable is open.
6. The form is identical for either type of stem vowel (-*û*- or -*î*-).

28.3 Hollow Verbs in Hifil & Hofal (H, Hp)

		קוּם√	**H**	**Hp**	**Q (II-י)**	**Q (II-ו)**
P	3ms		הֵקִים	הוּקַם	שָׂם	קָם
	1cp		הֲקִימֹנוּ	הוּקַמְנוּ	שַׂמְנוּ	קַמְנוּ
	3cp		הֵקִימוּ	הוּקְמוּ	שָׂמוּ	קָמוּ
F	3ms		יָקִים	יוּקַם	יָשִׂים	יָקוּם
	2fs		תָּקִימִי	תּוּקְמִי	תָּשִׂימִי	תָּקוּמִי
	2fp		תְּקִימֶינָה	תּוּקַמְנָה	תְּשִׂימֶינָה	תָּקֹמְנָה
Pr	3ms		וַיָּקֶם	וַיּוּקַם	וַיָּשֶׂם	וַיָּקָם
	3mp		וַיָּקִימוּ	וַיּוּקְמוּ	וַיָּשִׂימוּ	וַיָּקוּמוּ
V	2ms		הָקֵם	---	שִׂים	קוּם
	2mp		הָקִימוּ	---	שִׂימוּ	קוּמוּ
NC			הָקֵם	הוּקַם	שִׂים	קוּם
NA			הָקֵם	הוּקַם	שׂוֹם	קוֹם
Ptc	ms		מֵקִים	מוּקָם	שָׂם	קָם
	fs		מְקִימָה	מוּקָמָה	שָׂמָה	קָמָה

Hifil

1. The stem vowel in *hifil* is *ḥireq* in all forms except infinitive absolute and 2ms imperative (which have *ṣere*).
2. Its prefix vowel is *qameṣ* (H F, V, NC, NA) and *ṣere* (H P, Ptc).
3. In *hifil*, a helping vowel (וֹ) joins consonantal PGN endings to the verbal root.
4. Q F and H F look alike in II-י verbs, and must be distinguished by context; in the II-ו verbs they are distinguished by the stem (central) vowel, which will be a *u-/o-*vowel in Q and an *i-/e-*vowel in H.

Hofal

1. In Hp, the prefix vowel is always *šureq* (וּ). Its stem vowel is *pataḥ* or *šewa*. This skeleton paradigm displays the H-stems with *qal* of two hollow verbs.

28.4 Hollow Verbs in Polel, Polal, Hitpolel (P, Pp, Pt)

In the hollow verbs the D-stems are usually replaced by another set of stems in which the second radical is reduplicated to create a tri-radical "root".

These stems, *polel* (P), *polal* (Pp), and *hitpolel* (Pt) correspond in function to *piel* (D), *pual* (Dp), and *hitpael* (Dt), respectively.

	√קוּם	Polel	Polal	Hitpolel
P	3ms	קוֹמֵם	קוֹמַם	הִתְקוֹמֵם
	1cs	קוֹמַמְתִּי	קוֹמַמְתִּי	הִתְקוֹמַמְתִּי
	3cp	קוֹמְמוּ	קוֹמְמוּ	הִתְקוֹמְמוּ
F	3ms	יְקוֹמֵם	יְקוֹמַם	יִתְקוֹמֵם
	3mp	יְקוֹמְמוּ	יְקוֹמְמוּ	יִתְקוֹמְמוּ
V	2ms	קוֹמֵם	---	הִתְקוֹמֵם
	2mp	קוֹמְמוּ	---	הִתְקוֹמְמוּ
NC		קוֹמֵם	קוֹמַם	הִתְקוֹמֵם
Ptc	ms	מְקוֹמֵם	מְקוֹמָם	מִתְקוֹמֵם
	fs	מְקוֹמְמָה	מְקוֹמְמָה	מִתְקוֹמְמִים

1. *Šewa* is the prefix vowel in the imperfect, preterite, and participle of both *polel* and *polal*.
2. *Ḥolem* follows the first radical, either with or without the vowel letter (וֹ).
3. If the form has a sufformative, *polel* and *polal* are identical, and can only be distinguished by context.
4. *Hitpolel* is directly analogous to Dt (*hitpael*), looking just like P with prefixed -הִת. As in Dt, the -ת- of the prefix switches places (metathesizes) with the initial sibilant of the verbal root:

מַה־תִּשְׁתּוֹחֲחִי נַפְשִׁי   Why do you despair [melt?], my soul? (Ps 42.6; שׁח)

וָאֶשְׁתּוֹמֵם עַל־הַמַּרְאֶה   ... and I was astonished at the vision (Dn 8.27; שׁמם)

5. Hollow verbs rarely occur in D, Dp, or Dt. When they do, their middle radical is doubled *yod* (י):

קַיְּמֵנִי כִּדְבָרֶךָ:   *Restore me* according to your word (Ps 119.28b); 2ms D V + 1cs

28.5 Frequency

This table lists all **twenty-three** hollow verbs that occur fifty times or more in Biblical Hebrew.

בּוֹא	come, go (in), enter	2530x	בּוֹשׁ	be(come) ashamed	126x
שׁוּב	turn, turn back, return; repent	1055x	רוּץ	run	103x
מוּת	die	737x	טוֹב	be(come) good, pleasant	90x
קוּם	rise, stand	624x	שִׁיר	sing	88x
טוֹב	be good[187]	612x	שִׁית	put, place, set	87x
שִׂים	put, place, set	584x	גּוּר	reside as alien, sojourn	81x
סוּר	turn (aside); remove (H)	298x	עוּר	awake, arouse	76x
כּוּן	be established; prepare (H)	219x	לִין	spend the night, lodge	71x
רוּם	be(come) high, exalted	195x	פּוּץ	scatter, disperse (intrans.)	65x
בִּין	understand, perceive	171x	רִיב	sue, strive, contend	64x
נוּס	flee	160x	חִיל	be [writhe] in labor	57x
נוּחַ	rest (Q); deposit (H)	143x			

28.6 Vocabulary

die	מוּת	.427	come, go [in], enter	בּוֹא	.419
rest (Q); deposit (H)	נוּחַ	.428	be/become ashamed (st. vb.)	בּוֹשׁ	.420
flee	נוּס	.429	understand, discern	בִּין	.421
turn (aside); take away, remove (H)	סוּר	.430	reside as an alien (i.e., live in a land other than your native land; trad., sojourn)	גּוּר	.422
			alien; stranger (trad., sojourner)	גֵּר	
awake, arouse	עוּר	.431	writhe, tremble; [be in] labour	חִיל	.423
scatter, disperse (instrans.)	פּוּץ	.432	be/become good, pleasant (st. vb.)	טוֹב / טוֹב	.424
sue, strive, contend	רִיב	.433	be established, fixed (in place); prepare (H)	כּוּן	.425
[law]suit, strife, contention (n.)	רִיב	.434	lodge, spend the night	לִין	.426

N.B.: The lexical form of hollow verbs is *qal* infinitive construct (= ms *qal* imperative).

28.7 Exercises

After studying the hollow verbs, gloss these texts, parsing all verbal forms, *and then* locate and identify all hollow verbal forms in Genesis 14–15.

1. קוּמִי אוֹרִי כִּי בָא אוֹרֵךְ
וּכְבוֹד יְהוָה עָלַיִךְ זָרָח׃
Is 60.1; זרח *dawn, shine*; אוֹר *shine, give light*

2. יְהוָה בַּשָּׁמַיִם הֵכִין כִּסְאוֹ
וּמַלְכוּתוֹ בַּכֹּל מָשָׁלָה׃
Ps 103.19

---

187. It is often difficult to distinguish the verb from the (predicate) adjective טוֹב. Furthermore, this verb does not occur in the imperfect; the imperfect function uses the I-י root יטב.

3. בֹּאוּ שְׁעָרָיו בְּתוֹדָה   Ps 100.4; תּוֹדָה *thanks, thanksgiving*; חָצֵר
   חֲצֵרֹתָיו בִּתְהִלָּה   *court*; 2mp H V < ידה *praise, profess; thank* (H)
   הוֹדוּ־לוֹ
   בָּרֲכוּ שְׁמוֹ׃

4. שִׁירוּ לַיהוה שִׁיר חָדָשׁ   Ps 96.1-2; בשׂר *proclaim, announce*; תְּשׁוּעָה
   שִׁירוּ לַיהוה כָּל־הָאָרֶץ׃   *victory, salvation*
   שִׁירוּ לַיהוה
   בָּרֲכוּ שְׁמוֹ
   בַּשְּׂרוּ מִיּוֹם־לְיוֹם יְשׁוּעָתוֹ׃

5. וַיֹּאמֶר קַיִן אֶל־הֶבֶל אָחִיו   Gn 4.8; Cain, Abel
   וַיְהִי בִּהְיוֹתָם בַּשָּׂדֶה
   וַיָּקָם קַיִן אֶל־הֶבֶל אָחִיו וַיַּהַרְגֵהוּ׃

6. וּמֵעֵץ הַדַּעַת טוֹב וָרָע לֹא תֹאכַל מִמֶּנּוּ   Gn 2.17
   כִּי בְּיוֹם אֲכָלְךָ מִמֶּנּוּ מוֹת תָּמוּת׃

7. וַיַּךְ אֶת־הַפְּלִשְׁתִּי וַיְמִיתֵהוּ   2 Sam 21.17; Philistine

8. נַפְשִׁי יְשׁוֹבֵב   Ps 23.3; מַעְגָּל *path, track*
   יַנְחֵנִי בְמַעְגְּלֵי־צֶדֶק לְמַעַן שְׁמוֹ׃

9. כַּשּׁוֹפָר הָרֵם קוֹלֶךָ   Is 58.1; שׁוֹפָר *ram's horn; trumpet;* רום *be high,*
   וְהַגֵּד לְעַמִּי פִּשְׁעָם   *exalted;* Jacob
   וּלְבֵית יַעֲקֹב חַטֹּאתָם׃

10. הִנֵּה־מֵת שָׁאוּל   2 Sam 4.10; Saul

11. וַיֹּאמְרוּ אֶל־יְהוֹשֻׁעַ עֲבָדֶיךָ אֲנָחְנוּ   Josh 9.8; מֵאַיִן *from where?*; Joshua
    וַיֹּאמֶר אֲלֵהֶם יְהוֹשֻׁעַ מִי אַתֶּם וּמֵאַיִן תָּבֹאוּ׃

12. וַיֹּאמְרוּ אֵלָיו הִנֵּה אַתָּה זָקַנְתָּ   1 Sam 8.5
    וּבָנֶיךָ לֹא הָלְכוּ בִּדְרָכֶיךָ
    עַתָּה שִׂימָה־לָּנוּ מֶלֶךְ לְשָׁפְטֵנוּ כְּכָל־הַגּוֹיִם׃

13. וַיִּשָּׂאֵהוּ וַיְבִיאֵהוּ אֶל־אִמּוֹ   2 Kgs 4.20; 3ms Q Pr < ישׁב *stay, sit*; בֶּרֶךְ *knee*;
    וַיֵּשֶׁב עַל־בִּרְכֶּיהָ עַד־הַצָּהֳרַיִם וַיָּמֹת׃   צָהֳרַיִם *noon*

14. וַיִּבֶן יְהוָה אֱלֹהִים אֶת־הַצֵּלָע אֲשֶׁר־לָקַח   Gn 2.22; צֵלָע *piece* [trad., *rib*]
    מִן־הָאָדָם לְאִשָּׁה וַיְבִאֶהָ אֶל־הָאָדָם׃

15. הִנֵּה יָמִים בָּאִים וְגָדַעְתִּי אֶת־זְרֹעֲךָ   1 Sam 2.31; גדע *cut/chop off*
    וְאֶת־זְרֹעַ בֵּית אָבִיךָ מִהְיוֹת זָקֵן בְּבֵיתֶךָ׃

16. בְּכָל־הַמָּקוֹם אֲשֶׁר אַזְכִּיר אֶת־שְׁמִי   Ex 20.24
    אָבוֹא אֵלֶיךָ וּבֵרַכְתִּיךָ׃

17. וַיֹּאמְרוּ נָקוּם וּבָנִינוּ וַיְחַזְּקוּ יְדֵיהֶם לַטּוֹבָה׃   Ne 2.18

18. שִׂים לֶחֶם וָמַיִם לִפְנֵיהֶם וְיֹאכְלוּ וְיִשְׁתּוּ   2 Kgs 6.22; when *waw*+imperfect follows an
    וְיֵלְכוּ אֶל־אֲדֹנֵיהֶם׃   imperative, it is often telic (purpose or result)

Ps 119.73	יָדֶיךָ עָשׂוּנִי וַיְכוֹנְנוּנִי הֲבִינֵנִי וְאֶלְמְדָה מִצְוֺתֶיךָ:	19.
Ps 1.5-6	עַל־כֵּן לֹא־יָקֻמוּ רְשָׁעִים בַּמִּשְׁפָּט וְחַטָּאִים בַּעֲדַת צַדִּיקִים: כִּי־יוֹדֵעַ יְהוָה דֶּרֶךְ צַדִּיקִים וְדֶרֶךְ רְשָׁעִים תֹּאבֵד:	20.
Is 40.9; גבה high (not III-ה); מְבַשֶּׂרֶת messenger (f.s. D Ptc); Zion, Jerusalem	עַל הַר־גָּבֹהַּ עֲלִי־לָךְ מְבַשֶּׂרֶת צִיּוֹן הָרִימִי בַכֹּחַ קוֹלֵךְ מְבַשֶּׂרֶת יְרוּשָׁלִָם הָרִימִי אַל־תִּירָאִי אִמְרִי לְעָרֵי יְהוּדָה הִנֵּה אֱלֹהֵיכֶם:	21.

28.8 *Enrichment: Dating Haggai*

One of the most carefully dated biblical books contains the prophecy of Haggai, חַגַּי (Ezekiel is a close second), with five date formulae in thirty-eight verses (the second and third are divided between two verses).

לַחֹדֶשׁ בִּשְׁנַת שְׁתַּיִם לְדָרְיָוֶשׁ הַמֶּלֶךְ בַּחֹדֶשׁ הַשִּׁשִּׁי בְּיוֹם אֶחָד	In the second year of Darius the king, in the sixth month, on the first day of the month, ... (Hg 1.1)	29 August 520
בְּיוֹם עֶשְׂרִים וְאַרְבָּעָה לַחֹדֶשׁ בַּשִּׁשִּׁי	... on the twenty-fourth day of the sixth month (Hg 1.15a).	21 September 520
לַחֹדֶשׁ בִּשְׁנַת שְׁתַּיִם לְדָרְיָוֶשׁ הַמֶּלֶךְ: בַּשְּׁבִיעִי בְּעֶשְׂרִים וְאֶחָד	In the second year of Darius the king, in the seventh [month], on the twenty-first day of the month (Hg 1.15b–2.1)	17 October 520
בְּעֶשְׂרִים וְאַרְבָּעָה לַתְּשִׁיעִי בִּשְׁנַת שְׁתַּיִם לְדָרְיָוֶשׁ	In the twenty-fourth [day] of the ninth [month], in the second year of Darius ... (Hg 2.10)	18 December 520
וַיְהִי דְבַר־יְהוָה שֵׁנִית אֶל־חַגַּי בְּעֶשְׂרִים וְאַרְבָּעָה לַחֹדֶשׁ	The word of Yhwh came a second time to Haggai on the twenty-fourth [day] of the ninth [month] (Hg 2.20)	18 December 520

Such careful dating allows us to identify precisely the time of Haggai's ministry, and demonstrates the ancient Near Eastern tendency to date events by the king (cf. also Dn 1.1; Ezk *passim*) and other important figures (cf. the cross-references to the kings of Israel and Judah in the book of Kings), and events (cf. Amos 1.1). Although the result is not always a precise chronology in the modern sense, it nonetheless lets us see Israel's development and some of their history (or, in this case, the circumstances of the Persian province of Yehud).

In this case (as also in, e.g. the books of Ezekiel and Jeremiah), it establishes a relative chronology for the prophet's messages, and allows us to see how he adapted his message to the changing times (even if we do not know exactly what changes he was addressing).

Lesson 29

The *Masora*

In the outer margin and directly below the text block of BHS lie two sets of notes. The *masora*[188] *marginalis* (marginal *masora*)—also called *Masora parva* ([Mp]; "Small Masora")—consists of single letters, and unpointed words and expressions in Hebrew and Palestinian Aramaic, often with overhead dots, along with occasional superscript Arabic numerals. Below the text block, the first set of footnotes, which in BHS consists largely of "Mm" followed by a numeral, is a cross-reference system, the *Masora magna* ([Mm]; "Great Masora"), which directed the scribe to similar occurrences of the same or similar word(s).

Both parts of the *masora* are parts of an elaborate system designed to encourage scribal accuracy in copying the text, by telling the scribe to copy the word or phrase just as it stood in the text. The Masoretes—the "scribes" who copied biblical manuscripts, and developed the masora. were thus concerned to protect the text from scribes who might take it upon themselves to correct what they thought were mistakes. Masoretic notes, in essence, admit that the textual form was strange, unusual, disputed, or even wrong, but warn the copyist that it was better to leave a known error than for every scribe to begin "correcting" the text as he saw fit.[189] The Masoretes were saying in essence, "We know that this form is unusual—it only occurs a few other times in the Bible—but copy it as it stands. Don't change it to something more familiar or 'correct'."

29.1 *Reading the Masora*

29.1.1 *The Masora Marginalis*

1. A *circellus* ("little circle") over a word or between words refer to notes in Mp. A *circellus* over a word (מֵרָחֹק; Gn 37.18) means that the note refers only to that word; a *circellus* between two words (אֶל־בְּנֵי; Gn 37.35), or a series of *circelli* between more than two words means that the note refers to that sequence of words. These are occasionally interwoven, so that a note refers to a single word in the middle of a marked series of words. You have to sort out which note refers to which piece of the text.

    In Gn 13.10 (כְּגַן־יהוה) the circles mean that the first note is to כְּגַן and the second to the entire phrase (כְּגַן־יהוה). In Gn 37.25, seven consecutive words are marked, but the circles are over the words, not between them. There are seven marginal notes, one for each word.

2. The usual syntax of a masoretic note is the main statistic first, followed by any further explanation or discussion, including real or apparent exceptions or limitations to the number. The first example in Gn 37.18 (זֹ חֹס בתוֹר), above, restricts the statistic to the Torah (בתוֹר ≈ *in Torah*).

3. Heavy dots separate masoretic notes, which are read from right to left. The rightmost note, therefore, refers to the first marked word or group of words in the line, *in the order of the Hebrew text*.

4. Superscript dots have several purposes:
    a. A dot over a *single* letter means that it is a *numeral*, and that the form in the text occurs that many times (e.g., Gn 37.18 זֹ = 7 times).

---

188. It seems that the *masora* was originally so-called because the notes restricted the interpretation of the text (מָסֹרֶת, "fetter" or "bond", occurs only in Ezk 20.37) by eliminating discrepancies (as they thought). It was later connected to the root מסר ("to assign", "hand down/over"; it occurs only in Nu 31.5, 16) in the sense of "received tradition".

189. For an extended description of the *masora* and how to read and use it, see Kelley, Mynatt, & Crawford (1998).

b. A dot over *every* letter in a group of letters means that it is a compound *numeral* (e.g., in Gn 37.18 יֹ׳ = 17 (10 + 7); Gn 37.22 הֹ֗י = 15 (10 + 5)).

c. A dot over the *last* letter in a group of letters means that the word is *abbreviated* (e.g., in Gn 37.18 חֹס בתוֹר represents, respectively, חסר (*lacking* or *defective*; i.e., without the expected vowel letter) and בתורה (*in Torah*).

5. Numerals mean that the particular form of the word (morphological form, along with any prefixes and suffixes) occurs only that number of times (e.g., the 1cp Q F + 3ms suffix + *w* of the verb הרג occurs only in Gn 37.20; the root הרג occurs 168 times in all).

6. In the *Prolegomena* of BHS is the *Index siglorum et abbreviationum masorae parvae* ("Index of the Signs & Abbreviations of the Mp"). This lists most of the words and abbreviations used in Mp in alphabetical order, and glosses them into Latin. Glosses for these Latin terms are listed in "An English Key to the Latin Words and Abbreviations and Symbols of Biblia Hebraica Stuttgartensia" (Rüger 1985), which is printed as a separate booklet, or included in newer printings of BHS immediately following the Latin index.

7. Superscript numerals in Mp (cf. Gn 37.20: ²⁰ד׳) refer to the first set of footnotes in BHS, which consists of a list of notes in the form: "Mm" followed by a numeral (in this case "Mm 276"). These refer in turn to numbered lists in G. Weil (*Massorah Gedolah*. Vol. 1. Rome: Pontifical Biblical Institute, 1971), which lists the verses containing the occurrences of the form described in the note. You can check this quickly with a modern concordance (e.g., Even-Shoshan).

8. קֹ in Mp stands for *qere*, Aramaic for "Read!" (קְרָא, ms imperative), and means that the vowels in the text should be read with the consonants written above the קֹ in the margin. The consonants in the text are known as the *ketib* (כְּתִיב, "[that which is] written"), which is a combination of consonants and vowel points that cannot be pronounced as written. The *qere* "corrects" the problem by suggesting the appropriate reading, but putting it in the margin meant that they did not have to change the consonantal text. These *qere/ketib* readings are important in textual criticism; they are referred to as Q and K, respectively, in the textual footnotes. In Gn 39.20, for example:

Interpretation	Masora	Lemma
Read אֲסוּרֵי as though it were written אֲסִירֵי. The text (K) has the consonants of the Qp Ptc (אֲסוּרֵי, *prisoners*; as in Gn 40.3, 5); the Masoretes preferred the tradition that read this as mp of the noun אָסִיר, *prisoner*, which occurs in Gn 39.22. [For further examples, see "Enrichment", below.]	אסירי קֹ	אֲסוּרֵי

9. Finally, remember that although you can use a lexicon, Hebrew concordance (e.g., Even-Shoshan, Mandelkern), or electronic database to look up the form that is described in the note, such resources had not yet been invented when the Masoretes were at work—a testimony to their knowledge of the text!

29.1.2 *The Ending Masora*

1. At the end of every biblical document, the Masoretes appended a list of statistics for that text. In order to help them ensure that they had not left out or doubled any verses, the scribes counted the number of verses (הפסוקים *pasûqîm*, marked off by *sof pasûq*), and wrote the total at the end, as well as the first word(s) of the middle verse (וחציו, *and its half*). A scribe could thus determine which half of the document had an extra or missing *pasûq*. [*Pasûqîm* do not always correspond to verses, since a few "verses" do not end with *sof pasûq*).

2. They also totaled the *sᵉdarîm* (סדרים) for each text, "reading sections" for reading through the Torah on the Sabbath in three years, which are marked by a large *samek* in the inner margin, "crowned" by a sideways *qamesi*, and numbered by small Hebrew letters within square brackets. One of these (#33) comes at Gn 37.1, which also coincides with the beginning of a much larger unit called a *paraš* (marked פרש in the inner margin), which were used to read through the Torah on the Sabbath in one year (*pᵉrašôt* were not listed in the final

Masora). Within the text block a Hebrew numeral in small letters records the number of *pasûqîm* in the previous *paras̆* (קנ֗ד = 154 *pasûqîm*).
3. Since the Masoretes treated the Minor Prophets as a single entity—"The Twelve"—their final masora lists only the number of verses; Malachi also lists the central verse for the entire prophetic corpus (Joshua – Malachi) and the number of *sᵉdarîm* for the Twelve. More elaborate lists follow Deuteronomy and Chronicles.
4. This is the ending *masora* for Qohelet (Ecclesiastes):

סכום הפסוקים	*The total of the "verses"*
של ספר ר֗כ֗ב	*of the work [is] 222*
וחציו מה שהיה כבר²¹	*and its middle/half [is the verse that begins]*
מה שהיה כבר²¹	
וסדרים ד֗	*and sedarim [are] 4.*

The superscript (²¹) at the end of the line that identifies the middle verse (וחציו) directs us to #21 in the first set of notes at the bottom of the page—the apparatus for the *Masora Magna*, which then sends us to Qo 6.10; where Mp reads חצי הספר בפסוקים ("the middle of the work in verses").

29.2 *Masoretic Numerals*

These are the values of the letters of the alphabet in the *masora* (note the superlinear dot that indicates their numerical function).

Numeral	Value	Notes	Numeral	Value	Notes
א֗	1	used in combinations only (see ל, below)	ק֗ - ת֗	100-400	
ב֗	2	On מ֗ב֗ see below.	ך֗	500	
ג֗ - ט֗	3-9		ם֗	600	
י֗	10		ן֗	700	
כ֗	20		ף֗	800	
ל	1	used alone for unique forms	ץ֗	900	
	30	used in combinations for 31-39 (e.g., לא֗ = 31)	א֗	1000	The dot is supposed to be slightly larger than the numeral for "one" (and so down the alphabet); some traditions use two dots to show thousands; in BHS the letter's *position* shows that it refers to thousands.
מ֗	40	This can also be an abbreviation for מִן, *from*; the combination מ֗ב֗ means either "two of" or "except for, with the exception of".			
נ	50		ב֗	2000	
ס֗ - צ֗	60-90			etc.	

29.3 *Summary*

The Masoretes' aim was to safeguard the continued integrity of the biblical text as it was copied by hand from one MS to another. Thus was the biblical text preserved for many centuries until the printing press began to make their work superfluous. With the passage of time, the masora came to be viewed as more ornamental than helpful, and [at least some of] its purpose and function was lost. We pay attention to the masoretic notes because they offer ancient suggestions about difficult readings (e.g., *qere/ketib*), because they signal unusual forms (e.g., *malē'/hasēr*), and because they may point out interesting statistical coincidences that we might otherwise overlook (e.g., the clause וַיְהִי רָעָב בָּאָרֶץ, "there was a famine in the land", occurs twice in the Bible, Gn 12.10; Ru 1.1).

29.4 Vocabulary

.443	קוּם	rise, stand	.435	עֵז	goat; goat hair
.444	רוּם	be/become high, exalted	.436	פָּלָא	be wonderful, amazing, miraculous
.445	רוּץ	run	.437	קִיר	wall, city
.446	שִׂים	put, place, set (cf. שִׁית)[190]	.438	רָחַץ	wash (oneself)
.447	שׁוּב	turn (back), return, repent	.439	שָׁבַת	rest; stop (doing something)
.448	שִׁיר	sing, chant	.440	שׁוֹפָר	ram's horn ("trumpet")
.448	שִׁיר	song, chant (n.)	.441	אֲחֻזָּה	inherited/owned property (real estate)
.449	שִׁית	put, place, set (cf. שִׂים)	.442	אַלּוּף	friend (n), familiar (adj); chief (n)

29.5 Exercises

1. Using the final masora, how many verses (פסוקים) and reading sections (סדרים) are in each of these biblical books? Locate the middle verse and its page no.

Book	פסוקים ("Verses")	סדרים ("Sections")	Middle verse (חצי)	
			Ref.	Page no.
Genesis				
Kings				
Ezra-Nehemiah				

2. Interpret one or two masoretic notes on the assigned reading passage, and check their accuracy with a concordance or electronic database (see the example on the next page). Do any of them affect the reading or function of the text? If so, how, and how will you determine which reading to prefer?

29.6 Enrichment: The Masora Marginalis to Genesis 37.18-22

Interpretation	Masora	Lemma	V.
[This word is written] seven times "defectively" [חסר] (i.e., with *holem* rather than *holem-waw*]) in Torah. You could find the other six occurrences (Gn 22.4; Ex 2.4; 20.18, 21; 24.1; Nu 9.10) in a Hebrew concordance. Checking all of its occurrences shows that the note refers to the entire form (preposition + adjective).	ז חס בתור	מֵרָחֹק	18
[This word occurs] three times in the Bible (cf. Jr 1.5; 13.16).	ג	וּבְטֶרֶם	
[This word is written] seventeen times "full" [מלא] (also called *plene*, Latin for "full"), i.e., with the vowel letter י. The occurrences are listed in Mm #250 (the same form and note occur in cf. Gn 37.6).	יז מל בתור[9]	אֲלֵיהֶם	

---

190. Although these two verbs are nearly synonymous, שִׂים occurs more than 550 times, whereas שִׁית occurs only about 80 times (and never in a book in which שִׂים does not also occur).

	This is the only occurrence of this form in the Bible.	ל	וַיִּתְנַכְּלוּ
19	[This word is written] two times *defectively* [חסר] (i.e., without the vowel letter [*ḥolem* without *waw*]) in the Bible (cf. Gn 42.9).	ב׳ חס	הַחֲלֹמוֹת
	This form occurs twice in the Bible (cf. Gn 24.65)	ב׳	הַלָּזֶה
20	This is the only occurrence of this form in the Bible.	ל	וְנַהַרְגֵהוּ
	This form occurs four times in the Bible (cf. Gn 37.33; Ezk 15.5; 19.12).	ד׳	אֲכָלָתְהוּ
	This form occurs four times in the Bible, listed in #276 (cf. 2Kg 7.13; Is 41.23; 66.5).	ד׳ [20]	וְנִרְאֶה
	This form occurs three times in the Bible (cf. Gn 37.8; Dn 2.2).	ג׳	חֲלֹמֹתָיו
21	This is the only defective occurrence of this word (i.e., without the vowel letter י) in the Bible. Even-Shoshan's concordance shows that this is the only time that a form of נצל could have the *yod* but does not.	ל׳ וחס	וַיַּצִּלֵהוּ
22	This form occurs twice closely following [i.e., immediately after] the accent *zarqa* (over רְאוּבֵן; it is the "hook", and occurs right before words marked with *segolta*—the "upside-down supra-linear *segol*).	לזרקא [21] ב׳ דסמיכ	דָּם
	This form occurs three times in the Bible (cf. Ezk 18.31; 20.7).	ג׳	הַשְׁלִיכוּ
	This form occurs fifteen times in the Bible (the numerals are reversed to avoid abbreviating the divine name), three of which [מנה] have *qames* (abbreviated קמׂ).	הי ג׳ מנה קמׂ	וְיָד

None of these notes affects the readings or interpretation (content) of the text, although they should keep a scribe from changing less common forms to match what was more familiar. This may seem mere pedantry in a world after Gutenberg; it is nonetheless a reminder of the faithfulness of many generations of now-unknown scribes without whose work the Bible as we know it would not exist.

Lesson 30

I-י/ו Verbs

Like I-נ roots (Lesson 26), I-י/ו verbs are weak whenever the initial letter of the root is followed by silent *šewa*—that is, throughout the H-stems, as well as in some forms of *qal* (F, Pr, V, NC) and *nifal* (P, Ptc). They are strong throughout the D-stems. Some I-נ forms therefore look just like I-י forms, but whereas I-נ forms tend to have two radicals with *dageš forte* in the first letter, I-י forms tend to have a *long* prefix vowel, *without* a doubled second radical.[191]

Stem	Weak Forms	Strong Forms
Q	F, Pr, V [NC,NA]	P, Ptc [NC, NA]
N	P, Ptc	F, Pr, V [NC,NA]
D, Dp, Dt	None	All forms
H, Hp	All forms	None

30.1 *Nifal, Hifil, Hofal (N, H, Hp)*

The original initial -י appears as a long vowel in N P and Ptc (-וֹ-), and throughout H (-וֹ-) and Hp (-וּ-). The other forms of N are strong, with doubled *waw* [+ *qameṣ*] (-וָּ-) as the first radical. The long prefix vowel, or the doubled *waw*, is the main clue to the presence of a I-י root:

Prefix/ Prefix Vowel	Stem	Conjugations
- נוֹ	N	perfect, participle
	H	1cs imperfect, preterite
- יִוָּ	N	imperfect, preterite (strong, with doubled -וָּ- for initial -י)
- הִוָּ	N	imperative, infinitive construct
- וֹ -	H	all forms
- וּ -	Hp	

The skeleton paradigm of these stems illustrates the basic principle:

	√ישב		Q	N	H	Hp
P	3ms		יָשַׁב	נוֹשַׁב	הוֹשִׁיב	הוּשַׁב
F	3ms		יֵשֵׁב	יִוָּשֵׁב	יוֹשִׁיב	יוּשַׁב
V	2ms		שֵׁב	הִוָּשֵׁב	הוֹשֵׁב	---
NC			שֶׁבֶת	הִוָּשֵׁב	הוֹשִׁיב	הוּשַׁב
Ptc	ms		יֹשֵׁב	נוֹשָׁב	מוֹשִׁיב	מוּשָׁב

---

191. This chart of weak and strong forms is identical to that for I-נ roots.

30.2 Qal (F, Pr, V, NC)

I-י verbs are **strong** in the *qal* perfect and participle, which are therefore not discussed. I-י verbs have three forms in *qal* F, Pr, V, & NC. Some verbs are mixed in type.

1. **Type I** (*qal* imperfect with *ṣere*). The prefix and stem vowels are both *ṣere*, and the initial -י of the verbal root is missing in Q F, Pr, V, NC. הלך is not I-י, but follows this pattern as well (it is the only non-I-י verbal root that does this). The skeleton paradigm shows forms that *differ* from the basic verb.

		Qal	√ישב	√הלך
F	3ms		יֵשֵׁב	יֵלֵךְ
	2fs		תֵּשְׁבִי	תֵּלְכִי
	3mp		יֵשְׁבוּ	יֵלְכוּ
Pr	3ms		וַיֵּשֶׁב	וַיֵּלֶךְ
V	2ms		שֵׁב	לֵךְ
	2mp		שְׁבוּ	לְכוּ
NC			שֶׁבֶת	לֶכֶת

N.B.: Some forms of these roots look just like forms from I-נ roots, and can be distinguished from them only by knowing the vocabulary, or from the context. There is a paradigm of similar forms from different roots in Appendix D.

2. **Type II** (*qal* imperfect with *pataḥ*). In these roots the initial י is a vowel letter in Q F, but disappears in Q V and NC of some verbs. The prefix vowel is *ḥireq* and the stem vowel *pataḥ*.

		Qal	√יבשׁ	√ירשׁ
F	3ms		יִיבַשׁ	יִירַשׁ
	2fs		---	תִּירְשִׁי
	3mp		יִיבְשׁוּ	יִירְשׁוּ
Pr	3ms		וַיִּיבַשׁ	וַיִּירַשׁ
V	2ms		יְבַשׁ	רַשׁ
	2mp		---	רְשׁוּ
NC			יְבֹשׁ	רֶשֶׁת

3. **Type III** (original I-י roots). There are only six verbs of this type (ימן, יקץ, ישׁר, ילל, ינק, יטב). They all occur primarily in Q and H. Since the initial -י is present in all forms, either as a vowel letter or consonant, these are also called I-י roots. The prefix vowel is *ḥireq-yod* in Q (like Type II, above), and *ṣere-yod* in H.

	√יטב		Qal	Hifil
P	3ms		יָטַב	הֵיטִיב
	3cp		יָטְבוּ	הֵיטִיבוּ
F	3ms		יִיטַב	יֵיטִיב
	2fs		תִּיטְבִי	תֵּיטִיבִי
	3mp		יִיטְבוּ	יֵיטִיבוּ
Pr	3ms		וַיִּיטַב	וַיֵּיטֶב
V	2ms		יְטַב	הֵיטֵב
	2mp		יְטְבוּ	הֵיטִיבוּ
NC			יְטֹב	הֵיטִיב
Ptc	ms		יֹטֵב	מֵיטִיב

30.3 Frequency

These are all **nineteen** I-י verbs that occur fifty times or more in Biblical Hebrew, listed by frequency.

יָשַׁב	sit, dwell, remain	1078x	יָטַב	be(come) good	120x
יָצָא	leave, go out	1055x	יָדָה	throw (D); thank (H)	115x
יָדַע	know	924x	יָתַר	remain, be left (N), leave (H)	106x
יָלַד	bear, give birth, beget	488x	יָעַץ	counsel, advise	82x
יָרַד	go down, descend	380x	יָצַר	shape, form, mold	64x
יָרֵא	fear, be afraid [of]	377x	יָכַח	dispute (N); rebuke (H)	56x
יָרַשׁ	subdue, [dis]possess	231x	יָבֵשׁ	be(come) dry	55x
יָסַף	add (Q), repeat (H)	212x	יָרָה	throw; teach (H)	54x
יָשַׁע	save (H)	205x	יָצַק	serve (food); pour (liquid)	53x
יָכֹל	be able, prevail	194x			

30.4 Vocabulary

serve (food); pour (liquid)	יָצַק	.457	be[come] dry, dry up (st. vb.)	יָבֵשׁ	.450
shape, form, mold	יָצַר	.458	know, understand	יָדַע	.451
inhabitant, citizen, dweller (Q Ptc)	יֹשֵׁב	.459	be[come] good (cf. טוֹב, טוּב)	יָטַב	.452
save, deliver (implied: by winning a victory) (H)	יָשַׁע	.460	dispute (N); correct, rebuke (H)	יָכַח	.453
deliverance, salvation; victory	יְשׁוּעָה		repeat, do again (with inf. const.); add (H); add (Q)	יָסַף	.454
remain, be left [behind/over] (N)	יָתַר	.461	counsel, advise	יָעַץ	.455
be[come] small, insignificant (st. vb.); small, insignificant (adj.)	קָטֹן	.462	advice, counsel	עֵצָה	
			leave, go out, exit, depart	יָצָא	.456

30.5 Exercises

1. After learning to recognize the I-י verbs, locate and identify (parse) any I-י verbs in whatever biblical passage your teacher assigns.
2. Gloss these verses, parsing all verbal forms.

1. לָמָּה תֵלֵךְ גַּם־אַתָּה אִתָּנוּ
שׁוּב וְשֵׁב עִם־הַמֶּלֶךְ כִּי־נָכְרִי אָתָּה

S2 15.19; נָכְרִי foreigner

2. דְּעוּ כִּי־יְהוָה הוּא אֱלֹהִים
הוּא־עָשָׂנוּ וְלוֹ אֲנַחְנוּ
עַמּוֹ וְצֹאן מַרְעִיתוֹ׃

Ps 100.3; מַרְעִית flock; pasturing, shepherding; pasturage

3. בֹּאוּ שְׁעָרָיו בְּתוֹדָה
חֲצֵרֹתָיו בִּתְהִלָּה
הוֹדוּ־לוֹ בָּרֲכוּ שְׁמוֹ׃

Ps 100.4

Jg 7.4	4. וַיֹּאמֶר יְהוָה אֶל־גִּדְעוֹן עוֹד הָעָם רָב הוֹרֵד אוֹתָם אֶל־הַמָּיִם ... וְהָיָה אֲשֶׁר אֹמַר אֵלֶיךָ זֶה יֵלֵךְ אִתָּךְ הוּא יֵלֵךְ אִתָּךְ וְכֹל אֲשֶׁר־אֹמַר אֵלֶיךָ זֶה לֹא־יֵלֵךְ עִמָּךְ הוּא לֹא יֵלֵךְ:
Josh 7.12; עֹרֶף [back of] neck	5. וְלֹא יָכְלוּ בְּנֵי יִשְׂרָאֵל לָקוּם לִפְנֵי אֹיְבֵיהֶם עֹרֶף יִפְנוּ לִפְנֵי אֹיְבֵיהֶם
Dt 31.2	6. וַיֹּאמֶר אֲלֵהֶם בֶּן־מֵאָה וְעֶשְׂרִים שָׁנָה אָנֹכִי הַיּוֹם לֹא־אוּכַל עוֹד לָצֵאת וְלָבוֹא וַיהוָה אָמַר אֵלַי לֹא תַעֲבֹר אֶת־הַיַּרְדֵּן הַזֶּה:
1 Sam 9.16; נָגִיד leader; Benjamin, Israel, Philistines	7. כָּעֵת מָחָר אֶשְׁלַח אֵלֶיךָ אִישׁ מֵאֶרֶץ בִּנְיָמִן וּמְשַׁחְתּוֹ לְנָגִיד עַל־עַמִּי יִשְׂרָאֵל וְהוֹשִׁיעַ אֶת־עַמִּי מִיַּד פְּלִשְׁתִּים כִּי רָאִיתִי אֶת־עַמִּי כִּי בָּאָה צַעֲקָתוֹ אֵלָי:
Gn 39.11	8. וַיְהִי כְּהַיּוֹם הַזֶּה וַיָּבֹא הַבַּיְתָה לַעֲשׂוֹת מְלַאכְתּוֹ וְאֵין אִישׁ מֵאַנְשֵׁי הַבַּיִת שָׁם בַּבָּיִת:
Gn 25.19; Abraham, Isaac	9. אַבְרָהָם הוֹלִיד אֶת־יִצְחָק:
Jg 13.9; Manoah	10. וַיִּשְׁמַע הָאֱלֹהִים בְּקוֹל מָנוֹחַ וַיָּבֹא מַלְאַךְ הָאֱלֹהִים עוֹד אֶל־הָאִשָּׁה וְהִיא יוֹשֶׁבֶת בַּשָּׂדֶה וּמָנוֹחַ אִישָׁהּ אֵין עִמָּהּ:
Jr 15.20; בְּצוּרָה fortified; יכל overcome (without a complementary NC)	11. וּנְתַתִּיךָ לָעָם הַזֶּה לְחוֹמַת נְחֹשֶׁת בְּצוּרָה וְנִלְחֲמוּ אֵלֶיךָ וְלֹא־יוּכְלוּ לָךְ כִּי־אִתְּךָ אֲנִי לְהוֹשִׁיעֲךָ וּלְהַצִּילֶךָ נְאֻם־יְהוָה:
Gn 46.4; Egypt	12. אָנֹכִי אֵרֵד עִמְּךָ מִצְרַיְמָה וְאָנֹכִי אַעַלְךָ
Is 9.5; מִשְׂרָה, rule, dominion; שְׁכֶם, shoulder; עַד + אָב < אֲבִיעַד, Eternal Father	13. כִּי־יֶלֶד יֻלַּד־לָנוּ בֵּן נִתַּן־לָנוּ וַתְּהִי הַמִּשְׂרָה עַל־שִׁכְמוֹ וַיִּקְרָא שְׁמוֹ פֶּלֶא יוֹעֵץ אֵל גִּבּוֹר אֲבִיעַד שַׂר־שָׁלוֹם:
Gn 3.5; פקח, open (vb.)	14. כִּי יֹדֵעַ אֱלֹהִים כִּי בְּיוֹם אֲכָלְכֶם מִמֶּנּוּ וְנִפְקְחוּ עֵינֵיכֶם וִהְיִיתֶם כֵּאלֹהִים יֹדְעֵי טוֹב וָרָע:
Ezk 39.7; חלל, pollute, defile (1cs H F)	15. וְאֶת־שֵׁם קָדְשִׁי אוֹדִיעַ בְּתוֹךְ עַמִּי יִשְׂרָאֵל וְלֹא־אַחֵל אֶת־שֵׁם־קָדְשִׁי עוֹד וְיָדְעוּ הַגּוֹיִם כִּי־אֲנִי יְהוָה קָדוֹשׁ בְּיִשְׂרָאֵל:
Jg 10.13	16. וְאַתֶּם עֲזַבְתֶּם אוֹתִי וַתַּעַבְדוּ אֱלֹהִים אֲחֵרִים לָכֵן לֹא־אוֹסִיף לְהוֹשִׁיעַ אֶתְכֶם:
Josh 17.12; יאל, be determined; Manasseh, Canaanite(s)	17. וְלֹא יָכְלוּ בְּנֵי מְנַשֶּׁה לְהוֹרִישׁ אֶת־הֶעָרִים הָאֵלֶּה וַיּוֹאֶל הַכְּנַעֲנִי לָשֶׁבֶת בָּאָרֶץ הַזֹּאת:
1 Kgs 19.11; פרק, tear/break off (D)	18. וַיֹּאמֶר צֵא וְעָמַדְתָּ בָהָר לִפְנֵי יְהוָה וְהִנֵּה יְהוָה עֹבֵר וְרוּחַ גְּדוֹלָה וְחָזָק מְפָרֵק הָרִים

Pr 27.1; מָחָר, tomorrow

19. אַל־תִּתְהַלֵּל בְּיוֹם מָחָר
כִּי לֹא־תֵדַע מַה־יֵּלֶד יוֹם׃

Gn 12.19

20. לָמָה אָמַרְתָּ אֲחֹתִי הִוא וָאֶקַּח אֹתָהּ לִי לְאִשָּׁה
וְעַתָּה הִנֵּה אִשְׁתְּךָ קַח וָלֵךְ׃

30.6 *Enrichment: Pay Attention While Reading*

One way to strengthen our grasp of Biblical Hebrew is to choose some aspect of grammar or syntax, note its occurrences as we read, and analyze its function. Paying attention to one aspect of the text will encourage you to pay attention to other things as well, but—and far more important—it will help you form a view of how Hebrew actually functions, as opposed to merely reading a description in a book and translating a few exercises. If we then write a brief description of our results; we have a resource on the grammar or syntax (or even vocabulary) of a biblical book (with a cross-reference in your favourite reference grammar or lexicon), so that we can interact with statements like "The participle in ... always/never/rarely ..." based on our knowledge of what actually happens in the text.

We might, for example, try to note all of the asyndetic clauses in a passage to see if they have anything in common, such as type of material, morphology, syntax, or some other characteristic. Or to describe the function of the infinitive construct in the book of Judges, or the participle in Jonah (below).

This is an example of how you might describe all of the participles in the book of Jonah.

Participles in the Book of Jonah

As noted in Lessons 11 and 12, the participle (so-called) in Biblical Hebrew has three functions, which are precisely the same as the functions of the adjective, hence it is often called a "verbal adjective". Its three functions are: (1) verbal/predicate; (2) nominal/substantive; and (3) adjectival/attributive. In a syntagm of a different type, it (4) accompanies the verbal root *hyh*, apparently as a temporally specific parallel to the verbal/predicate function.[192]

This paper tests the validity of the three-fold division of participial function in Biblical Hebrew by reviewing all of the participles in the biblical book of Jonah. Only the first three functions occur in the book of Jonah, as this table shows:

Attrib.	Pred.	Subst.	*hyh*
2	10	1	---
15%	77%	7.5%	

Description

The first and last participles in the book are *attributive/adjectival;* both are anarthrous, describing a grammatically indefinite noun: "a ship [that was] *going* to Tarshish (1.3). The second modifies Yhwh, but here Jonah refers to him as "a god ... *relenting* [*who relents*] over the evil" (4.2), which follows four other attributes: "a god [who is] gracious and compassionate, slow to anger and great in lovingkindness". Since the phrases all modify the anarthrous אֵל "god", they are themselves anarthrous and attributive.

The single *substantive/nominal* occurs in the poem found in Jonah 2. The participle מְשַׁמְּרִים "those who regard" is the only *piel* occurrence of the root שׁמר/*šmr* in the Bible. (This substantive function of the participle is extremely frequent in biblical poetry, apparently as a means of syntactic compression.)

---

192. The "predicate adjective" function is rarely fulfilled by *hyh* + adjective, but rather by the verbal/predicate function of stative verbs. This (the fourth) function does not occur in the book of Jonah.

The majority of participles in Jonah (8 or 10/11) are *predicate/verbal*, functioning as the predicate of their clauses. The repeated hendiadys הוֹלֵךְ וְסֹעֵר "continuing to rage/storm" (1.11, 13) accounts for four of these occurrences. If they are counted individually, they account for ten of thirteen occurrences; if they are counted as "compound" forms (i.e., as genuine cases of hendiadys), they account for eight of eleven.

These predicate participles modify pronominal subjects (1.10, 12; 3.2, 9), nominal subjects (1.11a-b, 13a-b, 3.4); one occurs in a syntagm that is difficult to identify: מַה־לְּךָ נִרְדָּם "What's with you—asleep?" (perhaps i.e., "Why are you sleeping?"), but in which the participle, being masculine singular, seems to modify the 2 ms pronominal suffix that is the object of the preposition.

All of the participles in Jonah can be assigned to one of the three functions (above); there are no "exceptions" or unexplained "remainders".

Examples (all)

A	P	S	H		
A				וַיִּמְצָא אֳנִיָּה בָּאָה תַרְשִׁישׁ	1.3
	P			וַיֹּאמֶר לוֹ מַה־לְּךָ נִרְדָּם	1.6
	P			כִּי מִלִּפְנֵי יהוה הוּא בֹרֵחַ	1.10
	P(*bis*)			כִּי הַיָּם הוֹלֵךְ וְסֹעֵר:	1.11a-b
	P			כִּי יוֹדֵעַ אָנִי כִּי ...	1.12
	P(*bis*)			כִּי הַיָּם הוֹלֵךְ וְסֹעֵר עֲלֵיהֶם:	1.13a-b
		S		מְשַׁמְּרִים הַבְלֵי־שָׁוְא חַסְדָּם יַעֲזֹבוּ:	2.9
	P			אֲשֶׁר אָנֹכִי דֹבֵר אֵלֶיךָ:	3.2
	P			וַיֹּאמַר עוֹד אַרְבָּעִים יוֹם וְנִינְוֵה נֶהְפָּכֶת:	3.4
	P			מִי־יוֹדֵעַ יָשׁוּב וְנִחַם הָאֱלֹהִים וְשָׁב מֵחֲרוֹן אַפּוֹ	3.9
A				יָדַעְתִּי כִּי אַתָּה אֵל־חַנּוּן וְרַחוּם אֶרֶךְ אַפַּיִם וְרַב־חֶסֶד וְנִחָם עַל־הָרָעָה:	4.2

In this case, the goal is not to establish a new theory of participial function, but rather to force ourselves to pay attention to how the text means what it says, how the author used his language to convey his message, and thus allow us to learn how we ought to expect that language to function as we read other parts of the Bible. It is obviously much easier to do this for a short book like Jonah than for, e.g., the book of Judges, with nearly two hundred participles. But the work that we do on Jonah ought to prepare us for the larger task of studying Judges.

Nor is it necessary to do this for an entire (long) book. Looking at the function of *wayhî* or of the participle (as here), or of any particular aspect of syntax or morphology for a few chapters will both stretch and strengthen our understanding of how Biblical Hebrew "works".

Lesson 31

Geminate (ע"ע) Verbs

Geminate verbs have the same consonant as their second and third radicals, such as רעע and סבב (the term "geminate", or "twinned", reflects the theory that they were coined from biradical roots by repeating the second radical). They are strong in three forms of Q P (3ms, 3fs, 3cp), and in Q Ptc and NA. They are weak in all other stems and conjugations. Some verbs occur in *polel*, *polal*, and *hitpolel*, like the hollow verbs (above), others (e.g., הלל, *praise*, פלל, *pray*) occur primarily in the regular D-stems and so look like the basic verb (i.e., all three radicals are present in all forms).

31.1 *Forms*

The prefix vowel of the geminate verbs is nearly always the same as that of the hollow verbs (Lesson 28); a "helping [anaptyctic] vowel" joins PGN endings to the verbal root (-וֹ- in perfect; -ֶי- in imperfect, preterite, & imperative). The second and third radicals often coalesce and are written once with *dageš forte*. The verbal root occurs in three basic forms:

Form of the Verbal Root	Occurs in
סֹב	forms without PGN endings
סַבּ-	forms with PGN endings (but not imperative)
סבב	a few forms (*all* forms in the D-stems)

This skeleton paradigm illustrates these characteristics:

√סבב		Q		N	H	Hp	Po
P	2ms	סַבּוֹתָ		נְסַבּוֹתָ	הֲסִבּוֹתָ	הוּסַבּוֹתָ	סוֹבַבְתָּ
	3ms	סָבַב	קַל	נָסַב	הֵסֵב	הוּסַב	סֹבֵב
	3cp	סָבְבוּ	קָלוּ	נָסַבּוּ	הֵסֵבּוּ	הוּסַבּוּ	סֹבְבוּ
F	3ms	יָסֹב	יֵקַל	יִסַּב	יָסֵב	יוּסַב	יְסוֹבֵב
		יִסֹּב					
	2fs	תָּסֹבִּי		תִּסַּבִּי	תָּסֵבִּי	תּוּסַבִּי	תְּסוֹבְבִי
	2fp	תְּסֻבֶּינָה		תִּסַּבֶּינָה	תְּסִבֶּינָה	תּוּסַבֶּינָה	תְּסוֹבֵבְנָה
V	2ms	סֹב		הִסַּב	הָסֵב		סוֹבֵב
NC		סֹב		הִסֵּב	הָסֵב		סוֹבֵב

31.2 Geminate Verbs in Qal

Qal		√סבב		√קלל
P	1cs	סַבּוֹתִי		קַלּוֹתִי
	2ms	סַבּוֹתָ		קַלּוֹתָ
	2fs	סַבּוֹת		קַלּוֹת
	3ms	סַב	סָבַב	קַל
	3fs	סַבָּה	סָבְבָה	קַלָּה
	1cp	סַבּוֹנוּ		קַלּוֹנוּ
	2mp	סַבּוֹתֶם		קַלּוֹתֶם
	2fp	סַבּוֹתֶן		קַלּוֹתֶן
	3cp	סַבּוּ	סָבְבוּ	קַלּוּ
F	1cs	אָסֹב	אֶסֹּב	אֵקַל
	2ms	תָּסֹב	תִּסֹּב	תֵּקַל
	2fs	תָּסֹבִּי	תִּסְּבִי	תֵּקַלִּי
	3ms	יָסֹב	יִסֹּב	יֵקַל
	3fs	תָּסֹב	תִּסֹּב	תֵּקַל
	1cp	נָסֹב	נִסֹּב	נֵקַל
	2mp	תָּסֹבּוּ	תִּסְּבוּ	תֵּקַלּוּ
	2fp	תְּסֻבֶּינָה	תִּסֹּבְנָה	תְּקַלֶּינָה
	3mp	יָסֹבּוּ	יִסְּבוּ	יֵקַלּוּ
	3fp	תְּסֻבֶּינָה	תִּסֹּבְנָה	תְּקַלֶּינָה
Pr	3ms	וַיָּסָב	וַיִּסֹּב	וַיֵּקַל
V	2ms	סֹב		
	2fs	סֹבִּי		
	2mp	סֹבּוּ		
	2fp	סֻבֶּינָה		
NC		סֹב		קַל
Ptc	ms	סֹבֵב		קַל

1. *Qal* participle and infinitive absolute are **strong**, as are *qal* perfect forms with vocalic or no PGN sufformative (i.e., 3ms, 3fs, 3cp).
2. The stem syllable looks like the second syllable of the basic verb (*pataḥ* in Q P, *ḥolem* in Q F and V).
3. The three forms of the *qal* are compared in this table (their vertical alignment is merely for convenience; it does *not* imply that these would have been thought of as "types").
4. The middle column shows alternate forms, which in Q imperfect, look exactly like I-נ roots (cf. נפל, §26.1); they can be distinguished only in context by knowing the vocabulary.

31.3 Geminate Verbs in Nifal

This is a skeletal paradigm (the full paradigm is in Appendix D).

		Nifal	√סבב
P	3ms		נָסַב
	1cp		נְסַבּוֹנוּ
F	3ms		יִסַּב
	3mp		יִסַּבּוּ
Pr	3ms		וַיִּסַּב
V	2ms		הִסַּב
	2mp		הִסַּבּוּ
NC			הִסֵּב
Ptc	ms		נָסָב

1. The prefix looks exactly like the hollow verbs (*qameṣ* or *šewa* in *nifal* perfect and participle; *ḥireq* with doubled first radical in all other forms).
2. Some forms (e.g., 3ms N F) look exactly like 3ms Q F of a I-נ verbal root (cf. יִפֹּל, *he will fall*).
3. The stem vowel is *pataḥ*, except in N P forms with consonantal PGN endings (see paradigm, above).

31.4 Geminate Verbs in Hifil & Hofal

This skeleton paradigm lists the H-stems of both סבב and שׁוב for comparison.

		Hifil		Hofal	
		√סבב	√שׁוב	√סבב	√שׁוב
P	1cs	הֲסִבּוֹתִי	הֲשִׁיבוֹתִי	הוּסַבּוֹתִי	הוּשַׁבְתִּי
	3ms	הֵסֵב	הֵשִׁיב	הוּסַב	הוּשַׁב
F	3ms	יָסֵב	יָשִׁיב	יוּסַב	יוּשַׁב
	3mp	יָסֵבּוּ	יָשִׁיבוּ	יוּסַבּוּ	יוּשְׁבוּ
Pr	3ms	וַיָּסֵב	וַיָּשָׁב	וַיּוּסַב	וַיּוּשַׁב
V	2ms	הָסֵב	שׁוּב		
	2mp	הָסֵבּוּ	שׁוּבוּ		
NC		הָסֵב	שׁוּב	הוּשַׁב	
Ptc	ms	מֵסֵב	שָׁב	מוּסָב	מוּקָם

1. The prefix in *hifil* looks exactly like the hollow verbs (*ṣere* in H P and Ptc; *qameṣ* in all other forms).
2. The stem vowel is *ṣere* or *ḥireq* (before consonantal PGN endings). It is similar to the hollow verbs; geminate verbs tend to have *ṣere* rather than *ḥireq* as a stem vowel.
3. In *hofal*, the prefix vowel is always *šureq*, as in the I-י verbs, and the stem vowel is *pataḥ* in all forms, so that Hp geminates without PGN endings look exactly like Hp of I-י verbs without endings.

31.5 *Geminate Verbs in Polel, Polal, & Hitpolel*

Geminate verbs that use these forms look just like hollow verbs. This skeleton paradigm lists forms of a hollow verb (קוּם) for comparison. *Hitpolel* (Pt) looks exactly like *polel* with the prefixes הִתְ- (perfect, etc.) and יִתְ- (etc.).

P-stems		√סבב	√קוּם	Pt (both roots)
P	1cs	סֹבַבְתִּי	קֹמַמְתִּי	הִתְסֹבַבְתִּי
	3ms	סֹבֵב	קֹמֵם	הִתְסֹבֵב
	1cp	סֹבַבְנוּ	קֹמַמְנוּ	הִתְסֹבַבְנוּ
F	3ms	יְסֹבֵב	יְקֹמֵם	יִתְסֹבֵב
	3mp	יְסֹבְבוּ	יְקֹמְמוּ	יִתְסֹבְבוּ
Pr	3ms	וַיְסֹבֵב	וַיְקֹמֵם	וַיִּתְסֹבְבוּ
V	2ms	סֹבֵב	קֹמֵם	
	2mp	סֹבְבוּ	קֹמְמוּ	
NC		סֹבֵב	קֹמֵם	
Ptc	ms	מְסֹבֵב	מְקֹמֵם	

1. The only way to know whether a form in *polel*, *polal*, or *hitpolel* is from a hollow or geminate root is to know the vocabulary (which word best fits the context) or check a lexicon (most lexica cross-reference these forms to their putative root).
2. *Polal, et al.* occur with and without the vowel letter (וֹ). The stem vowel only distinguishes the active (*polel*) from the passive (*polal*; not listed) when there is no ending, so that the function of most forms must be determined from the context.

31.6 *"Double" Verbs*

A number of hollow, III-ה, and geminate roots are apparently "double" verbs—different roots that share some of their consonants and overlap in function. For example,

הוּם	המם	be in turmoil
פּוּר	פרר	break, destroy
צוּר	צרר	bind, be in distress
רבה	רבב	be numerous, many
שׁנה	שׁגג	go astray, sin

31.7 *Identical & "Ambiguous" Verbal Forms*

The results of the particular weaknesses of weak verbal roots creates two additional complications:

1. Forms can appear to be based on different verbal roots (one of which may not be attested). For example,

   וַיָּסֹב 3ms *qal* preterite < סבב   *He went around*
   looks like 3ms *qal* preterite < נסב   [The root does not exist in Biblical Hebrew.]

2. Some forms of a verbal root can be parsed in more than one way—that is, they are ambiguous *apart from a context*. A form may be located in more than one conjugation (below, שָׁר, מֵת) or stem (below, וַיֵּשֶׁב, וַיַּעַל). A form does not have several functions in a given context—its cotext restricts every form's function, but the same form may be ambiguous *apart from its context*. This means that a form must be read and its function identified only within the requirements of its context.

מֵת	3ms *qal* perfect ms *qal* participle	*He died* *[one who] [is] dead*
שָׁר	3ms *qal* perfect ms *qal* participle	*He sang* *[one who] sings*
וַיָּשֶׂם	3ms *qal* preterite 3ms *hifil* preterite	*He placed/set* [someone/something] *(one object)* *He caused* [someone] *to place/set* [something] *(two objects)*
וַיַּעַל	3ms *qal* preterite 3ms *hifil* preterite	*He went up* (intransitive—no object) *He brought up* (transitive)

31.8 *Frequency*

This is a list of all **sixteen** geminate verbs that occur fifty times or more in Biblical Hebrew, in descending order of frequency.

סבב	*surround, go around*	162x	תמם	*be complete, have integrity*	64x
הלל	*praise* (P); *boast* (Dt)	145x	צרר	*wrap up, be hostile to, confine*	61x
חלל	*be defiled* (N); *defile* (D); *begin* (H)	134x	ארר	*curse*	59x
רעע	*be evil, wicked, bad*	99x	שדד	*devastate, destroy, lay waste*	56x
שמם	*be astonished, desolate*	95x	חתת	*be shattered, dismayed*	53x
קלל	*be light, swift;* *slight, trifling, accursed*	82x	מדד	*measure*	52x
פלל	*pray* (Dt)	80x	רנן	*shout (in joy, triumph)*	52x
חנן	*be gracious to, favor*	77x	פרר	*break out, burst forth* (H)	50x

31.9 *Concepts*

anaptyctic   coalesce   double verbs   gemination

31.10 *Vocabulary*

confine, constrain, wrap up, be hostile to	צָרַר	.469	*curse*	אָרַר	.463
distress, trouble; confinement	צָרָה		*praise, exult in* (D); *boast* (Dt)	הָלַל	.464
enemy, foe	צַר		*praise, glory*	תְּהִלָּה	
be[come] light, swift; slight, trifling, accursed (st. vb.)	קָלַל	.470	*measure*	מָדַד	.465
shout (in joy, triumph, celebration)	רָנַן	.471	*surround, go around; encircle; turn around*	סָבַב	.466
be[come] bad, evil, wicked (st. vb.)	רָעַע	.472	*pray* (Dt)	פָּלַל	.467
devastate, lay waste; cf. §21.1	שָׁדַד	.472	*prayer*	תְּפִלָּה	
be[come] astounded, astonished, dumbfounded; desolate	שָׁמַם	.473	*break out, burst forth* (H)	פָּרַר	.468

31.11 Exercises

1. After learning to recognize geminate verbs, identify any geminate verbal forms in whatever biblical passage your teacher assigns.
2. Gloss these verses, parsing all verbal forms.

Jb 31.40; Job	1. תַּמּוּ דִּבְרֵי אִיּוֹב:
Nu 22.12; Balaam	2. וַיֹּאמֶר אֱלֹהִים אֶל־בִּלְעָם לֹא תֵלֵךְ עִמָּהֶם לֹא תָאֹר אֶת־הָעָם כִּי בָרוּךְ הוּא:
Lv 9.24	3. וַתֵּצֵא אֵשׁ מִלִּפְנֵי יְהוָה וַתֹּאכַל עַל־הַמִּזְבֵּחַ אֶת־הָעֹלָה וְאֶת־הַחֲלָבִים וַיַּרְא כָּל־הָעָם וַיָּרֹנּוּ וַיִּפְּלוּ עַל־פְּנֵיהֶם:
Ps 146.1; נַפְשִׁי is vocative	4. הַלְלוּ־יָהּ הַלְלִי נַפְשִׁי אֶת־יְהוָה:
Gn 12.3	5. וַאֲבָרֲכָה מְבָרְכֶיךָ וּמְקַלֶּלְךָ אָאֹר וְנִבְרְכוּ בְךָ כֹּל מִשְׁפְּחֹת הָאֲדָמָה:
Ps 145.3; גְּדֻלָּה, greatness; חֵקֶר, searchable; searching	6. גָּדוֹל יְהוָה וּמְהֻלָּל מְאֹד וְלִגְדֻלָּתוֹ אֵין חֵקֶר:
Josh 6.7	7. וַיֹּאמֶר אֶל־הָעָם עִבְרוּ וְסֹבּוּ אֶת־הָעִיר
Ps 114.3; אָחוֹר, back, rear (n.); Jordan	8. הַיָּם רָאָה וַיָּנֹס הַיַּרְדֵּן יִסֹּב לְאָחוֹר:
Nu 11.11; מצא lacks its final א; מַשָּׂא, burden	9. וַיֹּאמֶר מֹשֶׁה אֶל־יְהוָה לָמָה הֲרֵעֹתָ לְעַבְדֶּךָ וְלָמָּה לֹא־מָצָתִי חֵן בְּעֵינֶיךָ לָשׂוּם אֶת־מַשָּׂא כָּל־הָעָם הַזֶּה עָלָי:
Lv 26.32	10. וַהֲשִׁמֹּתִי אֲנִי אֶת־הָאָרֶץ וְשָׁמְמוּ עָלֶיהָ אֹיְבֵיכֶם הַיֹּשְׁבִים בָּהּ:
Ps 145.2; עַד, age (a duration of time)	11. בְּכָל־יוֹם אֲבָרֲכֶךָּ וַאֲהַלְלָה שִׁמְךָ לְעוֹלָם וָעֶד:
Zp 3.14; רוּעַ, shout; עלז, exult; Zion	12. רָנִּי בַּת־צִיּוֹן הָרִיעוּ יִשְׂרָאֵל שִׂמְחִי וְעָלְזִי בְּכָל־לֵב בַּת יְרוּשָׁלָם:
Jr 2.12; חרב, dry up; שׂער, bristle [with horror]	13. שֹׁמּוּ שָׁמַיִם עַל־זֹאת וְשַׂעֲרוּ חָרְבוּ מְאֹד נְאֻם־יְהוָה:
Ps 37.22	14. כִּי מְבֹרָכָיו יִירְשׁוּ אָרֶץ וּמְקֻלָּלָיו יִכָּרֵתוּ:
Jr 7.26; עֹרֶף, neck	15. וְלוֹא שָׁמְעוּ אֵלַי וְלֹא הִטּוּ אֶת־אָזְנָם וַיַּקְשׁוּ אֶת־עָרְפָּם הֵרֵעוּ מֵאֲבוֹתָם:
S2 22.6; חֶבֶל, cord; קדם, precede, go before; מוֹקֵשׁ snare; bait, lure; Sheol	16. חֶבְלֵי שְׁאוֹל סַבֻּנִי קִדְּמֻנִי מֹקְשֵׁי־מָוֶת:
Jn 2.4; מִשְׁבָּר, breaker (wave); גַּל, heap (wave)	17. וְנָהָר יְסֹבְבֵנִי כָּל־מִשְׁבָּרֶיךָ וְגַלֶּיךָ עָלַי עָבָרוּ:
Jr 21.4; סבב, turn back, reverse [Most of this v. is a quotation.]	18. כֹּה־אָמַר יְהוָה אֱלֹהֵי יִשְׂרָאֵל הִנְנִי מֵסֵב אֶת־כְּלֵי הַמִּלְחָמָה אֲשֶׁר בְּיֶדְכֶם אֲשֶׁר אַתֶּם נִלְחָמִים בָּם אֶת־מֶלֶךְ בָּבֶל וְאֶת־הַכַּשְׂדִּים הַצָּרִים עֲלֵיכֶם מִחוּץ לַחוֹמָה וְאָסַפְתִּי אוֹתָם אֶל־תּוֹךְ הָעִיר הַזֹּאת:

Dt 3.24; גֹּדֶל, *greatness* (n.); the first occurrence of אשר is probably causal (*because*)	.19 אֲדֹנָי יְהוִה אַתָּה הַחִלּוֹתָ לְהַרְאוֹת אֶת־עַבְדְּךָ אֶת־גָּדְלְךָ וְאֶת־יָדְךָ הַחֲזָקָה אֲשֶׁר מִי־אֵל בַּשָּׁמַיִם וּבָאָרֶץ אֲשֶׁר־יַעֲשֶׂה כְמַעֲשֶׂיךָ וְכִגְבוּרֹתֶךָ׃
Dt 15.10; בִּגְלַל, *on account of, because of*; מִשְׁלַח, *outstretching* (i.e., *attempt*)	.20 נָתוֹן תִּתֵּן לוֹ וְלֹא־יֵרַע לְבָבְךָ בְּתִתְּךָ לוֹ כִּי בִּגְלַל הַדָּבָר הַזֶּה יְבָרֶכְךָ יְהוָה אֱלֹהֶיךָ בְּכָל־מַעֲשֶׂךָ וּבְכֹל מִשְׁלַח יָדֶךָ׃
K1 8.35; עצר, *be closed, shut up* (N); מטר, *rain*; this is not a complete sentence, but the protasis ["if"-clause] of a conditional sentence; the next verse contains the the apodosis ["then"-clause]	.21 בְּהֵעָצֵר שָׁמַיִם וְלֹא־יִהְיֶה מָטָר כִּי יֶחֶטְאוּ־לָךְ וְהִתְפַּלְלוּ אֶל־הַמָּקוֹם הַזֶּה וְהוֹדוּ אֶת־שְׁמֶךָ וּמֵחַטָּאתָם יְשׁוּבוּן כִּי תַעֲנֵם׃

31.12 *Some Encouragement*

Congratulations! Having invested a great deal of time, effort, and energy (not to mention money) on Biblical Hebrew, how can you continue to grow in your ability to use what you have learned?

1. Continue to *read* the Hebrew text *aloud*, in order to strengthen your ability to see and hear "in Hebrew".
2. Continue to *gloss* the Hebrew text into another language, preferably *in writing*, but orally is better than nothing. Don't worry at this point about getting every word, or even getting every word "right" (when I first did this, I just skipped words that I didn't yet know or couldn't recognize and often ran into the same root in another context and recognized it there, so that I could go back and "insert" it in its earlier occurrence). It is more important that you see as much text as possible.
3. Continue to develop a *vocabulary* base by learning the words in the passage that you are reading. As you come across unknown words, check a tool such as Armstrong, Busby, & Carr (1988) or a concordance to see how frequently they occur in Biblical Hebrew. If they are relatively infrequent (fewer than ten times), you may not want to invest the time to learn them, but if they have the same root of a word that you already know, you can add them to your stock of vocabulary without much effort.
4. Use the *reading notes* (online at www.fredputnam.org) to review what you have already read, and to explore new passages.
5. The most important contribution to growing in your understanding of Biblical Hebrew is continued exposure to *passages* of text, not merely to a verse here or there. This is because the minimal unit of communication is not the word, but the sentence, and in order to think about *how* the biblical writers communicated, it is necessary to read their communications as they intended them to be read—as stories, poems, songs, oracles, &c., not as isolated phrases, clauses, or even verses.

The main benefit of seeing a lot of Hebrew is that you will gradually begin to say, "I've never seen that before", or "That's the fourth time in this chapter that the author repeated that word [syntagm, etc.]"—that is, you will begin to sense what is and is not significant, and to gain appreciation for the craft of the biblical authors. Since much of intepretation is asking questions about the text, the greater your familiarity with that text, the more appropriate—and therefore helpful—the questions will be.

You will also gain the ability to understand commentators' remarks, since you will have a fund of information on which to draw in interpreting both the accuracy and significance of what they say.

Appendices

A. **Supplementary Vocabulary**. Ten lists that, together with the vocabulary lists in the lessons, entail all words that occur *fifty times or more* in Biblical Hebrew.

B. **Hebrew – English Glossary**. An alphabetic list of all words in the lessons and Appendix A of this grammar.

C. **Glossary**. Grammatical and linguistic terms used in this grammar.

D. **Paradigms**. Pronominal and verbal forms, including a brief comparison of the forms of several weak verbs that may be confused due to their similarity.

E. **Bibliography**. An annotated list of [primarily] reference works on Biblical Hebrew and the Hebrew Bible.

Appendix A

Supplementary Vocabulary

Supplementary Vocabulary 1

.475	אָוֶן	wickedness, guilt, iniquity	.483	נְאֻם	declaration, utterance; often in the prophets as נְאֻם יהוה
.476	בְּלִי	not	.484	שָׁם	there, in that place
.477	גַּם	also, even, indeed (adv., cj.)	.485	תָּוֶךְ	area inside something else
.478	הֲ-	prefixed interrogative particle (not directly translated)		בְּתוֹךְ	in, within, inside [always construct to the following word]; trad. in the midst of
.479	יוֹמָם	daily, by day, daytime (cf. יוֹם)	.486	תָּפַשׂ	seize, take hold of
.480	יָלַד	bear, give birth [to] (of women); father; become the father of (of men)	.487	תִּפְאֶרֶת	ornament, decoration
.481	כָּנָף	wing; edge/end of, e.g., garment (hem) or the earth/land	.488	תְּרוּמָה	tribute; [heave-] offering
.482	לָמָה לָמָּה	why? (מָה + לְ)			

Supplementary Vocabulary 2

.489	אוֹצָר	treasury, storehouse	.496	חֹשֶׁךְ	[the] dark, darkness
.490	אוֹת	[miraclous] sign	.497	עֵדָה עֵדוּת	testimony, command, precept (of divine law)
.491	אָסַר	bind, tie, imprison	.498	עָזַר	help, assist
.492	אֲרִי אַרְיֵה	lion	.499	צוּר	cliff, crag, outcropping; rock
.493	בַּרְזֶל	iron	.500	קָצָה	end, edge; border
.494	הֵיכָל	large building; palace, temple (cf. בַּיִת)	.501	קָרְבָּן	offering, gift (cf. Mk 7.11)
.495	זָכָר	man (male); male being (animal)	.502	שָׁחַט	slaughter, kill

Supplementary Vocabulary 3

cedar	אֶרֶז	.503	bury	קָבַר	.511
belly, abdomen; womb	בֶּטֶן	.504	horn (oft. as symbol of strength)	קֶרֶן	.512
lot; allotment (what the lot reveals/awards)	גּוֹרָל	.505	bow (weapon); rainbow	קֶשֶׁת	.513
property, possession(s)	מִקְנֶה	.506	ride	רָכַב	.514
guard; obligation, duty	מִשְׁמֶרֶת	.507	succeed, prosper; understand (H)	שָׂכַל	.515
afflicted, poor, humble	עָנִי	.508	remainder, what is left (cf. שׁאר)	שְׁאֵרִית	.516
arrange, set in order	עָרַךְ	.509	table	שֻׁלְחָן	.517
valley, lowland	עֵמֶק	.510	plunder, booty, spoil	שָׁלָל	.518

Supplementary Vocabulary 4

cistern, well (i.e., a hole dug for water; cf. Gn 37.22; Jr 2.13)	בּוֹר	.519	shoulder[blade]	כָּתֵף	.527
man (male)	גֶּבֶר	.520	anoint	מָשַׁח	.528
dream	חֲלוֹם	.521	here, in this place	פּוֹ פֹּא פֹּה	.529
favor, grace	חֵן	.522	spread out	פָּרַשׂ	.530
remainder, left-over (n.)	יֶתֶר	.523	tomb, grave (usually hollowed out of rock, not dug in soil)	קֶבֶר	.531
loaf, talent, region (all were, or could be, roughly "circular")	כִּכָּר	.524	assembly, congregation; refers to assembly of Israelite adult males	קָהָל	.532
foolish, insolent (often substantive)	כְּסִיל	.525	heal, cure (vb.)	רָפָא	.533
according to (כְּ- + פֶּה + לְ-, פֶּה + כְּ-); always followed by a noun	לְפִי כְּפִי	.526	female slave/servant	שִׁפְחָה	.534

Supplementary Vocabulary 5

grasp, sieze, hold	אָחַז	.535	stumble, fall, sway, rock, waver	כָּשַׁל	.543
burnt offering, offering by fire (contrast אִשָּׁה, woman, wife)	אִשֶּׁה	.536	shield	מָגֵן	.544
hill; [cultic] high place; Gibeah	גִּבְעָה	.537	[young] girl, maid	נַעֲרָה	.545
be defiled, polluted (N); defile, pollute (D); begin (H)	חָלַל	.538	end; limit, boundary	קֵץ	.546
share, portion, part (cf. חָלַק)	חֵלֶק	.539	succeed, be effective/strong	צָלַח	.547
be gracious to, compassionate toward, favour; request favor/compassion (Dt)	חָנַן	.540	Sheol	שְׁאוֹל	.548
be shattered, dismayed (st. vb.)	חָתַת	.541	be complete, have integrity (st. vb.)	תָּמַם	.549
large river (esp. the Nile)	יְאֹר	.542	whole, blameless, entire	תָּמִים	

Appendix A

Supplementary Vocabulary 6

feast, festival; procession	חַג	.557	poor, needy, destitute, oppressed	אֶבְיוֹן	.550
violence, wrong, injury	חָמָס	.558	end, outcome	אַחֲרִית	.551
vow, oath	נֶדֶר נֵדֶר	.559	How? How! (either interrogative or exclamatory); אֵיכָה is the first word in Lam 1, 2, 4, and the Hebrew title of Lam	אֵיךְ אֵיכָה	.552
[to] vow; swear an oath/vow	נָדַר				
inherit, obtain	נָחַל	.560	side (n.); beside, near (prp.)	אֵצֶל	.553
drink offering, libation	נֶסֶךְ	.561	flee, run away	בָּרַח	.554
pour [out] (as a drink offering)	נָסַךְ		strength, power (cf. גֶּבֶר, גִּבּוֹר)	גְּבוּרָה	.555
plain, desert (often Jordan plain or valley & wilderness of Judah)	עֲרָבָה	.562	love, loved one, beloved	דּוֹד	.556

Supplementary Vocabulary 7

before, not yet (a following imperfect functions as past: וְטֶרֶם יִגָּלֶה אֵלָיו דְּבַר־יהוה: Yahwh's word had not yet been revealed to him (Sam 3:7)	טֶרֶם בְּטֶרֶם	.572	drive, thrust (a weapon); blow (a horn/trumpet)	תָּקַע	.563
			widow	אַלְמָנָה	.564
			female slave/servant	אָמָה	.565
undergrowth, thicket, woods	יַעַר	.573	path, way	אֹרַח	.566
thought, intention, plan	מַחְשָׁבָה	.574	grapevine	גֶּפֶן	.567
rock, crag, cliff	סֶלַע	.575	sow, plant (cf. זֶרַע, seed)	זָרַע	.568
highest (trad. Most High); upper	עֶלְיוֹן	.576	strong; hard	חָזָק	.569
distress, trouble; labour	עָמָל	.577	divide, apportion, assign (cf. חֶלְקָה)	חָלַק	.570
incense; smoke (from incense)	קְטֹרֶת	.578	arrow; arrows חִצִּים	חֵץ	.571

Supplementary Vocabulary 8

cease, stop (with inf. const.)	חָדַל	.587	prp. after, behind; last (adj.)	אַחֲרוֹן	.579
new, renewed; fresh	חָדָשׁ	.588	Where [is/are]?	אַיֵּה	.580
shadow, shade	צֵל	.589	trustworthiness, faithfulness	אֱמוּנָה	.581
be angry, furious	כָּעַס	.590	split, cleave	בָּקַע	.582
horseman (coll.); horse	פָּרָשׁ	.591	virgin, [marriageable] young woman	בְּתוּלָה	.583
reed (for measuring)	קָנֶה	.592	camel	גָּמָל	.584
tear (esp. clothing)	קָרַע	.593	cling/stick to	דָּבַק	.585
fellowship [trad., peace] offering	שֶׁלֶם	.594	honey	דְּבַשׁ	.586

Supplementary Vocabulary 9

.595	חָרַם	destroy utterly [as belonging to Yhwh] (trad. devote to the ban)	.602	פָּרַץ	break through, burst out (cf. Perez; Gn 38.29))
.596	כָּבַס	wash, clean	.603	רֵיחַ	smell, odor, scent
.597	מִדָּה	measure (n.) (cf. מדד)	.604	שְׂמֹאל	left [side/hand]
.598	מוּסָר	correction, discipline, instruction	.605	שָׁוְא	worthlessness, in vain
.599	מָחָר	tomorrow	.606	שְׁמָמָה	desolation, devastation; horror (cf. שׁמם)
.600	מַצָּה	unleavened bread	.607	שֵׁן	tooth; crag, outcropping
.601	מָרוֹם	height (cf. רום)	.608	פָּעַל	do, make

Supplementary Vocabulary 10[193]

.609	אֶדֶן	pedestal, socket [Ex] (N.B.: not "Eden", which is עֵדֶן]	.616	סֶלָה	The function of this word is unknown. [Pss]
.610	אוּלָם	porch, vestibule (of the Temple [1 Kg, 2 Chr, Ezk])	.617	סֹלֶת	finely ground wheat flour [43/53 in Lv, Nu]
.611	אֵילָם	porch, vestibule [Ezk]	.618	עֶרְוָה	nakedness [Lv (32/54)]
.612	יְרִיעָה	[tent] fabric/curtain [44/54 in Ex]	.619	פֵּאָה	corner, rim, side [Ex & Ezk (63/86)]
.613	מִגְרָשׁ	pasture, uncultivated land [Josh & 1 Chr (98/110)]	.620	קָדִים	east [Ezk (53/67)]
.614	מִזְמוֹר	psalm (this transliterates LX: *yavlmo*") [Ps]	.621	קֶרֶשׁ	plank, board, beam [Ex (48/51)]
.615	מְנַצֵּחַ	choir leader, conductor(?) [Ps]			

193. The words in this list occur fifty times or more, but they occur entirely or primarily in one or two biblical "books" (identified in brackets [Ps]); the number of occurrences is given as a fraction following the abbreviation of the title of the "book" (e.g., "Lv 35/54" עֶרְוָה) means that עֶרְוָה occurrs 35 times in Leviticus out of a total of 54 occurrences in Biblical Hebrew).

Appendix B

Hebrew – English Glossary

1. An alphabetical list of all Hebrew words in the lessons and Appendix A of this grammar (i.e., all words that occur fifty times or more in Biblical Hebrew), together with one or more glosses. [This is not intended to replace the need to learn to use the lexicon.]
2. Each gloss is preceded by an abbreviation ("n.", "v.", etc.) identifying its main function as, e.g., "noun", "verb", etc.
3. followed by the number of the vocabulary list in which which the word is introduced (e.g., (**3**) = Lesson 3). An "**S**" before the numeral means that it appears in a supplementary list (Appendix A).
4. Multiple forms are either alternate forms or singular and plural of the same word.
5. Unpredictable plurals (e.g., אִשָּׁה / נָשִׁים) are listed twice—with their singular and alphabetically.
6. Occasionally nouns that occur with both masculine and feminine forms are listed with both (e.g., סוּס, סוּסָה).
7. Gender is indicated only when the grammatical and morphological gender do not match. Feminine nouns that do not end in ה ָ- or ת ְ/ָ, etc. are marked as "(f.)" (e.g., עִיר); masculine nouns with those endings are marked "(m.)" (e.g., לַיְלָה).
8. If no stem is marked for the verb, the gloss reflects its function in the *qal*.
9. If a verb does not occur in *qal*, it is listed without vowels (e.g., שכב).
10. Words listed with a numeral followed by "x" occur that many times in Biblical Hebrew (e.g., (2x) = two occurrences).

Abbreviations

adj.	adjective	N	N-stem (*nifal*)
adv.	adverb	pl.	plural
D	D-active (*piel*)	prn.	pronoun
Dp	D-passive (*pual*)	prp.	preposition
Dt	D-t-infix (*hitpael*)	Q	*qal*
f.	feminine	Qp	*qal*-passive
H	H-active (*hifil*)	st. vb.	stative verb
Hp	H-passive (*hofal*)	trad.	"traditionally translated by/as …"
m.	masculine	us.	usually
n.	noun	v.	verb

N.B.: Other abbreviations may be added as needed.

n. *father, male ancestor* (**2**) (pl. אָבוֹת)	אָב	*Where is/are ...?*	אֵיפֹה
v. *perish* (**10**)	אבד	n. *man* (not *Man*), *husband* each (as subject of a plural verb) (pl. אֲנָשִׁים) (**2**)	אִישׁ
v. *be willing, agree* (often with NC) (**25**)	אבה		
n. *fathers* (pl. of אָב) (**2**)	אָבוֹת	n. *pupil* [of eye] (3x); *darkness* (2x)	אִישׁוֹן
n. *poor, needy, destitute, oppressed* (**S6**)	אֶבְיוֹן	adv. *only, surely* (adv.) (**18**)	אַךְ
n. *stone* (cf. אֶבֶן הָעֵזֶר, Ebenezer, "the stone of help") (**8**)	אֶבֶן	v. *eat, devour, consume* (**3**)	אָכַל
		there is/are not/no; without (וְאֵין) (**16**)	אֵין, אַיִן
n. *lord, master*; (*my*) *Lord, Master* (**4**)	אֲדֹנָי אָדוֹן	adv. *no, not* (**5**)	אַל
n. *humanity, humankind, man*; *Adam* (**3**)	אָדָם	prp. *to, toward* (**7**)	אֶל
		n. *God; god, gods* (used of YHWH, the God of Israel, and of pagan gods) (**2**)	אֱלֹהִים אֵל
n. *ground* (cf. אָדָם, Gn 3.19) (**8**)	אֲדָמָה		
n. *pedestal, socket* [Ex] (**S10**)	אֶדֶן	dem. *these* (cp) (**13**)	אֵלֶּה
v. *love, like; desire* (cf. Amnon & Tamar) (**9**)	אהב	n. *friend*; adj. *familiar*; n. *chief* (**29**)	אַלּוּף
		n. *widow* (**S7**)	אַלְמָנָה
n. *tent*; occasionally *home, house* (**4**)	אֹהֶל	*thousand* (**17**)	אֶלֶף
cj. *or* (**18**)	אוֹ	*two thousand* (**17**)	אַלְפַּיִם
n. *enemy* (ms Q Ptc < איב) (**6**)	אוֹיֵב	cj. *if, then* (**15**)	אִם
n. *porch, vestibule* [Ezk]; also אֵילָם (**S10**)	אוּלָם	n. *mother; ancestress* (**9**)	אֵם
n. *wickedness, guilt, iniquity* (**S1**)	אָוֶן	n. *female slave/servant* (**S7**)	אָמָה
n. *treasury, storehouse* (**S2**)	אוֹצָר	n. *cubit; forearm* (**7**)	אַמָּה
n. *light* (**18**)	אוֹר	n. *trustworthiness, faithfulness* (**S8**)	אֱמוּנָה
n. [*miraclous*] *sign* (pl. אֹתוֹת) (**S2**)	אוֹת	v. *be trustworthy, faithful; steady, firm* (N); *believe, trust* (H)f (**20**)	אמן
adv./cj. *then, at that time; formerly, since*; cf. מֵאָז (**20**)	אָז	st. v. *be[come] strong, bold*	אמץ
n. *ear, hearing* (**10**)	אֹזֶן	v. *say, speak; think* (**3**)	אָמַר
n. *brother, male relative* (**3**)	אָח	n. *truth; trustworthiness* (**20**)	אֱמֶת
n. *one* (**17**)	אֶחָד	prn. *we* (1cp) (**13**)	אֲנַחְנוּ
n. *inherited/owned property* (real estate) (**29**)	אֲחֻזָּה	prn. *I* (1cs); also אָנֹכִי (**13**)	אֲנִי
		prn. *I* (1cs); also אֲנִי (**13**)	אָנֹכִי
n. *sister, female relative* (**21**)	אָחוֹת	n. *men, husbands* (**2**)	אֲנָשִׁים
v. *grasp, sieze, hold* (**S5**)	אָחַז	v. *gather, take in* (**9**)	אָסַף
n./adj. *other, another* (**11**)	אַחֵר	v. *bind, tie, imprison* (**S2**)	אָסַר
prp. *behind, after* (**7**)	אַחֲרֵי אַחַר	(I) *even, also; all the more* (cj.) (**6**)	אַף
prp. *after, behind*; adj. *last* (**S8**)	אַחֲרוֹן	n. (II) *nose, nostril; anger* (**6**)	אַף
n. *end, outcome* (**S6**)	אַחֲרִית	n. *end, edge, limit*; אֶפֶס כִּי *but*)	אֶפֶס
Where [*is/are*]? (**S8**)	אַיֵּה אִי	n. *side*; pr. *beside, near* (**S6**)	אֵצֶל
n. *enemy* (m.s. Q Ptc < איב) (**6**)	אֹיֵב	n. *treasure; treasury, storehouse* (pl. אוֹצָרוֹת)	אוֹצָר
How? How! (interrogative & exclamatory); אֵיכָה is the Hebrew title of Lamentations (**S6**)	אֵיכָה אֵיךְ		
		four (**17**)	אַרְבַּע
n. *ram* (**12**)	אַיִל	n. *chest, box; ark* (of the covenant) (**9**)	אֲרוֹן
n. *porch, vestibule* [Ezk]; also אוּלָם (**S10**)	אֵילָם	n. *cedar* (**S3**)	אֶרֶז
		n. *path, way* (**S7**)	אֹרַח
adv. *no, not; There is/was not* (opp. of יֵשׁ); can occur with pronominal suffixes (**16**)	אֵין אַיִן	n. *lion* (**S2**)	אֲרִי
		n. *lion*	אַרְיֵה
		n. *length* (**22**)	אֹרֶךְ

n. *land* (geo-political region), *earth* (as in "heaven and earth") (f.) (**2**)	אֶרֶץ
v. *curse* (**31**)	אָרַר
n. *fire* (**4**)	אֵשׁ
n. *woman, wife* (pl. נָשִׁים) (**2**)	אִשָּׁה
n. *burnt offering, offering by fire* (not אִשָּׁה) (**S5**)	אִשֶּׁה
rel. *who, which, what; that, because, …* (**11**)	אֲשֶׁר
prp. *with*; sign of the direct object (not translated); with suffixes -אֹת or -אֵת (**5**)	אֵת־ אֵת
prn. *you* (2ms) (**13**)	אַתָּה
prn. *you* (2fs) (**13**)	אַתְּ
prn. *you* (2mp) (**13**)	אַתֶּם
prn. *you* (2fp) [4/5x are in Ezekiel] (**13**)	אַתֵּנָה אַתֵּן
prp. *in, by, on, against, …* (**7**)	בְּ-
n. *garment, clothing* (**9**)	בֶּגֶד
prp.+n. *on account of, because of*	בִּגְלַל
v. *divide, separate* (H)	בָּדַל
n. *cistern, well* (hole dug for water) (**S4**)	בּוֹר
st. v. *be/become ashamed* (**28**)	בּוֹשׁ
v. *choose* (often introduces object with בְּ) (**12**)	בָּחַר
v. *trust, be confident in/of* (**21**)	בָּטַח
n. *security*; also as adv., *securely*	בֶּטַח
n. *cattle; animals* (**10**)	בְּהֵמָה
v. *come, go* [*in*], *enter* (**28**)	בּוֹא
n. *belly, abdomen; womb* (**S3**)	בֶּטֶן
before, not yet (טֶרֶם + בְּ) (**S7**)	בְּטֶרֶם
prp. *between* (**7**)	בֵּין
v. *understand, discern* (cf. תְּבוּנָה) (**28**)	בִּין
n. *house, home, household* (pl. בָּתִּים) (**2**)	בַּיִת
v. *weep, mourn, wail* (**25**)	בָּכָה
n. [the] *firstborn* (**20**)	בְּכוֹר
adv. *no, not* (poetic) (**16**)	בַּל
adv. *not* (**S1**)	בְּלִי
prp. *apart from, except for, without* (16x)	בִּלְעֲדֵי
adv. *not*; cj. *except, unless*; us. לְבִלְתִּי or מִבִּלְתִּי (with inf. const.) (**16**)	בִּלְתִּי
n. *cult center* (trad., "high place") (**23**)	בָּמָה
n. *son, male descendant* (cf. בִּנְיָמִין, Benjamin, "son of [my] right hand") (**2**)	בֵּן
v. *build* (**24**)	בָּנָה
n. *daughters* (pl. of בַּת) (**3**)	בָּנוֹת
prp. *on behalf of, about; away from; behind* (**7**)	בְּעַד
n. *master, owner, husband, Baal* (**10**)	בַּעַל
v. *burn, consume* (Q, D) (**21**)	בָּעַר
v. *fortify, reinforced* (4x)	בָּצַר
n. *morning* (**9**)	בֹּקֶר
n. *herd* (large cattle) (**10**)	בָּקָר
prp.+n. *inside, within* (בְּ + קֶרֶב [q.v.]) (**9**)	בְּקֶרֶב
v. *search, seek* (D) (**19**)	בָּקַשׁ
v. *flee, run away* (**S6**)	בָּרַח
n. *knee*	בֶּרֶךְ
v. *kneel* (I: Q); *bless* (II: D) (**19**)	בָּרַךְ
n. *blessing* (**27**)	בְּרָכָה
n. *covenant, treaty, agreement* (**6**)	בְּרִית
v. *split, cleave* (**S8**)	בָּקַע
v. *look for, seek, search* (D) (**19**)	בָּקַשׁ
n. *iron* (**S2**)	בַּרְזֶל
n. *flesh, meat* (**6**)	בָּשָׂר
v. *proclaim, report, announce* (D)	בָּשַׂר
n. *daughter, female descendant* (pl. בָּנוֹת) (**3**)	בַּת
prp.+n. *within, inside* (בְּ + תָּוֶךְ) (**S1**)	בְּתוֹךְ
n. *virgin, young woman* (**S8**)	בְּתוּלָה
n. *houses* (pl. of בַּיִת) (**2**)	בָּתִּים
v. *redeem, purchase as a kinsman-redeemer; redeemer* (Q Ptc.) (**23**)	גָּאַל גֹּאֵל
st. v. *be/become high, exalted* (**23**)	גָּבַהּ
n. *boundary, territory* (**8**)	גְּבוּל
n. *mighty man, warrior* (**12**)	גִּבּוֹר
n. *strength, power* (cf. 147) (**S6**)	גְּבוּרָה
n. *hill*; [cultic] *high place* (**S5**)	גִּבְעָה
st. v. *be strong, mighty; prevail over* (-בְּ, עַל) (24x)	גָּבַר
n. *man* (male) (**S4**)	גֶּבֶר
n. *band, troop(s)*	גְּדוּד
st. v. *be[come] large, great*; adj. *large, big, great* (adj.) (**11**)	גָּדוֹל
n. *greatness*	גְּדֻלָּה
v. *chop/cut off*	גָּדַע

גּוֹי	n. *people* [group], *nation, folk* (**3**)
גּוּר	v. *reside as an alien; immigrate* (trad., *sojourn*) (**28**)
גּוֹרָל	n. *lot; allotment* (what the lot reveals) (**S3**)
גַּל	n. *heap* (*wave*)
גָּלָה	v. *uncover, reveal* [I] (**24**)
גָּלָה	v. *go into captivity/exile* [II] (**24**)
גַּם	adv./cj. *also, even, indeed* (**S1**)
גָּמָל	n. *camel* (**S8**)
גָּנַב	v. *steal*
גַּנָּב	n. *thief*
גְּנֵבָה	n. *stolen thing*
גֶּפֶן	n. *grapevine* (**S7**)
גֵּר	n. *alien; stranger; immigrant* [a non-native] (trad., *sojourner*) (**28**)
גָּרַשׁ	v. *drive away/out* (mainly D)
דָּבַק	v. *cling/stick to* (**S8**)
דבר	v. *speak* (D; in Q only as ptc.) (**19**)
דָּבָר	n. *word, thing; event, affair, matter* (**2**)
דְּבַשׁ	n. *honey* (**S8**)
דָּגָן	n. *grain* (i.e., wheat, spelt, rye, barley)
דּוֹד	n. *love, loved one, beloved* (**S6**)
דּוֹר	n. *generation, life-span* (**12**)
דֶּלֶת	n. *door*[*way*] (**14**)
דָּם	n. *blood* (**8**)
דָּמָה	v. *destroy, cut off*
דַּעַת	n. *knowledge, understanding* (**14**)
דָּרַךְ	v. *walk, step on, tramp; cause to march, tread down, tread* [string] *a bow* (H) (**21**)
דֶּרֶךְ	n. *road, way, path, journey; custom* (f.) (**3**)
דָּרַשׁ	v. *seek, inquire* (cf. מִדְרָשׁ) (**12**)
הַ-	art. *the* (also -הֶ, -הָ) (**4**)
הֲ-	pref. interrogative particle (untranslated) (**S1**)
הֶבֶל	n. *breath, idol; vanity* (**27**)
הוּא	prn. *he* (3ms); dem. *That* (**13**)
הוּא / הִיא	*she* (3fs pers. pron.); *that* (dem.) [the first form occurs primarily in the Torah] (**13**)
הָיָה	*be, become* (often with ל), *happen* (**10**)
הֵיכָל	n. *large building; palace, temple* (usually called בַּיִת) (**S2**)
הֲלֹא	*Is not …?* (לֹא + interrogative -הֲ]) (**13**)
הָלַךְ	v. *come, go, walk, travel* (**3**)
הָלַל	v. *praise, exult in* (D); *boast* (Dt) (**31**)
הֲלֹם	[*to*] *here*
הֵם / הֵנָּה	*they* (3mp pers. pron.); *those* (dem. pron.) (**13**)
הָמוֹן	n. *tumult, uproar; crowd, multitude* (**14**)
הֵן / הֵנָּה	*they* (3fp pers. pron.); *those* (dem. pron.) (**13**)
הִנֵּה	*there is/was, here is/was* (trad., *Behold!*) (**20**)
הָפַךְ	*turn, overturn, destroy; change* (**22**)
הַר	n. *mountain, mountain range, hill country, highlands* (i.e., not level land, valleys) (**13**)
הרג	v. *kill* (**12**)
וּ וְ וָ	*and, but, or, also, even …* (**4**)
זֹאת	*this* (fs dem.) (**13**)
זְבֻל	n. *dwelling* (5x)
זֶבַח	n. *sacrifice* (**12**)
זבח	v. *slaughter; sacrifice* (**14**)
זָהָב	n. *gold* (**8**)
זֶה	*this* (ms dem.) (**13**)
זכר	v. *remember* (**8**)
זָכָר	n. *man* (male); *male being* (animal) (**S2**)
זנה	v. *fornicate, engage in illicit sex* (**25**)
זעק	v. *cry out* [for help], *shout* (cf. צָעַק) (**27**)
זָקֵן	st. v. *be/become old*; adj. *old; elder* (**11**)
זָר	*strange, foreign; illicit* (**27**)
זְרוֹעַ	n. *arm, forearm; strength* (**14**)
זרח	v. *dawn, shine, rise* (cf. מִזְרָח)
זרע	v. *sow, plant* (cf. זֶרַע) (**S7**)
זֶרַע	n. *seed* (sg. & coll.) (**8**)
חֶבֶל	n. *cord; property* (area measured by cord)
חַג	n. *feast, festival; pilgrimage* (cf. hajj—the Muslim's journey to Mecca) (**S6**)
חדל	v. *cease, stop* (with inf. const.); *hold back, withhold* (**S8**)
חָדָשׁ	*new, renewed; fresh* (**S8**)
חֹדֶשׁ	n. *month, new moon* (**6**)
חוֹמָה	n. [*city*] *wall* (**20**)
חוּץ	*outside* (noun & prp.); *street* (**12**)

v. see, observe, gaze [at] (**25**)	חזה	v. dry up	חרב
v. be[come] strong (st. vb.) (**6**)	חזק	st. v. be[come] angry, hot (always 3ms with "subject" indicated by -לְ) (**25**)	חָרָה
adj. strong; hard (**S7**)	חָזָק	v. destroy utterly [as belonging to Yhwh] (trad. devote to the ban) (**S9**)	חרם
v. sin, miss [a mark] (**27**)	חטא	n. disgrace, reproach, embarrassment (**27**)	חֶרְפָּה
n. sin, error, fault; sin-offering (**27**)	חַטָּאת	v. account, regard, value, reckon (**19**)	חשב
adj. living, alive (**19**)	חַי	n. [the] dark; darkness (**S2**)	חֹשֶׁךְ
v. live, be/stay alive (**24**)	חיה	st. v. be shattered, dismayed (**S5**)	חתת
n. animal(s) [coll.] (**22**)	חַיָּה		
n. life, lifetime (always plural) (**19**)	חַיִּים	[ceremonially] clean, pure (**15**)	טָהֹר
n. strength; army; wealth (**8**)	חַיִל	st. v. be/become [ceremonially] clean, pure (**15**)	טָהֵר
v. writhe, tremble; [be in] labour (**28**)	חִיל	adj. good (**11**)	טוֹב
v. wait [for] (D)	חכה	st. v. be[come] good, pleasant (**28**)	טוֹב טוב
adj. wise, skilled (**18**)	חָכָם	st. v. be/become [ceremonially] unclean, impure; adj. unclean, impure (**15**)	טמא
n. wisdom, skill (cf. 243) (**12**)	חָכְמָה		
n. fat (**14**)	חֵלֶב	n. uncleanness, impurity	טֻמְאָה
v. be/become weak, sick, ill (**25**)	חלה	before, not yet (often as בְּטֶרֶם) (**S7**)	טֶרֶם
n. dream (cf. חָלַם) (**S4**)	חֲלוֹם		
adj. wounded, slain, dead (**22**)	חָלָל	v. [II] be determined/pleased; undertake (H; with inf. const.)	יאל
v. be defiled, polluted (N); defile, pollute, stain (D); begin (H) (**S5**)	חלל	n. [large?] river (esp. the *Nile*) (**S5**)	יְאֹר
v. dream (cf. חֲלוֹם) (25x)	חלם	st. v. be[come] dry, dry up (**30**)	יָבֵשׁ
n. share, portion, part (cf. חָלַק) (**S5**)	חֵלֶק	n. dry land (i.e., not the sea; cf. יָבֵשׁ)	יַבָּשָׁה
v. divide, apportion, assign (cf. חֵלֶק) (**S7**)	חלק	n. ram's horn; jubilee [marked by blowing the ram's horn]	יוֹבֵל
n. wrath, anger; heat (**19**)	חֵמָה	n. hand, power, authority (**2**)	יָד
n. male donkey/ass (**22**)	חֲמוֹר	v. thank, praise, acclaim (H); cf. יְהוּדָה (**25**)	ידה
n. violence, wrong, injury (**S6**)	חָמָס		
five (**17**)	חָמֵשׁ	v. know, understand; recognize (**30**)	ידע
n. favor, grace (cf. חָנַן) (**S4**)	חֵן	n. Yhwh (proper name of Israel's god); also *Yah*, יָהּ (**4**)	יהוה
v. camp, encamp (cf. מַחֲנֶה) (**25**)	חנה		
n. javelin, spear (40x)	חֲנִית	n. day; when (e.g., בְּיוֹם + inf. const. constructions); pl. יָמִים) (**2**)	יוֹם
v. be gracious to, compassionate toward, favour; ask for favor, compassion (Dt) (cf. חֵן) (**S5**)	חנן		
		daily, by day, daytime (יוֹם + "adverbial" ending) (**S1**)	יוֹמָם
n. love, loyalty, kindness (trad. "lovingkindness") (**8**)	חֶסֶד	together; simultaneously (adv.) (**20**)	יַחַד יַחְדָּו
pious, godly (32x)	חָסִיד	st. v. be[come] good; cf. טוֹב (**30**)	יטב
st. v. be pleased [with], delight [in] (**14**)	חָפֵץ	n. wine (**16**)	יַיִן
n. arrow(s); pl. חִצִּים (**S7**)	חֵץ	v. dispute (N); correct, rebuke (H) (**30**)	יכח
n. half (**17**)	חֲצִי	st. v. be able [to] (with infinitive construct; Lesson 14) (**15**)	יכל
n. court, enclosure, settlement (**18**)	חָצֵר		
n. ordinance, rule, prescription [sthg. prescribed, required, commanded] (**20**)	חֹק	v. bear, give birth [to], become the mother/ancestress of (of women); become the father/ancestor of (of men) (**S1**)	ילד
n. searching; understanding, comprehending	חֵקֶר		
n.f. sword, dagger, knife (**4**)	חֶרֶב		

n. (male or female) *child* (**14**)	יֶלֶד יַלְדָּה	n. *strength, power* (**14**)	כֹּחַ
n. *sea* (Mediterranean, Gulf of Aqaba, Red Sea); *west* (pl. יָמִים) (**4**)	יָם	cj. *for, because; that; but; since; when, if* (**15**)	כִּי
n. *right* (hand, side); *south* (**16**)	יָמִין	n. *loaf, talent, region* (all ≈ "circular") (**S4**)	כִּכָּר
v. *repeat, do again* (with inf. const.) (H); *add* (**30**)	יסף	n. *all, each, every* (n., *not* an adj.); -כָּל with suffixes (**2**)	כֹּל כָּל
prp. *on account of, for the sake of; because* [*of*] (cj.) (**22**)	יַעַן	v. *cease, finish, end, complete* (often with inf. const.) (**24**)	כלה
v. *counsel, advise*; cf. עֵצָה (**30**)	יעץ	n. *utensil, tool; container* (**5**)	כְּלִי
n. *undergrowth, thicket, woods* (**S7**)	יַעַר	v. *humiliate, trouble*	כלם
adj. *attractive, beautiful* (fem. sg. יָפָה)	יָפֶה	*like, just like; as; when* (adv. & cj.) (**21**)	כְּמוֹ
v. *leave, go out, exit* (**30**)	יצא	*honest, upright, right* (adj.); *thus, so, in this/that way* (adv.) (**11**)	כֵּן
v. *serve/dish out* (food); *pour* (liquid) (**30**)	יצק	n. *wing; hem* (of garment) (**S1**)	כָּנָף
v. *shape, form, mold* (**30**)	יצר	n. *seat, throne* (**16**)	כִּסֵּא
st. v. *fear, be afraid of* (thing or person introduced by אֶת, מִפְּנֵי, מִן) (**15**)	ירא	v. *cover, conceal* (D) (**24**)	כסה
v. *go down, descend* (**5**)	ירד	*foolish, insolent* (often substantive) (**S4**)	כְּסִיל
n. *moon, month*	יָרֵחַ	n. *silver* (**8**)	כֶּסֶף
n. [tent] *fabric/curtain* [Ex] (**S10**)	יְרִיעָה	v. *be angry, furious* (**S8**)	כעס
v. *possess, subdue; dispossess* [someone] (H) (**8**)	ירש	n. *palm of hand, sole of foot* (**10**)	כַּף
there is/are (opposite of אֵין) (**12**)	יֵשׁ	*according to; as, just as* (כְּ + פֶּה); cf. לְפִי (**S4**)	כְּפִי
v. *sit, live* [dwell], *settle, stay, remain* (**3**)	ישב	v. *cover* (Q); *atone* [for] (D) (**19**)	כפר
n. *inhabitant, citizen, dweller* (Q Ptc) (**30**)	יֹשֵׁב	n. *cherub* (probably a winged bull with human head; *not* winged baby!) (**14**)	כְּרוּב
n. *deliverance, salvation; victory*; cf. יֶשַׁע	יְשׁוּעָה	n. *vineyard* (**22**)	כֶּרֶם
v. *save, deliver* (implied: by winning a victory); cf. יְשׁוּעָה (**30**)	ישע	v. *stumble, fall, sway, rock, waver* (**S5**)	כשל
straight, upright; honest (adj.) (**23**)	יָשָׁר	v. *cut, cut off; make a treaty* (**6**)	כרת
v. *remain, be left* [behind/over] (N) (**30**)	יתר	v. *write* (**8**)	כתב
n. *remainder, left-over* (**S4**)	יֶתֶר	n. *shoulder* [blade] (**S4**)	כָּתֵף
		prp. *to, for* (**7**)	לְ-
like, as, according to; approximately (with numbers); *when* (with infinitive construct) (**7**)	כְּ-	adv. *no, not* (**5**)	לֹא
		n. *heart* (the center of the person, often used where English uses "mind") (**2**)	לֵבָב לֵב
as, just as, like; when (כְּ + אֲשֶׁר) (**11**)	כַּאֲשֶׁר	v. *put on, clothe* (oneself); *wear* (**23**)	לבש
st. v. *be/become heavy, severe; wealthy, honored*; adj. *heavy, severe*, etc. (**15**)	כָּבֵד	v. *fight* (N) (**20**)	לחם
n. *glory, honor, wealth* (**9**)	כָּבוֹד	n. *bread, food* (**6**)	לֶחֶם
v. *wash,* [make physically] *clean* (**S9**)	כבס	n. *night* (**8**)	לַיְלָה לֵיל
n. *young sheep: young ram* (m.; also written כֶּסֶב); *ewe-lamb* (f.) (**19**)	כֶּבֶשׂ כִּבְשָׂה	v. *lodge, spend the night* (**28**)	לין
		v. *capture, seize* (**19**)	לכד
in this way/manner, thus, so (**19**)	כֹּה	*therefore* (לְ + כֵּן; cj); not usually volitional); *for the sake of, on account of* (prp.); *in order that/to* (cj.) (**18**)	לָכֵן
n. *priest* (**2**)	כֹּהֵן		
v. *be established, fixed* (in place) (Q); *prepare* (H) (**28**)	כון	v. *learn* (Q); *teach* (D) (**19**)	למד

Appendix B

why? (also לָמָה) (S1)	לָמָּה
in order that, so that (18)	לְמַעַן
according to; as, just as (לְ + פֶּה); cf. כְּפִי (S4)	לְפִי
before (temporal & locative), in the presence of, in front of (לְ + פָּנִים) (11)	לִפְנֵי
v. take, get, acquire; buy; marry (4)	לָקַח
[prp.] toward, against, opposite (Q inf. const. + לְ) (21)	לִקְרַאת
n. tongue, language (23)	לָשׁוֹן
very, exceedingly (adv.); power, might (n.) (18)	מְאֹד
num. hundred (17)	מֵאָה
then, at that time; formerly; since (אָז + מִן) (20)	מֵאָז
v. refuse (D)	מאן
v. reject, refuse (23)	מאס
n. anything	מְאוּמָה
n. light [-source] (pl. מְאֹרֵי & מְאֹרוֹת)	מָאוֹר
prp. from (אֵת [with] + מִן)	מֵאֵת
num. two hundred; cf. מֵאָה (17)	מָאתַיִם
n. entrance; west (of the sun)	מָבוֹא
n. flood (only in Gn 6–11 and Ps 29.10)	מַבּוּל
n. shield (S5)	מָגֵן
n. pasture, uncultivated land; produce (S10)	מִגְרָשׁ
n. wilderness (uncultivated or "unclaimed" land) (6)	מִדְבָּר
v. measure; cf. מִדָּה (31)	מדד
n. measure; cf. מַדַּד (S9)	מִדָּה
Why? (27)	מַדּוּעַ
What? How? (also מַה־, מֶה־) (13)	מָה
v. hasten, act quickly (D) [often in adverbial hendiadys] (19)	מהר
v. move, totter, slip [metonymy for death or destruction]	מוט
n. correction, discipline, instruction (S9)	מוּסָר
n. something appointed (place, time); season (8)	מוֹעֵד
v. die, be[come] dead; cf. מָת (28)	מות
n. death; מוֹת ≈ death of (12)	מָוֶת
n. altar (4)	מִזְבֵּחַ
n. psalm (this transliterates LX) [Ps only] (S10)	מִזְמוֹר
n. sunrise; east (27)	מִזְרָח
n. camp, army (9)	מַחֲנֶה

n. tomorrow (S9)	מָחָר
n. thought, intention, plan; cf. חָשַׁב (S7)	מַחְשָׁבָה
m.n. rod, staff (sign of office); tribe (10)	מַטֶּה
n. rain	מָטָר
Who? (13)	מִי
n. waters of (const. of מַיִם) (4)	מֵי
n. water (4)	מַיִם
v. sell (22)	מכר
st. v. be/become full; adj. full (15)	מָלֵא
n. messenger (cf. מַלְאָכִי, Malachi, "my messenger") (9)	מַלְאָךְ
n. work, occupation (12)	מְלָאכָה
n. war, battle (5)	מִלְחָמָה
v. escape (N); rescue, deliver (D) (20)	מלט
v. reign, rule (as monarch, king), be king (5)	מלך
n. king, monarch (2)	מֶלֶךְ
n. kingdom, realm; kingship, dominion, royal power/authority; cf. מֶלֶךְ (23)	מַלְכוּת
n. kingdom, realm; kingship, dominion, royal power/authority; cf. מֶלֶךְ (23)	מַמְלָכָה
prp. from; than … (מִן + prn. suffix) (7)	מִמֶּנּ-
prp. from, out of; some of; than (7)	מִן
n. flight (cf. נוּס)	מָנוֹס
n. gift, offering, tribute (7)	מִנְחָה
n. choir leader, conductor(?) [Ps] (S10)	מְנַצֵּחַ
n. number, total; cf. סָפַר (16)	מִסְפָּר
n. path, track	מַעְגָּל
adj. [a] few, little (15)	מְעַט
prp. above (usually מִמַּעַל); higher (adv., usually מַעְלָה) (19)	מַעַל
m.n. work, deed, thing done; cf. עָשָׂה (8)	מַעֲשֶׂה
n. key(?); sthg. used to open (3x)	מַפְתֵּחַ
v. find (18)	מצא
n. standing stone, monolith	מַצֵּבָה
n. unleavened bread (S9)	מַצָּה
n. command[ment], order; cf. צָוָה (10)	מִצְוָה
n. sanctuary, holy place; cf. קָדַשׁ (27)	מִקְדָּשׁ
n. place (5)	מָקוֹם
n. property, possession(s); cf. קָנָה (S3)	מִקְנֶה
adj. bitter (cf. Marah)	מַר
sight, appearance; cf. רָאָה (22)	מַרְאֶה
n. spy (D Ptc; see רגל)	מְרַגֵּל
n. height; cf. רוּם (S9)	מָרוֹם

n. *open place* (cf. רחב)	מֶרְחָב	v. *stretch out; turn* (**24**)	נטה
n. *pasture, shepherding; pasturage*	מַרְעִית	v. *plant* (**26**)	נטע
n. *oracle; burden* (us. prophetic speech)	מַשָּׂא	v. *hit, wound, defeat* (H) (**24**)	נכה
n. *breaker* (i.e., wave)	מִשְׁבָּר	v. *pretend* (N); *recognize* (H) (**26**)	נכר
v. *anoint* (**S4**)	משח	n. *foreigner*	נָכְרִי
v. *draw, pull* [out]	משך	v. *depart, break camp, travel* (**26**)	נסע
n. *dwelling; Tabernacle* (**6**)	מִשְׁכָּן	n. *young man* (upper class) (**9**)	נַעַר
v. *rule, reign* (does not imply kingship; cf. מָלַךְ) (**5**)	משל	n. *young, girl, maid* (**S5**)	נַעֲרָה
n. *rule, reign, dominion*	מָשָׁל	v. *pour* [out] (as a drink offering) (**S6**)	נסך
n. *guard; obligation, duty*; cf. שָׁמַר (**S3**)	מִשְׁמֶרֶת	n. *drink offering, libation* (wine poured/offered to a god) (**S6**)	נֶסֶךְ
n. *clan, extended family* (smaller than a tribe) (**6**)	מִשְׁפָּחָה	v. *fall* (**26**)	נפל
n. *judgment, justice; justly; custom*; cf. שָׁפַט (**4**)	מִשְׁפָּט	n. *life, self* (f.); trad., *soul* (**2**)	נֶפֶשׁ
adj. *dead*; cf. מות (**27**)	מֵת	v. *take one's stand/place; be assigned* (N) (**26**)	נצב
		v. *lead* (D) (**26**)	נצח
		v. *rescue, deliver; snatch* (H) (**26**)	נצל
untranslatable particle indicating volition (trad. "please") (**8**)	נָא	v. *watch, guard, keep, protect* (**26**)	נצר
n. *declaration, utterance* (**S1**)	נְאֻם	v. *lift, carry; forgive* (**26**)	נשא
v. *prophesy* (N); cf. נָבִיא (**26**)	נבא	v. *reach, overtake* (H) (**27**)	נשג
v. *look at, pay attention to* (H) (**26**)	נבט	n. *leader, member of ruling class* (**21**)	נָשִׂיא
n. *prophet*; cf. נָבָא (**9**)	נָבִיא	n. *piece* [of a cut-up carcass] (11/12x = pl.)	נֵתַח
n. *south, Negev* (**22**)	נֶגֶב	n. *women, wives* (pl. of אִשָּׁה) (**2**)	נָשִׁים
v. *report, declare, announce* (**26**)	נגד	n. *path, way*	נָתִיב
prp. *in front of, before, opposite* (**16**)	נֶגֶד	v. *give; put, set; make* (sthg. into …) (**26**)	נתן
v. *shine* (not a III-ה verb)	נגה		
n. *leader*	נָגִיד	v. *surround, go around; encircle; turn around* (**31**)	סבב
v. *touch; reach, come to* (**26**)	נגע	adv. *surrounding,* [all] *around* (**21**)	סָבִיב מִסָּבִיב
n. *blow, assault; plague* (**26**)	נֶגַע	v. *close, shut* (Q); *give into someone's power* (H) (**21**)	סגר
v. *come near, approach* (**26**)	נגש	n. *horse, stallion* (m.), *mare* (f.) (**11**)	סוּסָה סוּס
v. *be scattered* (**26**)	נדח		
v. [to] *vow; swear an oath/a vow* (**S6**)	נדר	v. *turn* (aside); *remove* (H) (**28**)	סור
n. *vow, oath* (also נֵדֶר) (**S6**)	נֶדֶר	mng. unknown [Pss]; trad., *Selah* (**S10**)	סלה
n. [permanent] *river*; הַנָּהָר refers to Euphrates (rarely נְהַר פְּרָת) (**23**)	נָהָר	n. *rock, crag, cliff* (**S7**)	סֶלַע
v. *rest* (Q); *deposit* (H) (**23**)	נוח	n. *fine wheat flour* [Lv, Nu] (**S10**)	סֹלֶת
v. *flee* (**28**)	נוס	v. *lean on; support*	סמך
n. *wadi* (temporary stream *or* its valley) (**11**)	נַחַל	v. *count, number; tell* [recount]; *record* (**12**)	ספר
v. *inherit, obtain* (**S6**)	נחל	n. *scribe, writer, secretary; recorder* (ms Q Ptc of סָפַר) (**12**)	סֹפֵר
n. *inheritance, property* (**9**)	נַחֲלָה	n. *scroll, document* (trad., "book") (**10**)	סֵפֶר
v. *relent, be sorry, rue* (N); *comfort, console* (D) (**20**)	נחם	v. *hide, conceal* [oneself] (N, Dt); *be hidden/concealed* (N); *hide* [someone] (H) (**20**)	סתר
n. *snake*	נָחָשׁ		
n. *copper, bronze* (**11**)	נְחֹשֶׁת		

Appendix B

v. *serve* (cf. עֲבוֹדָה; עָבַד) (**6**)	עבד
n. *servant, slave*; cf. עָבַד (**2**)	עֶבֶד
n. *service, servitude, labour, work* (**11**)	עֲבוֹדָה
v. *cross over, pass through/by* (**4**)	עבר
n. *other side; region beyond* [sthg.] (**14**)	עֵבֶר
n. *Hebrew* (gentilic); *Eber* (proper name)	עִבְרִי
n. *calf*	עֵגֶל
n. *cart, wagon, chariot*	עֲגָלָה
n. *age* (duration of time)	עַד
prp./adv. *to, as far as; until, while* (**7**)	עַד
n. *witness* (**27**)	עֵד עֵדָה
n. *testimony, command, precept* (of divine law) (**S2**)	עֵדָה
n. *assembly* (trad. "congregation") (**16**)	עֵדוּת עֵדָה
adv. *still, yet, again* (**18**)	עוֹד
n. *long/remote time; ages past* (trad. "forever") (**4**)	עוֹלָם
n. *guilt, trespass, sin* (**4**)	עָוֹן
n. *bird, insect* [any flying thing]; collective (**27**)	עוֹף
v. *awake, arouse* (**28**)	עוּר
n. *skin, leather* (**22**)	עוֹר
n. *goat; goat hair* (**29**)	עֵז
n. *power, strength* (**14**)	עֹז עַז
v. *leave, forsake, abandon* (**7**)	עזב
v. *help, assist* (**S2**)	עזר
n. *eye; water-source, well* (cf. עֵין־גֶּדִי, En-gedi, "the well of the kid") (**3**)	עַיִן
n. *city* (f.); pl. עָרִים (**2**)	עִיר
prp. *on, upon, over; against; concerning* (**7**)	עַל
v. *go up, ascend* (**24**)	עלה
n. [whole] *burnt offering* (**18**)	עֹלָה
v. *exult, rejoice* (cf. עָלִיז)	עלז
adj.? *highest* (trad. *Most High*); *upper* (**S7**)	עֶלְיוֹן
prp. *with* (**7**)	עִם
n. *people* [group], *nation* (**10**)	עַם
v. *stand; stop* (**4**)	עמד
n. *pillar, column*; cf. עָמַד (**21**)	עַמּוּד
n. *distress, trouble; labour* (**S7**)	עָמָל
n. *valley, lowland* (**S3**)	עֵמֶק
v. *answer* (I) (**24**)	ענה
st. v. *be humbled, afflicted; humble, afflict* (D) (II) (**24**)	ענה
n. *afflicted, poor, humble*; cf. עָנָה (II) (**S3**)	עָנִי
n. *cloud*(s) (**22**)	עָנָן
n. *dust, dirt, soil* (**23**)	עָפָר
n. *tree* (sg. & coll.), *wood* (**5**)	עֵץ
n. *idol* (only pl.)	עֲצַבִּים
n. *advice, counsel*; cf. יָעַץ (**30**)	עֵצָה
n. *bone; essence* (i.e., the inmost part) (**23**)	עֶצֶם
v. *be closed, shut; restrain* (N) (**2**)	עצר
n. *evening* (**6**)	עֶרֶב
n. *plain, desert* (often of Jordan plain/valley & wilderness of Judah) (**S6**)	עֲרָבָה
n. *nakedness, weakness* [Lv, Nu] (**S10**)	עֶרְוָה
n. *cities*; pl. of עִיר (**2**)	עָרִים
v. *arrange, set in order* (**S3**)	ערך
n. [back of] *neck*	עֹרֶף
v. *do, make; act* (**24**)	עשה
ten (**17**)	עָשָׂר עֶשֶׂר
twenty (**17**)	עֶשְׂרִים
n. *time* (i.e., a particular moment) (**6**)	עֵת
now; וְעַתָּה ≈ *therefore* (us.), followed by a volitional form (**18**)	עַתָּה
n. *corner, rim, side* (**S10**)	פֵּאָה
v. *ransom, buy* (back) (**25**)	פדה
here, in this place (**S4**)	פֹּה פֹא פּוֹ
n. *mouth* (const. פִּי) (**11**)	פֶּה
v. *scatter, disperse* (instrans.) (**28**)	פוץ
n. *mouth of* (cf. פֶּה) (**11**)	פִּי
st. v. *be wonderful, amazing, miraculous* (**29**)	פלא
v. *pray* (Dt); cf. תְּפִלָּה (**31**)	פלל
so that not (i.e., פֶּן is a negative telic particle, trad., "lest") (**19**)	פֶּן־
v. *turn* (**25**)	פנה
n. *face, presence* (alw. pl.) (**3**)	פָּנִים
v. *do, make* (**S9**)	פעל
n. *foot, step; time* (i.e., once, three times); *twice* (dual) (**22**)	פַּעַם פַּעֲמַיִם
v. *do something* [good or bad] *for/to* [someone]; trad. "visit" (**6**)	פקד
n. *bull*; פָּרָה *cow* (fem.; 22x) (**20**)	פַּר
v. *be fruitful, produce fruit*; cf. פְּרִי	פרה
n. *fruit; descendants* (**23**)	פְּרִי
v. *break through, burst out* (cf. Perez) (**S9**)	פרץ

v. break/tear off (D)	פרק	n. voice, sound (5)	קוֹל
v. break out, burst forth (H) (31)	פרר	v. rise, stand (29)	קוּם
v. spread out (S4)	פרשׂ	st. v. be[come] small, insignificant; adj. small, insignificant (30)	קָטוֹן
n. horseman (coll.); horse (S8)	פָּרָשׁ	v. cause a sacrifice or incense to smoke (D, H) (21)	קטר
n. rebellion, revolt; transgression (14)	פֶּשַׁע	n. incense; smoke (from incense) (S7)	קְטֹרֶת
v. open (16)	פתח	v. vomit, spit up/out	קיא
n. opening, entrance (12)	פֶּתַח	n. wall, city (cf. Carthage < קִיר חָדָשׁ, "new city") (129)	קִיר
n. flock (sheep, goats) (6)	צֹאן	adj. swift, light	קַל
n. army, host; military duty (4)	צָבָא	st. v. be[come] light, swift; slight, trifling, accursed (31)	קלל
adj. innocent, just; righteous (7)	צַדִּיק	n. reed (for measuring); cf. canon (S8)	קָנֶה
st. v. be[come] innocent, righteous, just; justify, declare innocent, etc. (H)	צדק	v. acquire, get, buy; cf. מִקְנֶה (25)	קנה
n. that which is right, just, innocent; righteousness (7)	צֶדֶק	n. end; limit, boundary (S5)	קֵץ
n. innocence, righteousness (16)	צְדָקָה	n. end, edge; border (S2)	קָצֶה
n. noon, mid-day	צָהֳרַיִם	v. break, shatter (D)	קצץ
v. command, order (D); cf. מִצְוָה (24)	צוה	v. call, invite, summon; name; read; proclaim (15)	קרא
n. cliff, crag, outcropping; rock (S2)	צוּר	v. meet, encounter (cf. לִקְרַאת as qal NC: to meet); happen, occur (21)	קרא
n. shadow, shade (S8)	צֵל	v. approach, come near; offer (H); קָרְבָּן (6)	קרב
v. succeed, prosper; be effective/strong (S5)	צלח	n. inward part (9)	קֶרֶב
n. piece (trad. "rib")	צֵלָע	n. offering, gift; cf. Mk 7.11; קָרַב (H) (S2)	קָרְבָּן
v. cry out [for help], shout (≈ צעק) (27)	צעק	adj. near, close; cf. קָרַב (15)	קָרוֹב
n. north (16)	צָפוֹן	n. horn (oft. as symbol of strength) (S3)	קֶרֶן
n. enemy, foe (31)	צַר	v. tear (esp. clothing) (S8)	קרע
n. distress, confinement (31)	צָרָה	n. plank, board, beam [Ex] (S10)	קֶרֶשׁ
v. confine, constrain, wrap up; be hostile (31)	צרר	n. bow (weapon); rainbow (S3)	קֶשֶׁת
v. gather, assemble (21)	קבץ	v. see (24)	ראה
v. bury; lay in tomb/grave (see קֶבֶר) (S3)	קבר	n. head; peak, top (of a hill or mountain) (4)	רֹאשׁ
n. tomb, grave (rock-hewn, rarely dug) (S4)	קֶבֶר	first (ord.) (17)	רִאשׁוֹן
holy (11)	קָדוֹשׁ	n. first; beginning (17)	רֵאשִׁית
n. east (S10)	קָדִים	v. increase, multiply (24)	רבה
v. precede, go in front of (D)	קדם	n. abundance, multitude, great quantity (16)	רֹב
in front, east; eastward; also קֵדְמָה (14)	קֶדֶם	much, many (adj.) (11)	רַב
st. v. be/become holy; restricted in use (15)	קדשׁ	n. foot, leg; [male] genitals (9)	רֶגֶל
adj./n. holy (11)	קֹדֶשׁ	v. spy (D; cf. מְרַגֵּל)	רגל
n. [national] assembly (prob. males over 20 years old); trad. "congregation" (S4)	קָהָל	v. chase, persecute, pursue (16)	רדף
v. I wait for (D)	קוה	n. breath, wind, spirit (5)	רוּחַ
v. II be gathered, collect (N) (3x)	קוה	st. v. be[come] high, exalted (29)	רום

Appendix B

v. *run* (**29**)	רוּץ	n. *Sheol* (**S5**)	שְׁאוֹל
n. *womb, belly, abdomen*	רֶחֶם	v. *ask* [for], *request* (**12**)	שָׁאַל
v. *wash* (oneself) (**29**)	רָחַץ	v. *remain, be left over* (N); *spare, leave* (H) (**19**)	שָׁאַר
st. v. *be/become far, remote, distant* (**15**)	רחק	n. *remainder, what is left* (**S3**)	שְׁאֵרִית
far, remote, distant (adj.) (**15**)	רָחֹק	n. *rod, staff; tribe* (**10**)	שֵׁבֶט
v. *sue, strive, contend* (**28**)	רִיב	v. *swear* [an oath] (N) (**10**)	שָׁבַע
n. [law]*suit, strife, contention* (**28**)	רִיב	*seven* (**17**)	שֶׁבַע
n. *smell, odor, scent* (**S9**)	רֵיחַ	v. *break, smash* (Q, D) (**16**)	שָׁבַר
v. *ride* (**S3**)	רכב	v. *cease, stop* [doing sthg.]; *rest* (**29**)	שׁבת
n. *chariot(s); chariot force;* cf. מֶרְכָּבָה; רֶכֶב (**S3**)	רֶכֶב	n. *rest, sabbath* (**22**)	שַׁבָּת
n. *creeping animal/reptile*	רֶמֶשׂ	v. *devastate, lay waste* (**31**)	שׁדד
v. *shout* (in joy, triumph, celebration) (**31**)	רנן	n. *worthlessness, in vain, to no purpose* (**S9**)	שָׁוְא
adj. *bad, disastrous; evil, wicked;* cf. רָעַע (**11**)	רַע	v. *turn* (back), *return, repent* (**29**)	שׁוּב
n. *friend, companion* (**10**)	רֵעַ	n. *ram's horn* ("*trumpet*") (**29**)	שׁוֹפָר
n. *hunger, famine* (**21**)	רָעָב	n. *bull, young bull; steer* (**14**)	שׁוֹר
v. *feed, graze, tend; herd* (**24**)	רעה	v. *do obeisance* [only Dt, with metathesis and final וְ־: (הִשְׁתַּחֲוָה) (**27**)	שׁחה
n. *shepherd* (Q Ptc) (**18**)	רֹעֶה	v. *slaughter, kill* (**S2**)	שׁחט
st. v. *be/become bad, evil, wicked* (**31**)	רעע	v. *be ruined, corrupt* (N); *ruin, spoil* (D); *destroy* (H) (**20**)	שׁחת
v. *heal* (**S4**)	רפא	v. *sing, chant* (**29**)	שִׁיר
v. *be pleased with, like;* cf. רָצוֹן (**25**)	רצה	n. *song, chant* (**29**)	שִׁיר
n. *pleasure, favour;* cf. רָצָה (**25**)	רָצוֹן	v. *put, place, set* (≈ שִׂים) (**29**)	שׁית
only, surely (often begins clause) (**27**)	רַק	v. *lie down, sleep* (with), *have sexual relations with* (**7**)	שׁכב
bad, disastrous, evil, wicked (adj.) (**11**)	רָשָׁע	v. *forget* (**22**)	שׁכח
		v. *rise early* (H; often in hendiadys: "do X early") (**21**)	שׁכם
v. *be satisfied, satiated* (**14**)	שׂבע	n. *shoulder; Shechem*	שְׁכֶם
n. *cultivated ground* (trad. "field"); contrast מִדְבָּר (**5**)	שָׂדֶה	n. *peace, health, welfare* (**29**)	שָׁלוֹם
v. *put, place, set* (≈ שִׁית) (**29**)	שִׂים	v. *stretch out, reach; let go, send* (away) (**3**)	שׁלח
v. *succeed, prosper; understand* (H) (cf. שֶׂכֶל) (**S3**)	שׂכל	n. *table* (**S3**)	שֻׁלְחָן
n. *success, prosperity, well-being; prudence* (cf. שׂכל)	שֵׂכֶל	v. *throw, cast, hurl* (H) (**21**)	שׁלך
v. *rejoice, be glad* (**16**)	שׂמח	n. *plunder, booty, spoil* (**S3**)	שָׁלָל
n. *joy, rejoicing, gladness* (**18**)	שִׂמְחָה	n. *fellowship offering* (trad., *peace offering*) (**S8**)	שֶׁלֶם
n. *left* [side/hand] (**S9**)	שְׂמֹאל	st/ v. *be/become whole, complete;* [re]*pay* (D) (**15**)	שָׁלֵם
v. *hate* (**16**)	שׂנא	*three* (**17**)	שָׁלֹשׁ
v. *bristle* [with horror] (4x)	שׂער	n. *name; fame, reputation* (**3**)	שֵׁם
n. *lip, language; edge, shore* (**10**)	שָׂפָה	*there, in that place* (**S1**)	שָׁם
n. *official, leader, ruler* (**5**)	שַׂר	v. *be destroyed, exterminated* (N); *destroy, exterminate* (H) (**20**)	שׁמד
v. *burn* (oft. specified with בָּאֵשׁ) (**21**)	שׂרף		
who, which, what (with dageš forte in the following consonant); = אֲשֶׁר (**23**)	־שֶׁ		

eight (**17**)	שְׁמוֹנֶה
n. *report; rumor* (sthg. heard)	שְׁמוּעָה
n. *heaven(s), sky* (**5**)	שָׁמַיִם
st. v. *be[come] astounded, astonished, dumfounded; desolate* (**31**)	שמם
n. *desolation, devastation; horror* (**S9**)	שְׁמָמָה
n. *[olive] oil* (**12**)	שֶׁמֶן
v. *hear, listen, obey* (**3**)	שמע
v. *watch, guard, protect* (**5**)	שמר
n. *sun* (**18**)	שֶׁמֶשׁ
n. *tooth; crag, outcropping* (**S9**)	שֵׁן
n. *year* (cf. רֹאשׁ הַשָּׁנָה) (**3**)	שָׁנָה
second (ord.) (**18**)	שֵׁנִי
two; שְׁנֵי *both* (const.) (**17**)	שְׁנַיִם
n. *gate* (of a city) (**11**)	שַׁעַר
n. *female slave/servant* (**2S4**)	שִׁפְחָה
v. *judge* (**10**)	שפט
n. *judge* (Q Ptc) (**18**)	שֹׁפֵט
v. *pour [out]; shed [blood]* (**23**)	שפך
v. *water, give a drink [to]* (H) (**25**)	שקה
n. *shekel* (approx. 11.4g, 0.5 oz.) (**17**)	שֶׁקֶל
n. *lie, falsehood; deception* (**23**)	שֶׁקֶר
v. *serve, minister to* (D) (**19**)	שרת
six (**17**)	שֵׁשׁ
v. *drink* (**24**)	שתה
num. *two* (f.) (**17**)	שְׁתַּיִם
n. *insight, understanding, realization* (cf. בִּין)	תְּבוּנָה
n. *praise, glory;* cf. הָלַל (**31**)	תְּהִלָּה
n. *thanks[giving]*	תּוֹדָה
n. *area inside something else* (cf. בְּתוֹךְ) (**S1**)	תּוֹךְ
n. *abomination; something horrific* (**23**)	תּוֹעֵבָה
n. *teaching, instruction; law* (trad., "law") (**9**)	תּוֹרָה
under, beneath; instead of, in [the] place of (**7**)	תַּחַת
n. *[new] wine*	תִּירוֹשׁ
[adv.] *regularly, continually, always;* a noun ending a construct chain, referring to sthg. that is repeated, continual, or regular (e.g., עֹלָה תָּמִיד *perpetual offering*) (**22**)	תָּמִיד
whole, blameless, entire (**S5**)	תָּמִים
st. v. *be complete, have integrity* (st. vb.) (**S5**)	תמם
v. *wander, be lost* (**25**)	תעה
n. *ornament, decoration* (**S1**)	תִּפְאֶרֶת
n. *prayer;* cf. פָּלַל (**31**)	תְּפִלָּה
v. *seize, take hold of* (in order to use) (**31**)	תפש
v. *drive, thrust* (a weapon); *blow* (a horn) (**S7**)	תקע
n. *tribute; [heave-] offering* (**S1**)	תְּרוּמָה
num. *nine* (**17**)	תֵּשַׁע

The *Most Common "Proper" Nouns*

This lists all personal, national, gentilic, and locational names that occur fifty times or more in Biblical Hebrew, in alphabetical order. The numeral with "x" in parentheses after the name is the number of occurrences.

Abimelech (67x)	אֲבִימֶלֶךְ	Elisha (58x)	אֱלִישָׁע
Abner (63x)	אַבְנֵר	Eleazar (72x)	אֶלְעָזָר
Abram, Abraham (235x)	אַבְרָם אַבְרָהָם	Amorite(sx) (86x)	אֱמֹרִי
		Asa (58x)	אָסָא
Absalom (107x)	אַבְשָׁלוֹם	Esther (55x)	אֶסְתֵּר
Edom (112x)	אֱדוֹם	Ephraim (182x)	אֶפְרַיִם
Aaron (347x)	אַהֲרֹן	Aram ("Syria"; 155x)	אֲרָם
Ahab (93x)	אַחְאָב	Assyria (152x)	אַשּׁוּר
Job (58x)	אִיּוֹב	Babylon (288x)	בָּבֶל
Elijah (71x)	אֵלִיָּה אֵלִיָּהוּ	Benjamin (180x)	בִּנְיָמִן
		Balaam (64x)	בִּלְעָם

Appendix B

Bashan (60x)	בָּשָׁן	Chaldea [Mesopotamia] (89x)	כַּשְׂדִּים
Gad (85x)	גָּד	Laban (54x)	לָבָן
Gilead (108x)	גִּלְעָד	Lebanon (71x)	לְבָנוֹן
David (1031x)	דָּוִד	Levi (353x)	לֵוִי
Dan (78x)	דָּן	Midian (67x)	מִדְיָן
Haman (54x)	הָמָן	Moab (199x)	מוֹאָב
Hezekiah (131x)	חִזְקִיָּה	Micah (3 spellings; 63x)	מִיכָה
Heth; Hittite (62x)	חֵת חִתִּי	Manasseh (150x)	מְנַשֶּׁה
Hebron (77x)	חֶבְרוֹן	Egypt (708x)	מִצְרַיִם
Josiah (51x)	יֹאשִׁיָּה	Mordecai (60x)	מָרְדֳּכַי
Jehu (58x)	יֵהוּא	Moses (763x)	מֹשֶׁה
Judah (889x)	יְהוּדָה	Nebuchadnezzar (5 spellings; 91x)	נְבוּכַדְנֶאצַּר
Jehoiada (56x)	יְהוֹיָדָע	Naphtali (50x)	נַפְתָּלִי
Jonathan (124x)	יְהוֹנָתָן	Ammon (122x)	עַמּוֹן
Joshua (247x)	יְהוֹשֻׁעַ	Amalek (51x)	עֲמָלֵק
Jehoshaphat (86x)	יְהוֹשָׁפָט	Esau (96x)	עֵשָׂו
Joab (146x)	יוֹאָב	Philistine (294x)	פְּלִשְׁתִּי
Joash (64x)	יוֹאָשׁ	Pharaoh (273x)	פַּרְעֹה
Joseph (214x)	יוֹסֵף	Zadok (53x)	צָדוֹק
Jacob (348x)	יַעֲקֹב	Zedekiah (2 spellings; 63x)	צִדְקִיָּה
Isaac (112x)	יִצְחָק	Zion (154x)	צִיּוֹן
Jeroboam (104x)	יָרְבְעָם	Reuben (87x)	רְאוּבֵן
Jordan (181x)	יַרְדֵּן	Rehoboam (50x)	רְחַבְעָם
Jerusalem (667x)	יְרוּשָׁלַםִ	Sarai; Sarah (53x)	שָׂרָה שָׂרַי
Jericho (57x)	יְרִחוֹ	Saul (406x)	שָׁאוּל
Jeremiah (147x)	יִרְמְיָה	Shechem (64x)	שְׁכֶם
Israel (person, nation; 2513x)	יִשְׂרָאֵל	Solomon (293x)	שְׁלֹמֹה
Ishmael (56x)	יִשְׁמָעֵאל	Samuel (139x)	שְׁמוּאֵל
Cush [Ethiopia] (54x)	כּוּשׁ	Samaria (112x)	שֹׁמְרוֹן
Canaan (163x)	כְּנַעַן		

Appendix C

Glossary of Morphosyntactical Terms

The numeral in parentheses (6) indicates the lesson in which the term is introduced.

absolute	a word or phrase that is not "connected" to the rest of a sentence; i.e., not dependent on anything else (9)
accent(s)	mark(s) in the text that indicate the accented [tone] syllable of a word, as well as its logical relationship to the following word (27)
accusative	the supposed original function of the LOCATIVE ה- (7)
acrostic	a poem or text in which each line or group of lines begins with the next letter of the Hebrew alphabet; e.g., Pss 111, 112, 119; La 1-4 (1)
active	another term for FIENTIVE (12)
adjectival/adjective	any word used to modify another (9, 11)
Adonai	"lord/master/Lord"; the vowels of this word were combined with the TETRAGRAMMATON, producing the form יְהֹוָה, misinterpreted as "Jehovah" (3)
affix	any morphological unit attached directly to another (e.g., the ARTICLE), so that a WORD can be made up of as many as five ELEMENTS—a base or root, plus four affixes (4)
alphabet	the collection of symbols, usually in a static [traditional] order, that are used to represent a language visually (1)
anaptyctic	a phonetic element (vowel or syllable) added to a word, either to aid in pronouncing it, or to make it more like other forms (31)
anarthrous	lacking the article (4)
antecedent	the word (usually a noun or other SUBSTANTIVE) to which a PRONOUN refers (10)
apposition/apposed	a noun or noun phrase placed next to another noun or noun phrase in order to modify or define it; e.g., *David the king* (11)
article	a prefixed -ה with *dageš forte* in the first letter of the word (4)
articular	having the article (4)
ascender	a portion of a letter that projects above the basic shape of other letters; ל is the only letter with an ascender in Biblical Hebrew (1)
assimilation	the process of one thing—in phonetics, one sound—becoming like another; assimilation may be partial or complete (7)
attribution	to assign a quality or characteristic to something, to describe it (9)
bilabial	a sound made with both lips: /b/, /m/ (4)
cardinal numeral	the numerals used in all numerical descriptions exception descriptions of order or sequence; see ORDINAL (17)
causative	an activity in which the subject causes an object to do something (which may be a second object; see DOUBLY TRANSITIVE) (20)
circumstantial clause	a clause that identifies the temporal (usually) or locative (rarely) circumstances in which an event occurs (16)
clause	a syntagm with at least two main components: a topic (subject) and comment (predicate) (11)
closed syllable	a syllable that ends in a consonant; if unaccented, with a short vowel (3)
coalesce	to merge, or join (31)

cohortative	a first-person VOLITIONAL verbal form; in Biblical Hebrew usually indicating determination or desire; sometimes indicated by suffixed הָ - (8)
command	see IMPERATIVE (8)
comment	a clause's PREDICATE; what the clause says *about* its TOPIC (11)
complementary	a function of the INFINITIVE CONSTRUCT, in which it "completes" a VAGUE VERB (e.g., יכל, חדל, כלה)
compound form(s)	a "word" with more than one ELEMENT, such as preposition+lexeme+suffix (4)
conjugation	a pattern of verbal formation that designates or identifies the verb's function; the major conjugations in Biblical Hebrew are the imperfect, preterite, and perfect (5)
conjunction	a word or element that links or joins two or more words, phrases, or clauses (4)
conjunctive accent	a masoretic accent that joins a word to the following; the main conjunctive accent is munahi (27)
consonant	letters that represent the non-vocalic "sounds" of the language (1)
construct (chain)	an uninterrupted series of substantives in which each defines or modifies the preceding word by the "of" relationship (9)
content	the function and semantics of any distinguishable segment of text (word, phrase, etc.) (10)
context	the entire setting of an UTTERANCE, including, e.g., its historical circumstance, culture, language (10)
cotext	the *linguistic* material surrounding a [portion of an] UTTERANCE (10)
dageš forte	a *dot* in the "bosom" of a letter, showing that the letter is doubled [i.e., to be read twice]; does not occur in the GUTTURALS or *reš* (3)
dageš lene	a *dot* in the "bosom" of ב, ג, ד, כ, פ, ת to indicate a different pronounciation (3)
defective spelling	see ḤASER SPELLING (2)
definiteness	the quality of specificity, with or without the article (14)
demonstrative	a DEICTIC form or expression that, specifying something by "pointing to" it, depends heavily on the context for its function (13)
denominative	a verb that supposedly derived from a noun; i.e., the root first occurred as a noun, and then as a verb; e.g., דבר (*word* → *say/speak*) (19)
descender	a portion of a letter that is lower than the basic shape of other letters; in Biblical Hebrew only ק and four of five final forms (ך, ן, ף, ץ) have descenders (1)
diagnostic(s)	those vowel points (including doubling) and prefixes that distinguish verbal STEMS (6)
directional	LOCATIVE; ACCUSATIVE (7)
disjunctive accent	a MASORETIC ACCENT that separates ("disjoins") a word from the following; major disjunctive accents call for such a significant separation that they are called "pausal" (27)
disjunctive clause	any CLAUSE that begins with *waw* prefixed to a non-verbal form (וְאַבְרָהָם זָקֵן); used in narrative for ancillary (background or proleptic), contrasive, or summary information (6)
double-status	an action described by a verb, in which the subject both does the action verb and is affected by that activity; also called "reflexive", "middle", "reciprocal" "tolerative" (18)
double verbs	pairs of verbal roots that seem to be semantic synonyms; פור/פרר, *break* (31)
doubly transitive	a verb with two objects one of which causes the other to do something (20)
dual	the יִם - ending used on some nouns to show that there are two of the referent, especially parts of the body and certain numerals (4, 17)
dynamic	a verb that describes or identifies an event (i.e., *not* STATIVE or STATIC); also FIENTIVE
dynamic equivalence	a theory of translation that defines the translator's responsibility as making the translation as accessible as possible to the reader, emphasizing ease of understanding; assumes that we ought to translate "thought for thought" rather than "word by word" (5)

element	any morphological unit that can be combined with (AFFIXED to) another to form a larger word; the maximum number of elements in Biblical Hebrew is five (root, plural, pronominal suffix, preposition, conjunction)
factitive	a verbal function associated with D & H that describes an activity that brings about a change of state or condition (19)
feminine	see GENDER (4)
fientive	any verb that describes an ACTION, rather than a STATE (15)
final form	a form of a letter that occurs only when that letter is the final letter in the word; this applies only to five forms in Biblical Hebrew: ם, ן, ף, ץ, ך (1)
flashback	information about a former event; i.e., past non-sequential narrative material (6)
full vowel	any vowel except the HATEF-VOWELS (2)
functional equivalence	a newer term for DYNAMIC EQUIVALENCE (5)
furtive pataḥ	a pataḥ placed by the Masoretes between a final long [non-a] vowel and a final guttural, e.g., the pataḥ in [:Abl.GI, Gilboa (3)
gemination	the doubling of a sound, either a consonant or syllable (22)
gender	part of a language's concord system, used to indicate which words in a syntagm refer to or modify each other; the term "gender" reflects the tendency for one set of endings to be used for nouns that refer to male and female beings (4)
genre	"type" (Fr.); often distinguished because each kind of discourse in Biblical Hebrew (e.g., NARRATIVE, INSTRUCTION) makes its own use of the verbal system (6)
gerundive	a verbal function of the INFINITIVE CONSTRUCT, by which it specifies the manner or means of accomplishing an activity named by a preceding verb (16)
gloss	an English word that "represents" or "stands for" a Hebrew word; N.B.: A gloss is *not* a definition, nor does it represent the word's reference or function. (2)
guttural	"throat" (Lat.); the radicals א, ה, ח, or ע; ר is sometimes called a guttural, but is not, sharing only the characteristic of not doubling (1, 22)
guttural verbs	verbal roots with one or more of the above radicals
half vowel	a non-descript vowel (e.g., the sound represented by final 'a' in "umbrell*a*"); represented in Biblical Hebrew by vocal šewa and the HATEF VOWELS (2)
ḥaser spelling	"lacking" (Hb.); an occurrence of a word (usually written PLENE) that lacks the vowel letter (2)
ḥatef-vowel	any one of four vowel signs representing a HALF VOWEL; vocal šewa and three signs that combine šewa with a sign for a full vowel (ḥatef-qameṣ, ḥatef-pataḥ, ḥatef-segol) (2)
I-guttural	verbal roots with א, ה, ח, or ע as their initial consonant; GUTTURAL VERBS (22)
II-guttural	verbal roots with א, ה, ח, or ע as their middle consonant; verbs with middle ר occasionally resemble verbs with a middle guttural; GUTTURAL VERBS (22)
III-guttural	verbal roots with ה, ח, or ע as their final consonant; GUTTURAL VERBS (22)
imperative	second-person VOLITIONAL verbal forms directing the hearer to do the will of the speaker; formed like the IMPERFECT without the PGN prefix (8)
imperfect	one of two prefix verbal CONJUGATIONS in Biblical Hebrew, generally representing the present, future, or some MODAL function (5)
independent pronoun	pronouns that function as separate words (i.e., not suffixed); independent pronouns in Biblical Hebrew are primarily clausal SUBJECTS (13)
infinitive absolute	a verbal CONJUGATION that primarily modifies a verbal clausal PREDICATE, apparently by "strenthening" it; it has no single functional GLOSS (16)
infinitive construct	a verbal CONJUGATION that occurs often with prepositions in temporal clauses, or with the preposition -ל with TELIC or COMPLEMENTARY force (16)
inseparable	ELEMENTS that do not function as independent WORDS, but only as affixes (4)
inseparable preposition	three prepositions (ב, כ, ל) that only occur as prefixes (7)
instructional material	a genre of biblical prose that explains how a task is to be done; e.g., the laws of sacrifice in Lv 1-7 (10)

interlinear	a word-by-word gloss and [usually] analysis of a text from one language into another, purportedly to enable people who do not know the language of the original to understand it more fully (5)
interrogative	a question, whether indicated in Biblical Hebrew by the prefixed -הֲ, an interrogative verb (e.g., שׁאל, דרשׁ), or the context (13)
intransitive	any verb that describes a state (STATIVE) or an activity that does not immediately or directly affect an object; e.g., verbs of motion (15)
jussive	a MODAL function of the IMPERFECT by which the speaker directs a third party to do something (8)
lemma	the word(s) in the text that are under discussion; a common term in textual criticism (29)
lexeme	a member of the LEXICON of a language; a "word" as listed in the lexicon [book] (2)
lexicon	all the words [lexemes] of a language; a bilingual reference book (2)
locative	an ending on selected nouns indicating that motion or direction is *toward* that object [a.k.a. ACCUSATIVE] (7)
long vowel	any vowel that can stand in an open or closed & accented syllable; vowel signs with *MATRES LECTIONIS* are always long (ḥireq-yod, ṣere-yod, ḥolem-waw, qibbuṣ); others mark both long and short vowels (qameṣ, ṣere, ḥireq, qibbuṣ); ṣere and ḥolem are always long, with or without the MATER (3)
malē' spelling	"full" (Hb.); = PLENE (2)
mappiq	a dot in a final ה- showing that the ה- is a consonant rather than a MATER (3)
maqqef	a horizontal line, at the level of the top "surface" of the "letter square", linking two or more words into one accentual unit (5)
masculine	see GENDER (4)
masora marginalis	notes written in the margin by the Masoretes to note unexpected forms, or to offer alternate readings of the text (29)
Masoretes	the scribes who copied the biblical text (c. AD 500-1000), adding vowel points, accent marks, and other notes to the pages; the Hebrew Bible in use today is an example of the Masoretic Text (29)
mater lectionis	a consonantal sign used more or less sporadically to indicate the presence of a preceding long vowel (pl., *MATRES LECTIONIS*) (2)
medial form	the forms of consonants used at the beginning of or within a word; contrast FINAL FORM (1)
middle voice	an event in which the activity directly affects or necessarily involves the actor; primarily signalled in Biblical Hebrew by *nifal* and *hitpael* (18)
modal	any non-indicative verbal function, such as IMPERATIVE, COHORTATIVE, JUSSIVE
modify/modification	to define something by describing it more closely (4)
narrative	the GENRE used to tell stories (10)
narrative backbone	the primary sequence of events as outlined by the narrator; indicated in Biblical Hebrew by the PRETERITE (6)
negation	a statement that an event did *not* happen; *irrealis* (17)
non-verbal clause	a CLAUSE without a finite verbal form as its predicate (17)
number	morphological information indicating how many of the referent are being identified; Biblical Hebrew has three numbers—singular, dual, plural (4)
objective construct	a CONSTRUCT chain in which the second [later] element of the chain might be described as the OBJECT, result, or goal of the preceding element; e.g., in the phrase *Saul's death*, Saul is the one who died (9)
open syllable	a syllable that ends in a vowel; its vowel is [usually] long (3)
ordinal numeral	the numerals used in describing something's position in an order; first, second, etc.; in Biblical Hebrew, the ordinals end in יִ- , e.g., שִׁשִּׁי, sixth (17)
parenthetic information	material that stands apart from the flow of the narrative, generally supplying information needed to understand what has just been, or is about to be, described (6)

parse	to analyze a word's morphology by identifying, e.g., a verb's subject [PGN], stem, conjugation, etc. (5)
participle	verbal conjugation with primarily adjectival function (12)
passive	an event in which the subject is the object or recipient of the activity described by the verb; signalled in Biblical Hebrew by *nifal*, *pual*, and *hofal* (18)
penult	the next-to-last syllable of a word (2)
perfect	the suffixed verbal CONJUGATIONS in Biblical Hebrew, generally representing the past, unless *waw* is prefixed (10)
permissive	a MODAL function in which the SUBJECT allows ("permits") the activity (20)
person	the relationship of the subject to the activity described by the verb; there are three persons in both English and Biblical Hebrew (5)
PGN	a verb's inflection to show the person, gender, and number of its subject (5)
plene spelling	"full" (Lat.); a word spelled with a vowel letter; = MALĒ' (2)
plural	reference to more than one of an entity; the grammatical forms that indicate such reference (4)
pointing	marks added to the consonantal text that indicate vowels ("vowel points") and accentuation ("accents")
polar question	a question that expects an answer of either "yes" or "no" (17)
possessive	showing that one entity belongs to another (9)
predicate	the COMMENT portion of a clause; what the clause says *about* its TOPIC (11)
prefix	define as both noun & verb (4)
preposition	a "pre-posed" form that indicates a word's function in the CLAUSE or SENTENCE (4)
prepositional phrase	a non-clausal string of word(s) governed by the PREPOSITION (7)
prohibition	a negative command (8)
proleptic	"clues"; information anticipating a future development, especially in narrative (10)
pronominal subject	a non-nominal SUBJECT of a CLAUSE; indicated by either an INDEPENDENT PRONOUN, PRONOMINAL SUFFIX (on INFINITIVE CONSTRUCT), or the PGN affixes of the prefix and suffix CONJUGATIONS (13)
pronominal suffix	a shortened form of an independent pronoun, used to show pronominal possession, objects of verbs or prepositions, and subjects of infinitive constructs (14)
radical	another name for the consonants that make up the ROOT of a word; e.g., "second radical" is shorthand for "the second consonant of the root"
range of reference	a word's relative specificity; e.g., "animal" has a much wider range than "dog" (2)
reciprocal	an activity in which two or more parties simultaneously participate (e.g., fighting) (18)
reflexive	an activity in which the actor more or less directs the action toward him or herself (18)
relative	that which relates information to or about something else (11)
resultative	a verbal function associated with D & H that describes an activity that brings about a change of state or condition; see CAUSATIVE, FACTITIVE (19)
rhetorical question	a question asked, not seeking information, but in order to make an assertion (17)
root	the theoretical reconstructed base—usually of three RADICALS-that is common to a group of forms (5)
separable preposition	the preposition מִן, *from*, which is often—but not necessarily—prefixed to the word that it governs (7)
šewa	see VOCAL ŠEWA (2)
short vowel	any vowel that can stand in a closed, unaccented syllable (i.e., *pataḥ, segol, qameṣ ḥatuf*); some vowel signs (*ḥireq, qibbuṣ*) mark both long and short vowels; their function must be determined from their phonetic environment (3)
silent *šewa*	a sign (֖) used to mark the *absence* of a vowel between consonants, and unvocalized final *kaf* (ךְ-) (3)

singular	something referred to that consists of one, or a group considered collectively, or the form that identifies the referent as singular (4)
stative	a verb that describes the state or condition of its subject, rather than an ACTION; contrasted with DYNAMIC (10); also called "static"
status, change of	a change in the condition or situation of a clausal subject (15)
stem	a combination of prefixes, infixes (doubling), and vowels that indicate a verb's function (5)
strong verb	any verbal root in which all three radicals are present in all forms of the verb (24)
subject	the TOPIC of a clause—what the clause *describes* (5)
subjective construct	a CONSTRUCT chain in which the second [later] element of the chain might be described as the SUBJECT or source of the preceding element; e.g., in the phrase *Saul's death*, Saul is the one who died (9)
substantive	any form that can serve as a clausal SUBJECT, OBJECT, or PREDICATE NOMINATIVE, or function within a CONSTRUCT chain (11)
syllable	a cluster of sounds, both consonant and vowel; all syllables in Biblical Hebrew begin with a consonant (except the prefixed conjunction -וּ); syllables are OPEN or CLOSED
syntagm	one of the syntactical patterns of a language; any identifiable *syntactical* combination of specific grammatical forms which may be specific (e.g., *w*+perfect; היה + לְ-) or general (e.g., "construct chain", "sequential preterites"; disjunctive clause")
telic	a clause that identifies the intended or desired outcome—purpose or result—of an event or state
temporal clause/phrase	a clause or phrase that describes the *time at which* something happened (16)
Tetragrammaton	"four letters" (Greek); the divine name יהוה; see YHWH (3)
tittle	the small horizontal stroke that distinguishes, e.g., ב from כ, and ר from ד (1)
tolerative	a function of the *nifal* in which someone *allows* or *permits* something to be done (18)
topic	the SUBJECT of a clause—what the clause is *about* (11)
toponym	place name
transitive	any FIENTIVE verb that can direct its action toward an OBJECT (15)
translate	the process of attempting to present in one language a message originally expressed in another (5)
transliterate	to represent the *sounds* of one language in the *alphabet* of another; transliteration can be phonetically technical or exact, or relatively casual (1)
ultima	the final syllable of a word; in Biblical Hebrew, the ultima is usually the accented syllable (2)
utterance	any product of a linguistic act, whether written or oral
vague verb	a verb that is functionally/semantically incomplete, and thus requires another form (usually an infinitive construct in Biblical Hebrew); e.g., "be able", "finish" (16)
virtual doubling	when a letter that is normally doubled in a given form lacks *dageš forte*, but the preceding vowel is short, as though the letter had been doubled (22)
vocal *šewa*	the main HALF-VOWEL (3)
volitional	verbal forms that indicate the imposition of someone's will on another person; a collective term for the JUSSIVE, COHORTATIVE, and IMPERATIVE (8)
vowel letter	letters of the alphabet used to indicate the presence of a long vowel (2)
VSO	verb-subject-object as the usual word order of main narrative [PRETERITE] clauses (6)
weak verb	verbal roots with consonants or vowel letters that are in the lexical form, but do not appear in all verbal forms (24)
word	any form in Biblical Hebrew separated by a blank space or joined to another by MAQQEF
YHWH	the TETRAGRAMMATON ("four letters") the traditionally unpronounced proper name of the God of the Bible, pointed יְהוָה in BHS (3)

Appendix D

Paradigms

Pronouns

Person Gender Number	**Independent** (subject)	Basic Form	w/MS Noun	w/MP Noun	w/FS Noun	w/FP Noun
1cs	אֲנִי אָנֹכִי	־ִי	סוּסִי	סוּסַי	סוּסָתִי	סוּסוֹתַי
2ms	אַתָּה	־ְךָ	סוּסְךָ	סוּסֶיךָ	סוּסָתְךָ	סוּסוֹתֶיךָ
2fs	אַתְּ	־ֵךְ	סוּסֵךְ	סוּסַיִךְ	סוּסָתֵךְ	סוּסוֹתַיִךְ
3ms	הוּא	־וֹ	סוּסוֹ		סוּסָתוֹ	
		־ָה	סוּסֹה			
		־ֵהוּ	סוּסֵהוּ			
		־ָיו		סוּסָיו		סוּסוֹתָיו
3fs	הִיא	־ָהּ	סוּסָהּ		סוּסָתָהּ	
	הִוא	־ָהָ		סוּסֶיהָ		סוּסוֹתֶיהָ
1cp	אֲנַחְנוּ נַחְנוּ	־ֵנוּ	סוּסֵנוּ	סוּסֵינוּ	סוּסָתֵנוּ	סוּסוֹתֵינוּ
2mp	אַתֶּם	־ְכֶם	סוּסְכֶם	סוּסֵיכֶם	סוּסַתְכֶם	סוּסוֹתֵיכֶם
2fp	אַתֵּן אַתֵּנָה	־ְכֶן	סוּסְכֶן	סוּסֵיכֶן	סוּסַתְכֶן	סוּסוֹתֵיכֶן
3mp	הֵם	־ֶהֶם		סוּסֵיהֶם	סוּסָתָהֶם	סוּסוֹתֵיהֶם
	הֵמָּה	־ָם	סוּסָם			סוּסוֹתָם
		־ָמוֹ				
3fp	הֵנָּה	־ֶהֶן		סוּסֵיהֶן	סוּסָתָהֶן	סוּסוֹתֵיהֶן
		־ָן	סוּסָן			

1. Throughout the *Pentateuch*, הִיא (3fs) is written הִוא, with only eleven exceptions (e.g., Gn 14.2).
2. These suffixes are used with nouns, prepositions, infinitives construct, and participles. Suffixes on finite verbs and the imperative are similar, but show greater variety in form.
   a. if the verb ends in a vowel, the suffix either begins with or consists of a consonant (the 1cs verbal suffix is ־נִי):

   שָׂאוּנִי וַהֲטִילֻנִי אֶל־הַיָּם   Pick *me* up and throw *me* into the sea (Jon 1.12)

   b. if the verb ends in a consonant, either silent *šewa* or a vowel links the consonantal suffix to the verb; vocalic suffixes are affixed directly to the verb:

   וַיַּהַרְגֵהוּ   He killed *him* (Gn 4.8).
   לָכַד יְהוֹשֻׁעַ אֶת־הָעַי וַיַּחֲרִימָהּ   Joshua had captured Ai and destroyed *it* (Jos 10.1)

Strong Verb, I

	Forms	Qal	Nifal	Hifil	Hofal	Piel	Pual	Hitpael
P	1cs	מָשַׁלְתִּי	נִמְשַׁלְתִּי	הִמְשַׁלְתִּי	הָמְשַׁלְתִּי	מִשַּׁלְתִּי	מֻשַּׁלְתִּי	הִתְמַשַּׁלְתִּי
	2ms	מָשַׁלְתָּ	נִמְשַׁלְתָּ	הִמְשַׁלְתָּ	הָמְשַׁלְתָּ	מִשַּׁלְתָּ	מֻשַּׁלְתָּ	הִתְמַשַּׁלְתָּ
	2fs	מָשַׁלְתְּ	נִמְשַׁלְתְּ	הִמְשַׁלְתְּ	הָמְשַׁלְתְּ	מִשַּׁלְתְּ	מֻשַּׁלְתְּ	הִתְמַשַּׁלְתְּ
	3ms	מָשַׁל	נִמְשַׁל	הִמְשִׁיל	הָמְשַׁל	מִשֵּׁל	מֻשַּׁל	הִתְמַשֵּׁל
	3fs	מָשְׁלָה	נִמְשְׁלָה	הִמְשִׁילָה	הָמְשְׁלָה	מִשְּׁלָה	מֻשְּׁלָה	הִתְמַשְּׁלָה
	1cp	מָשַׁלְנוּ	נִמְשַׁלְנוּ	הִמְשַׁלְנוּ	הָמְשַׁלְנוּ	מִשַּׁלְנוּ	מֻשַּׁלְנוּ	הִתְמַשַּׁלְנוּ
	2mp	מְשַׁלְתֶּם	נִמְשַׁלְתֶּם	הִמְשַׁלְתֶּם	הָמְשַׁלְתֶּם	מִשַּׁלְתֶּם	מֻשַּׁלְתֶּם	הִתְמַשַּׁלְתֶּם
	2fp	מְשַׁלְתֶּן	נִמְשַׁלְתֶּן	הִמְשַׁלְתֶּן	הָמְשַׁלְתֶּן	מִשַּׁלְתֶּן	מֻשַּׁלְתֶּן	הִתְמַשַּׁלְתֶּן
	3cp	מָשְׁלוּ	נִמְשְׁלוּ	הִמְשִׁילוּ	הָמְשְׁלוּ	מִשְּׁלוּ	מֻשְּׁלוּ	הִתְמַשְּׁלוּ
F	1cs	אֶמְשֹׁל	אֶמָּשֵׁל	אַמְשִׁיל	אָמְשַׁל	אֲמַשֵּׁל	אֲמֻשַּׁל	אֶתְמַשֵּׁל
	2ms/3fs	תִּמְשֹׁל	תִּמָּשֵׁל	תַּמְשִׁיל	תָּמְשַׁל	תְּמַשֵּׁל	תְּמֻשַּׁל	תִּתְמַשֵּׁל
	2fs	תִּמְשְׁלִי	תִּמָּשְׁלִי	תַּמְשִׁילִי	תָּמְשְׁלִי	תְּמַשְּׁלִי	תְּמֻשְּׁלִי	תִּתְמַשְּׁלִי
	3ms	יִמְשֹׁל	יִמָּשֵׁל	יַמְשִׁיל	יָמְשַׁל	יְמַשֵּׁל	יְמֻשַּׁל	יִתְמַשֵּׁל
	1cp	נִמְשֹׁל	נִמָּשֵׁל	נַמְשִׁיל	נָמְשַׁל	נְמַשֵּׁל	נְמֻשַּׁל	נִתְמַשֵּׁל
	2mp	תִּמְשְׁלוּ	תִּמָּשְׁלוּ	תַּמְשִׁילוּ	תָּמְשְׁלוּ	תְּמַשְּׁלוּ	תְּמֻשְּׁלוּ	תִּתְמַשְּׁלוּ
	2/3fp	תִּמְשֹׁלְנָה	תִּמָּשַׁלְנָה	תַּמְשֵׁלְנָה	תָּמְשַׁלְנָה	תְּמַשֵּׁלְנָה	תְּמֻשַּׁלְנָה	תִּתְמַשֵּׁלְנָה
	3mp	יִמְשְׁלוּ	יִמָּשְׁלוּ	יַמְשִׁילוּ	יָמְשְׁלוּ	יְמַשְּׁלוּ	יְמֻשְּׁלוּ	יִתְמַשְּׁלוּ
V	ms	מְשֹׁל	הִמָּשֵׁל	הַמְשֵׁל		מַשֵּׁל		הִתְמַשֵּׁל
	fs	מִשְׁלִי	הִמָּשְׁלִי	הַמְשִׁילִי		מַשְּׁלִי		הִתְמַשְּׁלִי
	mp	מִשְׁלוּ	הִמָּשְׁלוּ	הַמְשִׁילוּ		מַשְּׁלוּ		הִתְמַשְּׁלוּ
	fp	מְשֹׁלְנָה	הִמָּשַׁלְנָה	הַמְשֵׁלְנָה		מַשֵּׁלְנָה		הִתְמַשֵּׁלְנָה
NC		מְשֹׁל	הִמָּשֵׁל	הַמְשִׁיל	הָמְשַׁל	מַשֵּׁל		הִתְמַשֵּׁל
NA		מָשׁוֹל	נִמְשֹׁל	הַמְשֵׁל	הָמְשֵׁל	מַשֵּׁל	מֻשָּׁל	הִתְמַשֵּׁל
Participle	ms	מֹשֵׁל	נִמְשָׁל	מַמְשִׁיל	מָמְשָׁל	מְמַשֵּׁל	מְמֻשָּׁל	מִתְמַשֵּׁל
	fs	מֹשְׁלָה / מֹשֶׁלֶת	נִמְשָׁלָה	מַמְשִׁילָה	מָמְשָׁלָה	מְמַשְּׁלָה	מְמֻשָּׁלָה	מִתְמַשְּׁלָה
	mp	מֹשְׁלִים	נִמְשָׁלִים	מַמְשִׁילִים	מָמְשָׁלִים	מְמַשְּׁלִים	מְמֻשָּׁלִים	מִתְמַשְּׁלִים
	fp	מֹשְׁלוֹת	נִמְשָׁלוֹת	מַמְשִׁילוֹת	מָמְשָׁלוֹת	מְמַשְּׁלוֹת	מְמֻשָּׁלוֹת	מִתְמַשְּׁלוֹת

1. If the verbal root begins with a sibilant (ז, ס, צ, שׁ, שׂ), the ת of the *hitpael* prefix and the sibilant exchange positions (metathesize): הִשְׁתַּמַּרְתִּי, "I kept myself"; if the root begins with צ, the ת both metathesizes and becomes ט (partial assimilation): הִצְטַדֵּק, "he sanctified himself".

2. If the verbal root ends with ת, this assimilates to the ת of the perfect endings (e.g., 1cs, 2ms), which is then written with *dageš forte*: כָּרַתָּ, "you (ms) cut". In some III-נ verbs, final נ occasionally assimilates to the consonant of the ending: נָתַתָּ (< נתן, for which this is especially true); שָׁכַנּוּ (< שכן).

Strong Verb, II
(with medial *bᵉgad-kᵉfat* letter [occasional *dageš lene*])

Conj/Sbj		Qal	Nifal	Hifil	Hofal	Piel	Pual	Hitpael
P	1cs	כָּתַבְתִּי	נִכְתַּבְתִּי	הִכְתַּבְתִּי	הָכְתַּבְתִּי	כִּתַּבְתִּי	כֻּתַּבְתִּי	הִתְכַּתַּבְתִּי
	2ms	כָּתַבְתָּ	נִכְתַּבְתָּ	הִכְתַּבְתָּ	הָכְתַּבְתָּ	כִּתַּבְתָּ	כֻּתַּבְתָּ	הִתְכַּתַּבְתָּ
	2fs	כָּתַבְתְּ	נִכְתַּבְתְּ	הִכְתַּבְתְּ	הָכְתַּבְתְּ	כִּתַּבְתְּ	כֻּתַּבְתְּ	הִתְכַּתַּבְתְּ
	3ms	כָּתַב	נִכְתַּב	הִכְתִּיב	הָכְתַּב	כִּתֵּב	כֻּתַּב	הִתְכַּתֵּב
	3fs	כָּתְבָה	נִכְתְּבָה	הִכְתִּיבָה	הָכְתְּבָה	כִּתְּבָה	כֻּתְּבָה	הִתְכַּתְּבָה
	1cp	כָּתַבְנוּ	נִכְתַּבְנוּ	הִכְתַּבְנוּ	הָכְתַּבְנוּ	כִּתַּבְנוּ	כֻּתַּבְנוּ	הִתְכַּתַּבְנוּ
	2mp	כְּתַבְתֶּם	נִכְתַּבְתֶּם	הִכְתַּבְתֶּם	הָכְתַּבְתֶּם	כִּתַּבְתֶּם	כֻּתַּבְתֶּם	הִתְכַּתַּבְתֶּם
	2fp	כְּתַבְתֶּן	נִכְתַּבְתֶּן	הִכְתַּבְתֶּן	הָכְתַּבְתֶּן	כִּתַּבְתֶּן	כֻּתַּבְתֶּן	הִתְכַּתַּבְתֶּן
	3cp	כָּתְבוּ	נִכְתְּבוּ	הִכְתִּיבוּ	הָכְתְּבוּ	כִּתְּבוּ	כֻּתְּבוּ	הִתְכַּתְּבוּ
F	1cs	אֶכְתֹּב	אֶכָּתֵב	אַכְתִּיב	אָכְתַּב	אֲכַתֵּב	אֲכֻתַּב	אֶתְכַּתֵּב
	2m/3fs	תִּכְתֹּב	תִּכָּתֵב	תַּכְתִּיב	תָּכְתַּב	תְּכַתֵּב	תְּכֻתַּב	תִּתְכַּתֵּב
	2fs	תִּכְתְּבִי	תִּכָּתְבִי	תַּכְתִּיבִי	תָּכְתְּבִי	תְּכַתְּבִי	תְּכֻתְּבִי	תִּתְכַּתְּבִי
	3ms	יִכְתֹּב	יִכָּתֵב	יַכְתִּיב	יָכְתַּב	יְכַתֵּב	יְכֻתַּב	יִתְכַּתֵּב
	1cp	נִכְתֹּב	נִכָּתֵב	נַכְתִּיב	נָכְתַּב	נְכַתֵּב	נְכֻתַּב	נִתְכַּתֵּב
	2mp	תִּכְתְּבוּ	תִּכָּתְבוּ	תַּכְתִּיבוּ	תָּכְתְּבוּ	תְּכַתְּבוּ	תְּכֻתְּבוּ	תִּתְכַּתְּבוּ
	2/3fp	תִּכְתֹּבְנָה	תִּכָּתֵבְנָה	תַּכְתֵּבְנָה	תָּכְתַּבְנָה	תְּכַתֵּבְנָה	תְּכֻתַּבְנָה	תִּתְכַּתֵּבְנָה
	3mp	יִכְתְּבוּ	יִכָּתְבוּ	יַכְתִּיבוּ	יָכְתְּבוּ	יְכַתְּבוּ	יְכֻתְּבוּ	יִתְכַּתְּבוּ
V	ms	כְּתֹב	הִכָּתֵב	הַכְתֵּב		כַּתֵּב		הִתְכַּתֵּב
	fs	כִּתְבִי	הִכָּתְבִי	הַכְתִּיבִי		כַּתְּבִי		הִתְכַּתְּבִי
	mp	כִּתְבוּ	הִכָּתְבוּ	הַכְתִּיבוּ		כַּתְּבוּ		הִתְכַּתְּבוּ
	fp	כְּתֹבְנָה	הִכָּתֵבְנָה	הַכְתֵּבְנָה		כַּתֵּבְנָה		הִתְכַּתֵּבְנָה
NC		כְּתֹב	הִכָּתֵב	הַכְתִּיב	הָכְתַּב	כַּתֵּב		הִתְכַּתֵּב
NA		כָּתוֹב	נִכְתֹּב	הַכְתֵּב	הָכְתֵּב	כַּתֹּב	כֻּתֹּב	הִתְכַּתֵּב
Participle	ms	כֹּתֵב	נִכְתָּב	מַכְתִּיב	מָכְתָּב	מְכַתֵּב	מְכֻתָּב	מִתְכַּתֵּב
	fs	כֹּתְבָה / כֹּתֶבֶת	נִכְתָּבָה	מַכְתִּיבָה	מָכְתָּבָה	מְכַתְּבָה	מְכֻתָּבָה	מִתְכַּתְּבָה
	mp	כֹּתְבִים	נִכְתָּבִים	מַכְתִּיבִים	מָכְתָּבִים	מְכַתְּבִים	מְכֻתָּבִים	מִתְכַּתְּבִים
	fp	כֹּתְבוֹת	נִכְתָּבוֹת	מַכְתִּיבוֹת	מָכְתָּבוֹת	מְכַתְּבוֹת	מְכֻתָּבוֹת	מִתְכַּתְּבוֹת

1. When a verbal root begins with a sibilant (ז, ס, צ, שׂ, שׁ), the ת of the *hitpael* prefix and the sibilant exchange positions (metathesize): הִשְׁתַּמַּרְתִּי, "I kept myself"; if the root begins with צ, the ת both metathesizes and becomes ט (partial assimilation): הִצְטַדֵּק, "Sanctify yourself!".
2. When a verbal root ends with ת, this assimilates to the ת of the perfect endings (e.g., 1cs, 2ms), which is then written with *dageš forte*: כָּרַתָּ, "you (ms) cut". The final ן- of some III-נ verbs occasionally assimilates to the consonant of the ending: נָתַתָּ (< נתן, for which this is especially true).

Guttural Verbs

Verbs with gutturals (א, ה, ח, ע) are strong (i.e., all three radicals of the root are present), except for occasional forms of III-א roots (below). They differ from the strong verb for four reasons:

(1) The gutturals (and ר) do not double
(2) The gutturals are followed by *hatef*-vowels rather than vocal *šewa*
(3) The gutturals tend to occur with *a*-vowels.
(4) When א comes at the end of a syllable, it becomes silent and the preceding vowel is long.

These characteristics mean that they differ from the strong verb in six ways (non-guttural forms in [ ] for comparison):

1. *long* vowels instead of short; gutturals don't double, so syllables that are closed in non-guttural forms are *open* and short vowels *lengthen*:

    יַעֲמֹד   3ms N F   [יִשָּׁמֵר]   בֵּרֵךְ   3ms D P   [כִּבֵּד]

2. *a*-vowels (especially *patach* and *patach furtivum*):

    יִשְׁמַע   3ms Q F   [יִכְתֹּב]   יְשַׁמַּע   3ms D F   [יְשַׁמֵּר]

3. *hatef*-vowels instead of vocal *shewa* under gutturals:

    בָּחֲרוּ   3cp Q P   [כָּתְבוּ]   עֲמַדְתֶּם   2mp Q P   [כְּתַבְתֶּם]

4. *segol* instead of *hireq* before non-final gutturals, especially in prefix:

    יֶחְדַּל   3ms Q F   [יִכְתֹּב]

5. short prefix vowel followed by *hatef*-vowel instead of silent *shewa*:

    יַעֲמֹד   3ms Q F   [יִכְתֹּב]   יַעֲמִיד   3ms H F   [יַמְשִׁיל]

6. III-א forms generally have the vowel of the basic verb after the second radical of the verbal root, if that vowel is long. The ת of PGN endings lacks *dageš lene* since it is preceded by a vowel (silent א is not counted as a consonant).

    מָצָאתִי   1cs Q P   [שָׁמַרְתִּי]   יִמָּצֵא   3ms Dp F   [יְשֻׁמַּר]

Some III-א forms lack the א completely (this is usually noted in the *masora marginalis*, as, e.g., in Ru 2.9, where וְצָמִת is noted as a unique occurrence [i.e., lacking final א]):

   וְצָמִית   2fs Q P   [שָׁמַרְתְּ]   מָצִתִי   1cs Q P   [שָׁמַרְתִּי]
   וַיָּבֹו   3ms Q Pr   [*Qere*: וַיָּבוֹא]

III-ה (ל״ה) Verbs

Conj/Sbj		Qal	Nifal	Hifil	Hofal	Piel	Pual	Hitpael
P	1cs	בָּנִיתִי	נִבְנֵיתִי	הִבְנֵיתִי	הָבְנֵיתִי	בִּנִּיתִי	בֻּנֵּיתִי	הִתְבַּנֵּיתִי
	2ms	בָּנִיתָ	נִבְנֵיתָ	הִבְנֵיתָ	הָבְנֵיתָ	בִּנִּיתָ	בֻּנֵּיתָ	הִתְבַּנֵּיתָ
	2fs	בָּנִית	נִבְנֵית	הִבְנֵית	הָבְנֵית	בִּנִּית	בֻּנֵּית	הִתְבַּנֵּית
	3ms	בָּנָה	נִבְנָה	הִבְנָה	הָבְנָה	בִּנָּה	בֻּנָּה	הִתְבַּנָּה
	3fs	בָּנְתָה	נִבְנְתָה	הִבְנְתָה	הָבְנְתָה	בִּנְּתָה	בֻּנְּתָה	הִתְבַּנְּתָה
	1cp	בָּנִינוּ	נִבְנֵינוּ	הִבְנֵינוּ	הָבְנֵינוּ	בִּנִּינוּ	בֻּנֵּינוּ	הִתְבַּנֵּינוּ
	2mp	בְּנִיתֶם	נִבְנֵיתֶם	הִבְנֵיתֶם	הָבְנֵיתֶם	בִּנִּיתֶם	בֻּנֵּיתֶם	הִתְבַּנֵּיתֶם
	2fp	בְּנִיתֶן	נִבְנֵיתֶן	הִבְנֵיתֶן	הָבְנֵיתֶן	בִּנִּיתֶן	בֻּנֵּיתֶן	הִתְבַּנֵּיתֶן
	3cp	בָּנוּ	נִבְנוּ	הִבְנוּ	הָבְנוּ	בִּנּוּ	בֻּנּוּ	הִתְבַּנּוּ
F	1cs	אֶבְנֶה	אֶבָּנֶה	אַבְנֶה	אָבְנֶה	אֲבַנֶּה	אֲבֻנֶּה	אֶתְבַּנֶּה
	2m/3f	תִּבְנֶה	תִּבָּנֶה	תַּבְנֶה	תָּבְנֶה	תְּבַנֶּה	תְּבֻנֶּה	תִּתְבַּנֶּה
	2fs	תִּבְנִי	תִּבָּנִי	תַּבְנִי	תָּבְנִי	תְּבַנִּי	תְּבֻנִּי	תִּתְבַּנִּי
	3ms	יִבְנֶה	יִבָּנֶה	יַבְנֶה	יָבְנֶה	יְבַנֶּה	יְבֻנֶּה	יִתְבַּנֶּה
	1cp	נִבְנֶה	נִבָּנֶה	נַבְנֶה	נָבְנֶה	נְבַנֶּה	נְבֻנֶּה	נִתְבַּנֶּה
	2mp	תִּבְנוּ	תִּבָּנוּ	תַּבְנוּ	תָּבְנוּ	תְּבַנּוּ	תְּבֻנּוּ	תִּתְבַּנּוּ
	2/3fp	תִּבְנֶינָה	תִּבָּנֶינָה	תַּבְנֶינָה	תָּבְנֶינָה	תְּבַנֶּינָה	תְּבֻנֶּינָה	תִּתְבַּנֶּינָה
	3mp	יִבְנוּ	יִבָּנוּ	יַבְנוּ	יָבְנוּ	יְבַנּוּ	יְבֻנּוּ	יִתְבַּנּוּ
V	ms	בְּנֵה	הִבָּנֵה	הַבְנֵה		בַּנֵּה		הִתְבַּנֵּה
	fs	בְּנִי	הִבָּנִי	הַבְנִי		בַּנִּי		הִתְבַּנִּי
	mp	בְּנוּ	הִבָּנוּ	הַבְנוּ		בַּנּוּ		הִתְבַּנּוּ
	fp	בְּנֶינָה	הִבָּנֶינָה	הַבְנֶינָה		בַּנֶּינָה		הִתְבַּנֶּינָה
NC		בְּנוֹת	הִבָּנוֹת	הַבְנוֹת	הָבְנוֹת	בַּנּוֹת	בֻּנּוֹת	הִתְבַּנּוֹת
NA		בָּנֹה	הִבָּנֹה	הַבְנֵה	הָבְנֵה	בַּנֹּה	בֻּנֹּה	הִתְבַּנֹּה
Participle	ms	בֹּנֶה	נִבְנֶה	מַבְנֶה	מָבְנֶה	מְבַנֶּה	מְבֻנֶּה	מִתְבַּנֶּה
	fs	בֹּנָה	נִבְנָה	מַבְנָה	מָבְנָה	מְבַנָּה	מְבֻנָּה	מִתְבַּנָּה
	mp	בֹּנִים	נִבְנִים	מַבְנִים	מָבְנִים	מְבַנִּים	מְבֻנִּים	מִתְבַּנִּים
	fp	בֹּנוֹת	נִבְנוֹת	מַבְנוֹת	מָבְנוֹת	מְבַנּוֹת	מְבֻנּוֹת	מִתְבַּנּוֹת

III-ה Verbal Roots

1. The final ה- (originally י-) "appears" as י between the second radical and consonantal endings, and is replaced by vocalic endings and the וֹת- of NC. Because the weakness lies at the end of the verbal root, it affects all stems equally, but only the pointing *after* the *second* radical of the verbal root.
2. If there is no PGN ending, the ending is ה -, preceded by the following vowels (all stems):

    הָ - perfect
    הֵ - imperative
    הֶ - imperative, participle (ms)
    הֹ - infinitive absolute

3. NC of all stems replaces final ה with וֹת-.
4. Some forms of *qal* and *hifil* imperfect and preterite look exactly alike in roots which are both III-ה and I-guttural (especially I-ע); the stem can be determined only from the context (e.g., if וַיַּעַל has a direct object, it is H, if not, it is Q).

I-נ (פ"נ) Verbs (see next page for נתן)

Conj/Sbj		Qal		Nifal	Hifil	Hofal	D-Stems
P	1cs	These forms are the same as the strong verb in *qal* perfect.		נִפַּלְתִּי	הִפַּלְתִּי	הֻפַּלְתִּי	
	2ms			נִפַּלְתָּ	הִפַּלְתָּ	הֻפַּלְתָּ	
	2fs			נִפַּלְתְּ	הִפַּלְתְּ	הֻפַּלְתְּ	
	3ms			נִפַּל	הִפִּיל	הֻפַּל	
	3fs			נִפְּלָה	הִפִּילָה	הֻפְּלָה	
	1cp			נִפַּלְנוּ	הִפַּלְנוּ	הֻפַּלְנוּ	
	2mp			נִפַּלְתֶּם	הִפַּלְתֶּם	הֻפַּלְתֶּם	
	2fp			נִפַּלְתֶּן	הִפַּלְתֶּן	הֻפַּלְתֶּן	
	3cp			נִפְּלוּ	הִפִּילוּ	הֻפְּלוּ	
F	1cs	אֶפֹּל	אֶגַּשׁ		אַפִּיל	אֻפַּל	Verbs based on I-נ roots are strong in all forms of the D-stems.
	2m/3f	תִּפֹּל	תִּגַּשׁ		תַּפִּיל	תֻּפַּל	
	2fs	תִּפְּלִי	תִּגְּשִׁי		תַּפִּילִי	תֻּפְּלִי	
	3ms	יִפֹּל	יִגַּשׁ		יַפִּיל	יֻפַּל	
	1cp	נִפֹּל	נִגַּשׁ	*Nifal* imperfect, imperative, and infinitives are the same as the strong verb in N.	נַפִּיל	נֻפַּל	
	2mp	תִּפְּלוּ	תִּגְּשׁוּ		תַּפִּילוּ	תֻּפְּלוּ	
	2/3fp	תִּפֹּלְנָה	תִּגַּשְׁנָה		תַּפֵּלְנָה	תֻּפַּלְנָה	
	3mp	יִפְּלוּ	יִגְּשׁוּ		יַפִּילוּ	יֻפְּלוּ	
V	ms		גַּשׁ		הַפֵּל		
	fs		גְּשִׁי		הַפִּילִי		
	mp	In *qal*, the imperative, infinitives, and participles of *o*-imperfect I-נ verbs are the same as the strong verb in Q.	גְּשׁוּ		הַפִּילוּ		
	fp		גַּשְׁנָה		הַפֵּלְנָה		
NC			גֶּשֶׁת		הַפִּיל	הֻפַּל	
NA			נָגוֹשׁ		הַפֵּל	הֻפֵּל	
Participle	ms			The participles are the same as the strong verb.	נִפָּל	מַפִּיל	מֻפָּל	
	fs				נִפָּלָה	מַפִּילָה	מֻפָּלָה	
	mp				נִפָּלִים	מַפִּילִים	מֻפָּלִים	
	fp				נִפָּלוֹת	מַפִּילוֹת	מֻפָּלוֹת	

1. These roots are weak whenever the first radical of the verbal root is followed by silent *shewa* (*qal* F,V; N P, Ptc; all forms of *hifil* and *hofal*); they are strong throughout the D-stems.
2. When followed by silent *šewa*, initial -נ assimilates to the second radical, doubling it. In *qal* V and NC of *holem*-imperfect roots, -נ drops off; תְּ or תַ is added to NC (just as in some I-י verbs).
3. לקח is formed just like נגש throughout the verbal system; *any verbal form* with -קח- is from לקח.

Appendix D

נתן *(all attested forms)*

Conj/Sbj		Qal	Qal Passive	Nifal
P	1cs	נָתַתִּי		
	2ms	נָתַתָּ		
	2fs	נָתַתְּ		
	3ms	נָתַן		נִתַּן
	3fs	נָתְנָה		נִתְּנָה
	1cp	נָתַנּוּ		נִתַּנּוּ
	2mp	נְתַתֶּם		
	3cp	נָתְנוּ		
F	1cs	אֶתֵּן		
	2m/3f	תִּתֵּן		תִּנָּתֵן
	2fs	תִּתְּנִי		
	3ms	יִתֵּן	יֻתַּן	יִנָּתֵן
	1cp	נִתֵּן		
	2mp	תִּתְּנוּ		
	3mp	יִתְּנוּ		יִנָּתְנוּ
V	ms	תֵּן		
		תְּנָה		
	fs	תְּנִי		
	mp	תְּנוּ		
NC		תֵּת		הִנָּתֵן
		תִּת–		
		(with suffixes)		
NA		נָתוֹן		הִנָּתוֹן
Participle	ms	נֹתֵן	נָתוּן	נִתָּן
	mp	נֹתְנִים	נְתוּנִים	
	fp		נְתוּנוֹת	

1. Forms listed do not occur; several forms occur only once or twice (e.g., 2fs *qal* P of נתן occurs only twice, in Ezk 16.33, 36).
2. The final ן- assimilates into all consonantal endings, doubling the consonant.
3. The initial –נ assimilates into the medial -ת- whenever silent *šewa* follows the first radical.
4. The stem-vowel in *qal* F, V, NC is *ṣere*.

I-י (פ"י) Verbs

Conj/Sbj		Qal		Nifal	Hifil	Hifil (I-י)	Hofal	D-Stems
P	1cs			נוֹרַשְׁתִּי	הוֹרַשְׁתִּי	הֵיטַבְתִּי	הוּרַשְׁתִּי	
	2ms			נוֹרַשְׁתָּ	הוֹרַשְׁתָּ	הֵיטַבְתָּ	הוּרַשְׁתָּ	
	2fs	These forms		נוֹרַשְׁתְּ	הוֹרַשְׁתְּ	הֵיטַבְתְּ	הוּרַשְׁתְּ	
	3ms	are the same		נוֹרַשׁ	הוֹרִישׁ	הֵיטִיב	הוּרַשׁ	
	3fs	as the strong		נוֹרְשָׁה	הוֹרִישָׁה	הֵיטִיבָה	הוּרְשָׁה	
	1cp	verb in *qal*		נוֹרַשְׁנוּ	הוֹרַשְׁנוּ	הֵיטַבְנוּ	הוּרַשְׁנוּ	
	2mp	perfect.		נוֹרַשְׁתֶּם	הוֹרַשְׁתֶּם	הֵיטַבְתֶּם	הוּרַשְׁתֶּם	
	2fp			נוֹרַשְׁתֶּן	הוֹרַשְׁתֶּן	הֵיטַבְתֶּן	הוּרַשְׁתֶּן	
	3cp			נוֹרְשׁוּ	הוֹרִישׁוּ	הֵיטִיבוּ	הוּרְשׁוּ	
F	1cs	אִירַשׁ	אֵשֵׁב	אִוָּרֵשׁ	אוֹרִישׁ	אֵיטִיב	אוּרַשׁ	
	2m/3f	תִּירַשׁ	תֵּשֵׁב	תִּוָּרֵשׁ	תּוֹרִישׁ	תֵּיטִיב	תּוּרַשׁ	
	2fs	תִּירְשִׁי	תֵּשְׁבִי	תִּוָּרְשִׁי	תּוֹרִישִׁי	תֵּיטִיבִי	תּוּרְשִׁי	
	3ms	יִירַשׁ	יֵשֵׁב	יִוָּרֵשׁ	יוֹרִישׁ	יֵיטִיב	יוּרַשׁ	Verbs based on
	1cp	נִירַשׁ	נֵשֵׁב	נִוָּרֵשׁ	נוֹרִישׁ	נֵיטִיב	נוּרַשׁ	I-י roots are
	2mp	תִּירְשׁוּ	תֵּשְׁבוּ	תִּוָּרְשׁוּ	תּוֹרִישׁוּ	תֵּיטִיבוּ	תּוּרְשׁוּ	strong in all
	2/3fp	תִּירַשְׁנָה	תֵּשַׁבְנָה	תִּוָּרַשְׁנָה	תּוֹרִישְׁנָה	תֵּיטַבְנָה	תּוּרַשְׁנָה	forms of the
	3mp	יִירְשׁוּ	יֵשְׁבוּ	יִוָּרְשׁוּ	יוֹרִישׁוּ	יֵיטִיבוּ	יוּרְשׁוּ	D-stems.
V	ms	רַשׁ	שֵׁב	הִוָּרֵשׁ	הוֹרֵשׁ	הֵיטֵב		
	fs	רְשִׁי	שְׁבִי	הִוָּרְשִׁי	הוֹרִישִׁי	הֵיטִיבִי		
	mp	רְשׁוּ	שְׁבוּ	הִוָּרְשׁוּ	הוֹרִישׁוּ	הֵיטִיבוּ		
	fp	רַשְׁנָה	שֵׁבְנָה	הִוָּרַשְׁנָה	הוֹרֵשְׁנָה	הֵיטֵבְנָה		
NC		רֶשֶׁת	שֶׁבֶת	הִוָּרֵשׁ	הוֹרִישׁ	הֵיטִיב	הוּרַשׁ	
NA		יָרוֹשׁ	יָשׁוֹב	הִוָּרֵשׁ	הוֹרֵשׁ	הֵיטֵב	הוּרֵשׁ	
Participle	ms	יֹרֵשׁ	יֹשֵׁב	נוֹרָשׁ	מוֹרִישׁ	מֵיטִיב	מוּרָשׁ	
	fs	יֹרֶשֶׁת / יֹרְשָׁה	יֹשֶׁבֶת / יֹשְׁבָה	נוֹרָשָׁה	מוֹרִישָׁה	מֵיטִיבָה	מוּרָשָׁה	
	mp	יֹרְשִׁים	יֹשְׁבִים	נוֹרָשִׁים	מוֹרִישִׁים	מֵיטִיבִים	מוּרָשִׁים	
	fp	יֹרְשׁוֹת	יֹשְׁבוֹת	נוֹרָשׁוֹת	מוֹרִישׁוֹת	מֵיטִיבוֹת	מוּרָשׁוֹת	

1. These roots are weak whenever the first radical of the verbal root is followed by silent *šewa* (Q F, V; N P, Ptc; all forms of H, Hp); strong throughout D, Dp, Dt.
2. When followed by silent *šewa*, initial -י assimilates to the preceding vowel, which becomes long; the initial -י may become a vowel letter or disappear.
3. In Q V and NC of many verbs the initial -י drops off and ת ִ - or תְ - is added to *qal* NC, so that some forms look exactly like the corresponding forms of I-נ roots.
4. הלך is formed like ישׁב (all forms).

Appendix D

*Hollow Verbs (II-*י/ו *or* ע-י/ו*; "monosyllabic roots")*

Conj/Sbj		Qal	Nifal	Hifil	Hofal	Polel	Polal	Hitpolel
P	1cs	קַמְתִּי	נְקוּמֹתִי	הֲקִמֹתִי	הוּקַמְתִּי	קֹמַמְתִּי	קֹמַמְתִּי	הִתְקֹמַמְתִּי
	2ms	קַמְתָּ	נְקוּמוֹתָ	הֲקִמוֹתָ	הוּקַמְתָּ	קֹמַמְתָּ	קֹמַמְתָּ	הִתְקֹמַמְתָּ
	2fs	קַמְתְּ	נְקוּמוֹת	הֲקִמוֹת	הוּקַמְתְּ	קֹמַמְתְּ	קֹמַמְתְּ	הִתְקֹמַמְתְּ
	3ms	קָם	נָקוֹם	הֵקִים	הוּקַם	קֹמֵם	קֹמַם	הִתְקֹמֵם
	3fs	קָמָה	נָקוֹמָה	הֵקִימָה	הוּקְמָה	קֹמְמָה	קֹמְמָה	הִתְקֹמֲמָה
	1cp	קַמְנוּ	נְקוּמוֹנוּ	הֲקִמוֹנוּ	הוּקַמְנוּ	קֹמַמְנוּ	קֹמַמְנוּ	הִתְקֹמַמְנוּ
	2mp	קַמְתֶּם	נְקוּמוֹתֶם	הֲקִמוֹתֶם	הוּקַמְתֶּם	קֹמַמְתֶּם	קֹמַמְתֶּם	הִתְקֹמַמְתֶּם
	2fp	קַמְתֶּן	נְקוּמוֹתֶן	הֲקִמוֹתֶן	הוּקַמְתֶּן	קֹמַמְתֶּן	קֹמַמְתֶּן	הִתְקֹמַמְתֶּן
	3cp	קָמוּ	נָקוֹמוּ	הֵקִימוּ	הוּקְמוּ	קֹמְמוּ	קֹמְמוּ	הִתְקֹמֲמוּ
F	1cs	אָקוּם	אֶקּוֹם	אָקִים	אוּקַם	אֲקֹמֵם	אֲקֹמַם	אֶתְקֹמֵם
	2m/3f	תָּקוּם	תִּקּוֹם	תָּקִים	תּוּקַם	תְּקֹמֵם	תְּקֹמַם	תִּתְקֹמֵם
	2fs	תָּקוּמִי	תִּקּוֹמִי	תָּקִימִי	תּוּקְמִי	תְּקֹמְמִי	תְּקֹמְמִי	תִּתְקֹמֲמִי
	3ms	יָקוּם	יִקּוֹם	יָקִים	יוּקַם	יְקֹמֵם	יְקֹמַם	יִתְקֹמֵם
	1cp	נָקוּם	נִקּוֹם	נָקִים	נוּקַם	נְקֹמֵם	נְקֹמַם	נִתְקֹמֵם
	2mp	תָּקוּמוּ	תִּקּוֹמוּ	תָּקִימוּ	תּוּקְמוּ	תְּקֹמְמוּ	תְּקֹמְמוּ	תִּתְקֹמֲמוּ
	2/3fp	תְּקֹמְנָה / תְּקוּמֶינָה	תִּקּוֹמְנָה	תְּקַמֶּנָה / תְּקִימֶינָה	תּוּקַמְנָה	תְּקֹמֵמְנָה	תְּקֹמַמְנָה	תִּתְקֹמֵמְנָה
	3mp	יָקוּמוּ	יִקּוֹמוּ	יָקִימוּ	יוּקְמוּ	יְקֹמְמוּ	יְקֹמְמוּ	יִתְקֹמֲמוּ
V	ms	קוּם	הִקּוֹם	הָקֵם		קֹמֵם		הִתְקֹמֵם
	fs	קוּמִי	הִקּוֹמִי	הָקִימִי		קֹמְמִי		הִתְקֹמֲמִי
	mp	קוּמוּ	הִקּוֹמוּ	הָקִימוּ		קֹמְמוּ		הִתְקֹמֲמוּ
	fp	קֹמְנָה	הִקּוֹמְנָה	הֲקֵמְנָה		קֹמֵמְנָה		הִתְקֹמֵמְנָה
NC		קוּם	הִקּוֹם	הָקִים	הוּקַם	קֹמֵם	קֹמַם	הִתְקֹמֵם
NA		קוֹם	הִקּוֹם / נָקוֹם	הָקֵם				
Participle	ms	קָם	נָקוֹם	מֵקִים	מוּקָם	מְקֹמֵם	מְקֹמָם	מִתְקֹמֵם
	fs	קָמָה		מְקִימָה	מוּקָמָה			
	mp	קָמִים			מוּקָמִים			
	fp	קָמוֹת			מוּקָמוֹת			

1. II-י verbs (e.g., שִׁיר, *sing*) look just like the II-ו verbs (קוּם), except that they have *ḥireq-yod* in the *qal* where קוּם has *šureq* (*qal* F, V, NC).
2. *Polel, polal, & hitpolel* substitute for D, Dp, and Dt (and thus look like geminates). Most forms of *polel* and *polal* look alike; *hitpolel* = *polel* with prefixed מִתְ- / יִתְ- / הִתְ-.
3. The jussive and preterite of the hollow verbs have shorter vowels than the imperfect:

	Qal	Hifil
3ms Jussive	יָקֹם	יָקֵם
3ms Preterite	וַיָּקָם	וַיָּקֶם

Geminate (ע"ע) Verbs

Conj/Sbj		Qal		Nifal	Hifil	Hofal	D-stems
P	1cs	סַבּוֹתִי		נְסַבּוֹתִי	הֲסִבּוֹתִי	הוּסַבּוֹתִי	
	2ms	סַבּוֹתָ		נְסַבּוֹתָ	הֲסִבּוֹתָ	הוּסַבּוֹתָ	
	2fs	סַבּוֹת		נְסַבּוֹת	הֲסִבּוֹת	הוּסַבּוֹת	
	3ms	סָבַב		נָסַב	הֵסֵב	הוּסַב	
	3fs	סָבָה		נָסַבָּה	הֵסֵבָּה	הוּסַבָּה	
	1cp	סַבּוֹנוּ		נְסַבּוֹנוּ	הֲסִבּוֹנוּ	הוּסַבּוֹנוּ	
	2mp	סַבּוֹתֶם		נְסַבּוֹתֶם	הֲסִבּוֹתֶם	הוּסַבּוֹתֶם	
	2fp	סַבּוֹתֶן		נְסַבּוֹתֶן	הֲסִבּוֹתֶן	הוּסַבּוֹתֶן	
	3cp	סָבּוּ		נָסַבּוּ	הֵסֵבּוּ	הוּסַבּוּ	
F	1cs	אָסֹב	אֶסֹּב	אֶסַּב	אָסֵב	אוּסַב	Geminate verbs have either the same forms in the D-stems as the *strong* verb or occur in *po'el*, *po'al*, and *hitpo'el* (these forms cannot be distinguished from the *polel*, *polal*, and *hitpolel* of the *hollow* verbal roots).
	2m/3f	תָּסֹב	תִּסֹּב	תִּסַּב	תָּסֵב	תּוּסַב	
	2fs	תָּסֹבִּי	תִּסְּבִי	תִּסַּבִּי	תָּסֵבִּי	תּוּסַבִּי	
	3ms	יָסֹב	יִסֹּב	יִסַּב	יָסֵב	יוּסַב	
	1cp	נָסֹב	נִסֹּב	נִסַּב	נָסֵב	נוּסַב	
	2mp	תָּסֹבּוּ	תִּסְּבוּ	תִּסַּבּוּ	תָּסֵבּוּ	תּוּסַבּוּ	
	2/3fp	תְּסֻבֶּינָה	תִּסְבֹּנָה	תִּסַּבֶּינָה	תְּסִבֶּינָה	תּוּסַבֶּינָה	
	3mp	יָסֹבּוּ	יִסְּבוּ	יִסַּבּוּ	יָסֵבּוּ	יוּסַבּוּ	
V	ms	סֹב		הִסַּב	הָסֵב		
	fs	סֹבִּי		הִסַּבִּי	הָסֵבִּי		
	mp	סֹבּוּ		הִסַּבּוּ	הָסֵבּוּ		
	fp	סֻבֶּינָה		הִסַּבֶּינָה	הָסֵבֶּינָה		
NC		סֹב		הִסַּב	הָסֵב		
NA		סָבוֹב		הִסֵּב	הָסֵב		
Participle	ms	סֹבֵב		נָסָב	מֵסֵב	מוּסָב	
	fs	סֹבְבָה		נָסַבָּה	מְסִבָּה	מוּסַבָּה	
	mp	סֹבְבִים		נְסַבִּים	מְסִבִּים	מוּסַבִּים	
	fp	סֹבְבוֹת		נְסַבּוֹת	מְסִבּוֹת	מוּסַבּוֹת	

1. There are three base forms of the geminates (סֹב [forms without PGN endings], סַבּ- [forms with PGN endings (except imperative)]; סבב [a few forms]).
2. Geminates are weak throughout Q, N, H, Hp. The D-stems either substitute *polel*, etc. (and thus look like *hollow* verbs), or look like the strong verb.
3. -וֹ- joins the verbal stem to consonantal endings.
4. An alternate form of *qal* imperfect looks just like verbs I-נ.
5. *Hofal* may have either *šureq* or *qibbuṣ* as its prefix vowel.
6. The *preterite* of geminates has shorter vowels than the imperfect (accent is on the PGN prefix).

        וַיָּסָב   3ms Q Pr   וַיָּסֵב   3ms H Pr

Appendix D

Some Easily Confused Forms.[194] Certain pairs of weak verbs which have two radicals in common can be difficult to distinguish. These charts compare יָשַׁב/שׁוּב (*return/sit, dwell*) and יָרֵא/רָאָה (*see/fear*). Only forms that actually occur are listed (but not all forms of each verb are listed).

Although these charts may be memorized (with difficulty!), it is more helpful to remember that these verbs will not occur in the same contexts, since "return" and "sit" describe very different actions, as do "seeing" and "fearing".

√ישׁב / √שׁוּב		Q		H		Hp	
		שׁוּב	ישׁב	שׁוּב	ישׁב	שׁוּב	ישׁב
P	3ms	שָׁב	יָשַׁב	הֵשִׁיב	הוֹשִׁיב	הוּשַׁב	הוּשַׁב
F	3ms	יָשׁוּב	יֵשֵׁב	יָשִׁיב	יוֹשִׁיב		יוּשַׁב
Pr	3ms	וַיָּשָׁב	וַיֵּשֶׁב	וַיָּשֶׁב	וַיּוֹשֶׁב		וַיּוּשַׁב
V	2ms	שׁוּב	שֵׁב	הָשֵׁב	הוֹשֵׁב		
NC		שׁוּב	שֶׁבֶת	הָשִׁיב	הוֹשִׁיב		
NA		שׁוֹב	יָשׁוֹב	הָשֵׁב			
Ptc	ms	שָׁב	יֹשֵׁב	מֵשִׁיב	מוֹשִׁיב		מוּשָׁב

√ירא / √ראה		Q		N		H
		ראה	ירא	ראה	ירא	ראה
P	3ms	רָאָה	יָרֵא	נִרְאָה		הֶרְאָה
F	3ms	יִרְאֶה	יִירָא	יֵרָאֶה		יַרְאֶה
Pr	3ms	וַיַּרְא	וַיִּירָא	וַיֵּרָא	וַיִּוָּרֵא	וַיַּרְא
V	2ms	רְאֵה	יְרָא	הֵרָאֵה		
NC		רְאוֹת	יְרֹא	הֵרָאוֹת		הַרְאוֹת
NA		רָאֹה				
Ptc	ms	רֹאֶה	יָרֵא	נִרְאֶה	נוֹרָא	מַרְאֶה

---

194. This comparison was suggested by my former colleague Mr. Eric Houseknecht, Th.M.

Appendix E

BIBLIOGRAPHY

Grammar & Syntax
*works indexed in Putnam (1996a)

Ben Zvi, Ehud, Maxine Hancock, & Richard Beinert. 1993 *Readings in Biblical Hebrew: An Intermediate Textbook*. New Haven: Yale University.
  Annotated biblical texts with notes on morphsyntax. This would be especially helpful for someone trying to regain competency in reading Biblical Hebrew.
Chisholm, Robert B., Jr. 1998. *From Exegesis to Exposition: A Practical Guide to Using Biblical Hebrew*. Grand Rapids: Baker.
Davidson, A.B. 1996. *Hebrew Syntax*. Edinburgh: T. & T. Clark, 1901; 3rd ed. Book International.
  A traditional approach to syntax, now revised as Gibson (1994).
Davis, John J. 1995. *Hebrew Language: An Analysis of the Strong Verb*. Quakertown, PA: Stylus Publishing.
  A laminated card-guide to the strong verb (only), punched for a three-ring binder.
Driver, S.R. 1998. *A Treatise on the Use of the Tenses in Hebrew and Some Other Syntactical Questions*. Oxford: Oxford Universtiy, 1892; reprinted, Grand Rapids: Eerdmans, 1998.
  The classic work, presenting a clausal approach to the verbal system, describing the conjugations as primarily aspectual (e.g., perfect ≈ completed action; imperfect ≈ non-complete).
*Gibson, J.C.L. 1994. *Davidson's Introductory Hebrew Grammar ~ Syntax*. 4th ed. Edinburgh: T. & T. Clark.
  A clarification and update of Davidson (1996), largely traditional in approach.
Horsnell, Malcolm J.A. 1998. *A Review and Reference Grammar for Biblical Hebrew*. Hamilton, Ontario: McMaster University Press.
  A traditional grammar, designed to help second-year students to review first-year grammar, but without exercises or indices. Students who have neglected Hebrew for a year or two may find this helpful.
*Joüon, Paul. 1991. *A Grammar of Biblical Hebrew*. 2 vols. Editrice Pontificio Instituto Biblico; 1927; trans. & rev., T. Muraoka. *Subsidia Biblica* 14/1-2. Rome.
  An translation and extensive revision of Joüon's grammar of 1927, which closely parallels GKC (below).
*Kautzsch, E. 1910. Ed., *Gesenius' Hebrew Grammar*. 2nd English ed., trans. & rev. A.E. Cowley. Oxford: Clarendon.
  Despite its age, still the standard in Hebrew morphology, although often out-of-date, especially with regard to cognate information and overall approach to syntax (although many of his basic insights remain valid). Abbreviated as GKC.
Putnam, Frederic Clarke. 1996a. *A Cumulative Index to the Grammar and Syntax of Biblical Hebrew*. Winona Lake, IN: Eisenbrauns.
  A verse-by-verse index to standard reference works in English (Gibson (1994), Joüon-Muraoka (1991), Kautzsch (1901), Walter & O'Connor (1995), Williams (1976)), & German (Bauer-Leander (1962), Beer (1972), Bergsträsser (1962), Brockelmann (1956), Richter (1980), Jenni (1981), Schneider (1974)), including some not otherwise indexed. Works indexed are marked with * in this bibliography.
____.1996b. *Card-Guide to Biblical Hebrew*. Quakertown, PA: Stylus.
  Laminated card with nominal, pronominal, and verbal paradigms of the complete verbal system; punched for three-ring binders. Far more extensive than Davis (1995), which covers only the strong verb.
____. 1996c. *Hebrew Bible Insert: A Student's Guide to the Syntax of Biblical Hebrew*. Ridley Park, PA: Stylus.
  Booklet covering nominal, adjectival, pronominal, verbal, and clausal syntax, as well as the "major" masoretic accents and complete verbal paradigms.

van der Merwe, Christo H.J., Jackie A. Naudé, & Jan H. Kroeze. 2000. *A Biblical Hebrew Reference Grammar*. Biblical Languages: Hebrew, ed., Stanley E. Porter & Richard S. Hess, 3. Sheffield: Sheffield Academic.
    An "intermediate" grammar, somewhat based on discourse principles of language; much more useful than Horsnell (1998).
*Waltke, Bruce K., & M. O'Connor. 1995. *An Introduction to Biblical Hebrew Syntax*. Winona Lake: Eisenbrauns, 1990; 5th printing with corrections.
    Massively detailed application of traditional analytical methods to syntax; the chapters that introduce each section are helpful.
Watts, James Washington. 1964. *A Survey of Syntax in the Hebrew Old Testament*. Rev. ed. Grand Rapids: Eerdmans.
*Williams, R.J. 1976. *Hebrew Syntax: An Outline*. Toronto: University of Toronto, 1967; 2nd ed.
    Essentially bound class notes, listing traditionally-derived functions for nouns, adjectives, etc., with copious examples, but little or no discussion or explanation.

Discourse & Text Linguistics

Bergen, Robert D., ed. 1994. *Biblical Hebrew and Discourse Linguistics*. Winona Lake: Eisenbrauns.
Bodine, Walter R., ed. 1992. *Linguistics & Biblical Hebrew*. Winona Lake: Eisenbrauns.
___, ed. 1995. *Discourse Analysis of Biblical Literature. What It Is and What It Offers*. Atlanta: Scholars Press.
Dooley, Robert A., & Stephen H. Levinsohn. 2001. *Analyzing Discourse. A Manual of Basic Concepts*. Dallas: SIL.
Grimes, Joseph E. 1975. *The Thread of Discourse*. Janua Linguarum Minor. The Hague: Mouton.
Longacre, Robert E. 2004. *Joseph: A Story of Divine Providence: A Text Theoretical and Textlinguistic Analysis of Genesis 37 and 39-48*. 2nd edition. Winona Lake: Eisenbrauns.
___. 1996. *The Grammar of Discourse*. Topics in Language and Linguistics. 2nd ed. New York: Plenum.

Lexica

Brown, Francis, S.R. Driver, & C.A. Briggs. 1907. *A Hebrew and English Lexicon of the Old Testament*. Oxford: Clarendon.
    Still the standard Hebrew-English lexicon, despite its age (it predates, e.g., the discovery of Ugaritic), arranged by "root".
Clines, David J.A., ed. 1993-2002. *The Dictionary of Classical Hebrew*. 5 vols. [incomplete] Sheffield, England: Sheffield Academic Press.
    A new type of concordance, DCH—ordered alphabetically—offers complete collocations for every word (e.g., under a particular verb, every occurrence of every subject modified by, and every object governed by, that verb, as well as every preposition with which it occurs). Incomplete & discontinued.
Davidson, Benjamin. 1970. *The Analytical Hebrew & Chaldee Lexicon*. London: Bagster & Sons, 1850; reprinted, Grand Rapids: Zondervan.
    Lists and parses [nearly] every verbal form in Biblical Hebrew.
Feyerabend, Karl. 1965. *Langenscheidt's Pocket Hebrew Dictionary to the Old Testament*. 5th ed. New York: Barnes & Noble.
    Offers one- or two-word gloss for each word, arranged by "root" (cf. BDB); glosses generally reflect KJV or RV/ASV.
Holladay, William L. 1971. *A Concise Hebrew and Aramaic Lexicon of the Old Testament Based upon the Lexical Work of Ludwig Koehler & Walter Baumgartner*. Grand Rapids: Eerdmans.
    The first edition of Koehler-Baumgartner, minus the German and etymological/comparative data, and a minimal listing of lemmas for each word. Ordered alphabetically. Easy to use, and for that reason popular, but quickly outgrown by diligent students.
Koehler, Ludwig, & Walter Baumgartner. 2001. *The Hebrew and Aramaic Lexicon of the Old Testament*. 3rd ed. Ed., Walter Baumgartner & Johann Jakob Stamm. Study ed. 2 vols. Leiden, The Netherlands: E.J. Brill.
    The best modern lexicon of Biblical Hebrew, with entries arranged alphabetically (i.e., not by "root"), with an extensive bibliography. One- or two-word glosses (which can be difficult to find in longer articles).

Vocabulary

Andersen, Francis I., & A. Dean Forbes. 1989. *The Vocabulary of the Old Testament*. Rome: Pontifical Biblical Institute.
> The basis of the statistics used in this grammar, this shows how grammatical forms (e.g., participles) and "frequent" words are distributed among the books and genres of the Hebrew Bible, correlates the three major concordances (Even-Shoshan, Mandelkern, Lisowsky), and lists all verbs according to their distribution among the roots (e.g., all verbs that occur in two stems, by those stems, and how many times in each stem).

Armstrong, Terry A., Douglas L. Busby, & Cyril E. Carr. 1989. *A Reader's Hebrew-English Lexicon of the Old Testament*. Four volumes in one. Grand Rapids: Zondervan.
> Verse-by-verse list of all vocabulary that occurs fifty times or less in the Bible, with statistics on occurrence and page number in BDB. Sections on the latter prophets and Writings include idioms and glosses that are more context-sensitive.

Beall, Todd S., William A. Banks, & Colin Smith. 1990. *Old Testament Parsing Guide*. Chicago: Moody.
> Verse-by-verse morphology [parsing] of every verb in the text of BHS, along with page numbers in BDB and KBL, and a suggested gloss.

Einspahr, Bruce. 1976. *Index to Brown, Driver & Briggs Lexicon*. Chicago: Moody Press.
> Verse-by-verse list of all words indexed in BDB, with gloss (BDB's primary listing) and location (page and quadrant number).

Landes, George M. 1961. *A Student's Vocabulary of Biblical Hebrew Listed According to Frequency and Cognate*. New York: Charles Scribner's Sons.
> A list of Hebrew words and glosses that occur ten times or more, arranged for self-study in order of descending frequency; the cognate listings are helpful.

Mitchell Larry A. 1984. *A Student's Vocabulary for Biblical Hebrew & Aramaic*. Grand Rapids: Zondervan.
> Essentially an update of Landes (1961) that lists Hebrew words used ten times or more with a gloss in order of descending frequency; includes the vocabulary of Biblical Aramaic. Indexed.

Owens, John Joseph. 1990. *Analytical Key to the Old Testament*. 4 vols. Grand Rapids: Baker.
> Verse-by-verse morphology of every word in the text of BHS, along with the correespondng page number in BDB, and a suggested gloss (based on RSV).

Watts, James Washington. 1967. *Lists of Words Occurring Frequently in the Hebrew Bible*. Grand Rapids/Leiden: Eerdmans (1960) / E.J. Brill.

Concordances

Although electronic [computer-based] databases have begun to replace concordances, it is still wise to have one or more of the following as a check on the electronic information, since the various programs can yield different results.

Even-Shoshan, Abraham, ed. 1989. *A New Concordance of the Old Testament*. 2nd ed. Grand Rapids: Baker.
> Modern concordance of the entire vocabulary of Biblical Hebrew, arranged alphabetically and analyzed (you can look up, e.g., every occurrence of the 2ms H P + *waw* of a particular verb); glosses, book titles, chapter numerals in [Modern] Hebrew.

Lisowsky, Gerhard. 1981. *Konkordanz zum hebräischen Alten Testaments*. 2nd ed. Stuttgart: Deutsche Bibelgesellschaft, 1958.
> A hand-written concordance of the nouns, verbs, adjectives, and aderbs of Biblical Hebrew, arranged alphabetically.

Mandelkern, Solomon. 1967. *Concordance on the Bible*. 2 vols. rev., F. Margolin (Berlin, 1925); rev., Moshe Henry Goshen-Gottstein. New York: Shulsinger Brothers.
> Analytical (cf. Even-Shoshan, above) concordance of the vocabulary of Biblical Hebrew, arranged by "root". Glosses in Latin; multiple "editions" and "publications", some abridged. Beware!

Wigram, George V., ed. 1843. *The Englishman's Hebrew and Chaldee Concordance of the Old Testament*. 2 vols. London (often reprinted).

Textual Criticism & Masora

Brotzman, Ellis R. 1994. *Old Testament Textual Criticism: A Practical Introduction*. Grand Rapids: Baker.
> A basic and learner-friendly introduction to textual criticism. The most helpful part may be the final chapter, in which he discusses every textual note in BHS for the book of Ruth.

Ginsburg, Christian D. 1966. *The Massorah*. 4 vols. London, 1880-1905; reprint ed. New York: KTAV.

_____. 1966. *Introduction to the Massoretico-Critical Edition of the Hebrew Bible*. London: Trinitarian Bible Society, 1897; reprint ed. New York: KTAV.
> The classic introduction to the Masoretes and their concerns, with helpful discussions of many aspects of the text merely referred to in later works. Eminently readable, this provides source material and statistics for many later works.

Goshen-Gottstein, Moshe H. 1983. "The Textual Criticism of the Old Testament: Rise, Decline, Rebirth" *JBL* 102, 365-99.

The Göttingen Septuagint. 1922-.
> The standard critical edition LX (not yet complete); individually edited volumes (one biblical book per volume) contain an eclectic text and thorough textual apparatus. Companion volumes on the translation technique of some books are also available (but not listed separately in this bibliography).

Greenberg, Moshe. 1977. "The Use of the Ancient Versions for Interpreting the Hebrew Text" *Congress Volume*, pp. 131-48. *Vetus Testamentum Supplement* 29. Leiden: Brill, 1978.

Kelley, Page H., Daniel S. Mynatt, & Timothy G. Crawford. 1998. *The Masorah of Biblia Hebraica Stuttgartensia. Introduction and Annotated Glossary*. Grand Rapids: Eerdmans.
> The first three chapters comprise the most helpful introduction to the subject available in English; Chapter Four lists the notes of *mp* alphabetically, and translates and explains examples for each listing. Yeivin (1980) also does this (and in more detail), but Kelley's material is much more clear and easier to use.

Klein, Michael L. 1974. *Textual Criticism of the Old Testament: From the Septuagint to Qumran*. Guides to Biblical Scholarship. Old Testament Series. Philadelphia: Fortress.
> Another basic guide, without as much information or detail as Brotzman, focussing far more on the value and use of LX.

McCarter, Kyle P., Jr. 1986. *Textual Criticism: Recovering the Text of the Hebrew Bible*. Guides to Biblical Scholarsip. Old Testament Series. Philadelphia: Fortress.

Mynatt, Daniel S. 1994. *The Sub Loco Notes in the Torah of Biblia Hebraica Stuttgartensia*. BIBAL Dissertation Series, 2. Berkeley: BIBAL.
> Explains a particular type of reference in the Torah of BHS, e.g., the footnote referred to by the superscript "21" on the first note on Gn 37.22. The note reads "Mp sub loco", which means "see Mp at the [appropriate] location", referring to a projected supplement to *BHS* that was never produced.

Rahlfs, Alfred, ed. 1935. *Septuaginta*. 2 vols. Stuttgart: Württembergische Bibelanstalt.
> The first modern eclectic edition of LX, based on a handful of MSS; underlies most electronic databases.

Scott, William R. 1990. *A Simplified Guide to BHS: Critical Apparatus, Masora, Accents, Unusual Letters & Other Markings*. 2nd ed. Berkeley: BIBAL, 1987.
> Briefly explains how to read *Mp* (pp. 1-17), with notes on other masoretic materials.

Talmon, Shemaryahu. 1970. "The Old Testament Text". The Cambridge History of the Bible. vol. 1: *From Beginnings to Jerome*, pp. 159-99. Ed., Peter R. Ackroyd & Christopher F. Evans. Cambridge: Cambridge University.

Tov, Emanuel. 1992. *Textual Criticism of the Hebrew Bible*. Minneapolis: Fortress.
> The primary and standard introduction to textual criticism, far more detailed, technical, and theoretical than Brotzman.

Vasholz, R.I. 1983. *Data for the Sigla of BHS*. Winona Lake: Eisenbrauns.
> A pamphlet with a table of information about the sources used in the text-critical footnotes of BHS.

Waltke, Bruce K. 1989. "Aims of OT Textual Criticism" *WTJ* 51, 93-108.

_____. 1979. "The Textual Criticism of the Old Testament" *The Expositor's Bible Commentary*, ed., Franke E. Gaebelein, 1, pp. 211-28. Grand Rapids: Zonderan.

Weil, Gerhard. 1971. *Massorah Gedolah*, vol. I. Rome: Pontifical Biblical Institute.
> Conceived as Volume Two of BHS, this contains lists of all of the *Masora gedola* (including Weil's corrections). The appropriate list can be found *via* the "Mm" footnotes in BHS, referred to by the raised numerals in the *masora marginalis*. Some of this data can be retrieved more quickly with a Hebrew concordance or electronic database.

Williams, Prescott H., Jr. 1965. *An English Key to the Symbols and Latin Words and Abbreviations of Biblia Hebraica*. Stuttgart: Wurttenbergischen Bibelanstalt Stuttgart.
> Printed as part of the forematter in the newest permutation of BHS.

Wonneberger, Reinhard. 1984. *Understanding BHS. A Manual for the Users of Biblia Hebraica Stuttgartensia*, trans. Dwight R. Daniels. *Subsidia Biblica*, 8. Rome: Biblical Institute Press.
> Explains the logic and syntax of the text-critical footnotes of BHS, with a brief discussion of Mp (61-68).

Würthwein, Ernst. 1995. *The Text of the Old Testament.* Trans. Erroll F. Rhodes. 2nd ed. Grand Rapids: Eerdmans.
: Explains the symbols used in the text-critical footnotes of BHS, with a brief discussion of Mp and textual criticism. The second half of the book consists of two-page spreads of a photograph and description of various manuscripts (Hebrew, Greek, DSS, Samaritan, etc.).

Yeivin, Israel. 1980. *Introduction to the Tiberian Masorah.* Trans. & ed., E.J. Revell. *Masoretic Studies,* ed., Harry M. Orlinsky, 5. Scholars Press.
: Covers the same ground as pp. 33-156 of Kelley, *et al.* (1998), but adds extensive discussions of the Masoretic accents.

History of Hebrew; Modern Hebrew

Bennett, Patrick R. 1998. *Comparative Semitic Linguistics: A Manual.* Winonah Lake: Eisenbrauns.
: A serious workbook of exercises designed to illustrate the relationships between the various Semitic languages and dialects. It seems to assume that you know something about comparative linguistics.

Bergsträsser, Gotthelf. 1995. *Introduction to the Semitic Languages: Text Specimens and Grammatical Sketches.* Trans. Peter T. Daniels. 2nd ed. Winonah Lake: Eisenbrauns.
: Perhaps the best place to begin examining the Semitic languages; includes Akkadian, Hebrew, Aramaic, Arabic (South and North).

Chomsky, William. 1957. *Hebrew: The Eternal Language.* Philadelphia: JPS.

Healey, John F. 1990. *The Early Alphabet.* Reading the Past. Berkeley/London: University of California/British Museum.

Muraoka, Takamitsu. 1982. *Modern Hebrew for Biblical Scholars. An Annotated Chrestomathy with an Outline Grammar and a Glossary.* JSOT Manuals, 2. Sheffield: JSOT.
: Sketches basic differences between Biblical Hebrew and Modern Israeli, followed by three sets of articles (grouped by field—language, Biblical studies, and archaeology), in which the first is fully pointed (with an English translation included in the appendices), the second less so, and the rest unpointed. All reading selections have some morphosyntactical notes.

Sáenz-Badillos, Angel. 1996. *A History of the Hebrew Language.* Trans. John Elwode. New York: Cambridge University.
: The best history of Hebrew in print—beginning with a discussion of Hebrew's emergence among the Semitic languages and extending to the twentieth century.

Sivan, Reuven, & Edward A. Levenston. 1975. *The New Bantam-Megiddo Hebrew & English Dictionary.* New York: Bantam.
: A pocket dictionary of Modern Hebrew, based on *The Megiddo Modern Dictionary* (same authors), one of the standard dictionaries of Modern Hebrew. A brief "preface" sketches verbal and nominal morphology, and lists the numerals. The "dictionary" indicates each word's gender and offers a one- or two-word gloss.

A New Grammar of Biblical Hebrew features a master teacher's skills coming from a lifetime commitment to the Hebrew Bible. Students facing the challenge of learning Biblical Hebrew need to gain an understanding of the way the language works within its discourse structures. Putnam provides those students with a grammar that is both traditional (as in his explanation of Hebrew's two conjugational verb forms) and non-traditional (the grammar's linguistic orientation and careful attention to clausal syntax). This volume represents a pragmatic pedagogy that will produce proficiency in the acquisition of Biblical Hebrew and preparation for an ongoing exegetical examination of the biblical text.

William D. Barrick, Th.D.
Professor of Old Testament
The Master's Seminary
Sun Valley, CA

www.ingramcontent.com/pod-product-compliance
Lightning Source LLC
Chambersburg PA
CBHW080542230426
43663CB00015B/2685